Stage 1

Cost Accounting and
Quantitative Methods

Textbook

5617/J97

British Library Cataloguing-in-Publication Data

A catalogue record for this book is available from the British Library.

Published by AT Foulks Lynch Ltd
Number 4
The Griffin Centre
Staines Road
Feltham
Middlesex
TW14 0HS

ISBN 0 7483 3561 7

© AT Foulks Lynch Ltd, 1997

Acknowledgements

We are grateful to the Chartered Institute of Management Accountants, the Association of Chartered Certified Accountants and the Institute of Chartered Accountants in England and Wales for permission to reproduce past examination questions. The answers have been prepared by AT Foulks Lynch Ltd.

Printed by Ashford Colour Press, Gosport, Hants

CONTENTS

PREFACE

The 1997 edition of this textbook has been specifically written for paper 2, Cost Accounting and Quantitative Methods for the CIMA examinations.

CIMA base the examinations set in November 1997 and May 1998 on legislation at 1 June 1997, and this Textbook has been fully updated where necessary for such legislation.

We have also analysed the syllabus guidance notes and the various clarifications issued by CIMA to ensure that all the appropriate items contained therein have been incorporated into the text. CIMA have also kindly provided us with an advance copy of the new syllabus guidance notes to be published in August 1997, and we have incorporated these into the text where appropriate.

The text has been written to cover the syllabus in great detail giving appropriate weighting to the various topics. Our texts are, however, very different from a reference book or a more traditional style text book. The texts are focused very closely on the examinations and are written in a way that will help you assimilate the information easily and give you plenty of practice at the various techniques involved.

Particular attention has been paid to producing an interactive text that will maintain your interest with a series of carefully designed features.

- **Activities**. The text involves you in the learning process with a series of activities designed to arrest your attention and make you concentrate and respond.

- **Definitions**. The text clearly defines key words or concepts and where relevant we do of course use CIMA's new official terminology, published in 1996. The purpose of including these definitions is **not** that you should learn them - rote learning is not required and is positively harmful. The definitions are included to focus your attention on the point being covered.

- **Conclusions**. Where helpful, the text includes conclusions that summarise important points as you read through the chapter rather than leaving the conclusion to the chapter end. The purpose of this is to summarise concisely the key material that has just been covered so that you can constantly monitor your understanding of the material as you read it.

- **Self test questions**. At the end of each chapter there is a series of self test questions. The purpose of these is to help you revise some of the key elements of the chapter. The answer to each is a paragraph reference, encouraging you to go back and re-read and revise that point.

- **End of chapter questions**. At the end of each chapter we include examination style questions. These will give you a very good idea of the sort of thing the examiner will ask and will test your understanding of what has been covered.

All in all a textbook which will teach you, involve you, interest you and help you revise and, most importantly of all, a textbook that is focused on the examinations.

THE SYLLABUS

ABILITIES REQUIRED IN THE EXAMINATION

Each examination paper contains a number of topics. Each topic has been given a number to indicate the level of ability required of the candidate.

The numbers range from 1 to 4 and represent the following ability levels:

Ability level

Appreciation

To understand a knowledge area at an early stage of learning, or outside the core of management accounting, at a level which enables the accountant to communicate and work with other members of the management team.

1

Knowledge

To have detailed knowledge of such matters as laws, standards, facts and techniques so as to advise at a level appropriate to a management accounting specialist.

2

Skill

To apply theoretical knowledge, concepts and techniques to the solution of problems where it is clear what technique has to be used and the information needed is clearly indicated.

3

Application

To apply knowledge and skills where candidates have to determine from a number of techniques which is the most appropriate and select the information required from a fairly wide range of data, some of which might not be relevant; to exercise professional judgement and to communicate and work with members of the management team and other recipients of financial reports.

4

EXAMINATION PROCEDURE

The examination will be set in accordance with the provisions of relevant UK legislation passed and case law established *up to and including 1 June* preceding the examination. This is especially relevant to the following five papers:

- Business Environment and Information Technology (Stage 1)
- Financial Accounting & Business and Company Law (Stage 2)
- Financial Reporting & Business Taxation (Stage 3)

This means that the Business Taxation paper will be set in accordance with the Finance Act 1997 for both the November 1997 and May 1998 examinations and with the Finance Act 1998 for the November 1998 examination.

The examination will also be set in accordance with relevant Statements of Standard Accounting Practice and Financial Reporting Standards issued up to and including 1 June preceding the examination. These are especially relevant to the following papers:

- Financial Accounting
- Financial Reporting

This criterion also applies to material contained in Exposure Drafts which are especially relevant to the Financial Reporting paper.

Students are advised to refer to the notice of examinable legislation published in *CIMA Student.* Information specific to the May examination appears in the February issue and that for the November examination in the August issue.

Where examinations are not based on UK legislation and practice, overseas candidates may take appropriate opportunities to cite examples of local practice in their answers. Such examples should be supported with references which will validate the answers.

Stage 1, Paper 2: COST ACCOUNTING AND QUANTITATIVE METHODS

Syllabus overview

This syllabus contains the two complementary areas of cost accounting and quantitative methods. In each area great importance will be attached to fundamental numeracy, analytical techniques and computer literacy. Students will be expected to understand the basic methods and techniques of cost accounting, and when and why they are used in practice. They should also have the ability to understand and interpret statistical and mathematical information. The syllabus as a whole provides the essential background techniques for Operational Cost Accounting and Management Science Applications at Stage 2.

Aims

To test the candidate's ability to:

- understand how component elements of cost make up the total cost of an activity, service or product

- prepare cost accounting records and statements of profit for management from cost accounting records, in particular operational environments

- explain the purpose of various cost accounting methods and activities; explain their relevance to management and decision making

- recognise when a quantitative approach is applicable

- use quantitative methods to obtain accurate and reliable management information; explain and present results.

Content	*Ability required*	*Chapter where covered in this text*
2a ELEMENTS OF COST (study weighting 15%)		
How and why costs are classified	2	1
Cost behaviour	2	1
Materials: cost collection	3	2
Stock valuation methods; the effect on profit of the valuation method selected	3	2
Labour: cost allocation; payroll routine	3	3
Overhead cost: classification and analysis	3	4
Principles of apportionment and absorption into cost centres and units; departmental accounts	3	4
Application of marginal costing principles to management reporting and the preparation of profit and loss accounts	3	5
Relevant cost concepts	2	6

SYLLABUS GUIDANCE NOTES

Stage 1

Paper 2

Cost Accounting and Quantitative Methods (CQM)

Introduction

For the convenience of study and presentation, this syllabus is divided into eight sections, **(a)** to **(h)**. However, candidates must remember that real problems in management accounting do not come in watertight boxes and, in order to reflect this, questions may be set which range across more than one area of the syllabus. This means that the divisions of the syllabus are to an extent arbitrary and the study weightings are an approximate guide only. For example, sections **(a)** and **(b)**, elements of cost and cost accounting systems, are very closely interrelated.

The overall aim of the cost accounting section of the syllabus is to ensure that candidates have a sound grasp of the fundamentals of cost accounting. They must demonstrate not only a detailed understanding of how basic principles are used, but also why they are used and their advantages and shortcomings. The development of a questioning, critical attitude to traditional methods and techniques is important preparation for a would-be Chartered Management Accountant. An awareness of recent developments is required, particularly in terms of their effects on cost accounting systems.

The major objective of the quantitative methods section of the syllabus is to develop the three areas of competence that are all vital to the successful training and education of a Chartered Management Accountant:

- knowledge of available quantitative methods
- understanding of how and why the methods are used
- understanding and appreciation of the significance of the solutions provided by such quantitative methods.

The quantitative methods syllabus is not intended to produce mathematicians or statisticians. It sets out to develop numeracy and the confidence to use basic, but essential, quantitative tools.

The examination paper

The examination paper will be divided into two sections, Cost Accounting and Quantitative Methods. Each section will be worth 50 marks and each will have a compulsory question consisting of ten multiple-choice sub-questions. These will range over the whole of the respective syllabuses. The other questions in each section will be worth 15 marks each and candidates will have the choice of two questions out of three within each section. Although the paper is in two sections, performance will be judged on the basis of the total mark for the paper as a whole.

In general, cost accounting questions and quantitative methods questions will be separated into the two respective sections of the examination. However, because cost accounting is a numerical subject, it is inevitable that some basic mathematical or quantitative techniques which are listed in the quantitative methods section of the syllabus may be used within a cost accounting question. Examples include: handling formulae, percentages, interest and discounting calculations, graphs and diagrams.

Questions in the cost accounting section may require either numerical or discursive answers, or a mixture of the two. Although much basic cost accounting is carried out nowadays by computers, Chartered Management Accountants still need numerical ability and this will be tested from time to time.

Applications other than manufacturing may form the background to questions. These may include: service industries, not-for-profit organisations, public sector organisations, etc. Specific knowledge of these areas is **not** required.

Content

2 (a) Elements of cost (study weighting 15%)

This section deals with the various classifications of costs, eg labour/material/overheads, direct/indirect, fixed/semi-fixed/variable and how material, labour and overhead costs are collected.

In the examination, candidates may be required to:

- demonstrate a knowledge of the documentation and procedures associated with materials and labour including: storage, reception and issue, issue pricing, wage payment systems, the treatment of waste and idle time and so on

- demonstrate a knowledge of stock control levels

- demonstrate a thorough knowledge of the analysis of cost and the build-up of product cost using a conventional absorption approach

- demonstrate an appreciation of activity based costing (ABC)

- carry out the apportionment of service department costs to production or operating departments

- apply a knowledge of marginal costing principles in the presentation of reports and statements, in decision making or in stock valuation

- identify relevant costs and carry out basic decision analysis including make or buy, choice of product, special order acceptance and single limiting factor decisions. These decisions would be based on contribution analysis, but an appreciation of other possible relevant costs, eg differential costs and opportunity costs, is required.

The following items are **not** examinable:

- numerical calculations using ABC
- reciprocal servicing within overhead apportionment
- derivation/calculation of the economic order quantity (EOQ)
- breakeven analysis, breakeven charts and profit charts.

2 (b) Cost accounting systems (study weighting 20%)

Candidates must be able to deal with the detailed accounting entries for all the types of systems mentioned in the syllabus. Profit and loss accounts and other accounts may be based on either marginal or absorption costing principles.

In the examination, candidates may be required to:

- prepare accounting entries for standard cost systems

- deal with process losses, process gains and closing work-in-progress in a system of process costing

- demonstrate an awareness of the distinction between joint products and by-products and of their accounting treatment.

The following items are **not** examinable:

- opening work-in-progress in a system of process costing

- standard process costing

- the apportionment of joint costs between joint products.

2 (c) Budgets and variance accounting (study weighting 15%)

In the examination, candidates may be required to:

- prepare budgets, including flexible budgets

- calculate budget variances by comparing actual results with an appropriate flexed budget

- calculate basic variances as detailed in the syllabus, using absorption costing principles

- demonstrate an awareness of the arguments regarding the appropriateness, or otherwise, of standard costing in the modern industrial environment

- reconcile the profit and cash flow for a period, demonstrating a thorough understanding of the difference between them.

The following items are **not** examinable:

- the behavioural aspects of budgeting

- zero-base budgeting

- detailed overhead variance analysis and materials mix and yield variances.

2 (d) Basic mathematics (study weighting 5%)

The skills required for this section are fundamental and underpin all other parts. It is unlikely that a whole question would be based on this single section, but questions from other sections will draw on these skills.

In the examination, candidates may be required to:

- use the four rules of number: addition, subtraction, multiplication and division

- handle formulae and equations including simultaneous and quadratic equations.

2 (e) Summarising and analysing data (study weighting 15%)

In the examination, candidates may be required to:

- demonstrate a knowledge of the characteristics of various sampling methods used to collect data, such as simple random sampling, multi-stage sampling, stratified sampling, quota and cluster sampling, and when they are appropriate

- answer numeric questions on sampling, based on simple random samples

- demonstrate an awareness of the main characteristics of interviewing and questionnaires

- summarise a set of raw data into a frequency table and from this
  - draw up a histogram and cumulative frequency table
  - calculate the arithmetic mean, the variance and the standard deviation

- derive or identify the median, the mode, upper and lower quartiles and deciles

- plot and interpret a range of charts and diagrams, eg various forms of bar chart, pie charts, Z charts, time series, semi-logarithmic charts and so on

- demonstrate a familiarity with the basic structure of price and quantity indexes, both base and current weighted

- use an index number series to take into account the effects of inflation, ie time series deflation.

The following item is **not** examinable:

- calculations involving either the harmonic mean or the geometric mean.

2 (f) Sampling and probability (study weighting 10%)

Managers have to cope with risk and uncertainty, and probability is a major tool to handle this. Furthermore, many decisions are made on the basis of sample information.

In the examination, candidates may be required to:

- make an inference about a population mean or proportion based on sample evidence and to calculate the appropriate confidence interval, for simple random samples only

- apply a knowledge of the properties and characteristics of the Normal Distribution

- demonstrate an understanding of the factors that determine an appropriate sample size both from a statistical and administrative viewpoint

- demonstrate knowledge of permutations and combinations.

The following item is **not** examinable:

- Bayes Theorem.

2 (g) Introduction to financial mathematics (study weighting 10%)

In the examination, candidates may be required to:

- demonstrate a sound working knowledge of simple and compound interest and the progressions which underlie these concepts

- use and interpret introductory discounted cash flow techniques such as net present value and internal rate of return. The discount rate will always be supplied

- use discount tables to deal with various cash flow patterns, both irregular and regular, ie annuities

- calculate and use perpetuity factors.

The following items are **not** examinable:

- the calculation of the annual percentage rate (APR) on loans

- the measurement of the cost of capital.

2 (h) Introduction to forecasting (study weighting 10%)

In the examination, candidates may be required to:

- construct a short-term forecast by calculating the trend using moving averages, the seasonal factors and the random fluctuations using either the additive or multiplicative models. Questions will specify the approach to be used

- fit and extrapolate a linear least-squares line of best fit to a time series for making longer term forecasts or to make forecasts of movements in one variable based on movements in an associated variable, eg predictions of sales based on advertising expenditure

- calculate the co-efficient of linear correlation and co-efficient of determination between two sets of variables and comment on the quality of a forecast based on linear regression

- in addition, although not a forecasting technique, be able to calculate and use Spearman's Rank Correlation Coefficient.

HOTLINE TO THE EXAMINER

AT Foulks Lynch, in common with other training organisations, maintains regular contact with the CIMA examiners to seek clarification of the syllabus. CIMA publishes all such questions and the examiners' answers, and we are grateful to CIMA for permission to reproduce the key questions and answers below.

1   **To what extent will the topic of cost behaviour be examined (2a)?**

Cost behaviour may be examined based on simple linear (eg, $y = a + bx$) or non-linear (eg, $y = a + bx + cx^3$) functions. Arithmetic and or graphical solutions may be required.

2   **Are learning curves examinable (2a)?**

No

3   **Will students be expected to have knowledge of just-in-time (JIT)?   If so, what level of knowledge would be required (2a)?**

No.

4   **Is the derivation and/or calculation of economic order quantity (EOQ) examinable (2a)?**

No.

5   **Will students be tested on stock control levels (2a)?**

Yes.

6   **Please confirm, or otherwise indicate, that decision-making situations involving limiting factors are not examinable (2a).**

Single limiting factors are examinable in a decision-making situation.

7   **Could you please clarify what is meant by 'departmental accounts' with respect to overhead absorption (2a)?**

Collection of overheads by department.

8   **Will students need to know how to account for scrap in process costing systems (2b)?**

Yes.

9   **Might losses and closing work-in-progress be examined within the same process (2b)?**

Yes

10   **Is contract costing examinable (2b)?**

No.

11   **Will questions be set on the reconciliation of cost and financial profits in a system of interlocking accounts (2b)?**

Pro forma reconciliation only ie, no accounting entries.

12   **Will candidates be required to prepare functional budgets (2c)?**

Yes, at a simple level.

13   **To what extent are flexible budgets examinable (2c)?**

Flexible budgets are examinable at an elementary level, with variable items flexed on volume.

14   **Are candidates expected to be able to integrate conditions into spreadsheet formulae (2c)?**

No.

15   **Could any of the following be incorporated into cash budgeting questions (a) debtors and creditors collection periods (b) provisions for bad and doubtful debts (c) build up/reduction of stock levels (2c)?**

Yes, all of them.

16   **Will candidates be expected to know how to formulate a spreadsheet (2d)?**

Not in a detailed, technical sense - only a general knowledge of the principles is required.

17   **What is meant by 'discounts' (2d)?**

The normal meaning applies ie, 5% discount for quantities above 100 etc.

18   **Are Lorenz and Pareto charts examinable (2e)?**

No.

19   **Will calculations of median and mode of grouped data be required (2e)?**

No, although they may have to be found graphically.

20   **Are P_1/P_0 and $P_1/P_0 \times 100$ both acceptable as price relative indices (2e)?**

Yes.

21   **Are significance tests examinable (2f)?**

No.

22   **Will questions be set on the estimation of the population variance from two samples (2f)?**

No.

23   **Are candidates expected to be aware of the concept of permutations and combinations (2f)?**

Yes.

24   **To what extent are annuities examinable (2g)?**

Candidates should know the meaning of annuities, how to find the present value, how to convert irregular series into an equivalent annuity.

25   **What is the scope of likely investment appraisal questions (2g)?**

Simple risk analysis using expected value may be incorporated.

26   **Do candidates need to be aware of, and be able to use, Spearman's Rank correlation coefficient (2h)?**

Yes.

27   Is the poisson distribution examinable at any stage in the syllabus - ie, CQM, MSA or any other paper? (Because formulae and tables are still in the formulae booklet.)

Not in CQM.

28   Is the binomial distribution examinable at any stage in the syllabus - ie CQM, MSA or any other paper? (Because formulae and tables are still in the formulae booklet.)

Not in CQM.

29   The normal distribution is obviously to be studied (because of the sampling aspects), although it is not mentioned in the syllabus anywhere, but will the normal distribution be examined in CQM or MSA in its own right (ie, as in the previous stage 1 syllabus)?

Normal distribution may be examined in CQM.

30   The 'Queuing theory' formulae are still given - is queueing theory examinable in any part of the CIMA syllabus?

Not in CQM.

Table 4   **A R E A   U N D E R   T H E   N O R M A L   C U R V E**

This table gives the area under the normal curve between the mean and a point Z standard deviations above the mean. The corresponding area for deviations below the mean can be found by symmetry.

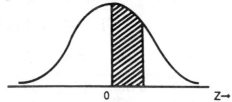

$Z = \dfrac{(x-\mu)}{\sigma}$	0·00	0·01	0·02	0·03	0·04	0·05	0·06	0·07	0·08	0·09
0·0	·0000	·0040	·0080	·0120	·0159	·0199	·0239	·0279	·0319	·0359
0·1	·0398	·0438	·0478	·0517	·0557	·0596	·0636	·0675	·0714	·0753
0·2	·0793	·0832	·0871	·0910	·0948	·0987	·1026	·1064	·1103	·1141
0·3	·1179	·1217	·1255	·1293	·1331	·1368	·1406	·1443	·1480	·1517
0·4	·1554	·1591	·1628	·1664	·1700	·1736	·1772	·1808	·1844	·1879
0·5	·1915	·1950	·1985	·2019	·2054	·2088	·2123	·2157	·2190	·2224
0·6	·2257	·2291	·2324	·2357	·2389	·2422	·2454	·2486	·2518	·2549
0·7	·2580	·2611	·2642	·2673	·2704	·2734	·2764	·2794	·2823	·2852
0·8	·2881	·2910	·2939	·2967	·2995	·3023	·3051	·3078	·3106	·3133
0·9	·3159	·3186	·3212	·3238	·3264	·3289	·3315	·3340	·3365	·3389
1·0	·3413	·3438	·3461	·3485	·3508	·3531	·3554	·3577	·3599	·3621
1·1	·3643	·3665	·3686	·3708	·3729	·3749	·3770	·3790	·3810	·3830
1·2	·3849	·3869	·3888	·3907	·3925	·3944	·3962	·3980	·3997	·4015
1·3	·4032	·4049	·4066	·4082	·4099	·4115	·4131	·4147	·4162	·4177
1·4	·4192	·4207	·4222	·4236	·4251	·4265	·4279	·4292	·4306	·4319
1·5	·4332	·4345	·4357	·4370	·4382	·4394	·4406	·4418	·4430	·4441
1·6	·4452	·4463	·4474	·4485	·4495	·4505	·4515	·4525	·4535	·4545
1·7	·4554	·4564	·4573	·4582	·4591	·4599	·4608	·4616	·4625	·4633
1·8	·4641	·4649	·4656	·4664	·4671	·4678	·4686	·4693	·4699	·4706
1·9	·4713	·4719	·4726	·4732	·4738	·4744	·4750	·4756	·4762	·4767
2·0	·4772	·4778	·4783	·4788	·4793	·4798	·4803	·4808	·4812	·4817
2·1	·4821	·4826	·4830	·4834	·4838	·4842	·4846	·4850	·4854	·4857
2·2	·4861	·4865	·4868	·4871	·4875	·4878	·4881	·4884	·4887	·4890
2·3	·4893	·4896	·4898	·4901	·4904	·4906	·4909	·4911	·4913	·4916
2·4	·4918	·4920	·4922	·4925	·4927	·4929	·4931	·4932	·4934	·4936
2·5	·4938	·4940	·4941	·4943	·4945	·4946	·4948	·4949	·4951	·4952
2·6	·4953	·4955	·4956	·4957	·4959	·4960	·4961	·4962	·4963	·4964
2·7	·4965	·4966	·4967	·4968	·4969	·4970	·4971	·4972	·4973	·4974
2·8	·4974	·4975	·4976	·4977	·4977	·4978	·4979	·4980	·4980	·4981
2·9	·4981	·4982	·4983	·4983	·4984	·4984	·4985	·4985	·4986	·4986
3·0	·49865	·4987	·4987	·4988	·4988	·4989	·4989	·4989	·4990	·4990
3·1	·49903	·4991	·4991	·4991	·4992	·4992	·4992	·4992	·4993	·4993
3·2	·49931	·4993	·4994	·4994	·4994	·4994	·4994	·4995	·4995	·4995
3·3	·49952	·4995	·4995	·4996	·4996	·4996	·4996	·4996	·4996	·4997
3·4	·49966	·4997	·4997	·4997	·4997	·4997	·4997	·4997	·4997	·4998
3·5	·49977									

Table 11

PRESENT VALUE TABLE

Present value of 1 ie $(1 + r)^{-n}$ where r = discount rate, n = number of periods until payment.

Periods (n)	Discount rates (r)									
	1%	2%	3%	4%	5%	6%	7%	8%	9%	10%
1	0·990	0·980	0·971	0·962	0·952	0·943	0·935	0·926	0·917	0·909
2	0·980	0·961	0·943	0·925	0·907	0·890	0·873	0·857	0·842	0·826
3	0·971	0·942	0·915	0·889	0·864	0·840	0·816	0·794	0·772	0·751
4	0·961	0·924	0·888	0·855	0·823	0·792	0·763	0·735	0·708	0·683
5	0·951	0·906	0·863	0·822	0·784	0·747	0·713	0·681	0·650	0·621
6	0·942	0·888	0·837	0·790	0·746	0·705	0·666	0·630	0·596	0·564
7	0·933	0·871	0·813	0·760	0·711	0·665	0·623	0·583	0·547	0·513
8	0·923	0·853	0·789	0·731	0·677	0·627	0·582	0·540	0·502	0·467
9	0·914	0·837	0·766	0·703	0·645	0·592	0·544	0·500	0·460	0·424
10	0·905	0·820	0·744	0·676	0·614	0·558	0·508	0·463	0·422	0·386
11	0·896	0·804	0·722	0·650	0·585	0·527	0·475	0·429	0·388	0·350
12	0·887	0·788	0·702	0·625	0·557	0·497	0·444	0·397	0·356	0·319
13	0·879	0·773	0·681	0·601	0·530	0·469	0·415	0·368	0·326	0·290
14	0·870	0·758	0·661	0·577	0·505	0·442	0·388	0·340	0·299	0·263
15	0·861	0·743	0·642	0·555	0·481	0·417	0·362	0·315	0·275	0·239

Periods (n)	Discount rates (r)									
	11%	12%	13%	14%	15%	16%	17%	18%	19%	20%
1	0·901	0·893	0·885	0·877	0·870	0·862	0·855	0·847	0·840	0·833
2	0·812	0·797	0·783	0·769	0·756	0·743	0·731	0·718	0·706	0·694
3	0·731	0·712	0·693	0·675	0·658	0·641	0·624	0·609	0·593	0·579
4	0·659	0·636	0·613	0·592	0·572	0·552	0·534	0·516	0·499	0·482
5	0·593	0·567	0·543	0·519	0·497	0·476	0·456	0·437	0·419	0·402
6	0·535	0·507	0·480	0·456	0·432	0·410	0·390	0·370	0·352	0·335
7	0·482	0·452	0·425	0·400	0·376	0·354	0·333	0·314	0·296	0·279
8	0·434	0·404	0·376	0·351	0·327	0·305	0·285	0·266	0·249	0·233
9	0·391	0·361	0·333	0·308	0·284	0·263	0·243	0·225	0·209	0·194
10	0·352	0·322	0·295	0·270	0·247	0·227	0·208	0·191	0·176	0·162
11	0·317	0·287	0·261	0·237	0·215	0·195	0·178	0·162	0·148	0·135
12	0·286	0·257	0·231	0·208	0·187	0·168	0·152	0·137	0·124	0·112
13	0·258	0·229	0·204	0·182	0·163	0·145	0·130	0·116	0·104	0·093
14	0·232	0·205	0·181	0·160	0·141	0·125	0·111	0·099	0·088	0·078
15	0·209	0·183	0·160	0·140	0·123	0·108	0·095	0·084	0·074	0·065

Table 12   CUMULATIVE PRESENT VALUE OF £1

This table shows the Present Value of £1 per annum, Receivable or Payable at the end of each year for *n* years.

Present (n)	Interest rates r									
	1%	2%	3%	4%	5%	6%	7%	8%	9%	10%
1	0·990	0·980	0·971	0·962	0·952	0·943	0·935	0·926	0·917	0·909
2	1·970	1·942	1·913	1·886	1·859	1·833	1·808	1·783	1·759	1·736
3	2·941	2·884	2·829	2·775	2·723	2·673	2·624	2·577	2·531	2·487
4	3·902	3·808	3·717	3·630	3·546	3·465	3·387	3·312	3·240	3·170
5	4·853	4·713	4·580	4·452	4·329	4·212	4·100	3·993	3·890	3·791
6	5·795	5·601	5·417	5·242	5·076	4·917	4·767	4·623	4·486	4·355
7	6·728	6·472	6·230	6·002	5·786	5·582	5·389	5·206	5·033	4·868
8	7·652	7·325	7·020	6·733	6·463	6·210	5·971	5·747	5·535	5·335
9	8·566	8·162	7·786	7·435	7·108	6·802	6·515	6·247	5·995	5·759
10	9·471	8·983	8·530	8·111	7·722	7·360	7·024	6·710	6·418	6·145
11	10·37	9·787	9·253	8·760	8·306	7·887	7·499	7·139	6·805	6·495
12	11·26	10·58	9·954	9·385	8·863	8·384	7·943	7·536	7·161	6·814
13	12·13	11·35	10·63	9·986	9·394	8·853	8·358	7·904	7·487	7·103
14	13·00	12·11	11·30	10·56	9·899	9·295	8·745	8·244	7·786	7·367
15	13·87	12·85	11·94	11·12	10·38	9·712	9·108	8·559	8·061	7·606

Present (n)	Interest rates (r)									
	11%	12%	13%	14%	15%	16%	17%	18%	19%	20%
1	0·901	0·893	0·885	0·877	0·870	0·862	0·855	0·847	0·840	0·833
2	1·713	1·690	1·668	1·647	1·626	1·605	1·585	1·566	1·547	1·528
3	2·444	2·402	2·361	2·322	2·283	2·246	2·210	2·174	2·140	2·106
4	3·102	3·037	2·974	2·914	2·855	2·798	2·743	2·690	2·639	2·589
5	3·696	3·605	3·517	3·433	3·352	3·274	3·199	3·127	3·058	2·991
6	4·231	4·111	3·998	3·889	3·784	3·685	3·589	3·498	3·410	3·326
7	4·712	4·564	4·423	4·288	4·160	4·039	3·922	3·812	3·706	3·605
8	5·146	4·968	4·799	4·639	4·487	4·344	4·207	4·078	3·954	3·837
9	5·537	5·328	5·132	4·946	4·772	4·607	4·451	4·303	4·163	4·031
10	5·889	5·650	5·426	5·216	5·019	4·833	4·659	4·494	4·339	4·192
11	6·207	5·938	5·687	5·453	5·234	5·028	4·836	4·656	4·486	4·327
12	6·492	6·194	5·918	5·660	5·421	5·197	4·988	4·793	4·611	4·439
13	6·750	6·424	6·122	5·842	5·583	5·342	5·118	4·910	4·715	4·533
14	6·982	6·628	6·302	6·002	5·724	5·468	5·229	5·008	4·802	4·611
15	7·191	6·811	6·462	6·142	5·847	5·575	5·324	5·092	4·876	4·675

LOGARITHMS

	0	1	2	3	4	5	6	7	8	9	1	2	3	4	5	6	7	8	9
10	0000	0043	0086	0128	0170	0212	0253	0294	0334	0374	4	9	13	17	21	26	30	34	38
											4	8	12	16	20	24	28	32	37
11	0414	0453	0492	0531	0569	0607	0645	0682	0719	0755	4	8	12	15	19	23	27	31	35
											4	7	11	15	19	22	26	30	33
12	0792	0828	0864	0899	0934	0969	1004	1038	1072	1106	3	7	11	14	18	21	25	28	32
											3	7	10	14	17	20	24	27	31
13	1139	1173	1206	1239	1271	1303	1335	1367	1399	1430	3	7	10	13	16	20	23	26	30
											3	7	10	12	16	19	22	25	29
14	1461	1492	1523	1553	1584	1614	1644	1673	1703	1732	3	6	9	12	15	18	21	24	28
											3	6	9	12	15	17	20	23	26
15	1761	1790	1818	1847	1875	1903	1931	1959	1987	2014	3	6	9	11	14	17	20	23	26
											3	5	8	11	14	16	19	22	25
16	2041	2068	2095	2122	2148	2175	2201	2227	2253	2279	3	5	8	11	14	16	19	22	24
											3	5	8	10	13	15	18	21	23
17	2304	2330	2355	2380	2405	2430	2455	2480	2504	2529	3	5	8	10	13	15	18	20	23
											2	5	7	10	12	15	17	19	22
18	2553	2577	2601	2625	2648	2672	2695	2718	2742	2765	2	5	7	9	12	14	16	19	21
											2	5	7	9	11	14	16	18	21
19	2788	2810	2833	2856	2878	2900	2923	2945	2967	2989	2	4	7	9	11	13	16	18	20
											2	4	6	8	11	13	15	17	19
20	3010	3032	3054	3075	3096	3118	3139	3160	3181	3201	2	4	6	8	11	13	15	17	19
21	3222	3243	3263	3284	3304	3324	3345	3365	3385	3404	2	4	6	8	10	12	14	16	18
22	3424	3444	3464	3483	3502	3522	3541	3560	3579	3598	2	4	6	8	10	12	14	15	17
23	3617	3636	3655	3674	3692	3711	3729	3747	3766	3784	2	4	6	7	9	11	13	15	17
24	3802	3820	3838	3856	3874	3892	3909	3927	3945	3962	2	4	5	7	9	11	12	14	16
25	3979	3997	4014	4031	4048	4065	4082	4099	4116	4133	2	3	5	7	9	10	12	14	15
26	4150	4166	4183	4200	4216	4232	4249	4265	4281	4298	2	3	5	7	8	10	11	13	15
27	4314	4330	4346	4362	4378	4393	4409	4425	4440	4456	2	3	5	6	8	9	11	13	14
28	4472	4487	4502	4518	4533	4548	4564	4579	4594	4609	2	3	5	6	8	9	11	12	14
29	4624	4639	4654	4669	4683	4698	4713	4728	4742	4757	1	3	4	6	7	9	10	12	13
30	4771	4786	4800	4814	4829	4843	4857	4871	4886	4900	1	3	4	6	7	9	10	11	13
31	4914	4928	4942	4955	4969	4983	4997	5011	5024	5038	1	3	4	6	7	8	10	11	12
32	5051	5065	5079	5092	5105	5119	5132	5145	5159	5172	1	3	4	5	7	8	9	11	12
33	5185	5198	5211	5224	5237	5250	5263	5276	5289	5302	1	3	4	5	7	8	9	11	12
34	5315	5328	5340	5353	5366	5378	5391	5403	5416	5428	1	3	4	5	6	8	9	10	11
35	5441	5453	5465	5478	5490	5502	5514	5527	5539	5551	1	2	4	5	6	7	9	10	11
36	5563	5575	5587	5599	5611	5623	5635	5647	5658	5670	1	2	4	5	6	7	8	10	11
37	5682	5694	5705	5717	5729	5740	5752	5763	5775	5786	1	2	3	5	6	7	8	9	10
38	5798	5809	5821	5832	5843	5855	5866	5877	5888	5899	1	2	3	5	6	7	8	9	10
39	5911	5922	5933	5944	5955	5966	5977	5988	5999	6010	1	2	3	4	5	7	8	9	10
40	6021	6031	6042	6053	6064	6075	6085	6096	6107	6117	1	2	3	4	5	6	8	9	10
41	6128	6138	6149	6160	6170	6180	6191	6201	6212	6222	1	2	3	4	5	6	7	8	9
42	6232	6243	6253	6263	6274	6284	6294	6304	6314	6325	1	2	3	4	5	6	7	8	9
43	6335	6345	6355	6365	6375	6385	6395	6405	6415	6425	1	2	3	4	5	6	7	8	9
44	6435	6444	6454	6464	6474	6484	6493	6503	6513	6522	1	2	3	4	5	6	7	8	9
45	6532	6542	6551	6561	6571	6580	6590	6599	6609	6618	1	2	3	4	5	6	7	8	9
46	6628	6637	6646	6656	6665	6675	6684	6693	6702	6712	1	2	3	4	5	6	7	7	8
47	6721	6730	6739	6749	6758	6767	6776	6785	6794	6803	1	2	3	4	5	5	6	7	8
48	6812	6821	6830	6839	6848	6857	6866	6875	6884	6893	1	2	3	4	5	5	6	7	8
49	6902	6911	6920	6928	6937	6946	6955	6964	6972	6981	1	2	3	4	4	5	6	7	8

LOGARITHMS

	0	1	2	3	4	5	6	7	8	9	1	2	3	4	5	6	7	8	9
50	6990	6998	7007	7016	7024	7033	7042	7050	7059	7067	1	2	3	3	4	5	6	7	8
51	7076	7084	7093	7101	7110	7118	7126	7135	7143	7152	1	2	3	3	4	5	6	7	8
52	7160	7168	7177	7185	7193	7202	7210	7218	7226	7235	1	2	2	3	4	5	6	7	7
53	7243	7251	7259	7267	7275	7284	7292	7300	7308	7316	1	2	2	3	4	5	6	6	7
54	7324	7332	7340	7348	7356	7364	7372	7380	7388	7396	1	2	2	3	4	5	6	6	7
55	7404	7412	7419	7427	7435	7443	7451	7459	7466	7474	1	2	2	3	4	5	5	6	7
56	7482	7490	7497	7505	7513	7520	7528	7536	7543	7551	1	2	2	3	4	5	5	6	7
57	7559	7566	7574	7582	7589	7597	7604	7612	7619	7627	1	2	2	3	4	5	5	6	7
58	7634	7642	7649	7657	7664	7672	7679	7686	7694	7701	1	1	2	3	4	4	5	6	7
59	7709	7716	7723	7731	7738	7745	7752	7760	7767	7774	1	1	2	3	4	4	5	6	7
60	7782	7789	7796	7803	7810	7818	7825	7832	7839	7846	1	1	2	3	4	4	5	6	6
61	7853	7860	7868	7875	7882	7889	7896	7903	7910	7917	1	1	2	3	4	4	5	6	6
62	7924	7931	7938	7945	7952	7959	7966	7973	7980	7987	1	1	2	3	3	4	5	6	6
63	7993	8000	8007	8014	8021	8028	8035	8041	8048	8055	1	1	2	3	3	4	5	5	6
64	8062	8069	8075	8082	8089	8096	8102	8109	8116	8122	1	1	2	3	3	4	5	5	6
65	8129	8136	8142	8149	8156	8162	8169	8176	8182	8189	1	1	2	3	3	4	5	5	6
66	8195	8202	8209	8215	8222	8228	8235	8241	8248	8254	1	1	2	3	3	4	5	5	6
67	8261	8267	8274	8280	8287	8293	8299	8306	8312	8319	1	1	2	3	3	4	5	5	6
68	8325	8331	8338	8344	8351	8357	8363	8370	8376	8382	1	1	2	3	3	4	4	5	6
69	8388	8395	8401	8407	8414	8420	8426	8432	8439	8445	1	1	2	2	3	4	4	5	6
70	8451	8457	8463	8470	8476	8482	8488	8494	8500	8506	1	1	2	2	3	4	4	5	6
71	8513	8519	8525	8531	8537	8543	8549	8555	8561	8567	1	1	2	2	3	4	4	5	5
72	8573	8579	8585	8591	8597	8603	8609	8615	8621	8627	1	1	2	2	3	4	4	5	5
73	8633	8639	8645	8651	8657	8663	8669	8675	8681	8686	1	1	2	2	3	4	4	5	5
74	8692	8698	8704	8710	8716	8722	8727	8733	8739	8745	1	1	2	2	3	4	4	5	5
75	8751	8756	8762	8768	8774	8779	8785	8791	8797	8802	1	1	2	2	3	3	4	5	5
76	8808	8814	8820	8825	8831	8837	8842	8848	8854	8859	1	1	2	2	3	3	4	5	5
77	8865	8871	8876	8882	8887	8893	8899	8904	8910	8915	1	1	2	2	3	3	4	4	5
78	8921	8927	8932	8938	8943	8949	8954	8960	8965	8971	1	1	2	2	3	3	4	4	5
79	8976	8982	8987	8993	8998	9004	9009	9015	9020	9025	1	1	2	2	3	3	4	4	5
80	9031	9036	9042	9047	9053	9058	9063	9069	9074	9079	1	1	2	2	3	3	4	4	5
81	9085	9090	9096	9101	9106	9112	9117	9122	9128	9133	1	1	2	2	3	3	4	4	5
82	9138	9143	9149	9154	9159	9165	9170	9175	9180	9186	1	1	2	2	3	3	4	4	5
83	9191	9196	9201	9206	9212	9217	9222	9227	9232	9238	1	1	2	2	3	3	4	4	5
84	9243	9248	9253	9258	9263	9269	9274	9279	9284	9289	1	1	2	2	3	3	4	4	5
85	9294	9299	9304	9309	9315	9320	9325	9330	9335	9340	1	1	2	2	3	3	4	4	5
86	9345	9350	9355	9360	9365	9370	9375	9380	9385	9390	1	1	2	2	3	3	4	4	5
87	9395	9400	9405	9410	9415	9420	9425	9430	9435	9440	0	1	1	2	2	3	3	4	4
88	9445	9450	9455	9460	9465	9469	9474	9479	9484	9489	0	1	1	2	2	3	3	4	4
89	9494	9499	9504	9509	9513	9518	9523	9528	9533	9538	0	1	1	2	2	3	3	4	4
90	9542	9547	9552	9557	9562	9566	9571	9576	9581	9586	0	1	1	2	2	3	3	4	4
91	9590	9595	9600	9605	9609	9614	9619	9624	9628	9633	0	1	1	2	2	3	3	4	4
92	9638	9643	9647	9652	9657	9661	9666	9671	9675	9680	0	1	1	2	2	3	3	4	4
93	9685	9689	9694	9699	9703	9708	9713	9717	9722	9727	0	1	1	2	2	3	3	4	4
94	9731	9736	9741	9745	9750	9754	9759	9763	9768	9773	0	1	1	2	2	3	3	4	4
95	9777	9782	9786	9791	9795	9800	9805	9809	9814	9818	0	1	1	2	2	3	3	4	4
96	9823	9827	9832	9836	9841	9845	9850	9854	9859	9863	0	1	1	2	2	3	3	4	4
97	9868	9872	9877	9881	9886	9890	9894	9899	9903	9908	0	1	1	2	2	3	3	4	4
98	9912	9917	9921	9926	9930	9934	9939	9943	9948	9952	0	1	1	2	2	3	3	4	4
99	9956	9961	9965	9969	9974	9978	9983	9987	9991	9996	0	1	1	2	2	3	3	3	4

14. FORMULAE AND SYMBOLS

General section

± plus *or* minus; positive *or* negative

≠ not equal

≏ or ≐ approximately equal

> greater than

< less than

$a > b > c, c < b < a$ value of middle term lies between outer values

≥ greater than *or* equal to

$\log_e$ N; Natural logarithm of N. Note that if $e^x = N$, $\log_e N = x$

$\log N$ $\log_{10}N$ common (Briggsian) logarithm of N. Note that if $10^x = N$, $\log N = x$

$e^x = 1 + \dfrac{x}{1!} + \dfrac{x^2}{2!} + \ldots$

xy or $x.y$ product of x and y; x multiplied by y; $(x)(y) = xy$

* multiplied by

A * B A times B

$y = f(x)$ y is a function of x

dy/dx or $f'(x)$ differential coefficient of $y = f(x)$; 1st derivative

d^2y/dx^2 or $f''(x)$ 2nd derivative

x/y or $x \div y$ x divided by y

x^n x to power n; the product $xx \ldots$ to n factors; nth power of x

$\sqrt{x} = x^{1/2}$ square root of x

$\sqrt[n]{x} = x^{1/n}$ nth root of x

$x^{-n} = \dfrac{1}{x^n}$ reciprocal of nth power of x

$|x|$ absolute value of x (sign ignored)

Σx summed values of variable x

$\displaystyle\sum_{i=1}^{n} x_i$ summed values of variable x over range x_1 to x_n inclusive

$x!$ factorial x; the product $1,2,3,\ldots x$

$P(n,x)$ $_nP_x$ number of permutations of x things from n

$C(n,x)$ $_nC_x$ ^nC_x number of combinations of x things from n

101_2 subscript $_2$ indicates binary number system

534_n subscript $_n$ indicates number system based on n

$\int f(x)dx$ indefinite integral of $f(x)$

$\displaystyle\int_a^b f(x)dx$ definite integral of $f(x)$ between limits $x=a$, $x=b$

Sets and Probability

A=B   set A equals set B

ε   is an element of

⊂   inclusion; A⊂B means set A is included in set B

∩(cap) conjunction, intersection; A∩B defines all elements included in *both* A and B

∪(cup) Union; A∪B defines all elements in A *plus* all elements in B, no element being counted twice

A′ or $\overline{A}$ negation; the set of all elements *not* in A

n(A)   number of elements in set A

U   universe of discourse, sample space; note that for any set A+A′=U=1

Φ( )   null or empty set
p(A)   probability of event A

p(A|B)   probability of event A, given B

General Rules
P(A∪B)=P(A)+P(B)−P(A∩B)

P(A∩B)=P(A).P(B|A)=P(B).P(A|B)

Statistics and Quantitative methods

μ   population mean

$\overline{x}$ sample mean

$Q_1 \ldots Q_n$ first ... nth quantile

cum x cumulative total of variable x

d.f.   degrees of freedom

χ^2 chi-squared

F F ratio

t   Student's t-statistic

n number in the sample

N   population size

s   sample standard deviation

s^2 sample variance

σ   population standard deviation

σ^2 population variance

$s/\overline{x}$ coefficient of variation

r   coefficient of correlation

r^2 (or R^2)   coefficient of determination

E(X)   expectation of X
= probability * pay off

p($X=x_1$)   probability that X equals x_1

Distributions

Normal Distribution

$$Z = \frac{x-\mu}{\sigma}$$

Descriptive Statistics
Arithmetic Mean

$$\bar{x} = \frac{\Sigma x}{n} \quad or \quad \bar{x} = \frac{\Sigma f x}{\Sigma f}$$

Standard Deviation

$$SD = \sqrt{\frac{\Sigma(x-\bar{x})^2}{n-1}} \quad or \quad \sqrt{\frac{\Sigma(x-\bar{x})^2}{n}}$$

if n is 'large'.

$$SD = \sqrt{\frac{\Sigma f x^2}{\Sigma f} - \bar{x}^2} \quad \text{(frequency distribution)}$$

Index numbers

Laspeyres quantity $\quad 100 \times \dfrac{\Sigma Q_1 P_0}{\Sigma Q_0 P_0}$

Paasche quantity $\quad 100 \times \dfrac{\Sigma Q_1 P_1}{\Sigma Q_0 P_1}$

Laspeyres price $\quad 100 \times \dfrac{\Sigma Q_0 P_1}{\Sigma Q_0 P_0}$

Paasche price $\quad 100 \times \dfrac{\Sigma Q_1 P_1}{\Sigma Q_1 P_0}$

Time series

Additive Model:
   Series = Trend + Seasonal + Random

Multiplicative Model:
   Series = Trend * Seasonal * Random

Statistical inference
Estimated Standard Errors —

Sample mean: $\quad \dfrac{s}{\sqrt{n}}$

Sample proportion: $\sqrt{\dfrac{pq}{n}}$

Regression Analysis
The linear regression equation of Y on X is given by:

$Y = a + bX \quad or$
$Y - \bar{Y} = b(X - \bar{X})$, where

$$b = \frac{\text{Covariance (XY)}}{\text{Variance (X)}} = \frac{n\Sigma XY - (\Sigma X)(\Sigma Y)}{n\Sigma X^2 - (\Sigma X)^2}$$

and $a = \bar{Y} - b\bar{X}$,
or solve $\Sigma Y = na + b\Sigma X$
$\quad\quad \Sigma XY = a\Sigma X + b\Sigma X^2$

Exponential $\quad Y = ab^x$
Geometric $\quad Y = aX^b$

Coefficient of Correlation (r)

$$r = \frac{\text{Covariance (XY)}}{\sqrt{VAR(X).VAR(Y)}}$$

$$= \frac{n\Sigma XY - (\Sigma X)(\Sigma Y)}{\sqrt{\{n\Sigma X^2 - (\Sigma X)^2\}\{n\Sigma Y^2 - (\Sigma Y)^2\}}}$$

15. FINANCIAL MATHEMATICS

GENERAL

Annuity

The value of annuity of £1 per period for t years (t-year annuity factor) is:

$$PV = \frac{1}{r} - \frac{1}{r(1+r)^t}$$

Perpetuity

The value of a perpetuity of £1 per year is:

$$PV = \frac{1}{r}$$

Growing Perpetuity (Gordon model)

If the initial cash flow is £1 at year 1 and if cash flows thereafter grow at a constant rate of g in perpetuity,

$$PV = \frac{1}{r-g}$$

Values and Sums

The value, V, attained by a single sum X, after n periods at $r\%$ is

$$V = X(1+r)^n$$

The sum, S, of a geometric series of n terms, with first term A and common ratio R, is

$$S = A + AR + AR^2 + AR^3 + \ldots + AR^{n-1}$$

$$S = A\frac{(R^n - 1)}{R-1}$$

Equivalent Annual Cost

An asset with a life of t years has an equivalent annual cost of:

$$\frac{PV\ (costs)}{t\text{-year annuity factor}}$$

1 INTRODUCTION TO COST ACCOUNTING

INTRODUCTION & LEARNING OBJECTIVES

Syllabus area 2a. How and why costs are classified. (Ability required 2).

Cost behaviour. (Ability required 2).

In this chapter the basic principles of cost accounting and why it exists will be introduced. Much of the chapter concentrates on the terminology that will be encountered throughout cost accounting studies and in particular on the different classifications and definitions of costs.

When you have studied this chapter you should be able to do the following:

- Understand the need for cost accounting as well as financial accounting.

- Be able to classify costs as direct or indirect and according to their function or activity group.

- Understand the terminology of cost centres and cost units.

- Be able to identify costs as fixed, variable, semi-fixed or semi-variable.

1 COST ACCOUNTING

1.1 Financial, cost and management accounting

The financial accounts record transactions between the business and its customers, suppliers, employees and owners, eg, shareholders. The managers of the business must account for the way in which funds entrusted to them have been used and, therefore, records of assets and liabilities are required as well as a statement of any increase in the total wealth of the business. This is done by presenting a balance sheet and a profit and loss account at least once a year.

However, in performing their task, managers will need to know a great deal about the detailed workings of the business. This knowledge must embrace production methods and the cost of processes, products etc.

Cost accounting involves the application of a comprehensive set of principles, methods and techniques to the determination and appropriate analysis of costs to suit the various parts of the organisation structure within a business.

Cost accounting is defined in the **CIMA Official Terminology** as:

'The establishment of budgets, standard costs and actual costs of operations, processes, activities or products; and the analysis of variances, profitability or the social use of funds'.

Management accounting is a wider concept involving professional knowledge and skill in the preparation and particularly the presentation of information to all levels of management in the organisation structure. The source of such information is the financial and cost accounts. The information is intended to assist management in its policy and decision-making, planning and control activities.

1.2   Financial accounts and management

It may be helpful at this stage to examine a simple set of financial accounts to consider the work of the cost accountant:

XYZ Company
Trading and profit and loss account

	£	£
Sales		200,000
Cost of sales:		
Materials consumed	80,000	
Wages	40,000	
Production expenses	15,000	
		135,000
Gross profit		65,000
Marketing expenses	15,000	
General administrative expenses	10,000	
Financing costs	4,000	
		29,000
Net profit		36,000

This statement may be adequate to provide outsiders with a superficial picture of the trading results of the whole business, but it is obvious that managers would need much more detail to answer questions such as:

(a)   What are the major products and which are most profitable?
(b)   How much have stocks of raw materials increased?
(c)   How does labour cost per unit compare with the last period?
(d)   Are personnel department expenses more than expected?

The cost accountant will aim to maintain a system which will provide the answers to these (and many other) questions on a regular and ad hoc basis. In addition, the cost accounts will contain detailed information concerning stocks of raw materials, work in progress and finished goods as a basis for the valuation necessary to prepare final accounts.

1.3   Cost ascertainment

Cost accounting systems are primarily designed to ascertain costs: costs of operating identifiable sections of the business and the cost of output products or units or service. The system thus represents a **data bank** which can be referred to and adapted to suit the needs of people throughout the organisation. In developing a system, guidelines should be recognised so that the basic objective does not become obscured:

(a)   **Utility of information** - procedures involved in cost accounting should be examined to confirm that the information provided is of specific benefit, ie, it is uneconomic to carry out analysis and presentation on the basis that 'it may be useful to someone at some time'.

(b)   **Accuracy and expedience** - the cost of obtaining a high degree of accuracy must be measured against the purpose of the exercise. To take an extreme example, it would be possible (in theory) to ascertain the cost of each nut and bolt used on a particular job of work but it is unlikely that such a precise calculation would be necessary.

(c)   **Actual cost** - you are advised to avoid thinking in terms of **actual costs**. The concept is entirely theoretical, since in ascertaining the cost of a cost centre or cost unit, many estimates will be made based upon experienced judgement. The charge for depreciation is an obvious example, but the charge for materials also depends upon the pricing method used, as will be shown later. Many overheads are arbitrarily apportioned to cost centres and a cost per unit will depend upon the number of units used as the denominator.

(d)   **Normality** - costs will be used for a variety of purposes eg, settling selling prices or choosing between alternative production methods. Unless a distinction is made between normal and abnormal costs, the information may be misleading.

1.4   Benefits of cost accounting

The overriding benefit is the provision of information which can be used specifically to:

(a)   disclose profitable and unprofitable activities;
(b)   identify waste and inefficiency;
(c)   analyse movements in profit;
(d)   estimate and fix selling prices;
(e)   value stocks;
(f)   develop budgets and standards to assist planning and control;
(g)   evaluate the cost effects of policy decisions.

1.5   Costing principles, techniques and methods

The following diagram provides a summary.

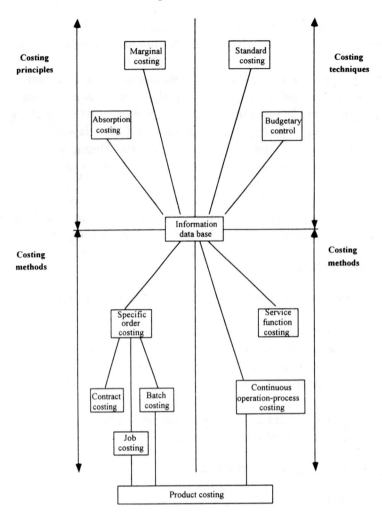

All of the principles, and some of the methods, are studied in this course.

2   ANALYSIS OF COSTS

2.1   Cost units

At this stage, it is helpful to consider cost accounting procedures in relation to a single aim:

> ascertaining the cost of the output/product of the business

Definition   A cost unit is a unit of product or service in relation to which costs are ascertained.

The physical measure of product or service for which costs can be determined, is a cost unit. In a printing firm, the cost unit would be the specific customer order. For a paint manufacturer, the unit would be a litre (or a thousand litres) of paint.

The ascertainment of the cost per cost unit is important for a variety of reasons:

(a)   making decisions about pricing, acceptance of orders, and so on
(b)   measuring changes in costs and relative levels of efficiency
(c)   inventory valuation for financial reporting
(d)   planning future costs (budgeting and standard costs).

The process of ascertaining unit costs involves analysis, classification and grouping of costs. In the remainder of this section, we will introduce the main terms encountered in cost accounting.

2.2   Examples of cost units

Industry or activity	Cost unit
Manufacturing industries	
Brewers	Barrel/hectolitre
Brick-making	1,000 bricks
Coal mining	Ton/tonne
Paper	Ream
Sand and gravel	Cubic yard/metre
Service industries	
Hospitals	(a) Bed occupied
	(b) Out-patient
Professional service eg, accountants	Chargeable man-hour
Individual departments	
Personnel departments and welfare	Employee
Materials storage/handling	(a) Requisition units issued/received
	(b) Material movement values issued/received

2.3   Cost classification

Classification is a means of analysing costs into logical groups so that they may be summarised into meaningful information for management.

Management will require information concerning a variety of issues, each of which may require different cost summaries, for example costs may be required for a particular department, or for a product. For this reason there are many different classifications of cost which may be used - these are explained below.

2.4   Elements of cost

The initial classification of costs is according to the **elements** upon which expenditure is incurred:

(a)   Materials
(b)   Labour
(c)   Services.

Within cost elements, costs can be further classified according to the **nature** of expenditure. This is the usual analysis in a financial accounting system, eg, raw materials, consumable stores, wages, salaries, rent, rates, depreciation.

2.5   Direct and indirect costs

The following definitions are taken from the CIMA *Official Terminology*:

Definition   A direct cost is expenditure which can be economically identified with and specifically measured in respect to a relevant cost object.

Definition   Prime cost is the total cost of direct material, direct labour and direct expenses.

Definition | An overhead or indirect cost is expenditure on labour, materials or services which cannot be economically identified with a specific saleable cost unit.

Summary

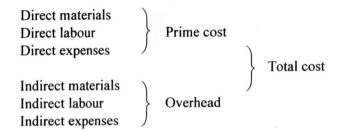

To ascertain the total cost of a cost unit, indirect costs are allotted to cost centres and cost centre costs are shared over (absorbed by) cost units. The subject of allotment and absorption of overhead costs is explained later.

2.6   Activity

Consider direct and indirect costs and note down in particular the types of factors that are likely to influence whether a cost is treated as direct or indirect in relation to a cost unit.

2.7   Activity solution

Direct costs are all costs which are 'physically traceable to the finished goods in an economically feasible manner' (CT Horngren). All other costs are indirect. There are several factors which will affect whether a cost is direct or whether it is treated as being indirect. For example, as the definition suggests, certain costs may be traceable to finished goods but it may not be economically worthwhile to do so.

If the cost unit is very large, eg, contract costing, then the majority of costs, including depreciation of plant and machinery and foreman's salary will be direct costs for a particular contract. For 'small' cost units where for example, cost units are processed on a machine, the depreciation of the machine is not traceable to individual cost units. It would, therefore, be treated as production overhead and included in unit cost via the overhead absorption rate.

Another cost which may be direct or indirect is overtime premium. It may be possible to, for example, trace which jobs are carried out during overtime hours, and charge the premium to those jobs. However, if overtime is worked to increase the overall volume of production it would not be equitable to charge the premium to certain units. The premium would therefore be treated as a production overhead unless the overtime is worked at the specific request of a customer in which case it would be treated as direct.

Hence, whether costs are direct or indirect depends on the individual circumstances.

2.8   Functional analysis of cost

Overheads are usually categorised into the principal activity groups:

(a)   manufacturing;
(b)   administration;
(c)   selling;
(d)   distribution;

(e)   research.

Prime costs are usually regarded as being solely related to manufacturing, and so are not classified.

2.9   Manufacturing and service industries

Whereas manufacturing industries are concerned with converting raw materials into a product which they sell, service industries do not have a manufactured output. Instead, their output consists of services to a customer. Nevertheless, in the process of providing such services, they may use considerable quantities of consumable materials.

Since there is no manufacturing element, service industries cannot have factory, prime or overhead costs.

2.10   Cost centres

> **Definition**   A cost centre is a production or service location, function, activity or item of equipment for which costs are accumulated (**CIMA Official Terminology**).

A **cost centre** is a small part of a business in respect of which costs may be determined and then related to cost units. Terminology varies from organisation to organisation, but the small part of a business could be a whole department or merely a sub-division of a department. A number of departments together would comprise a function. Thus a cost centre could be a location, function or item of equipment or a group or combination of any of these.

It is important to recognise that the ascertainment of cost centre costs, apart from the aspect of calculating unit costs, is necessary for control purposes.

The terms **direct** and **indirect** may be used in relation to a cost centre. For example, a supervisor's salary would be a direct charge to the cost centre in which he is employed, whereas rent would need to be shared between a number of cost centres. Both of these items are, of course, indirect as regards specific cost units.

2.11   Basic costing methods

Two fundamental types of business activity exist - where the cost is unique, eg a job made to the customer's specification; or where cost units are identical or basically similar, eg, cans of paint. Consequently basic costing methods fall into two categories:

(a)   specific order costing;
(b)   operation costing.

Specific order costing is applicable where the work consists of separate contracts, jobs or batches, each of which is authorised by a specific order or contract. The type of business applicable to operation costing is where standardised goods or services are produced by repetition. The crucial test in deciding if operation costing is appropriate is whether unit costs are ascertained by dividing cost for a period by the units produced in that period.

2.12   Activity

Give some examples of business activities where each of specific order costing and operation costing would be appropriate.

2.13   Activity solution

Specific order	*Operation*
Building contractor	Oil refining
Printer	Food processing
Specialist aircraft equipment	Power generation

2.14   Further analysis of costing methods

In subsequent studies these two basic costing methods are further sub-divided into major costing methods, so that **job, batch** and **contract** costing are three types of application of the more general **specific order** costing.

Operation costing can be split into **process** and **service** costing.

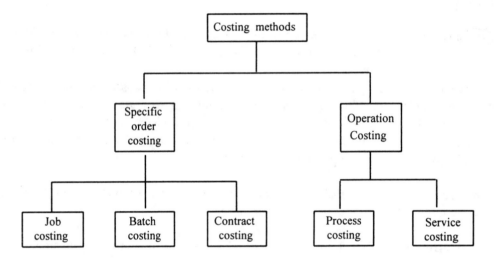

3   COST BEHAVIOUR

3.1   Total cost

It has been shown that production cost comprises three elements - materials, wages and expenses; it can also be noted that production cost includes both fixed and variable segment elements. It is useful to look at the way costs behave in response to changes in production volume.

Definition   Cost behaviour is the variability of input costs with activity undertaken (**CIMA Official Terminology**).

3.2   Example

	Production	
	500 units	*1,000 units*
	£	£
Sales (@ £3 per unit)	1,500	3,000
Total costs	1,000	1,500
Profit	500	1,500
Average unit cost	£2.00	£1.50
Average unit profit	£1.00	£1.50

Total costs have increased by only 50% although production has doubled. This is because some costs will not rise in relation to the increase in volume.

Suppose the product is widgets and the only costs are:

(a)   rental of a fully equipped factory, £500 pa;

(b)   raw materials, £1 per widget.

3.3   Solution

Then the way these two costs react to producing varying numbers of widgets is as follows:

(a)   **Factory rental - a fixed cost**

Although production rises, the same rent is payable.

Definition   A fixed cost is a cost which is incurred for an accounting period, and which, within certain output or turnover limits, tends to be unaffected by fluctuations in the levels of activity (output or turnover) **(CIMA Official Terminology)**

Graph showing relationship between rent and output

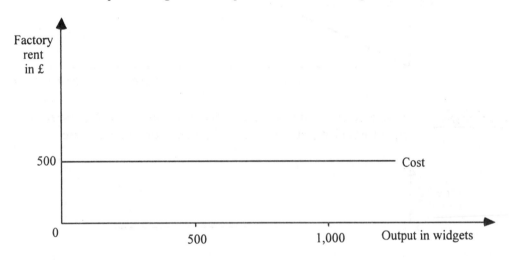

This may be also shown by plotting the average fixed cost per unit on a graph.

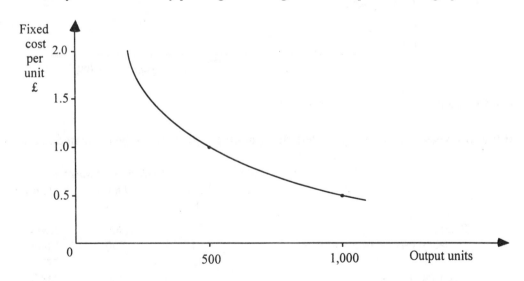

Conclusion   As output increases, unit fixed costs decline.

This only changes if a new or larger factory is rented.

(b)   Raw materials - a variable cost

Every widget has a raw material cost of £1; therefore, the cost varies directly with the level of production.

Definition   A variable cost is a cost which varies with a measure of activity. **(CIMA Official Terminology)**.

Graph showing relationship between raw materials, costs and output

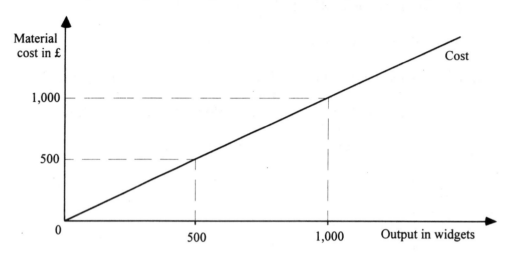

Conclusion   In the case of variable costs unit cost remains constant irrespective of the level of output (provided that there are no discounts for bulk purchase).

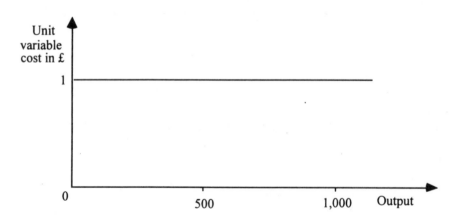

3.4   Contribution

If the two types of cost are segregated, the operating statement can be presented in a different way:

| | Production of widgets | | |
| | *1 unit* | *500 units* | *1,000 units* |
	£	*£*	*£*
Sales	3	1,500	3,000
Variable costs - Raw materials	1	500	1,000
Contribution	2	1,000	2,000
Fixed costs - Factory rent	500	500	500
Profit/(loss)	(498)	500	1,500

The revised presentation is based on the concept that each unit sold **contributes** a selling price less the variable cost per unit. Total contribution provides a fund to cover fixed costs and net profit.

Definition   Contribution is the sales value less variable cost of sales. **(CIMA Official Terminology).**

Thus: Sales – Variable cost of sales =   Contribution
        Contribution – Fixed costs   =   Net profit

Note that unit contribution is a constant number unless prices or the specification for variable costs change.

Conclusion   As output increases total unit costs gravitate towards the unit variable cost:

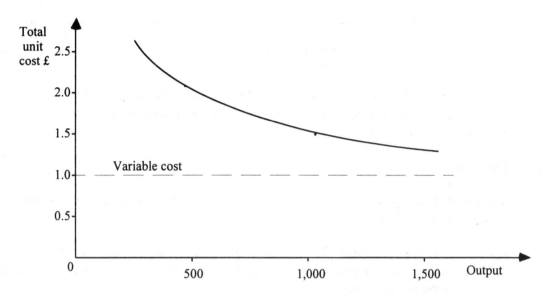

3.5   Relevant range of activity

The analysis of cost behaviour is only appropriate when considering the kind of movement in activity which could reasonably be expected, ie, within the relevant range of volume (output) levels. A number of simplifying assumptions are, therefore, usually made.

3.6   Costs which change per unit

When buying items such as tyres, it is normal to obtain special prices for larger orders. Thus, the more tyres ordered, the lower the price paid for each tyre.

Graph showing relationship between the total cost of tyres and the output of cars

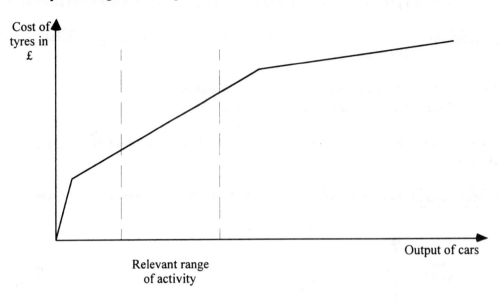

However, in practice it is likely that only relatively limited changes in the level of production will be considered. This is described as the **relevant range of activity**, and within that range unit prices are likely to be constant.

3.7   Step costs

Some costs rise in a series of steps. Large steps (renting a second factory) or small steps (renting a typewriter) may occur.

(a)   If the steps are large, the concept of the relevant range of activity usually applies ie, only occasionally is a new factory considered and therefore one can assume the cost to be fixed for the relevant range.

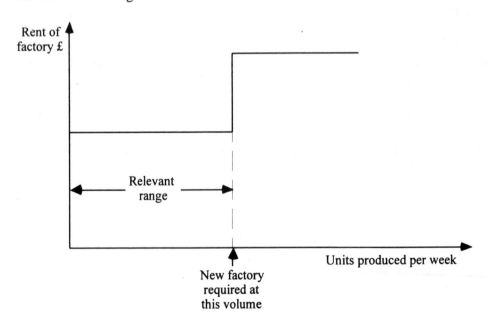

(b)   If the steps are small they may be ignored, ie, the cost may be treated as a variable cost.

Graph showing relationship between total rent of typewriters and output

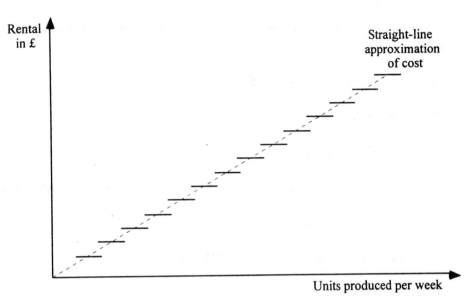

3.8   Semi-variable costs (also referred to as semi-fixed costs)

Definition   A semi-variable cost is a cost containing both fixed and variable components and which is thus partly affected by a change in the level of activity **(CIMA Official Terminology)**.

An example is maintenance costs: even at zero output **standby** maintenance costs are incurred. As output rises so do maintenance costs.

Graph showing relationship between machine maintenance costs and output

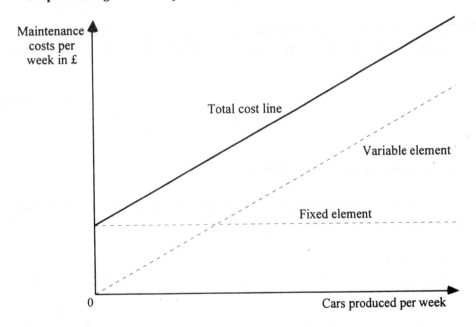

4   CHAPTER SUMMARY

This chapter was an important introduction to much of the terminology involved in dealing with costs and cost accounting. In order to understand cost accounting processes it is vital that an understanding is gained of the different types of costs and the different possible classifications and groupings of those costs.

5   SELF TEST QUESTIONS

5.1   What guidelines should be recognised in the development of a cost accounting system? (1.3)

5.2   Name two costing techniques (1.5)

5.3   What is a cost unit? (2.1)

5.4   What are indirect costs? (2.5)

5.5   What are the principal activity groups into which overheads are usually categorised? (2.8)

5.6   What are the three types of specific order costing? (2.14)

5.7   What are the two types of operation costing? (2.14)

5.8   What is a fixed cost? (3.3)

5.9   What is the effect on variable cost per unit of output increasing? (3.3)

5.10   What are step costs? (3.7)

6   EXAMINATION TYPE QUESTIONS

6.1   Definitions

(a)   Define the terms 'cost centre' and 'cost unit'.

(4 marks)

(b)   Distinguish between direct and indirect costs and discuss the factors which should influence whether a particular cost is treated as direct or indirect in relation to a cost unit.

(7 marks)

(Total: 11 marks)

6.2   Classify

A company manufactures and retails clothing.

Group the costs which are listed as (1) - (10) below into the following classifications (each cost is intended to belong to only one classification):

(i)   direct materials;

(ii)   direct labour;

(iii)   direct expenses;

(iv)   indirect production overhead;

(v)   research and development costs;

(vi)   selling and distribution costs;

(vii)   administration costs; and

(viii)   finance costs.

(1)   lubricant for sewing machines;

(2)   floppy discs for general office computer;

(3)   wages of operatives in the cutting department;;

(4)   telephone rental plus metered calls;

(5)   interest on bank overdraft;

(6)   Performing Rights Society charge for music broadcast throughout the factory;

(7)   market research undertaken prior to a new product launch;

(8)   wages of security guards for factory;

(9)   carriage on purchases of basic raw material;

(10)   royalty payable on number of units of product XY produced;

7   ANSWERS TO EXAMINATION TYPE QUESTIONS

7.1   Definitions

(a)   A **cost centre** is a production or service location, function, activity or item of equipment for which costs are accumulated. **(CIMA Official Terminology)**

A **cost unit** is a unit of product or service in relation to which costs are ascertained. **(CIMA Official Terminology).**

(b)   **Direct costs** are items of expenditure which can be economically identified with and specifically measured in respect to a relevant cost object **(CIMA Official Terminology).**

There are several factors which will affect whether a cost is direct or whether it is treated as being direct. For example, as the definition suggests, certain costs may be traceable to finished goods but it may not be economically worthwhile to do so.

If the cost unit is very large eg, contract costing, then the majority of costs, including depreciation of plant and machinery and foreman's salary will be direct costs for a particular contract. For 'small' cost units where for example, cost units are processed on a machine, the depreciation of the machine is not traceable to individual cost units. It would, therefore, be treated as production overhead and included in unit cost via the overhead absorption rate.

Another cost which may be direct or indirect is overtime premium. It may be possible to, for example, trace which jobs are carried out during overtime hours, and charge the premium to those jobs. However, if overtime is worked to increase the overall volume of production it would be equitable to charge the premium to certain units. The premium would, therefore, be treated as production overhead unless the overtime is worked at the specific request of a customer in which it would be treated as direct.

Hence, whether costs are direct or indirect depends on the individual circumstances.

7.2   Classify

Cost number	Classification number
1	iv
2	vii
3	ii
4	vii
5	viii
6	iv
7	vi
8	iv
9	i or iv
10	iii

2 MATERIALS

INTRODUCTION & LEARNING OBJECTIVES

Syllabus area 2a. Materials: cost collection. (Ability required 3).

Stock valuation methods : the effect on profit of the valuation method selected. (Ability required 3).

In this chapter consideration will be given to the control of and accounting for the materials purchases of an organisation. This ranges from the initial order, purchase and receipt of goods through to the storekeeping function, recording of receipts and classification and coding of materials.

When you have studied this chapter you should be able to do the following:

- Understand the processes required for the order, purchase, receipt and storage of goods.
- Understand and be able to draw up a stores ledger card.
- Calculate the value of goods transferred to production and closing stock using a variety of different methods.
- Be able to compare the different methods of stock valuation.
- Describe how materials might be classified and coded.

---

1 CONTROL OF MATERIALS

1.1 Types of materials

In a manufacturing business, materials purchased fall into three main categories:

(a) raw materials from which the product is made eg, sheet steel from which car body sections are made;

(b) consumable stores used in production eg, grease, nuts, screws;

(c) materials used in operating the business as opposed to making the product eg, machine parts and fuel for power generation.

Categories (b) and (c) are generally treated as indirect materials which form part of overhead costs, so the remainder of this chapter will concentrate on the costing and control procedures relating to direct materials.

1.2 Procedures and documentation for purchasing materials

Materials can form the largest single item of cost so it is essential that the material purchased is the most suitable for the intended purpose from the aspects of utility and cost. Purchasing a great variety of materials is expensive and ideally the business should seek to use standard materials wherever possible; classification and coding of all materials used will help to this end.

1.3   Purchase requisition

It is important to control the placing of orders with suppliers which normally is centralised in the purchasing department.   Any request for material must therefore be made on a **purchase requisition**. The purchasing manager will verify that requisitions are authorised in accordance with established policy before placing orders.

1.4   Specimen purchase requisition

PURCHASE REQUISITION								
Date 19						Serial No:		
Purpose*: stock/special production/consumables capital equipment/ (budget reference *Delete as appropriate.								
Quantity and units	Description	Material code	Job or dept. code	Delivery required		Purchase order		
				Date	Place	No.	Date	Supplier
Origination department: . . . . Authorisation								

1.5   Ordering procedure

On receipt of a properly authorised requisition, the purchasing manager will select a supplier and place an order. The selection will be based upon price, delivery promise, quality and past performance.

1.6 Specimen purchase order

PURCHASE ORDER

To: . . . . Serial No: . . . .

. . . . Date: . . . .

. . . . Purchase Req. No: . . . .

Please supply, in accordance with the attached conditions of purchase

Quantity	Description	Code	Delivery date	Price	Per

Your quotation . . . .

To be delivered, carriage paid, to . . . . Terms

Please quote our Purchase Order number on all correspondence, advice notes, and invoices

For ABC Ltd

. . . .

Buyer

A copy of the purchase order is sent to the goods receiving department as confirmation of expected delivery.

If a supplier fails to meet a delivery promise, sections of the factory may be brought to a standstill and prevent the company from keeping its delivery promises to its own customers. It is essential that close contact is maintained with suppliers to obtain advance warning of delayed delivery.

1.7 Goods receiving procedure

When goods are received, the goods receiving department will:

(i)   determine what they are, in terms of quantity, apparent quality, the supplier and purchase order number to which they relate;

(ii)   check the advice or delivery note accompanying the materials to see that it agrees with the goods sent and then check the order copy to see that the goods are as ordered. Full details of the goods are entered on a **goods received note (GRN)**.

1.8 Activity

Design a goods received note.

1.9   Activity solution

GOODS RECEIVED NOTE				
Supplier:		Serial No:		
. . . .		Date issued:		
Carrier:		Purchase Order No:		
Date of delivery:				

Description	Code	Quantity	Packages	Gross weight

INSPECTION REPORT			Received by:	
Quantity passed	Quantity rejected	Remarks	Required by:	
Inspector . . . . Date			Accepted: . . . . Date:	

The goods received note (GRN) is the basis for entering receipts in the stores record.

Certain goods will need to be critically inspected and/or possibly chemically analysed. Normally inspection will be on a sampling basis ie, a number of items selected at random will be investigated and checked against the detailed specification in the purchase order.

1.10   Purchase invoices

A copy of the GRN will be sent to the purchasing department attached to the copy purchase order. When the supplier's invoice is received, the three documents will be passed to the appropriate individual to approve payment of the invoice.

1.11   Storekeeping and storage

The storekeeper is responsible for ensuring that materials are accessible for use, protected from deterioration, fire and theft, and handled economically. To those ends an efficient stores layout is essential, the principles of which are:

(a)   Materials should be close to the point where they are most frequently used.

(b)   Racks and gangways should be so arranged that mechanical handling equipment is able to gain easy access to any point.

(c)   Since floor space is expensive, use should be made of the height of the stores.

(d)   Materials should be packed in the normal quantities that are issued, eg, a dozen, hundred, gross, etc.

(e)   Use should be made of pallets so that materials can be put into store and removed on the same pallet by fork-lift trucks, etc.

(f)   Racks and bins must be properly labelled to ensure identification of the materials.

(g)   Materials must be put into store in such a way that old stocks are issued first.

(h)   Bulk materials must be stored in such a way that an assessment of the quantity in stock is facilitated. Thus, instead of putting all the material in a large heap, it should be arranged in a number of smaller heaps of known quantity.

(i)   Materials that move relatively slowly can be stored in close-packed racks which are arranged on rails so that those at the front move from side to side to give access to racks at the rear.

Since some of the above principles may in practice conflict, relative benefits need assessment before a given layout is adopted.

1.12   Internal transport and mechanical handling

Handling of materials can be costly and is to be avoided where possible. Gravity feed and conveyor belt production lines will be employed where the nature of the materials and production methods make them appropriate. The location of stores in relation to factory departments will be a vital factor in handling arrangements and careful planning is essential when a factory is first set up. The stores manager is often made responsible for internal transport, but the whole area of material handling is really a specialist subject. When material is moved from point A to point B, it is necessary to consider the eventual operation and disposal of material at point B. It is costly to load material in small units onto a truck, move it, work on it and then load it again for further movement. A study of related movement and operations and the use of pallets can lead to great savings.

1.13   Centralised, decentralised and sub-stores

Each business will have factors peculiar to itself that will favour a central store or many sub-stores. In many cases management will decide to keep some materials centrally - probably those of high value - and others on a decentralised basis. Materials of small value but of rapid turnover would probably be kept in sub-stores. The advantages of having departmental sub-stores in addition to the main store are:

(a)   the cost of internal transport is minimised, materials being transported in bulk between the main and sub-stores;

(b)   materials are stored in the department using them: thereby specialist technical knowledge is on hand;

(c)   batching of materials or components for manufacture or assembly may be carried out in advance.

The disadvantages are:

(a)   increased staffing and therefore an increase in indirect labour cost;

(b)   supervision of storekeepers is more difficult;

(c)   larger stocks may be carried because buffer stock of the same item is required in a number of sub-stores entailing increased storage space, additional working capital, increased administration costs and greater risks;

(d)   a physical stocktake is more complex.

1.14   Use of bin cards

Definition   A bin card is a record of receipts, issues and balances of the quantity of an item of stock handled by a store. **(CIMA Official Terminology)**

The bin card is a duplication of the quantity information recorded in the stores ledger but storekeepers frequently find that such a ready record is a very useful aid in carrying out their duties.

1.15   Materials requisition and issues

Materials issued to production departments (and to other departments for internal use) are controlled by a materials requisition. This document performs two functions - it authorises the storekeeper to release the goods and acts as a posting medium to the stores ledger and bin card.

1.16   Specimen materials requisition

			Cost office only				
Code No.	Description	Quantity or weight	Rate	Unit	£	£	Stores ledger

MATERIAL REQUISITION   Serial No: . . . .

Charge Job/ Cost Centre No: . . . .   Date: . . . .

Authorised by:	Storekeeper:	Prices entered by:
Received by:	Bin card entered:	Calculations checked:

When unused materials are returned to store, the transaction will be recorded on a document of similar format to the materials requisition but printed in a different colour.

Similarly, materials which are transferred from one production order to another (or from one department to another) should be documented for control and accounting purposes.

Items such as nails and screws are in theory direct materials which could be related to specific production orders, but they are usually treated as overhead costs of the production department. A bulk requisition would be placed to cover the requirements for a period.

2   ACCOUNTING FOR MATERIALS: COST COLLECTION

2.1   Stores ledger

Accounting for direct materials is carried out in the stores ledger, which contains a detailed record for each class of material handled. The ledger may be in the form of a loose-leaf binder, a card index or, more commonly perhaps, a computer print-out.

This record of materials is often referred to as a 'perpetual inventory'.

Definition   Perpetual inventory is the recording **as they occur** of receipts, issues, and the resulting balances of individual items of stock in either quantity or quantity and value.

2.2   Specimen stores ledger card

STORES LEDGER CARD									
Description . . . . Unit . . . . .Location . . . . Code									
Maximum . . . . Minimum . . . . Reorder level . . . . Reorder quantity									
Receipts			Issues				On order		
Date	Ref.	Quantity	Date	Ref.	Quantity	Physical balance	Date	Ref.	Quantity

In the above illustration values have been omitted. Materials are frequently valued at standard or predetermined prices; this allows value columns to be dispensed with.

The stores ledger, in addition to its function as part of the cost accounting system, is the basis for stock control procedures (see below).

2.3   Direct materials cost

In theory the cost of materials received is obtained from the supplier's invoice, but the inevitable time-lag between receipt of the goods and paying the invoice would make the stores ledger out of date as a basis for information. Consequently, receipts are posted to the ledger from GRNs; actual prices, if required, are transcribed from purchase orders.

The value of receipts includes any related costs incurred, such as customs duty, carriage and packaging. Where an extra charge covers several items of material, the charge would be apportioned on an equitable basis, probably by weight. If such charges are not significant in relation to the actual cost of materials, they may be treated as indirect costs.

2.4   Example

An invoice of £500 for carriage covers a delivery of Material A (cost £2,000), Material B (cost £3,000) and Material C (cost £5,000); carriage represents 5% of materials cost. The value of the receipts posted to the stores ledger might be:

	£	£	£
Material A	2,000 +	100 =	2,100
Material B	3,000 +	150 =	3,150
Material C	5,000 +	250 =	5,250
	10,000	500	10,500

If, however, the carriage cost was £50 not £500, it would probably be treated not as part of materials cost, but as an overhead cost (see below) of the receiving cost centre.

2.5   Allocating direct materials cost to production

If materials were purchased exactly as required for production, the cost of a particular consignment could be immediately attributed to a specific job or production order. Frequently, however, materials are purchased in large quantities at different prices and issued to production in smaller lots. In attempting to ascertain unit costs of output, therefore, the cost accountant is faced with the problem of identifying the material cost of a particular issue.

2.6   Stock valuation methods (issue pricing)

There are five different methods which may be used by the cost accountant in order to solve the problem of allocating direct materials cost to production. The five methods are:-

- FIFO (first in, first out)
- LIFO (last in, first out)
- Weighted average cost
- NIFO (next in, first out)
- Standard cost

The following example is used to illustrate each of these methods.

2.7   Example

In November 1,000 tonnes of 'Grotti' were purchased in three lots:

3 November	400 tonnes at £60 per tonne
11 November	300 tonnes at £70 per tonne
21 November	300 tonnes at £80 per tonne

During the same period four materials requisitions were completed for 200 tonnes each, on 5, 14, 22 and 27 November.

In order to calculate the actual material cost of each requisition the cost accountant would need to identify physically from which consignment(s) each issued batch of 200 was drawn. Such precision is uneconomic as well as impractical, so a conventional method of pricing materials issues is adopted.

Using the data in the above example, the following sub-sections will examine and illustrate the conventional methods which are available and how they are applied. The methods which will be examined are:

- (a)   first in first out (FIFO) price;
- (b)   last in first out (LIFO) price;
- (c)   weighted average price;
- (d)   next in first out (NIFO) price;
- (e)   standard cost.

2.8   Solution - First in first out (FIFO) price

Each issue is valued at the price paid for the material first taken into the stocks from which the issue could have been drawn.

The stores ledger account (in abbreviated form) would appear as below:

GROTTI

Date	Quantity	Price £	Value £	@ £60	@ £70	@ £80
3 Nov	400	60	24,000	400		
5 Nov	(200)	60	(12,000)	(200)		
11 Nov	300	70	21,000		300	
14 Nov	(200)	60	(12,000)	(200)		
21 Nov	300	80	24,000			300
22 Nov	(200)	70	(14,000)		(200)	
27 Nov	(200)	75	(15,000)		(100)	(100)
30 Nov (bal)	200	80	16,000	-	-	200

Receipts (issues) and *Balance (quantity)* are column group headers.

Conclusion Note that the value of the stock at 30 November is at the latest price. Note also that the balance at any time requires analysis by purchase price so that each consignment is exhausted before charging issues at the next price.

2.9 Solution - Last in first out (LIFO) price

Each issue is valued at the price paid for the material last taken into the stock from which the issue could have been drawn.

GROTTI

Date	Quantity	Price £	Value £	@ £60	@ £70	@ £80
3 Nov	400	60	24,000	400		
5 Nov	(200)	60	(12,000)	(200)		
11 Nov	300	70	21,000		300	
14 Nov	(200)	70	(14,000)		(200)	
21 Nov	300	80	24,000			300
22 Nov	(200)	80	(16,000)			(200)
27 Nov	(200)	75	(15,000)		(100)	(100)
30 Nov (bal)	200	60	12,000	200	-	-

Conclusion Under LIFO the closing stock is now valued at £60 per tonne, the earliest price. The issue on 27 November exhausts the latest receipt (at £80) so that the previous latest is used to price the remaining 100 tonnes issued.

2.10 Weighted average price

Each time a consignment is received a weighted average price is calculated as:

$$\frac{\text{Stock value} + \text{Receipt value}}{\text{Quantity in stock} + \text{Quantity received}}$$

The price so calculated is used to value subsequent issues until the next consignment is received.

GROTTI

Date	Quantity	Receipts (issues) Price	Value	Weighted average price
		£	£	£
3 Nov	400	60	24,000	
5 Nov	(200)	60	(12,000)	
11 Nov	300	70	21,000	
Balance	500		33,000	66
14 Nov	(200)	66	(13,200)	
21 Nov	300	80	24,000	
Balance	600		43,800	73
22 Nov	(200)	73	(14,600)	
27 Nov	(200)	73	(14,600)	
30 Nov (bal)	200	73	14,600	

A fresh calculation is required after each receipt but analysis of the balance is unnecessary.

In a computer system, where data is stored for, say, a month and then processed all at once, an average price for the month could be calculated and used to value all issues during the month, irrespective of sequence.

This average can be based on either of the following:

(a)   **Periodic simple average.** Average of all the prices of the period irrespective of quantity delivered (only used where prices do not fluctuate significantly).

(b)   **Periodic weighted average.** Average of all the prices of the period weighted by quantity delivered at each price.

For both alternatives, opening stock is treated as the first delivery of the month.

(a)   Periodic simple average $= \dfrac{£(60 + 70 + 80)}{3}$ $=$ £70 per tonne.

(b)   Periodic weighted average $= \dfrac{£(24,000 + 21,000 + 24,000)}{(400 + 300 + 300)} =$ £69 per tonne

The closing balance, 200 tonnes at £70 or at £69, would be treated as the first receipt in the following month to be included in that month's average.

2.11   Next in first out (NIFO) price

Under this method, each issue would be valued at the price which is assessed as the cost which will be paid for the next order to replace the materials issued at the date it is issued to production. Adjustments will be required to equate the issue values with the receipt value. Differences are adjusted in the costing ledger through a stock adjustment account.

Next order cost for period November 26-30 was £90.

		£	£
Cost of receipts:			
3 November	400 @ £60	24,000	
11 November	300 @ £70	21,000	
21 November	300 @ £80	24,000	
		——	
			69,000
Value of issues:			
5 November	200 @ £70	14,000	
14 November	200 @ £80	16,000	
22 November	200 @ £80	16,000	
27 November	200 @ £90	18,000	
Stock:			
30 November	200 @ £90	18,000	
		——	
			82,000
			——
Credit stock revaluation reserve			13,000

Conclusion   Note that next in first out is similar to **replacement cost accounting**. In replacement cost accounting each issue is valued at the cost which would be incurred to replace the materials at the **date it is issued to production**. If stock is reordered at frequent intervals this price will be the same as the next order price.

2.12   Standard cost

Issues to production and stock balances would be valued at their standard price or cost. Differences between the actual price and the standard price of purchases are accumulated in a separate **variance account** for action outside the stores ledger system.

The method avoids the fluctuations in ascertaining material costs caused by timing and provides the considerable benefit of obviating the need to maintain value records in the stores ledger.

Standard cost is £70 per unit.

		£	£
Cost of receipts:			
3 November	400 @ £60	24,000	
11 November	300 @ £70	21,000	
21 November	300 @ £80	24,000	
		——	
			69,000
Value of issues	800 @ £70	56,000	
Stock	200 @ £70	14,000	
		——	
			70,000
			——
Credit materials price variance account			1,000

2.13   Activity

You are given the following information about one line of stock held by Tolley plc:

		Units	Cost £	Sales price £
Opening stock	1 January	50	7	
Purchase	1 February	60	8	
Sale	1 March	40		10
Purchase	1 April	70	9	
Sale	1 May	60		12

Assuming that there are no further transactions in the month of May, and that the replacement cost of the line at 31 May was £10, what would be the stock valuation at that date, using a FIFO valuation method?

2.14   Activity solution

FIFO results in later purchases remaining in stock.

	Units
Opening stock	50
Purchases	130
Sales	(100)
Closing stock	80

		£
Comprising		
1 April	70 × £9 =	630
1 February	10 × £8 =	80
		710

2.15   Comparison of methods - the effect on profit of the stock valuation method selected

The relative advantages and disadvantages of each system are discussed below, particularly in relation to inflationary situations which are now accepted as being normality.

2.16   FIFO

Advantage:

Produces realistic stock values.

Disadvantages:

(a)   Produces out of date production costs and therefore potentially overstates profits.

(b)   Complicates stock records as stock must be analysed by delivery.

2.17   LIFO

Advantage:

Produces realistic production costs and therefore more realistic/prudent profit figures.

Disadvantages:

(a)   Produces unrealistically low stock values.

(b)   Complicates stock records as stock must be analysed by delivery.

2.18   Weighted average price

Advantage:

Simple to operate - calculations within the stock records are minimised.

Disadvantage:

Produces both stock values and production costs which are far from current values.

2.19   NIFO

Advantage:

Produces stock values and production costs which are realistic.

Disadvantages:

(a)   The complexity and effort of estimating next order prices for each issue.

(b)   Adjustments to equate issue values with receipt values are required continuously.

(c)   The validity of the approach is part of the wider consideration of replacement cost accounting as opposed to actual cost ascertainment.

2.20   Standard cost

Advantage:

Simplifies stock records as no values need to be maintained.

Disadvantage:

Standard may not reflect current values: if so, stock values and production costs may be unrealistic.

2.21   Conclusion   Whichever method is adopted it should be applied consistently from period to period and its limitations should be recognised when material cost information is being used. For example, if FIFO is in use and a business is tendering for a special order, it may be dangerous to estimate on the basis of past costs. Such costs probably include the cost of materials purchased some time ago. Additionally, if selling prices are based on ascertained costs, the use of FIFO or weighted average price could lead to under-pricing, since costs may reflect out of date material prices.

Note that for financial accounting purposes, **SSAP 9** restricts the range of possible methods to FIFO and weighted average, with standard cost also being acceptable as long as it approximates to one of the first two methods.

2.22   Stock losses and waste

Stock losses may be quantified by comparing the physical quantity of an item held with the balance quantity recorded on the bin card and/or stores ledger card.

There are two categories of loss:-

- those which have occurred because of theft, pilferage, damage or similar means; and
- those which occur because of the breaking of bulk receipts into smaller quantities.

It is the second of these which are more commonly referred to as waste.

2.23   Accounting treatment of stock losses

Stock losses must be written off as soon as they occur against profits. If the value to be written off is significant then an investigation should be made of the cause.

2.24   Accounting treatment of waste

When waste occurs as a result of breaking bulk it is reasonable to expect that the extent of such wastage could be estimated in advance based upon past records. Two accounting treatments could then be used:-

- issues continue to be made and priced without any adjustment and the difference at the end of the period is written off; or

- the issue price is increased to compensate for the expected waste, for example:

Suppose that a 100 metre length of copper is bought for £99. The estimated loss caused by cutting into shorter lengths as required is 1%.

The issue price could be based on the expected issues of 99 metres ie, £1 per metre rather than pricing the copper at

$$\frac{£99}{100} \quad = \quad £0.99/\text{metre}$$

and then having to write off the loss of £1 when the 99 metres have been issued.

3   MATERIALS CLASSIFICATION AND CODING

3.1   Materials coding system

Where a business uses many types of material there are often at least two ways of describing any one material and a **coding system** becomes necessary.

Definition   A code is a system of symbols designed to be applied to a classified set of items to give a brief, accurate reference, facilitating entry, collation and analysis **(CIMA Official Terminology)**.

The advantages of using a materials code are:

(a)   clerical effort is reduced because the writing out of precise descriptions becomes unnecessary;

(b)   ambiguity is avoided because everyone knows what material is being referred to;

(c)   it becomes easier to refer to items and to categorise them;

(d)   it is normally essential when handling material data in mechanical or electronic processing systems.

3.2   Classifications of materials

Definition   Classification is the arrangement of items in logical groups having regard to their nature (subjective classification) or purpose (objective classification).   **(CIMA Official Terminology)**.

(a)   Raw materials - materials which are converted by production processes into a saleable product.

(b)   Packing materials - materials which do not form part of the product being sold but are necessary to enable the product to be distributed to the customer.

(c).   Maintenance materials - materials which are not required for production or distribution but are necessary to keep machines and plant in working order.

(d)   Patterns and tools - materials which do not form part of the product but are necessary in its production.

(e)   Other indirect materials - among these would be stationery, protective clothing, fuels, etc.

3.3   Allocation of code

The code may be allocated in ascending order, ie 1, 2, 3, 4, so that the actual code depends on when the material first came to be used. The disadvantage with this method is the danger that a material purchased in the past may be given another code because the coding clerk was not aware of its existence. This is a common problem where different descriptions may be given to the same material. The alternative is to code the material according to its characteristics. Careful analysis of each material is required, but the method is more satisfactory since it avoids duplication, assists storekeeping and can be structured to aid the memory.

3.4   Continuous stocktaking

The stores ledger will show, at any time, the quantity which should be in stock.

> **Definition**   Continuous stocktaking is the process of counting and valuing selected items at different times on a rotating basis. **(CIMA Official Terminology)**

Items are checked at random throughout the year but, for guidance, it is recommended that:

(i)   all items are checked at least once a year;

(ii)   items subject to specially frequent use are checked at least twice a year;

(iii)   checks are carried out by staff unconnected with the stores, being those responsible to the chief accountant or internal auditor.

If stock checking regularly disclosed significant differences between book and physical stocks, the recording system and/or security arrangements should be reviewed. If differences are within acceptable limits, however, the need for an annual stocktaking, with its consequent disruption, is avoided, since the stock shown by the stores ledger can be assumed to be sufficiently accurate.

3.5   Accounting for stock differences

In theory any differences between 'book' stock and physical stock has arisen through faulty recording. The stores ledger, therefore, should be adjusted to the physical balance by posting a correcting document for the discrepancy once it has been identified. If the error cannot be traced, the value of the difference (calculated on a FIFO or LIFO, etc basis) will be recorded as an issue in the stores ledger but charged to a special account pending authority for write-off.

3.6   Slow-moving and obsolete stocks

These may arise through faulty purchasing and/or storekeeping and also as a result of changing circumstances. It is important that such stocks should not be allowed to accumulate as they will tie up space and capital. The stock controller must regularly bring slow-moving and obsolete stocks to the attention of production and sales management for decisions to be taken as to their disposal if necessary. Certain items, eg maintenance materials or product spares, must be kept although they are slow-moving.

4   STOCK CONTROL LEVELS

4.1   Inventory control systems

It is important that inventory levels are maintained at a high enough level to service the production facility and at a level which minimises working capital tied up in inventory. The following sections look at both the physical aspects of different control systems.

4.2   Two-bin system

Under this system the existence of two bins is assumed, say A and B. Stock is taken from A until A is empty. A is then replenished with the economic order quantity. During the lead-time stock is used from B. The standard stock for B is the expected demand in the lead-time, plus the buffer stock. When the new order arrives, B is filled up to its standard stock and the rest placed in A. Stock is then drawn as required from A, and the process repeated.

The same sort of approach is adopted by some firms for a single bin. In such cases a red line is painted round the inside of the bin, such that when sufficient stock is removed to expose the red line, this indicates the need to re-order. The stock in the bin up to the red line therefore represents bin B, that above the red line bin A.

In considering the costs of stock control, the actual costs of operating the system must be recognised. The costs of a continual review as implied by the two-bin system may be excessive, and it may be more economic to operate a **periodic review system**. (see 4.5)

4.3   Reorder level system - stock control levels

This is a more sophisticated version of the two-bin system, which involves the setting of three control levels, as defined in CIMA Official Terminology:

Reorder level - a level of stock at which a replenishment order should be placed.

Minimum stock level - a stock level below which stockholding should not fall without being highlighted. (If the stocks fall below that level the storekeeper will consider the need for an emergency order.)

Maximum stock level - a stock level which actual stockholding should never exceed. (If the stock rises above this level, it is an indication of decline in usage/demand, and the reorder quantity may need to be reviewed.)

The following diagram illustrates the reorder level system:

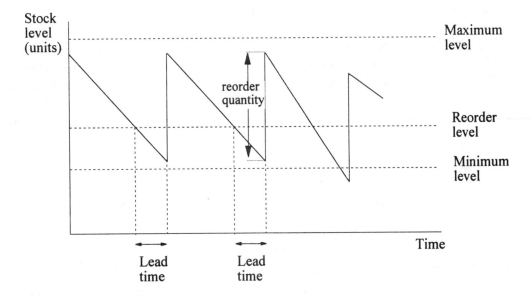

4.4   Calculation of stock control levels - example

The formulae for the minimum and maximum levels described above are as follows:

Minimum level =   reorder level - (maximum lead time × maximum rate of usage)
Maximum level =   reorder level + reorder quantity - (minimum lead time × minimum rate of usage)

The following information is given in respect of **Material X**:

	Weekly usage (units)	Lead time (weeks)
Maximum	1,500	5
Minimum	500	3

Reorder quantity = 12,000 units   Reorder level = 8,000 units

Minimum level =   8,000 − (5 × 1,500) = 500 units
Maximum level =   8,000 + 12,000 − (3 × 500) = 18,500 units

4.5   Periodic review system

Under this system the stock levels are reviewed at fixed intervals eg, every four weeks. The stock in hand is then made up to a predetermined level, which takes account of likely demand before the next review and during the lead-time. Thus, a four-weekly review in a system where the lead-time was two weeks would demand that stock be made up to the likely maximum demand for the next six weeks.

This system is described in some textbooks as the **constant order cycle system**.

| Conclusion |

Advantages of two-bin system

Stock can be kept at a lower level because of the ability to order whenever stocks fall to a low level, rather than having to wait for the next re-order date.

Advantages of periodic review system

Order load is more evenly spread and easier to plan. For this reason the system is popular with suppliers.

5   CHAPTER SUMMARY

Materials are likely to be the most significant cost of most manufacturing organisations and therefore it is essential that control is exercised over all aspects of materials from their purchase through to their issue to production departments. This chapter has looked at many of those aspects of control and most specifically the important area of valuation of materials and closing stock. This valuation and the comparison of the various methods of valuation tends to be a popular examination topic.

6   SELF TEST QUESTIONS

6.1   What are the three main categories of materials purchases in a manufacturing business? (1.1)

6.2   What are the advantages of having departmental sub-stores? (1.13)

6.3   What is a perpetual inventory? (2.1)

6.4   Under the LIFO method of stock valuation at what price is closing stock valued? (2.9)

6.5   What are the advantages and disadvantages of the weighted average price method of stock valuation? (2.18)

7   EXAMINATION TYPE QUESTION

7.1   Coding System

(a)   In connection with control of materials, you are required to:

(i)   explain the meaning of classification;
(ii)   explain the principles of coding; and
(iii)   state **four** advantages of using a coding system.

(b)   A company manufactures shoes and slippers in half-sizes in the following ranges:

	Sizes
Mens	6 to 9½
Ladies	3 to 9
Boys	1 to 5½
Girls	1 to 5

The company uses a seven-digit code to identify its finished products, which, reading from left to right, is built up as follows:

Digit **one** indicates whether the products are mens, ladies, boys or girls. The numbers used are:

        1 - mens
        2 - ladies
        3 - boys
        4 - girls

Digit **two** denotes type of footwear (shoes or slippers).
Digit **three** denotes colour (5 is green; 6 is burgundy).
Digit **four** denotes the material of the upper part of the product.
Digit **five** denotes the material of the sole.
Digits **six** and **seven** denote size.

Examples:

(1)   Code 1613275 represents a pair of mens slippers, brown suede, rubber sole, size 7½.
(2)   Code 1324195 represents a pair of mens shoes, black leather, leather sole, size 9½.

You are required to set suitable code numbers to the following, stating any assumptions you make:

(i)   boys shoes, brown leather uppers, rubber soles, size 4;
(ii)   ladies slippers, green felt uppers, rubber soles, size 4½; and
(iii)   girls shoes, burgundy leather uppers, leather soles, size 3½.

(20 marks)

8   **ANSWER TO EXAMINATION TYPE QUESTION**

8.1   **Coding System**

(a)   (i)   CIMA defines classification as the arrangement of items in logical groups having regard to their nature (subjective classification) or purpose (objective classification).

The following are examples of classifications which may be used in the context of material control:

(1)   Nature, eg wire, chemicals, resistors, screws. This should be used as a basis for the stores layout - all types of wire kept in one section, all types of chemicals in another section.

Stock can then be accessed more quickly and appropriate storage containers can be organised more easily.

(2)   ABC/pareto analysis. Stock may be analysed into categories based on

value. High value items warrant closer control than low value items.

(3) Direct/indirect. Direct materials are those materials which are incorporated in the product. Indirect materials include for example spare parts for fixed assets, cooling oil for machines.

This classification is used, for example, to aid accurate calculation of the cost per unit, ie direct materials are charged straight to the cost unit in job costing by inclusion on the job card. Indirect materials are charged to production overhead and included in unit cost via the overhead absorption rate.

(ii) A code is a system of symbols designed to be applied to a classified set of items, to give a brief accurate reference facilitating entry, collation and analysis.

When designing a coding system the following principles should be borne in mind:

(1) **Simplicity.** To ensure the code is easy to use - to minimise the likelihood of errors.

(2) **Unambiguity.** Each code should only refer to one item.

(3) **Flexibility.** It should be possible to add further categories.

(4) **Brevity.** Codes should be kept short for ease of use and to reduce the chance of errors.

(iii) A coding system can have the following advantages:

(1) It provides a quick, accurate way of identifying materials ie, should avoid incorrect materials being issued to production or ordered from suppliers.

(2) It can provide a suitable basis for stores layout.

(3) It can reduce clerical effort by assisting in the sorting and preparation of reports for material control.

(4) It can assist in the computerisation of the materials control systems.

(b) (i) Boys shoes, brown leather uppers, rubber soles, size 4.

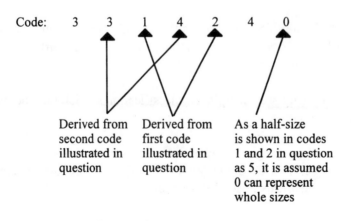

Code: 3 3 1 4 2 4 0

Derived from second code illustrated in question

Derived from first code illustrated in question

As a half-size is shown in codes 1 and 2 in question as 5, it is assumed 0 can represent whole sizes

(ii)   Ladies slippers, green felt uppers, rubber soles, size 4½.

Code: 2   6   5   7   2   4   5

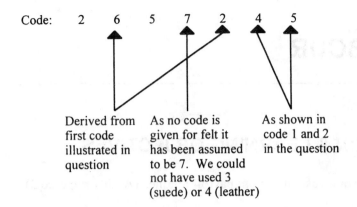

Derived from   As no code is   As shown in
first code   given for felt it   code 1 and 2
illustrated in   has been assumed   in the question
question   to be 7. We could
                    not have used 3
                    (suede) or 4 (leather)

(iii)   Girls shoes, burgundy leather uppers, leather soles, size 3½

Code: 4   3   6   4   1   3   5

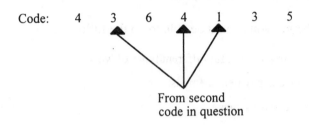

From second
code in question

3 LABOUR

INTRODUCTION & LEARNING OBJECTIVES

Syllabus area 2a. Labour: cost allocation; payroll routine. (Ability required 3).

The three components of production cost are materials, labour and services. In this chapter the control and accounting required for labour costs will be examined.

When you have studied this chapter you should be able to do the following:

- Describe how labour costs are recorded for different types of work.

- Describe the payroll routine and payment methods.

- Discuss various forms of incentive scheme.

---

1 LABOUR COSTS AND DOCUMENTATION

1.1 Personal history

The personnel department will maintain a history record for each employee. The record will include such details as:

(a)   full name and address;
(b)   previous employment;
(c)   clock number issued;
(d)   date engaged;
(e)   department, job title and pay rate upon engagement;
(f)   amendments to (e) above, recorded as and when they occur;
(g)   on the termination of employment, the date and reason for leaving.

1.2 Clock cards

 A clock card is a document on which is recorded the starting and finishing time of an employee, eg, by insertion into a time-recording device, for ascertaining total actual attendance time. (**CIMA Official Terminology**).

Wages cost represents payments for **direct** and **indirect** labour. Both types of workers will be supplied with clock cards or other records on which to record their time of arrival and departure from the factory. Such records will provide the basis for wages calculation at time rates. For direct workers **job cards** may also be maintained to record the time spent on particular orders as a basis for cost accounting.

1.3 Job cost sheet (or card)

 A job cost sheet is a detailed record of the amount, and cost, of the labour, material and overhead charged to a specific job. (**CIMA Official Terminology**).

Where possible, time recording clocks should be used to ensure the accuracy of time records.

The precise arrangements for job-time recording should be adapted to the nature and organisation of production, and so will vary from one factory to another. In some cases a card for each job may accompany that job through the factory, each worker involved noting or 'clocking' the time spent on the one card. Alternatively, a separate job card or ticket may be issued to each worker for each job.

Where the card travels with the work, calculation of the total wages cost of the job is made easier since the times spent by all employees on that order are recorded on the one card. This arrangement may also be advantageous for control purposes. Where a separate ticket is issued to each worker, reconciliation of gate and job times is made easier; particulars are pre-printed on the ticket as far as possible and times are recorded by a wages clerk, so that a clear and accurate record is available for costing purposes. The system, however, is relatively expensive.

1.4   Time sheets

Definition   A time sheet is a record of how a person's time has been spent.

Daily or weekly time-sheets on which the employee enters all particulars himself are commonly issued to indirect workers, eg, maintenance staff. The worker enters his clock number, name and cost centre at the head of the sheet, and details of the work upon which he is engaged, together with the starting and finishing times, are entered in the appropriate columns of the form. By contrast with the job cards in the systems mentioned above, a time-sheet provides a complete record of how an employee has spent the working day or week. On the other hand, a disadvantage of using time-sheets is that they tend to be entered up at the end of the day or week, rather that at the times when the jobs were started and finished.

Conclusion   Time sheets are not as accurate as individual job cards which have to be returned to the office immediately the worker has concluded the job. Idle time may not be fully disclosed when time-sheets are used.

1.5   Preparing the payroll

Definition   The payroll is a record showing for each employee, gross pay, deductions and net pay.

The payroll is the basic document used in accounting for wages. It is prepared from:

(a)   personal history card;
(b)   time records;
(c)   employee deduction records;
(d)   supplementary information.

Each employee is listed and his gross wage calculated from time records and record cards. Deductions for PAYE, voluntary contributions, etc, are entered to arrive at net pay. The payroll provides supplementary analysis for entries in the financial accounts and the gross wage total is a control figure for cost analysis.

1.6   Wage payment methods

There are two basic approaches to remuneration, **time-related** or **output-related**. However, since output ultimately depends on time, the 'remuneration-syllogism' is:

> *Wages depend on output*
> *Output depends on time worked*
> *Therefore, wages depend on time.*

(Baggott)

The two basic methods are time rate and piece rates.

1.7   Time rates

The most common method of payment is time rate, whereby employees are paid a basic rate per hour, day, or week irrespective of production achieved. Basic time rate provides no incentive to improve productivity and close supervision is necessary.

A variation is known as 'higher time rates', where rates above the basic level are offered and paid, to attract more enthusiastic and skilled employees.

1.8   Piece-work

The direct alternative to time rate is piece-work, whereby a fixed amount is paid per unit of output achieved, irrespective of time spent. Rigid inspection procedures are required to ensure work is of an adequate standard.

Straight piece-work is almost extinct today as a result of employment legislation and trade union resistance.

Piece-workers are usually required to keep time records for disciplinary and security purposes.

A variable is 'differential piece rates'. This is almost a penal system, with a low piece rate for the first units of production, and a high piece rate for subsequent units.

1.9   Payment incentive schemes

These have developed from the piece rate approach, but attempt to avoid the crudities of the system described above.

The variety of approaches are all explained in the sections below.

1.10   Activity

What do you think are the essential requirements of an incentive scheme?

1.11   Activity solution

As a general rule, any incentive scheme should satisfy the following requirements:

(a)   Related closely to effort.
(b)   Agreed by prior consultation between employer and employees.
(c)   Understandable and simple to operate.
(d)   Capable of being beneficial to the average worker.

1.12   Premium bonus plans

The basic idea of all premium bonus plans is to pay a basic time rate, plus a portion of the time saved as compared to some agreed allowed time. Examples of such schemes are Halsey and Rowan.

1.13   Halsey plan

The employee receives 50% of the time saving, ie,

$$\text{Bonus} = \frac{\text{Time allowed} - \text{Time taken}}{2} \times \text{Time rate}$$

1.14   Example

Employee's basic rate	=	£4.80 per hour
Allowed time for job A	=	1 hour
Time taken for Job A	=	36 minutes

1.15   Solution

			£
Bonus	=	$\dfrac{60-36}{2} \times \dfrac{£4.80}{60}$	0.96
Basic rate	=	$\dfrac{36}{60} \times £4.80$	2.88
Total payment for Job A			3.84

1.16   Rowan plan

The proportion paid to the employee is based on the ratio of time taken to time allowed, ie

$$\text{Bonus} = \frac{\text{Time taken}}{\text{Time allowed}} \times \text{Time saved} \times \text{Time rate}$$

1.17   Example

Using the facts in 1.14 above.

1.18   Solution

			£
Bonus	=	$\dfrac{36}{60} \times 24 \times \dfrac{£4.80}{60}$	1.15
Basic rate	=	$\dfrac{36}{60} \times £4.80$	2.88
Total payment for Job A			4.03

1.19   Activity

What would be the bonus under each plan if the time taken in the previous example was 18 minutes?

1.20   Activity solution

Halsey

$$\text{Bonus} = \frac{60-18}{2} \times \frac{£4.80}{60}$$

$$= £1.68$$

Rowan

$$\text{Bonus} = \frac{18}{60} \times 42 \times \frac{£4.80}{60}$$

$$= \quad £1.00$$

Conclusion   Premium bonus schemes of the type described are really only appropriate for skilled craftsmen. In continuous production the output of the individual worker is largely governed by the speed of the flowline, although such schemes may be suitable for special jobs eg, fitting radios in motor car assembly. As with straight piece-work, production under bonus for time-saving requires strict inspection to prevent slapdash work.

1.21   Measured day work

The concept of this approach is to pay a high time rate, but this rate is based on an analysis of past performance. Initially, work measurement is used to calculate the allowed time per unit. This allowed time is compared to the time actually taken in the past by the employee, and if this is better than the allowed time an incentive is agreed.

1.22   Example

Allowed time - 1 hour.

Average time taken by employee over last three months - 50 minutes.

Normal rate - £4.80/hour.

Agreed incentive rate (say) - £5.00/hour.

Note: the incentive rate will be a matter of negotiation. This incentive wage rate will be reviewed periodically in the light of the employee's actual performance.

1.23   Share of production plans

In order to understand this plan, it is necessary to introduce the concept of value added. This is explained below:

	£
Sales	X
Less: Costs of external inputs	
(ie, all costs except payroll)	X
Value added	X

Generally, wages tends to maintain a constant relationship to value added, usually about 40%.

Share of production plans are based on acceptance by both management and labour representatives of a constant share of value added for payroll. Thus, any gains in value added - whether by improved production performance or cost savings - are shared by employees in this ratio.

1.24   Example

A company might have the following result for the year:

	£
Sales	100,000
Less: External inputs	55,000
Value added	45,000

1.25   Solution

	£
Agreed wages share (40% × £45,000)	18,000
Wages paid	15,000
Balance paid as bonus	3,000

1.26   Group incentive schemes

All of the schemes discussed above can be operated as group incentive schemes. This more closely relates to reality, in that improved performance is the result of group rather than individual effort.

1.27   Example

Ten men work as a group. When production of the group exceeds the standard - 200 pieces per hour - each man in the group is paid a bonus for the excess production in addition to his wages at hourly rates.

The bonus is computed thus: the percentage of production in excess of the standard quantity is found, and one half of the percentage is regarded as the men's share. Each man in the group is paid as a bonus this percentage of a wage rate of £5.20 per hour. There is no relationship between the individual workman's hourly rate and the bonus rate.

The following is one week's record:

	Hours worked	Production
Monday	90	24,500
Tuesday	88	20,600
Wednesday	90	24,200
Thursday	84	20,100
Friday	88	20,400
Saturday	40	10,200
	480	120,000

You are required

(a)   to compute the rate and amount of bonus for the week;

(b)   to calculate the total pay of Jones, who worked 42 hours and was paid £3.00 per hour basic; and that of Smith, who worked 44 hours and was paid £3.75 per hour basic.

1.28   Solution

(a)   Standard production for the week = 480 hours × 200   =   96,000 pieces
      Actual production for the week   =   120,000 pieces

$$\text{Bonus rate} = \frac{24,000}{96,000} \times 0.5 \times £5.20$$

$$= \text{65p per hour}$$

$$\text{Total bonus} = \text{480 hours} \times \text{65p}$$

$$= £312$$

(b)

		Jones £		Smith £
Basic	42 × £3.00	126.00	44 × £3.75	165.00
Bonus	42 × £0.65	27.30	44 × £0.65	28.60
Total pay		153.30		193.60

2   LABOUR COST ACCOUNTING

2.1   Time recording

Time recording is required both for payment purposes, and also for determining costs to be charged to specific jobs. These may be described diagrammatically:

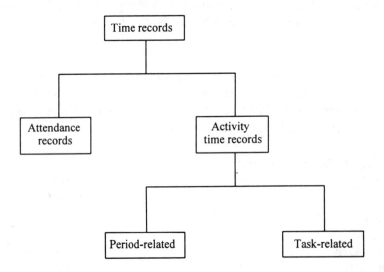

2.2   Attendance records

These are usually either a register, or mechanical/electronic time recorder. The most sophisticated time recorders use plastic identity cards and are directly linked to a central computer.

2.3   Period-related activity time records

These may be for daily, weekly, or sometimes longer periods. An example of a weekly time sheet is given below:

Weekly Time Sheet				Dept:		
Employee No			**Name**	**Wk Edg**		
To be completed by employee				*For Office Use*		
Day	*Start*	*Finish*	*Job*	*Code*	*Hrs*	*Amounts* £ p
Foreman's Signature:				**Gross Wages**		

2.4   Task-related activity time records

Known variously as job sheets, operations charts or piecework tickets, these are generally more accurate and reliable than time-related activity time records, and are essential for use with incentive schemes. An example is given below:

Time Sheet						
Employee name: **Start date:** **Department:**				**No:** **Finish date:** **Operation:**		
Day	*Start*	*Finish*	*Time*	*Production*		*Foreman's signature*
1						
2						
3						
4						
5						
Total						
Time allowed						
Time saved						

	Hours	*Rate* £ p	*Paid* £ p
Time wages			
Bonus			
Total wages			

2.5   Reconciliation of activity time and attendance time

This is essential to ensure the accuracy of the information.

2.6   Payroll preparation

Because of the sums of money involved, security control is necessary at all stages of the task of payroll preparation and payment. One major area of risk is the introduction of fictitious employees ('dummies' or 'ghosting') in the payroll.

The payroll preparation involves:

(a)   calculating gross wages from time and activity records;

(b)   calculating net wages after PAYE and other deductions, and properly recording the deductions; and

(c)   preparing a cash analysis of total cash required for payment.

2.7   Making up pay-packets

The cash is made up into pay-packets for each employee, together with a pay-slip.

2.8   Paying out wages

This is an area where physical security is very important. Another problem is unclaimed wages (eg, if the employee is sick). Procedures are required for proper control and alternative means of distributing such unclaimed wages.

2.9   Functional analysis of wages

Under a costing system, it will be necessary to functionally analyse the gross wages and post these to the cost accounts. This is done from the activity time records:

(a)   Weekly time sheets - no problem.

(b)   Daily time sheets - usually posted from daily sheets, any discrepancy with payroll being charged to an adjustment account.

(c)   Job sheets - again these may lead to small differences, because jobs overlap payweeks. These are also usually written off to an adjustment account.

Indirect wages are usually analysed according to activity - supervision, inspection, etc.

Finally, note that overtime premium is charged as an overhead, not to the job on which it is worked.

2.10   Direct/indirect wages control ratios

Within any company, and with consistent classification, this ratio should stay fairly constant.

As an example:

	This week £	Last week £
Direct wages	4,700	4,500
Indirect wages	2,600	2,700
Total	7,300	7,200
Ratio of direct to indirect wages	1.81	1.67

This provides a very crude control over indirect wages.

2.11   Idle time

Idle time may also be referred to as non-productive time. It represents 'the period for which a workstation is available for production but is not used due to, eg, shortage of tooling, material or operators' **(CIMA Official Terminology)**.

There are a number of causes of idle time:-

- lack of work
- poor supervision
- lack of materials
- machine breakdown

The causes of idle time should be monitored and the costs analysed between these causes so that action may be taken by management as appropriate.

The costs of idle time are treated as production overhead costs, which are explained in more detail later.

3   CHAPTER SUMMARY

The purpose of this chapter has been to consider the recording, calculation and payment of labour costs in a manufacturing organisation.

4   SELF TEST QUESTIONS

4.1   What is a clock card? (1.2)

4.2   What is a job cost sheet? (1.3)

4.3   What is a time-sheet? (1.4)

4.4   What are the two main approaches to calculating the remuneration paid to employees? (1.6)

4.5   What is measured day work? (1.21)

4.6   What is value added? (1.23)

4.7   What is a group incentive scheme? (1.26)

4.8   What does payroll preparation involve? (2.6)

4.9   How are indirect wages normally analysed? (2.9)

4.10   How is an overtime premium treated? (2.9)

5   EXAMINATION TYPE QUESTIONS

5.1   Control of labour costs

How can the cost accountant help to control labour costs in an organisation?

(15 marks)

5.2   Components A, B and C

A factory manufactures three components A, B and C.

During week 26, the following was recorded:

Labour grade	Number of employees	Rate per hour £	Individual hours worked
I	6	4.00	40
II	18	3.20	42
III	4	2.80	40
IV	1	1.60	44

Output and standard times during the same week were:

Component	Output	Standard minutes (each)
A	444	30
B	900	54
C	480	66

The normal working week is 38 hours, and overtime is paid at a premium of 50% of the normal hourly rate.

A group incentive scheme is in operation. The time saved is expressed as a percentage of hours worked and is shared between the group as a proportion of the hours worked by each grade.

The rate paid is 75% of the normal hourly rate.

You are required

(a)   To calculate the total payroll showing the basic pay, overtime premium and bonus pay as a separate total for each grade of labour.

(18 marks)

(b)   To journalise the payroll assuming: income tax deducted is £884.00; national insurance payable by employee is 6% of gross pay; national insurance payable by employer is 5% of gross pay; 12 employees are members of the Social Club whose weekly subscription is 25 pence.

(6 marks)

(c)   To summarise two advantages and two disadvantages of group incentive schemes.

(4 marks)

(Total: 28 marks)

6   **ANSWERS TO EXAMINATION TYPE QUESTIONS**

6.1   **Control of labour costs**

In cost and management accounting the word 'control' has many different meanings. The overall aim of control is to ensure that, for a given level of sales, costs are kept as low as possible hence that profit is as high as possible.

In this question we are focusing on the ways in which information prepared by the cost accountant or systems implemented by the cost accountant can assist in the control of labour related costs. These may be summarised as follows:

(a)   **Labour turnover**

$$\frac{\text{Number of people who leave who require replacement}}{\text{Average number employed}} \times 100$$

This provides an indication of whether an unacceptably high number of people are leaving the company. This can cause costs of recruitment and training to be unnecessarily high.

(b)   **Incentive schemes**

A way of improving efficiency and reducing the need for supervision is to use some form of incentive scheme. The cost accountant would be needed to quantify the costs and benefits of schemes.

(c)   **Payroll preparation and wage payment procedures**

The cost accountant is in a position to implement control procedures to minimise the risk of fraud or errors in the payroll department.

(d)   **Wage analysis**

When analysing wage costs care should be taken to ensure all costs are accounted for eg, charged to the appropriate job. Any controllable idle time which arises should be analysed into causes and reported to management.

(e)   **Standard costing**

Three major benefits of implementing a standard costing system are:

(i)   In the process of preparing standard costs production methods should be reviewed to try to achieve reductions in cost eg, to make use of newly available technology which may reduce the amount of labour time required.

(ii)   The standard provides a target for the production manager to work to.

(iii)   The standard provides a basis for comparison with actual results. This enables the cost accountant to calculate labour efficiency, rate and idle time variances, providing management with valuable feedback.

(f)   **Clock cards**

Employees' attendance times may be recorded using a properly supervised clock card system. This will facilitate recording lateness and absenteeism of employees.

(g)   **Authorisation**

Procedures should be implemented to ensure that:

(i)   Overtime is only worked when authorised by the appropriate manager.

(ii)   Output of employees on piece-rates is recorded and checked.   Arrangements whether employees are paid for any rejects should be built into any scheme.

When setting up any system, procedure or report, consideration should be given as to whether it is cost effective ie, do the potential savings exceed the cost of operating the system/procedure or the cost of preparing the report?

6.2   Components A, B and C

(a)   **Calculation of total payroll cost**

		Grade of labour				
		I	*II*	*III*	*IV*	*Total*
		£	£	£	£	£
Basic pay:						
I	$6 \times £4.00 \times 40$	960.00				
II	$18 \times £3.20 \times 42$		2,419.20			
III	$4 \times £2.80 \times 40$			448.00		
IV	$1 \times £1.60 \times 44$				70.40	
		960.00	2,419.20	448.00	70.40	3,897.60

		I	*II*	*III*	*IV*	
		£	£	£	£	
Overtime premium:						
I	$6 \times £2.00 \times (40 - 38)$	24.00				
II	$18 \times £1.60 \times (42 - 38)$		115.20			
III	$4 \times £1.40 \times (40 - 38)$			11.20		
IV	$1 \times £0.80 \times (44 - 38)$				4.80	
		24.00	115.20	11.20	4.80	155.20

Bonus payable (see working):

		Grade of labour				
		I	*II*	*III*	*IV*	
		£	£	£	£	
I	$\dfrac{6 \times 40}{1,200} \times 360 \times (75\% \times £4)$	216.00				
II	$\dfrac{18 \times 42}{1,200} \times 360 \times (75\% \times £3.20)$		544.32			
III	$\dfrac{4 \times 40}{1,200} \times 360 \times (75\% \times £2.80)$			100.80		
IV	$\dfrac{1 \times 44}{1,200} \times 360 \times (75\% \times £1.60)$				15.84	
		216.00	544.32	100.80	15.84	876.96
Total (gross pay)		1,200.00	3,078.72	560.00	91.04	4,929.76

WORKING

Standard time for actual output:

Component			Std hrs
A	$444 \times 0.5 =$		222
B	$900 \times 0.9 =$		810
C	$480 \times 1.1 =$		528
	Total standard hours		1,560

Actual time:

Grade		Std hrs
I	6×40	240
II	18×42	756
III	4×40	160
IV	1×44	44
Total standard hours		1,200
Total hours saved		360

(b)   **Journal**

	Dr	Cr
	£	£
Wages	4,929.76	
National insurance (paid by company):		
$5\% \times £4,929.76$	246.48	
Income tax payable		884.00
National insurance payable		
$£246.48 + (6\% \times £4,929.76)$		542.26
Social club $(12 \times £0.25)$		3.00
Bank		3,746.98
	5,176.24	5,176.24

Being the payroll with deductions and national insurance for Week 26.

(c)   Advantages of a group incentive scheme:

(i)   Emphasises the need for worker cooperation to achieve required targets for the company.

(ii)   Applicable when a production line exists or when operatives work in crews or gangs.

Disadvantages of a group incentive scheme:

(i)   The more conscientious members of the group create the benefit that has to be shared with the less efficient members of the group.   This can have a demotivational effect on the former.

(ii)   Where there are different degrees of skill required by members of the group it may be difficult to recognise this easily and objectively in allocating the bonus between the group members.

4 OVERHEADS

INTRODUCTION & LEARNING OBJECTIVES

Syllabus area 2a. Overhead cost: classification and analysis. (Ability required 3).

Principles of apportionment and absorption into cost centres and units; departmental accounts. (Ability required 3).

Overhead is the general term used to describe costs which are not directly related to production. They are also known as indirect costs. When a cost accountant is trying to ascertain the cost of a product there are two possible approaches available.

Firstly he can use only direct costs and leave indirect costs as a general overhead not related to units of output. This approach is generally known as marginal costing and will be dealt with in the next chapter.

In this chapter the alternative approach is considered where apportionment and allocation of all production overheads is used to arrive at a 'full' cost per unit. This is known as absorption costing.

Definition Absorption costing is a method of costing that, in addition to direct costs, assigns all, or a proportion of, production overhead costs to cost units by means of one or a number of overhead absorption rates (**CIMA Official Terminology**).

When you have studied this chapter you should be able to do the following:

- Understand the process of collecting and allocating all of the costs that relate to a unit of production.
- Allocate overheads, including the cost of service departments, to production departments.
- Apportion overheads to cost centres on a sensible basis.
- Calculate absorption rates.
- Understand and deal with any under or over-absorption of overhead.
- Compare activity based costing to cost centre absorption methods.

1 OVERHEAD ALLOTMENT

1.1 Overhead cost classification and analysis

Overhead costs are those costs incurred which cannot be economically attributed to the cost unit. Therefore they are incurred in many different parts of the organisation.

Overhead costs are classified by function, for example production, selling, administration. This then enables them to be attributed to unit costs in the case of production overhead and to be treated as period costs in respect of the other organisational functions.

1.2   Production overhead

[Definition]   Overhead is expenditure on labour, materials or services which cannot be economically identified with a specific saleable cost unit.

Overhead represents indirect materials, indirect wages and indirect expenses attributable to production and the service activities associated with production. Marketing, general administration, research and development costs which are not associated with production are not usually treated as overheads for this purpose; consequently, the term 'overhead' may be assumed to mean **production overhead** unless otherwise stated.

Indirect production costs are incurred in three main ways:

(a)   **Production activities** - costs arising in production departments such as fuel, protective clothing, depreciation and supervision.

(b)   **Service activities** - the cost of operating non-producing departments or sections within the factory, eg materials handling, production control, canteen.

(c)   **Establishment costs** - general production overhead such as factory rent/rates, heating and lighting and production management salaries.

It is important to note that analysis of overhead may be used for two purposes, viz:

(i)   to facilitate allotment to cost units;
(ii)   to relate costs to responsibility as an aid to control.

1.3   Cost allotment

One of the purposes of cost accounting is to provide a basis for valuing work in progress and finished stocks. SSAP 9 requires that the financial accounts should reflect a stock value including a share of indirect costs. An objective of absorption costing is to arrive at such stock valuations.

So far the allocation of direct costs to cost units has been discussed. Now it is necessary to examine the sharing (or allotment) of indirect costs to cost units. A sequence of procedures is undertaken:

[Step 1]   Collecting production overhead costs by item.

[Step 2]   Establishing cost centres.

[Step 3]   Allocating and apportioning overhead costs to cost centres.

[Step 4]   Apportioning service cost centre costs to production cost centres.

[Step 5]   Absorbing production cost centre costs into cost units.

...trated diagrammatically:

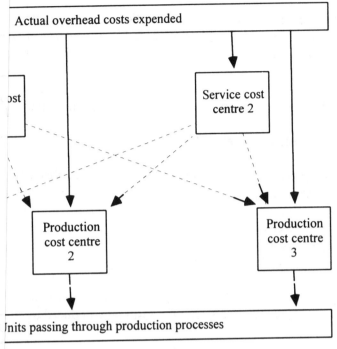

...rect cost allocation

...location of service centre costs to production centres

...bsorption of costs into units of output

...s by item

...rect materials costs were obtained by analysing materials requisitions and that indirect wages cost was derived from an analysis of the payroll. Indirect expenses are recorded from invoices, petty cash vouchers and journal entries (eg, for depreciation) and classified firstly by nature (subjective).

1.5   Step 2: Establishment of cost centres

In analysing the production activity, the twofold purpose of allotment to cost centres and allocation of responsibility for costs should be recognised. Thus, the cost centres established should ideally combine an identifiable activity with a specific person responsible. For example, if Department A comprises three machine groups - I, II and III - under the overall supervision of a departmental supervisor, then it would help responsibility accounting to have only one cost centre for Department A. The three machine groups may, however, perform entirely different production activities, in which case three separate cost centres may be necessary for cost allotment purposes. The cost accountant must decide which alternative to implement.

Service cost centres are usually set up to represent individual service departments eg, stores; but in a large factory a department may combine a number of cost centres related to the responsibility of section heads within the department, eg, each sub-store would be a separate cost centre.

1.6   Step 3: Cost allocation and apportionment

The total cost of production overhead needs to be distributed among specific cost centres. Some items can be **allocated** immediately, eg, the salary of a cost centre supervisor or indirect materials issued to a cost centre; other items need to be **apportioned** between a number of centres eg, factory rent and rates or the factory manager's salary.

The basis for apportioning a total amount will be selected so that the charge to a specific centre will reflect, with reasonable accuracy, the benefit obtained by that centre from the cost incurred.

1.7   Step 4: Apportioning service cost centre costs to production cost centres

Part of the total factory overhead will be allotted to cost centres which do not actually produce the saleable output. In order to reflect the cost of services in unit costs, service cost centre costs must be allotted to production cost centres (remember these are production services only ie, not marketing, etc).

Once again the basis of apportionment should reflect the benefit derived.

1.8   Step 5: Absorption in cost units

Finally, the production cost centres will have been allotted with the total amount of factory overhead, representing:

(a)   allocated costs;
(b)   apportioned costs;
(c)   share of service department costs.

The overhead to be absorbed by a particular cost unit will be calculated by dividing the production cost centre overhead for a period by the cost units produced by that centre in the period.

When a cost centre produces dissimilar units eg, jobs to customer order, the volume of production must be expressed in a common measurement eg, direct labour hours. When a cost unit passes through several centres, the overhead absorbed should be calculated separately for each centre.

1.9   Example

The ABC Washing Machine Co produces a standard washing machine in three production departments (Machining, Assembling and Finishing) and two service departments (Materials handling and Production control).

Costs for last year, when 2,000 machines were produced, were as follows:

Materials:

Machine shop	£240,000
Assembly	£160,000
Finishing	£40,000
Materials handling	£4,000

Wages:

Machining	10,000 hours at £3.72
Assembly	5,000 hours at £2.88
Finishing	3,000 hours at £3.60
Materials handling	£8,000
Production control	£11,200

Other costs:

Machine shop	£41,920
Assembly	£12,960
Finishing	£7,920
Materials handling	£8,000
Production control	£2,400

It is estimated that the benefit derived from the service departments is as follows:

Materials handling:

Machine shop	60%
Assembly	30%
Finishing	10%

Production control:

Machine shop	40%
Assembly	30%
Finishing	20%
Materials handling	10%

You are required

(a)   to prepare a statement showing the overhead allotted to each of the production departments;

(b)   to calculate the unit cost of a washing machine.

1.10   Solution

(a)   Overhead allotment

Materials and wages incurred by the production departments may be assumed to be direct costs and are therefore excluded from the overhead distribution.

	Total £	Machining £	Assembly £	Finishing £	Production control £	Materials handling £
Indirect materials	4,000	-	-	-	-	4,000
Indirect wages	19,200	-	-	-	11,200	8,000
Other	73,200	41,920	12,960	7,920	2,400	8,000
	96,400	41,920	12,960	7,920	13,600	20,000
Production control	-	5,440	4,080	2,720	(13,600)	1,360
Materials handling	-	12,816	6,408	2,136	-	(21,360)
	96,400	60,176	23,448	12,776	-	-

Service department costs have been apportioned to production departments using the percentage benefit shown in the question. As 10% of the production control overhead is to be charged to materials handling this must be done first.

(b)   Unit cost

	Machining £	Assembly £	Finishing £	Total £
Direct materials	240,000	160,000	40,000	440,000
Direct wages	37,200	14,400	10,800	62,400
Production overheads (from above)	60,176	23,448	12,776	96,400
	337,376	197,848	63,576	598,800
Units produced				2,000
Cost per unit				£299.40

1.11   Overhead distribution summary

The illustration above showed a total amount of production overhead of £96,400, which had been allotted to the five cost centres in the production function.

The usual way of recording the details of overhead allotment is to prepare a tabulated overhead distribution summary in the following format:

Overhead distribution summary

Overhead item	Total	Basis of distribution	Cost centres				
			A	B	C	D	E
	£		£	£	£	£	£
Indirect wages		Payroll					
Indirect materials		Requisition					
Rent		Floor area					
Depreciation		Plant register					

Conclusion   The guiding principle is that the total charge for an item should be shared to reflect, with reasonable accuracy, the relative benefit derived by particular cost centres.

Generally, allocation will be more accurate than apportionment but absolute accuracy must often be sacrificed in the interests of economy. For example, an employer's National Insurance contributions should be strictly analysed according to employee to obtain the exact amounts attributed to each cost centre; the amount involved would probably not justify such analysis and the total charge would be apportioned on the basis of the number of employees in each centre.

2   OVERHEAD APPORTIONMENT

2.1   Bases for apportioning costs

In selecting a basis for apportioning an overhead item, the cost of obtaining a high degree of accuracy must be considered. For example, the charge for heat and light could be shared on the basis of a complex formula incorporating power points, light bulbs and wattage but you should be aware that the end-result will still be open to question. When answering examination questions, you may have to use your own judgement in relation to the information given as it is impracticable to provide a comprehensive list of bases to cover every situation.

2.2   Activity

The overhead budget for the month together with data relating to cost centres is as follows:

	£
Supervision	7,525
Indirect workers	6,000
Holiday pay and National Insurance	6,200
Tooling cost	9,400
Machine maintenance labour cost	4,500
Power	1,944
Small tools and supplies	1,171
Insurance of machinery	185
Insurance of building	150
Rent and rates	2,500
Depreciation of machinery	9,250
	48,825

	Machine groups				
	Q	*R*	*S*	*T*	*Total*
Floor space (sq ft)	1,800	1,500	800	900	5,000
Kilowatt hours	270,000	66,000	85,000	65,000	486,000
Capital cost of machines (£)	30,000	20,000	8,000	16,000	74,000
Indirect workers (persons)	3	3	1	1	8
Total workers (persons)	19	24	12	7	62
Machine maintenance hours	3,000	2,000	3,000	1,000	9,000
Tooling costs (£)	3,500	4,300	1,000	600	9,400
Supervision costs (£)	2,050	2,200	1,775	1,500	7,525
Small tools and supplies (£)	491	441	66	173	1,171
Machine running hours	30,000	36,000	19,000	8,000	93,000

Apportion each of the costs given to the four groups of machines on a suitable basis and then calculate a machine hour rate for each of the four groups of machines.

2.3   Activity solution

	Basis (see below for code)	Q	R	S	T	Total
			Machine groups			
Supervision	A	2,050	2,200	1,775	1,500	7,525
Indirect workers	4	2,250	2,250	750	750	6,000
Holiday pay and NI	5	1,900	2,400	1,200	700	6,200
Tooling cost	A	3,500	4,300	1,000	600	9,400
Machine maintenance labour	6	1,500	1,000	1,500	500	4,500
Power	2	1,080	264	340	260	1,944
Small tools, etc	A	491	441	66	173	1,171
Insurance of machines	3	75	50	20	40	185
Insurance of buildings	1	54	45	24	27	150
Rent and rates	1	900	750	400	450	2,500
Depreciation of machinery	3	3,750	2,500	1,000	2,000	9,250
		17,550	16,200	8,075	7,000	48,825
Machine running hours		30,000	36,000	19,000	8,000	93,000
Machine hour rate		£0.585	£0.450	£0.425	£0.875	£0.525

Bases of apportionment:

1	Floor space	5	Total workers	
2	Kilowatt hours	6	Machine maintenance hours	
3	Capital cost of machines	A	Direct - allocated	
4	No of indirect workers			

Note that depreciation is apportioned on the basis of capital cost. The usage of machines will be reflected in the machine hour rate.

2.4   Responsibility criterion

Overhead allotment has so far been looked at from the point of view of benefit obtained. Much of the information is only relevant, however, for cost control purposes, by segregating those cost centre costs which are controllable by the centre manager.

The above overhead distribution could be adapted to achieve that object by adding a **general** cost centre; items which cannot be controlled by machine group supervisors (such as rent and insurance) would be charged to the general centre as the responsibility of, say, the factory manager. Cost centres would then be allotted overhead in two stages:

(a)   allocation of controllable costs;

(b)   apportioned costs transferred from the general cost centre.

The sub-total of allocated costs would be suitable for control information and the grand total would be used for absorption purposes.

2.5   Example

Speed Manufacturing Co Ltd has three production departments (two machine shops and one assembly shop) and three service departments, one of which - the Engineering Service Department - serves the machine shops only.

The annual budgeted overhead costs for the year are:

	Indirect wages £	Consumable. supplies £
Machine shop A	23,260	6,300
Machine shop B	20,670	9,100
Assembly	8,110	2,100
Stores	4,100	1,400
Engineering service	2,670	2,100
General services	3,760	1,600
	62,570	22,600

	£
Depreciation of machinery	22,000
Insurance of machinery	4,000
Insurance of building	1,800 (Note 1)
Power	3,600
Light and heat	3,000
Rent and rates	7,050 (Note 2)

Notes:

(1)   Because of special fire risks, Machine shop A is responsible for a special loading of insurance on the building. This results in a total building insurance cost for Machine shop A of one-third of the annual premium.

(2)   The general services department is located in a building owned by the company. It is valued at £6,000 and is charged into costs at a notional value of 8% pa. This cost is additional to the rent and rates shown above.

(3)   The values of issues of materials to the production departments are in the same proportions as shown above for consumable supplies.

The following data is also available:

Departments	Book value of machinery £	Area (sq ft)	Effective HP hours %	Production capacity Direct labour hours	Machine hours
Productive:					
Machine shop A	60,000	5,000	50	200,000	40,000
Machine shop B	45,000	6,000	$33\frac{1}{3}$	150,000	50,000
Assembly	15,000	8,000	$4\frac{1}{6}$	300,000	
Service:					
Stores	6,000	2,000	-		
Engineering service	18,000	2,500	$12\frac{1}{2}$		
General services	6,000	1,500	-		
	150,000	25,000	100		

You are required

(a)   to prepare an overhead analysis sheet showing the bases of any apportionments of overhead to departments

(b)   to calculate suitable overhead absorption rates for the production departments; ignoring the apportionment of service department costs amongst service departments;

(c)   to calculate the overhead to be absorbed by two products, PSK and SGM, with cost sheets showing the following times spent in different departments:

	PSK	SGM
Machine shop A	6 machine hours	3 machine hours
Machine shop B	2 machine hours	8 machine hours
Assembly	5 direct labour hours	7 direct labour hours

2.6   Solution

(a)   Overhead analysis sheet

	Total £	Machine shop A £	B £	Assembly £	Stores £	Engineering service £	General service £
Indirect wages	62,570	23,260	20,670	8,110	4,100	2,670	3,760
Consumable supplies	22,600	6,300	9,100	2,100	1,400	2,100	1,600
Depreciation of machinery	22,000	8,800	6,600	2,200	880	2,640	880
Insurance of machinery	4,000	1,600	1,200	400	160	480	160
Insurance of building	1,800	600	360	480	120	150	90
Power	3,600	1,800	1,200	150	-	450	-
Light and heat	3,000	600	720	960	240	300	180
Rent and rates	7,050	1,500	1,800	2,400	600	750	-
Notional rent	480	-	-	-	-	-	480
	127,100	44,460	41,650	16,800	7,500	9,540	7,150

Bases of apportionment:

Depreciation and insurance of machinery	:	Book value of machinery
Insurance of building	:	One-third to machine shop A,
	:	balance apportioned on area
Power	:	Effective HP hours
Light and heat	:	Area
Rent and rates	:	Area excluding general service

(b)   **Production departments**

	Machine shop A £	Machine shop B £	Assembly £	Total £
Total from overhead analysis sheet	44,460	41,650	16,800	102,910
Apportionment of service departments:				
Stores (consumable supplies)	2,700	3,900	900	7,500
Engineering service (machine hours)	4,240	5,300	-	9,540
General services (direct labour hours)	2,200	1,650	3,300	7,150
	53,600	52,500	21,000	127,100
Absorption basis (hours)	40,000 (M/C)	50,000 (M/C)	300,000 (D Lab)	
Overhead absorption rates	£1.34 per machine hour	£1.05 per machine hour	£0.07 per direct labour hour	

(c)   **Absorption of production overhead**

		Product PSK £	Product SGM £
Machine shop A:			
PSK	6 machine hours @ £1.34	8.04	
SGM	3 machine hours @ £1.34		4.02
Machine shop B:			
PSK	2 machine hours @ £1.05	2.10	
SGM	8 machine hours @ £1.05		8.40
Assembly:			
PSK	5 direct labour hours @ £0.07	0.35	
SGM	7 direct labour hours @ £0.07		0.49
Overhead absorbed		10.49	12.91

3   OVERHEAD ABSORPTION

3.1   Measurement of volume

Definition   The overhead absorption rate is a means of attributing overhead to a product or service based for example on direct labour hours, direct labour cost or machine hours. (**CIMA Official Terminology**). It may be calculated by the fraction:

$$\frac{\text{Cost centre overhead in £s}}{\text{Cost centre volume in units}}$$

where the cost centre volume is expressed in hours or cost as appropriate to the basis being used.

3.2 Absorption bases

Overhead can be absorbed in cost units by means of:

(a)   rate per unit;
(b)   percentage of prime cost (direct labour, direct material and direct expenses);
(c)   percentage of direct wages;
(d)   direct labour hour rate;
(e)   machine hour rate.

3.3 Example

Facts as in the ABC Washing Machine Co. example above. A separate absorption rate for each cost centre is to be calculated as follows:

(a)   Machining   Machine hour rate (each machine is manned by four operatives).
(b)   Assembly   Direct labour hour rate.
(c)   Finishing   Percentage of direct wages.

3.4 Solution

Absorption rates:

$$\text{Machining} \quad \frac{\text{Cost centre overhead}}{\text{Machine hours}} = \frac{£60,176}{10,000 \div 4}$$

$$= £24.07 \text{ per machine hour}$$

$$\text{Assembly} \quad \frac{\text{Cost centre overhead}}{\text{Direct labour hours}} = \frac{£23,448}{5,000}$$

$$= £4.69 \text{ per labour hour}$$

$$\text{Finishing} \quad \frac{\text{Cost centre overhead} \times 100}{\text{Direct wages}} = \frac{£12,776 \times 100}{£10,800}$$

$$= 118.3\% \text{ of direct wages}$$

The overhead absorbed by a particular washing machine could then be accumulated.

3.5 Activity

Assuming that a regular machine takes 1 hour machining, 2 hours assembly and 1 hour finishing, what is the total overhead absorbed by that machine?

3.6 Activity solution

Overhead absorbed:

		£
Machining	1 hour × £24.07	24.07
Assembly	2 hours × £4.69	9.38
Finishing	118.3% of (1 × £3.60)	4.25
		37.70

3.7   Predetermined absorption rates

The washing machine example implies that absorption rates are calculated after the event, ie, when overhead and volume for the period have been ascertained. This is not so. Unit costs are a continuous requirement for management information and will invariably reflect overhead absorption on a predetermined basis.

[Definition]   Predetermined absorption rate $= \dfrac{\text{Budgeted overhead}}{\text{Budgeted volume}}$

Generally, the rate is derived from the annual budget to avoid distortion caused by seasonal fluctuation and to provide a consistent basis for measuring variations.

It is obvious that actual overhead and/or volume will rarely coincide exactly with budget and therefore a difference between overhead absorbed and overhead incurred will arise.

3.8   Activity

In year 9 the budget for the machine shop shows:

Overhead   £60,000
Volume of activity   12,000 machine hours

In January Year 9 the machine shop incurred £5,400 of overhead and 1,050 machine hours were worked.

Calculate the pre-determined absorption rate and the overhead under or over absorbed in January.

3.9   Activity solution

Absorption rate $= \dfrac{\text{Budgeted overhead}}{\text{Budgeted volume}}$

$= \dfrac{£60,000}{12,000 \text{ machine hours}}$

$=$ £5.00 per machine hour.

	£
Overhead incurred	5,400
Overhead absorbed (1,050 hours × £5.00)	5,250
Under absorbed overhead	150

3.10   Under/over absorption

The net under absorption arises from a combination of two compensating factors:

(a)   overhead costs were higher than budget (£60,000 ÷ 12) for the month;
(b)   volume was greater than budget (12,000 hours ÷ 12) for the month.

In practice a separate absorption rate may be calculated for fixed and variable overhead to enable the effect of cost and volume changes to be shown more clearly. Analysis of over/under absorbed overhead is perhaps covered more appropriately under standard costing.

Conclusion   Overhead absorbed (sometimes called **recovered**) represents:

$$\text{Actual production (machine hours in this instance)} \times \text{Predetermined rate per unit (machine hours)}$$

3.11   Treatment of under/over absorption

The unit cost of production will include overhead at the predetermined rate and, generally, overhead under or over absorbed will be shown as a separate item in the costing profit and loss account.

Costing profit and loss account

	£
Sales	100
Cost of sales (units sold × unit cost including overheads)	70
Margin	30
Under/(over) absorption	(5)
Operating profit	25

A large balance in the over/under absorbed account indicates that unit costs are inaccurate and management should be made aware that such costs must be used with care.

3.12   Accounting for overhead absorption

The following example will illustrate the cost accounting entries relating to overhead absorbed.

3.13   Example

From the following data relating to four departments of a factory you are required to:

(a)   journalise departmental overheads incurred;
(b)   journalise departmental overheads recovered;
(c)   give the journal entry recording under or over absorbed overhead expenditure.

	Actual expenses £	Absorption rates (based on predetermined annual estimates)
Department A	1,000	£0.10 per machine hour
Department B	4,000	£0.75 per direct labour hour
Department C	7,000	100% on direct wages
Department D	3,500	£0.25 per unit

	Machine hours worked	Direct labour hours worked	Direct wages £	Units produced
Department A	10,000	11,000	6,000	100,000
Department B	3,000	5,300	6,000	48,900
Department C	6,000	18,000	6,800	52,000
Department D	14,000	30,000	10,000	13,800

3.14   Solution

		Dr £	Cr £
(a)	Department A overhead account	1,000	
	Department B overhead account	4,000	
	Department C overhead account	7,000	
	Department D overhead account	3,500	
	Factory overhead control account		15,500
	Transfer of actual departmental expenses for period	15,500	15,500
(b)	Work in progress account	15,225	
	Department A overhead account		1,000
	Department B overhead account		3,975
	Department C overhead account		6,800
	Department D overhead account		3,450
	Transfer of absorbed departmental expenses for period	15,225	15,225
(c)	Profit and loss account	275	
	Department B overhead account		25
	Department C overhead account		200
	Department D overhead account		50
	Transfer of under absorbed departmental expenses for period	275	275

Note: absorbed expenses:

		£
Department A	10,000 machine hours × £0.10	1,000
Department B	5,300 labour hours × £0.75	3,975
Department C	100% of £6,800	6,800
Department D	13,800 units × £0.25	3,450

3.15   Example

A machine has a potential capacity per annum of 48 weeks at 40 hours per week. It is forecast, however, that the machine will have an actual capacity usage of only 90% because of normal idle time. When the machine is in operation, two operatives who are paid on a time basis of £1.20 per hour each are required. Fixed expenses directly associated with the use of the machine, such as depreciation and maintenance, etc, are £3,840 and general factory overhead totals £30,000. General overhead is allocated to machines on the basis of normal capacity which for the factory as a whole is 25,920 machine hours. During the year the machine was actually in operation for 1,650 hours. The abnormal idle time records indicate that time lost was as follows:

Shortage of materials	10 hours
Excess repairs	50 hours
Labour dispute	5 hours
Re-runs	20 hours

From the above information you are required to prepare a statement analysing the cost of abnormal idle time.

3.16   Solution

Cost of abnormal idle time

	Hours lost		Machine idle time @ £3.38 (W3) per hour		Labour idle time (@ £2.40 per hour)		Total idle time	
	Hrs	Hrs	£	£	£	£	£	£
Normal (10% × 1,920) (W1)		192		-		-		-
Abnormal:								
Shortage of materials (W2)	10		34				34	
Excess repairs (W2)	50		169				169	
Labour dispute (W2)	5		17		12		29	
Re-runs (W2)	20		68		48		116	
Unaccounted losses (W2)	13		44				44	
Total abnormal	98		332		60		392	

Note: it is assumed:

(a)   that the operatives were employed on another machine during the times when the machine was not in operation, with the exception of the five hours lost owing to the labour dispute;

(b)   that the operatives were paid during the hours of the labour dispute; and

(c)   that the operatives were not in attendance during the hours of unaccounted losses.

WORKINGS

		Hours	Hours
(1)	**Analysis of capacity utilisation**		
	Potential capacity, 48 weeks @ 40 hours per week		1,920
	Total operated hours	1,650	
	Less: Re-run hours	20	
	Productive operating hours		1,630
	Total idle time (including non-productive operating hours)		290
(2)	**Analysis of idle time**		
	Normal (10%)		192
	Abnormal:		
	Shortage of materials	10	
	Excess repairs	50	
	Labour dispute	5	
	Re-runs	20	
	Unaccounted losses (bal fig)	13	
	Total abnormal		98
	Total idle time		290

(3)   **Overhead rate on basis of potential capacity**

Fixed expenses:

Direct allocation	3,840
General apportionment $\dfrac{(1,920 \times 90\%)}{25,920} \times £30,000$	2,000
Total fixed expenses	5,840

Normal capacity (hours)	1,728
Rate per hour	£3.38 approx

This rate has been applied to the hours in (2) above to arrive at the cost of idle time. Operatives' wages have been added for the hours of labour dispute and re-runs as follows:

Labour dispute	5 hours @ £2.40	= £12
Re-runs	20 hours @ £2.40	= £48

4   COSTS OF NON-PRODUCTION FUNCTIONS

4.1   Absorption of non-production costs

In the past many businesses attempted to ensure that unit costs included a charge for the administration, selling and distribution costs, usually calculated as a fixed percentage of production costs.

The practice has largely been discontinued but that is not to say that such costs should be ignored. The cost of administration, marketing, research and development, etc has a great impact on the fortunes of a business.

The cost accounting emphasis is to provide information for cost control and to disclose the effect of management decisions on other function costs, and *vice versa.*

4.2   Marketing

Marketing comprises the activities of selling, publicity and distribution. The cost accounting system should show:

(a)   suitable cost centre analysis to identify costs with responsibility;

(b)   analysis between fixed and variable, especially for distribution costs, eg, packaging and delivery;

(c)   statistical bases to measure and compare costs, eg, salemen's calls, number of orders.

4.3   General administration

This function represents the costs of general management, secretarial, accounting and administrative services, except for any such costs which can be directly related to production, marketing, research or development.

Once again the cost accounting emphasis will be on analysis by cost centre for control.

4.4   Research and development

Research costs are those incurred in seeking new or improved products or methods. Development costs are those incurred by those stages from decision implementation to production. Cost analysis will usually relate to natural classification, such as materials or laboratory services and will accumulate costs by specific project.

5   ACTIVITY BASED COSTING (ABC)

5.1   Introduction

ABC has been developed from Professor Kaplan's ideas. A number of companies, are now using ABC including for example, Hewlett Packard and Siemens.

The essence of ABC is that it is **activities** which cause cost, not products, and it is products which consume activities. If the cost of activities and their relationship to products is understood there can be established a basis for product costing performance measurement and profitability analysis.

The important activities in a business are known as **cost drivers.**

> **Definition**   A cost driver is any factor which causes a change in the cost of an activity. (**CIMA Official Terminology**).

Cost drivers represent the allocation bases in an ABC system, and there will often be more than one cost driver used to attribute costs to products.

Before examining examples of cost drivers, the ABC view of costs needs to be considered. Traditional costing splits costs into fixed and variable. In an advanced manufacturing environment the variable costs may be only a small proportion of total costs. Also the non-production overheads eg, design and marketing can be high.

ABC splits costs between short-term and long-term variable costs. Short-term variable costs equate with variable costs under traditional cost accounting. Their characteristic is that they are volume related and change proportionately with the volume of production.

Long-term variable costs are equivalent to fixed costs under traditional cost accounting. It should be noted that this is not just a change in name. The terminology reflects the fact that such costs do vary with activity but with a time lag. For example salaried production engineers will not be immediately made redundant if the number of production runs declines but may be if the decline continues. In addition the cost classification does not stop with factory overheads; non-production overheads such as design and marketing costs are included in product costs and profitability analysis by the ABC system.

5.2   Examples of cost drivers

Short-term variable costs can be routed to products using **volume related** cost drivers such as direct labour hours, machine hours or direct materials used. The cost drivers may be different depending upon how the cost is driven. Thus the cost of power will be related to (ie, driven by) the number of machine hours. Other costs may, however, be related to direct materials. This analysis is similar to traditional cost accounting.

For long-term variable costs however, **volume related** cost drivers will tend to be inappropriate. For example the number and cost of salaried production engineers is not a function of direct labour hours or machine hours but a function of the number of times a machine has to be set up for a production run. The **activity** which drives the cost is the number of set ups. Costs should thus be allocated to products on this number. This contrasts with traditional practice which absorbs all overheads based on (often) direct labour hours and has no regard to the activity which causes the cost.

5.3   Example

There are two identical plants. Plant X produces 500,000 units of Product A. Plant Y produces 50,000 units of Product A and 450,000 units of many products which are similar to A.

The variable cost structure of the two plants are similar but Plant Y has more overheads in the following areas:

Set up costs	(for each production run of a similar product).
Inspection costs	(for each production run of a similar product).
Inventory costs	(due to range of products).
Purchasing goods	(extra staff to buy the greater range of raw materials).
Despatching costs	(more complex due to range of products).

If volume related cost drivers are used to allocate the overheads Product A will suffer about 10% of these additional overheads and a small run of another product, say 1,000, will be allocated 0.2%. This cost allocation is misleading as the additional overheads in Plant Y compared to Plant X arise due to the complexity of the operations. The products which contribute to the complexity should thus bear the additional costs. Put another way, the costs of producing Product A in Plants X and Y should be similar.

5.4   Mechanics of ABC

The mechanics of operating an ABC system are similar to a traditional costing system. The significant cost drivers need to be ascertained and a cost centre is established for each cost driver. Costs are allocated to products by dividing the cost centre costs by the number of transactions undertaken.

For example in Plant Y a set up of a production run would be a cost driver. The cost of the engineers who do the set ups would be a cost centre. If the cost of the engineers is say £280,000 and the number of set ups is 500, then the charging out rate is $\frac{280,000}{500} = £560$. A product which has a number of small production runs will thus have a greater proportion of these costs relative to the quantity of the product produced than a product with large production runs.

Other overheads will be allocated to products in a different way; which way depends upon the cost drivers which have been ascertained.

5.5   Example

(**Note**: numerical calculations using ABC are not examinable in this paper; the following example should be used to get a better appreciation of the principles.)

Plant Y produces about one hundred products. Its largest selling product is Product A; its smallest is Product B. Relevant data is given below:

	Product A	Product B	Total products
Units produced pa	50,000	1,000	500,000
Material cost per unit	£1.00	£1.00	
Direct labour per unit	15 minutes	15 minutes	
Machine time per unit	1 hour	1 hour	
Number of set ups pa	24	2	500
Number of purchase orders for materials	36	6	2,800
Number of times material handled	200	15	12,000
Direct labour cost per hour			£5

Overhead costs:

	£
Set up	280,000
Purchasing	145,000
Materials handling	130,000
Machines	660,000
	1,215,000

Total machine hours are 600,000 hours.

Traditional costing (absorbing overheads on machine hours)

Unit cost	A £	B £
Material cost	1.00	1.00
Labour cost	1.25	1.25
Overhead per machine hour		

$$\frac{1,215,000}{600,000} = 2.025$$

	A	B
	2.025	2.025
	4.275	4.275

The above costings imply that we are indifferent between producing Product A and Product B.

Using an ABC approach would show:

Unit cost	A £	B £

Step 1   Calculate the direct material and labour costs as for the traditional approach.

	A	B
Material cost	1.00	1.00
Labour cost	1.25	1.25
	2.25	2.25

Step 2 Calculate the overheads that will be charged to each product by

(a) Calculating the overhead cost per cost driver for each type of overhead (eg, cost per set-up)

(b) Charge cost to each unit by

- Calculating the total overhead incurred by the production of Product A and Product B.

- Calculating the unit cost accordingly.

Overheads:	A £	B £
Set-up		
$\dfrac{280,000}{500} = £560$ per set up		
$\dfrac{560 \times 24}{50,000}$	0.27	
$\dfrac{560 \times 2}{1,000}$		1.12
Purchasing:		
$\dfrac{145,000}{2,800} = £51.786$ per purchase order		
$\dfrac{36 \times 51.786}{50,000}$	0.04	
$\dfrac{6 \times 51.786}{1,000}$		0.31
Material handling:		
$\dfrac{130,000}{12,000} = 10.833$ per time		
$\dfrac{200 \times 10.833}{50,000}$	0.04	
$\dfrac{15 \times 10.833}{1,000}$		0.16
Machines:		
$\dfrac{660,000}{600,000} = 1.10$ per machine hour	1.10	1.10
	1.45	2.69
Add: Direct material and labour costs	2.25	2.25
	£3.70	£4.94

Common-sense would lead us to conclude that the ABC is a more accurate representation of the relative real costs of the two products.

What must be borne in mind however is whether the benefits of this approach outweigh the costs of implementing and applying the system.

5.6   Activity

Calculate the unit cost of products X and Y this example, (where products X and Y are the sole output of the business)

	Product X	Product Y
Units produced p.a	45,000	5,000
Material cost per unit	£1.50	£4.00
Direct labour per unit	£7.00	£3.50
Direct labour time per unit	1 hr	30 mins
Number of set ups p.a.	30	10
Number of purchase orders for materials	70	10

Overhead costs	£
Set up	20,000
Purchasing	16,000
Labour supervision	23,750

5.7   Activity solution

	X £	Y £
Material cost	1.50	4.00
Labour cost	7.00	3.50
	8.50	7.50

Overhead cost:

Set-up

$$\frac{20,000}{40} = £500 \text{ per set - up}$$

$$\frac{500 \times 30}{45,000} \qquad 0.33$$

$$\frac{500 \times 10}{5,000} \qquad\qquad\qquad 1.00$$

Purchasing

$$\frac{16,000}{800} = £200 \text{ per order}$$

$$\frac{70 \times 200}{45,000} \qquad 0.31$$

$$\frac{10 \times 200}{5,000} \qquad\qquad\qquad 0.40$$

Labour supervision

$$\frac{23,750}{47,500} = £0.50 \text{ per labour hour} \qquad 0.50 \qquad 0.25$$

Total unit cost	9.64	9.15

5.8   Activity based costing and cost centre absorption compared

The main difference between activity based costing and cost centre absorption methods is that activity based costing recognises that costs are caused by many different measure of activity and attributes costs to cost units accordingly.

Cost centre absorption rates use a single measure of activity to attribute production overhead costs to cost units.

The perceived benefit of introducing an activity based costing system is that the unit costs should more accurately reflect the usage of resources, though it is questionable whether the cost of the system can be justified.

6   CHAPTER SUMMARY

In order for management to take many decisions about their products, such as stock valuations, pricing decisions and production decisions, then they must be given information on the cost of the items that are being produced. Cost will include not only the direct costs of production such as direct materials and direct labour but also indirect costs or overhead.

In this chapter much thought has been given to the process of collecting all of the overhead relevant to a cost centre and cost unit and then allocating those overheads to the cost centres. The allocation of these overheads may be by means of an apportionment of the overhead to a number of departments on a common sense basis. Finally the costs allocated and apportioned to the cost centres must then be absorbed into the cost units in a sensible manner.

This approach was then compared with activity based costing, the differences explained and the arguments for and against the use of activity based costing compared to the use of cost centre absorption rates discussed.

7   SELF TEST QUESTIONS

7.1   What is overhead? (1.2)

7.2   What are the three ways in which indirect production costs are incurred? (1.2)

7.3   What are the five steps in the allotment of indirect costs to cost units? (1.3)

7.4   How would the depreciation of machines normally be apportioned to cost centres? (2.3)

7.5   How is the overhead absorption rate calculated? (3.1)

7.6   For overhead absorption purposes how is volume normally measured? (3.1)

7.7   How is a pre-determined absorption rate calculated? (3.7)

7.8   How does an under absorption of overhead arise? (3.10)

7.9   How is the overhead actually absorbed calculated? (3.10)

7.10   What is the usual treatment of an under or over absorption of overhead? (3.11)

7.11   What is activity based costing? (5.1)

7.12   What is a cost driver? (5.1)

8   EXAMINATION TYPE QUESTIONS

8.1   Fibrex Ltd

Shown below are next year's budgeted operating costs for Fibrex Ltd, a company with three production and two service departments.

| | Production departments | | | Service departments | | |
	Weaving dept	Proofing dept	Finishing dept	Personnel dept	Equipment maintenance	Total
	£'000	£'000	£'000	£'000	£'000	£'000
Direct materials	7,000	2,000	1,500	-	-	10,500
Direct wages	2,500	5,500	2,000	-	-	10,000
Indirect materials and wages	1,100	900	300	1,500	3,800	7,600
Power	5,200	1,000	200	100	800	7,300
Rent and rates						8,000
Factory administration and supervision						10,000
Machine insurance						2,400

Additional data extracted from next year's budget is shown below:

	Weaving dept	Proofing dept	Finishing dept	Personnel dept	Equipment maintenance	Total
Floor area, square metres	12,000	27,000	6,000	12,000	3,000	60,000
Machine hours	1,600,000	400,000	400,000	-	-	2,400,000
Direct labour hours	1,200,000	1,800,000	600,000	-	-	3,600,000
Number of employees	600	1,000	400	100	400	2,500
Gross book value of equipment	£4.0m	£1.0m	£1.0m	-	-	£6.0m

You are required as follows:

(a)   Calculate the budgeted overhead absorption rates for each production department using the following methods:

   (i)   a machine hour rate in the weaving department;
   (ii)   a direct labour hour rate in the proofing department; and
   (iii) another suitable method in the finishing department.

It may be assumed that the equipment maintenance department does not service the personnel department.

All workings should be clearly shown.

(17 marks)

(b)   It has been suggested that, instead of calculating department overhead absorption rates, one blanket rate for a factory may be adequate. Identify the circumstances where such a blanket rate may be suitable.

(5 marks)

(Total: 22 marks)

8.2   ABC Manufacturing Company

One of the budget centres of the ABC Manufacturing Company is the boiler house, which raises and supplies steam for all manufacturing budget centres in the company.

The foreman of one of the manufacturing budget centres has complained to the works manager that in his accounts he is charged at different rates each month per lb of steam used. The highest rates have been as much as 20% above the lowest.

You are required to explain in a report to the works manager:

(a)   how such different rates per lb of steam can be incurred in the boiler house;

(5 marks)

(b)   why being charged at different rates could present a difficulty to the foreman of the manufacturing budget centre;

(5 marks)

(c)   what procedure, as cost accountant of the ABC Manufacturing Company, you would propose to install to remedy this position.

(5 marks)

(Total: 15 marks)

9   ANSWERS TO EXAMINATION TYPE QUESTIONS

9.1   Fibrex Ltd

Note: Overheads are **indirect** costs so take care to ensure that the direct materials and wages are **not** included in the overhead calculations.

(a)   The first step is to allocate and apportion total overheads to the cost centres:

Overhead item	Basis of apportionment	Weaving dept	Proofing dept	Finishing dept	Personnel dept	Maint- enance	Total
Indirect materials and wages	Given	1,100	900	300	1,500	3,800	7,600
Power	Given	5,200	1,000	200	100	800	7,300
Rent and rates	Floor area	1,600	3,600	800	1,600	400	8,000
Factory admin & supervision	Number of employees	2,400	4,000	1,600	400	1,600	10,000
Machine insurance	Gross book value	1,600	400	400	-	-	2,400
		11,900	9,900	3,300	3,600	6,600	35,300
Reapportionments: Personnel	(see Tutorial note) Number of employees 6:10:4:4	900	1,500	600	(3,600)	600	
					-		7,200

Equipment maintenance	Gross book value (or machine hours) 4:1:1	4,800	1,200	1,200	(7,200)
		17,600	12,600	5,100	

	Weaving Dept	*Proofing Dept*	*Finishing Dept*

Overhead absorption rate

$$= \frac{\text{Budgeted overhead}}{\text{Budgeted machine hours}} \quad \frac{\text{Budgeted overhead}}{\text{Budgeted labour hours}} \quad \frac{\text{Budgeted overhead}}{\text{Budgeted wage cost}} \times 100$$

$$= \frac{17,600}{1,600} \quad \frac{12,600}{1,800} \quad \frac{5,100}{2,000} \times 100$$

£11 per machine hour	£7 per direct labour hour	255% of direct wage cost

(Tutorial note:

Reapportionment of service cost centres

As personnel provides a service to another service department (equipment maintenance) the quickest approach is first to reapportion the service cost centre which services other service cost centres, ie, in this case personnel. Otherwise the apportionment for equipment maintenance would be slightly longer.*)*

(b)   The circumstances under which a blanket overhead rate may be suitable include the following:

(i)   Where the company offers only a single product or service which must therefore absorb all overheads irrespective of where they are incurred. This does not obviate the need for charging overheads to functional cost centres for cost control purposes.

(ii)   Where all products are similar in nature and use approximately the same amount of the services provided by each department.

(iii)   Where overhead costs are relatively insignificant and the costs of calculating more detailed absorption rates would exceed the benefits resulting from the exercise (eg, under contract costing the majority of costs are direct).

9.2   ABC Manufacturing Co

REPORT

To: Works Manager

From: Cost Accountant

Date: X-X-19XX

Subject: Steam Costs

(a)   The complaint that the cost per lb of steam charged to manufacturing budget centres fluctuates probably arises because the rate is calculated by dividing the month's cost of the boiler house by the total steam raised during the month. Therefore, if either the cost or demand for steam varies each month, the cost per lb will vary. Due to the heavy incidence of fixed costs in the boiler house, in a month when total demand is low, the cost per lb will be higher even though total boiler house costs remain the same.

Consequently the rate charged to a specific manufacturing budget centre will be affected by the use of steam in other centres as well as by boiler house cost fluctuations.

(b)   The problem encountered by the foreman of the budget centre is that he is held accountable for the level of costs incurred in his centre. The unit cost of steam, however, is beyond his control and even though he makes a determined attempt to economise in the use of steam, it may not be reflected in the charge to his centre because the cost per lb may have increased. Any excess spending by the boiler house foreman is automatically passed on to the manufacturing departments.

(c)   The charge for steam must be based upon a budgeted rate. To calculate the rate, the budgeted annual expenditure of the boiler house is divided by the budgeted demand for steam during this year. The charge to cost centres would then be calculated by multiplying the actual steam used by each centre by the budgeted rate.

The expenditure incurred in the boiler house is thus controlled against a budget and any difference between the actual cost and the amounts charged to manufacturing centres would be analysed between cost increases/savings and under/over-utilisation of steam by the manufacturing centres. Such differences would be charged or credited to profit and loss and serve as useful control information.

5 MARGINAL COSTING

INTRODUCTION & LEARNING OBJECTIVES

Syllabus area 2a. Application of marginal costing principles to management reporting and the preparation of profit and loss accounts. (Ability required 3).

In the previous chapter the techniques of allocating, apportioning and absorbing of overheads into the cost of units were examined. In this chapter the alternative method of valuing production and stocks using only variable costs rather than total costs is considered.

When you have studied this chapter you should be able to do the following:

- Understand the term marginal costing.

- Compare marginal costing to absorption costing.

- Reconcile the operating profit under marginal costing principles to that under absorption costing principles.

- Understand the use of contribution in comparison of products.

1 MARGINAL COSTING

1.1 Introduction

Marginal cost is essentially an economist's concept.

> **Definition** Marginal cost is the part of the cost of one unit of product or service which would be avoided if that unit were not produced, or which would increase if one extra unit were produced **(CIMA Official Terminology)**.

1.2 Marginal costing as an alternative to absorption costing

> **Definition** Marginal costing is the accounting system in which variable costs are charged to cost units and fixed costs of the period are written off in full against the aggregate contribution. **(CIMA Official Terminology)**

When absorption costing was examined, it was noted that overhead absorption rates could be analysed between fixed and variable, but that unit cost included an absorption rate based on total overhead, ie, fixed plus variable.

1.3 Marginal costing reports and statements

Marginal costing may be used for internal management reporting as an alternative to absorption costing.

The following example illustrates the preparation of such a statement. Note how the layouts differ, under absorption costing the fixed costs are included in cost of sales (by using the predetermined absorption rate) whereas under marginal costing they are treated as a period cost and shown as a deduction from contribution.

Definition Contribution is sales value less variable cost of sales. **(CIMA Official Terminology).**

1.4 Example

Company A produces a single product with the following budget:

Selling price	£10
Direct materials	£3 per unit
Direct wages	£2 per unit
Variable overhead	£1 per unit
Fixed overhead	£10,000 per month.

The fixed overhead absorption rate is based on volume of 5,000 units per month.

1.5 Activity

Show the operating statement for the month, when 4,800 units were produced and sold under absorption costing principles.

Assume that costs were as budget.

1.6 Activity solution

Absorption costing

	£
Sales (4,800 units)	48,000
Cost of sales (4,800 × £8) (W1)	38,400
Operating margin	9,600
Under absorbed overhead (W2)	(400)
Operating profit	9,200

WORKINGS

(1) Unit cost represents materials (£3) + wages (£2) + variable overhead (£1) + fixed overhead absorbed $(\frac{£10,000}{5,000})$ = £8 per unit.

		£
(2)	Fixed overhead incurred	10,000
	Fixed overhead absorbed	9,600 (4,800 × £2)
	Under absorption	400

(3) Variable overhead is, by definition, budgeted at £1 **per unit**; costs are as budget. Therefore total variable overhead is £4,800.

1.7 Example

In contrast the operating statement will now be shown under marginal costing principles.

1.8 Solution

	£
Sales	48,000
Variable cost of sales (4,800 × £6)	28,800
Contribution	19,200
Fixed costs	10,000
Operating profit	9,200

In this example operating profit is the same under both methods. That will not be so, however, when production is more or less than sales, ie, stocks of finished goods are maintained.

1.9 Marginal costing and stock valuation

Stock valuation under marginal costing is based on variable production costs only. This is in contrast to absorption costing where fixed production overhead costs are included in stock valuations using the predetermined absorption rate.

The following example illustrates the effects of the different stock valuations on profit.

1.10 Activity

Suppose that in the previous example production was in fact 6,000 units ie, 4,800 units sold and 1,200 units left in closing stock.

Prepare the profit statement for the month under absorption costing principles.

1.11 Activity solution

	£	£
Sales		48,000
Cost of sales:		
Production (6,000 × £8)	48,000	
Closing stock (1,200 × £8)	9,600	
		38,400
Operating margin		9,600
Over absorbed fixed overhead ((6,000 × £2) − £10,000)		2,000
Operating profit		11,600

1.12 Activity

Now show the profit statement for the month under marginal costing principles.

1.13   Activity solution

		£	£
Sales			48,000
Variable cost of sales:			
Production costs (6,000 × £6)		36,000	
Closing stock (1,200 × £6)		7,200	
			28,800
Contribution			19,200
Fixed costs			10,000
Operating profit			9,200

1.14   Reconciliation of absorption cost profit and marginal cost profit

The difference in profit under the two methods (£11,600 – 9,200 = £2,400) arises because of the difference in the amount of fixed overhead included in stock under the absorption costing system.

The closing stock of 1,200 units includes in its absorption cost valuation £2 per unit of fixed costs. This £2,400 is therefore being carried forward to the next accounting period rather than being charged in this accounting period giving a profit figure in this period £2,400 higher under absorption rather than marginal costing.

1.15   Marginal costing - advantages over absorption costing

Preparation of routine operating statements using absorption costing is considered less informative because:

(a)   Profit per unit is a misleading figure: in the example the operating margin of £2 per unit arises because fixed overhead per unit is based on 5,000 units. If another basis were used, margin per unit would differ even though fixed overhead was the same amount in total.

(b)   Build-up or run-down of stocks of finished goods can distort comparison of period operating statements and obscure the effect of increasing or decreasing sales.

(c)   Comparison between products can be misleading because of the effect of arbitrary apportionment of fixed costs.

1.16   Defence of absorption costing

Absorption costing is widely used and you must understand both principles. Defenders of the absorption principle point out that:

(a)   it is necessary to include fixed overhead in stock values for financial statements; routine cost accounting using absorption costing produces stock values which include a share of fixed overhead;

(b)   for small jobbing business, overhead allotment is the only practicable way of obtaining job costs for estimating and profit analysis;

(c)   analysis of under/over absorbed overhead is useful to identify inefficient utilisation of production resources.

Conclusion If marginal costing is adopted, then stocks of work in progress and finished products will be valued at variable costs only. Where production and sales levels are not in sympathy and stock levels are fluctuating, the net profit will be different from that disclosed by an absorption method of costing.

1.17   Example

A company sells ¿ product for £10, and incurs £4 of variable costs in its manufacture. The fixed costs are £900 per year and are absorbed on the basis of the normal production volume of 250 units per year. The results for the last four years, when no expenditure variances arose, were as follows:

Item	1st year units	2nd year units	3rd year units	4th year units	Total units
Opening stock	-	200	300	300	-
Production	300	250	200	200	950
	300	450	500	500	950
Closing stock	200	300	300	200	200
Sales	100	150	200	300	750
	£	£	£	£	£
Sales value	1,000	1,500	2,000	3,000	7,500

1.18   Solution

The profit statement under absorption costing would be as follows:

	£	£	£	£	£
Opening stock @ £7.60	-	1,520	2,280	2,280	-
Variable costs of production @ £4	1,200	1,000	800	800	3,800
Fixed costs @ $\frac{900}{250}$ = £3.60	1,080	900	720	720	3,420
	2,280	3,420	3,800	3,800	7,220
Closing stock £7.60	1,520	2,280	2,280	1,520	1,520
Cost of sales	(760)	(1,140)	(1,520)	(2,280)	(5,700)
(Under)/over absorption (W)	180	Nil	(180)	(180)	(180)
Net profit	420	360	300	540	1,620

WORKING

Calculation of over/under absorption

Fixed cost control account

	£		£
Incurred:		Absorbed:	
Year 1	900	300 × £3.60	1,080
Over absorption	180		
	1,080		1,080
Year 2	900	250 × £3.60	900
Year 3	900	200 × £3.60	720
		Under absorption	180
	900		900
Year 4	900	200 × £3.60	720
		Under absorption	180
	900		900

If marginal costing had been used instead of absorption, the results would have been shown as:

Item	1st year £	2nd year £	3rd year £	4th year £	Total £
Sales	1,000	1,500	2,000	3,000	7,500
Variable cost of sales (@ £4)	400	600	800	1,200	3,000
Contribution	600	900	1,200	1,800	4,500
Fixed costs	900	900	900	900	3,600
Net profit/(loss)	(300)	-	300	900	900

The marginal presentation indicates clearly that the business must sell at least 150 units per year to break even, ie, £900 ÷ (10 − 4) whereas it appeared, using absorption costing, that even at 100 units it was making a healthy profit.

The total profit for the four years is less under the marginal principle because the stocks are valued at £800 (£4 × 200) instead of £1,520, ie, £720 of the fixed costs are being carried forward under the absorption principle.

The profit figures shown may be reconciled as follows:

	Year 1 £		Year 2 £	Year 3 £		Year 4 £		Total £
Profit/(loss) under marginal costing	(300)		Nil	300		900		900
Add: Distortion from stock increase								
200 × £3.60	720	100 × £3.60 =	360	-		200 × £3.60 =	720	
Less: Distortion from stock decrease				-	100 × £3.60 =	360		
Profit per absorption	420		360	300		540		1,620

Conclusion The under/over absorption figures have nothing to do with the difference in the profit figures. The difference is simply due to changes in stock levels and the fixed cost included in those stock valuations.

1.19 Marginal costing and decision-making

Marginal costing emphasises variable costs per unit and fixed costs in total whereas absorption costing unitises all production costs.

Marginal costing therefore reflects the behaviour of costs in relation to activity. Since most decision-making problems involve changes to activity, marginal costing is more appropriate for short-run decision-making than absorption costing.

1.20 Product comparison

It is considered more informative to present comparison statements on a contribution basis. Remember,

Definition Contribution is sales value less variable cost of sales. **(CIMA Official Terminology)**

The term **contribution** describes the amount which a product provides or contributes towards a fund out of which fixed overhead may be paid, the balance being net profit. Where two or more products are manufactured in a factory and share all production facilities, the fixed overhead can only be apportioned on an arbitrary basis.

1.21 Example

A factory manufactures three components – X, Y and Z – and the budgeted production for the year is 1,000 units, 1,500 units and 2,000 units respectively. Fixed overhead amounts to £6,750 and has been apportioned on the basis of budgeted units: £1,500 to X, £2,250 to Y and £3,000 to Z. Sales and variable costs are as follows:

	Component X	Component Y	Component Z
Selling price	£4	£6	£5
Variable cost	£1	£4	£4

1.22 Solution

The budgeted profit and loss account based on the above is as follows:

	Component X		Component Y		Component Z		Total	
Sales units	1,000		1,500		2,000		4,500	
	£	£	£	£	£	£	£	£
Sales value		4,000		9,000		10,000		23,000
Variable cost	1,000		6,000		8,000		15,000	
Fixed overhead	1,500		2,250		3,000		6,750	
		2,500		8,250		11,000		21,750
Net profit/(loss)		1,500		750		(1,000)		1,250

Clearly, there is little value in comparing products in this way. If the fixed overhead is common to all three products, there is no point in apportioning it. A better presentation is as follows:

	Component X	Component Y	Component Z	Total
Sales units	1,000	1,500	2,000	4,500
	£	£	£	£
Sales value	4,000	9,000	10,000	23,000
Variable cost	1,000	6,000	8,000	15,000
Contribution	3,000	3,000	2,000	8,000
Fixed overhead				6,750
Net profit				1,250

Analysis may show, however, that certain fixed costs may be associated with a specific product and the statement can be amended to differentiate specific fixed costs (under products) from general fixed costs (under total).

1.23   Example

A company that manufactures one product has calculated its cost on a quarterly production budget of 10,000 units. The selling price was £5 per unit.

Sales in the four successive quarters of the last year were:

Quarter 1	10,000 units
Quarter 2	9,000 units
Quarter 3	7,000 units
Quarter 4	5,500 units

The level of stock at the beginning of the year was 1,000 units and the company maintained its stock of finished products at the same level at the end of each of the four quarters.

Based on its quarterly production budget, the cost per unit was:

	£
Prime cost	3.50
Production overhead	0.75
Selling and administration overhead	0.30
Total	4.55

Fixed production overhead, which has been taken into account in calculating the above figures, was £5,000 per quarter. Selling and administration overhead was treated as fixed, and was charged against sales in the period in which it was incurred.

You are required to present a tabular statement to bring out the effect on net profit of the declining volume of sales over the four quarters given, assuming in respect of fixed production overhead that the company:

(a)   absorbs it at the budgeted rate per unit;

(b)   does not absorb it into the product cost, but charges it against sales in each quarter.

1.24 Solution

(a) **Net profit statement (fixed overhead absorbed)**

	1st quarter	2nd quarter	3rd quarter	4th quarter
Sales units	10,000	9,000	7,000	5,500
	£	£	£	£
Sales value (£5 per unit)	50,000	45,000	35,000	27,500
Cost of sales:				
Prime costs (£3.50 per unit)	35,000	31,500	24,500	19,250
Production overhead absorbed (£0.75 per unit)	7,500	6,750	5,250	4,125
Under absorbed production overhead (W)	-	500	1,500	2,250
	42,500	38,750	31,250	25,625
Gross profit	7,500	6,250	3,750	1,875
Less: Selling and administration overhead (10,000 × 0.30)	3,000	3,000	3,000	3,000
Net profit/(loss)	4,500	3,250	750	(1,125)

WORKING

Fixed production overhead absorption rate:

$$\frac{\text{Fixed production overhead}}{\text{Budgeted production}} = \frac{£5,000}{10,000 \text{ units}} = £0.50 \text{ per unit}$$

As finished stock is maintained at 1,000 units, fixed overhead under absorbed in each quarter = £5,000 − (Sales units × £0.50).

(b) **Net profit statement (fixed overhead charged against period sales)**

	1st quarter	2nd quarter	3rd quarter	4th quarter
Sales units	10,000	9,000	7,000	5,500
	£	£	£	£
Sales value	50,000	45,000	35,000	27,500
Less: Variable cost of sales (£3.75 per unit)	37,500	33,750	26,250	20,625
Contribution	12,500	11,250	8,750	6,875
Less: Fixed production selling and administration overhead	8,000	8,000	8,000	8,000
Net profit/(loss)	4,500	3,250	750	(1,125)

2 CHAPTER SUMMARY

Under marginal costing principles, only the variable production costs are charged against turnover to give contribution for the period. These variable production costs will include direct materials, labour and expenses as well as variable production overhead. All of the fixed costs of the business, including fixed production overhead, is then charged against contribution for the period in order to give net profit.

This also means that the closing stocks carried forward are valued at their variable cost only. The whole of the period's fixed costs are charged to the profit and loss account for the period and none carried forward to later periods.

3 SELF TEST QUESTIONS

3.1   What is marginal cost? (1.1)

3.2   What is marginal costing? (1.2)

3.3   What is the difference between marginal costing and absorption costing? (1.2)

3.4   What is contribution? (1.3)

3.5   What is the reason for the difference in operating profit under marginal and absorption costing? (1.14)

3.6   What are the advantages of marginal costing? (1.15)

3.7   What are the advantages of absorption costing? (1.16)

3.8   What is the best figure to use for comparison of products? (1.20)

3.9   How is the fixed production overhead absorption rate calculated? (1.24)

4 EXAMINATION TYPE QUESTIONS

4.1 Rayners plc

Rayners plc manufactures and sells electric blankets. The selling price is £12. Each blanket has the following unit cost:

	£
Direct material	2
Direct labour	1
Variable production overhead	2
Fixed production overhead	3
	8

Administration costs are incurred at the rate of £20 per annum.

The company achieved the following production and sales of blankets:

Year	1	2	3
Production	100	110	90
Sales	90	110	95

The following information is also relevant:

(1)   The overhead costs of £2 and £3 per unit have been calculated on the basis of a budgeted production volume of 90 units.

(2)   There was no inflation.

(3)   There was no opening stock.

You are required

(a)   to prepare an operating statement for each year using:

    (i)   marginal costing; and

    (ii)   absorption costing.

(10 marks)

(b)   to explain why the profit figures reported under the two techniques disagree.

(6 marks)

(Total: 16 marks)

4.2   Stock valuation - fixed overhead costs

The valuation of stocks in a manufacturing and trading company is dependent on a number of factors, not least of which is the company's policy concerning its treatment of fixed overhead costs, which is an important part of a company's cost accounting procedures.

You are required

(a)   to discuss the principles of marginal and absorption costing, explaining clearly the difference between them;

(10 marks)

(b)   to explain the use of pre-determined rates to absorb overhead costs into product costs.

(10 marks)

(Total: 20 marks)

Use numerical examples to illustrate your answers, for which 8 of the total marks are available.

(CIMA May 1988)

5   ANSWERS TO EXAMINATION TYPE QUESTIONS

5.1   Rayners plc

(a)   **Operating statement**

		Year 1		Year 2		Year 3	
		£	£	£	£	£	£
(i)	**Marginal costing**						
	Sales		1,080		1,320		1,140
	Opening stock @ £5	Nil		50		50	
	Add: Production cost @ £5	500		550		450	
		500		600		500	
	Less: Closing stock @ £5	50		50		25	
	Cost of sales		(450)		(550)		(475)
	Contribution		630		770		665
	Less: Fixed costs:						
	Production overhead	270		270		270	
	Administration overhead	20		20		20	
			(290)		(290)		(290)
	Profit		340		480		375

		Year 1		Year 2		Year 3	
(ii)	**Absorption costing**						
	Sales		1,080		1,320		1,140
	Opening stock @ £8	Nil		80		80	
	Add: Production cost @ £8	800		880		720	
		800		960		800	
	Less: Closing stock @ £8	80		80		40	
	Cost of sales		(720)		(880)		(760)
			360		440		380
	(Under)/over absorption (see working)		30		60		Nil
	Administration overhead		(20)		(20)		(20)
	Profit		370		480		360

Note: the control account below includes variable overhead for information ie, the under/over recovery only occurs on fixed overheads - it is a 'fixed overhead volume variance'.

WORKING

Production overhead control account

		£		£
Year 1	Incurred: Fixed: 90 × £3 =	270	Absorbed to work-in progress:	
	Variable: 100 × £2 =	200	100 × (2 + 3)	500
	Over-recovery			
	(90 − 100) × 3	30		
		500		500
Year 2	Incurred: Fixed: 90 × £3	270	Absorbed to work-in-progress:	
	Variable: 110 × 2	220	110 × 5	550
	Over-recovery			
	(90 − 110) × 3	60		
		550		550
Year 3	Incurred: Fixed: 90 × £3	270	Absorbed to work-in-progress:	
	Variable: 90 × 2	180	90 × 5	450
		450		450

(b)   The difference in profit arises because of the difference in the amount of fixed overhead included in stock under the absorption costing system.

When the opening and closing stock includes the same amount of fixed overheads (ie, here when the volume of opening and closing stock is the same, in year 2) profit is the same under both techniques. Where volume of stock has gone up (year 1) and the amount of fixed overhead in stock has increased then profit is higher under absorption costing and *vice versa*.

This may be summarised as follows:

		Year 1 £	*Year 2* £	*Year 3* £
Profit per marginal costing		340	480	375
Add:	Increase in fixed overhead included in stock under absorption costing: 10 units @ 3	30	-	-
Less:	Decrease in fixed overhead included in stock under absorption costing: 5 units @ 3	-	-	(15)
Profit per absorption costing		370	480	360

5.2   Stock valuation - fixed overhead costs

Note: the narrative in the question refers to stock valuation. It is thus necessary to refer in the answer to the effect the methods have on the closing stock value.

(a)   Marginal and absorption costing are two different principles that can be used to determine the costs that are taken into account in calculating the cost of a unit of output.

Marginal costing only includes those costs which are variable. Fixed costs are a function of time and not different levels of output.

Absorption costing includes all costs which are incurred in the production process. Fixed costs are 'absorbed' into units of output by collecting the costs in convenient cost centres and then absorbing them into units of output on this basis, for example by direct labour hours or machine hours.

It follows that stocks will often be a (significantly) higher value using absorption costing compared to marginal costing. If there is a high number of units in stock at the year end compared to the previous year, profit will also be significantly different.

Example

A new business produces 1,500 units in the year. Sales are 1,000 units. Variable costs are 40% of the selling price (£10 per unit).

Contribution is thus:

		£
Sales	$1,000 \times £10$	10,000
Variable cost	£4	4,000
Contribution		6,000

Suppose that fixed production costs are £6,000.

Under marginal costing the fixed costs are charged to the profit and loss account. Closing stocks are valued at:

$500 \times £4 = £2,000.$

Under absorption costing the fixed costs are absorbed into both the units sold and the closing stock.

Profit is:

	£
Contribution	6,000
Less: Fixed costs $\dfrac{1,000}{1,500} \times 6,000$	(4,000)
Profit	2,000

Closing stock is valued at:

	£
$500 \times £4 =$	2,000
Add: Fixed costs $\dfrac{500}{1,500} \times 6,000$	2,000
	4,000

(b) **The use of pre-determined rates to absorb overhead costs**

A pre-determined rate is used:

(i)   to smooth out seasonal fluctuations in overhead costs;
(ii)   to enable cost to be calculated quickly.

The pre-determined rate is calculated by:

$$\frac{\text{Budgeted overheads}}{\text{Budgeted volume}}$$

The budgeted volume can be expressed using a number of different measures, the most common being:

(i)   number of units
(ii)   number of labour hours
(iii)   number of machine hours.

The pre-determined rate will be applied to actual units produced (or hours worked).

The use of estimates usually means that at the end of the period there is a difference between the fixed production overhead incurred and the amount absorbed into product costs. This difference must be debited or credited to cost accounting profit and loss. The individual product costs are not altered.

Example

In the example in part (a) assume that a pre-determined absorption rate was calculated at the start of the year.

$$\frac{\text{Budgeted fixed overheads say £6,500}}{\text{Budgeted production say 1,600 units}} = £4.06 \text{ per unit}$$

Overheads absorbed would be:

	£
$1,500 \times £4.06 =$	6,090
Actual overheads are	6,000
Over absorbed	90

The profit and loss account is:

	£
Sales	10,000
Cost of sales $1,000 \times (£4 + 4.06)$	(8,060)
	1,940
Over absorbed overhead	90
Profit	2,030
Closing stock $500 \times (£4 + 4.06)$	4,030

6 DECISION MAKING

INTRODUCTION & LEARNING OBJECTIVES

Syllabus area 2a. Relevant cost concepts. (Ability required 2).

This chapter is concerned with the provision of cost accounting information relevant to decisions made by management.

Different types of decision are explained by examples which identify the factors to be considered when making the decision.

Most decisions rely on the use of contribution theory and an understanding of cost behaviour which was dealt with earlier.

When you have studied this chapter you should be able to do the following:

- Identify relevant costs for a particular decision.

- Evaluate a decision on financial grounds.

- Identify other non-financial factors which should be considered when making a decision.

1 RELEVANT COSTS FOR DECISIONS

1.1 Structure of a decision

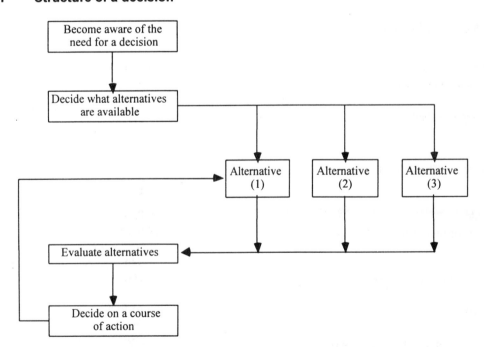

Although the cost accountant may be involved in all four stages, the main concern is with the evaluation process.

1.2   Quantitative and qualitative factors

In an evaluation of the alternatives the manager will take account of factors of two types:

(a)   those which may be quantified in monetary terms;

(b)   those which may not as easily be quantified eg, effect on customer relations.

1.3   Short and long term decisions

The decisions faced by management may affect the future of the business in the long term, the short term or both.

Factors which are relevant in the short term may be irrelevant in the long term or *vice versa;* but in evaluating the factors, only the revenues and costs which are affected by the decision are relevant.

Factors which are **not** relevant to decision-making include:

(a)   **Sunk costs.** Costs which have already been incurred eg, costs already incurred in market research. The information gained from the research will be useful in making the decision, but the costs are irrelevant as the decision will not change them.

(b)   **Book values and accounting depreciation.** Both of these figures are determined by accounting conventions. For decision-making purposes it is the economic considerations which are important.

   Illustration

   A machine which cost £10,000 four years ago has a written down value of £6,000 and the depreciation to be charged this year is £1,000. Assuming that it has no alternative use, could be sold now for £3,000, but in one year's time will be unsaleable, the cost of keeping it and using it for a further year will be £3,000.

(c)   **Common costs.** Costs which are common to all alternative courses of action are irrelevant to decision-making.

1.4   General approach to decision-making problems

In the examples which follow, remember the key question:

Do the relevant revenues exceed the relevant costs? If they do, the proposals are to be recommended, at least on financial grounds.

1.5   Example

A decision has to be made whether to use production method A or B.

The cost figures are as follows:

	Method A		Method B	
	Costs last year	*Expected costs next year*	*Costs last year*	*Expected costs next year*
	£	*£*	*£*	*£*
Fixed costs	5,000	7,000	5,000	7,000
Variable costs per unit:				
Labour	2	6	4	12
Materials	12	8	15	10

Which costs are relevant to the decision?

(a)   First, reject past costs (though in practice they may be used as a guide to future costs).

(b)   Second, reject expected fixed costs because, although they are not past, they are the same for both alternatives and may therefore be ignored.

(c)   Hence the only relevant costs are:

	Method A £	*Method B* £
Expected future variable costs:		
Labour	6	12
Materials	8	10
	14	22

It is concluded that the analysis should eliminate all irrelevant figures ie, those unaffected by the decision.

This, of course, considerably simplifies the decision, because it eliminates from consideration many irrelevant costs.

Note that fixed cost are not always irrelevant. If they vary between decision alternatives, they are relevant and must be taken into account.

1.6   Problems of uncertainty

The approach presupposes that the relevant costs and revenues are known. In fact, it is never possible to know future costs or revenues with certainty. Estimates may have varying degrees of confidence attached to them.

The examples in this lesson will use single figure estimates of costs and revenues. In practice it may be more desirable to use a range of figures, and to give probability weightings to the various values. These can be used to compute 'expected values' or a table of possible outcomes with their probabilities.

These techniques are covered in Chapter 23 'Probability'.

1.7   Determining the relevant costs of materials

In any decision situation the cost of materials relevant to a particular decision is their opportunity cost. This can be represented by a decision tree:

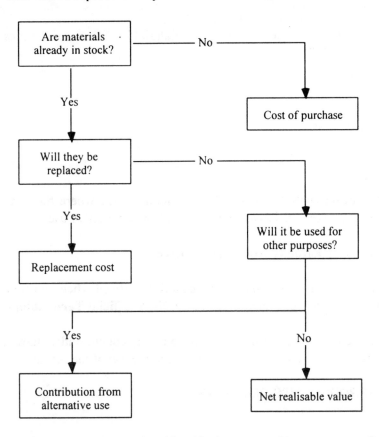

This decision tree can be used to identify the appropriate cost to use for materials.

1.8   Determining the relevant costs of labour

A similar problem exists in determining the relevant costs of labour. In this case the key question is whether spare capacity exists and on this basis another decision tree can be produced:

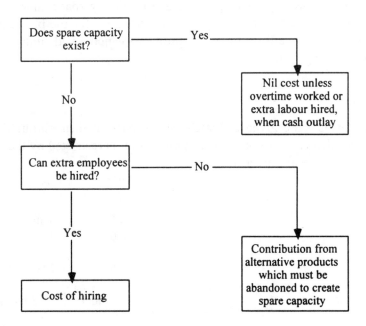

Again this can be used to identify the relevant cost.

1.9   Activity

Z Ltd has 50kg of material P in stock which was bought five years ago for £70. It is no longer used but could be sold for £3/kg.

Z Ltd is currently pricing a job which could use 40kg of material P. What is the relevant cost of P which should be included in the price?

1.10   Solution to activity

40kg @ £3/kg = £120

1.11   Opportunity costs

In the determination of relevant costs for materials and labour above where the resource was in short supply its relevant cost was referred to as 'contribution from alternative use'.

This may be referred to as the opportunity cost of the resource.

Definition   An opportunity cost is the value of the benefit sacrificed when one course of action is chosen, in preference to an alternative. **(CIMA Official Terminology)**.

Opportunity costs are sometimes referred to as an economic idea, they represent the benefit foregone as a consequence of an alternative use of the resource.

2   CHOICE OF PRODUCT (PRODUCT MIX) DECISIONS

2.1   Limiting factors

All businesses which aim to maximise profit find that the volume of output and sales is restricted. For many, sales demand is the limiting factor and therefore the business will seek to make the maximum profit by concentrating its selling efforts on those products which yield high contributions.

Other limiting factors may prevent sales growth eg, shortage of building space, machine capacity, skilled labour, or the necessary materials. In such cases it is important for the business to obtain maximum profit by concentrating its efforts on those products which yield high contributions relative to the amount of the limiting factor they consume.

2.2   Example

Two products - Alpha and Gama - are given a final finish by passing them through a spraying process. There is considerable demand for both products but output is restricted by the capacity of the spraying process. The product details are as follows:

	Alpha £	Gama £
Selling price	10.00	15.00
Variable cost	6.00	7.50
Contribution	4.00	7.50
Finishing time in spraying process	1 hour	3 hours

Without any restriction in the capacity of the spraying process, Gama is the more profitable product and should be promoted (assuming that the sales of each product do not affect the other). However, as the spraying process is the limiting factor, it is important for the business to use the capacity of the process as profitably as possible ie, to earn the maximum profit for each spraying hour. The contributions per spraying hour are £4.00 for Alpha and £2.50 for Gama and, therefore, it is Alpha which should be promoted. This can be proved by assuming a fixed number of spraying hours per week, say 45:

	Alpha	*Gama*
Number of units to be sprayed in 45 hours	45	15
Contribution per unit	£4.00	£7.50
Total contribution	£180.00	£112.50

2.3   Differential cost approach

The proof in the above example illustrates an application of differential costing, a technique in which only cost and income differences between alternative courses of action are considered.

The difference between the two alternatives (viz product Alpha alone and product Gama alone) is £67.50.

2.4   Other considerations regarding limiting factors

(a)   In the long run management must seek to remove the limiting factor. In the example above, management should be attempting to increase the capacity of the spraying process. Thus, any one limiting factor should only be a short term problem. However, as soon as it is removed, it will be replaced by another limiting factor.

(b)   Even in the short run management may be able to find ways round the bottleneck eg, overtime working or sub-contracting might be solutions to the situations described.

(c)   It may not always be easy to identify the limiting factor. In practice, as already stated, several limiting factors may operate simultaneously. Even in examination questions where there is only one limiting factor, it may be necessary to investigate several possible limiting factors.

(d)   Other parameters may set minimum production levels eg, there may be a contract to supply Gama so that certain minimum quantities must be produced.

2.5   Example

X Ltd makes three products - A, B and C - of which unit costs, machine hours and selling prices are as follows:

	Product A	*Product B*	*Product C*
Machine hours	10	12	14
	£	£	£
Direct materials £1 per lb	14 (14 lbs)	12 (12 lbs)	10 (10 lbs)
Variable overhead	18 (12 hours)	12 (8 hours)	6 (4 hours)
Marginal cost	38	30	22
Selling price	50	40	30
Contribution	12	10	8

Sales demand for the period is limited as follows:

A	4,000
B	6,000
C	6,000

However, as a matter of company policy it is decided to produce a minimum of 1,000 units of Product A. The supply of materials in the period is unlimited but machine hours are restricted to 200,000 and direct labour hours to 50,000.

Indicate the production levels that should be adopted for the three products in order to maximise profitability, and state the maximum contribution.

2.6   Solution

First, determine which is the limiting factor. At potential sales level:

	Sales potential (units)	Total machine hours	Total labour hours
Product A	4,000	40,000	48,000
Product B	6,000	72,000	48,000
Product C	6,000	84,000	24,000
		196,000	120,000

Thus the limiting factor is the labour hours. The next stage is to calculate contribution per labour hour:

Product A $\dfrac{£12}{12} = £1.00$

Product B $\dfrac{£10}{8} = £1.25$

Product C $\dfrac{£8}{4} = £2.00$

Thus, production should be concentrated on C up to maximum available sales, then B and finally A.

However, a minimum of 1,000 units of A must be produced. Taking these factors into account, the production schedule becomes:

	Units produced	Labour hours	Cumulative labour hours	Limiting factor
Product A	1,000	12,000	12,000	Policy to produce 1,000 units
Product C	6,000	24,000	36,000	Sales
Product B	1,750	14,000	50,000	Labour hours

3   MAKE OR BUY DECISIONS

3.1   Types of make or buy decisions

Occasionally a business may have the opportunity to purchase, from another company, a component part or assembly which it currently produces from its own resources.

In examining the choice, management must first consider the following questions:

(a)   Is the alternative source of supply available only temporarily or for the foreseeable future?

(b)   Is there spare production capacity available now and/or in the future?

3.2 Spare capacity

If the business is operating below maximum capacity, production resources will be idle if the component is purchased from outside. The fixed costs of those resources are irrelevant to the decision in the short term as they will be incurred whether the component is made or purchased. Purchase would be recommended, therefore, only if the buying price were less than the variable costs of internal manufacture.

In the long term, however, the business may dispense with or transfer some of its resources and may purchase from outside if it thereby saves more than the extra cost of purchasing.

3.3 Example

A company manufactures an assembly used in the production of one of its product lines. The department in which the assembly is produced incurs fixed costs of £24,000 pa. The variable costs of production are £2.55 per unit. The assembly could be bought outside at a cost of £2.65 per unit.

The current annual requirement is for 80,000 assemblies per year. Should the company continue to manufacture the assembly, or should it be purchased from the outside suppliers?

3.4 Solution

A decision to purchase outside would cost the company £(2.65 - 2.55) = 10p per unit, which for 80,000 assemblies would amount to £8,000 pa. Thus, the fixed costs of £24,000 will require analysis to determine if more than £8,000 would actually be saved if production of the assembly were discontinued.

3.5 Other considerations affecting the decision

Management would need to consider other factors before reaching a decision. Some would be quantifiable and some not:

(a)   **Continuity and control of supply.** Can the outside company be relied upon to meet the requirements in terms of quantity, quality, delivery dates and price stability?

(b)   **Alternative use of resources.** Can the resources used to make this article be transferred to another activity which will save cost or increase revenue?

(c)   **Social/legal.** Will the decision affect contractual or ethical obligations to employees or business connections.

3.6 Capacity exhausted

If a business cannot fulfil orders because it has used up all available capacity, it may be forced to purchase from outside in the short term (unless it is cheaper to refuse sales). In the longer term management may look to other alternatives, such as capital expenditure.

It may be, however, that a variety of components is produced from common resources and management would try to arrange manufacture or purchase to use its available capacity most profitably. In such a situation the limiting factor concept makes it easier to formulate the optimum plans; priority for purchase would be indicated by ranking components in relation to the excess purchasing cost per unit of limiting factor.

3.7   Example

Fidgets Ltd manufactures three components used in its finished product. The component workshop is currently unable to meet the demand for components and the possibility of sub-contracting part of the requirement is being investigated on the basis of the following data:

	Component A	Component B	Component C
	£	£	£
Variable costs of production	3.00	4.00	7.00
Outside purchase price	2.50	6.00	13.00
Excess cost per unit	(0.50)	2.00	6.00
Machine hours per unit	1	0.5	2
Labour hours per unit	2	2	4

You are required:

(a)   to decide which component should be bought out if the company is operating at full capacity;

(b)   to decide which component should be bought out if production is limited to 4,000 machine hours per week;

(c)   to decide which component should be bought out if production is limited to 4,000 labour hours per week.

3.8   Solution

(a)   Component A should always be bought out regardless of any limiting factors, as its variable cost of production is higher than the outside purchase price.

(b)   If machine hours are limited to 4,000 hours:

	Component B	Component C
Excess cost	£2	£6
Machine hours per unit	0.5	2
Excess cost per machine hour	£4	£3

Component C has the lowest excess cost per limiting factor and should, therefore, be bought out.

Proof:

	Component B	Component C
Units produced in 4,000 hours	8,000	2,000
	£	£
Production costs	32,000	14,000
Purchase costs	48,000	26,000
Excess cost of purchase	16,000	12,000

(c)   If labour hours are limited to 4,000 hours:

	Component B	*Component C*
Excess cost	£2	£6
Labour hours	2	4
Excess cost per labour hour	£1	£1.50

Therefore, component B has the lowest excess cost per limiting factor and should be bought out.

Proof:

	Component B	*Component C*
Units produced in 4,000 hours	2,000	1,000
	£	£
Production costs	8,000	7,000
Purchase costs	12,000	13,000
Excess cost of purchase	4,000	6,000

4   EVALUATING PROPOSALS

4.1   Volume and cost structure changes

Management will require information to evaluate proposals aimed to increase profit by changing operating strategy. The cost accountant will need to show clearly the effect of the proposals on profit by pin-pointing the changes in costs and revenues and by quantifying the margin of error which will cause the proposal to be unviable.

4.2   Example

A company produces and sells one product and its forecast for the next financial year is as follows:

	£'000	£'000
Sales 100,000 units @ £8		800
Variable costs:		
Material	300	
Labour	200	
		500
Contribution (£3 per unit)		300
Fixed costs		150
Net profit		150

As an attempt to increase net profit, two proposals have been put forward:

(a)   to launch an advertising campaign costing £14,000. This will increase the sales to 150,000 units, although the price will have to be reduced to £7;

(b)   to produce some components at present purchased from suppliers.   This will reduce material costs by 20% but will increase fixed costs by £72,000.

Proposal (a) will increase the sales revenue but the increase in costs will be greater:

	£'000
Sales 150,000 × £7	1,050
Variable costs	750
	300
Fixed costs plus advertising	164
	136

4.3   Solution

Proposal (a) is therefore of no value and sales must be increased by a further 7,000 units to maintain net profit:

Advertising cost	=	£14,000
Contribution per unit	=	£2
∴ Additional volume required	=	7,000 units

Proposal (b) reduces variable costs by £60,000 but increases fixed costs by £72,000 and is therefore not to be recommended unless the total volume increases as a result of the policy (eg, if the supply of the components were previously a limiting factor).   The increase in sales needed to maintain profit at £150,000 (assuming the price remains at £8) would be:

Reduced profits at 100,000 units	=	£12,000
Revised contribution per unit	=	£3.60
∴ Additional volume required	=	3,333 units

4.4   Utilisation of spare capacity and special order acceptance

Where production is below capacity, opportunities may arise for sales at a specially reduced price, for example, export orders or manufacturing under another brand name (eg, 'St Michael').   Such opportunities are worthwhile if the answer to two key questions is 'Yes':

(a)   Is spare capacity available?

(b)   Does additional revenue (Units × Price) exceed additional costs (Units × Variable cost)?

However, the evaluation should also consider:

(i)   Is there an alternative more profitable way of utilising spare capacity (eg, sales promotion, making an alternative product)?

(ii)   Will fixed costs be unchanged if the order is accepted?

(iii)   Will accepting one order at below normal selling price lead other customers to ask for price cuts?

The longer the time period in question, the more important are these other factors.

4.5 Example

At a production level of 8,000 units per month, which is 80% of capacity, the budget of Export Ltd is:

	Per unit £	8,000 units £
Sales	5.00	40,000
Variable costs:		
Direct labour	1.00	8,000
Raw materials	1.50	12,000
Variable overheads	0.50	4,000
	3.00	24,000
Fixed costs	1.50	12,000
Total	4.50	36,000
Budgeted profit	0.50	4,000

An opportunity arises to export 1,000 units per month at a price of £4 per unit.

Should the contract be accepted?

4.6 Solution

(a) Is spare capacity available?   Yes

			£
(b)	Additional revenue	1,000 × £4	4,000
	Additional costs	1,000 × £3	3,000
			1,000

Increased profitability

Therefore, the contract should be accepted.

Note that fixed costs are not relevant to the decision and are therefore ignored.

4.7 Special contract pricing

A business which produces to customer's order may be working to full capacity. Any additional orders must be considered on the basis of the following questions:

(a) What price must be quoted to make the contract profitable?
(b) Can other orders be fulfilled if this contract is accepted?

In such a situation the limiting factor needs to be recognised so that the contract price quoted will at least maintain the existing rate of contribution per unit of limiting factor.

4.8 **Example**

Oddjobs Ltd manufactures special purpose gauges to customers' specifications. The highly skilled labour force is always working to full capacity and the budget for the next year shows:

	£	£
Sales		40,000
Direct materials	4,000	
Direct wages 3,200 hours @ £5	16,000	
Fixed overhead	10,000	
		30,000
Profit		10,000

An enquiry is received from XY Ltd for a gauge which would use £60 of direct materials and 40 labour hours.

(a)   What is the minimum price to quote to XY Ltd?

(b)   Would the minimum price be different if spare capacity were available but materials were subject to a quota of £4,000 per year?

4.9 **Solution**

(a)   The limiting factor is 3,200 labour hours and the budgeted contribution per hour is £20,000 ÷ 3,200 hours = £6.25 per hour. Minimum price is therefore:

	£
Materials	60
Wages 40 hours @ £5	200
	260
Add: Contribution 40 hours @ £6.25	250
Contract price	510

At the above price the contract will maintain the budgeted contribution (check by calculating the effect of devoting the whole 3,200 hours to XY Ltd.)

Note, however, that the budget probably represents a mixture of orders, some of which earn more than £6.25 per hour and some less. Acceptance of the XY order must displace other contracts, so the contribution rate of contracts displaced should be checked.

(b)   If the limiting factor is materials, budgeted contribution per £ of materials is £20,000 ÷ £4,000 = £5 per £1 of materials.

Minimum price is therefore:

	£
Materials/wages (as above)	260
Contribution £60 × 5	300
Contract price	560

Because materials are scarce, Oddjobs must aim to earn the maximum profit from its limited supply.

4.10   Closure of a business segment

Part of a business may appear to be unprofitable. The segment may, for example, be a product, a department or a channel of distribution. In evaluating closure the cost accountant should identify:

(a)   loss of contribution from the segment;
(b)   savings in specific fixed costs from closure;
(c)   penalties eg, redundancy, compensation to customers etc;
(d)   alternative use for resources released;
(e)   non-quantifiable effects.

4.11   Example

Harolds department store comprises three departments - Menswear, Ladies' Wear and Unisex. The store budget is as follows:

	Mens £	Ladies £	Unisex £	Total £
Sales	40,000	60,000	20,000	120,000
Direct cost of sales	20,000	36,000	15,000	71,000
Department costs	5,000	10,000	3,000	18,000
Apportioned store costs	5,000	5,000	5,000	15,000
Profit/(loss)	10,000	9,000	(3,000)	16,000

It is suggested that Unisex be closed to increase the size of Mens and Ladies.

What information is relevant or required?

4.12   Solution

Possible answers are:

(a)   Unisex earns £2,000 net contribution (store costs will be re-apportioned to Mens/Ladies).

(b)   Possible increase in Mens/Ladies sales volume.

(c)   Will Unisex staff be dismissed or transferred to Mens/Ladies?

(d)   Reorganisation costs eg, repartitioning, stock disposal.

(e)   Loss of custom because Unisex attracts certain types of customer who will not buy in Mens/Ladies.

4.13   Calculation of basic selling price

When a business manufactures a limited range of repetitive products, initial estimation of economic selling prices is most useful.

4.14   Example

The Dainty Dolly Co manufactures a single product, the Dainty, which is a life-size doll selling in the high-price toy market through approved dealers.

The standard cost of the doll is as follows:

	£
Direct material	9
Direct labour	7
Variable factory overhead	4
Variable selling overhead	2

Production capacity is 60,000 pa and market research suggests that with an aggressive sales effort this quantity could be sold.

Inflation is expected to be as follows for the variable costs:

Direct material	2%
Direct labour	5%
Variable factory overhead	2%

Fixed costs are not affected by inflation and will be:

Production	£80,100
Selling and administration	£63,300

The company's assets involved in the product are as follows:

Land and buildings	£135,000
Plant and equipment	£125,000
Fixtures and fittings	£40,000

In addition, there will be a working capital requirement which the company estimates will be £10 for each unit produced and sold in the year.

The company expects a return on capital employed of 20% before tax.

Calculate the list selling price for the Dainty which will cover a dealership discount of 20% on list price and enable the company to achieve its profit objective.

4.15   Solution

	£	£ per unit
Variable costs:		
Direct materials £9 + 2%		9.18
Direct labour £7 + 5%		7.35
Factory overhead £4 + 2%		4.08
Selling overhead		2.00
		22.61
Fixed costs:		
Production	80,100	
Selling and administration	63,300	
	143,400	
Units of production	60,000	
Fixed cost per unit		2.39
Total cost		25.00
Profit required (see workings)		3.00
Sales price to dealer		28.00
20% dealer discount $\frac{20}{80} \times £28.00$		7.00
List price		35.00

WORKINGS

The company requires 20% return on capital employed.

	£
Capital employed:	
Land and buildings	135,000
Plant and equipment	125,000
Fixtures and fittings	40,000
Current assets 60,000 units × £10	600,000
	900,000
20% return	180,000
Return per unit of production	£3.00

4.16   Segment profitability

When presenting information for comparing results or plans for different products, departments etc, it is useful to show gross and net contribution for each segment. The information in the example above would be presented in the following form.

	Menswear	Ladies Wear	Unisex	Total
	£'000	£'000	£'000	£'000
Sales	40	60	20	120
Direct cost of sales	20	36	15	71
Gross contribution	20	24	5	49
Department costs	5	10	3	18
Net contribution	15	14	2	31

Note that the store costs if shown would only appear in the total column. In addition, the statement should include performance indicators relevant to the type of operation. For a department store, such indicators would include:

(a)   C/S ratios (based on **gross** contribution);
(b)   gross and net contribution per unit of floor space;
(c)   gross and net contribution per employee.

For a manufacturing company, more relevant indicators would include:

(a)   contribution per labour/machine hour;
(b)   added value/conversion cost per hour;
(c)   added/value conversion cost per employee.

4.17   Temporary shut-down

When a business has experienced trading difficulties which do not appear likely to improve in the immediate future, consideration may be given to closing down operations temporarily. Factors other than cost which will influence the decision are:

(a)   suspending production and sales of products will result in their **leaving the public eye;**

(b)   dismissal of the labour force will entail bad feeling and possible difficulty in recruitment when operations are restarted;

(c)   danger of plant obsolescence;

(d)   difficulty and cost of closing down and restarting operations in certain industries eg, a blast furnace.

The temporary closure of a business will result in additional expenditure eg, plant will require protective coverings, services will be disconnected. In the same way, additional expenditure will be incurred when the business restarts.

On the other hand, a temporary closure may enable the business to reorganise efficiently to take full advantage of improved trading conditions when they return.

In the short term a business can continue to operate while marginal contribution equals fixed expenses. In periods of trading difficulty, as long as some contribution is made towards fixed expenses, it will generally be worthwhile continuing operations.

4.18   **Example**

A company is operating at 40% capacity and is considering closing down its factory for one year, after which time the demand for its product is expected to increase substantially. The following data applies:

	£
Sales value at 40% capacity	60,000
Marginal costs of sales at 40% capacity	40,000
Fixed costs	50,000

Fixed costs which will remain if the factory is closed amount to £20,000. The cost of closing down operations will amount to £4,000.

Prepare a statement to show the best course of action.

4.19   **Solution**

Statement of profit or loss

Continuing operation	£	*Temporary closure*	£
Sales	60,000	Fixed expenses	20,000
Marginal cost of sales	40,000	Closing down costs	4,000
	——		
Contribution to fixed costs	20,000		
Fixed costs	50,000		——
	——		
Net loss	30,000		24,000
	——		——

Ignoring non-cost considerations, the company will minimise its losses by closing down for one year.

Students should note that the marginal contribution of £20,000 does not cover the difference between existing fixed costs and those that remain on closure (ie, £(50,000 − 24,000) = £26,000 compared to £20,000).

5   **CHAPTER SUMMARY**

This chapter has shown examples of the different kinds of decisions which must be made in order to maximise profitability.

Relevant costs for decisions have been identified and the techniques used to evaluate decision options illustrated.

6   **SELF TEST QUESTIONS**

6.1   What is an opportunity cost? (1.11)

6.2   What is a limiting factor? (2.1)

6.3   In a closure decision, what five factors should be considered? (4.10)

7   EXAMINATION TYPE QUESTIONS

7.1   Hard and soft

A company produces a hard grade and, by additional processing, a soft grade of its product.

A market research study for next year has indicated very good prospects not only for both the hard and soft grades but also for a light grade produced after still further processing.

The raw material is imported and there is a possibility that a quota system will be introduced allowing only a maximum of £300,000 pa of material to be imported.

The company's marketing policy has been to sell 60% of its capacity (or of its allocation of material if the quota is introduced) in the most profitable grade. It has been decided that this policy should continue if it is to produce three grades, but that only 15% of its capacity (or material allocation) should be sold in the least profitable grade.

The budgeted prime costs and selling prices per ton for each grade are as follows:

	Hard	*Soft*	*Light*
	£	£	£
Selling price	70	95	150
Direct material cost	15	20	25
Direct wages (@ £2.50 per hour)	15	25	45

For next year the company's annual production capacity is 225,000 direct labour hours and its fixed overhead is £500,000. Variable overhead is 20% of direct wages.

Fixed overhead is at present absorbed by a rate per ton produced.

You are required:

(a)   to state which of the three grades of product will be most profitable and which will be least profitable in the short term assuming that such volume as can be produced can be sold:

(i)   if the materials quota does not operate;
(ii)   if the materials quota does come into force.

(b)   if the materials quota does come into force, to calculate the budgeted profit for next year from the company's marketing policy if:

(i)   only light grade is produced;
(ii)   all three grades are produced in accordance with present policy.

7.2   Tools

In a manufacturing company the normal practice for ordering tools is for the production manager to compare cost estimates prepared by the tool shop foreman with quotations from an outside tool-making company which is able to produce tools to an acceptable standard. The manager then places the order where the cost is lowest.

On 29 October the manager places an enquiry with the tool shop and the outside company for two tools which will be required during December.

The tool shop foreman establishes the following facts:

	Tool A.100	*Tool B.105*
Material cost	£169	£352
Operator and machine time	140 hours	90 hours

The budgeted costs (excluding direct material) for the tool shop for the month of December are as follows:

	£
Direct wages	13,000
Foreman's salary	1,850
Electricity	4,000
Depreciation	4,200
Heating, rent and rates	500
Service department apportionments:	
Maintenance department	550
Canteen and welfare	1,900
Central administration	2,000

The budgeted activity for the year is 24,000 hours.

Electricity is used solely to drive machines.

You are required:

(a)   to calculate the cost of each tool if it is to be made by the tool shop on an absorption cost basis;

(b)   to advise the production manager where the tools should be produced if the outside company has quoted £1,750 for tool A.100 and £1,000 for tool B.105. Briefly give your reasons;

(c)   to state whether the production manager should take a different decision if the production hours worked from the beginning of the year to 29 October are 1,500 per month.

7.3   Moonshine Co Ltd

The Moonshine Co Ltd manufactures three products, each of which is made in a separate factory. The company sets target profit levels for its products. For Product A the target for budget period 5 (a twelve month period) has been set at the level of £2,500.

The budgeted profitability of Product A is indicated in the summarised statement below:

Product A - budget period 5

	£	£
Sales (all domestic) - 10,000 units		25,000
Less: Variable costs	15,000	
Fixed costs	9,000	
		24,000
Profit		1,000
Profit as percentage of sales		4%
Profit required		£2,500

In the statement above fixed costs consist of £2,000 allocated head office expenses and £7,000 direct fixed costs ie, costs which need be incurred only if Product A is to be produced but which do not alter according to variations in the actual quantity produced. In view of the deviation between the budgeted and target profit levels for Product A, it had been decided to increase the selling price in order to close the gap. However, because of the national economic situation this course of action was subsequently abandoned.

You are required to examine the situation, indicating possible ways in which the problem of raising the profit of Product A to the target level for budget period 5 might be solved and giving your views briefly on the relevance of the allocation of head office expenses to a solution of the problem.

7.4   Minute

You are the management accountant of a company operating a simple chemical process making four different products from a single raw material: Minute, Small, Medium and Large. Your production director is considering proposals to discontinue certain work at present done on these products and has therefore asked you to prepare a report, giving:

(a)   a statement of the profit made or loss incurred on each of the four products, Minute, Small, Medium and Large, under present conditions;

(b)   an assessment of the change in the profit or loss, given in answer to (a) above, if the proposals being considered were adopted;

(c)   any recommendations you consider you should put forward arising out of the assessment.

Your report should be based on the information given below.

The cost of raw material for the year just ended was £67,000 and initial processing costs amounted to a further £128,200. All the four products, Minute, Small, Medium and Large, are produced simultaneously at a single split-off point. Product Medium is sold immediately without further processing. The other three products are subject to further processing before being sold. It is the company's policy to apportion the costs prior to the split-off point on a suitable sales value basis.

The output, sales and additional processing costs for the past year were as follows:

Product	Output in units	Sales £	Additional processing cost £
Minute	800,000	192,000	40,000
Small	179,450	58,000	32,000
Medium	10,000	8,000	-
Large	18,000	60,000	2,000

The proposals being considered by the production director are to sell the products to other processors immediately after the split-off point without any of the present additional processing being done. The additional processing facilities for products Minute, Small and Large would then either no longer be used or be put to an alternative profitable use. The prices per unit to be obtained from the other processors would be:

	£
Minute	0.16
Small	0.20
Medium	0.80
Large	2.50

8   ANSWERS TO EXAMINATION TYPE QUESTIONS

8.1   Hard and soft

(a)   In the short term, whatever decision the company makes regarding the mix of products to be produced and sold, the fixed overhead can be assumed to remain the same. It is necessary, therefore, to base the decision on the contribution earned by each product.

	Hard		Soft		Light	
	£	£	£	£	£	£
Selling price		70		95		150
Direct material	15		20		25	
Direct wages	15		25		45	
Variable overhead	3		5		9	
		33		50		79
Contribution		37		45		71
Hours per unit		6		10		18
Contribution per hour		£6.167		£4.500		£3.944
Contribution per £1 material		£2.467		£2.25		£2.84

(i)   If the materials quota does not operate, the company's production capacity is limited to 225,000 labour hours, in which case it must seek to obtain the greatest contribution for each labour hour. The hard grade gives the greatest contribution per hour and therefore this is the most profitable.

(ii)   If the materials quota comes into force, the company must obtain the maximum contribution from each £1 spent on material. The light grade gives the greatest contribution per £1 of material and this is therefore the most profitable.

Note: this applies only if the materials quota provides production which is within the production capacity of 900,000 hours. To test this:

$$\frac{£300,000}{£25} \times 18 = 216,000 \text{ hours}$$

As this is within the labour constraint, conclusion (ii) is correct.

(b)   (i)

	Light
Material	£300,000
Budgeted units	12,000
Contribution per unit	£71
	£
Total contribution	852,000
Fixed overhead	500,000
Budgeted profit for year	352,000

(ii)

	Hard	Soft	Light	Total
				£
Material allocation	£75,000 (25%)	£45,000 (15%)	£180,000 (60%)	300,000
Budgeted units	5,000	2,250	7,200	
Contribution per unit	£37	£45	£71	
Total contribution	£185,000	£101,250	£511,200	797,450
Fixed overhead				500,000
Budgeted profit for year				297,450

8.2   Tools

(a)   **Tool cost estimates**

	Tool A.100	Tool B.105
	£	£
Material	169	352
Direct wages	910 (140 × £6.50)	585 (90 × £6.50)
Electricity	280 (140 × £2.00)	180 (90 × £2.00)
Variable cost	1,359	1,117
Fixed overhead	770 (140 × £5.50)	495 (90 × £5.50)
Total cost	2,129	1,612

(b)   Tool A.100 should be produced by the tool room as the additional costs incurred on manufacture (£1,359) are about £400 less than the cost of buying the tool.

Tool B.105 should be purchased as the additional costs (£1,117) are more than £100 above the purchase price.

(c)   As the hours actually worked are 1,500 per month and this is less than the budget, it may indicate that there is some difficulty in obtaining orders. If it is thought that the direct operatives would be idle unless the order for tool B.105 were given to the tool shop, it should be given the order as the additional costs would be only £532 ie, material and electricity. This assumes that employees would be paid during the idle time, not laid off.

WORKINGS

(i)   Direct wages per hour $= \dfrac{£13,000}{2,000}$

$= £6.50$

(ii)   Electricity cost per hour $= \dfrac{£4,000}{2,000}$

$= £2.00$

(iii)   Fixed overhead (all other costs) per hour $= \dfrac{£11,000}{2,000}$

$= £5.50$

8.3   Moonshine Ltd

The Moonshine Co Ltd
Profit report for Product A, period 5

	Units £	Total £
Sales 10,000 units @	2.50	25,000
Variable costs 10,000 units @	1.50	15,000
Contribution to fixed costs and profit	1.00	10,000
Direct fixed costs	0.70	7,000
Contribution to head office expenses and profit	0.30	3,000
Allocated head office costs		2,000
		1,000

An extra £1,500 of profit must be made to raise profit to the level of £2,500 required. There are four ways in which this end can be achieved, since an increase in selling prices in the home market is precluded by the economic situation:

(a)   increase in units sold, at the existing price;
(b)   reduction in variable costs;
(c)   reduction in fixed costs;
(d)   diversification into the export market.

(a)   An increase in units sold

Every unit sold makes a contribution of £1 to fixed costs and profits, so that in order to increase profits by £1,500, an extra 1,500 units will have to be sold. This is a 15% increase in sales. Such an increase may only be possible after an advertising campaign has been undertaken, which will cause direct fixed costs to increase. Any increase in the direct fixed costs must be added to the additional revenue required, and extra units must be sold to compensate for it, at a contribution rate of £1 per unit. For example, if advertising costing £500 is undertaken to increase sales, the extra units sold must bring in £1,500 (the extra profit required) plus £500 to cover the increased fixed costs ie, at least 2,000 extra units must be sold.

(b)   Reduction of variable costs

A 10% reduction of variable costs would increase profit by the £1,500 required. Keen buying, cheaper alternative materials, or greater productivity from the labour force are required to reduce the variable unit cost by 15p from its present level of £1.50.

(c)   Reduction in fixed costs

To increase profits a reduction in fixed costs could be made. Such costs cannot be reduced in the short run when they are fixed by definition. It may be possible, however, to prune them by careful budgeting in the next financial year. It is difficult to see how the direct fixed costs can be reduced, but a detailed examination of the budget may indicate economies which can be made. A reduction of 21.4% would be required to increase profits to a satisfactory level.

At present Product A contributes £2,000 pa to general head office expenses. If this cost allocation were reduced by 75% to £500, the profit on Product A would reach the desired level. This is a false economy insofar as it does not reduce the level of head office costs, but merely redistributes them. There is no case for discontinuing the production of Product A as it contributes £3,000 towards profit and overhead during the period, unless the capacity involved in the production of A could be devoted to some alternative which is more profitable.

(d)   **The export market**

There are two alternatives open to the company:

(i)   To make all sales in the export market, where there is no bar to increased prices. A market survey should be undertaken to discover if, after a 6% increase in selling prices, a similar volume could be sold.

(ii)   Dumping. The minimum acceptable price in an overseas market which has no connection with the home market would be a unit price in excess of the variable cost burden ie, any price in excess of £1.50 would make a contribution towards fixed costs, assuming that the variable cost of exported products is the same for those sold at home. Sufficient units must be sold for the total contribution to equal the £1,500 of extra profit required. If a 10% margin is required on extra export sales, the price computation would be as follows:

$$\text{Variable cost} \times \frac{10}{9} = £1.50 \times \frac{10}{9} =$$

£	
1.667	Price
1.500	Less: Variable cost
0.167	Profit @ 10% on sales

At this price 9,000 (£1,500 ÷ £0.167) must be sold before the required extra profits are obtained.

8.4   Minute

Report

To: Production director

From: Management accountant

Date:

Subject: Product profitability

The profitability of the company's products is shown in the following statement. It is, of course, impossible to identify the costs of the initial process for particular products with any degree of accuracy, and they have been apportioned on the basis of sales value less further processing costs.

(a)

	1 Sales value	*2* Additional processing costs	*3* (1-2)	*4* Joint costs apportioned	*5* Total cost (2 + 4)	*6* Profit (1 − 5)
	£	£	£	£	£	£
Minute	192,000	40,000	152,000	121,600	161,600	30,400
Small	58,000	32,000	26,000	20,800	52,800	5,200
Medium	8,000	-	8,000	6,400	6,400	1,600
Large	60,000	2,000	58,000	46,400	48,400	11,600
	318,000	74,000	244,000	195,200	269,200	48,800

(b) The proposal to sell the products to other processors immediately the products are separated from the initial process would reduce the sales income by £101,110 and eliminate the additional processing costs of £74,000, thus giving a net reduction in profit of £27,110.

	Production units	Price to processors £	Sales value £
Minute	800,000	0.16	128,000
Small	179,450	0.20	35,890
Medium	10,000	0.80	8,000
Large	18,000	2.50	45,000
			216,890
Less: Costs of initial process			195,200
Net profit			21,690

(c) A study of individual products shows that the sales value lost on Minute and Large is greater than the additional processing costs saved; it is therefore better to continue the present policy. However, the sales value lost on Small is less than the additional processing costs saved and therefore it would be better to adopt the proposal for that product. The Medium product's profitability is the same under both arrangements.

	Present sales value £	New sales value £	Sales reduction £	Costs saved £	Reduction in profit £
Minute	192,000	128,000	64,000	40,000	(24,000)
Small	58,000	35,890	22,110	32,000	9,890
Medium	8,000	8,000	-	-	-
Large	60,000	45,000	15,000	2,000	(13,000)
	318,000	216,890	101,110	74,000	(27,110)

The following statement shows that by adopting the policy suggested above, the company's total profit will increase from the existing £48,800 to £58,690.

	£	£	£
Sales value: Minute	192,000		
Small	35,890		
Medium	8,000		
Large	60,000		
			295,890
Less: Initial process costs		195,200	
Additional process costs (Minute and Large)		42,000	
			237,200
			58,690

However, if the alternative uses of the additional processing facilities for products Minute and Large were to yield a contribution towards the additional processing costs of at least £64,000 and £15,000 respectively, then it would be better to sell the products unprocessed. An investigation into the alternative uses of the additional processing facilities should be initiated forthwith. It is assumed that the additional processing facilities for each product can operate independently of each other.

Signed ....
Management Accountant

7 JOB COSTING

INTRODUCTION & LEARNING OBJECTIVES

Syllabus area 2b. Work-in-progress accounts for job costing. (Ability required 3).

Profit and loss accounts for job costing systems. (Ability required 3).

This chapter is concerned with the type of costing sometimes known as specific order costing. As its name suggests, this is used where the unit(s) produced can be related to a specific production order as opposed to a continuous production process where items are made for stock.

When you have studied this chapter you should be able to do the following:

- Explain when it is appropriate to use job costing.
- Explain how a job costing system operates.
- Explain when it is appropriate to use batch costing.
- Discuss the similarities and differences of job costing and batch costing.
- Value work-in-progress in accordance with SSAP 9 under systems of job costing and batch costing.

---

1 APPLICATIONS OF SPECIFIC ORDER COSTING

1.1 Specific order costing

Definition **Specific order costing** is the basic cost accounting method applicable where work consists of separately identifiable contracts, jobs or batches. **(CIMA Official Terminology).**

The distinguishing features are:

(a) work is separated as opposed to a continuous flow;
(b) work can be identified with a particular customer's order or contract.

Note that contract costing is not examinable in this paper.

1.2 Introduction to job costing

Definition Job costing is a form of specific order costing in which costs are attributed to individual jobs **(CIMA Official Terminology).**

This method of costing is adopted when the factory issues an order to produce one cost unit for a customer. Jobbing firms are engaged in 'one-off' products of a specialist nature such as tools, machines, replacement parts, etc. The firm may meet a demand for products which need to be of a much higher standard than mass-produced equivalents or where the quantity required is so small that the planning and setting up involved for other firms would not be worthwhile.

Jobbing firms normally operate with a variety of machines in order to be able to tackle the majority of operations that will be required in the product. They will handle a wide range of work and are often used as sub-contractors to larger firms which have to off-load work where they have not the resources required for particular products or operations. The jobbing firm, therefore, probably has only a small amount of work of a repetitive nature which means that production plans may be prepared for just a few weeks or months ahead, and have to be flexible to meet urgent orders.

1.3   Introduction to batch costing

[Definition]   Batch costing is a form of specific order costing in which costs are attributed to batches of products (**CIMA Official Terminology**).

Businesses which manufacture a variety of products, eg, household electrical goods, to be held in stock prior to sale, will operate **batch costing.** Jobbing methods are still used and the costing system is practically the same as for job costing. The only difference is that instead of charging costs to each separate cost unit, they are charged to the one production order which covers a quantity of cost units. When the order is completed the unit cost is found by dividing the quantity into the total batch cost.

1.4   Costing principles

Either direct or absorption costing can be applied in job and batch costing. Again the decision is influenced by **SSAP 9**, which requires absorption costing for stock valuation purposes, and therefore encourages its application for all costing. The assumption made in the following sections is that absorption costing is to be applied. This is the more complex situation, in that it involves the use of pre-determined overhead rates, and the problems of over-or under-absorption. If marginal costing is applied, then only variable overheads are charged to the production units; other costs are expensed on a time basis.

2   JOB COSTING

2.1   Job cost sheet (or card)

The focal point of a job costing system is the cost sheet (or card). A separate sheet will be opened for each customer's order, on which will be recorded:

(a)   materials purchased specifically for the job (from GRNs or suppliers' invoices);
(b)   materials drawn from stock (from requisitions);
(c)   direct wages (from time sheet/job cards);
(d)   direct expenses (from invoices, etc)

When the job is finished, the cost sheet gives the total direct cost, and overhead can be calculated and entered using one of the accepted methods. If the job is unfinished at the end of an accounting period the total cost recorded to date on the cost sheets will give the work in progress figure. The job cost can be compared with the estimate to analyse the difference between actual and estimated cost. Where the product contains a number of components it is advisable to check that the costs of all the components have been recorded.

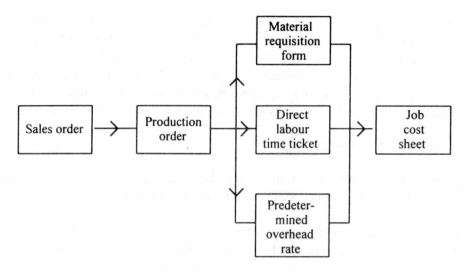

2.2   Example of a job cost

Jobbers Ltd undertakes jobbing engineering work. Among the requests for quotations received in December was one from A for a small machine to be manufactured according to the customer's drawings supplied. Jobbers Ltd prepared an estimate of the material and labour content based on the drawings, and amounts were added for overhead and profit. The estimate indicated a price of £600 and this price was quoted to, and accepted by, A.

The work on A's order was put in hand in January on the authority of Production Order No. 1001 signed by the works manager and was completed in that month. The abstract of stores requisitions issued in January showed the following against Production Order No. 1001:

Stores requisition	£
D57	48
D61	24
D70	26
Total	98

Two operatives paid at £2.20 per hour each had been employed in separate cost centres on Production Order No. 1001 during January and their time-sheets showed that each had worked for thirty hours on that order. The overhead rates for the cost centres in which the operatives are employed are in one centre £2.00 per direct labour hour and 100% on direct wages in the other. Administration and other overhead is recovered at the rate of 30% on production cost.

You are required to prepare a statement showing the cost and profitability of the order from A.

2.3   Solution

Statement of cost and profitability - production order number 1001
machine for A per customer's drawing

	£	£	£
Selling price per estimate			600
Costs:			
Direct materials, per stores abstract		98	
Direct wages, 60 hours @ £2.20		132	
Prime cost		230	
Production overhead:			
30 hours @ £2.00	60		
100% of 30 hours @ £2.20	66		
		126	
Production cost		356	
Administration and other overhead, 30% of production cost		107	
Total cost of sales			463
Net profit			137

Note: actual and estimated profit on the order would be compared and any significant difference reported to management. The estimate should have been compiled on the same lines as the actual cost in the above statement to assist in locating the particular costs which were not as estimated.

2.4   Defective work and rectification

A business may incur extra cost by producing replacements for units scrapped as defective, or by rectifying the units. Two main objectives must be considered when accounting for the cost of defective output:

(a)   control of the level of defective work and rectification;

(b)   ensuring that selling prices cover, among other factors, the production cost including normal defective work and rectification.

For the first objective it is important to determine the costs already incurred, or additional costs spent in rectifying sub-standard units. The decision regarding whether units are to be scrapped or reworked is normally taken by the production manager on notification by the inspection department by means of a **rejection note.** The decision will be affected by the costs of the raw material and the setting-up costs of machines. It may be simpler and cheaper to scrap sub-standard units and increase the size of a later batch of units rather than arrange for a small rectification order to be processed separately through the factory. The cost of defective work can be isolated by using special job numbers to which the costs are charged. If units are scrapped and not replaced on the original order, the rejection note can be used by the cost department as a voucher with which to credit the job cost account and debit the defective work account. If the units are to be replaced on the original order by processing a small replacement batch, theoretically it is this replacement order which should be charged to the defective work account to give a more accurate figure of the cost of defectives. If units are to be rectified, the costs of rectification will be charged to the rectified account.

In connection with selling prices, it is important for the cost accountant to appreciate the estimating system. The estimator may anticipate a certain level of scrap for a particular job but the cost accountant may have already allowed for normal scrap in setting overhead rates. Thus, it is possible that an excessive allowance for scrap may be built into the estimated cost.

The cost accountant is likely to express the overhead rate for defectives in terms of a rate per machine or labour hour. This assumes, therefore, that the cost of scrap is related to the number of hours worked on a job. This is inaccurate because the cost of scrap is more likely to be related to the total value of material handled. It is better, therefore, to exclude scrap from the overhead rate and calculate a separate scrap allowance to be included in the direct cost estimates.

If the scrap has any realisable value either by sale or by re-use as a raw material substitutive, the sale proceeds or the normal cost of the raw material should be credited to the defective work account.

2.5   Setting up costs

When a business makes a variety of products in batches, the costs of clearing and re-setting machines are likely to be significant and worthy of comprehensive analysis and control. The costing procedure should be aimed to reflect, as accurately as possible, such costs in individual product costs without incurring excessive clerical expense to attain accuracy. Methods available are:

(a)   **Include setting up costs with direct labour costs**

Setting up costs for a period will thus be apportioned over products on the basis of units produced in the period. This method is simple to operate but will ignore effect on cost of different lengths of production run.

(b)   **Treat setting up costs as a production overhead**

The apportionment will be the same as in (a) above if overhead is absorbed in relation to direct labour. If, however, overhead is recovered in a machine hour rate, the charge will reflect the varying incidence of setting up costs between machines.

(c)   **Cost each batch separately**

Actual set up time will be booked to particular batches from time sheets. This method will result in accurate product costs but may cause clerical work when a large number of batches pass through a process.

(d)   **Analyse set-up time by product, accumulate for a period and apply product costs**

Accurate product costs will be provided which will tend to fluctuate from period to period depending on the incidence of long or short production runs. In addition, this method will require special time recording and analysis.

(e)   **Develop standard set up costs for each product and apply the standard as a cost per batch processed**

The set up cost per unit will vary according to the batch size which will disclose the cost effect of long or short runs. In addition, actual set up costs can be compared with standard to measure efficiency. Use of a standard, however, will leave a balance of over or under-absorbed cost to be dealt with in the accounts.

2.6   Effect of inaccurate overhead absorption rates

The above illustration shows that selling prices can reflect estimates and that the major uncertainty in estimating is calculation of an accurate figure for overhead recovery. Inaccurate estimating can seriously harm the business because:

(a)   if jobs are over-priced, customers will go elsewhere;

(b)   if jobs are under-priced, sales revenue will fail to cover costs and/or provide an adequate return.

2.7   Inaccurate estimate of volume

Predetermined overhead rates are based on a volume estimate. If actual volume is significantly higher or lower than expected, then estimates, and consequently selling prices, will be inaccurate.

2.8   Example

Company A's budget for the year is as follows:

	£
Prime costs	50,000
Overhead	30,000
	80,000
Profit (40% on cost)	32,000
Sales	112,000
Volume	3,000 labour hours

If volume is half budget, ie, 1,500 hours, actual results would show:

	£
Prime costs (half budget)	25,000
Overhead absorbed	15,000 (1,500 hours $\times \frac{£30,000}{3,000}$)
	40,000
Profit (40% on cost)	16,000
Sales	56,000

Actual overhead incurred would not fall to half the budget, however, because of the fixed element. It may fall to, perhaps, £24,000 but job costs would reflect overhead at the predetermined rate of £10 per hour, leaving £9,000 under-absorbed.

Actual profit would therefore be £(16,000 − 9,000) = £7,000.

2.9   Inaccurate absorption basis

Estimated costs should reflect overhead in relation to the way it is incurred, so that selling prices are competitive but profitable.

2.10   Example

Company B bases its estimates on the following formulae:

Total cost	=	Prime cost plus 40% for overhead
Selling price	=	Total cost plus 25% for profit

Estimates for two jobs show:

Item	Job X £	Job Y £
Direct materials	200	100
Direct wages @ £2 per hour	200	300
Prime cost	400	400
Overhead absorbed (40%)	160	160
Total cost	560	560
Profit (25%)	140	140
Selling price	700	700

Thus both jobs will be priced the same even though it would appear from the direct wages estimate that Job Y takes 50% more time to complete and therefore uses much more of the factory's resources.

Job X may be over-priced in relation to competitors whereas Job Y is under-priced and the business would lose its Job X customers and get more orders for Job Y.

Consider what would happen if 1,500 hours were available. The factory could produce 10 of Job Y compared to 15 of Job X.

2.11   Insufficient analysis by cost centre

A similar effect could arise if overhead rates do not recognise use of more or less expensive resources.

2.12   Example

Company C uses a 'blanket' overhead rate calculated as follows:

	Overhead cost £	Labour hours
Cost centre Y	40,000	4,000
Cost centre Z	80,000	4,000
	120,000	8,000

$$\text{Absorption rate} = \frac{£120,000}{8,000}$$

$$= £15 \text{ per labour hour}$$

Thus a job which takes one hour in Y will be charged the same amount for overhead as a job which takes an hour in Z even though the latter centre costs twice as much per hour to operate.

Once again, estimates would not reflect a realistic charge for the use of resources and over or under-pricing may result.

2.13 Reconciling job costs with profit and loss account

In many small businesses job costing is carried on in a seemingly haphazard way and little attempt is made to relate the work of estimating and price-fixing to accounting principles. Consequently it may be difficult to reconcile the profit shown by the accounts with that shown by job cards.

2.14 Example

The Industrial Refurbishing Company undertakes repair and reconditioning work on agricultural machinery and it is the practice to charge out each job at a profit of 15% of the invoice value. Cost cards relating to complete jobs for the year ended 31 May 19X4 have been summarised as follows:

	£	£
Materials issued		46,400
Direct labour		34,000
Overhead:		
20% on material	9,280	
100% on direct labour	34,000	
		43,280
Carriage		1,270
Profit		22,050
Sales		147,000

The job costing work in progress account is as follows:

Work in progress

	£		£
Balance b/d	12,000	Cost of jobs completed	124,950
Materials	46,500	Balance c/d	13,900
Direct labour	35,800		
Overhead	43,280		
Carriage	1,270		
	138,850		138,850

The firm's accountants have summarised the financial accounts for the year as follows:

	£	£	£
Sales			147,000
Less: Stocks and work in progress 1 June 19X3	18,000		
Purchase of materials	51,300		
	69,300		
Less: Stocks and work in progress 31 May 19X4	20,100		
		49,200	
Factory wages		51,000	
Factory expenses		20,000	
			120,200
Gross profit			26,800
Less: General office expenses		8,400	
Estimating and selling expenses		3,600	

Carriage on completed jobs	1,200	
	——	13,200
Net profit		13,600

You have been asked to explain the difference between the profit shown by the completed jobs summary and that shown by the annual accounts. To assist you the accountants have provided the following analyses:

(a)   The composition of the stocks and work in progress figures is as follows:

	1 June 19X3	31 May 19X4
	£	£
Stocks of materials	6,000	6,200
Work in progress:		
Material	9,000	9,100
Labour	3,000	4,800

(b)   Factory wages consist of £38,800 for direct labour and £12,200 for indirect labour.

2.15   Solution

Item	Financial accounts £	£	Cost cards £	Differences £
Opening stock of materials	6,000			
Work in progress	9,000			
	15,000			
Purchases	51,300			
	66,300			
Less: Closing stocks	15,300			
Materials issued		51,000	46,400	4,600
Opening work in progress wages	3,000			
Direct labour paid	38,800			
	41,800			
Less: Closing work in progress wages	4,800			
Direct labour		37,000	34,000	3,000
Indirect labour	12,200			
Factory expenses	20,000			
General office	8,400			
Estimating/selling	3,600			
Overhead		44,200	43,280	920
Carriage		1,200	1,270	(70)

Reconciliation:

	£	£
Profit per cost cards		22,050
Less: Materials not booked	4,600	
Wages not allocated	3,000	
Overhead not absorbed	920	
		8,520
		13,530
Add: Carriage over-recovered		70
Profit per financial accounts		13,600

2.16   Activity

List some causes of discrepancies summarised in the above reconciliation.

2.17   Activity solution

Examples are:

(a)   materials requisition not recorded;

(b)   direct labour shown as indirect;

(c)   over/under-absorption of overhead from various causes.

2.18   Treatment as direct or indirect costs

Instances may arise when analyses for cost ascertainment can conflict with the analyses required for control.

2.19   Example

Jones is paid £4 per hour for a basic week of 40 hours. In one week he worked four hours overtime at double rates and received £28 under a group bonus scheme. His time sheet for that week shows:

	Hours
Job A	20
Job B	10
Job C	8
Training	6
	44

Jones' gross wage may be allocated in two ways:

(a)   As an average direct wage per hour ie:

	£
Basic 40 × £4	160
Overtime 4 × £8	32
Bonus	28
	220

$$\text{Hourly rate} \quad = \quad \frac{£220}{44 \text{ hours}}$$

$$= \quad £5.00 \text{ per hour}$$

(b)   Basic rate used for costing and overtime premium/bonus treated as indirect wages. Different allocations would result as follows:

		Method (a) £		*Method (b)* £
Job A	20 × £5.00	100	20 × £4.00	80
Job B	10 × £5.00	50	10 × £4.00	40
Job C	8 × £5.00	40	8 × £4.00	32
		190		152
Overhead:				
Training	6 × £5.00	30	6 × £4.00	24
Overtime		-	4 × £4.00	16
Bonus		-		28
		220		220

Method (a) should give more accurate job costs but the total costs of overtime and bonus will be more difficult to identify for management information purposes.

In answering examination questions concerning problematic items, the student should recognise the different requirements for cost information as well as the practical implications of the suggested treatment.

2.20   Activity

Discuss how a company manufacturing products on a jobbing basis should deal with the following cost accounting problems.

(a) It employs a draughtsman from whose drawings templates are produced which are used in the production process. These drawings are only made against firm orders. Hitherto the salary and other costs of the draughtsman have been included in factory overhead and absorbed into the cost of the job as part of total factory overhead.

Discuss whether this method of dealing with the draughtsman's costs is satisfactory and suggest what alternative approach might be taken.

(b) The company is at present operating a day and evening shift. It now proposes a night shift whose average wage rate would involve a premium. This night shift would concentrate on one particular contract which would continue over a period of two to three years.

Discuss how the company should deal with the night shift premium in calculating the costs of its products.

(c) One of the major production cost centres involves a chemical process which is very complex. The time required to produce any particular quantity of output depends rather unpredictably on a wide range of factors, some of which are outside the control of the operator.

As a result, a subsidiary smaller machine to do 'touching up' work as and when products require it has been installed in that cost centre.

Discuss the case for treating the wages of the operator of the subsidiary machine as an overhead of the cost centre rather than as direct wages.

2.21   Activity solution

(a) As drawings are only made against firm orders, the cost of producing the drawings may be considered as a direct cost rather than as a production overhead. More accurate information, at little expense, could be obtained by an analysis of time spent by the draughtsman; an hourly rate, including associated costs, could be developed for charging to jobs. The hourly rate could incorporate normal idle time or, alternatively, hours not attributable to a specific order could be charged to drawing office overhead at the rate developed.

(b) It appears that the night shift will be operated to fulfil the one particular long-term contract. Consequently, there would be no justification for including the night-shift premium in factory overhead as that would unfairly burden jobs completed during the day and evening shift. In fact it could be appropriate to separate this particular contract from the normal costing routine and treat it as a marginal contract by only charging costs directly incurred.

(c) The alternative methods for dealing with the wages of the operator of the subsidiary machine are:

　　(i)　**Charge as direct wages**

　　　　This method implies that the operator's time can conveniently be analysed between products. In addition, the machine operating costs should be charged in conjunction with the operator's wages ie, a composite machine hour rate will be developed.

(ii) Charge as overhead of the production cost centre

Machine operating costs would be charge similarly.

The first method would achieve greater accuracy of product costs and provide useful information on the cost of the 'touching up' machine but would involve additional clerical work analysing the operator's time and developing a machine hour rate.

2.22 Cost control

When production is related to a specification or to customers' orders, the costing system will be interlocked with estimating so that the estimate can be used as a standard to locate excessive usage of materials and time.

Control will be assisted by:

(a) Detailed production orders

These should be subject to serial number control. The production order is the authority to obtain or allocate specific resources in the form of materials, labour and machines.

(b) Excess material requisitions

Additional requirements for material would be supplied only on presentation of a properly authorised document which would show the reason for additional need.

(c) Route cards

Each production order can be supported by route cards which specify the sequence of operations and the estimated time for each operation or stage. Actual time would be recorded and causes of excess time noted where appropriate.

(d) Regular reports

The above documents will form the basis of a report to show the incidence of excess usage together with an analysis of main causes. The aim would be to prevent recurrence, where possible by appropriate action, eg:

- amendment of existing methods of estimating usage's;
- change of supplier;
- increased labour training;
- introduction of incentive payment to all grades of works labour;
- improved system of preventive plant maintenance.

2.23 Job profitability and pricing

Management of a jobbing firm would be very interested in comparing the profitability of different types of work to assist:

(a) selection of the most profitable mix, possibly by rejection of some jobs, giving priority to others and by sub-contracting;

(b)   identification of work where prices could be shaded or where increases may be necessary.

One of the major obstacles to accurate job cost ascertainment is the calculation of a reasonable proportion of fixed overhead to be recovered. Accurate estimation of volumes and costs is difficult and the diversity of production methods in a jobbing business complicates any attempt to establish an equitable basis for apportionment and absorption of costs. It may be more realistic for price fixing purposes, therefore, to ignore indirect costs and to base selling prices on direct cost plus contribution; control of fixed costs will, of course, still be a vital area. The following report format indicates the kind of information management would need for pricing and control.

An inherent danger when prices are based on contribution is the tendency to under-price because 'any contribution is better than losing the order'. That approach may be justifiable in exceptional circumstances but in the long run selling prices must cover all costs and provide an acceptable return.

3   BATCH COSTING

3.1   Combined job and batch costing

Many businesses combine job costing with batch costing. This occurs where the business assembles a product to meet a customer's specification, but the assembly contains a number of components that can also be used in other assemblies. The components will be produced in batches and a batch cost sheet will record the costs. When the components are finished the order will be closed and the components will be transferred into a finished parts store at, say, the average cost of the batch. When the customer orders his particular assembly, a new order number will be raised and the required components drawn from store and charged against the assembly order.

3.2   Economic batch quantity

Where products are made in batches for stock to await sale or use in assemblies, the quantity to be produced in any one batch is a recurring and major problem, which involves consideration of:

(a)   Rate of consumption.

(b)   Storage costs and availability.

(c)   Time required to set up and take down production facilities.

.(d)   Capacity available in terms of machines, labour and services in relation to requirements for other products.

3.3   Product line information

Batch costing is typically employed where a wide variety of products are held in stock. The cost accountant will be called upon for detailed information on product costs to satisfy the following needs:

(a)   **Production planning/control**

Scheduling to maintain stock levels and to meet demand fluctuations could be a major problem requiring continuous information on set up costs, machine utilisation and stock movements.

(b)   **Product profitability pricing**

Management are likely to require regular analyses of product costs and profits;

maintenance or improvement of margins will be a recurring problem. The information will also assist in directing sales effort and formulating sales policy.

(c)   **Research**

Cost information, perhaps on an **ad hoc** basis, will be required in the development of new products or in improving operations.

4   CHAPTER SUMMARY

This chapter has considered the two methods of specific order costing and identified when each of them is to be used.

5   SELF TEST QUESTIONS

5.1   What is job costing? (1.2)

5.2   What is batch costing? (1.3)

5.3   Explain how setting up costs may be incorporated into job costs (2.5)

6   EXAMINATION TYPE QUESTION

6.1   Job number 123

In order to identify the costs incurred in carrying out a range of work to customer specification in its factory, a company has a job costing system. This system identifies costs directly with a job where this is possible and reasonable. In addition, production overhead costs are absorbed into the cost of jobs at the end of each month, at an actual rate per direct labour hour for each of the two production departments.

One of the jobs carried out in the factory during the month just ended was Job No. 123. The following information has been collected relating specifically to this job:

(1)   400 kilos of Material Y were issued from stores to Department A.

(2)   76 direct labour hours were worked in Department A at a basic wage of £4.50 per hour. 6 of these hours were classified as overtime at a premium of 50%.

(3)   300 kilos of Material Z were issued from stores to Department B. Department B returned 30 kilos of Material Z to the storeroom being excess to requirements for the job.

(4)   110 direct labour hours were worked in Department B at a basic wage of £4.00 per hour. 30 of these hours were classified as overtime at a premium of 50%. All overtime worked in Department B in the month is a result of the request of a customer for early completion of another job which had been originally scheduled for completion in the month following.

(5)   Department B discovered defects in some of the work, which was returned to Department A for rectification. 3 labour hours were worked in Department A on rectification (these are additional to the 76 direct labour hours in Department A noted above). Such rectification is regarded as a normal part of the work carried out generally in the department.

(6)   Department B damaged 5 kilos of Material Z which then had to be disposed of. Such losses of material are not expected to occur.

Total costs incurred during the month on all jobs in the two production departments were as follows:

	Dept A £	Dept B £
Direct materials issued from stores*	6,500	13,730
Direct materials returned to stores	135	275
Direct labour, at basic wage rate**	9,090	11,200
Indirect labour, at basic wage rate	2,420	2,960
Overtime premium	450	120
Lubricants and cleaning compounds	520	680
Maintenance	720	510
Other	1,200	2,150

Materials are priced at the end of each month on a weighted average basis. Relevant information of material stock movements during the month, for materials Y and Z, is as follows:

	Material Y	*Material Z*
Opening stock	1,050 kilos (value £529.75)	6,970 kilos (value £9,946.50)
Purchases	600 kilos at £0.50 per kilo	16,000 kilos at £1.46 per kilo
	500 kilos at £0.50 per kilo	
	400 kilos at £0.52 per kilo	
Issues from stores	1,430 kilos	8,100 kilos
Returns to stores	-	30 kilos

* This includes, in Department B, the scrapped Material Z. This was the only material scrapped in the month.

** All direct labour in Department A is paid a basic wage of £4.50 per hour, and in Department B £4.00 per hour. Department A direct labour includes a total of 20 hours spent on rectification work.

You are required

(a) to prepare a list of the costs that should be assigned to Job No. 123. Provide an explanation of your treatment of each item.

(17 marks)

(b) to discuss briefly how information concerning the cost of individual jobs can be used.

(5 marks)

(Total: 22 marks)

7   ANSWER TO EXAMINATION TYPE QUESTION

7.1   Job number 123

Notes:

(1) One point to note is that overhead is absorbed at an **actual** rate. The normal approach is to use a pre-determined rate.

(2)   The examiner has presented the information in three sections:

   (a)   quantities specifically related to Job 123 in the 'box'
   (b)   actual costs of Departments A and B;
   (c)   information concerning Materials Y and Z.

   The approach in answering is to go through the items in the 'box' one at a time and select the relevant information from the other parts of the question as needed.

(3)   The weighted average used here is a periodic average, ie, calculated monthly as opposed to continuous - valuing each issue as it occurs during the month. The latter approach is normally used in questions concerning valuation of issues.

(4)   There does not appear to be any reason for the examiner stating the value of direct materials issued from stores - £6,500 and £13,730. Note that this must include materials other than Y and Z because the value of issues of Y is: £0.505 × 1,430 = £722.15 and Z is £1.45 × 8,100 = £11,745.

(a)   **List of costs which should be assigned to job number 123**

(1)

		Kilos	£
Material Y:			
	Opening stock	1,050	529.75
	Purchases	600	300.00
		500	250.00
		400	208.00
		2,550	1,287.75

Weighted average price $= \dfrac{1,287.75}{2,550} = 0.505$

	£
Value of material issued to this job: 400 kilos @ £0.505 =	202.00

(2)   Department A labour: 76 hours @ £4.50 =   342.00

It is assumed that the overtime is not worked at the specific request of the customer for Job 123 and hence the premium has been excluded from direct cost and therefore included in production overhead.

Rectification work:

As this is regarded as a normal part of the work carried out **generally** by the department, it is assumed to be non-controllable and should therefore be included in the cost of jobs. It is assumed most equitable to do this, not by charging each specific job with rectification costs but to charge this cost to jobs via the overhead absorption rate.

	Kilos	Value £
(3) Material Z	6,970	9,946.50
	16,000	23,360.00
	22,970	33,306.50

Weighted average price $= \dfrac{33,306.50}{22,970} = 1.45$

Value of material issued to this job: $(300 - 30 - 5) \times £1.45 =$ 384.25

Material damaged:

As this loss is not expected to occur, it is controllable/abnormal. The cost should, therefore, be charged to the profit and loss account and excluded from the cost of jobs.

(4)   Department B labour: 110 hours @ £4 =   440.00

The cost of the overtime premium should be charged to the other customer's jobs.

(5)   Production overhead:

	Dept A £	Dept B £
Amount incurred:		
Rectification labour cost:		
20×4.50	90	-
Indirect labour	2,420	2,960
Overtime premium	450	-
Lubricants and cleaning		
compounds	520	680
Maintenance	720	510
Other	1,200	2,150
	5,400	6,300

Actual labour hours	$\dfrac{9,090}{4.50} = 2,020$	$\dfrac{11,200}{4} = 2,800$
Less: Rectification hours	20	
	2,000	2,800

Overhead recovery rate:

$\dfrac{\text{Actual overhead}}{\text{Actual labour hours}} =$	$\dfrac{5,400}{2,000}$	$\dfrac{6,300}{2,800}$
	= £2.70 per labour hour	= £2.25 per labour hour

Production overhead absorbed by Job number 123:	
Department A: 76 hours @ £2.70	205.20
Department B: 110 hours @ £2.25	247.50
	———
Cost of Job No. 123	1,820.95

(b)   The cost of individual jobs may be used in the following ways:

(i)   the estimated cost can be calculated in advance in order to provide a basis for fixing the selling price. In this case it would be necessary to use a pre-determined overhead absorption rate.

(ii)   The estimated budgeted cost can be used as a guideline while the work is being carried out so as to try to ensure that actual costs are kept within the original estimate.

(iii)   The actual cost of jobs can be used for valuing work-in-progress stock if the job is on hand at the end of the accounting period.

(iv)   Actual cost can be compared with the estimated cost in order to identify variances on individual cost items. This should help to control costs and to improve the quality of future estimates.

(v)   Actual cost can be compared with the selling price of the job in order to assess profitability of the job.

8 PROCESS COSTING

INTRODUCTION & LEARNING OBJECTIVES

Syllabus area 2b. Work-in-progress accounts for process costing. (Ability required 3).

Profit and loss accounts for process costing systems. (Ability required 3).

This chapter is concerned with the methods of costing used in situations where the units produced are homogeneous, and the operations used to achieve the final result are continuous.

This type of costing method may be used in situations where the final result is a product (output costing and process costing) or is a service (service costing).

This chapter shows when to use output costing and process costing, and how to use each method to value cost units. Service costing is dealt with later in this text.

Finally the use of values derived from these methods is considered in the area of decision making and the inherent problems discussed.

When you have studied this chapter you should be able to do the following:

- Distinguish between output costing and process costing.

- Explain the meaning of and differences between normal losses and abnormal losses/gains.

- Account for process costs involving losses.

- Explain and apply the equivalent units concept to closing work in process.

- Distinguish between joint and by-products.

---

1 OUTPUT VERSUS PROCESS COSTING

1.1 Continuous production

In the previous chapter costs were directly allocated to a particular job or batch. When standardised goods or services result from a sequence of repetitive and continuous operations, it is useful to work out the cost of each operation. Then, because every unit produced may be assumed to have involved the same amount of work, costs for a period are charged to processes or operations, and unit costs are ascertained by dividing process costs by units produced. This is known as **process costing.**

1.2 Output costing

> **Definition** Output costing applies when standardised goods are produced from a single operation eg, mining, quarrying.

1.3 Process costing

> [Definition]   Process costing is the costing method applicable where goods or services result from a sequence of continuous or repetitive operations or processes (**CIMA Official Terminology**).

For example

     (a)   oil refining;
     (b)   breweries;
     (c)   canned food.

2 OUTPUT COSTING

2.1 Special features of output costing

The basic physical feature of output costing is that only a single operation is required to obtain the final product. Examples of output costing include the extraction of minerals. Output costing applies where such minerals are sold as the final product immediately after extraction, if they are, instead, further processed within the same organisation; then process costing (see below) should be used.

The finished product, such as the minerals extracted, are homogeneous (that is one tonne of mineral extracted is indistinguishable from another). As a consequence it is assumed that each unit of the product will require the same level of resources to acquire as the next unit. It is therefore not necessary to identify the cost of each tonne, (if this were possible, its cost could not be justified). Instead the total cost of a particular time period is divided by the output of the period and an average cost per unit calculated. In this respect the same principles are used as discussed under process costing (later in this chapter).

2.2 Calculating the unit cost

Assume that Z Ltd extracts clay from the ground in a single process and sells it to a local pottery.

During June costs incurred amount to £19,500 and output was 6,500 tonnes of clay.

The cost per tonne is:

$$\frac{\text{Cost incurred}}{\text{Output in tonnes}} = \frac{£19,500}{6,500}$$

$$= £3 \text{ per tonne.}$$

This would be used to evaluate stock and prepare profit statements.

2.3 Activity

Calculate the cost per tonne given that:-

      Costs incurred   =   £46,740
      Output   =   16,400 tonnes

2.4 Activity solution

Cost per tonne = £46,740/16,400 = £2.85.

3   **PROCESS COSTING**

3.1   **Special features of process costing**

The basic physical feature of a processing system is that as products pass from the raw material input stage to becoming finished products they pass through a number of distinct stages or **processes** of manufacture. In such a situation it is not feasible to link the cost of specific inputs to specific units of output. For example, in the production of paint it would be impossible to isolate one unit of output (a litre can of paint) and determine precisely which inputs have finished up in that particular litre of paint. The nature of a processing business is such that inputs are being added continuously to the manufacturing process, losing their identity, and a continuous output of production is being achieved.

Ascertaining the cost of production involves:

(a)   determination of the costs (direct and indirect) associated with each process;

(b)   calculation of the average process unit cost by dividing the appropriate costs by the appropriate number of units of output;

(c)   valuation of the units of output transferred from one process to the next and any work in process by applying the unit costs;

(d)   the cost of output from the first process becomes the cost of input to the second process and so on until output from the final process has accumulated the cost of all processes.

This procedure is complicated by the following factors:

(a)   output units will not equal input units to the extent that losses are sustained during processing;

(b)   the existence of partially processed units, ie, work in process, at the end of the period;

Each of these factors will be considered in this chapter.

3.2   **Basic principles**

The nature of the processing operation is such that the input volume rarely equals the output volume, the difference, or loss, is analysed between that which is expected (and considered to be unavoidable) and any additional loss (or lack of loss) which actually occurs.

3.3   **Normal loss and process losses**

 Normal loss is the amount of loss expected from the operation of a process. This expectation is based on past experience, and this loss is considered to be unavoidable.

The normal loss is usually expressed as a percentage of the input volume, in accounting for the normal loss the cost of its production is borne by the remaining forms of output.

3.4   Example

The following data relates to process one during March:

Input materials 1,000 kg costing	£9,000
Labour cost	£18,000
Overhead cost	£13,500

A normal loss equal to 10% of input was expected. Actual output was 900 kg.

Solution

Step 1   Calculate the number of normal loss units.

The normal loss equals 10% of 1,000 kg = 100 kg.

Step 2   Calculate the expected number of output units.

The expected output units equals the input less the normal loss = 1,000 kg – 100 kg = 900 kg.

Step 3   Total the process costs.

The total process costs = £40,500.

Step 4   Calculate the cost per unit.

The cost per unit equals:

$$\frac{£40,500}{900} = £45 \text{ per kg}$$

Step 5   Write up the process account and normal loss account.

Process account

	Kg	£		Kg	£/kg	£
Material input	1,000	9,000	Normal loss	100	-	-
Labour		18,000	Output	900	45	40,500
Overhead		13,500				
	1,000	40,500		1,000		40,500

Note:

(a)   that the process account contains columns to record both quantities and values which are both balanced off.

(b)   that no value is attributed to the normal loss units in this example (later the effect of scrap and similar values will be shown).

3.5   Scrap value of process losses

When losses have a scrap value, two alternative accounting treatments exist:

(a)   credit the income from such sales to a miscellaneous income account, transferring the balance directly to the profit and loss account; or

(b)   reduce the cost of the process by the income anticipated from the normal loss.

Method (b) is the preferred method and should be used in examinations. Its effect on the example above can be illustrated.

3.6   Example

Suppose that the normal loss of 100 kg could be sold as scrap for £9/kg.

Step three is now amended to recognise the reduction in process costs caused by the income anticipated from the normal loss.

Step 3   becomes:

$$£40,500 \text{ (as before)} - (100 \text{ kg} \times £9/\text{kg}) = £39,600$$

Step 4   The cost per unit is now:

$$\frac{£39,600}{900} = £44 / \text{kg}$$

Step 5

Process account

19XX	Units	£	19XX	Units	£/Unit	£
Material input	1,000	9,000	Normal loss	100	9	900
Labour		18,000	Output	900	44	39,600
Overhead		13,500				
	1,000	40,500		1,000		40,500

Note that the normal loss now has a value equal to its scrap value.

Since the process account is part of the cost book-keeping system (see later in this text), the corresponding debit entry must be made for the normal loss:

Normal loss

19XX	Units	£	19XX	Units	£
Process account	100	900	Cash/bank	100	900

3.7   Activity

Calculate the cost per tonne from the following data:

Input 5,000 tonnes costing	£15,000
Labour cost	£6,000
Overhead cost	£10,000

Normal loss is 10% of input and has a scrap value of £4/tonne.

3.8   Activity solution

Normal loss = 500 tonnes and has a value of £2,000 (500 × £4)

$$\text{Process costs} = £31,000 - £2,000$$
$$= £29,000$$

$$\text{Cost per tonne} = \frac{£29,000}{4,500} = £6.44$$

3.9   Actual loss exceeds normal loss

[Definition] The extent to which the actual loss exceeds the normal loss is referred to as the abnormal loss. This loss is unexpected and considered to be avoidable consequently the cost of producing abnormal loss units is not treated in the same way as the cost of the normal loss.

The following example shows how to account for abnormal losses.

3.10   Example

The following data relates to one process during April:

Input materials 1,000 kg costing	£9,000
Labour cost	£18,000
Overhead cost	£13,500

A normal loss equal to 10% of input was expected.
Actual output was 850 kg.
Losses are sold as scrap for £9/kg.

3.11   Solution

The steps are the same as in the earlier example, only the entries in the ledger accounts differ:

[Step 1]   The normal loss equals 10% of 1,000 kg = 100 kg.

[Step 2]   The expected output units equals the input less the normal loss
= 1,000 kg – 100 kg = 900 kg.

[Step 3]   The process costs equal
£40,500 – (100 kg × £9) = £39,600.

[Step 4]   The cost per unit equals

$$\frac{£39,600}{900} = £44$$

[Step 5]

Process account

	Units	£		Units	£/Unit	£
Material input	1,000	9,000	Normal loss	100	9	900
Labour		18,000	Abnormal loss			
			(W1)	50	44	2,200
Overhead		13,500	Output	850	44	37,400
	1,000	40,500		1,000		40,500

WORKINGS

(W1)   The abnormal loss units equals the difference between the actual and expected output. These are then valued at the cost per unit calculated in step four.

Normal loss

	Units	£		Units	£
Process account	100	900	Cash/bank (W2)	150	1,350
Abnormal loss (W2)	50	450			
	150	1,350		150	1,350

Abnormal loss

	Units	£		Units	£
Process account	50	2,200	Normal loss	50	450
			Profit & Loss		1,750
	50	2,200		50	2,200

(W2)   The distinction between normal and abnormal losses is purely an accounting one, all of the loss may be sold as scrap for £9/kg. All of these proceeds are credited to the normal loss account and any balance on this account is transferred to the abnormal loss account.

Note that the transfer to profit and loss shown in the abnormal loss account is the net cost of producing the unexpected loss (after deducting its scrap value). This is used to control the costs of excess losses.

3.12   Activity

Calculate the net cost of the abnormal loss from the following data:

Input quantity	5,000 kg
Normal loss	5% of input
Process costs	£16,500
Actual output	4,600 kg

Losses are sold for £2.35 per kg.

3.13   Activity solution

Step 1   Normal loss = 250 kg

Step 2   Scrap value of normal loss = £587.50

Step 3   Net process cost = £15,912.50

Step 4   Cost per unit = £3.35

Step 5   Net cost of abnormal loss/kg = £1.00
Volume of abnormal loss
= 4,750 kg – 4,600 kg
= 150 kg

Answer: net cost of abnormal loss = £150

3.14   Losses having a disposal cost

Sometimes, instead of having a sale value losses have a disposal cost (this occurs particularly when toxic chemicals are processed). From an accounting viewpoint the treatment is the same as that shown above for losses having a sale value except that the value is negative.

The disposal cost of the normal loss must be entered in the process account either alongside the normal loss quantity as a negative value on the credit side or as a debit (ie, an extra cost). In either case the quantity MUST be entered on the credit side.

3.15   Actual loss is less than normal loss: abnormal gain

> Definition   The extent to which the actual loss is less than the normal loss is referred to as an abnormal gain.

The following example shows how to account for abnormal gains.

3.16   Example

The following data relates to one process during May:

Input materials 1,000 kg costing	£9,000
Labour cost	£18,000
Overhead cost	£13,500

A normal loss equal to 10% of input was expected.
Actual output was 920 kg.
Losses are sold as scrap for £9/kg.

3.17   Solution

The steps are the same as was shown earlier:

> Step 1   The normal loss equals 10% of 1,000 kg = 100 kg.

> Step 2   The expected output units equals the input less the normal loss
> = 1,000 kg – 100 kg = 900 kg

> Step 3   The process costs equal £40,500 – (100 kg × £9) = £39,600.

> Step 4   The cost per unit equals

$$\frac{£39,600}{900} = £44$$

> Step 5

Process account

	Units	£		Units	£/Unit	£
Material input	1,000	9,000	Normal loss	100	9	900
Labour		18,000	Output	920	44	40,480
Overhead		13,500				
Abnormal gain	20	880				
	1,020	41,380		1,020		41,380

WORKINGS

(W1)   The abnormal gain units equals the difference between the actual and expected output. These are then valued at the cost per unit calculated in step four. Note that these entries are made on the debit side of the process account, thus causing it to balance.

Normal loss

	Units	£		Units	£
Process account	100	900	Cash bank	80(W2)	720
			Abnormal gain	20	180
	───	───		───	───
	100	900		100	900
	───	───		───	───

Abnormal loss

	Units	£		Units	£
Normal loss	20	180	Process account	20	880
Profic and los (W3)		700			
	───	───		───	───
	20	880		20	880
	───	───		───	───

(W2)   This is the actual loss being sold at £9/kg.

(W3)   This represents the net benefit of producing less loss than expected (after deducting the lost income from the anticipated scrap sales).

3.18   Partially processed units

At the end of a period there may be some units which have been started but have not been completed. These are said to be closing work in process units.

Assuming at this stage that there is no opening work in process, the output for a period will consist of:

(a)   units of production that have been started and fully processed within the period;

(b)   units of production that have been started in the period but which are only part-processed at the end of the period; this closing work in process will be completed next period when further costs will be incurred in completing it.

3.19   Equivalent units

Costs in a process costing system are allocated to units of production on the basis of **equivalent units.** The idea behind this concept is that once processing has started on a unit of output, to the extent that it remains in an uncompleted state it can be expressed as a proportion of a completed unit. For example, if 100 units are exactly half-way through the production process in terms of the amount of cost they have absorbed, they are effectively equal to 50 complete units. Therefore, 100 units which are half-complete can be regarded as 50 equivalent units that are complete.

3.20   Example

A manufacturer starts processing on 1 March. In the month of March he starts work on 20,000 units of production. At the end of March there are 1,500 units still in process and it is estimated that each is two thirds complete. Costs for the period total £19,500.

Calculate the value of the completed units and the work in process at 31 March.

3.21   Solution

	Units	Proportion complete	Equivalent units
	(a)	(b)	(c)=(a)×(b)
Started and completed	18,500	1	18,500
Work in process	1,500	$\frac{2}{3}$	1,000
			19,500

$$\text{Cost per equivalent unit} = \frac{£19,500}{19,500} = £1$$

	Equivalent units	Cost £
Finished production	18,500 × £1	18,500
Work in process	1,000 × £1	1,000
Total costs for period		19,500

The 1,500 physical units in process at the end of the period have a value (based on 1,000 equivalent units) of £1,000.

3.22   Extension of the equivalent units approach

In practice it is unlikely that all inputs to production will take place at the same time, as was suggested in the example above. For instance, materials are frequently added at the beginning of a process, whereas labour may be applied throughout the process. Thus, work in process may be **more complete** as regards one input or cost element than as regards another. Equivalent units must thus be calculated for each input and costs applied on that basis.

3.23   Example

As in the example above, except that:

(a)   all materials have been input to the process;
(b)   work in process is only one-third complete as regards labour;
(c)   costs for the period are:

	£
Materials	10,000
Labour	9,500
Total	19,500

3.24   Solution

	Units	Materials		Labour	
		Proportion complete	Equivalent units	Proportion complete	Equivalent units
Started and completed	18,500	1	18,500	1	18,500
Work in process	1,500	1	1,500	$\frac{1}{3}$	500
Total equivalent units			20,000		19,000
Cost per equivalent unit			$\frac{£10,000}{20,000} = 50p$		$\frac{£9,500}{19,000} = 50p$

	Materials	*Labour*	*Total*
			£
Cost of finished production	18,500 × £0.50 = £9,250	18,500 × £0.50 = £9,250	18,500
Cost of work in process	1,500 × £0.50 = £750	500 × £0.50 = £250	1,000
Total costs for period			19,500

3.25   Six-step method for process costing

The five step method shown earlier can now be modified. The approach used in the last two examples can be summarised into a six-step technique which can be generally used in process costing problems:

Step 1   Trace the physical flow of units so that units input to the production process are reconciled with units output or in process at the end of the period.

Step 2   Convert the physical units determined in Step 1 into equivalent units of production for each factor of production (ie, materials, labour, etc.)

Step 3   Calculate the total cost for each factor for the period.

Step 4   Divide the total costs by equivalent units to establish a cost per equivalent unit.

Step 5   Multiply equivalent units by the cost per equivalent unit to cost out finished production and work in process. Reconcile these values to the total costs for the period as calculated in Step 3.

Step 6   Write up the ledger accounts.

3.26   Example

The Excelsior Co Ltd manufactures a single product in two successive processes. The following information is available for the month of July:

Process 1

(a)   No opening work in process on 1 July.

(b)   During the month 815 units costing £2,415 were put into process.

(c)   Labour and overhead incurred amounted to £1,600.

(d)   During the month 600 units were finished and passed to Process 2.

(e)   On 31 July 190 units remained in process, the operations on which were half completed, but the materials for the whole process have been charged to the process.

Process 2

(a)   No opening work in process on 1 July.

(b)   The cost of labour and overhead in this process was £900, and material costing £350 was added at the end of operations.

(c)   On 31 July 400 units had been transferred to finished stock.

(d)   At that date 180 units remained in process, and it was estimated that one-third of the operations had been completed.

You are required to show the process accounts, treating any process losses as a normal loss.

3.27   **Solution**

Process 1

	Units	£		Units	£
Input	815	2,415	Process 2	600	3,216
Labour and overhead		1,600	Work in process c/d	190	799
			Process loss	25	-
	815	4,015		815	4,015

Process 2

	Units	£		Units	£
Process 1	600	3,216	Finished stock	400	3,351
Labour and overhead		900	Work in process c/d	180	1,115
Material added		350	Process loss	20	-
	600	4,466		600	4,466

WORKINGS

Valuation of work in process

Process 1

	Input effective units	Labour and overhead effective units	Total
Work in process	190	95	
Transferred to Process 2	600	600	
Total effective units	790	695	
Total costs	£2,415	£1,600	
Cost per unit	$\dfrac{2,415}{790} = £3.057$	$\dfrac{1,600}{695} = £2.302$	£5.359
Value of work in process	190 × £3.057 = £580	95 × £2.302 = £219	£799
Value of output		600 × £5.359 = £3,216	

Process 2

	Input *effective units*	*Labour and overhead* *effective units*
Work in process	180	60
Transferred to finished stock	400	400
Total effective units	580	460
Total costs	£3,216	£900

Cost of work in process

$$(\frac{180}{580} \times £3,216) + (\frac{60}{460} \times £900) \quad = \quad £(998 + 117)$$

$$= \quad £1,115$$

Notes:

(1)   The cost of normal losses is borne **pro rata** by the effective units.

(2)   The 190 units of work in process on 31 July in Process 1 are counted as 95 units for the purpose of apportioning labour and overhead since operations on these units were only half-completed. Similarly, the 180 units of work in process in Process 2 are counted as 60 units for the purpose of apportioning the labour and overhead costs of that process.

(3)   As the material costing £350 was added **at the end** of operations in Process 2, none of it relates to the work in process units.

In addition to the individual process accounts the cost ledger would include a 'work in progress control account' which would be as follows:

Work in progress control

	£		£
Input	2,415	Finished stock	3,351
Other materials	350	Work in process c/d	1,914
Labour and overhead	2,500		
	5,265		5,265

3.28   Losses in process - interaction with work in process

In a chemical process, losses may occur as a result of chemical change or evaporation; in machining, scrap arises. The generally accepted costing treatment for process losses dealt with earlier is to

(a)   establish a normal (or acceptable or expected) loss level, usually expressed as a percentage of input; the cost of normal losses is absorbed as part of unit cost. The normal loss is generally assumed to be unavoidable or non-controllable;

(b)   losses above or below normal (abnormal losses/gains) are valued at the average unit cost and written off to costing profit and loss account.

3.29   Example

Input to Process A was 1,000 units costing £4,500. Conversion costs were £3,400. The normal process loss is estimated as 10% of input. At the end of the period 780 units were transferred to Process B and 100 units were in process, 50% complete as regards conversion. There was no opening work in process.

Process A - unit costs

	Materials units	Conversion equivalent units
Input to Process A	1,000	
Less: Normal loss (10%)	100	
	900	
Transfer to Process B	780	780
Work in process	100	50
Abnormal loss	20	20
Total units/equivalent units	900	850
Costs incurred	£4,500	£3,400
Cost per unit	£5	
Cost per equivalent unit		£4

Notes:

(1)   The **normal** loss of 100 units is excluded from the output units. By doing so the cost of such a loss is absorbed into the unit cost. The unit cost is thus increased.

(2)   Losses are usually assumed to occur at the end of a process ie, when the units involved are fully processed.

Process A - cost allocation to inter-process transfers and work in process

		£	£
Input costs:			
Materials			4,500
Conversion			3,400
Total costs incurred			7,900
Total costs allocated to:			
Transfer to Process B	780 × £9		7,020
Abnormal loss	20 × £9		180
Work in process carried down:			
Materials	100 × £5	500	
Conversion	50 × £4	200	
			700
Total (agrees with costs incurred)			7,900

3.30   Abnormal gains

If, in the previous example, 820 units had been transferred to Process B, an abnormal gain (ie, a lower than normal loss) would have arisen. Unit cost would, however, be the same because the normal loss of 100 units is absorbed and the abnormal **gain** is valued at normal unit cost as a **credit** to the process.

		£
Input costs (as above)		7,900
Transfer to Process B	820 × £9	7,380
Abnormal gain	−20 × £9	(180)
Work in process (as before)		700
		7,900

Note that unit cost represents $\dfrac{\text{Normal process cost}}{\text{Normal output}}$

3.31   Scrap value of process losses

Remember that where the losses (normal or abnormal) are in the form of scrap they may be sold to generate revenue.

The treatment of such revenue is consistent with that of losses:

(a)   revenue from normal losses is **deducted** from process costs;

(b)   revenue from abnormal losses (or forgone if there is an abnormal gain) is deducted from the value debited (or credited) to profit and loss account.

3.32   Example

Data as per example above but the normal loss is sold as scrap for £1.80 per unit.

Process A - unit costs

	Materials	*Conversion*
Output in units (as before)	900	850
	£	£
Costs	4,500	3,400
Less: Revenue from scrap sales (100 × £1.80)	180	-
	4,320	3,400
Cost per unit	£4.80	£4.00

Note: the recovery is deducted from materials cost since the value of scrap is related to its material content, thus reducing the cost per unit for materials. The cost per unit for conversion remains unchanged.

Process A - cost allocation

		£	£
Input costs net of revenue from scrap sales			7,720
Allocated to:			
Transfer to Process B	780 × £8.80		6,864
Abnormal loss	20 × £8.80		176
Work in process:			
Materials	100 × £4.80	480	
Conversion	50 × £4.00	200	
			680
Total (agrees with net costs incurred)			7,720

Revenue from the abnormal loss of 20 units will be credited to profit and loss account, so that the net cost of abnormal losses is £176 − (20 × £1.80) = £140.

3.33   Partially completed losses

The example above assumed that losses occurred at the end of the process and, therefore, were completed units. If a question indicates that losses occur part way through the process, the following procedure can be adopted:

Step 1   calculate the equivalent units for normal and abnormal losses;

Step 2   divide costs by output units (including losses) to find unit costs by cost element;

Step 3   multiply normal losses by the unit cost in step 2;

Step 4   divide step 3 by the total units **excluding** normal losses;

Step 5   now step 2 + step 4 = unit cost including normal loss; step 5 can be used for cost allocation.

3.34   Example

Input to Process A was 1,000 units. Process costs for the month were £3,608.

780 units were transferred to Process B in the month and 100 units were in progress at the end of the month (50% complete). Normal loss is estimated as 10% of input and losses occur when the process is 60% complete.

Normal loss is 100 units and abnormal loss is:

(1,000 − (780 + 100 + 100)) = 20 units

Unit costs may be calculated:

	Equivalent units
Transfer to B	780
WIP (50%)	50
Normal loss (100 × 60%)	60
Abnormal loss (20 × 60%)	12
	902

	£
Process costs	3,608
Per unit	4.00

The cost value attributable to normal loss is:

60 @ £4 = £240

and the cost per unit is increased by:

$$\frac{£240}{(902-60)} = 28.5\text{p approximately}$$

Process cost is thus allocated:

	£
Transfer to B 780 units × £4.285	3,342.30
WIP 50 equivalent units × £4.285	214.25
Abnormal loss 12 equivalent units × £4.285	51.42
Rounding-off	0.03
	3,608.00

The rounding would normally be added to the output value, thus increasing it to £3,342.33.

It may be suggested that if WIP is less advanced than the point where losses occur, then the valuation should exclude any share of normal loss. This seems to be rather an academic point, however, since:

(a)   normal loss may reasonably be anticipated; and

(b)   the difference in valuation is unlikely to be significant enough to warrant cumbersome calculation.

If the example is extended by considering process B to be a packaging process which costs £2 per unit, with no losses expected this would appear:

Process B

	Units	£		Units	£
Process A	780	3,342.33	Finished goods	780	4,902.33
Packaging costs		1,560.00			
	780	4,902.33		780	4,902.33

3.35 Profit and loss

If 700 units were sold for £8 each, the profit and loss account would be as follows:

	£	£
Sales		5,600.00
Production cost of finished goods	4,902.33	
Less closing stock of finished goods		
(80/780 × £4,902.33)	(502.80)	
		(4,399.53)
Gross profit		1,200.47
Abnormal loss		(51.42)
Net profit		1,149.05

3.36 Ledger entries - a summary

When drawing up process cost accounts it is important to include columns for the appropriate physical units involved in addition to the usual debit and credit value columns. The physical unit columns should be balanced in the same manner as the value columns.

The bookkeeping entries in the ledger accounts to record process costing transactions are as follows:

(a) Process accounts are debited with all the appropriate costs incurred and the appropriate physical units associated with the material input.

(b) For any normal loss in process, the process account is credited with the physical units involved. If the loss has a recoverable value (eg, as scrap), the process account is also credited with the appropriate value. The debit is in the normal process loss account.

(c) Units of production that have finished being processed and have been transferred to the next process (or to finished stock) are credited to the process account they have left and debited to next process account (or finished stock account). The physical units involved are evaluated at the process cost per unit.

(d) Any closing work in process will be evaluated at the process cost per unit (due recognition having been taken of the equivalent units involved) and the balance carried down in the process account.

(e) Any abnormal loss in process is credited to the physical units column of the process account. The units are evaluated at the process cost per unit. The debit is to the abnormal loss account. If an abnormal gain is involved the entries are, of course, reversed.

(f) The accumulated balance of physical units in the abnormal loss account is valued at the recoverable value for losses, if any, and credited to the account. The debit is to the normal process loss account. The physical units columns in the abnormal loss account are thus balanced and the balancing value is transferred to the profit and loss account, thereby finally closing off the abnormal loss account.

(g) Any sums received from the sale of losses should be credited to the normal loss account along with the physical units involved. Any stock of losses (scrap) deemed to be saleable will be evaluated at its expected recoverable value.

Any balance of value on the normal loss account would represent a difference between the expected and the actual sums recovered, and would be transferred to the profit and loss account. It is the expected recoverable value that is used to credit the original process account (and debit the normal loss account) when losses arise.

4   JOINT PRODUCTS AND BY PRODUCTS

4.1   Introduction

The nature of process costing is that the process often produces more than one product. These additional products may be described as either **joint** or **by-products**. The distinction is of great importance, and is a matter of drawing a dividing line. Essentially joint products are both main products whereas by-products are incidental to the main products. Rules as to drawing the dividing line are provided by the CIMA's Terminology (1996).

4.2   Joint products

Definition   Two or more products separated in processing, each having a sufficiently high saleable value to merit recognition as a main product.   **(CIMA Official Terminology)**.

4.3   By-product

Definition   Output of some value produced incidentally in manufacturing something else (main product). **(CIMA Official Terminology)**.

These definitions still leave scope for subjective judgement, but they provide a basis for such judgement. The distinction is important because the accounting treatment of joint and by products differs.

4.4   Relationship between processes, joint and by-products

The following diagram illustrates the relationships:

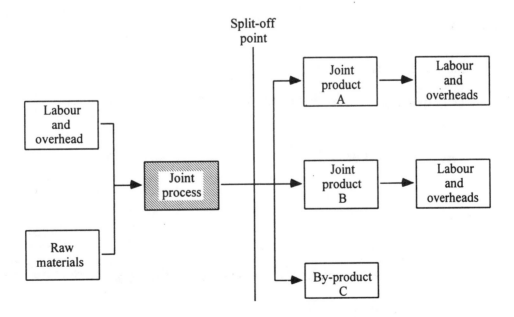

4.5 Accounting for by-products

Either of the following methods may be adopted:

(a) the proceeds from the sale of the by-product may be treated as pure profit;

(b) the proceeds from the sale, less any handling and selling expenses, may be applied in reducing the cost of the main products.

If a by-product needs further processing to improve its marketability, such cost will be deducted in arriving at net revenue, treated as in (a) or (b) above.

Note that recorded profits will be affected by the method adopted if stocks of the main product are maintained.

4.6 Example

Output from a process was 1,300 kilos of the main product and 100 kilos of a by-product. Sales of the main product were 1,000 kilos realising £6,000; sales of the by-product realised £160 but incurred £30 distribution cost. Process costs were £5,200.

Method (a)

	£	£
Main product sales		6,000
Process costs	5,200	
Less: Closing stock $\dfrac{300}{1,300} \times £5,200$	1,200	
	——	4,000
		2,000
Add: Net profit of by-product sales (£160 – 30)		130
Net profit		2,130

Method (b)

	£	£
Main product sales		6,000
Process costs	5,200	
Less: By-product revenue	130	
	——	
	5,070	
Less: Closing stock $300 \times \dfrac{£5,070}{1,300}$	1,170	
	——	
Cost of sales		3,900
Net profit		2,100

Under method (b), a portion of by-product revenue is deferred in the stock value of the main product.

4.7 Accounting for joint products

Joint products are, by definition, subject to individual accounting procedures. Joint costs may require apportionment between products if only for joint valuation purposes.

The main bases for apportionment are:

(a)   **Physical measurement of joint products**

When the unit of measurement is different eg, litres and kilos, some method should be found of expressing them in a common unit. Some joint costs are not incurred strictly equally for all joint products: such costs can be separated and apportioned by introducing weighting factors.

(b)   **Market value**

The effect is to make each product appear to be equally profitable. Where certain products are processed after the point of separation, further processing costs must be deducted from the market values before joint costs are apportioned.

(c)   **Technical estimates of relative use of common resources**

Apportionment is, of necessity, an arbitrary calculation and product costs which include such an apportionment can be misleading if used as a basis for decision making.

4.8   Relevance of joint costs

Definition   A joint cost is the cost of a process which results in more than one main product. **(CIMA Official Terminology)**.

Even if careful technical estimates are made of relative benefits, joint costs apportionment will inevitably be an arbitrary calculation. When providing information to assist decision making, therefore, the cost accountant will emphasise cost revenue differences arising from the decision.

Examples of decisions involving joint products are:

(a)   withdrawing, or adding, a product;
(b)   special pricing;
(c)   economics of further processing.

Apportioned joint costs are **not** relevant to any of the above decisions although a change in marketing strategy may affect total joint costs eg, withdrawing a product may allow capacity of the joint process to be reduced.

In the short or medium term, it is probably impractical and/or uneconomic to alter the processing structure. The relation benefit derived by joint products is, therefore, irrelevant when considering profitability or marketing opportunities.

4.9   Joint costs and decisions

(a)   **Decisions regarding joint process**

The joint process should, as stated above, be evaluated by looking at the **total** revenue and **total** cost for that process. However, it is important also to note that further processing may well increase profits. This further processing is only possible **if** the joint process is carried out.

(b)   **Decision regarding further processing of individual products**

For this purpose it is assumed that further processing of products is independent, ie, a decision to process one joint product in no way affects the decision to process further the other joint products. It should also be noted that joint costs are not affected by whether individual products are further processed, and are therefore not relevant.

To evaluate processing of the individual products it is necessary to identify the **incremental** costs and **incremental** revenues relating to that further processing, ie, the **additional** costs and revenue brought about directly as a result of that further processing.

5   CHAPTER SUMMARY

This chapter has explained output costing and process costing and the distinction between them.

These methods are used in organisations whose operations produce a finished product and are continuous. The operations are only artificially stopped and restarted by the preparation of monthly cost accounts.

In dealing with process costing the problems of losses and closing work in process have been illustrated and their solution methods shown.

Finally joint and by-products have been distinguished and their different accounting treatment explained.

6   SELF TEST QUESTIONS

6.1   What is output costing? (1.2)

6.2   What is process costing? (1.3)

6.3   Explain the special features of output costing (2.1)

6.4   What is a normal loss? (3.3)

6.5   What is an abnormal loss? (3.9)

6.6   What is an abnormal gain? (3.15)

6.7   Explain the concept of equivalent units (3.19)

6.8   What is a joint product? (4.2)

6.9   What is a by-product? (4.3)

7   EXAMINATION TYPE QUESTIONS

7.1   Alpha

The manufacture of product Alpha is completed by means of three consecutive processes. **You are required** to prepare, for the month of April, using the following information:

(a)   the work in process accounts for Processes 1, 2 and 3; and

(b)   the accounts for:

> abnormal loss
> abnormal gain
> normal loss
> finished goods stock

During April the input to Process 1 of basic raw material was 5,000 units at a cost of £0.2 per unit. Total production overhead of £3,200 was charged to the costs of each process for the month as a percentage of the direct wages incurred. There was no opening or closing work in process stocks. There were, however, in the finished goods stock the following balances:

1 April	£1,200
30 April	£1,500

Information for the month for the individual processes was as follows:

	Process 1	Process 2	Process 3
Normal loss, as percentage of input	5%	10%	5%
Output, in units	4,700	4,300	4,050
	£	£	£
Scrap value, per unit	0.10	0.50	0.60
Additional direct materials consumed	700	800	1,300
Direct wages incurred	300	500	800
Direct expenses incurred	275	191	256

(20 marks)

7.2 Process

A product is produced as a result of a continuous process.

The raw material issued to the process is shown in the following uncompleted account:

Raw material account

	Units	£		Units	£
Opening balance	3,000	600	To Process account	10,000	
Creditors	12,000	3,000	Closing balance	5,000	1,250
	15,000	3,600		15,000	3,600

The raw material is issued to a process where it is converted to finished products after the processing operation.

Details of the process for Month 1 are:

Opening work-in-progress	Nil
Input of raw materials	10,000 units
Conversion costs	£8,000
Normal loss expected	5% of input
Output of finished goods	9,200 units
Closing work-in-progress	200 units:
	Fully complete for material costs
	60% complete for conversion costs

Sale of scrapped units expected to bring in 10p per unit

The finished goods account appeared as follows:

Finished goods account

	Units		Units
Opening balance	1,200		
Process account	9,200	Closing balance	1,400
	10,400		10,400

You are required to prepare:

(a)   a completed raw materials account;

(1 mark)

(b)   a completed process account;

(10 marks)

(c)   a completed finished goods account;

(2 marks)

(d)   any other necessary accounts.

(4 marks)

(Total: 17 marks)

8   ANSWERS TO EXAMINATION TYPE QUESTIONS

8.1   Alpha

(a)   **Work in process accounts**

Process 1

	Units	£		Units	£
Raw materials	5,000	1,000	Normal loss (5%) (note 1)	250	25
Additional materials		700	Output to Process 2		
Direct wages		300	(note 2)	4,700	2,820
Direct expenses		275	Abnormal loss	50	30
Production overhead					
(note 3)		600			
	5,000	2,875		5,000	2,875

Process 2

	Units	£		Units	£
Process 2	4,700	2,820	Normal loss (10%)		
Direct materials		800	(note 1)	470	235
Direct wages		500	Output to Process 3		
Direct expenses		191	(note 2)	4,300	5,160
Production overhead					
(note 3)		1,000			
Abnormal gain (note 2)	70	84			
	4,770	5,395		4,770	5,395

Process 3

	Units	£		Units	£
Process 2	4,300	5,160	Normal loss (5%)		
Direct materials		1,300	(note 1)	215	129
Direct wages		800	Output to finished goods		
Direct expenses		256	(note 2)	4,050	8,910
Production overhead			Abnormal loss (note 2)	35	77
(note 3)		1,600			
	4,300	9,116		4,300	9,116

(b)

Abnormal loss account

	Units	£		Units	£
Process 1	50	30	Scrap receivable account	50	5
Process 3	35	77	Scrap receivable account	35	21
			Net loss to profit and		
			loss account	-	81
	85	107		85	107

Abnormal gain account

	Units	£		Units	£
Normal loss account			Process 2	70	84
(scrap value) (note 4)	70	35			
Net gain to profit and					
loss account	-	49			
	70	84		70	84

Normal loss account

	£		£
Process 1	25	Abnormal gain account (note 4)	35
Process 2	235	Scrap receivable account	354
Process 3	129		
	389		389

Finished goods stock account

	£		£
Opening stock	1,200	Cost of sales (note 5)	8,610
Process 3	8,910	Closing stock	1,500
	10,110		10,110

Notes

(1)   The scrap value of normal losses is credited to the process account.

(2)   The cost per unit for each process represents:

$$\frac{\text{Process input cost - Scrap value of normal loss}}{\text{Output + Abnormal losses/ gains}}$$

ie,   Process 1 $\dfrac{£2,875-25}{4,700+50}$ = £0.6

         Process 2 $\dfrac{£5,311-235}{4,300-70}$ = £1.2

         Process 3 $\dfrac{£9,116-129}{4,050+35}$ = £2.2

The output transferred to the next process or to finished goods stock, and abnormal losses/gains are valued at the above costs per unit.

(3)   Production overhead is charged to each process at 200% of direct wages ie,

$$\frac{\text{Total overhead}}{\text{Total direct wages}} = \frac{£3,200}{1,600}$$

(4)   The scrap value not obtained as a result of the abnormal gain in Process 2 is debited to abnormal gain account and credited to normal loss account, thereby offsetting the cost gain credited to profit and loss and reducing the scrap value receivable from normal losses ie, the scrap value receivable in relation to Process 2 is the amount for the **actual** loss which is only 400 units.

(5)   Cost of sales = Opening stock + Output from Process 3 – Closing stock.

8.2   Process

(Tutorial notes:

(1)   This question is not difficult for the well-prepared student, but parts (a)(i) and (iii) are so easy that they might confuse the student into looking for a problem that does not exist. Note that the finished goods account can only be completed for units. No values are available.

(2)   Remember to use the concept of equivalent units for (a)(ii) and calculate the abnormal loss, in units, before starting your workings.*)

(a)

Raw material account

	Units	£		Units	£
Opening balance	3,000	600	To process account	10,000	2,350
Creditors	12,000	3,000	Closing balance	5,000	1,250
	15,000	3,600		15,000	3,600

(b)   **Equivalent unit calculations**

	Raw material	Conversion costs	
Good output	9,200	9,200	
Abnormal loss	100 (bal)	100	(assume 100%)
Closing work-in-progress	200	120	(60%)
Equivalent units	9,500	9,420	

	£	£
Costs:	2,350	8,000
Less: Scrap sale re normal loss	50	N/A
	2,300	8,000

Cost per equivalent unit $\dfrac{£2,300}{9,500} = £0.2421$ $\dfrac{£8,000}{9,420} = £0.8493$

Good output $= 9,200 \times £(0.2421 + 0.8493)$

$= £10,041$

Abnormal loss $= 100 \times £(0.2421 + 0.8493)$

$= £109$

Closing work-in-progress $= (200 \times £0.2421) + (120 \times £0.8493)$

$= £150$

Process account

	Units	£		Units	£
Raw materials	10,000	2,350	Normal loss	500	50
Conversion costs		8,000	Good output	9,200	10,041
			Closing work-in-progress	200	150
			Abnormal loss	100	109
	10,000	10,350		10,000	10,350

Note: The abnormal loss, in units, is the residual after accounting for the normal loss (5% × 10,000 units), the good output and the units not yet completed.

(c)

Finished goods account

	Units		Units
Opening balance	1,200	Cost of sales	9,000
Process account	9,200	Closing balance	1,400
	10,400		10,400

(d)

Scrap sales account

	£		£
Process account	50	Bank (or debtors)	60
Abnormal account	10		
	——		——
	60		60
	——		——

Abnormal loss account

	£		£
Process account	109	Scrap sales account	10
		Closing balance	99
	——		——
	109		109
	——		——

9 SERVICE COSTING

INTRODUCTION & LEARNING OBJECTIVES

Syllabus area 2b. Cost accounting statements for services and service industries. (Ability required 3).

This chapter is concerned with the application of cost accounting techniques to service departments and service organisations.

[Definition] Service (or function) costing is cost accounting for services or functions eg, canteens, maintenance, personnel. These may be referred to as service centres, departments or functions. **(CIMA Official Terminology)**.

When you have studied this chapter you should be able to do the following:

- Identify when it is appropriate to use service costing.

- Recognise the application of composite cost units in service industries.

- Classify costs in service industries so that meaningful management reports may be produced.

1 SERVICE COSTING METHODS

1.1 Application of service costing

Some of the principles explained earlier are appropriate to service costing in that costs are charged to activities and averaged over the units of service provided.

The method is appropriate when the service can be expressed in a standardised unit of measurement eg, an accountant in practice would provide an individual service to each client, but the service could be measured in man-hour units.

1.2 Cost units for service industries

A major problem in service industries is the selection of a suitable unit for measuring the service, ie, in deciding what service is actually being provided and what measures of performance are most appropriate to the control of costs. Some cost units used in different activities are:

Service	Cost unit
Electricity generation	Kilowatt hours*
Canteens and restaurants	Meals served
Carriers	Miles travelled/ton-miles*
Hospitals	Patient-days*
Passenger transport	Passenger-miles/seat-miles*

* These are examples of composite cost-units, where the cost depends not only upon the time or distance over which the service is offered, but also on the level at which the service is operated.

A service undertaking may use several different units to measure the various kinds of service provided eg, an hotel may use:

Service	*Cost unit*
Restaurant	Meals served
Hotel services	Guest-days
Function facilities	Hours

When appropriate cost units have been determined for a particular service, provision will need to be made for the collection of the appropriate statistical data. In a transport organisation this may involve the recording of mileages day-to-day for each vehicle in the fleet. For this each driver would be required to complete a log sheet. Fuel usage per vehicle and loads or weight carried may be appropriate for the business.

1.3   Collection, classification and ascertainment of costs

Costs will be classified under appropriate headings for the particular service. This will involve the issue of suitable cost codes to be used in the recording and, therefore, the collection of costs. For a transport undertaking the main cost classification may be based on the following activities:

(a)   operating and running the fleet;
(b)   repairs and maintenance;
(c)   fixed charges;
(d)   administration.

Within each of these there would need to be a sub-classification of costs, each with its own code, so that under (c) fixed charges, there might appear the following breakdown:

(a)   road fund licences;
(b)   insurances;
(c)   depreciation;
(d)   vehicle testing fees; and
(e)   others.

In service costing it is often important to classify costs into their fixed and variable elements. Many service applications involve high fixed costs and the higher the number of cost units the lower the fixed costs per unit. The variable cost per unit will indicate to management the additional cost involved in the provision of one extra unit of service. In the context of a transport undertaking, fixed and variable costs are often referred to as standing and running costs respectively.

1.4   Cost sheets for service industries

At appropriate intervals (usually weekly or monthly) cost sheets will be prepared by the costing department to provide information about the appropriate service to management. A typical cost sheet for a service would incorporate the following for the current period and the cumulative year to date:

(a)   Cost information over the appropriate expense or activity headings.

(b)   Cost units statistics.

(c)   Cost per unit calculations using the data in (a) and dividing by the data in (b). Different cost units may be used for different elements of costs and the same cost or group of costs may be related to different cost unit bases to provide additional control information to management. In the transport organisation, for example, the operating and running costs may be expressed in per mile and per day terms.

(d)   Analyses based on the physical cost units.

On a transport cost sheet, the following non-cost statistics may be shown:

- average miles covered per day;
- average miles per gallon of fuel.

1.5   Performance/cost reports

These reports are derived from the cost sheets and other data collected. Usually costs are presented as totals for the period, classified often into fixed and variable costs. The next section illustrates how such statements would be prepared for a number of difference service organisations.

2   EXAMPLES OF PERFORMANCE/COST REPORTS

2.1   Power supply industry

Example

The following figures were taken from the annual accounts of two electricity supply boards working on uniform costing methods:

Meter reading, billing and collection costs

	Board A £'000	Board B £'000
Salaries and wages of:		
Meter readers	150	240
Billing and collection staff	300	480
Transport and travelling	30	40
Collection agency charges	-	20
Bad debts	10	10
General charges	100	200
Miscellaneous	10	10
	600	1,000
Units sold (millions)	2,880	9,600
Number of consumers (thousands)	800	1,600
Sales of electricity (millions)	£18	£50
Size of area (square miles)	4,000	4,000

Prepare a comparative cost statement using suitable units of cost. Brief notes should be added, commenting on likely causes for major differences in unit costs so disclosed.

Solution to example

Electricity Boards A and B
Comparative costs – year ending ....

	Board A £'000	Board A % of total	Board B £'000	Board B % of total
Salaries and wages:				
Meter reading	150	25.0	240	24.0
Billing and collection	300	50.0	480	48.0
Transport/travelling	30	5.0	40	4.0
Collection agency	-	-	20	2.0
Bad debts	10	1.7	10	1.0
General charges	100	16.6	200	20.0
Miscellaneous	10	1.7	10	1.0
	600	100.0	1,000	100.0

	£	£
Cost per:		
Millions units sold	208	105
Thousand consumers	750	625
£m of sales	33,333	20,000
Square mile area	150	250

Possible reasons for unit cost differences include:

(a)   **Area density.** B covers the same size of area but has double the number of consumers, indicating that B is a more urban territory.

(b)   **Industrialisation.** Costs per unit are almost twice as high for A but the pattern is not continued for costs in relation to sales value. B, therefore, probably contains a higher proportion of industrial consumers at cheaper rates.

(c)   **Territory covered.** Comparative costs per square mile deviate from the pattern shown by the other measurement units, confirming that the bulk of costs is incurred in relation to consumers and usage.

2.2   Transport operations

Example

Remix Plc makes ready-mixed cement and operates a small fleet of vehicles which delivers the product to customers within its delivery area.

General data

Maintenance records for the previous five years reveal:

Year	Mileage of vehicles	Maintenance cost £
1	170,000	13,500
2	180,000	14,000
3	165,000	13,250
4	160,000	13,000
5	175,000	13,750

Transport statistics reveal:

Vehicle	Number of journeys each day	Average tonnage carried to customers tonnes	Average distance to customers miles
1	6	4	10
2	4	4	20
3	2	5	40
4	2	6	30
5	1	6	60

There are five vehicles operating a five-day week, for fifty weeks a year.

Inflation can be ignored.

Standard cost data include:

Drivers' wages are £150 each per week.
Supervisor/relief driver's wage is £200 per week.
Depreciation, on a straight-line basis with no residual value.

	Cost	Life
Loading equipment	£100,000	5 years
Vehicles	£30,000 each	5 years

Petrol/oil costs 20p per mile.
Repairs cost 7½p per mile.
Vehicle licences cost £400 p.a. for each vehicle.
Insurance costs £600 p.a. for each vehicle.
Tyres cost £3,000 p.a. in total.
Miscellaneous costs, £2,250 p.a. in total.

You are required to calculate a standard rate per tonne/mile of operating the vehicles.

Solution to example

Calculation of standard rate per tonne/mile:

Running costs	£	£
Maintenance costs (W(1))	0.05	
Petrol/oil	0.2	
Repairs cost	0.075	
	0.325	
Total per annum: 0.325 × 170,000 (W(2))		55,250

Sundry costs		
Maintenance costs (W(1))	5,000	
Drivers' wages: 150 × 52 × 5	39,000	
Supervisor/relief driver: 200 × 52	10,400	
Depreciation of loading equipment:		
100,000 ÷ 5	20,000	
Depreciation of vehicles 30,000 × 5 ÷ 5	30,000	
Vehicle licences 400 × 5	2,000	
Insurance: 600 × 5	3,000	
Tyres	3,000	
Miscellaneous costs	2,250	
		114,650
		169,900

$$\text{Therefore, standard rate per tonne/mile} = \frac{169,900}{420,000 \ (W(3))}$$

$$= \text{£0.4045 per tonne/mile}$$

WORKINGS

(1)   Maintenance cost, separation of fixed and variable element using high/low method:

	Mileage	Maintenance cost £
High	180,000	14,000
Low	160,000	13,000
Variable cost	20,000	1,000

$$\text{Variable/running cost per mile} = \frac{1,000}{20,000} = £0.05 \text{ per mile}$$

Total cost = Total fixed cost + Variable cost per mile × Number of miles

14,000 = Total fixed cost + (0.05 × 180,000)

Total fixed cost = 14,000 − 9,000 = 5,000

(2)   Distance travelled

Vehicle		
1	6 × 10 × 2	= 120
2	4 × 20 × 2	= 160
3	2 × 40 × 2	= 160
4	2 × 30 × 2	= 120
5	1 × 60 × 2	= 120

680 × 5 × 50 = 170,000

(3)   Number of tonne/miles

Vehicle		
1	6 × 4 × 10	= 240
2	4 × 4 × 20	= 320
3	2 × 5 × 40	= 400
4	2 × 6 × 30	= 360
5	1 × 6 × 60	= 360

1,680 × 5 × 50 = 420,000 tonne miles

3   CHAPTER SUMMARY

In this chapter the application of costing principles has been applied to service organisations.

You should now be able to explain how and when service costing should be used, and be able to prepare operating statements from cost and related data.

4   SELF TEST QUESTIONS

4.1   What is a composite cost unit? (1.2)

4.2   Give an example of a composite cost unit. (1.2)

5   EXAMINATION TYPE QUESTION

5.1   Hotel rooms

(a)   Describe the benefits which cost accounting provides for an organisation.

Note: You may refer to your own experience in answering this question.

(7 marks)

(b)   The following information is provided for a 30 day period for the Rooms Department of a hotel:

	Rooms with twin beds	Single rooms
Number of rooms in hotel	260	70
Number of rooms available to let	240	40
Average number of rooms occupied daily	200	30

Number of guests in period	6,450
Average length of stay	2 days
Total revenue in period	£774,000
Number of employees	200
Payroll costs for period	£100,000
Items laundered in period	15,000
Cost of cleaning supplies in period	£5,000
Total cost of laundering	£22,500
Listed daily rate for twin-bedded room	£110
Listed daily rate for single room	£70

The hotel calculates a number of statistics, including the following:

Room occupancy	Total number of rooms occupied as a percentage of rooms available to let.
Bed occupancy	Total number of beds occupied as a percentage of beds available.
Average guest rate	Total revenue divided by number of guests.
Revenue utilisation	Actual revenue as a percentage of maximum revenue from available rooms.
Average cost per occupied bed	Total cost divided by number of beds occupied.

You are required to

Prepare a table which contains the following statistics, calculated to one decimal place:

Room occupancy (%)
Bed occupancy (%)
Average guest rate (£)
Revenue utilisation (%)
Cost of cleaning supplies per occupied room per day (£)
Average cost per occupied bed per day (£)

(12 marks)

(c)   Explain what you understand by the following terms:

Cost unit
Cost centre

(4 marks)

(d)   Identify **one cost centre** which might exist in a hotel, excluding the Rooms Department. For the cost centre identified give an appropriate **cost unit**.

(2 marks)

(Total: 25 marks)

6   ANSWER TO EXAMINATION TYPE QUESTION

6.1   Hotel rooms

(Tutorial notes

(1)   Part (a) requires a general knowledge of cost accounting. Those students with practical experience will have little difficulty with this part of the question, but full-time students or those who do not work in a manufacturing environment will not find it easy to produce an answer worth seven marks.

(2)   Part (b) initially appears to be 'odd' and rather difficult. But read carefully the notes relating to the calculation of the statistics and this turns out to be an easy question.

(3)   Parts (c) and (d) are both basic cost accounting. Well-prepared students will not find these difficult.)

(a)   The cost accounting systems will take basic cost data and, by following the basic costing principles, using one or more of the costing techniques in accordance with one or more of the costing methods, will produce information which can be used by management for planning, controlling and decision-making. The establishment of budgets, standard costs and actual costs will aid in the management of the organisation.

A specific example would be the establishment of standard costs and the reporting of actuals against these standards, the resulting variances being used for the control of operations, processes and departments.

(b)   Room occupancy

$$\text{Room occupancy} = \frac{\text{Total number of rooms occupied}}{\text{Rooms available to be let}}$$

$$= \frac{200 + 30}{240 + 40}$$

$$= 82.1\%$$

Bed occupancy

$$= \frac{\text{Total number of beds occupied}}{\text{Total number of beds available}}$$

$$= \frac{6{,}450 \text{ guests} \times 2 \text{ days per guest}}{((240 \times 2) + (40 \times 1)) \times 30 \text{ days}}$$

$$= \frac{12{,}900}{15{,}600}$$

$$= 82.7\%$$

Average guest rate

$$= \frac{\text{Total revenue}}{\text{Number of guests}}$$

$$= \frac{£774{,}000}{6{,}450}$$

$$= £120$$

$$\text{Revenue utilisation} = \frac{\text{Actual revenue}}{\text{Maximum revenue from available rooms}}$$

$$= \frac{£774,000}{((240 \times £110) + (40 \times £70)) \times 30 \text{ days}}$$

$$= \frac{£774,000}{876,000}$$

$$= 88.4\%$$

$$\text{Cost of cleaning supplies per occupied room per day} = \frac{£5,000}{(200 + 30) \times 30 \text{ days}}$$

$$= £0.7$$

$$\text{Average cost per occupied bed per day} = \frac{\text{Total cost}}{\text{Number of beds occupied}}$$

$$= \frac{£100,000 + £5,000 + £22,500}{6,450 \times 2}$$

$$= £9.9$$

(c)   **Cost unit**

A unit of product or service in relation to which costs are ascertained **(CIMA Official Terminology)**. They can be used to help build up the cost of a unit of output. In manufacturing firms the cost unit will often be the unit product, while for servicing firms (eg, road haulage) it will relate to the type of service eg, cost per tonne/mile.

Cost centre

This is a production or service location, function, activity or item of equipment for which costs are accumulated **(CIMA Official Terminology)**. They often enable production costs to be related to cost units in a structured manner.

(d)   **Note:**   Students should try to consider all the separate activities that take place in a hotel and select one where they are carried out in a separately identifiable department or area.

Cost centre:	Kitchen	**or**	Restaurant
Cost unit:	Meals produced	**or**	Meals served

10 COST BOOKKEEPING

INTRODUCTION & LEARNING OBJECTIVES

Syllabus area 2b. Accounting entries for integrated and non-integrated accounting systems. (Ability required 3).

The basic principles of double entry and ledger accounts apply to cost accounting as well as to financial accounting. However the detailed application of these principles differs and the cost accounts must provide more detailed information than is normally required for financial accounts.

In this chapter the basic principles of the two main systems of cost accounting bookkeeping will be examined. These two systems are known as interlocking accounts (non-integrated accounting systems) and integrated accounts.

When you have studied this chapter you should be able to do the following:

- Describe a system of interlocking accounts and integrated accounts.

- Detail the differences between financial and costing profit in an interlocking system.

- Understand the ledger account entries in an interlocking system.

- Describe an integrated accounts system.

---

1 METHODS OF COST BOOKKEEPING

1.1 Interlocking accounts (non-integrated accounting)

Definition **Interlocking accounts** are a system in which the cost accounts are distinct from the financial accounts, the two sets of accounts being kept continuously in agreement by the use of control accounts or reconciled by other means. **(CIMA Official Terminology).**

The recording system may be arranged in two ways:

(a) Separate book records without control account: separate costing records are derived independently from the source documents, but are reconciled periodically with the financial records.

(b) Separate cost ledger with control account: a separate costing ledger is maintained under the control of the cost accountant, but integrated with the financial books by means of a cost ledger control account through which all cost and revenue information for re-analysis is transferred.

1.2 Reconciliation of financial and costing profit

Where the cost accounts are maintained independently in an interlocking system it is possible to reconcile the financial and costing results. The examiner has stated that you will be required to produce a pro-forma reconciliation only ie, you will not be required to make the accounting entries.

1.3   Activity

List the differences that you think there might be between the financial and costing profits under the following headings:

(a)   Appropriations of profit not dealt with in the costing system.

(b)   Income and expenditure of a purely financial nature (ie, nothing to do with manufacturing).

(c)   Items where financial and costing treatments differ.

1.4   Activity solution

(a)   **Appropriations of profit not dealt with in the costing system**

    (i)   Corporation tax;

    (ii)   transfers to reserves;

    (iii)   dividends paid and proposed;

    (iv)   amounts written off intangibles such as goodwill, discount on issue of debentures, expenses of capital issues, etc;

    (v)   appropriations to sinking funds for the repayment of loans;

    (vi)   charitable donations where no direct benefit is derived by the employees of the company.

(b)   **Income and expenditure of a purely financial nature** (ie, outside the scope of manufacture)

    (i)   Interest and dividends received;

    (ii)   rents receivable - however, if this arises from part of rented business premises which have been sublet, only the profit element should be excluded, the proportion representing cost being deducted from rents payable to determine the net rent of premises;

    (iii)   profits and losses on the sale of fixed assets and investments;

    (iv)   interest on bank loans, mortgages and debentures;

    (v)   damages payable at law, fines and penalties.

(c)   **Items where financial and costing treatments differ**

    (i)   Differences in the valuation of stocks and work in progress. The latter may, for costing purposes, be valued at factory cost (including production overhead), whereas prime cost may be employed in the financial accounts. Likewise, stocks of materials and finished goods may be written down in the financial accounts to net realisable value.

(ii)   Depreciation. In the financial accounts this charge is normally based solely upon the passage of time, whereas in the cost accounts it may be a variable charge based upon machine/man hours worked.

(iii)   Abnormal losses in production and storage. In the financial accounts, materials and wages will include any abnormal losses of material or time. In the cost accounts such losses may be excluded to avoid misleading comparisons.

(iv)   Interest on capital. Notional interest on capital employed in production is sometimes included in the cost accounts to reflect the nominal cost of employing the capital rather than investing it outside the business.

(v)   Charge in lieu of rent. Again a notional amount for rent may be included in costs in order to compare costs of production with costs of another business which occupies a rented or leasehold factory.

1.5   Integrated accounts

[Definition]   Integrated accounts are a set of accounting records which provides both financial and cost accounts using a common input of data for all accounting purposes. **(CIMA Official Terminology)**

These are studied a little later.

2   THE COST LEDGER IN AN INTERLOCKING SYSTEM

2.1   Cost ledger control account

In an interlocking system the cost accounts will only need to record transactions relating to operating revenue and costs; details of capital, debtors and creditors are part of the financial accounting routine. Frequently, however, such financial accounts are merged into a single account (cost ledger control) solely to maintain the double entry principle within the cost accounts.

2.2   Control accounts

The cost ledger for a manufacturing business will probably contain control accounts for:

(a)   stores;
(b)   work in progress;
(c)   finished stock;
(d)   production overhead;
(e)   general administration costs;
(f)   marketing costs.

2.3   Subsidiary ledgers

Each control account will be supported by a subsidiary ledger to provide the detail required for financial reporting and/or management information. Analysis will be by:

(a)   item of material;
(b)   job number (job costing), product (batch costing) or process (process costing);
(c)   job or production;
(d)   cost centres (there will be more than one of these).

2.4   Cost ledger accounts

In addition to the cost ledger control and the control accounts detailed above, separate accounts will be kept as required, particularly:

(a)   sales;
(b)   cost of sales;
(c)   wages;
(d)   profit and loss.

Subsidiary details in the form of a sub-ledger or analysis columns may be necessary.

2.5   Accounting entries

Entries to the cost ledger follow the sequence of transactions in the manufacturing business:

	Transaction	*Journal entry*	*Document*
(a)	Purchases	Dr Stores Cr Contra	Invoice/GRN
(b)	Gross wages	Dr Wages Cr Contra	Payroll
(c)	Expenses incurred	Dr Production overhead Dr General admin cost Dr Marketing cost Cr Contra	Invoices/ Petty cash/ Journal
(d)	Materials issued	Dr Work in progress (direct) Dr Production overhead (indirect) Cr Stores	Requisitions
(e)	Analysed wages	Dr (as (d) above) Cr Wages	Time sheets, etc
(f)	Overhead absorbed	Dr Work in progress Cr Production overhead	Cost journal
(g)	Completed work	Dr Finished stock Cr Work in progress	Production order
(h)	Goods sold	Dr Cost of sales/contra Cr Finished stock/sales	Delivery note/ Invoice

Notes:

(i)   (d) and (e) could affect general administration and marketing.

(ii)   Overhead absorbed (f) would be debited to finished stock if work in progress is valued at prime cost.

(iii)   In a marginal costing system entry (f) would be for variable overhead only.

2.6   Period end procedure

At the end of the reporting period a profit and loss account can be prepared from the cost ledger in the following format:

	£	£
Sales		X
Less: Cost of sales		(X)
Gross margin		X
Add/Less: Over/under-absorbed overhead		X/(X)
Less: General administration costs	X	
Marketing costs	X	(X)
Operating profit		X

Balances in stores, work in progress and finished stock represent stock valuations at cost. At the end of the financial year the costing profit and loss account will be closed by transfer to cost ledger contra and the balances in stock accounts carried forward with an offsetting credit in cost ledger contra.

2.7   Example

The following illustrates the double entry aspect of cost accounting. The entries relating to notional charges and absorption of non-production cost are unlikely to be encountered in practice, but will test your application of accounting procedure.

Details are given below of the operations during a period of one month of a manufacturing company which makes a single product.

You are required to show the entries in an interlocking set of cost accounts.

Data for a period of one month:

	Opening stock		Closing stock	
	Units	£	Units	£
Raw materials:				
Direct		15,000		20,000
Indirect production		1,700		3,000
Work in progress:				
Direct materials		3,000		3,500
Direct wages		1,000		1,200
Finished goods	7,500	9,000	10,000	12,000
Sales 150,000 units				225,000
Rent of offices				1,500
Advertising				2,000
Stationery				840
Rates on factory				2,700
Salesmen's commission and expenses				1,400
Insurance of offices				80
Depreciation of machinery				6,400
Warehouse rentals				800
Secretarial wages				3,000
Repairs to plant				1,850
Salesmen's salaries				6,000
Insurance of factory				1,100
Accounting staff wages				8,200
Delivery charges				450
Other factory expenses				7,950
Other administration expenses				2,480
Other marketing expenses				6,250
Purchase of materials:				
Direct				65,000
Indirect production				5,000
Direct wages				55,000
Factory indirect wages				15,000
Loan interest received				500
Included in factory expenses are:				
Notional charge for use of own premises				2,800
Notional interest on capital employed in the business				400

'Other marketing expenses' wrongly contains an amount of £4,500 which should be in 'Other factory expenses'.

The cost accounts are kept separately from the financial accounts. In the cost accounts the company absorbs factory overhead at 40% of prime cost of finished units produced, administration overhead at 10p per unit produced and marketing overhead at 9p per unit delivered.

2.8   Solution

The question should be tackled in logical sequence.

Step 1   Open the necessary cost accounts, which are:

       Direct raw materials
       Indirect production materials
       Work in progress
       Factory overhead
       Administration overhead
       Marketing overhead
       Finished goods
       Cost of sales
       Profit and loss
       Cost contra (memo to maintain double entry)

Step 2   Record the opening balances on the stock accounts, crediting cost contra, and post purchases of materials.

Step 3   Post the issues of material.

Step 4   Charge direct wages to work in progress and indirect wages to factory overhead.

Step 5   Charge the remaining costs for the period to appropriate overhead accounts.

Step 6   Complete the work in progress account. The balance, after posting the closing stock, represents the prime cost of finished units produced.

Step 7   Debit finished goods account with factory and administration overhead at the absorption rates given.

Step 8   Complete the finished goods account. The balance, after posting the closing stock, represents cost of goods sold. The number of units produced (required for Step 7 above) represents Sales + Closing stock − Opening stock, ie, 150,000 + 10,000 − 7,500 = 152,500.

Step 9   Debit cost of sales with absorbed marketing overhead.

Step 10   Compile the profit and loss account by posting sales, cost of sales, and the balances on overhead accounts (under/over-absorption).

Solution (for guidance, the entries have been referenced to the sequence above)

(a)

Direct raw materials

	£		£
Opening stock b/d (2)	15,000	WIP - issued to production (3)	60,000
Cost contra - purchases (2)	65,000	Closing stock c/d	20,000
	80,000		80,000

Indirect production materials

	£		£
Opening stock b/d (2)	1,700	Factory overhead - issues (3)	3,700
Cost contra - purchases (2)	5,000	Closing stock c/d	3,000
	6,700		6,700

Work in progress

	£		£
Opening stock b/d (2)	4,000	Finished goods - prime cost	
Direct raw materials (3)	60,000	of finished units (6) (bal fig)	114,300
Direct wages (4)	55,000	Closing stock c/d	4,700
	119,000		119,000

Factory overhead

	£		£
Indirect materials (3)	3,700	Finished goods - absorbed	
Indirect wages (4)	15,000	overhead @ 40% of £114,300	45,720
Factory rates (5)	2,700		
Depreciation of machinery (5)	6,400		
Repairs to plant (5)	1,850		
Factory insurance (5)	1,100		
Other factory expenses (5)	7,950		
Marketing overhead (error)	4,500		
	43,200		
Profit and loss over-absorbed			
overhead (10)	2,520		
	45,720		45,720

Administration overhead

	£		£
Rent of offices (5)	1,500	Finished goods - absorbed	
Stationery (5)	840	overhead: 152,500 units	
Insurance of offices (5)	80	@ 10p per unit (7)	15,250
Secretarial wages (5)	3,000	Profit and loss -	
Accounting staff wages (5)	8,200	under-absorbed (10)	850
Other admin expenses (5)	2,480		
	16,100		16,100

Marketing overhead

	£		£
Advertising (5)	2,000	Factory overhead (error)	4,500
Salesmen's commission/		Cost of sales - absorbed	
expenses (5)	1,400	overhead @ 9p per unit on	
Warehouse rentals (5)	800	150,000 units delivered (a)	13,500
Salesmen's salaries (5)	6,000		
Delivery charges (5)	450		
Other expenses (5)	6,250		
Profit and loss - over-absorbed			
overhead (10)	1,100		
	18,000		18,000

Finished goods

	Units	£		Units	£
Opening stock (2)	7,500	9,000	Cost of sales (8)		
Work in progress (6)	152,500	114,300	(bal fig)	150,000	172,270
Factory overhead (7)		45,720	Closing stock	10,000	12,000
Admin overhead (7)		15,250			
	160,000	184,270		160,000	184,270

Cost of sales

	£		£
Finished goods (8)	172,270	Profit and loss (10)	185,770
Marketing overhead (9)	13,500		
	185,770		185,770

Profit and loss

	£		£
Cost of sales (10)	185,770	Sales (10)	225,000
Admin overhead (10)	850	Factory overhead (10)	2,520
Balance - costing profit	42,000	Marketing overhead (10)	1,100
	228,620		228,620

Cost contra account

	£	£		£
Sales (10)		225,000	Balance b/d (2)	
Balance c/d:			(15,000 + 1,700 + 4,000	
Raw material	20,000		+ 9,000)	29,700
Indirect material	3,000		Purchases (2) (65,000 + 5,000)	70,000
Work in progress	4,700		Wages (4) (55,000 + 15,000)	70,000
Finished goods	12,000		Factory overhead (5)	20,000
		39,700	Admin overhead (5)	16,100
			Marketing overhead (5)	16,900
			Balance c/d	
			Costing profit (10)	42,000
		264,700		264,700

2.9 Activity

Take the costing profit of £42,000 and prepare a pro-forma statement showing any additional items necessary in order to give the financial accounting profit.

2.10 Activity solution

	£	£	£
Profit per costing profit and loss account			42,000
Add: Loan interest received (excluded from cost accounts)		-	
Notional charges not included in financial accounts:			
Rent	-		
Interest	-		
		-	
			-
Profit per financial accounts			-

3 INTEGRATED ACCOUNTS

3.1 Purpose of integration

Integration of the cost and financial accounts into one comprehensive system offers savings in work by avoiding:

(a)   Duplication of certain accounting entries, for example in an interlocking system, purchases of raw materials would be posted thus.

> **Financial account**   Dr Purchases   Cr Creditors
>
> **Cost account**   Dr Stores   Cr Cost Contra

In an integral system, a single entry would suffice, ie,

> Dr Stores   Cr Creditors

(b)   Reconciliation of costing with financial profit; only one profit and loss account would be prepared.

More importantly perhaps, integration should improve the usefulness of, and promote the reliance upon, the accounting system as an information base. The overall system will be subject to control by external, internal and management audit. Furthermore, the design of accounting procedures will have to co-ordinate the requirements for management and financial information.

3.2 Methods of integration

Various methods of integrating the financial and cost accounts exist and the system must take into account the structure, etc, of the company and the normal information requirements for management and outsiders, eg, shareholders and the Revenue. Some requirements will be met by a two-fold analysis of costs: by natural headings and by cost centres, products, etc.

The organisation of the accounting department can take the same form as if separate cost and financial accounting systems were in use. The cost department will become involved in a detailed analysis of WIP and overhead accounts (and probably sales as well), and will supply details of transfers from WIP to finished goods, of overhead recovery, and, where applicable, an analysis of variances.

Division of work can be incorporated in the accounting system by:

(a)   Creating a cost ledger control account in the main ledger. The account would operate in the same way as a debtors' control account, ie, all entries affecting the cost accounts would be posted to cost ledger control and the cost accountant would be responsible for maintaining all the subsidiary ledgers and accounts.

(b)   Opening cost control and financial control accounts. The accounts would perform a similar function to branch/head office accounts to separate cost and financial accounting. The cost control and financial control accounts would be kept in agreement except that balances would appear on opposite sides.

3.3   Accounting for production overhead

Production overhead costs are those costs incurred in the production function but which cannot be economically identified with the cost unit to which they relate.

The requirements of SSAP 9 for stock valuations used in financial accounting are that stocks should be valued at their total cost including an appropriate proportion of production overhead.

Since work-in-progress is a form of stock this valuation rule must also apply to work-in-progress.

To achieve this valuation production overhead absorption rates are used and applied to cost units as they are being completed (via the work-in-progress account). This ensures that finished units and work-in-progress at the end of a period are valued at their total cost.

3.4   Integrated system example

The following example illustrates the use of an integrated system within a processing organisation.

Note how this system includes accounts for debtors, creditors, bank, capital etc, which differs from the interlocking system example earlier.

From the following informations **you are required**

(a)   to write up the accounts in the cost ledger for June; and

(22 marks)

(b)   to extract a trial balance as at 30 June.

(6 marks)

(Total: 28 marks)

The trial balance of the cost ledger as at 31 May was as follows:

	£	£	£
Stores control		90,400	
Work-in-progress, Process 1:			
Direct materials	8,200		
Direct wages	6,400		
Production overhead	22,400		
		37,000	
Work-in-progress, Process 2:			
Direct materials	31,200		
Direct wages	8,800		
Production overhead	22,000		
		62,000	
Finished goods		89,000	
Production overhead, under-/over-absorbed			4,800
Sales			680,000
Cost of sales		529,200	
General ledger control			131,800
Abnormal loss		9,000	
		816,600	816,600

During June the following transactions took place:

	£
Materials returned to suppliers	1,560
Actual cost of materials purchased	42,500
Materials issued to:	
Process 1	21,200
Process 2	10,400
Materials issued to production maintenance department	1,280
Direct wages incurred in:	
Process 1	16,800
Process 2	21,600
Indirect wages and salaries incurred	48,200
Production indirect expenses incurred	72,000
Sales	300,000

Production reports include the following:

	Direct materials £	Direct wages £
Abnormal loss in:		
Process 1	480	400
Process 2	1,400	280
Transfer from:		
Process 1	24,600	19,600
Process 2	110,000	20,520

The value of finished goods in stock at 30 June was £98,200.

Overhead is absorbed by means of direct wages percentage rates.

Production transferred from Process 1 to Process 2 is treated as an item of materials cost in Process 2 accounts.

Stores control

	£		£
Balance, 31 May	90,400	Returns	1,560
Purchases	42,500	Process 1	21,200
		Process 2	10,400
		Production maintenance	1,280
		Balance, 30 June	98,460
	132,900		132,900

Work-in-progress - Process 1

	Material £	*Wages* £	*Overhead* £	*Total* £		*Material* £	*Wages* £	*Overhead* £	*Total* £
Balance, 31 May	8,200	6,400	22,400	37,000	Abnormal loss	480	400	1,400	2,280
Direct materials	21,200	-	-	21,200	Transfers to				
Direct wages	-	16,800	-	16,800	Process 2	24,600	19,600	68,600	112,800
Production					Balance 30 June	4,320	3,200	11,200	18,720
overhead	-	-	58,800	58,800					
	29,400	23,200	81,200	133,800		29,400	23,200	81,200	133,800

Work-in-progress - Process 2

	Material £	*Wages* £	*Overhead* £	*Total* £		*Material* £	*Wages* £	*Overhead* £	*Total* £
Balance, 31 May	31,200	8,800	22,000	62,000	Abnormal loss	1,400	280	700	2,380
Transfers in					Transfers to				
(Process 1)	112,800	-	-	112,800	finished goods	110,000	20,520	51,300	181,820
Direct materials	10,400	-	-	10,400	Balance, 30 June	43,000	9,600	24,000	76,600
Direct wages	-	21,600	-	21,600					
Production									
overhead	-	-	54,000	54,000					
	154,400	30,400	76,000	260,800		154,400	30,400	76,000	260,800

Finished goods

	£		£
Balance, 31 May	89,000	Cost of sales (bal. fig.)	172,620
Process 2	181,820	Balance, 30 June	98,200
	270,820		270,820

Production overhead control

	£		£
Indirect wages and salaries	48,200	Balance, 31 May	4,800
Production indirect expenses	72,000	WIP, Process 1	58,800
		WIP, Process 2	54,000
Maintenance	1,280	Balance, 30 June	3,880
	121,480		121,480

Sales

	£		£
Balance, 30 June	980,000	Balance, 31 May	680,000
		General ledger control	300,000
	980,000		980,000

Cost of sales

	£		£
Balance, 31 May	529,200	Balance, 30 June	701,820
Finished goods	172,620		
	701,820		701,820

General ledger control

	£		£
Returns	1,560	Balance, 30 May	131,800
Sales	300,000	Purchases	42,500
Balance, 30 June	31,340	Direct wages	38,400
		Indirect wages and salaries	48,200
		Production indirect expenses	72,000
	332,900		332,900

Abnormal loss

	£		£
Balance, 31 May	9,000	Balance, 30 June	13,660
Process 1	2,280		
Process 2	2,380		
	13,660		13,660

(b)   **Trial balance as at 30 June**

	£	£	£
Stores control		98,460	
Work-in-progress, Process 1:			
Direct materials	4,320		
Direct wages	3,200		
Production overhead	11,200		
		18,720	
Work-in-progress, Process 2:			
Direct materials	43,000		
Direct wages	9,600		
Production overhead	24,000		
		76,600	
Finished goods		98,200	
Production overhead, under-/over-absorbed		3,880	
Sales			980,000
Cost of sales		701,820	
General ledger control			31,340
Abnormal loss		13,660	
		1,011,340	1,011,340

4   EXAMPLE

The following illustrates the double entry aspect of recording transactions, firstly using an interlocking (non-integrated) system; and then using an integrated system.

4.1   Example

	£
Incurred direct wages	100,000
Incurred indirect production wages	41,200
Administration salaries paid	12,800
Purchased raw materials	46,500
Paid business rates	4,000
Paid creditor for materials	41,400
Paid wages	98,700
Paid PAYE creditor	40,900
Paid bank charges	420
Sales on credit	480,000
Production overhead costs (other than business rates) paid	81,400
Received from debtors	414,600

Notes: (re: Interlocking system)

(1)   In the cost ledgers production overhead costs are absorbed into cost units using an absorption rate of 100% of direct wage costs. Any under or over absorption is carried forward to the end of the year.

(2)   Stocks of raw material are valued using FIFO in the financial ledgers and LIFO in the cost ledgers. There was no opening stock, closing stock was valued:

FIFO   £6,300
LIFO   £4,800

(3)   There is no work-in-progress or stock of finished goods.

(4)   The amount payable to the PAYE creditor in respect of wages and salaries is £43,400.

(5)   Business rates are to be apportioned:

Production   80%
Administration   20%

4.2   Solution

Interlocking system

Financial ledger

Wages and salaries

	£		£
Wages control	154,000	Profit & loss	154,000

Wages control

	£		£
PAYE creditor	43,400	Wages &	
Bank	98,700	Salaries	154,000

PAYE creditor

	£		£
Bank	40,900	Wages control	43,400

Raw material purchases

	£		£
Creditor	46,500	Profit & loss	46,500

Creditor - Raw materials

	£		£
Bank	41,400	Purchases	46,500

Bank

	£		£
Debtors	414,600	Wages control	98,700
		PAYE creditor	40,900
		Creditor	
		- materials	41,400
		Rates	4,000
		Bank charges	420
		Overhead costs	81,400

Rates

	£		£
Bank	4,000	Profit & loss	4,000

Bank charges

	£		£
Bank	420	Profit & loss	420

Sales

	£		£
Profit & loss	480,000	Debtors	480,000

Debtors

	£		£
Sales	480,000	Bank	414,600

Overhead costs

	£		£
Bank	81,400	Profit & loss	81,400

Stock

	£		£
Profit & loss	6,300		

Profit & loss

	£		£
Raw material	46,500	Sales	480,000
Wages &		Raw material	
salaries	154,000	stock	6,300
Rates	4,000		
Bank charges	420		
Overhead costs	81,400		
Net profit	199,980		
	486,300		486,300

Cost ledger

Raw material control

	£		£
CLC	46,500	WIP	41,700
		Bal c/d	4,800
	46,500		46,500

Work in progress

	£		£
CLC	100,000	Cost of sales	241,700
Raw material	41,700		
Prod Ohd	100,000		
	241,700		241,700

Production overhead

	£		£
CLC	41,200	Work in	
CLC	3,200	progress	100,000
CLC	81,400	Bal c/d	25,800
	125,800		125,800

Administration overhead

	£		£
CLC	12,800	Profit & loss	13,600
CLC	800		
	13,600		13,600

Cost ledger control (CLC)

	£		£
Sales	480,000	Raw material	46,500
		WIP	100,000
		Prod Ohd	41,200
		Admin Ohd	12,800
		Prod Ohd	3,200
		Admin Ohd	800
		Prod Ohd	81,400

Sales

	£		£
Profit & loss	480,000	CLC	480,000

Cost of sales

	£		£
WIP	241,700	Profit & loss	241,700

Profit & loss

	£		£
Cost of sales	241,700	Sales	480,000
Admin Ohd	13,600		
Net profit	224,700		
	480,000		480,000

Profit reconciliation

(Note that in the exam you will only have to produce the pro-forma for this - you will not have to make the accounting entries. However, we show you the entries here to reinforce your understanding.)

	£	£
Net profit as per financial ledgers		199,980
Adjust for item not in cost ledger:		
Bank charges		420
Differences in treatment of:		
Production overhead costs	25,800	
Closing stock valuation	(1,500)	
		24,300
Net profit as per cost ledgers		224,700

Integrated system

(**Note.** Stocks are valued on a FIFO basis.)

Raw material control

	£		£
Creditor	46,500	WIP	40,200
		Bal c/d	6,300
	46,500		46,500

Creditor

	£		£
Bank	41,400	Raw materials	46,500

Work in progress

	£		£
Wages control	100,000	Cost of sales	240,200
Raw material	40,200		
Prod'n Ohd	100,000		
	240,200		240,200

Wages control

	£		£
Bank	98,700	Work in progress	100,000
PAYE creditor	43,400	Production Ohd	41,200

Production overhead			
	£		£
Wages control	41,200	WIP	100,000
Bank	3,200	Bal c/d	25,800
Bank	81,400		
	125,800		125,800

Administration overhead			
	£		£
Bank	12,800	Profit & loss	13,600
Bank	800		
	13,600		13,600

Bank			
	£		£
Debtors	414,600	Admin Ohd	12,800
		Admin Ohd	800
		Production Ohd	3,200
		Creditor	41,400
		Wages control	98,700
		PAYE creditor	40,900
		Bank charges	420
		Production Ohd	81,400

PAYE creditor			
	£		£
Bank	40,900	Wages control	43,400

Cost of sales			
	£		£
WIP	240,200	Profit & loss	240,200

Bank charges			
	£		£
Bank	420	Profit & loss	420

Debtors			
	£		£
Sales	480,000	Bank	414,600

Sales			
	£		£
Profit & loss	480,000	Debtors	480,000

Profit & loss			
	£		£
Cost of sales	240,200	Sales	480,000
Admin Ohd	13,600		
Bank charges	420		
Net profit	225,780		
	480,000		480,000

4.3   Interlocking and integrated systems - a comparison

The above example has identified the following differences between these systems:

- Many transactions are recorded twice when an interlocking system is used, once in the cost ledger and once in the financial ledger. This is an additional administrative cost.

- Some transactions are not recorded in the cost ledger when an interlocking system is used.

- Some items (eg, stock) may be valued differently in each set of ledgers when an interlocking system is used.

- An integrated system classifies costs similarly to the classifications used in the cost ledger of an interlocking system. The integrated ledger records all transactions and shows the asset and liability accounts similarly to those in the financial ledger of an interlocking system.

In summarising the above it can be shown that the interlocking system provides more flexibility because it is not constrained (in the cost ledger) by the regulations of financial accounting. However, this flexibility has a cost:

- the administrative burden of recording many transactions twice (referred to above); and

- the need to prepare a statement reconciling the profit shown by the cost and financial ledgers.

5   CHAPTER SUMMARY

The information required in cost accounting is often somewhat different to that required in a financial accounting system. The traditional method of dealing with this is to keep two separate sets of ledgers which are not integrated with each other. This is known as an interlocking system. The alternative is to integrate the two systems and this is known as an integrated system.

6   SELF TEST QUESTIONS

6.1   What is an interlocking system of accounts? (1.1)

6.2   What are the two ways in which an interlocking system can be arranged? (1.1)

6.3   What type of appropriations of profit might there be that are not dealt with in a costing system? (1.4)

6.4   What types of items might be treated differently in financial and costing accounts? (1.4)

6.5   What are integrated accounts? (1.5)

6.6   What is the name of the account used in the cost ledger of an interlocking system in order to maintain the double entry? (2.1)

6.7   What types of control accounts are likely to be kept in an interlocking system? (2.2)

6.8   What accounts, other than control accounts and the cost ledger contra, are likely to be kept in an interlocking system? (2.4)

6.9   What are the two main benefits of an integrated system of accounting? (3.1)

6.10   In an integrated system what would be the double entry for purchase of raw materials? (3.1)

7   EXAMINATION TYPE QUESTION

7.1   Accounting records

A company keeps cost accounting records which are quite separate from its financial accounting records, and prepares a profit and loss account from each of the two sets of records. For the financial year just ended, the figure of 'profit' in the cost accounting records is substantially different from the figure of 'profit' in financial accounting records.

List the items that might cause this difference.

(15 marks)

(CIMA November 1987)

8   ANSWER TO EXAMINATION TYPE QUESTION

8.1   Accounting records

Items included in financial accounts but not in cost accounts

Income:

> Cash, quantity and trade discounts
> Rents receivable
> Profit on sale of assets
> Income from non-trading activities
> Interest on investments
> Dividends on investments

Costs:

> Abnormal losses
> Goodwill written off
> Other intangible assets written down
> Corporation tax
> Donations

Note: dividends paid and proposed do not necessarily cause a 'difference' in the 'profit', only in the balance carried down.'

This also applies to transfers to reserves.

Items included in cost accounts but not in financial accounts

Notional charge for rent where premises are owned.

Notional charge for interest on capital employed.

Use of different stock valuation methods (note that this should be reflected in the financial accounts if an efficient stock records system is employed).

Under/over-absorption of overheads.

Depreciation rates/capital allowances for fixed assets.

11 BUDGETING

INTRODUCTION & LEARNING OBJECTIVES

Syllabus area 2c. Budget preparation, including a master budget and simple cash budget. (Ability required 3).

The use of computers for budgeting. (Ability required 2).

Reconciliation of operational cashflow with operating profit. (Ability required 3).

This chapter will concentrate on the techniques of preparing budgets and the process of comparing actual and budgeted results in a meaningful manner.

When you have studied this chapter you should be able to do the following:

- Discuss the purposes of budgets and the benefits of budgetary control.

- Prepare sales budgets, production budgets, purchases budgets, labour budgets and overhead budgets

- Prepare a budgeted operating statement.

- Prepare a cash budget.

- Understand and be able to use flexible budgets.

- Understand how computers may be used for budgeting.

- Reconcile operating cashflow with operating profit.

- Make meaningful comparisons of budget and actual results.

---

1 BUDGETARY CONTROL

1.1 The concept of budgeting

Definition A budget is a quantitative statement, for a defined period of time, which may include planned revenues, expenses, assets, liabilities and cash flows. **(CIMA Official Terminology).**

Thus, budgeting may be regarded as **predictive accounting**. A budget may stand on its own, but it is more useful if it is part of a control system. A simple closed control system is illustrated by an oven thermostat:

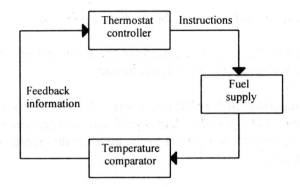

A budgetary control system is essentially similar:

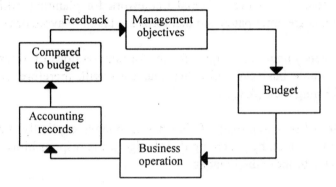

This is an oversimplified view, in that there are other factors and forecasts.

Definition   Budgetary control is the establishment of budgets relating the responsibilities of executives to the requirements of a policy, and the continuous comparison of actual with budgeted results, either to secure by individual action the objectives of that policy or to provide a basis for its revision. **(CIMA Official Terminology)**.

Conclusion   The subject of budgetary control is vital to management accounting and is an important management tool in practice.

1.2   The nature of budgets

In general, budgets are set for specific periods of time in the future, for example the budget for next year. Sometimes budgets are constructed for specific projects that are to be undertaken but again these can be analysed into the periods of time that the projects are expected to last. Thus, if a project is planned to last two years, the total budget for it can be split into that relating to the first year and that relating to the second year.

Budgets are plans expressed in financial and/or quantitative terms for either the whole of a business or for the various parts of a business for a specified period of time in the future. The budgets are prepared (**the planning activity**) within the framework of objectives (**targets** or **goals**) and policies that have been determined by senior management as part of its own planning activities.

1.3   Functions of budgetary control

Essentially the budgetary control process consists of two distinct elements:

(a)   **Planning** - This involves the setting of the various budgets for the appropriate future period. Management at the various levels in an organisation should be involved in the budgetary planning stage for its own area of responsibility. In many medium and large businesses this activity can take a considerable amount of time. There is a need to coordinate the budgets of the various parts of a business to ensure that they are all complementary and in line with overall company objectives and policies.

(b)   **Control** - Once the budgets have been set and agreed for the future period under review, the formal control element of budgetary control is ready to start.

This control involves the comparison of the plan in the form of the budget with the actual results achieved for the appropriate period. Any significant divergences between the budgeted and the actual results should be reported to the appropriate management so that the necessary action can be taken.

1.4   Benefits of budgetary control

(a)   **Planning** - budgetary control provides a formal framework for planning, which involves making sure that problems are anticipated and that steps are taken to avoid or reduce them.

(b)   **Coordination** - the system integrates budgets for the various sections of a business into a master budget for the whole business; individual managers will, therefore, recognise the overall objectives in forming their plans.

(c)   **Authorising and delegating** - approval of the master budget explicitly authorises the policy represented by the budget; by accepting their budgets, the responsibility for carrying out the policy is delegated to individual managers.

(d)   **Evaluating performance** - the budget represents a target against which the performance of managers can be assessed.

(e)   **Communicating and motivating** - preparing budgets involves communication between top management and lower levels on how to attain the objectives. Agreement motivates managers to achieve the targets set.

(f)   **Control** - continuous comparison of actual against plan indicates where control is needed.

1.5   Budget centres

Definition   A budget centre is a section of an entity for which control may be exercised and budgets prepared. **(CIMA Official Terminology)**.

A **budget centre** is a clearly defined part of an organisation for the purposes of operating a budgetary control system. Each function within an organisation will be sub-divided into appropriate budget centres. In determining budget centres it is important to be able to define them in terms of management responsibility. The manager responsible for a budget centre (eg, the machining department within the production function) will be involved in the planning stage of setting the budget for his area of responsibility and he will be the recipient of control information in due course.

1.6   Budget period

Definition   The **budget period** is the period for which a budget is prepared and used, which may then be subdivided into control periods. **(CIMA Official Terminology)**.

The length of a budget period will depend on:

(a)   **The nature of the business** - in the ship-building or power supply industries budget periods of ten to twenty years may be appropriate; periods of less than one year may be appropriate for firms in the clothing and fashion industries.

(b)   **The part of the business being budgeted** - capital expenditure will usually be budgeted for longer periods ahead than the production output.

(c)   **The basis of control** - many businesses use a twelve month period as their basic budget period, but at the same time it is very common to find the annual budget broken down into quarterly or monthly sub-units. Such a breakdown is usually for control purposes because actual and budgeted results need to be monitored continuously. It is not practicable to wait until the end of a twelve month budget period before making control comparisons.

2   BUDGET PREPARATION

2.1   How to budget - the seven steps

Preparation of the budget involves seven steps. These are illustrated diagrammatically below:

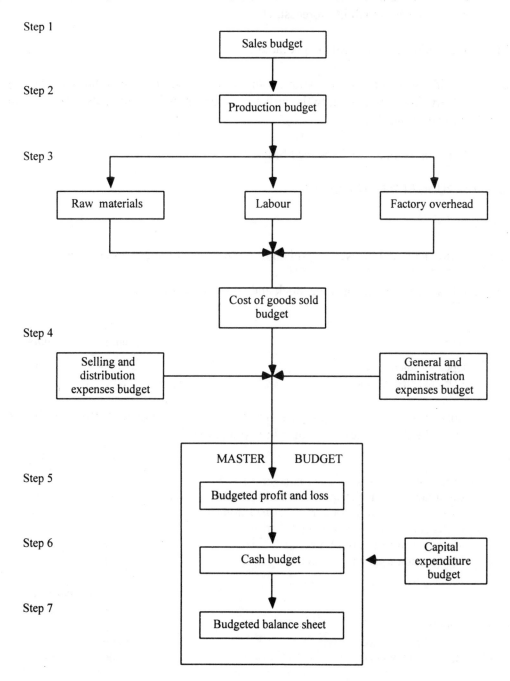

2.2   Principal budget factor

The sales budget is shown in the diagram because this is the pattern in most businesses, where it is the volume of the demand for the product which limits the scale of operation. It is possible, however, for there to be some other limiting factor eg, labour, material, cash or machinery. The limiting factor must be identified at the first stage of the budgeting process, since it will determine all the other budgets. In this context the limiting factor is referred to as the **principal budget factor.**

The budgeting process is, therefore, more fully described as follows:

(a)   Prepare:

- sales forecast;
- raw material availability forecast;
- cash availability forecast, etc.

(b)   Determine the principal budget factor.

(c)   Decide whether the limitations can be removed, and at what cost eg, by additional advertising expenditure, by intensive recruitment and training, etc. This is a matter for the budget committee.

(d)   Draw up budgets on the agreed basis.

3   MASTER BUDGET PREPARATION

3.1   Example

The following data will be used to explain the technique of budget preparation

Hash Ltd has the following opening stock and required closing stock.

	PS units	TG units
Opening stock	100	50
Required closing stock	1,100	50

You are also given the following data about the materials required to produce PS and TG and the Whittling and Fettling processes involved in production.

	PS	TG
Finished products:		
Kg of raw material X, per unit of finished product	12	12
Kg of raw material Y, per unit of finished product	6	8
Direct labour hours per unit of finished product	8	12
Machine hours per unit - Whittling	5	8
Machine hours per unit - Fettling	3	4

	Raw material X	Y
Direct materials:		
Desired closing stock in kg	6,000	1,000
Opening stock in kg	5,000	5,000

Standard rates and prices:

Direct labour	£2.20 per hour
Raw material X	£0.72 per kg
Raw material Y	£1.56 per kg

Production overheads:

Variable	£1.54 per labour hour
Fixed	£0.54 per labour hour
	£2.08 per labour hour

3.2   The sales budget

The sales budget represents the plan in terms of the quantity and value of sales, for sales management. In practice this is often the most difficult budget to calculate.

Hash Ltd makes two products - PS and TG. Sales for next year are budgeted at 5,000 units of PS and 1,000 units of TG. Planned selling prices are £65 and £100 respectively.

What is next year's sales budget?

The sales budget would be:

	Total	*PS*	*TG*
Sales units	6,000	5,000	1,000
Sales value	£425,000	£325,000	£100,000

In practice a business would market many more than two products. Moreover, the sales budget would probably be supported by subsidiary budgets to show analysis according to:

(a)   responsibility eg, Northern area, Western area, etc
(b)   type of customer eg, wholesale, retail, government, etc

3.3   The production budget

The production budget is usually expressed in quantity and represents the sales budget adjusted for opening/closing finished stocks and work in progress.

Production budget	*PS units*	*TG units*
Sales budget	5,000	1,000
Budgeted stock increase $(1,100 - 100)/(50 - 50)$	1,000	-
Production in units	6,000	1,000

The production budget needs to be translated into requirements for:

(a)   raw materials;
(b)   direct labour;
(c)   machine utilisation;
(d)   factory overheads;
(e)   closing stock levels.

3.4   The raw materials budget

(Remember that Hash Ltd is going to produce 6,000 units of PS and 1,000 units of TG.)

		X kg		Y kg
For production of PS	6,000 × 12 kg	72,000	6,000 × 6 kg	36,000
For production of TG	1,000 × 12 kg	12,000	1,000 × 8 kg	8,000
		84,000		44,000
Budgeted raw material stock increase/(decrease)	(6,000 – 5,000)	1,000	(1,000 – 5,000)	(4,000)
Raw materials required		85,000		40,000

		£	£
Budgeted value:			
X £0.72 per kg × 85,000		61,200	
Y £1.56 per kg × 40,000			62,400

3.5   The direct labour budget

		Hours		£
For PS	6,000 × 8 hrs	48,000		
For TG	1,000 × 12 hrs	12,000		
		60,000	@ £2.20	132,000

3.6   The machine utilisation budget

		Whittling hours		Fettling hours
For PS	6,000 × 5 hrs	30,000	6,000 × 3 hrs	18,000
For TG	1,000 × 8 hrs	8,000	1,000 × 4 hrs	4,000
		38,000		22,000
Total hours	=			60,000

3.7   Production overheads

		£
Variable costs	60,000 hours × £1.54	92,400
Fixed costs	60,000 hours × £0.54	32,400
		124,800

3.8   Opening and closing stocks

Remember that we are calculating the cost of sales. So far we have calculated the amounts of material, labour and overheads used in **production**. To arrive at the figures for cost of sales you have to remember that **production** is used not just for sales but also to increase/decrease stock levels - hence the need to adjust for the opening and closing stock position of both raw material and finished goods.

3.9   Closing stock of raw materials

		£
X	6,000 kg × £0.72	4,320
Y	1,000 kg × £1.56	1,560
		5,880

3.10   Closing stock of finished goods

		PS £		TG £
Standard cost of finished goods: Materials:				
X	12 kg × £0.72	8.64	12 kg × £0.72	8.64
Y	6 kg × £1.56	9.36	8 kg × £1.56	12.48
		18.00		21.12
Wages	8 hours × £2.20	17.60	12 hours × £2.20	26.40
Overhead	8 hours × £2.08	16.64	12 hours × £2.08	24.96
		52.24		72.48
Stock in units		1,100		50
Stock value		£57,464		£3,624

3.11   Activity

Calculate the values of the opening stocks of raw material and finished goods.

3.12   Activity solution

Raw material	X:	5,000 kg × £0.72	=	£3,600
Raw material	Y:	5,000 kg × £1.56	=	£7,800
Finished good	PS:	100 units × £52.24	=	£5,224
Finished good	TG:	50 units × £72.48	=	£3,624

3.13   Cost of sales budget

We can now bring all the above elements together.

	£	£
Opening stocks:		
Raw materials (3,600 + 7,800)	11,400	
Finished goods (5,224 + 3,624)	8,848	
		20,248
Raw materials (61,200 + 62,400)		123,600
Direct labour		132,000
Production overhead		124,800
		400,648
Less: Closing stocks:		
Raw materials	5,880	
Finished goods (57,464 + 3,624)	61,088	
		66,968
		333,680

3.14   Marketing and administration budget

Marketing and administration budgets will be a summary of the budget centres within those functions.

For the purposes of this example, the marketing/administration budget is assumed to be £45,000.

3.15   Budgeted profit and loss account

The budgeted profit and loss account is prepared by summarising the operating budgets.

Master budget - profit and loss account

	£	£
Sales		425,000
Cost of sales:		
Opening stocks	20,248	
Raw materials	123,600	
Direct labour	132,000	
Production overhead	124,800	
	400,648	
Closing stocks	66,968	
		333,680
Operating margin		91,320
Marketing/administration		45,000
Operating profit		46,320

Note: that the above budgets are presented to highlight planned requirements rather than for costing purposes. Most businesses will obviously be more complex than that illustrated and supporting analyses would be prepared as required eg,

> Production units by month or weeks
> Raw materials by supplier
> Direct labour by grade

3.16   Cash budgets

Cash budgets are illustrated later.

3.17   Budgeted balance sheet

The total company plan will include a statement to show the financial situation at the end of the budget period. Subsidiary budgets will be prepared to analyse movements in fixed and working capital during the budget period based on the operating budgets and reflecting financial policy formulated by the budget committee.

3.18   Other budgets - capital expenditure

Obtaining finance for investment and selecting capital investment projects are aspects of long-term planning which are outside the syllabus. The capital expenditure included in the master budget will essentially be an extract from the long-term capital budget.

The cash required to finance the capital expenditure will be incorporated in the cash budget as illustrated later.

3.19   Other miscellaneous budgets

Depending on the requirements of management, additional budgets may be prepared for:

(a)   **Purchasing** - consolidates purchases of raw materials, supplies and services in raw materials/expense budgets, analysed to show when the goods are received (for control of supply) and also when they are paid for (for cash budget).

(b)   **Personnel (manpower)** - shows detailed requirements, month by month, for production and administration personnel.

(c)   **Stocks** - itemises quantity and value, month by month, of planned stock levels for raw materials, work in progress and finished goods.

(d)   **Debtors** - details time analysis of collections from sales suitably analysed by type of customer or type of product.

4   CASH BUDGETS

4.1   Objectives of cash budgets

[Definition]   A cash budget is a detailed budget of cash inflows and outflows incorporating both revenue and capital items. **(CIMA Official Terminology).**

The objective of a cash budget is to anticipate cash shortages/surpluses and allow time to make plans for dealing with them.

4.2   Preparing a cash budget

(a)   Forecast sales.
(b)   Forecast time-lag on converting debtors to cash, and hence cash receipts.
(c)   Determine stock levels, and hence purchase requirements.
(d)   Forecast time-lag on paying suppliers, and thus cash payments.
(e)   Incorporate other cash payments and receipts, including such items as capital expenditure and tax payments.
(f)   Collate this information so as to find the net cash flows.

4.3   Layout of cash budget

A tabular layout should be used with columns for months and rows for receipts and payments.

4.4   Example

(a)   **Revenue budget (ie, trading and profit and loss account)**

Six months to 31 December (all revenue/costs accrue evenly over the six months):

	£'000	£'000
Sales (cash received one month in arrear)		1,200
Cost of sales:		
Paid one month in arrear	900	
Paid in month of purchase	144	
Depreciation	72	
	——	1,116
Budgeted profit		84

(b)   **Capital budget**

	£'000	£'000
Payments for new plant:		
July	12	
August	25	
September	13	
November	50	
	—	100
Increase in stocks, payable August		20
		120
Receipts: New issue of share capital (October)		30

(c)   **Balance sheet**

	Actual 1 July £'000
Assets side:	
Fixed assets	720
Stocks	100
Debtors	210
Cash	40
	1,070
Liabilities side:	
Capital and reserves	856
Taxation (payable December)	30
Creditors - trade	160
Dividends (payable August)	24
	1,070

Prepare a cash budget for the six months to 31 December.

4.5   Solution

Cash budget for six months to 31 December

	Jul £'000	Aug £'000	Sep £'000	Oct £'000	Nov £'000	Dec £'000	Total £'000
Receipts:							
Sales	210	200	200	200	200	200	1,210
New issue of share capital	-	-	-	30	-	-	30
Payments:							
Exps & purchases	160	150	150	150	150	150	910
Exps & purchases	24	24	24	24	24	24	144
Plant	12	25	13	-	50	-	100
Stock	-	20	-	-	-	-	20
Tax	-	-	-	-	-	30	30
Dividends	-	24	-	-	-	-	24
	196	243	187	174	224	204	1,228
Surplus/(deficiency)	14	(43)	13	56	(24)	(4)	12
Opening balance	40	54	11	24	80	56	40
Closing balance	54	11	24	80	56	52	52

4.6   Reconciliation of profit and cashflow

The cash budget prepared above shows that the balance at bank has increased from £40,000 at the beginning of July to £52,000 at the end of December, an increase of £12,000. During the same period the revenue budget shows a profit of £84,000. Why is there a difference of £72,000?

There are two broad categories of causes of difference between profits and cashflow:

- items which are **not** included in both budgets; and
- differences in timing which affect profit/cashflow comparisons over a specific period.

Examples of items which do not appear in both budgets include:

- payments for new plant;
- receipts from the issue of share capital;
- payments of dividends; and
- payments of taxation.

These are not included in the statement of budgeted profit.

In addition, depreciation does not appear in the cash budget, it is a cost which reflects a cashflow which occurred in the past when the asset was acquired.

Examples of timing differences include changes in the levels of:

- stocks;
- debtors; and
- creditors

during the period.

We will now explain the difference of £72,000 referred to earlier, but first we need to calculate the changes in the levels of stocks, debtors, and creditors.

(a)   **Stock**

There is a stock increase of £20,000 in August shown in the capital budget.

(b)   **Debtors**

	£'000
The opening debtors (per balance sheet - 1 July)	210
Sales are paid one month in arrear so closing debtors at 31 December equal December sales	200
A reduction of	10

(c)   **Creditors**

	£'000
The opening creditors (per balance sheet 1 July)	160
Closing creditors represent December cost of sales paid one month in arrears	150
A reduction of	10

(d)   **The reconciliation**

	£'000	£'000	£'000
Profit as per revenue budget			84
Add: Non-cashflow item:			
Depreciation			72
			156
Adjust for timing differences:			
Increase in level of stock		(20)	
Decrease in level of debtors		10	
Decrease in level of creditors		(10)	
			(20)
			136
Adjust for cashflows not affecting profit:			
Receipts: New share capital		30	
Payments: Plant	(100)		
Taxation	(30)		
Dividends	(24)		
		(154)	
			(124)
Increase in cash balance			12

4.7   Activity

The budgeted sales for an organisation are as follows:

	Jan £	Feb £	March £	April £
Sales	600	800	400	500

These are all sales on credit and debtors tend to pay in the following pattern.

	%
In month of sale	10
In month after sale	40
Two months after sale	45

The organisation expects a bad debt rate of 5%

What are the budgeted cash receipts from debtors in April?

4.8   Activity solution

	£
April sales 10% × 500	50
March sales 40% × 400	160
February sales 45% × 800	360
	570

4.9 Activity

You are given the following budgeted information about an organisation.

	Jan	*Feb*	*March*
Opening stock in units	100	150	120
Closing stock in units	150	120	180
Sales in units	400	450	420

The cost of materials is £2 per unit and 40% of purchases are for cash whilst 60% are on credit and are paid two months after the purchase. What are the payments for purchases in March?

4.10 Activity solution

Purchases in units	*Jan*	*Feb*	*March*
Sales	400	450	420
Less: Opening stock	(100)	(150)	(120)
Add: Closing stock	150	120	180
Production in units	450	420	480
	£	£	£
Purchases	900	840	960

Payment in March

	£
March purchases (960 × 40%)	384
January purchases (900 × 60%)	540
	924

5 FLEXIBLE BUDGETING

5.1 Contrast with fixed budgets

As individuals we tend to think of budgets as imposing ceilings on expenditure. This is not necessarily the most useful approach to business budgeting. To apply such a budget rigidly would mean, for example, turning down sales opportunities because the budget sets a ceiling on raw materials purchases.

In the business context the budget, will providing output targets, should also be able to cope with variations between actual and budgeted output. In particular it should continue to provide useful control information at different output levels.

So far only fixed (or static) budgets have been considered. Now it is necessary to consider how budgets can be developed and used to cope with varying output levels - flexible budgets.

Definition A flexible budget is a budget which, by recognising different cost behaviour patterns, is designed to change as volume of activity changes. **(CIMA Official Terminology).**

5.2   Activity

Distinguish between a fixed cost and a variable cost.

5.3   Activity solution

(a)   **Fixed** - no variation as volume varies (within the relevant range).
(b)   **Variable** - varies directly with volume.

This distinction is important in setting up flexible budgets.   One needs to know into which behaviour pattern individual costs fall.

5.4   The need for flexible budgets

The twin concepts of responsibility reporting and management by exception require reporting to managers when actual results for items under their control deviate from planned results.

[Definition]   Management by exception is the practice of focusing on activities which require attention and ignoring those which appear to be conforming to expectations. **(CIMA Official Terminology)**.

Many of the costs for which a manager is responsible are variable costs.   Since total variable cost is by definition dependent on the level of activity, a means must be found of eliminating that part of a cost variance which is due to activity level changes, so as to isolate the aspects of total variable cost for which the individual manager is responsible.   The key points to note are:

(a)   an original budget is set at the beginning of the period based on estimated production;
(b)   this is then **flexed** to correspond with the actual level of activity;
(c)   the result is compared with actual monetary costs and revenue, and differences (variances) are reported to the managers responsible.

5.5   Calculation of budget variances

The following example illustrates the comparison of actual and budget results firstly using a fixed budget and then using a flexible budget.

The differences between the budget and actual values are known as variances.   Where they relate to costs, if the actual cost is less than the budget cost the variance is described as favourable, if the actual cost is greater the variance is said to be adverse.

Bug Ltd manufactures one uniform product only and activity levels in the assembly department vary widely from month to month.   The following statement shows the departmental overhead budget based on an average level of activity of 20,000 units production per four week period, and the actual results for four weeks in October:

	Budget average for four week period £	Actual for 1 to 28 October £
Indirect labour - variable	20,000	19,540
Consumables - variable	800	1,000
Other variable overhead	4,200	3,660
Depreciation - fixed	10,000	10,000
Other fixed overhead	5,000	5,000
	40,000	39,200
Production (units)	20,000	17,600

You are required to

(a)   prepare a columnar flexible four week budget at 16,000, 20,000 and 24,000 unit levels of production;

(b)   prepare two performance reports, based on production of 17,600 units by the department in October comparing actual with:

(i)   average four week budget; and
(ii)   flexed four week budget for 17,600 units of production.

5.6   Solution

(a)

Production level (units)	16,000	20,000	24,000
	£	£	£
Variable costs:			
Indirect labour	16,000	20,000	24,000
Consumables	640	800	960
Other	3,360	4,200	5,040
	20,000	25,000	30,000
Fixed costs:			
Depreciation	10,000	10,000	10,000
Other	5,000	5,000	5,000
Total costs	35,000	40,000	45,000

(b)   (i)

	Average four week budget £	Actual results £	Variances favourable/ (adverse) £
Indirect labour	20,000	19,540	460
Consumables	800	1,000	(200)
Other variable	4,200	3,660	540
Depreciation	10,000	10,000	-
Other fixed	5,000	5,000	-
	40,000	39,200	800

(ii)

	Flexed four week budget £	Actual results £	Variances favourable/ (adverse) £
Sales (units)	17,600	17,600	-
	£	£	£
Indirect labour	17,600	19,540	(1,940)
Consumables	704	1,000	(296)
Other variable	3,696	3,660	36
Depreciation	10,000	10,000	-
Other fixed	5,000	5,000	-
	37,000	39,200	(2,200)

5.7 Activity

Decide which comparison, (b)(i) or (b)(ii) is more useful in assessing the foreman's effectiveness and why?

5.8 Activity solution

Clearly the flexed budget provides more useful data for comparison because:

(a)   the **fixed** budget makes no distinction between fixed and variable costs;

(b)   hence no data is available about the appropriate level of costs at the actual production level;

(c)   this would lead to the conclusion that the foreman had done well when in fact costs had not fallen as much as anticipated for the actual production;

(d)   responsibility for the production shortfall is not known.

5.9 The choice between fixed and flexible budgets

Despite these advantages of flexible budgets, many companies use fixed budgets for the following reasons:

(a)   flexible budgets involve more work, and hence are more expensive to operate;

(b)   in many businesses costs are largely fixed over the budget period - this tends to be particularly true in service industries.

| Conclusion | It should not therefore be automatically assumed that flexible budgets should be employed. The value of the additional information should be balanced against the incremental costs as compared to fixed budgeting.

6 USING COMPUTERS IN BUDGETING

6.1 The budgeting exercise

The nature of the budgeting exercise, as shown by the example earlier in this chapter, is that many of the resulting final values are dependent on the estimate made of sales units together with a few policy decisions (for example stockholding policies, payment period policies).

It is also true to say that budgets are a planning device designed to assist in the achievement of an organisation's longer term plans.

These two factors have the following consequences:-

(a)   there are likely to be a number of alterations made to the first draft of the budget to see the effects of such changes; and

(b)   the alteration of one value will cause many other values to alter.

It is these factors which have led to the preparation of budgets being computerised using spreadsheet packages.

6.2 Spreadsheets

The examiner has stated that you will not need to be able to formulate a spreadsheet in the 'detailed technical sense' - you will only require a general knowledge of the principles. We include here sufficient material to illustrate the principles. A spreadsheet is a computer package which stores data in a matrix format where the intersection of each row and column is referred to as a cell. Columns are referenced alphabetically and rows numerically with the result that a cell reference is a combination of these. This is illustrated below:

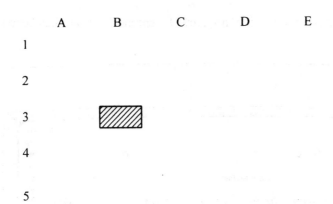

The reference of the shaded cell is B3 because it is the intersection of column B and row 3.

Each cell within a spreadsheet may be used to store:

(a) a label (description) eg, the title of the spreadsheet;
(b) a value; or
(c) a formula.

The formula is used to carry out calculations on values entered in other parts of the spreadsheet.

Chapter 16 looks at formulae in spreadsheets in greater depth.

6.3 Spreadsheets and budgeting

It has been explained earlier that the final budget results are dependent on the values entered for sales units and other factors. In addition there will be a number of alterations made to the initial budget before it is finalised. The use of a spreadsheet therefore allows these alterations to be made accurately and very quickly by the use of formulae. This is often referred to as 'What If' analysis.

A simple example of the use of a spreadsheet to prepare a production budget is shown below.

Example

X Ltd has estimated its sales for 19X5 to be 5,000 units, and sales for 19X6 are expected to be 6,000 units.

X Ltd's stockholding policy is to hold 10% of next years sales in stock at the end of the current year.

The spreadsheet would appear:

	A	B	C
1	Sales Units	5000	6000
2	Closing stock	C1*0.1	
3	Opening stock	B1*0.1	
4	Production	+B1+B2−B3	
5			

Note how an alteration to the input sales unit values in row 1 would automatically alter the results of the formulae in the other cells.

This example could be extended to include costs and revenues and to finally produce a master budget which is linked by the use of formulae to the basic data. In the example below, we show how a spreadsheet can be used to construct a cash budget.

6.4 Example of a cash budget

The following worksheet illustrates a screen showing part of a spreadsheet that has been set up for a cash budget.

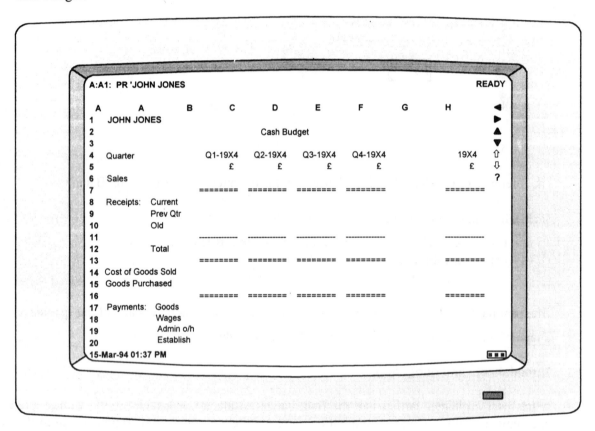

It is not the purpose of this examination or text to teach you how to use a spreadsheet. The following therefore simply attempts to give a good overview of how a spreadsheet can be used to produce part of a cash budget.

(a) Quarterly sales

Sales are expected to be £60,000 in quarter 1, increasing in volume by 10% per quarter.

Thus insert £60,000 in C6. A formula can then be inserted into D6:

+C6*1.1

This can be copied into E6 to G6 using:

/ C(opy) D6 ↵ E6..G6 ↵

The figures for quarters 2-4 should be:

£66,000, £72,600, £79,860 (and £87,846 for the first quarter of 19X5 which will be needed to find purchases below. This 19X5 quarter is shown in column G.)

Total sales revenue (@SUM(C6..F6)) is £278,460.

(b)   **Receipts**

50% of sales are expected to be received in the quarter that the sale is made, 40% is received one quarter later and 10% received two quarters later.)

The formulae: for cell F8 will be   F6*0.5

for cell F9 will be   E6*0.4

for cell F10 will be   D6*0.1

These can be copied into rows C, D and E.

In cells H8..H10 an @SUM function is required to add the total of columns C to F. In row 12 the three elements of receipts can be totalled. The result is shown below.

```
A:F10: U +D6/10                                                          READY

      A        A        B       C        D        E        F      G       H       ◄
 1  JOHN JONES                                                                    ►
 2                                      Cash Budget                               ▲
 3                                                                                ▼
 4  Quarter                          Q1-19X4  Q2-19X4  Q3-19X4  Q4-19X4    19X4   ⇧
 5                                        £        £        £        £       £    ⇩
 6  Sales                             60,000   66,000   72,600   79,860  87,846  278,460  ?
 7                                    ======== ======== ======== ========         ========
 8  Receipts: Current                30,000   33,000   36,300   39,930          139,230
 9            Prev Qtr                    0   24,000   26,400   29,040           79,440
10            Old                         0        0    6,000    6,600           12,600
11                                   -------- -------- -------- --------         --------
12            Total                  30,000   57,000   68,700   75,570          231,270
13                                   ======== ======== ======== ========         ========
14  Cost of Goods Sold
15  Goods Purchased
16                                   ======== ======== ======== ========         ========
17  Payments: Goods
18            Wages
19            Admin o/h
20            Establish
15-Mar-94 01:47 PM                                                         ▪▪▪
```

(c)   **Cost of sales and purchases**

The company will use a mark up on cost of 60%. 1½ months stock is to be held, therefore purchases in a quarter will correspond to 50% of the current quarter's cost of sales plus 50% of the next quarter's, the exception being quarter 1 of 19X4 when sufficient goods will be purchased to satisfy the next 4½ months.

The formula for cell C14 can be worked out by looking at the cost structure:

Cost of goods sold	+	profit	=	sales revenue
100	+	60	=	160

Cost of goods sold are $\dfrac{100}{160}$ times sales revenue.

The formula for cell C14 is:

+C6*100/160

When this is copied into rows D to G, the figures that appear are:

£37,500, £41,250, £45,375, £49,912.5 (and £54,903.75)

The cost of goods purchased shown in cell C15 must be:

+C14+D14/2

However in D15 (and copied into E and F) will be:

+D14/2 + E14/2

The totals can be shown in row H. The total of the Cost of Goods Sold is £174,037.50 (£278,460 × $\frac{100}{160}$) and of Goods Purchased £201,489.4.

(d)   **Payments for goods**

Assume that 50% of purchases in each quarter are paid for in the quarter in which the purchases were made and 50% in the following quarter.

A similar approach can be adopted as for receipts by entering a formula in cell C17:

+C15/2 + B15/2

This can be copied into cells D17..F17 and the row summed to give the following worksheet.

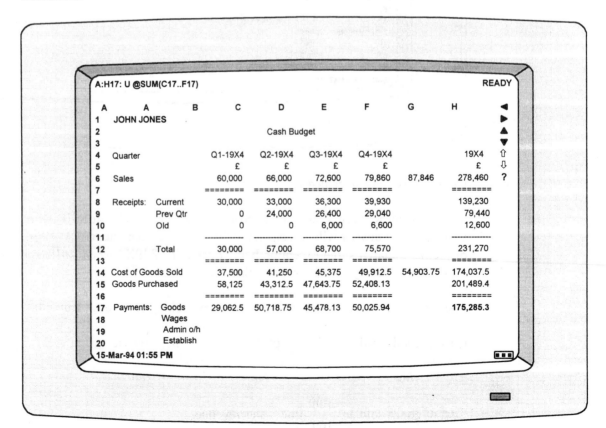

```
A:H17: U @SUM(C17..F17)                                              READY

   A        A        B       C        D        E        F       G        H
1  JOHN JONES
2                                   Cash Budget
3
4  Quarter             Q1-19X4  Q2-19X4  Q3-19X4  Q4-19X4          19X4
5                         £        £        £        £              £
6  Sales                60,000   66,000   72,600   79,860  87,846  278,460
7                      ======== ======== ======== ========        ========
8  Receipts: Current   30,000   33,000   36,300   39,930          139,230
9           Prev Qtr        0   24,000   26,400   29,040           79,440
10          Old             0        0    6,000    6,600           12,600
11                    -------- -------- -------- --------          --------
12          Total      30,000   57,000   68,700   75,570          231,270
13                    ======== ======== ======== ========        ========
14 Cost of Goods Sold  37,500   41,250   45,375  49,912.5 54,903.75 174,037.5
15 Goods Purchased     58,125  43,312.5 47,643.75 52,408.13       201,489.4
16                    ======== ======== ======== ========        ========
17 Payments: Goods    29,062.5 50,718.75 45,478.13 50,025.94      175,285.3
18           Wages
19           Admin o/h
20           Establish
15-Mar-94 01:55 PM
```

7   CHAPTER SUMMARY

The process of budgeting is an important management tool. The preparation of budgets assists in the planning activities of the organisation and by the use of flexed budgets comparison of actual and budgeted results can assist in the control of operations.

8   SELF TEST QUESTIONS

8.1   What is a budget? (1.1)

8.2   What is budgetary control? (1.1)

8.3   What are the benefits of budgetary control? (1.4)

8.4   What is a budget centre? (1.5)

8.5   What are the factors that will affect the length of a budget period? (1.6)

8.6   What is a limiting factor? (2.2)

8.7   What is a cash budget? (4.1)

8.8   How should a cash budget be laid out? (4.3)

8.9   What is a flexible budget? (5.1)

8.10   What is a flexed budget? (5.4)

9   EXAMINATION TYPE QUESTION

9.1   S Ltd

S Ltd manufactures three products - A, C and E - in two production departments - F and G - each of which employs two grades of labour. The cost accountant is preparing the annual budgets for Year 2 and he has asked you as his assistant to prepare, using the data given below:

(a)   the production budget in units for Products A, C and E;

(b)   the direct wages budget for Departments F and G with the labour costs of Products A, C and E and totals shown separately.

Data

	Total		Product	
		A	C	E
		£'000	£'000	£'000
Finished stocks:				
Budgeted stocks are:				
1 January, year 2		720	540	1,800
31 December, year 2		600	570	1,000
All stocks are valued at standard cost per unit		£24	£15	£20
Standard profit:				
Calculated as percentage of selling price		20%	25%	$16\frac{2}{3}$%

	£'000	£'000	£'000	£'000
Budgeted sales:				
South	6,600	1,200	1,800	3,600
Midlands	5,100	1,500	1,200	2,400
North	6,380	1,500	800	4,080
	18,080	4,200	3,800	10,080
Normal loss in production		10%	20%	5%

Standard labour times per unit and standard rates per hour	Rate £	Hours per unit	Hours per unit	Hours per unit
Department F:				
Grade 1	1.80	1.00	1.50	0.50
Grade 2	1.60	1.25	1.00	0.75
Department G:				
Grade 1	2.00	1.50	0.50	0.50
Grade 2	1.80	1.00	0.75	1.25

(15 marks)

10   ANSWER TO EXAMINATION TYPE QUESTION

10.1   S Ltd

(a)   **Production budget**

	Product		
	A	C	E
	000 units	000 units	000 units
Sales (W1)	140	190	420
Stock increase/(decrease) (W2)	(5)	2	(40)
Production required	135	192	380
Add: Excess to cover normal loss (W3)	15	48	20
Production budget	150	240	400

(b)   **Direct wages budget**

	Product						
	A		C		E		Total
	000 hours	£'000	000 hours	£'000	000 hours	£'000	£'000
Department F:							
Grade 1 (@ £1.80/hr)	150	270	360	648	200	360	1,278
Grade 2 (@ £1.60/hr)	187.5	180	240	384	300	480	1,044
		450		1,032		840	2,322
Department G:							
Grade 1 (@ £2.00/hr)	225	450	120	240	200	400	1,090
Grade 2 (@ £1.80/hr)	150	270	180	324	500	900	1,494
		720		564		1,300	2,584
Total budget		1,170		1,596		2,140	4,906

Note: Hours budgeted represent production budget units at standard labour times.

WORKINGS

(1)   Sales units $= \dfrac{\text{Budgeted sales value}}{\text{Standard selling price}}$

   A $= \dfrac{4,200}{24 \times \dfrac{100}{80}}$

   $=$ 140 units

   B $= \dfrac{3,800}{15 \times \dfrac{100}{75}}$

   $=$ 190 units

   C $= \dfrac{10,080}{20 \times \dfrac{100}{83.33}}$

   $=$ 420 units.

(2)   Stock units $= \dfrac{\text{Budgeted stock value}}{\text{Standard unit costs}}$

	Opening units	*Closing units*	*Increase/ (decrease) units*
A	30	25	(5)
B	36	38	2
C	90	50	(40)

(3)   Additional requirements to cover normal loss of production:

   $\text{Required production} \times \dfrac{\text{Loss percentage}}{\text{Normal production percentage}}$

   ie,   Product A $135 \times \dfrac{10}{90}$ $=$ 15

   Product C $192 \times \dfrac{20}{80}$ $=$ 48

   Product E $380 \times \dfrac{5}{95}$ $=$ 20

12 COST ESTIMATION

INTRODUCTION & LEARNING OBJECTIVES

Syllabus area 2c. Cost estimation and estimating techniques. (Ability required 3).

When you have studied this chapter you should be able to do the following:

- Recognise the need to estimate costs.

- Use past cost data to predict future costs.

- Recognise the limitations of using linear assumptions concerning costs.

- Recognise the importance of the relevant range.

---

1 COST PREDICTION

1.1 Introduction

The use of cost behaviour described in the previous sections rests on being able to predict costs associated with a given level of activity. Such data is not available from traditional cost analysis, and alternative approaches must be used. In this process historical information provides valuable guidance, but it must be recognised that the environment is not static, and what was relevant in the past may not be relevant in the future.

Five main approaches may be identified:

(a)   the engineering approach;
(b)   the account analysis approach;
(c)   the high-low (or range) method;
(d)   scatter charts; and
(e)   regression analysis.

In all of these approaches the assumption is made that the linear model of cost behaviour is valid, and therefore the relation between costs, y, and activity, x, is the form:

$$y = a + bx$$

Where y = total costs
          x = activity
          a = fixed costs
          b = unit variable (or marginal) cost

These five approaches are considered below, followed by the possibility of making less restrictive assumptions about cost behaviour.

1.2   The engineering approach

This approach is based on building up a complete specification of all inputs (eg, materials, labour, overheads) required to produce given levels of output. This approach is therefore based on technical specification, which is then costed out using expected input prices.

This approach works reasonably well in a single product or start-up situation - indeed in the latter it may be the only feasible approach. However, it is difficult to apply in a multi-product situation, especially where there are joint costs, or the exact output mix is not known.

1.3   The account analysis approach

Rather than using the technical information, this approach uses the information contained in the ledger accounts. These are analysed and categorised as either fixed or variable (or semi-fixed or semi-variable). Thus, for example, material purchase accounts would represent variable costs, office salaries at fixed cost. Since the ledger accounts are not designed for use in this way, some reorganisation and reclassification of accounts may be required.

Students should note that this is the approach implicit in many examination questions.

The problems with this approach are several:

(a)   Inspection does not always indicate the true nature of costs. For example, today factory wages would normally be a fixed cost, with only overtime and/or bonuses as the variable element.

(b)   Accounts are by their nature summaries, and often contain transactions of different categories.

(c)   It rests on historic information with the problems noted above.

1.4   High low (or range) method

This and the next two methods that follow are based on an analysis of historic information on costs at different activity levels. Students should relate the methods used to their studies of the statistical techniques being applied. To illustrate the methods the data below will be used as an example.

Example

A company wishes to establish the cost equation for its product inspection costs.

The data for the six months to 31 December 19X8 is as follows:

Month	Units	Total inspection cost
		£
July	340	2,260
August	300	2,160
September	380	2,320
October	420	2,400
November	400	2,300
December	360	2,266

The variable element of a cost item may be estimated by calculating the unit cost between high and low volumes during a period.

Six months to 31/12/X8	Units produced	Inspection costs
		£
Highest month	420	2,400
Lowest month	300	2,160
Range	120	240

The additional cost per unit between high and low is $\dfrac{£240}{120 \text{ units}} = £2$ per unit

which may be estimated as the variable content of inspection costs. Fixed inspection costs are, therefore:

$$£2,400 - (420 \times £2) = £1,560 \text{ per month}$$
$$\text{or} \quad £2,160 - (300 \times £2) = £1,560 \text{ per month.}$$

ie, the relationship is of the form $y = £(1,560 + 2x)$.

The limitations of the high low method are:

(a)   Its reliance on historic data, assuming that (i) activity is the only factor affecting costs and (ii) historic costs reliably predict future costs.

(b)   The use of only two values, the highest and the lowest, means that the results may be distorted due to random variations in these values.

1.5   Activity

Use the high-low points method to calculate the fixed and variable elements of the following cost:

	Activity	£
January	400	1,050
February	600	1,700
March	550	1,600
April	800	2,100
May	750	2,000
June	900	2,300

1.6   Activity solution

		£
High	900	2,300
Low	(400)	(1,050)
	500	1,250

Variable cost = £1,250/500 = £2.50/unit

Fixed cost = £1,050 − (400 × £2.50) = £50.

1.7   Scatter charts

If the data from the example was plotted on a graph, the result would be a scatter chart of inspections costs.

Scatter chart showing the relationship between total inspection costs and output

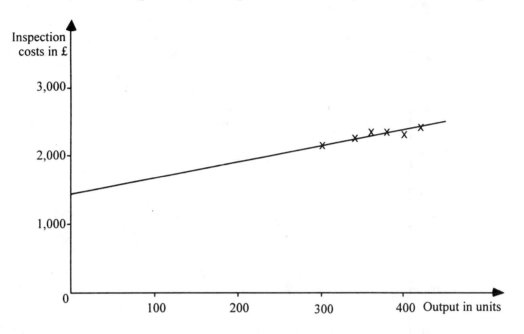

The **line of best fit** (a line which passes through the plotted points to equalise the number of points on each side and the aggregate distance from the line) may be drawn as accurately as possible by inspection. The point at which that line cuts the vertical axis indicates the fixed cost (about £1,460 in the illustration).

Scatter charts suffer from the general limitations of using historic data referred to above. In addition, their problem is that the estimate of the best linear relationship between the data is subjective. Finally, it should be noted that this can only be converted into a mathematical relationship by actual measurement.

1.8   Activity

Plot the data points from the previous activity on a scatter graph and draw a line of best fit to find the fixed cost. Measure the gradient of the line to determine the variable cost.

1.9 Activity solution

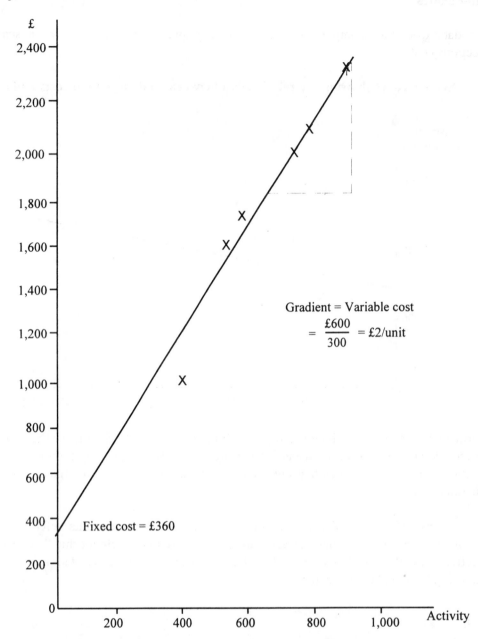

Gradient = Variable cost

$$= \frac{£600}{300} = £2/\text{unit}$$

Fixed cost = £360

1.10 Regression analysis

Regression analysis is a technique for estimating the line of best fit, given a series of data of the type in the example above. It is essentially a statistical technique, and is fully covered later in this text (Chapter 27).

1.11 Limitations of using predicted costs

The cost accountant must be careful when using analysis of historical costs as a basis for predicting future costs. This is true even if he is fully satisfied with the accuracy of the analysis. The reasons are:

(a)   It is difficult and costly to obtain sufficient data to be confident that a representative sample is used.

(b)   Prediction implies a continuing relationship of costs to volume. In practice, methods and efficiency change.

(c) The relationship between costs and volume may be obscured by time-lags, eg recruiting trainee labour in anticipation of increased production.

(d) Factors other than volume of production can influence costs, eg, purchasing in small lots could increase handling and incidental material costs.

(e) Prices of the input factors may change, eg, due to inflation or technical change.

(f) The analysis is based on the assumption that the cost/activity relationship is linear.

1.12 Comparison of accountant's and economist's cost behaviour models

The analysis above has been based on the accountant's model of cost behaviour patterns. This assumes that unit variable cost equals marginal cost. Indeed the CIMA thus defines marginal cost - 'the part of the cost of one unit of a product or service which would be avoided if that unit were not produced'. Thus, the unit marginal cost is a constant, and unit marginal and total costs can be presented thus:

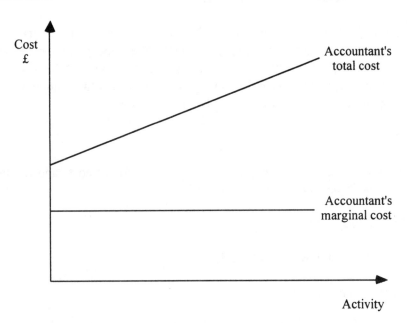

This contrasts with traditional economist's model of cost behaviour:

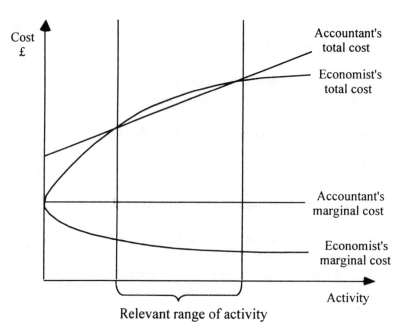

Relevant range of activity

It is apparent that though these represent cost behaviour patterns in different ways, over the 'relevant range' of activity they are substantially similar. The concept of the relevant range is intended to represent the range of activity levels within which management decisions are normally made. Therefore for practical management decision making the accountant's approximation may be regarded as a working approximation to actual cost behaviour patterns.

2   CHAPTER SUMMARY

This chapter has shown how past costs may be used to predict future costs and the limitations of using assumptions to enable such predictions to be made.

3   SELF ASSESSMENT QUESTIONS

3.1   Briefly explain the high low method. (1.4)

3.2   What is a scatter chart? (1.7)

3.3   Explain 'the relevant range'. (1.12)

13 STANDARD COSTING

INTRODUCTION & LEARNING OBJECTIVES

Syllabus area 2c. Principles of standard costs. (Ability required 2).

Preparation of a standard product cost. (Ability required 3).

Variances: materials - total, price and usage; labour - total, rate and efficiency; overheads - total. (Ability required 3).

In this chapter a particular form of budgetary control system known as standard costing will be considered. This is a method of analysing the elements that make up the difference between actual operating profit and budgeted operating profit.

When you have studied this chapter you should be able to do the following:

- Understand the meaning of standards and how they are set.

- Understand the purpose of variance analysis.

- Be able to calculate total cost variances for materials, labour and overheads.

- Be able to calculate price and usage variances for materials.

- Be able to calculate rate and efficiency variances for labour.

- Be able to discuss the use of standards in the modern industrial environment.

---

1 STANDARD COST

1.1 Principles of standard cost

A standard cost is used as a means of providing a target cost per unit which may be compared with the actual results which occur.

This comparison seeks to identify the causes of the differences and report them to the manager responsible. For this reason standard costing is usually regarded as part of a responsibility accounting system.

1.2 Standard cost

Definition   A standard cost is the planned unit cost of the products, components or services produced in a period (**CIMA Official Terminology**).

Standard costing is a specific approach to budgetary control. It involves setting budget targets, or 'standards' for each cost element per unit of production. Typically these will be in the form of a Standard Cost Card.

```
┌─────────────────────────────────────────────────────────────────────┐
│                          Standard Cost Card                            │
│                           Cost per Budget                              │
│                                                              £          │
│   Raw materials:      5 kgs P @ £2/kg                     10.00        │
│                       3 kgs Q @ £1.5/kg                    4.50        │
│                                                                        │
│   Labour              4 hrs grade A @ £4/hr              16.00         │
│                       1 hr grade B @ £5.50/hr             5.50         │
│                                                          ──────        │
│   Total                                                  36.00         │
│                                                          ──────        │
└─────────────────────────────────────────────────────────────────────┘
```

These standard costs are used as a basis of comparison with actual results.

1.3   Standard costing in budgetary control

Historically, standard costing evolved as a parallel system to budgetary control, representing a different approach to the problem. Today, standard costing has become a subset of budgetary control, and is commonly used within an organisation as part of a budgetary control system.

Nevertheless, it is important to identify three factors that differentiate standard costing from other approaches to budgetary control:

(1)   Under standard costing, for costing purposes all stocks are valued at their standard costs.

(2)   Standard costs are incorporated in the ledger accounts; budgets are a memorandum record outside the ledger accounts.

(3)   Standard costs are set as unit costs; budgets tend to be set as total costs.

Thus although standard costing is a subset of budgeting, it has certain distinct features of its own. For these reasons it tends to be studied as a separate subject.

1.4   Setting standards

In general, a standard cost will be set for each product, comprising:

(a)   **Direct materials:** Standard quantity (kgs, litres etc) × Standard price per unit (kg, litre etc).

(b)   **Direct wages:** Standard labour hours × Standard hourly rate.

(c)   **Variable overhead:** Standard hours (labour or machine) × Standard rate per hour.

(d)   **Fixed overhead:** Budgeted overhead for the period ÷ Budgeted standard hours (labour or machine) for the period.

1.5   Standard - definition

> **Definition**   A standard is a benchmark measurement of resource usage, set in defined conditions. **(CIMA Official Terminology)**.

The term implies a fixed relationship which is assumed to hold good for the budget period or until it is deliberately revised. By the use of standards one measurement can be converted into another. When it is said that a journey of 90 miles from A to B takes three hours, a standard speed under prevailing traffic conditions of 30 miles per hour is assumed. It is thus possible to express distance in hours.

Therefore, if our standard speed of production is 50 items per hour, a transfer of 5,000 items into finished store may be said to represent 100 hours of work. Again, if the standard cost of raw materials is £2.50 per lb and the standard usage per item is 2 lb, the 5,000 items may be regarded either as representing 10,000 lb of raw material or as having a raw material content of £25,000.

A standard cost is calculated in relation to a prescribed set of working conditions, ie, it reflects technical specifications and scientific measurement of the resources used to manufacture a product.

Standard costs represent target costs. As such they represent costs which are most likely to be useful for:

(a)   planning;

(b)   control;

(c)   motivation.

However carefully costs are predetermined (and one authority has referred to them as 'scientifically' predetermined costs), in the end they must be **somebody's** best estimate.

Nevertheless in one sense standard costs go beyond a best estimate: standard costs have been adopted as the firm's target - they become a statement of policy. For this reason it is necessary to think carefully about what sort of standards should be set.

> **Conclusion**   Standard costing can help an organisation in the planning and control of its operation and motivation of its staff.

1.6   Bases for standards

Three possible bases for setting standards are given below. These should be set against the three objectives above:

(a)   **Based on past achievements:** useful for control since a comparison is made with previous performance. Less useful for planning since the future is unlikely to reproduce the past, and counter-productive in terms of motivation.

(b)   **Ideal standard:** the theoretically best possible performance. Of some use for control because reasons for shortfalls can be isolated, but not suitable for planning because too optimistic. Neither are they likely to be useful for motivation since they will be recognised as unrealistic - and therefore ignored.

(c)   **High but attainable:** most commonly used in practice. They are suitable for planning (they are attainable), for control (a high standard) and for motivation (high but attainable). However, there is an inherent conflict in such standards between the questions 'how high?' and 'how attainable?'.

1.7   The standard hour

Output is often measured in terms of standard hours.

> **Definition**   A standard hour is the amount of work achievable, at standard efficiency levels, in an hour. **(CIMA Official Terminology).**

Thus, if 50 articles are estimated to be made in a 'clock' hour, an output of 150 should take three 'clock' hours and would be valued at the standard cost of those three hours, irrespective of the actual time taken to manufacture them.

1.8 Example

A factory in week 1 had an activity level of 120% with the following output:

	Units	Standard minutes each
Product F	5,100	6
Product C	2,520	10
Product A	3,150	12

The budgeted direct labour cost for budgeted output was £2,080.

You are required to calculate:

(a) budgeted standard hours;

(b) budgeted labour cost per standard hour.

1.9 Solution

(a) Actual standard hours produced were:

Product F	$5,100 \times \dfrac{6}{60} =$	510
Product C	$2,520 \times \dfrac{10}{60} =$	420
Product A	$3,150 \times \dfrac{12}{60} =$	630
		——
		1,560
		——

representing 120% of budgeted standard hours ie,

$$\text{Budgeted standard hours} = 1,560 \times \frac{100}{120} \quad = \quad 1,300$$

(b) Budgeted labour cost per standard hour $\quad = \quad \dfrac{\text{Budgeted cost}}{\text{Budgeted standard hours}}$

$$= \quad \frac{£2,080}{1,300}$$

$$= \quad £1.60 \text{ per hour.}$$

2 BASIC COST VARIANCE ANALYSIS

2.1 Cost variances

Definition A cost variance is a difference between a planned, budgeted or standard cost and the actual cost incurred. **(CIMA Official Terminology).**

Cost variances occur when standard costs are compared to actual costs. There is one important feature of standard costing which must be remembered: standard costing carries out variance analysis using the normal, double entry ledger accounts. This is done by recording in the ledgers:

(a) actual costs as inputs;

(b) standard costs as outputs;

(c) the difference as the variance.

2.2   CIMA Official Terminology

Each variance covered in this chapter is defined in the **CIMA Official Terminology** in the form of a general explanation of what the variance measures, followed by a formula for its calculation.

It is essential, however, that you do not simply learn formulae for variances without really understanding what they mean and the principles behind their calculation. The examiner may ask you to calculate non-standard variances, which will be testing your understanding rather than your ability to remember formulae.

In this section, therefore, we have initially considered each variance from a 'common sense' point of view, developing its calculation from basic principles. Make sure you work through this carefully.

The CIMA definitions are given at the end of the section relating to each type of cost, along with an illustration of the use of the formulae.

3   DIRECT MATERIAL COST VARIANCES

3.1   Introduction

The purpose of calculating direct material cost variances is to quantify the effect on profit of actual direct material costs differing from standard direct material costs. This total effect is then analysed to quantify how much has been caused by a difference in the price paid for the material and how much by a difference in the quantity of material used.

3.2   Example

The following standard costs relate to a single unit of product X:

	£
Direct materials	10
Direct labour	8
Production overhead	5
	23

On the basis of the above standard costs if a unit of product X is sold for £30, the expected (or standard) profit would be £7 (£30 − £23).

However, if the **actual** direct material cost of making the unit of X were £12 then (assuming the other costs to be as per standard) the actual cost of product X would be:

	£
Direct materials	12
Direct labour	8
Production overhead	5
	25

Thus when the product is sold, the profit is only £5 (£30 − £25).

This reduction in profit is the effect of the difference between the actual and standard direct material cost of £2 (£12 − £10).

This simple example considered only one unit of product X, but it is the principle upon which variance calculations are made.

3.3   Direct material total cost variance

The purpose of this variance is to show the effect on profit for an accounting period of the actual direct material cost being different from the standard direct material cost.

3.4   Example

In July, 1,000 units of product X were manufactured, and sold for £30 each.

Using the data above,

(i)   the standard direct material cost of these 1,000 units of product X would be:

$$1,000 \text{ units} \times £10/\text{unit} = £10,000$$

(ii)   the actual direct material cost of these 1,000 units of product X would be:

$$1,000 \text{ units} \times £12/\text{unit} = £12,000$$

Assuming the other actual costs to be as expected in the standard, the actual profit and loss account would appear:

	£	£
Sales (1,000 × £30)		30,000
Direct materials (1,000 × £12)	12,000	
Direct labour (1,000 × £8)	8,000	
Production overhead (1,000 × £5)	5,000	
		25,000
Profit		5,000

The expected profit was £7 per unit (£30 – £23) so on sales of 1,000 units this would be:

$$1,000 \text{ units} \times £7/\text{unit} = £7,000.$$

Actual profit is £2,000 less than expected. Note that this is the same as the difference between the actual and standard direct material cost calculated earlier (£12,000 – £10,000).

This is known as the direct material total cost variance, and because it causes actual profits to be less than expected it is said to be an **adverse** variance.

Note that this total variance for the period can be shown to be equal to the difference of £2 per unit of X (calculated earlier) multiplied by 1,000 units.

3.6   Activity solution

	£
Standard direct material cost of 600 units:	
£5 × 600	3,000
Actual direct material cost	3,200
Direct material total cost variance - Adverse	200

3.7   Analysing the direct material total cost variance

When a standard material cost is determined for a unit of a product it is made up of two parts. These are estimates of:

(a)   the quantity of material to be used; and
(b)   the price to be paid per unit of material.

If we return to the earlier example concerning product X, the standard direct material cost per unit was stated to be £10. This was based on using 5 kg of a particular material to make each unit of product X and paying £2/kg for the material.

You should remember that the actual direct material cost incurred in making 1,000 units of product X was £12,000. The invoice for these costs shows:

4,800 kg @ £2.50/kg = £12,000.

It should be noted that this form of analysis corresponds to the two estimates which form the basis of the standard cost. It is this which allows the direct material total cost variance to be analysed.

3.8   Direct material price variance

The purpose of calculating this variance is to identify the extent to which profits will differ from those expected by reason of the actual price paid for direct materials being different from the standard price.

The standard price per kg of material was stated above to be £2/kg. This can be used to calculate the expected cost of the actual materials used to make 1,000 units of product X. On this basis the 4,800 kg of material should have cost:

4,800 kg × £2/kg = £9,600.

The actual cost of these materials was £12,000 which is £2,400 (£12,000 – £9,600) more than expected. Since the actual price was greater than expected this will cause the profit to be lower than expected. This variance, known as the direct material price variance, is adverse.

3.9 Activity

A raw material, used in the manufacture of product F has a standard price of £1.30 per litre. During May 2,300 litres were bought at a cost of £3,128. Calculate the direct material price variance for May.

3.10 Activity solution

	£
Standard cost of 2,300 litres:	
2,300 litres × £1.30/litre	2,990
Actual cost of 2,300 litres	3,128
Direct material price variance - Adverse	138

3.11 Direct material usage variance

The purpose of this variance is to quantify the effect on profit of using a different quantity of raw material from that expected for the actual production achieved.

Returning to our example concerning product X, it was stated that each unit of product X had a standard direct material usage of 5 kgs. This can be used to calculate the amount of direct material (in kgs) which should be used for the actual production achieved.

1,000 units of X @ 5 kgs of direct material each = 5,000 kgs.

You should remember that the analysis of the actual cost showed that 4,800 kgs of direct material were actually used.

Thus a saving of 200 kgs (5,000 − 4,800) was achieved.

This saving of materials must be valued to show the effect on profit. If the original standard direct material cost were revised to reflect this saving of material it would become:

4.8 kgs (4,800/1,000) @ £2/kg = £9.60.

This is £0.40 per unit of product X less than the original standard and profit would therefore increase by this amount for every unit of product X produced. This has a total value of

1,000 units × £0.40 = £400.

We achieve the same result by multiplying the saving in quantity by the standard price:

200 kgs × £2/kg = £400.

In this case profits will be higher than expected because less material was used than expected in the standard. Therefore the variance is said to be **favourable**.

3.12   Activity

The standard direct material usage per unit of product K is 0.4 tonnes. The standard price of the material is £30/tonne.

During April 500 units of K were made using 223 tonnes of material costing £6,913. Calculate the direct material usage variance.

3.13   Activity solution

Standard usage of 500 units of K: 500 × 0.4 tonnes	200 tonnes
Actual usage	223 tonnes
Excess usage	23 tonnes

Valued at standard price of £30/tonne:

Direct material usage variance is:

23 tonnes × £30/tonne = £690 Adverse

3.14   Raw material stocks

The earlier example has assumed that the quantity of materials purchased equalled the quantity of materials used by production. Whilst this is possible it is not always certain to occur. Where this does not occur profit will be affected by the change in the level of stock. The extent to which this affects the calculation of direct material variances depends on the methods chosen to value stock. Stocks may be valued either using:

(a)   the standard price for the material; or
(b)   the actual price (as applies from using FIFO, LIFO, etc).

3.15   Stocks valued at standard price

This is the most common method when using a standard costing system because it eliminates the need to record value based movements of stock on stores ledger cards (since all movements, both receipts and issues, will be valued at the standard price).

The effect of this valuation method is that price variances are calculated based on the quantity purchased rather than the quantity of materials used. This is illustrated by the following example.

3.16   Example

Product P requires 4 kg of material Z per unit. The standard price of material Z is £8/kg. During September 16,000 kgs of Z were bought for £134,400. There was no opening stock of material Z but at the end of September 1,400 kgs of Z remained in stock. Stocks of Z are valued at standard prices.

The price variance is based on the quantity purchased (ie, 16,000 kgs). The standard cost of these materials can be calculated:

		£
16,000 kgs × £8/kg		128,000
Actual cost of 16,000 kgs		134,400
Direct material price variance - Adverse		6,400

3.17   Stock account

Continuing the above example the issues of material Z of 14,600 kgs (16,000 – 1,400) would be valued at the standard price of £8/kg.

The value of the issues debited to work in progress would thus be:

14,600 kgs × £8/kg = £116,800.

The stock account would appear thus:

Raw material Z

	£		£
Creditor	134,400	Work in progress	116,800
		Price variance	6,400
		Bal c/d	11,200
	134,400		134,400

Note that the balance c/d comprises the closing stock of 1,400 kgs valued at the standard price of £8/kg.

1,400 kgs × £8/kg = £11,200.

The entry representing the price variance is shown as a credit in the raw material account because it is an adverse variance. The corresponding entry is made to a price variance account, the balance of which is transferred to profit and loss at the end of the year. The price variance account is as follows:

Raw material price variance

	£		£
Raw material Z	6,400		

3.18   Stocks valued at actual price

If this stock valuation method is used it means that any price variance is recognised not at the time of purchase but at the time of issue.

When using this method issues are made from stock at actual prices (using FIFO, LIFO, etc) with the consequence that detailed stores ledger cards must be kept. The price variance is calculated based upon the quantity used.

3.19   Example

Using the data concerning material Z above, calculations of the value of issues and closing stock can be made as follows:

$$\text{Actual cost/kg} = \frac{£134,400}{16,000} \quad = \quad £8.40$$

Value of issues (at actual cost) $\quad = \quad$ 14,600 kgs × £8.40
$\quad = \quad$ £122,640

Closing stock value (at actual cost) $\quad = \quad$ 1,400 kgs × £8.40
$\quad = \quad$ £11,760.

The direct material price variance based on the issues quantity can be calculated:

	£
Standard cost of 14,600 kgs: 14,600 kgs × £8/kg	116,800
Actual cost of 14,600 kgs (above)	122,640
Direct material price variance - Adverse	5,840

3.20   Stock account

If stock is valued using actual prices, the stock account will be as follows:

Raw material Z

	£		£
Creditor	134,400	Work in progress	122,640
		Balance c/d	11,760
	134,400		134,400

Note that the closing balance comprises:

	£
1,400 kgs × standard price of £8/kg	11,200
Adverse price variance not yet recognised: 1,400 kgs × (£8.40 – £8.00)	560
	11,760

The price variance is shown in the work in progress account with the entry as before:

Work in progress

	£		£
Raw material Z	122,640	Direct material price variance	5,840

3.21   CIMA material cost variance definitions and illustrations

The material cost variances discussed above are defined in the **CIMA Official Terminology** as follows:

Direct material total cost variance

Definition   A measurement of the difference between the standard material cost of the output produced and the actual material cost incurred

(standard material cost of output produced - actual cost of material purchased)

Illustration   Using the Product X example in 3.2 and subsequent paragraphs:

$(1,000 \times £10 - 1,000 \times £12) = £2,000$ adverse

Definition   Where the quantities of material purchased and used are different, the total variance should be calculated as the sum of the usage and price variances

Direct material price variance

Definition   The difference between the actual price paid for purchased materials and their standard cost.

((actual quantity of material purchased × standard price) - actual cost of material purchased)

Illustration   Using the Product X example in 3.2 and subsequent paragraphs:

$(4,800 \times £2) - £12,000 = £2,400$ adverse

Definition   The material price variance may also be calculated at the time of material withdrawal from stores. In this case, the stock accounts are maintained at actual cost, price variances being extracted at the time of material usage rather than of purchase

((actual material used × standard cost) - actual cost of material used)

Illustration   This is illustrated in paragraph 3.19 (Material Z)

Direct material usage variance

Definition   Measures efficiency in the use of material, by comparing the standard cost of material used with the standard material cost of what has been produced.

((actual production × standard material cost per unit) - (actual material used × standard cost per unit))

Illustration   Using the Product X example in 3.2 and subsequent paragraphs:

$(1,000 \times £10) - (4,800 \times £2) = £400$ favourable

4   DIRECT LABOUR COST VARIANCES

4.1   Introduction

The purpose of calculating direct labour cost variances is to quantify the effect on profit of actual direct labour costs differing from standard direct labour costs.

This total effect is then analysed to quantify how much has been caused by a difference in the wage rate paid to employees and how much by a difference in the number of hours.

4.2 Example

The following standard costs relate to a single unit of product Q:

	£
Direct materials	8
Direct labour	12
Production overhead	6
	26

On the basis of these standard costs if a unit of product Q is sold for £35, the expected (or standard) profit would be £9 (£35 – £26).

However, if the actual direct labour cost of making the unit of Q were £10, then (assuming the other costs to be as per standard) the actual cost of product Q would be:

	£
Direct materials	8
Direct labour	10
Production overhead	6
	24

Thus when the product is sold the profit is £11 (£35 – £24).

This increase in profit is the effect of the difference between the actual and standard direct labour cost of £2 (£12 – £10).

This simple example considered only one unit of product Q, but it is the principle upon which variance calculations are made.

4.3 Direct labour total cost variance

The purpose of this variance is to show the effect on profit for an accounting period of the actual direct labour cost being different from the standard direct labour cost.

4.4 Example

In August, 800 units of product Q were manufactured, and sold for £35 each.

Using the data above,

(i)   the standard direct labour cost of these 800 units of product Q would be:

800 units × £12/unit = £9,600

(ii)   the actual direct labour cost of these 800 units of product Q would be:

800 units × £10/unit = £8,000.

Assuming the other actual costs to be as expected in the standard, the actual profit and loss account would appear:

	£	£
Sales (800 × £35)		28,000
Direct materials (800 × £8)	6,400	
Direct labour (800 × £10)	8,000	
Production overhead (800 × £6)	4,800	
		19,200
Profit		8,800

The expected profit was £9 per unit (£35 – £26) so on sales of 800 units this would be:

800 units × £9/unit = £7,200.

Actual profit is £1,600 more than expected. Note that this is the same as the difference between the actual and standard direct labour cost calculated earlier (£9,600 – £8,000).

This is known as the direct labour total cost variance, and because it causes actual profits to be more than expected it is said to be a favourable variance.

Note that this total variance for the period can be shown to be equal to the difference of £2 per unit of Q (calculated earlier) multiplied by 800 units.

4.5   Activity

The standard direct labour cost of product H is £7. During January 450 units of product H were made, and the actual direct labour cost was £3,450. Calculate the direct labour total cost variance of the period.

4.6   Activity solution

	£
Standard direct labour cost of 450 units:	
£7 × 450	3,150
Actual direct labour cost	3,450
Direct labour total cost variance - Adverse	300

4.7   Analysing the direct labour total cost variance

When a standard labour cost is determined for a unit of a product it is made up of two parts. These are estimates of:

(a)   the number of hours required per unit; and
(b)   the hourly wage rate.

If we return to the example concerning product Q, the standard direct labour cost per unit was stated to be £12. This was based on 4 direct labour hours being required per unit of Q and paying a wage rate of £3/hour.

You should remember that the actual direct labour cost incurred in making 800 units of product Q was £8,000. An analysis of the payroll records shows:

2,000 hours @ £4/hour = £8,000.

It should be noted that this corresponds to the two estimates which form the basis of the standard cost. It is this which allows the direct labour total cost variance to be analysed.

4.8   Direct labour rate variance

The purpose of calculating this variance is to identify the extent to which profits will differ from those expected by reason of the actual wage rate per hour being different from the standard.

The standard wage rate per hour was stated to be £3. This can be used to calculate the expected cost of the actual hours taken to make 800 units of product Q. On this basis the 2,000 hours should have cost:

2,000 hours × £3/hour = £6,000.

The actual labour cost was £8,000 which is £2,000 (£8,000 – £6,000) more than expected.

Since the actual rate was greater than expected, this will cause the profit to be lower than expected. This variance, known as the direct labour rate variance, is adverse.

4.9   Direct labour efficiency variance

The purpose of this variance is to quantify the effect on profit of using a different number of hours than expected for the actual production achieved.

Continuing with our example concerning product Q, it was stated that each unit of product Q would require 4 direct labour hours. This can be used to calculate the number of direct labour hours which should be required for the actual production achieved.

800 units of Q × 4 direct labour hours each = 3,200 direct labour hours

You should remember that the analysis of the actual cost showed that only 2,000 hours were used.

Thus a saving of 1,200 direct labour hours (3,200 – 2,000) was achieved.

This saving of labour hours must be valued to show the effect on profit. We do this by multiplying the difference in hours by the standard hourly rate:

1,200 direct labour hours × £3/hr = £3,600.

In this case profit will be higher than expected because fewer hours were used. Therefore the variance is favourable.

4.10   Activity

The following data relates to product C

Actual production of C (units)	700
Standard wage rate/hour	£4.00
Standard time allowance per unit of C (hours)	1.50
Actual hours worked	1,000
Actual wage cost	£4,200

Calculate the direct labour rate and efficiency variances from the above data.

4.11   Activity solution

	£
Expected cost of actual hours worked:	
1,000 hours × £4/hr	4,000
Actual wage cost	4,200
Direct labour rate variance - Adverse	200
Expected hours for actual production:	
700 units × 1.50 hours/unit	1,050
Actual hours	1,000
A saving (in hours) of	50

These are valued at the standard wage rate/hour.

Direct labour efficiency variance is:

50 hours × £4/hour = £200 Favourable.

4.12   CIMA labour cost variance definitions and illustrations

The labour cost variances discussed above are defined in the **CIMA Official Terminology** as follows:

Direct labour total cost variance

Definition   Indicates the difference between the standard direct labour cost of the output which has been produced and the actual direct labour cost incurred

((standard hours produced × standard direct labour hour rate per hour) - (actual hours paid × actual direct labour rate per hour))

Illustration   Using the Product Q example in 4.2 and subsequent paragraphs:

(3,200 × £3) - (2,000 × £4) = £1,600 favourable

Direct labour rate variance

Definition   Indicates the actual cost of any change from the standard labour rate of remuneration

((actual hours paid × standard direct labour hour rate per hour) - (actual hours paid × actual direct labour rate per hour))

Illustration   Using the Product Q example in 4.2 and subsequent paragraphs:

(2,000 × £3) - (2,000 × £4) = £2,000 adverse

Direct labour efficiency variance

Definition   Indicates the standard labour cost of any change from the standard level of labour efficiency

((actual production in standard hours × standard direct labour hour rate per hour) - (actual direct labour hours worked × standard direct labour rate per hour))

Illustration   Using the Product Q example in 4.2 and subsequent paragraphs:

$(3,200 \times £3) - (2,000 \times £3) = £3,600$ favourable

5   OVERHEAD VARIANCES

5.1   Introduction

In practice, most standard costing systems have been based on **absorption principles,** and certainly in the examination room you must expect to be faced with absorption standard costing.

Remember, when trying to pre-determine an overhead absorption rate, two estimates must be made:

(a)   The level of expenditure.
(b)   The number of units over which it is to be spread.

In standard costing terms this means that to arrive at an overhead absorption rate, standards must be set for:

(a)   Overhead expenditure.
(b)   Output.

Variances in either of these lead to an overhead variance.

5.2   Example

Budget:

Total overheads	£6,000
Output	100 units

Actual:

Overheads	£6,120
Output	90 units

5.3   Solution

(i)	Standard for overheads	£6,000
(ii)	Standard for output	100 units
(iii)	Overhead absorption rate $\dfrac{£6,000}{100} =$	£60 per unit

£

Actual expenditure	£6,120	Overhead total variance
Amount absorbed (90 × 60)	£5,400	£720 A

The adverse balance arises for two reasons:

(a)   Actual expenditure has exceeded budget by £120.

(b)   The overhead absorbed is less than budget as the **volume** of output is less, ie, 10 units at £60 = £600.

5.4   Standard hours of production

In the previous example, overheads were absorbed at a rate per unit:

$$\frac{£6,000}{100} = £60/\text{unit}.$$

This is perfectly satisfactory whilst all output consists of one type of product. However, this is not very likely.

Suppose a company has two products, A and B, with the following costs:

	A	B
Raw materials	£10	£50
Direct labour	£20 (10 hrs)	£160 (80 hrs)

It is extremely unlikely that both A and B will make equal demands on the overheads. Therefore, some method of absorbing the overheads which reasonably represents the products' respective consumptions is needed.

By its nature, this is an arbitrary and nebulous concept. Overheads are not 'consumed' by producing units. They are incurred whether units are produced or not. The best that can be hoped for is some reasonable basis for allocating overheads.

This is usually provided by labour hours (or sometimes machine hours). In the above example, product A represents 10 standard hours of production and B 80 standard hours of production. Therefore, it is possible to devise an overhead absorption rate based not on units but on budgeted hours. This is illustrated with the CIMA definition below.

5.5   CIMA overhead cost variance definition and illustration

The overhead cost variance discussed above is defined in two parts in the **CIMA Official Terminology** as follows:

Variable production overhead total cost variance

Definition   The difference between the amount of variable production overhead which has been absorbed by output, and the actual cost.

(actual cost incurred - (actual production in standard hours × variable production overhead absorption rate per hour))

Illustration   Using the example in 5.2. and assuming
- 1.6 standard hours per unit
- a split of overheads of   £2,000 variable, £4,000 fixed (budget)
                            £1,600 variable, £4,520 fixed (actual)

$$\text{absorption rate per hour} = \frac{\text{budgeted cost}}{\text{budgeted hours}} = \frac{£2,000}{100 \times 1.6} = £12.50/\text{hour}$$

$$1,600 - (90 \times 1.6 \times £12.50) = £200 \text{ favourable}$$

Fixed production overhead total cost variance

Definition   The difference between the actual fixed production overhead incurred and the amount absorbed by output produced.

((actual production in standard hours × fixed overhead absorption rate per hour) – actual fixed production overhead)

Illustration   Using the example in 5.2, and the further assumptions above,

$$\text{absorption rate per hour} = \frac{\text{budgeted cost}}{\text{budgeted hours}} = \frac{£4,000}{100 \times 1.6} = £25 \text{ per hour}$$

$$((90 \times 1.6 \times £25) - £4,520 = £920 \text{ adverse}$$

(the total of this and the variable overhead variance is £720 adverse, as in 5.3)

6   STANDARD COSTING AND THE MODERN INDUSTRIAL ENVIRONMENT

6.1   Introduction

Developments in modern manufacturing methods and organisational structures have changed the requirements for management control information compared to those which existed when standard costing was first developed.

When standard costing was first developed manufacturing methods were often labour intensive and where machinery was used, it was controlled manually.

It was therefore obvious to base a standard costing system on hours and the principle of a standard hour was developed for labour and overhead variances. At this time guarantees about numbers of hours and minimum weekly wages rarely existed and consequently labour costs were considered variable costs.

In the context of materials there was little interaction between the supplier and the user other than on the basis of individual arm's length transactions. It was therefore appropriate to set material cost standards based on price and usage and to make comparisons between these and the actual results and report them to the managers concerned.

The modern industrial environment is different in two ways, manufacturing methods, and supplier relationships.

6.2   Modern manufacturing methods

The first significant development was the introduction (following Trade Union pressure) of guaranteed minimum wages for employees. This had the effect of changing the total wage cost from being variable to being largely fixed. This led to problems in the reporting of labour efficiency and at the same time increased labour costs.

This increase in cost led to companies seeking alternative methods of manufacture involving computer technology to operate machines and robotics. This questions the validity of the use of labour hours as the basis of variance calculations. Many people argue that machine hour based calculations are more appropriate or indeed that labour costs should be regarded as fixed production overhead costs in industries which are significantly automated.

6.3   Supplier relationships

The growth in the size of organisations by formal integration has of course led to suppliers of materials being part of the manufacturing organisation, but even where this is not the case there have been significant changes in the conduct of business between manufacturers and suppliers.

It is now recognised that production planning is an essential part of manufacturing efficiency. Such planning will only succeed if the resource suppliers are aware of, and able to meet, the manufacturers' requirements.

This has led to a significant increase in the communications between manufacturers and suppliers. Often one order is placed in respect of the annual requirements with a delivery schedule for the supplier. This also means that the price is agreed for the duration of the order, consequently the price does not fluctuate and price variances are eliminated. In some instances suppliers are penalised for late delivery and this too will affect the reporting of variances relating to stops in production.

7   CHAPTER SUMMARY

This chapter has contained an introduction to a specific form of costing, standard costing, and in particular to basic variance analysis.

8   SELF TEST QUESTIONS

8.1   What is a standard cost? (1.2)

8.2   What are the differences between standard costing and general budgetary control? (1.3)

8.3   What are the three purposes of standard costing? (1.5)

8.4   What are three possible bases for setting standards? (1.6)

8.5   What is a standard hour? (1.7)

8.6   What is a cost variance? (2.1)

8.7   How is the total raw materials variance calculated? (3.2)

8.8   How is the total direct labour cost variance calculated? (4.4)

8.9   For which two items must standards be set for fixed overhead expenditure? (5.1)

9   EXAMINATION TYPE QUESTION

9.1   Company M

The following standard costs apply in Company M which manufactures a single product:

Standard weight to produce one unit	12 kgs
Standard price per kg	£9
Standard hours to produce one unit	10
Standard rate per hour	£4

Actual production and costs for one accounting period were:

Material used	3,770	kgs
Material cost	£35,815	
Hours worked	2,755	
Wages paid	£11,571	

The actual output was 290 units.

You are required

(a)   to calculate relevant material and labour cost variances, and present these in a format suitable for presentation to the management of the company;

(14 marks)

(b)   to explain how standard costs for material and labour might be compiled.

(5 marks)

(Total: 19 marks)

10   **ANSWER TO EXAMINATION TYPE QUESTION**

10.1   **Company M**

(a)   *(Tutorial note*

The question asks for a 'format suitable for presentation to management'. It is therefore recommended that the first part of the solution is a summary of the variances and the details workings are shown separately.*)*

Summary of variances for one accounting period

(F = Favourable; A = Adverse)

	£	
Materials:		
Price	1,885	A
Usage	2,610	A
Cost	4,495	A
Labour:		
Rate:	551	A
Efficiency	580	F
Cost	29	F

WORKINGS

Direct materials	£			£	
Actual cost	35,815				
Actual quantity purchased/ used at 3,770 × £9	33,930		Price variance	1,885	A
Standard quantity for actual production at standard price 290 × 12 × £9	31,320		Usage variance	2,610	A
Cost variance				4,495	A
Labour					
Actual cost	11,571				
Actual hours paid/worked at standard rate 2,755 × £4	11,020		Rate variance	551	A
Standard hours for actual production at standard rate 290 × 10 × £4	11,600		Efficiency variance	580	F
Cost variance				29	F

Assumptions

(1)   Quantity of material purchased = Quantity used.

(2)   Actual hours paid for = Actual hours worked.

(b)   To compile standard costs it is necessary to establish standards ie, planned amounts for each of the following:

Material

Price is established with the assistance of the buying department; it is necessary to take account of quantity discounts and price increases.

Quantity (including an allowance for wastage) should be available from the production department.

Quality/type. This is closely linked to quantity and design of the product and may involve a decision by the production department as to which material is most suitable.

Labour

It is first necessary to identify the tasks that are to be carried out on the product. Then for each tasks the following information is needed:

(i)   level of skill/grade of worker needed;

(ii)   time allowed - it may be necessary to use work study to decide on the production method and the associated standard time;

(iii)   rate of pay - this will be dependent on the grade of employee and may be subject to a company-wide or national wage agreement.

14 HANDLING FORMULAE

INTRODUCTION & LEARNING OBJECTIVES

Syllabus area 2d. Handling formulae (the use of positive and negative numbers, brackets and powers). (Ability required 3).

This chapter provides the background needed to tackle the later chapters on more specific areas of the syllabus.

Like many other areas of study, mathematics and statistics has its own 'shorthand' in order to enable faster and more efficient communication of information. Whilst there are a lot of symbols which are used to mean different things by different writers, many symbols and other notations do have a specific interpretation. These must be summarised and explained before the subject can be developed further.

When you have studied this chapter you should be able to do the following:

- Perform basic arithmetic procedures (ie, addition, subtraction, multiplication and division).

- Understand the basis of algebra and express data algebraically.

- Understand the order in which algebraic operations should be carried out.

- Substitute definite numbers into an algebraic expression to calculate numerical values.

- Understand and perform the basic rules governing indices ie,

$$a^m \times a^n = a^{m+n},$$

$$a^m \div a^n = a^{m-n},$$

$$a^{-n} = \frac{1}{a^n}$$

$$(ab)^m = a^m \times b^m$$

$$a^{\frac{1}{n}} = \sqrt[n]{a}$$

- Define and explain logarithms.
- Use log tables when necessary.
- Understand why logarithms are used.
- Understand and handle equations.

---

1   ARITHMETIC

The basic tool of mathematical method are the four rules of numbers, addition (+), subtraction (−), multiplication (×), and division (÷).

These four processes are used to perform the required operations on numbers in many different forms ie, integers, fractions, signed numbers, real numbers and indexed numbers.

1.1   Addition and subtraction

Addition

The addition of two or more numbers results in an answer which is termed the sum.

For example, the sum of the following numbers is 13600.

```
    123
   4567
   8910  +
  _____

  13600
  _____
```

This process is performed by listing the numbers one under the other, as above, and then by adding the digits in the units column first, followed by the tens column, the hundreds column and so on, until the addition is complete.

Subtraction

To subtract one number from another, the process is much the same. The numbers must be aligned correctly, and starting with the units column, subtract each pair of numbers eg,

```
   1298
    164  –
  _____

   1134
  _____
```

1.2   Multiplication and division

Multiplication

When two numbers are multiplied together the result is termed the product.

The multiplication is carried out in a number of stages. The multiplicand is multiplied by each digit of the multiplier in turn, starting with the right most digit. Each of these multiplications results in a partial product, with the results being moved one place further to the left than the previous multiplication, the final product being the sum of all the partial products.

For example:

342	Multiplicand
112	Multiplier
684	1st partial product
3420	2nd partial product
34200	3rd partial product
38304	Final product

Division

The process of division is slightly more complex than multiplication. The dividend is divided by the divisor and the result is termed the quotient.

The steps required are:

Step 1   Taking each digit of the dividend in turn, commencing with the left most digit, the process involves finding how many times the divisor goes into that digit.

Step 2   If the divisor is larger than the first digit of the dividend, then the 1st step is ignored, and instead the process now involves calculating how many times the divisor will go into the first two digits. If the divisor is still not larger than the dividend, then the process continues until it is large enough.

Step 3   The result of how many times the divisor goes into the dividend is written above the right most digit of the part of the dividend used to obtain the result.

Step 4   The result in step 3 is multiplied by the divisor and the total written below the dividend aligned with the left most digit.

Step 5   The value in step 4 is then subtracted from the dividend, and the next unused digit of the dividend is written next to it.

Step 6   This process is then repeated until the quotient is found.

For example:

```
          1 3
     _____
1 2 | 1 5 ³6
      1 2
      ─────
        3 6
        3 6
      ─────
          0
```

12 is the divisor

156 is the dividend

13 is the quotient

2   MATHEMATICAL SYMBOLS

Mathematical symbols are used in order that people can exchange ideas with a minimum of effort and maximum clarity. They are a form of shorthand. Mathematics has its own language - its vocabulary being symbols, some of which are explained below:

x   the collective symbol meaning all the individual values of a variable, ie, x_1, x_2, x_3, etc. The subscripts denote particular values of the variable x.

y   is an alternative symbol to x, and is used to denote one set of variables where two sets of variables are involved, x being used for the other set.

$\sum_{i=1}^{n} x_i$ (Sigma x) means the sum of the individual values of the variable x from x_1 to x_n. This is usually abbreviated to $\sum x$.

So: $\sum x = x_1 + x_2 + x_3 \ldots + x_n$

$\sum xy$ (Sigma xy) means the sum of the products of corresponding x and y values

So: $\sum xy = x_1 y_1 + x_2 y_2 + x_3 y_3 + \ldots + x_n y_n$

$\sum x^2$ (Sigma x squared) means the sum of the squares of the individual x values

So: $\sum x^2 = x_1^2 + x_2^2 + x_3^2 + \ldots + x_n^2$

$(\sum x^2)$ (Sigma x all squared) means the square of the sum of the individual x values

So: $(\sum x^2) = (x_1 + x_2 + x_3 + \ldots + x_n)^2$

$\sum(x-y)$ (Sigma x minus y) means the sum of the difference between corresponding x and y values.

So: $\sum(x - y) = (x_1 - y_1) + (x_2 - y_2) + (x_3 - y_3) + \ldots + (x_n - y_n)$

2.1   Example

$x_1 = 4$, $x_2 = 6$, $x_3 = 10$ and $y_1 = 2$, $y_2 = 11$, $y_3 = 20$

$\sum x$, $\sum y$, $\sum xy$, $\sum x^2$, $\sum y^2$, $(\sum x)^2$, $(\sum y)^2$, $\sum(x - y)$ will be calculated.

2.2   Solution

$\sum x$ = $4 + 6 + 10$

    = 20

$\sum y$ = $2 + 11 + 20$

    = 33

$\sum xy$ = $4 \times 2 + 6 \times 11 + 10 \times 20$

    = $8 + 66 + 200$

    = 274

$\sum x^2$ = $4^2 + 6^2 + 10^2$

    = $16 + 36 + 100$

    = 152

$\sum y^2$ = $2^2 + 11^2 + 20^2$

    = $4 + 121 + 400$

    = 525

$(\sum x)^2$ = $(4 + 6 + 10)^2$

    = $(20)^2$

    = 400

(Note: $\sum x^2$ does not equal $(\sum x)^2$.)

$(\sum y)^2$ = $(2 + 11 + 10)^2$

    = $(33)^2$

    = $1,089$

$$\Sigma(x - y) = (4 - 2) + (6 - 11) + (10 - 20)$$

$$= 2 + (-5) + (-10)$$

$$= -13$$

2.3   Statements and relationships

$\approx$	approximately equal to
$x \le y$	x is less than or equal to y
$x > y$	x is greater than y
$x \ne y$	x is not equal to y
$z \le x \le y$	x is greater than or equal to z, and less than or equal to y
$z < x < y$	x is greater than z but less than y
$x \to y$	the truth of statement x implies the truth of statement y
$\sqrt{x}$ or $x^{\frac{1}{2}}$	square root of x

3   FORMULATION AND EVALUATION OF FORMULAE

When letters are used to represent numbers it is helpful if suitable letters are chosen eg,:

$$A = L \times B$$

This is a well known formula for finding the area (A) of a rectangle of length (L) and breadth (B). Other letters could be used but these are obviously the most appropriate ones.

Whatever letters or symbols are used the following two points are important:

(a)   It must be clearly stated what each letter or symbol represents.

(b)   If any units of measurement are involved they must be clearly defined.

3.1   Illustration

The number of pence in x pounds and y pence is expressed as follows:

$$£x = x \times 100 \text{ pence}$$

$$= 100x \text{ pence}$$

So total number of pence $= (100x + y)$ pence.

3.2   Example

There are two numbers; the first is multiplied by 3, and 5 is then added to the product. The sum is divided by 4 times the second number. This is expressed algebraically as:

Let x = first number
and y = second number

'The first is multiplied by 3 . .'. This gives $x \times 3$ or $3x$ '. . and 5 is added to the product' ie, $3x + 5$ '..4 times the second number' is $y \times 4$ or $4y$.

The first expression divided by the second gives:

$$(3x + 5) \div 4y \ \text{ or } \ \frac{(3x + 5)}{4y}$$

3.3   Terms and coefficients

When an algebraic expression contains the symbols of operation . . . + or −, those parts of the expression which they separate are called **terms**.

Therefore the expression derived in 1.1 contains two terms 100x and y.

100 is called the **coefficient** of x, and the corresponding coefficient of y is 1 since
$1 \times y = y$.

If an expression contains terms which involve the same letter and differ only in the coefficients, then they are called **like terms**. The important point is that like terms can be added or subtracted by adding or subtracting the coefficients.

3.4   Example

Simplify the following expressions:

(a) $5a + 6b + 2a - 3b$

(b) $4x + 3x - 2x - x$

(c)   The sum of the three expressions $5x + 2y + 3z$, $x - y - 2z$, and $2x - y + z$

3.5   Solution

(a) $5a + 6b + 2a - 3b \quad = \quad (5 + 2)a + (6 - 3)b$

$$= \quad 7a + 3b$$

(b) $4x + 3x - 2x - x \quad = \quad (4 + 3 - 2 - 1)x$

$$= \quad 4x$$

(c) $(5x + 2y + 3z) + (x - y - 2z) + (2x - y + z)$

$$= \quad (5 + 1 + 2)x + (2 - 1 - 1)y + (3 - 2 + 1)z$$

$$= \quad 8x + 0y + 2z$$

$$= \quad 8x + 2z$$

3.6   Evaluation by substitution

Numerical values of algebraic expressions can be calculated by substituting definite numbers for the letters.

3.7   Example

Numerical values of the expressions simplified in 1.5 above will now be calculated using:

(a) $a = 3$, $b = -1$
(b) $x = 5$
(c) $x = -4$, $z = 7$

3.8   Solution

(a) $7a + 3b$ = $7 \times 3 + 3 \times (-1)$ (Remember $7a$ = $7 \times a$

               = $21 - 3$ and $3b$ = $3 \times b$)

               = 18

(b) $4x$ = 4×5 (Remember $4x$ = $4 \times x$)

               = 20

(c) $8x + 2z$ = $8 \times (-4) + 2 \times 7$ (Remember $8x$ = $8 \times x$

               = $-32 + 14$ and $2z$ = $2 \times z$)

               = -18

3.9   Order of operations

(a)   **Addition** - The order in which numbers are added is immaterial to the result eg,

        $2 + 3$ = 5 = $3 + 2$

        $5b + 2b$ = $7b$ = $2b + 5b$

(b)   **Multiplication** - The order in which numbers are multiplied is immaterial to the result eg,

        2×3 = 6 = 3×2

        $2 \times a \times 5$ = $10a$ = $2 \times 5 \times a$

        $3a \times 2b$ = $6ab$ = $3 \times 2 \times a \times b$

(c)   **Subtraction** - The order is important and affects the answer materially eg,

        $8 - 3$ = 5 but $3 - 8$ = -5

        $12x - 10x$ = $2x$ but $10x - 12x$ = $-2x$

(d)   **Division** - Again the order is important and the answer will be affected eg,

        $12 \div 6$ = 2 but $6 \div 12$ = $\dfrac{1}{2}$

        $3a \div 4$ = $\dfrac{3a}{4}$ but $4 \div 3a$ = $\dfrac{4}{3a}$

(e)   **Mixed operations**

        (1)   The contents of brackets must be evaluated first. The line dividing the numerator and denominator of a fraction acts as a bracket in this respect.

        (2)   Multiplication and division must be done before addition and subtraction.

                Eg,   (i) $2x + 3x \times 2$ = $2x + 6x$ = $8x$

                        (ii) $(2x + 3x) \times 2$ = $5x \times 2$ = $10x$

(iii) $\dfrac{4a + 3a \times 2}{7a - 4a \div 2}$ $=$ $(4a + 3a \times 2) \div (7a - 4a \div 2)$

$=$ $(4a + 6a) \div (7a - 2a)$

$=$ $10a \div 5a$

$=$ $\dfrac{10a}{5a}$

$=$ $\dfrac{2}{1}$ (cancelling 5a top and bottom)

$=$ 2

3.10   Brackets

(a)   Items outside brackets multiply **everything** within:

$$a(x + y + z) \quad = \quad ax + ay + az$$

eg, if $a = 3$, then:

$$3(x + y + z) \quad = \quad 3x + 3y + 3z$$

(b)   Signs outside brackets multiply everything within:

$$-a(x + y + z) \quad = \quad -ax + -ay + -az$$

eg if $a = 7$, and if the expression in the brackets is modified slightly, then:

$$-7(x + y - z) \quad = \quad -7x - 7y + 7z$$

3.11   Activity

Expand the following expressions:

(a) $5(2x + 3y - 4z)$

(b) $-x(2 + 3x)$

(c) $-4(x - 2y + 3z)$

3.12   Activity solution

(a)   Multiply everything within the bracket by 5. $10x + 15y - 20z$

(b)   Multiply everything within the bracket by $(-x)$. $-2x - 3x^2$

(c)   Multiply everything within the bracket by (-4). $-4x + 8y - 12z$

3.13   Fractions

(a)   Fractions may be added when reduced to a common denominator:

$$\frac{a}{x} + \frac{b}{y} \quad = \quad \frac{ay}{xy} + \frac{bx}{xy} \quad = \quad \frac{ay + bx}{xy}$$

eg, if a = 2, b = 1, x = 7 and y = 3, then:

$$\frac{2}{7}+\frac{1}{3} \quad = \quad \frac{2\times3+1\times7}{7\times3} \quad = \quad \frac{6+7}{21}$$

$$= \quad \frac{13}{21}$$

(b)   When multiplying fractions, numerators and denominators are dealt with separately:

$$\frac{a}{x}\times\frac{b}{y} \quad = \quad \frac{ab}{xy}$$

eg, if a = 3, b = 4, x = 5 and y = 7, then:

$$\frac{3}{5}\times\frac{4}{7} \quad = \quad \frac{3\times4}{5\times7}$$

$$= \quad \frac{12}{35}$$

(c)   When dividing fractions, invert the divisor and multiply:

$$\frac{a}{x}\div\frac{b}{y} \quad = \quad \frac{a}{x}\times\frac{y}{b}$$

$$= \quad \frac{ay}{xb}$$

eg, if a = 2, b = 11, x = 5 and y = 9, then:

$$\frac{2}{5}\div\frac{11}{9} \quad = \quad \frac{2}{5}\times\frac{9}{11}$$

$$= \quad \frac{18}{55}$$

Students who find difficulty with the above elementary forms will probably find they need a text book of basic algebraic relationships to hand as they work through this manual.

4   INDICES AND POWERS OF NUMBERS

4.1   Rules

As noted above, when equal numbers are multiplied together the result is known as a **power** and is denoted by a superscript to the right or such a number, eg,

$2^3 = 2\times2\times2 = 8$ Therefore 8 is the third power of 2, or 2 to the power of three.

$a^2 = a\times a$ Therefore a^2 is the second power of a or a to the power of 2.

A number raised to the power of 2 is said to be squared, and if raised to the power of 3 is said to be cubed.

There are certain rules governing the use of such indices.

4.2   Multiplication of powers of a number

$$\text{eg,} \quad a^2 \times a^3 \quad = \quad (a \times a) \times (a \times a \times a) \quad = \quad a^5$$

But, more simply,

$$a^2 \times a^3 \quad = \quad a^{(2+3)} \quad = \quad a^5$$

$$\therefore \quad a^7 \times a^9 \quad = \quad a^{(7+9)} \quad = \quad a^{16}$$

So when two or more powers of the same number are multiplied the individual indices are added.

$\boxed{\text{Conclusion}}$ In general terms $a^m \times a^n = \qquad a^{m+n}$

4.3   Power of a product

$$\text{eg,} \qquad (ab)^2 \quad = \quad ab \times ab$$

$$= \quad a \times a \times b \times b$$

$$= \quad a^2 \times b^2$$

$$(2xy)^3 \quad = \quad 2xy \times 2xy \times 2xy$$

$$= \quad 2^3 \times x^3 \times y^3$$

$$= \quad 8x^3y^3$$

So when taking a power of a product the index is applied to each factor of the product.

$\boxed{\text{Conclusion}}$ In general terms: $\qquad (3ab)^m \quad = \qquad 3^m a^m b^m$

4.4   Example

Simplify the following expressions:

(i) $2a^2 \times a^3$

(ii) $3x^3 \times 2x^4$

(iii) $(3a^2b)^3$

(iv) $(2a^2x)^2$ and evaluate when $a = 2$, $x = 3$.

4.5   Solution

(i) $2a^2 \times a^3 \quad = \quad 2 \times a^{(2+3)} \qquad = \quad 2a^5$

(ii) $3x^3 \times 2x^4 \quad = \quad 3 \times 2 \times x^{(3+4)} \quad = \quad 6x^7$

(iii) $(3a^2b)^3 \quad = \quad 3^3 \times (a^2)^3 \times b^3 \quad = \quad 27a^6b^3$

Note: $(a^2)^3 \qquad = \quad a^2 \times a^2 \times a^2$

$$= \quad a^{(2+2+2)}$$

$$= \quad a^6$$

(iv) $(2a^2x)^2 = 2^2 \times (a^2)^2 \times x^2 = 4a^4x^2$

Evaluating gives:

$(2a^2x)^2 = 4 \times 2^4 \times 3^2$

$= 4 \times 16 \times 9$

$= 576$

4.6   Division of powers

eg, $a^5 \div a^2 = \dfrac{a^5}{a^2} = \dfrac{a \times a \times a \times \cancel{a} \times \cancel{a}}{\cancel{a} \times \cancel{a}} = a^3$

But more simply.

$a^5 \div a^2 = a^{(5-2)} = a^3$

$a^9 \div a^7 = a^{(9-7)} = a^2$

$15x^5 \div 3x^4 = 5x^{(5-4)} = 5x$

So when dividing a power of a number by another power of the same number the indices are subtracted in that order.

Conclusion   In general terms $a^m \div a^n = a^{(m-n)}$

Note: It is important to observe that in both multiplication and division, for these rules to be correct, both terms must have the same base eg, $a^2 \times b^3$ is **not** equal to $(ab)^{2+3}$ because the two bases, a and b, are different.

4.7   Special cases

(a)   **Zero index**

$a^6 \div a^6 = \dfrac{\cancel{a} \times \cancel{a} \times \cancel{a} \times \cancel{a} \times \cancel{a} \times \cancel{a}}{\cancel{a} \times \cancel{a} \times \cancel{a} \times \cancel{a} \times \cancel{a} \times \cancel{a}} = 1$

but $a^6 \div a^6 = a^{(6-6)} = a^0$

$\therefore \qquad a^0 = 1$

Conclusion   So any number of the power zero equals 1. (Confirm this on your calculator.)

(b)   **Fractional indices**

The meaning of fractional indices will be illustrated by the next examples:

$a^{\frac{1}{2}} = \sqrt{a}$

because $a^{\frac{1}{2}} \times a^{\frac{1}{2}} = a^1$, hence $a^{\frac{1}{2}}$ is that quantity that when squared, gives a, which is by definition the **square root of a**.

$a^{\frac{1}{3}} = \sqrt[3]{a}$

because $a^{1/3} \times a^{1/3} \times a^{1/3} = a^{(1/3+1/3+1/3)} = a^1$.

Conclusion   In general terms $a^{1/n} = \sqrt[n]{a}$

(c)   Negative indices

$$\text{Eg, } a^5 \div a^7 = \frac{\cancel{a} \times \cancel{a} \times \cancel{a} \times \cancel{a} \times \cancel{a}}{\cancel{a} \times \cancel{a} \times \cancel{a} \times \cancel{a} \times \cancel{a} \times a \times a} = \frac{1}{a^2}$$

but $a^5 \div a^7 = a^{5-7} = a^{-2}$

$$\therefore \quad a^{-2} = \frac{1}{a^2}$$

Similarly $a^{-6} = \dfrac{1}{a^6}$

Conclusion   In general terms $a^{-n} = \dfrac{1}{a^n}$

4.8   Example

Calculate the following values:

(i) $3^{1/2}$

(ii) $2^{0.5}$

(iii) $4^{1.5}$

(iv) 10^{-3}

(v) $36^{-0.5}$

4.9   Solution

(i) $3^{1/2}$ $= \sqrt{3}$ $= 1.732$

(ii) $2^{0.5}$ $= 2^{1/2}$ $= \sqrt{2}$ $= 1.414$

(iii) $4^{1.5}$ $= 4^{1\frac{1}{2}}$ $= 4^{3/2}$

$4^{3/2}$ $= \sqrt{4^3}$ $= \sqrt{64}$ $= 8$

or $4^{3/2}$ $= \left(\sqrt{4}\right)^3$ $= 2^3$ $= 8$

(iv) 10^{-3} $= \dfrac{1}{10^3}$ $= \dfrac{1}{1,000}$ $(= 0.001)$

(v) $36^{-0.5}$ $= \dfrac{1}{36^{0.5}}$ $= \dfrac{1}{36^{1/2}}$ $= \dfrac{1}{\sqrt{36}}$ $= \dfrac{1}{6}$

4.10   Activity

Calculate the following values:

(i) $9^{\frac{1}{2}}$

(ii) 10^2

(iii) $81^{-\frac{1}{2}}$

(iv) $25^{\frac{5}{2}}$

4.11   Activity solution

(i) $9^{\frac{1}{2}}$ $=$ $\sqrt{9}$ $=$ 3

(ii) 10^2 $=$ 10×10 $=$ 100

(iii) $81^{-\frac{1}{2}}$ $=$ $\dfrac{1}{\sqrt{81}}$ $=$ $\dfrac{1}{9}$

(iv) $25^{\frac{5}{2}}$ $=$ $\sqrt{25^5}$ $=$ $3,125$

5   LOGARITHMS

5.1   Definition of logarithms

Logarithms use the fact that:

$$x^a \times x^b = x^{a+b}$$

and $$(x^a)^b = x^{ab}$$

and give us a convenient method for multiplying numbers and finding powers and roots in the absence of a calculator.

By convention logarithms (logs) use $x = 10$, ie, they are to the base of 10.

Any number (n) can be expressed in the form: $n = 10^a$

eg, 10 $=$ 10^1

100 $=$ 10^2

3.1623 $=$ $\sqrt{10}$ $=$ $10^{\frac{1}{2}}$ $=$ $10^{0.5}$

1 $=$ 10^0

0.1 $=$ $\dfrac{1}{10}$ $=$ 10^{-1}

The power that 10 is raised to in each case is known as the log of n. Therefore:

log 10   = 1

log 100   = 2

log (3.1623) = 0.5

etc.

Logarithm tables are used to find the logs of any positive number. *Note:* first from the illustrations given above that the log of any number between 1 and 10 lies in the range 0 to 1. There are some log tables at the front of this text.

5.2   Use of log tables

(a)   **Logs of numbers greater than 1, less than 10**

The log is in the range 0 to 1.

eg, to find log 3.1623

$\boxed{\text{Step 1}}$ Read down left hand column to 31. The figure in the column headed 0 in this line is 4914.

So 0.4914 is log 3.1.

$\boxed{\text{Step 2}}$ Read across to column headed 6 to find 4997

So 0.4997 is log 3.16.

$\boxed{\text{Step 3}}$ Keeping a finger on 4997 read across again to the small columns to the column headed 2. This reads 3. Add this to 4997, giving 5000.

So 0.5 is log 3.162.

This agrees with our understanding of logs, since 3.162 is $\sqrt{10}$, ie, $10^{0.5}$.

Note: these log tables are only constructed to four significant figures. Therefore we can only find the log of 3.162, not 3.1623. The figure is rounded down. This is sufficiently accurate for most purposes and indeed in this case does give us the correct answer.

Now look up the logs of the following numbers:

(i)   5.764

(ii)   9.34

(iii)   1.615

(iv)   1.655

Solutions

(i)   log 5.764   =   0.7607 (7604 + 3)

(ii)   log 9.34   =   0.9703

(iii)   log 1.615   =   0.2082 (2068 + 14)

(iv)   log 1.655   =   0.2188 (2175 + 13)

In (iii) and (iv) we read along the same line to find the last digit. Therefore, in (iii) it is the top part of the 16 line since 161 is at the top, and in (iv) it is the lower part since 165 is at the bottom.

If you use your calculators to find logs, use the log button (rather than the nearby ln).

(b)   **Log of any number**

It will be seen that the log of any number consists of two parts, a decimal fraction, called the **mantissa**, and a whole number, called the **characteristic**. The mantissa is obtained from the log tables as we have just done, the characteristic from the following rule:

In the number whose logarithm is required, move the decimal point until it comes immediately after the first non-zero digit. The characteristic is equal to the number of places by which the decimal point is moved. If moved to the left, the characteristic is positive, and if moved to the right it is negative. Eg,

$$\log 211.6 = 2.3255$$

The characteristic is 2 because to get 2.116 from 211.6, the decimal point must be moved two places to the left.

$$\log 0.006236 = \bar{3}.7949$$

The characteristic is −3 because to get 6.236 from 0.006236, the decimal point must be moved three places to the right.

Note: $\bar{3}.7949$ means −3 + 0.7949, ie, the mantissa is still positive, only the characteristic being negative. This is why the minus sign is written over the three. $\bar{3}$ is said as 'bar 3'. (Calculators will produce the result - 2.2051, which = 3 + 0.7949.)

5.3   Activity

Find the logarithms to base 10 of the following numbers.

(a)   48

(b)   2.463

(c)   0.84

(d)   0.0047

5.4   Activity solution

(a)   1.6812

(b)   0.3909 + 0.0005 = 0.3914

(c) $\bar{1}.9243$

(d) $\bar{3}.6721$

5.5   Antilogarithm tables

The purpose of antilog tables is to convert back from the log to the number it represents. This is done using the log tables backwards. It would be easier to use antilog tables, but these are not available in the exam.

Antilog of 0.3564 = 2.272 (2270 + 2)

Because the characteristic is 0, the decimal point in the antilog comes immediately after the first digit.

Antilog of 1.389 = 24.49

Only the mantissa (.389) is looked up. The result is first written down as 2.449 and as the characteristic is 1, the decimal point is moved 1 place to the right.

5.6   Activity

Find the antilogs of the following numbers.

(a)   2.6444

(b)   0.3395

(c) $\bar{3}$.8261

5.7   Activity solution

(a)   441
(b)   2.185
(c)   0.0067

5.8   Use of logarithms

From the laws of indices, if numbers are to be multiplied, their logarithms must be added and if one number is to be divided by another, the logarithm of the second number must be subtracted from the logarithm of the first. The answer to the original calculation is then found by taking the antilogarithm of the result. The calculations should be set out as in the following examples:

(a)   Evaluate 5.436 × 0.31

No	*Log*	
5.436	0.7353	
0.31	$\bar{1}$.4914	add
1.686	0.2267	

Hence 5.436 × 0.31 = 1.686

Always check such calculations for reasonableness by doing a mental calculation with approximate values. In this case 5 × 0.3 = 1.5 showing that the answer is reasonable at least as far as the position of the decimal point is concerned.

Note: An electronic calculator would give the answer 1.68516. The difference between this and the above answer is due to the fact that the logarithm tables used have been rounded to four figures, introducing a small but unavoidable error.

(b)   Evaluate $0.07486 \times 0.985 \div 62.38$

No	Log	
0.07486	$\bar{2}.8742$	
0.985	$\bar{1}.9934$	add
0.073737	$\bar{2}.8676$	
62.38	1.7950	subtract
0.001182	$\bar{3}.0726$	

Hence $0.07486 \times 0.985 \div 62.38 = 0.001182$

Note:

(i)   In line 3, $\bar{2} + \bar{1} = \bar{3}$
                 $\bar{3} + 1$ (carried over) $= \bar{2}$

(ii)   In line 5, $\bar{2} - 1 = \bar{3}$ because subtracting 1 from -2 gives -3.

(iii)   Check for reasonableness by taking approximate values.

$$0.07 \times 1 \div 60 = 0.07 \div 60$$
$$= 0.001 \text{ (approx)}$$

5.9   Activity

Evaluate: 261×3.964

5.10   Activity solution

$\log 261 = 2.4166$

$\log 3.964 = 0.5981$ add

             3.0147

antilog $3.0147 = 1,034$

Check: $261 \times 4 = 1,044$ therefore the answer is reasonable.

5.11   Activity

Evaluate: $3.7 \div 0.051$

5.12   Activity solution

$\log 3.7 = 0.5682$

$\log 0.051 = \bar{2}.7076$ subtract

             1.8606

antilog $1.8606 = 72.55$

6   EQUATIONS

6.1   Equations with one unknown

Where an equation contains only one unknown, say x, its solution may be found by simply manipulating the equation until x appears on the left-hand (LH) side only, and then evaluating the right-hand (RH) side.   The manipulation depends on the fact that an equation is analogous to balanced weights on a pair of scales. The balance will be maintained provided both sides are increased or decreased by the same amount.

$$\text{eg, } 3x - 4 \quad = \quad 2 - 6x$$

Adding 6x to both sides gives:

$$3x - 4 + 6x \quad = \quad 2*$$

$$9x - 4 \quad = \quad 2$$

Adding 4 to both sides gives:

$$9x \quad = \quad 2 + 4*$$

$$9x \quad = \quad 6$$

$$x \quad = \quad \frac{6}{9} \; = \; \frac{2}{3} \qquad \text{(dividing both sides by 9)}$$

Note: that by adding the same term to both sides, it looks as if that term has been taken over to the other side of the equation and given the opposite sign. This is what is done in practice, leading to the well-known rule 'change the side, change the sign'.

$$\text{eg, } 7x + 2 \quad = \quad 10 - 5x$$

Take −5x over from RH side to LH side and change to +5x:

$$7x + 5x + 2 \quad = \quad 10$$

Take +2 over from LH side to RH side and change to −2:

$$7x + 5x \quad = \quad 10 - 2$$

$$12x \quad = \quad 8$$

Dividing both sides by 12 and cancel:

$$\frac{12x}{12} \quad = \quad \frac{8}{12}$$

$$x \quad = \quad \frac{2}{3}$$

Note: always check your result by substituting the value obtained into the *original* equation.

Thus if $x = \dfrac{2}{3}$,

$$7 \times \dfrac{2}{3} + 2 \quad = \quad 10 - 5 \times \dfrac{2}{3}$$

$$\dfrac{14}{3} + 2 \quad = \quad 10 - \dfrac{10}{3}$$

$$\dfrac{14 + 6}{3} \quad = \quad \dfrac{30 - 10}{3}$$

$$\dfrac{20}{3} \quad = \quad \dfrac{20}{3}$$

As this balances, the solution is correct.

6.2   Linear equations

In general we are required to find the value of more than one unknown. In order to be able to do this, it is a necessary, but not sufficient, condition that there are as many equations as there are unknowns.

The basic method is to eliminate one of the two unknowns between the equations. This is achieved by adding or subtracting the equations, this process is known as solving simultaneous equations.

6.3   Solving simultaneous equations with 2 unknowns

Step 1   By multiplying one or both of the equations, make the coefficients of either x or y equal.

Step 2   Eliminate one of the unknowns by addition or subtraction.

6.4   Example of simultaneous equations

Solve:

$$x + y \quad = \quad 10 \quad (1)$$

and $\quad x - 4y \quad = \quad 0 \quad (2)$

6.5   Solution

Step 1   The coefficients of x are already equal in this example, so there is no need to multiply either equation.

Step 2   By subtracting equation (2) from equation (1), x will be eliminated, leaving y.

(1): $\quad x + \ y \ = \quad 10$

(2): $\quad x - 4y \ = \quad\ \ 0$ *subtract*

$\qquad\qquad 5y \quad = \quad 10$

Note: that to subtract $(-4y)$ change to $(+4y)$ and add,

ie, $y - (-4y) \quad = \quad y + 4y \quad = \quad 5y.$

Step 3   Obtain a value for y.

$$\therefore \quad y \quad = \quad 2$$

Step 4   This value of y is now substituted in equation (1) or (2) - whichever is the easier.

Substituting in (1): $x + 2 \quad = \quad 10$

$$\therefore x \quad = \quad 10 - 2 \quad = \quad 8$$

So the solution is x = 8, y = 2.

The result should be checked by substituting the values of x and y in the *other* equations. The original form of this equation should be used as an error may have been made in transposing it.

Substituting x = 8, y = 2 in the equation x – 4y = 0:

$$8 - 4 \times 2 \quad = \quad 0$$

$$8 - 8 \quad = \quad 0$$

As this is a true statement, the answer is correct.

It is not always possible to eliminate one of the unknowns by simply adding or subtracting the equations. In such a case it will be necessary to multiply one or both of the equations to make the coefficients of x or y equal. One of the unknowns may then be eliminated by addition or subtraction of the amended equation(s).

6.6   Example

$$2x + 3y \quad = \quad 42 \quad (1)$$

$$5x - y \quad = \quad 20 \quad (2)$$

6.7   Solution

Step 1   By multiplying equation (2) by 3 the coefficients of y become equal.

(1): $2x + 3y \quad = \quad 42$

$3 \times$ (2): $15x - 3y \quad = \quad 60 \ldots$ (3) *add*

Step 2   Equation (2) when multiplied by 3 becomes equation (3). Add equation (1) to equation (3) to eliminate y.

(1) $2x + 3y \quad = \quad 42$

(3) $15x - 3y \quad = \quad 60$

$ \quad 17x 102$

Step 3   Obtain a value for x by rearranging the equation

$$17x = 102$$

$$x = \frac{102}{17}$$

$$x = 6$$

Step 4   Substitution into any of (1), (2) or (3) is possible but in this case (2) is most convenient giving:

$$(5 \times 6) - y = 20$$

$$30 - y = 20$$

$$y = 30 - 20 = 10$$

So the solution is x = 6, y = 10

Check by substituting in (1)

$$2 \times 6 + 3 \times 10 = 42$$

$$12 + 30 = 42$$

$$42 = 42$$

As this is a true statement, the solution is correct.

6.8   Activity

Solve the following:

$$\frac{x}{3} + \frac{y}{2} = \frac{2x}{3} - \frac{y}{6} = 7$$

6.9   Activity solution

This means $\dfrac{x}{3} + \dfrac{y}{2} = 7$ (1)

and $\dfrac{2x}{3} - \dfrac{y}{6} = 7$ (2)

The first objective is to multiply through each equation by the lowest common denominator of that equation to remove the fractions, no attempt being made to eliminate x or y until the fractions are removed. Once this has been completed, and the equations are in the correct form, steps 1 to 4 can then be followed.

$(1) \times 6$: $6 \times \dfrac{x}{3} + 6 \times \dfrac{y}{2} = 6 \times 7$ $\therefore 2x + 3y = 42$ (3)

$(2) \times 6$: $6 \times \dfrac{2x}{3} - 6 \times \dfrac{y}{6} = 6 \times 7$ $\therefore 4x - y = 42$ (4)

Step 1   Multiply equation (4) by 3 to make the coefficients of y equal

$$(3): \quad 2x + 3y \quad = \quad 42$$

$$3 \times (4): \quad 12x - 3y \quad = \quad 126 \quad (5)$$

Step 2   Add equation (3) to equation (5) to eliminate y.

$$(3) \quad 2x + 3y \quad = \quad 42$$

$$(5) \quad 12x - 3y \quad = \quad 126$$

$$\overline{\quad 14x \quad} \qquad \overline{\quad 168 \quad}$$

Step 3   Rearrange the equation to calculate a value for x.

$$14x \quad = \quad 168$$

$$x \quad = \quad \frac{168}{14}$$

$$\therefore x \quad = \quad 12$$

Step 4   Substitute the value for x into (4).

Substituting in (4):
$$4 \times 12 - y \quad = \quad 42$$
$$48 - y \quad = \quad 42$$
$$-y \quad = \quad 42 - 48$$
$$-y \quad = \quad -6$$
$$\therefore y \quad = \quad 6$$

So the solution is x = 12, y = 6.

Check by substituting in (1) not (3):

$$\frac{12}{3} + \frac{6}{2} \quad = \quad 7$$

$$4 + 3 \quad = \quad 7$$

$$7 \quad = \quad 7$$

As this is true the solution is correct.

6.10   Solving simultaneous equations with 3 unknowns

When faced with 3 unknowns, one of these must be eliminated, hence leaving 2 unknowns which can then be solved in the usual way.

6.11   Example

Solve the simultaneous equations:

$$2x + 3y + 4z \quad = \quad 9 \quad (1)$$
$$3x - 2y - 3z \quad = \quad 3 \quad (2)$$
$$4x + 5y - 2z \quad = \quad 25 \quad (3)$$

6.12   Solution

Eliminate x (either of the other variables would do) between (1) and (2):

$3 \times (1)$:	$6x + 9y + 12z$	$=$	27
$2 \times (2)$:	$6x - 4y - 6z$	$=$	6
Subtract:	$13y + 18z$	$=$	21 (4)

Eliminate x between (3) and (1), ((2) could have been used instead of (1)):

$2 \times (1)$:	$4x + 6y + 8z$	$=$	18
(3):	$4x + 5y - 2z$	$=$	25
Subtract:	$y + 10z$	$=$	-7 (5)

Step 1   Multiply equation (5) by 13

$$13y + 130z \quad = \quad -91 \quad (6)$$

Step 2   Subtract (4) from (6)

$$13y + 130z \quad = \quad -91 \quad (6)$$

$$13y + 18z \quad = \quad 21 \quad (4)$$

$$112z \quad = \quad -112$$

Step 3   Rearrange the equation to obtain a value for z.

$$112z \quad = \quad -112$$

$$z \quad = \quad \frac{-112}{112}$$

$$z \quad = \quad -1$$

Step 4   Substitute the value of z into equation (5)

$y + 10z$	$= -7$
$y + 10(-1)$	$= -7$
$y - 10$	$= -7$
y	$= -7 + 10$
y	$= 3$

Due to there being 3 unknowns, substitute the values for y and z into equation (1) to obtain a value for x.

$$2x + 3y + 4z \qquad = \quad 9 \quad (1)$$
$$2x + 3 \times (3) + 4 \times (-1) \quad = \quad 9$$
$$2x + 9 - 4 \qquad = \quad 9$$
$$2x \qquad = \quad 9 - 9 + 4$$
$$2x \qquad = \quad 4$$
$$x \qquad = \quad \frac{4}{2} \quad = \quad 2$$

Check in either (2) or (3):

$$\text{from (2):} \quad 3 \times 2 - 2 \times 3 - 3 \times (-1) \quad = \quad 3$$
$$6 - 6 + 3 \qquad = \quad 3$$
$$3 \qquad = \quad 3$$

Hence the solution is x = 2, y = 3, z = -1.

7   EQUATIONS OF THE FIRST DEGREE (LINEAR EQUATIONS)

7.1   Graphing linear equations

An equation of the first degree is an equation containing no higher powers than the first of x and y, and is of the type $y = a + bx$ where a and b are both constants.

Consider the three equations:

(1) y = 2x
(2) y = 4 + 2x
(3) y = -2 + 2x

In order to draw graphs of these three equations it is necessary to decide on a range of values for x, say from -3 to +3, and then to calculate the corresponding values for y.

This is best displayed in the form of a table.

	x	-3	-2	-1	0	1	2	3
(1)	y = 2x	-6	-4	-2	0	2	4	6
(2)	y = 4 + 2x	-2	0	2	4	6	8	10
(3)	y = -2 + 2x	-8	-6	-4	-2	0	2	4

The three graphs will appear as follows:

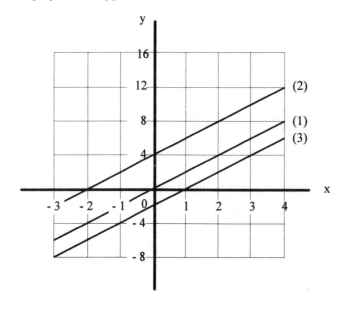

Several points are obvious from the graphs:

(a)   The graphs are all straight lines.

(b)   They are parallel to each other.

(c)   Line (1) crosses the y axis at $x = 0$, $y = 0$,   ie, (0, 0), called 'the origin'
         Line (2) crosses the y axis at $x = 0$, $y = 4$,   ie, (0, 4)
         Line (3) crosses the y axis at $x = 0$, $y = -2$, ie, (0, –2)

         The values of y are called the *intercepts on the y axis.*

(d)   Line (1) crosses the x axis at $x = 0$, $y = 0$,   ie, (0, 0)
         Line (2) crosses the x axis at $x = -2$, $y = 0$,   ie, (–2, 0)
         Line (3) crosses the x axis at $x = 1$, $y = 0$,   ie, (1, 0)

         These values of x are called the *intercepts on the x axis.*

7.2   The general equation of a straight line

Returning to the general form of the equation $y = a + bx$:

b   (the coefficient of x) is the *gradient* of the line, which is a measure of the 'steepness' of the line. This explains why the lines (1), (2) and (3) are parallel, since they all have a gradient of 2.

a   (the constant) is the *intercept* on the y axis ie, the value of y where the line cuts the y axis. For line (1) $a = 0$, line (2) $a = 4$, line (3) $a = -2$.

Equations of the first degree, ie, of the form $y = a + bx$, always result in straight line graphs.

However, equations of the first degree will sometimes not be given in this straightforward form and will need to be rearranged prior to plotting the graph.

7.3   Example

To plot $2(x - 3) = 4(y - 1)$, it is advisable to rearrange the expression so that y alone appears on the left hand side.

7.4   Solution

$2x - 6 = 4y - 4$ (multiplying out each bracket)

$2x - 2 = 4y$ (adding 4 to both sides)

$4y = -2 + 2x$ (transposing sides)

$y = -0.5 + 0.5x$ (dividing both sides by 4)

Hence it can be seen that the gradient is 0.5 and the intercept on the y axis is –0.5.

7.5   Example

Plot the graphs of the following equations and find the gradients and intercepts on the y axis.

(a) $4y = 6x - 5$ (x from 0 to +5)

(b) $\dfrac{x}{3}+\dfrac{y}{2} \;=\; 2$ (x from −2 to +3)

(c) $2(x-3) \;=\; 4(y-1)$ (x from −6 to +4 at even numbers only)

7.6   Solution

(a) $4y \;=\; 6x-5$

$y \;=\; \dfrac{6x}{4}-\dfrac{5}{4}$ (Dividing through by 4)

$y \;=\; 1.5x-1.25$ Comparing this with the general equation y = a + bx gives:

gradient = 1.5   (b)
intercept = −1.25   (a)

x	0	1	2	3	4	5
1.5x	0	1.5	3	4.5	6	7.5
y = 1.5x − 1.25	−1.25	0.25	1.75	3.25	4.75	6.25

(b) $\dfrac{x}{3}+\dfrac{y}{2} \;=\; 2$

$\dfrac{y}{2} \;=\; 2-\dfrac{x}{3}$

$\therefore y \;=\; 4-\dfrac{2x}{3}$ (Multiplying through by 2)

Gradient = $-\dfrac{2}{3}$;   intercept = 4

x	−2	−1	0	1	2	3
$\dfrac{-2x}{3}$	1.3	0.7	0	−0.7	−1.3	−2
$y = 4-\dfrac{2x}{3}$	5.3	4.7	4	3.3	2.7	2

(c) $2(x-3) \;=\; 4(y-1)$

$2x-6 \;=\; 4y-4$

$\therefore 2x-6+4 \;=\; 4y$

$2x-2 \;=\; 4y$

$\dfrac{2x}{4}-\dfrac{2}{4} \;=\; y$ (Dividing through by 4)

$y \;=\; 0.5x-0.5$

Gradient = 0.5, intercept = −0.5

x	−6	−4	−2	0	2	4
0.5x	−3	−2	−1	0	1	2
y = 0.5x − 0.5	−3.5	−2.5	−1.5	−0.5	0.5	1.5

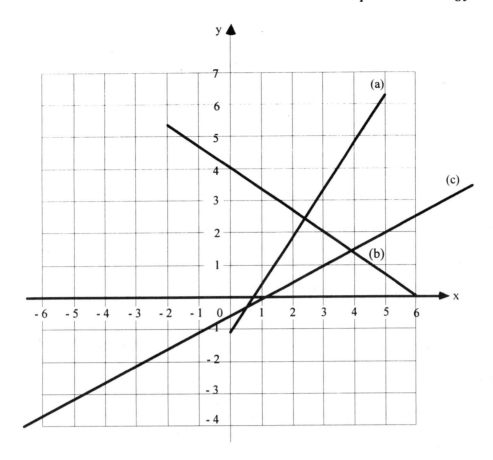

Note: in practice, once the equation is recognised as a straight line, it is only necessary to calculate and plot two points, as there is only one straight line that can pass through two given points. It is advisable, however, to plot three points as a check. If the three points do not lie on a straight line, a mistake has been made which must be located and corrected. It is never necessary to plot more than three points for a straight line graph. The points plotted must be well spaced out along the line. If the three points plotted are close together, the line cannot be drawn accurately.

8   QUADRATIC EQUATIONS

Whereas an expression of the first degree contains only terms in x, y, and constants, a quadratic, or second order, expression may also contain terms in x^2 and/or y^2.

A quadratic equation is simply a quadratic expression which is set to be equal to zero, for example:

$x^2 + 3x + 2 \quad = \quad 0 \qquad$ is a quadratic equation

The values of x that satisfy the equation are called the *roots* of the equation.

One method of solution of quadratic equations is by factorisation.

8.1   Factorisation

Factorisation is the reverse of multiplying out brackets. For example:

$3x(x + 2) \quad = \quad 3x^2 + 6x$

hence:

$3x^2 + 6x$ factorises to $3x(x + 2)$

Similarly,

$$(3x + 4)(2x - 5) \quad = \quad 3x(2x - 5) + 4(2x - 5)$$

$$= \quad 6x^2 - 15x + 8x - 20$$

$$= \quad 6x^2 - 7x - 20$$

Hence:

$6x^2 - 7x - 20$ factorises to $(3x + 4)(2x - 5)$

Three important factorisations that must be memorised are:

$$a^2 + 2ab + b^2 \quad = \quad (a + b)(a + b) \quad = \quad (a + b)^2$$
$$a^2 - 2ab + b^2 \quad = \quad (a - b)(a - b) \quad = \quad (a - b)^2$$
$$a^2 - b^2 \quad = \quad (a + b)(a - b)$$

(You can prove these to yourself by multiplying out the brackets.)

8.2   Example

The following expressions will be factorised:

(a) $12a^2m^3 - 15am^5$

(b) $am + bm + an + bn$

(c) $x^2 + 4x - 12$

(d) $10p^2 + 11pq - 6q^2$

8.3   Solutions

(a) $3am^3$ is a common factor of both terms, hence:

$$12a^2m^3 - 15am^5 \quad = \quad 3am^3 (4a - 5m^2)$$

(b)   m is a factor of the first two terms, and n is a factor of the last two terms, hence:

$$am + bm + an + bn \quad = \quad m(a + b) + n(a + b)$$

$(a + b)$ is now seen to be a factor of both terms, hence:

$$m(a + b) + n(a + b) \quad = \quad (a + b)(m + n)$$

(c)   In general, $(x + a)(x + b) \quad = \quad x^2 + (a + b)x + ab$

Two numbers are therefore required, whose product is −12 and whose sum is +4. By trial and error, these are found to be +6 and −2. Hence:

$$x^2 + 4x - 12 \quad = \quad (x + 6)(x - 2)$$

(d)   The factors will be of the form $(ap + bq)(cp + dq)$. On multiplying out, the coefficient of p^2 will be ac which equals 10, the coefficient of q^2 will be bd, which equals −6. The coefficient of pq will be ad + bc which equals 11. Trial and error then shows that the required values are:

$a = 5, b = -2, c = 2, d = 3$

hence: $10p^2 + 11pq - 6q^2 \quad = \quad (5p - 2q)(2p + 3q)$

8.4   Using factorisation to solve quadratic equations

If a quadratic expression can be seen to factorise then this gives a quick and neat way of solving the equation, eg, in the case of the above equation.

$$x^2 + 3x + 2 \quad = \quad 0$$

$$(x + 2)(x + 1) \quad = \quad 0$$

(If the product of two factors is zero, then one or both factors must be zero.)

$\therefore$ either $x + 2 = 0$ or $x + 1 = 0$

$\therefore$ $x = -2$ or $x = -1$

Not all quadratic equations factorise, and even if they do, factors will often be difficult to spot, and thus it is more usual to use a formula to solve the equation.

8.5   Solution of quadratics by formula

Consider the general quadratic equation

$$ax^2 + bx + c \quad = \quad 0$$

This has the solution:

$$x \quad = \quad \frac{-b \pm \sqrt{b^2 - 4ac}}{2a}$$

The most important part of this formula is $b^2 - 4ac$. There are three possibilities:

(a)   If $b^2 - 4ac$ is zero there is only one solution to the quadratic equation. (Strictly speaking there are two solutions (roots), but they both have the same value and are said to be coincident.)

or

(b)   If $b^2 - 4ac$ is positive there are two distinct solutions to the quadratic equations;

or

(c)   If $b^2 - 4ac$ is negative there are no real solutions to the quadratic equation since it is not possible to take the square root of a negative number (or not easily, as you can confirm on your calculator).

8.6   Example

The following equations will be solved using the formula:

(a) $9x^2 - 30x + 25 \quad = \quad 0$

(b) $(x + 3)^2 \quad = \quad 25$

8.7   Solution

(a) $9x^2 - 30x + 25 = 0$ so a = 9, b = –30, c = 25

then x $= \dfrac{-(-30) \pm \sqrt{(-30)^2 - 4 \times 9 \times 25}}{2 \times 9}$

$= \dfrac{30 \pm \sqrt{0}}{18}$ (remember that $(-30)^2 = +900$ as the product of two negative numbers is positive)

$= \dfrac{30}{18} = \dfrac{5}{3}$

$b^2 - 4ac$ is zero and there is only one solution to the quadratic equation. Also, the quadratic will factorise:

$9x^2 - 30x + 25 = 0$

$(3x - 5)(3x - 5) = 0$

$(3x - 5)^2 = 0$

$\therefore 3x - 5 = 0$

$\therefore 3x = 5$ so x = 5/3 (Twice, each factor giving the same root.)

(b) $(x + 3)^2 = 25$,   but $(x + 3)(x + 3) = x^2 + 6x + 9$

$\therefore x^2 + 6x + 9 = 25$

$x^2 + 6x + 9 - 25 = 0$

$x^2 + 6x - 16 = 0$ so a = 1, b = 6, c = –16

then   x $= \dfrac{-6 \pm \sqrt{6^2 - 4 \times 1 \times (-16)}}{2 \times 1}$

$= \dfrac{-6 \pm \sqrt{100}}{2}$

$= \dfrac{-6 \pm 10}{2}$

$= \dfrac{4}{2}$ ie, 2 or $-\dfrac{16}{2}$ ie, -8

8.8   Simultaneous equations - one linear, one quadratic

eg, $x + y = 1$ (1)

$3x^2 - xy + y^2 = 37$ (2)

The general method is to find an expression for one of the variables from the linear equation (1) and replace this in the quadratic equation (2).

ie, $x + y = 1$

$\therefore y = 1 - x$

Substituting for y in (2): $3x^2 - x(1-x) + (1-x)^2 = 37$

$$3x^2 - x + x^2 + (1 - 2x + x^2) = 37$$

$$5x^2 - 3x + 1 - 37 = 0$$

$$5x^2 - 3x - 36 = 0$$

It will now be necessary to solve this equation by factorisation or by using the formula.

By factorisation:

$(5x + 12)(x - 3) = 0$ check by multiplying out the brackets

Either $5x + 12 = 0$ $\therefore x = \dfrac{-12}{5}$

or $x - 3 = 0$ $\therefore x = 3$

When $x = \dfrac{-12}{5}$ or -2.4, $y = 1 - (-2.4) = 3.4$

When $x = 3$, $y = 1 - 3 = -2$

So the solutions are:

$(x, y) = (-2.4, 3.4)$

or $(x, y) = (3, -2)$

9   GRAPHS OF THE QUADRATIC FUNCTION

Graphs will now be drawn of:

(a) $y = 2x^2$

(b) $y = 2x^2 + 3$

(c) $y = 2x^2 - 4$

For the values of x from -3 to $+3$

	x	-3	-2	-1	0	1	2	3
(a)	x^2	9	4	1	0	1	4	9
	$y = 2x^2$	18	8	2	0	2	8	18
(b)	$y = 2x^2 + 3$	21	11	5	3	5	11	21
(c)	$y = 2x^2 - 4$	14	4	-2	-4	-2	4	14

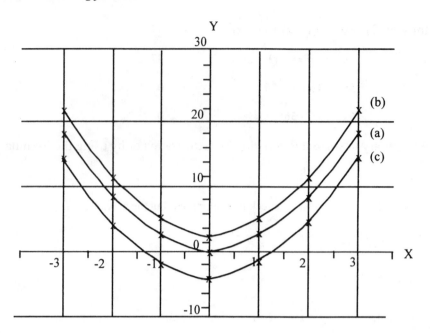

The graphs are symmetrical about the y axis, and they are clearly related to one another.

ie, (b)   y = 2x² + 3 is identical to (a)   y = 2x² but it is raised three units higher.

ie, (c)   y = 2x² – 4 is identical to (a)   y = 2x² but is it four units lower.

Therefore, the set of curves y = 2x² ± constant are identical except that they are higher or lower than the basic curve y = 2x² by the amount of the constant.

9.1   Example

The graph of y = x² + 3x + 2 will be drawn for values of x from –3 to +3.

x	-3	-2	-1	0	1	2	2
x^2	9	4	1	0	1	4	9
$3x$	-9	-6	-3	0	3	6	9
$y = x^2 + 3x + 2$	2	0	0	2	6	12	20

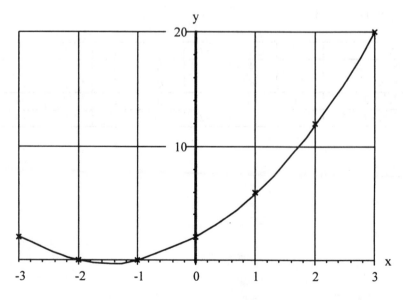

Although y = 0 at x = –2 and x = –1 the graph is a continuous curve between these points, it does not suddenly go flat.

9.2   Activity

The marketing department estimates that if the selling price of the new product A1 is set at £40 per unit then the sales will be 400 units per week, while, if the selling price is set at £20 per unit, the sales will be 800 units per week. Assume that the graph of this function is linear.

The production department estimates that the variable costs will be £7.50 per unit and that the fixed costs will be £10,000 per week.

(a)   Derive the cost, sales revenue, and profit equations.

(b)   Graph the three equations derived in (a).

(c)   From the graph, estimate the maximum profit that can be obtained, stating the number of sales units and the selling price necessary to achieve this profit.

Given: Selling price   =   £40/unit   Sales   =   400 units/week

Selling price   =   £20/unit   Sales   =   800 units/week

Variable costs   =   £7.50/unit

Fixed costs   =   £10,000/week

9.3   Activity solution

(a)   **Cost equation**

Let output = x units/week

then Total cost: T   =   10,000 + 7.5x

Sales revenue equation

Let price per unit = £p/unit

Then x = a + bp   since the graph of this function is linear.

Substituting each price and corresponding sales quantity into this equation,

when x   =   400, p   =   40   ∴   400   =   a + 40b   (1)

when x   =   800, p   =   20   ∴   800   =   a + 20b   (2)

(2) – (1):   400   =   –20b

∴ $\dfrac{400}{-20}$ =   b

–20   =   b

Substituting in (1):   400   =   a + 40 × (–20)

400   =   a – 800

400 + 800   =   a

1,200   =   a

So x = 1,200 – 20p   (3)

Rearranging: $20p = 1,200 - x$

$$\therefore \quad p = \frac{1,200 - x}{20} = 60 - \frac{x}{20}$$

But sales revenue R $= x \times p$ (ie, no of units sold × price per unit)

So sales revenue R $= x \times \left(60 - \frac{x}{20}\right)$

$$\therefore \quad R = 60x - \frac{x^2}{20}$$

Profit equation

Profit   P $= R - T$

$$= \left(60x - \frac{x^2}{20}\right) - (10,000 + 7.5x)$$

$$\therefore P = -\frac{x^2}{20} + 52.5x - 10,000$$

(b)   In order to draw graphs of the above equations it is necessary to calculate a range of values for x and T, R and P. Taking x from 0 to 1,200 units:

x	0	200	400	600	800	1,000	1,200
$7.5x$	0	1,500	3,000	4,500	6,000	7,500	9,000
$T = 10,000 + 7.5x$	10,000	11,500	13,000	14,500	16,000	17,500	19,000
$60x$	0	12,000	24,000	36,000	48,000	60,000	72,000
$x^2/20$	0	2,000	8,000	18,000	32,000	50,000	72,000
$R = 60x - x^2/20$	0	10,000	16,000	18,000	16,000	10,000	0
$P = R - T$	−10,000	-1,5000	3,000	3,500	0	−7,500	−19,000

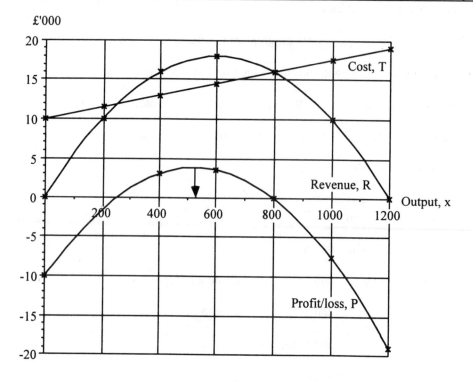

(c)   From the graph it can be seen that a maximum profit of about £3,800 occurs at an output of 525 units/week.

$$\text{Selling price p} \quad = \quad \frac{1,200 - x}{20}$$

$$= \quad \frac{1,200 - 525}{20}$$

$$= \quad £33.75/\text{unit}$$

9.4   Graphical solution of simultaneous equations

The solution of simultaneous equations with two unknowns can be found at the point or points of intersection of the graphs of the equations. In practice, it is essential to use graph paper, otherwise accurate readings cannot be taken from the graph. (Solving the equations of the lines simultaneously will provide a more accurate and reliable result, which can be checked with the graph.)

9.5   Examples

Solve the following pairs of equations graphically.

(a) $4x - 5y \quad = \quad -5$

$5x + 4y \quad = \quad 20$ (drawing graphs in the range 0 to 5)

(b) $2x + 3 - x^2 \quad = y$

$2x - 5y \quad = \quad -11$ (drawing graphs in the range -1 to 3)

9.6   Solutions

(a)   From $4x - 5y \quad = \quad -5$ we get $y \quad = \quad \dfrac{4x + 5}{5}$

x	0	2.5	5
$4x + 5$	5	15	25
$y = \dfrac{4x + 5}{5}$	1	3	5

From $5x + 4y = 20$ we get $y = \dfrac{20 - 5x}{4}$

x	0	2	4
$20 - 5x$	20	10	0
$y = \dfrac{20 + 5x}{4}$	5	2.5	0

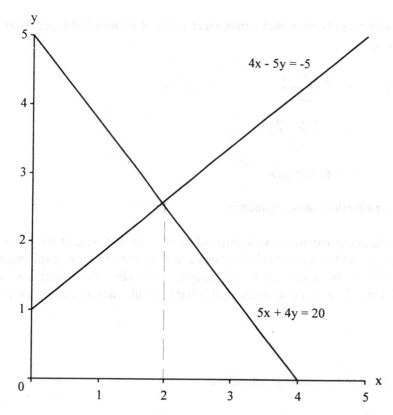

From the graph, the point of intersection of the lines is:

$$x \approx 2$$

$$y \approx 2\tfrac{1}{2}$$

Note: that if the two lines were parallel, they would not intersect and there would be no solution. (The true point of intersection found by solving the equations simultaneously, is $x = 1\tfrac{39}{41}, y = 2\tfrac{23}{41}$.)

(b) $y = 2x + 3 - x^2$

x	-1	0	1	2	3
$2x$	-2	0	2	4	6
3	3	3	3	3	3
$-x^2$	-1	0	-1	-4	-9
$y = 2x + 3 - x^2$	0	3	4	3	0

From $2x - 5y = -11$ we get $y = \dfrac{2x + 11}{5}$

x	0	1	2
$2x + 11$	11	13	15
$y = \dfrac{2x + 11}{5}$	2.2	2.6	3

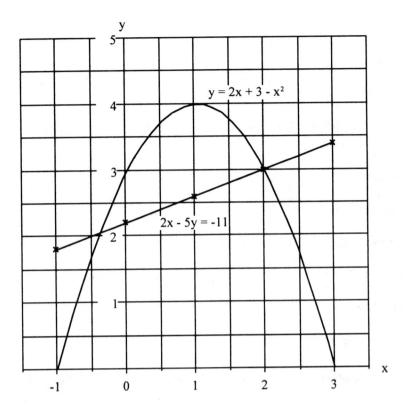

From the graph, the solutions are:

$x \approx -0.4,$ $y \approx 2.05$ and;

$x \approx 2.0,$ $y \approx 3.0$

Note: that there may be two solutions, one solution or no solution, depending on whether the straight line cuts the curve, just touches it or misses it altogether. These correspond to the three possibilities listed in section 3.4.

9.7   Activity

(a)   Factorise:

(i) $a^2 + 2a - 15$

(ii) $7b^2 + 10b + 3$

(b)   Solve the simultaneous equations:

$3p + 4q = 36$

$2p - 5q = 1$

(c)   Solve the following by factorisation if possible, otherwise by using the formula:

(i) $x^2 - 5x + 6 = 0$

(ii) $x^2 + 6x + 7 = 0$

(iii) $x^2 - 6x + 9 = 0$

(iv) $2x^2 + 5x - 20 = 0$

9.8   **Activity solution**

(a)   (i) $(a + 5)(a - 3)$

(ii) $(7b + 3)(b + 1)$

(b) $p = 8, q = 3$ (multiply the first equation by 2 and the second by 3 and subtract, eliminating p)

(c)   (i)   factorises, $x = 2$ or 3

(ii)   does not factorise, $x = -1.59$ or -4.41 (2dp)

(iii)   factorises, $x = 3$ twice

(iv)   does not factorise, $x = 2.15$ or -4.65 (2dp)

10   **SELF TEST QUESTIONS**

10.1   What is a coefficient? (3.3)

10.2   When two or more powers of the same number are multiplied together, what is the result? (4.2)

10.3   When dividing a power of a number by another power of the same number, what is the result? (4.6)

10.4   What does any number to the power of zero equal? (4.7)

10.5   Show a^{-n} in the form of a fraction. (4.7)

10.6   By convention, what number are logarithms to the base of? (5.1)

10.7   How many parts does a log consist of? (5.2)

10.8   What is the mantissa? (5.2)

10.9   Why are minus signs written over the characteristic? (5.2)

10.10   What is the purpose of an antilog table? (5.5)

10.11   What shape do graphs of linear equations take? (7)

10.12   What is the general equation of a straight line? Explain the significance of the constants involved (7.2)

10.13   What is the general form of a quadratic equation? (8.4)

10.14   What is the formula used to solve quadratic equations? (8.4)

10.15   With reference to the formula used to solve quadratic equations, how many solutions will there be if '$b^2 - 4ac$' is positive? (8.4)

11   EXAMINATION TYPE QUESTIONS

11.1

The quantity 10^{-2} means:

A -100

B $-2/10$

C $1/100$

D $2/10$

E $1/\sqrt{10}$.

11.2

There are two quantities, X and Y. $X = -1$ and $Y = -2$.

Therefore:

A $2X^2 > Y^2 < 0$

B $2X^2 < Y^2 < 0$

C $2X^2 < Y^2 > 0$

D $2X^2 > Y^2 > 0$

E $2X^2 = Y^2$

11.3   Exercises in solving equations

Solve the following equations:

(a) $3x - 2$ $=$ $4x - 4$;

(b) $4 - 5x$ $=$ $14 + 12x$;

(c) $\dfrac{12 - 3x}{4x + 5}$ $=$ 4;

(d) $12x + 2y$ $=$ 4 and

         $x - 2y$ $=$ 9

(e) $10x + 5y$ $=$ $3 - 2x$ and

         $4x + 10y$ $=$ $8 - 3x$

(f) $(2x + 5)(x + 1)$ $=$ 5;

(g) $6x^2 + 12x$ $=$ $4(5x + 2)$;

(h) $3x^2 - 2x + 7$ $=$ 0

(i) $2x^2 - 5x + 4xy$ $=$ 60

         $3x - y$ $=$ 9

11.4   Simultaneous equations

Solve the following equations simultaneously:

$$x + 2y - z = 12$$
$$x + y + 2z = 5$$
$$3x - y + z = 4$$

12   ANSWERS TO EXAMINATION TYPE QUESTIONS

12.1

C $10^{-2} = \dfrac{1}{10^2} = \dfrac{1}{100}$

12.2

C $2 < 4 > 0$

12.3   Exercises in solving equations

(a) $3x - 2 = 4x - 4$

$$3x - 4x = -4 + 2$$
$$-x = -2$$

(b) $4 - 5x = 14 + 12x$

$$-12x - 5x = 14 - 4$$
$$-17x = 10$$
$$x = -0.588$$

(c) $\dfrac{12 - 3x}{4x + 5} = 4$ (cross multiply by $(4x + 5)$)

$$12 - 3x = 4(4x + 5)$$ (multiply out bracket)

$$12 - 3x = 16x + 20$$ (subtract 16x and 12 from both sides)

$$-19x = 8$$

$$x = -0.421$$

(d)   Add equations

$$12x + 2y = 4 \quad (1)$$

$$\underline{x - 2y = 9} \quad (2)$$

$$13x = 13$$

$$\therefore x = 1$$

Substitute $x = 1$ into either equation: (for example equation 2)

$$x - 2y = 9$$

$$1 - 2y = 9$$

$$-2y = 8$$

$$y = -4$$

Check in other equation (ie, equation 1)

$$12 \times 1 + 2 \times (-4) \quad = \quad 12 - 8$$
$$= \quad 4$$

which is correct

Hence $(x, y) = (1, -4)$

(e) $10x + 5y \quad = \quad 3 - 2x$

rearrange to $12x + 5y \quad = \quad 3$ (1)

                              $4x + 10y \quad = \quad 8 - 3x$

rearrange to $7x + 10y \quad = \quad 8 - 3x$ (2)

Multiply equation (1) by 2

                              $24x + 10y \quad = \quad 6$ (1) $\times$ 2

Subtract $7x + 10y \quad = \quad 8$ (2)

                              $17x \quad = \quad -2$

$$\therefore x = \frac{-2}{17} \quad = \quad -0.118$$

Substitute value of x into equation (2)

$$(7 \times -{}^{2}\!/_{17}) + 10y \quad = \quad 8$$

$$10y \quad = \quad 8 + 0.823529$$

$$y \quad = \quad \frac{8.823529}{10}$$

$$y \quad = \quad 0.882$$

Check in equation (1) in its original form,

$10x + 5y$	$=$	$3 - 2x$
$10 \times (-0.118) + 5 \times 0.882$	$=$	$3 - 2 \times (-0.118)$
$-1.18 + 4.413$	$=$	$3 + 0.236$
3.23	$=$	3.236

The difference is due to rounding errors (which wouldn't occur if fractions were consistently used).

(f) $(2x + 5)(x + 1) \quad = \quad 5$ (multiply out brackets)

$2x^2 + 5x + 2x + 5 \quad = \quad 5$ (rearrange)

$2x^2 + 7x \quad = \quad 0$ (factorise)

$x(2x + 7) \quad = \quad 0$

$x = 0$ or $(2x + 7) \quad = \quad 0$

$x = 0$ or $x = -7/2$

(g) $6x^2 + 12x \quad = \quad 4(5x + 2)$ (multiply out brackets)

$6x^2 + 12x \quad = \quad 20x + 8$ (rearrange)

$6x^2 - 8x - 8 \quad = \quad 0$ Solve by formula:

$$x \quad = \quad \frac{-(-8) \pm \sqrt{(-8)^2 - (4 \times 6 \times (-8))}}{2 \times 6}$$

$$= \quad \frac{8 \pm \sqrt{64 + 192}}{12}$$

$$= \quad \frac{8}{12} \pm \frac{16}{12}$$

$$x \quad = \quad \frac{-2}{3} \text{ or } \quad x \quad = \quad 2$$

(h) $3x^2 - 2x + 7 \quad = \quad 0$ Solve by formula:

$$x \quad = \quad \frac{-(-2) \pm \sqrt{(-2)^2 - (4 \times 3 \times 7)}}{2 \times 3}$$

$$= \quad \frac{2 \pm \sqrt{(-80)}}{6}$$

There are no real roots to this equation, since the square root of (-80) cannot be found.

(i) $2x^2 - 5x + 4xy \qquad = \quad 60$ (1)

$3x - y \qquad = \quad 9$ (2)

From equation (2), $y \quad = \quad 3x - 9$ (3)

Substitute into (1) to get:

$2x^2 - 5x + 4x(3x - 9) \quad = \quad 60$ (multiply out bracket)

$2x^2 - 5x + 12x^2 - 36x \quad = \quad 60$ (rearrange)

$14x^2 - 41x - 60 \qquad = \quad 0$ (solve by formula)

$$x \quad = \quad \frac{41 \pm \sqrt{(41 \times 41) - (4 \times 14 \times -60)}}{2 \times 14}$$

$$= \quad \frac{41 \pm \sqrt{5,041}}{28}$$

$x = 4, \text{ or } x = \dfrac{-30}{28}$

Substitute into (3) to give:

$y = (3 \times 4 - 9) = 3$, or $y = (3 \times {}^{-30}\!/_{28} - 9) = -12{}^6\!/_{28}$ (or -12.21)

Hence $(x, y) = (4, 3)$ or $(x, y) = (-1.07, -12.21)$

12.4   Simultaneous equations

$$x + 2y - z = 12 \qquad (1)$$
$$x + y + 2z = 5 \qquad (2)$$
$$3x - y + z = 4 \qquad (3)$$

It is necessary to eliminate z between (1) and (2) and then (1) and (3).

$(1) \times 2 + (2)$
$$2(x + 2y - z) + (x + y + 2z) = 24 + 5$$
$$2x + 4y - 2z + x + y + 2z = 29$$
$$3x + 5y = 29 \qquad (4)$$

$(1) + (3)$
$$(x + 2y - z) + (3x - y + z) = 12 + 4$$
$$x + 2y - z + 3x - y + z = 16$$
$$4x + y = 16 \qquad (5)$$

$(4) - (5) \times 5$
$$3x + 5y - 5(4x + y) = 29 - 16 \times 5$$
$$3x + 5y - 20x - 5y = 29 - 80$$
$$-17x = -51$$
$$\therefore x = 3$$

Replacing $x = 3$ in (5) gives $4 \times 3 + y = 16$ $\qquad \therefore y = 4$

Replacing $x = 3$, $y = 4$ in (2) gives $3 + 4 + 2z = 5$ $\qquad \therefore z = -1$

So the solution is $x = 3$, $y = 4$, $z = -1$.

15 PERCENTAGES, RATIOS & DISCOUNTS

INTRODUCTION & LEARNING OBJECTIVES

Syllabus area 2d.   Percentages; ratios; discounts. (Ability required 3).

This chapter provides a basic knowledge of percentages, ratios and discounts and also explains permutations and combinations. This is background knowledge needed to tackle areas covered later in the text, and everyday in the accounting world.

When you have studied this chapter you should be able to do the following:

- Confidently calculate percentages, ratios and proportions.

- Explain the meaning of and difference between permutations and combinations.

- Calculate permutations.

- Understand and calculate discounts.

---

1   PERCENTAGES

1.1   Percentages

Definition   'Percent' means 'out of 100.' The rule is: to convert a fraction into a percentage, multiply the fraction by 100; to convert a percentage into a fraction, divide by 100, eg,:

$$40\% = \frac{40}{100}$$

$$= \frac{2}{5}$$

$$2\tfrac{1}{2}\% = \frac{2\tfrac{1}{2}}{100}$$

$$= \frac{1}{40}$$

We are well used to reading about percentages - wage increases may be, for example, restricted to 7%, in Britain VAT is levied at, for example, 17.5%. Eg, to find the amount of VAT on £250, assuming a VAT rate of 17.5%.

$$17.5\% \text{ of } £250 = \frac{17.5}{100} \times £250 = £43.75$$

Percentages are very easy to deal with, which is why they are frequently used when handling business data.

1.2   Example

Equipment is sold for £240 and makes a profit of 20% on cost. What is the cost price? What is the profit?

1.3   Solution

If cost price	=	100%
and profit	=	20% (as we are told it is 20% of cost)
Selling price	=	120% of cost

	120% of cost	=	£240
∴	100% of cost	=	$\dfrac{240}{120} \times 100$
	Cost price	=	£200
∴	Profit	=	£240 – £200
		=	£40

The figure of 20% on cost is usually referred to as a 'mark-up'.

1.4   Example

Profit percentages are often expressed as a percentage of selling price.

If stock is bought for £210, what should the selling price be to achieve a profit of 30% on the selling price?

1.5   Solution

If selling price	=	100%
and profit	=	30%
Cost		70%

	70% of selling price	=	£210
∴	100% of selling price	=	$£\dfrac{210}{70} \times 100$
	Selling price	=	£300
∴	Profit	=	£300 – £210
		=	£90

1.6   Example

A group of workers earn £120 per week. They want to negotiate an increase of £15 per week. What percentage increase should they claim?

1.7 Solution

$$\frac{15}{120} \times 100\% \qquad = \quad 12.5\%$$

1.8 Activity

A company buys a product from the manufacturer for £900. They feel that they need to make a profit of 35% on the selling price to cover overheads. At what price should the company sell the product?

1.9 Activity solution

	If selling price	=	100%
	and profit	=	35%
	Cost	=	65%
	65% of selling price	=	£900
∴	100% of selling price	=	$\dfrac{£900}{65} \times 100$
	Selling price	=	£1,384.62
∴	Profit	=	£1,384.62 – £900 = £484.62

2 RATIOS

2.1 What is a ratio?

A ratio is really an alternative way of expressing a fraction. For example:

Sales	500
Cost of sales	300
Gross profit	200

The gross profit to sales could be expressed in any of four ways:

(a)   Fraction $\dfrac{200}{500} = \dfrac{2}{5}$

(b)   Decimal $\dfrac{200}{500} = 0.4$

(c)   Percentage $\dfrac{200}{500} \times 100 = 40\%$

(d)   Ratio $200 : 500 \quad = \quad 2 : 5$

The colon sign indicates that the two sides are being expressed as ratios to each other.

To divide a number into separate parts in a given ratio, the ratios are converted into fractions as follows:

To divide 275 into three parts in the ratio 2 : 4 : 5.

Add the three ratio numbers: 2 + 4 + 5 = 11.

Express each as a fraction of the total: $\dfrac{2}{11}$, $\dfrac{4}{11}$, $\dfrac{5}{11}$

The three parts are therefore:

(a) $\dfrac{2}{11} \times 275 = 50$

(b) $\dfrac{4}{11} \times 275 = 100$

(c) $\dfrac{5}{11} \times 275 = 125$

Thus 50, 100 and 125 are in the ratio 2 : 4 : 5 and add up to 275.

2.2   Example

Tom, Bill and Fred are in business together and one year make a profit of £39,000. They had previously agreed to share profits in the ratio 7 : 2 : 4 respectively. How is the profit shared between them?

2.3   Solution

$7 + 2 + 4 = 13$

		£
Tom receives	$\dfrac{7}{13} \times 39,000$	= 21,000
Bill receives	$\dfrac{2}{13} \times 39,000$	= 6,000
Fred receives	$\dfrac{4}{13} \times 39,000$	= 12,000
		£39,000

How would it have been shared if the ratio was 4 : 3 : 3 respectively?

$4 + 3 + 3 = 10$

		£
Tom receives	$\dfrac{4}{10} \times 39,000$	= 15,600
Bill receives	$\dfrac{3}{10} \times 39,000$	= 11,700
Fred receives	$\dfrac{3}{10} \times 39,000$	= 11,700
		39,000

Notice how important it is to deal with ratio calculations in the correct order.

3   PROPORTIONS

3.1   What is a proportion?

A proportion is the ratio of a part to the whole. In the first part of Example 4.2 above, Tom received $\frac{7}{13}$ of the total profit.

The ratio of Tom's share to the total profit it is $\frac{7}{13}$ or 0.53846 as a decimal; this is the proportion of the total profit that Tom recieves.

3.2   Activity

If the population in the town of Medton is 278,000 and 54,000 of these are old age pensioners (OAPs):

(a)   What is the ratio of OAPs to non-OAPs?
(b)   What is the percentage of OAPs in the population?
(c)   What proportion of the population are OAPs?

3.3   Activity solution

(a)   OAPs   =   54,000

        Non-OAPs   =   278,000 – 54,000

                            =   224,000

        Ratio   =   54,000 : 224,000

                            =   27 : 112

(b)   Percentage of OAPs = $\dfrac{54,000}{278,000} \times 100\%$

                            =   19.4%

(c)   Proportion of OAPs = $\dfrac{54,000}{278,000}$

                            = $\dfrac{27}{139}$ or 0.194

4   PERMUTATIONS

4.1   Introduction

An area which is of importance when considering probability is determining the number of possible ways in which things might occur, and then the number of different ways which meet certain criteria. It is included in this chapter as it is a mathematical technique of general application - not merely limited to use as part of theoretical probability.

The basis of all such problems is the number of ways in which a given number of items can be arranged in a different order. For example, to find the number of ways in which six different people can be arranged in a row, imagine how they may be seated on six chairs. The first person has a choice of six chairs. Once he is seated, the second person has a choice of five chairs. So for each of the six positions in which the first is seated, the second has a choice of five positions, making $6 \times 5 = 30$ different positions. The third person has a choice of four chairs, and so on, down to the last person who has a choice of only one chair. The total number of ways in which the six can be arranged is therefore $6 \times 5 \times 4 \times 3 \times 2 \times 1 = 720$. This is called 'factorial six' and is denoted by 6!. In general,

Factorial n $=$ n! $=$ $n \times (n-1) \times (n-2) \times \ldots 3 \times 2 \times 1$

4.2   [Definition]   A permutation is a number of items, selected from a larger group of items, where the order in which the items are selected **is significant**.

If there are twelve applicants for four **different** vacancies in a factory and the recruitment officer, deciding they are all equally suitable for each vacancy, makes the appointments by drawing four names from a hat, how many different allocations are possible?

The first name out of the hat could be that of any of the twelve applicants, as there are twelve ways of drawing the first name. That leaves eleven names in the hat, so there are eleven ways of drawing the second name, and so on.

There are $12 \times 11 \times 10 \times 9$ ways of allocating the jobs $= 11,880$ in total.

Note that $12 \times 11 \times 10 \times 9$ can be expressed as:

$$\frac{12 \times 11 \times 10 \times 9 \times 8 \times 7 \times 6 \times 5 \times 4 \times 3 \times 2 \times 1}{8 \times 7 \times 6 \times 5 \times 4 \times 3 \times 2 \times 1} = \frac{12!}{8!} = \frac{12!}{(12-4)!}$$

the last eight factors in the numerator cancelling out with the denominator.

Expressed mathematically, this problem involves finding the number of **permutations** of size four from a group of items size twelve.

In general, the number of permutations of size r from a group of n items is:

$$^nP_r = n(n-1)(n-2)\ldots(n-r+1)$$

$$= \frac{n!}{(n-r)!}$$

It was stated that all the vacancies in the above problem were different. Two possible allocations are:

Vacancy   1 2 3 4   and   Vacancy   1 2 3 4
Applicant A B C D   Applicant D C B A

Just considering applicants, A, B, C and D, the number of ways they can be allocated to the four vacancies is:

$$^4P_4 = \frac{4!}{(4-4)!}$$

$$= \frac{4!}{0!}$$

$$= \frac{4!}{1}$$

$$= 4 \times 3 \times 2 \times 1$$

$$= 24$$

Note that $0! = 1$. This is so by definition to make factorials obey the ordinary rules of algebra. 1! is also of course 1.

4.3   Activity

Three marbles are put into a bag, the colours of the marbles being red, blue and yellow. How many possible ways/orders are there of pulling the marbles out of the bag?

4.4   Activity solution

$$^nP_r = \frac{n!}{(n-r)!}$$

$$^3P_3 = \frac{3!}{(3-3)!} = \frac{3!}{1} = 6$$

The permutations are:

(1)   Red, Blue, Yellow.
(2)   Red, Yellow, Blue.
(3)   Yellow, Blue, Red.
(4)   Yellow, Red, Blue.
(5)   Blue, Red, Yellow.
(6)   Blue, Yellow, Red.

5   COMBINATIONS

5.1

Definition   A combination is a number of items, selected from a larger group of items, where the order in which those items are selected **is not significant.**

If the four vacancies were for identical jobs, then the twenty-four arrangements ABCD, DCBA, etc are effectively the same: any distinction between them is meaningless. The order of drawing applicants does not now matter.

The collective name for all permutations which are the same is a **combination**. Taking all the four vacancies as identical, the number of combinations of four applicants from the group of twelve is:

$$^{12}C_4 = \frac{11,880}{24}$$

$$= 495$$

In general:

$$^nC_r = \frac{n(n-1)(n-2)(n-3)...(n-r+1)}{r(r-1)(r-2)...3.2.1}$$

$$= \frac{n!}{r!(n-r)!}$$

where $n! = n(n-1)(n-2) \ldots 3.2.1$

$(n-r)! = (n-r)(n-r-1)(n-r-2) \ldots 3.2.1$

$r! = r(r-1)(r-2) \ldots 3.2.1$

Note that both 0! and 1! are equal to 1.

5.2   Example

The board of directors, consisting of four persons, is to be formed from a group of ten senior managers. How many different ways can this be achieved?

5.3   Solution

Four specific candidates will constitute the same board, irrespective of the order in which they are chosen, hence combinations rather than permutations are required.

The number of different ways is:

$$\frac{10!}{(10-4)!4!}$$

$$= \frac{10!}{6!4!}$$

$$= \frac{10\times9\times8\times7}{4\times3\times2\times1}$$

$$= 210$$

5.4   Example

The board, in Example 5.2, consists of managing director, chairman and secretary, plus one other board member. How many different ways are possible now?

5.5   Solution

In this case each post on the board is distinct and therefore the number of permutations rather than combinations is required:

The number of different ways is:

$$\frac{10!}{(10-4)!}$$

$$= 10\times9\times8\times7$$

$$= 5,040$$

5.6   Example

An audit team is made up of a manager, 2 seniors and 4 assistants. There are 10 managers, 15 seniors and 20 assistants in Tickit & Co. How many different audit teams could be formed from these personnel?

5.7   Solution

It is necessary to calculate the number of teams of each grade of staff:

number of different managers $= 10$

number of different combinations of seniors $= \dfrac{15\times14}{2\times1} = 105$

number of different combinations of assistants $= \dfrac{20\times19\times18\times17}{4\times3\times2\times1} = 4,845$

Therefore number of different audit teams possible $10\times105\times4,845 = 5,087,250$

5.8   Activity

(a)   Calculate the number of ways of choosing 6 employees to fill 6 vacancies.

(b)   Ten people apply for 4 jobs. Calculate the number of ways of four of these people taking the 4 jobs offered (irrespective of order).

5.9   Activity solution

(a) $^6C_6 = \dfrac{6!}{(6-6)!6!} = \dfrac{720}{1 \times 720} = \dfrac{720}{720} = 1$

(b) $^{10}C_4 = \dfrac{10!}{(10-4)!4!} = \dfrac{3,628,800}{720 \times 24} = \dfrac{3,628,800}{17,280} = 210$

5.10   Activity

(a)   In how many different ways can vehicle registration numbers consisting of three letters and three digits be selected from twenty six letters and ten digits if no letter or digit can be used more than once in any one registration number?

(b)   In how many ways can four clerks be selected for promotion out of a group of fifteen clerks?

5.11   Activity solution

(a)   The same letters or digits in a different order will give different registration numbers, hence permutations must be used.

Number of different registration numbers $=\quad ^{26}P_3 \times \ ^{10}P_3$

$=\quad \dfrac{26!}{(26-3)!} \times \dfrac{10!}{(10-3)!}$

$=\quad 15,600 \times 720$

$=\quad 11,232,000$

(b)   It is immaterial in which order within the group the four clerks appear, hence combinations must be used.

Number of ways $=\quad ^{15}C_4$

$=\quad \dfrac{15!}{(15-4)!4!}$

$=\quad 1,365$

6   DISCOUNTS

6.1 $\boxed{\textbf{Definition}}$ A discount is a percentage or an amount deducted from the price, cost etc.

A business may offer its customers benefits in the form of discounts, the bigger (financially) the customer to the business, the bigger the discount usually given.

The discount is normally deducted by calculating a fixed percentage of the total value of the goods, and then deducting this value from the original total. For example, a business offers its customer a 10% discount on all orders over £500.

Customer X orders goods to a value of £700. The discount is calculated as follows:

	£
Original order value	700
Less 10% discount (700 × 0.10)	70 –
Amount invoiced to customer	630

6.2   Example

Company Y offers its customers a 12% discount on all orders over £500 and 15% discount on orders over £1000.

Customers A and B place orders for £1,010 and £620 respectively.

Calculate the value that company Y will invoice to both its customers.

6.3   Solution

Customer A:

Order value	1,010.00	
Less discount 15%	151.50	– (1,010 × 0.15)
Value invoiced	858.50	

Customer B:

Order value	620.00	
Less discount 12%	74.40	– (620 × 0.12)
Value invoiced	545.60	

7   SELF TEST QUESTIONS

7.1   What does 'percent' mean? (1.1)

7.2   In general, what are the number of permutations of size r from a group of n items? (4.2)

7.3   What is the value of 0!? (4.2)

7.4   What is the value of 1!? (4.2)

7.5   What is the formula for combinations? (5.1)

7.6   What is a discount? (6.1)

16 FORMULAE IN SPREADSHEETS

INTRODUCTION & LEARNING OBJECTIVES

Syllabus area 2d. Formulae in spreadsheets. (Ability required 3).

This chapter provides a basic knowledge of spreadsheets. It explains the uses of spreadsheet packages and gives an insight into the basic formulae which are used.

There are many different spreadsheets presently on the market, some being more powerful than others, and obviously some are a lot more expensive than others. Spreadsheets do however have an important use within businesses.

When you have studied this chapter you should be able to do the following:

●   Understand the uses of a spreadsheet.

●   Understand and explain how formulae are used within the spreadsheet.

---

1   SPREADSHEETS

1.1   **Definition**   A spreadsheet is a computer program that allows numbers to be entered and manipulated, as well as the use of text, and in most cases gives the ability to draw graphs.

1.2   **Blank spreadsheet**

The blank spreadsheet is made up of a number of vertical and horizontal lines.

The horizontal border, contains one or two letters as a heading to each column, and the vertical border contains a number for each row of the worksheet.

There is a control panel which is usually activated by pressing the '/' key. This panel is called upon for all commands (ie, copying, erasing, changing column widths, rounding to a number of decimal places, plotting a graph, saving data and exiting the spreadsheet).

Cell A1 is usually highlighted when a new spreadsheet is called upon, and the cursor can be moved around by the use of the four arrow keys (ie, $\uparrow$, $\rightarrow$, $\downarrow$, $\leftarrow$).

A spreadsheet has at times been referred to as a giant calculator, it allows a large amount of information to be entered, and calculations are carried out immediately formulae have been entered into the required cell.

1.3   How the spreadsheet works

Columns

A   B   C   D   E   etc,

1

2

Rows   3

4

5

etc

The spreadsheet is made up of a number of rows and columns, as shown above.

A cell is located at the intersection of a column and row. Thus the cell illustrated above is cell B2, ie, the cell in column B and row 2.

2   FORMULAE IN SPREADSHEETS

2.1   Symbols

The spreadsheet allows the user to perform addition, subtraction, multiplication and division by using formulae which relate to each of the cell references.

The following symbols are used within the formulae:

+	Addition
–	Subtraction
*	Multiplication
/	Division
@SUM( )	Add a range of cells
@AVERAGE( )	Calculate the average of a range of cells

2.2   Example

The values 2, 3 and 4 are entered into cells B2, B3, B4 respectively. They are to be added together, with the sum being entered into cell B7.

This would appear on the spreadsheet as follows:

2.3   Solution

	A	B	C	D	
1					
2		2			
3		3			
4		4			
5					
6					
7		+B2+B3+B4			
8					

Although the formulae is entered into cell B7, it will not be seen, only the value will appear ie, the number 9. (Note: it is possible to show the formula instead of the answer.)

2.4   Larger formulae

The formula can be of any size within the cell, but the answer must be able to fit within the cell. The cell width can obviously be widened if so needed.

2.5   Addition using '+' symbol

As with addition on a calculator, the '+' symbol is used. If you refer to example 1.5, note that the formula starts with a '+'.

2.6   Addition using '@SUM'

When addition of a range of cells is required ie, A1 to A100, a very large formula would need to be entered if the '+' symbol was to be used. Instead the '@SUM' method can be used. Hence if adding the range of cells A1 to A100, and the answer is to appear in cell A102, the following formula would be entered into cell A102:

@SUM(A1..A100)   The '..' means all cells between the two cell references.

2.7   Multiplication

Multiplication within a formula is specified using the '*' asterisk symbol.

Example:

To multiply cell A2 by cell A3, the answer would appear as +A2*A3.

2.8   Division

To divide a number by another number the '/' symbol is used.

Example:

To divide cell C2 by cell E2 it would appear as +C2/E2.

2.9   Activity

The numbers 10,000, 2,000 and 6,000 are entered into cells A1, A2 and A3. The sum of the three numbers should be entered into cell A5, and the value of A3 divided by A2 should be entered into cell A6.

Show how the spreadsheet should look when both formulae are entered onto it.

2.10   Activity solution

	A
1	10000
2	2000
3	6000
4	
5	@SUM(A1..A3)
6	+A3/A2

3   SPREADHSEET EXAMPLE

3.1   Introduction

The following example will show how these formulae can be used in an actual spreadsheet.

The illustration below is of a spreadsheet screen using Lotus 123. The 'Unit' and 'Qty' column will have been entered by an operator. The text that follows shows the formulae that are needed to produce the 'Total' column.

The text refers to various Lotus functions and facilities with which you may not be familiar. If this is the case, do not worry. The text is designed to give you a overview of how a spreadsheet can be used - it is not necessary for you to know the detail of how the spreadsheet works.

3.2   The formulae

The cost of two packets of OHP films and five batteries, etc, has to be found. This can be done by moving the cursor to cell G10 and typing:

   +E10*F10 (and pressing **ENTER**).

The * (asterisk) denotes multiply.

This formula can be copied for the remaining items on lines 11 to 14. To do this, with the cell pointer over cell G10, type:

   / C ↵

to indicate that the formula in cell G10 is to be copied, then moving the cursor down to cell G11 and typing a dot (.), to indicate that a range is required, then moving the cell pointer to G14 and pressing **ENTER**.

3.3   Using an @ function

To find the subtotal of the five prices one **could** move to cell G16 and enter a long and cumbersome formula:

   +G10+G11+G12+G13+G14

There is a quicker way.

The quick method involves using a function (or rather an @ function). The particular function needed here is one to add up a range of figures (in this case those in cells G10 to G14). The function, unsurprisingly, is called **@SUM**.

To find the subtotal, move to cell G16 and enter:

   @SUM(G10..G14)   (note the two dots) and press **ENTER**

The total will appear (139.67), which you may wish to check, leaving the invoice as follows.

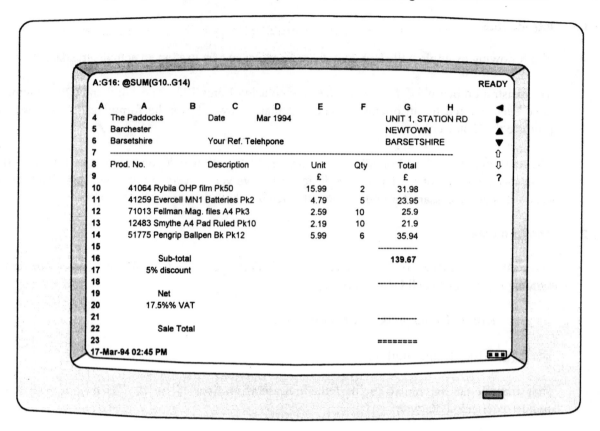

The range could have been typed as just G10.G14; Lotus will add the extra dot itself.

3.4   Including the remaining figures

Discount and VAT need to be calculated and the Sale Total found.

To find the size of the discount, 5% of 139.67 needs to be calculated. This requires a formula. In cell G17 enter:

+G16*A17/100

(Note that all A17 contains is the discount of 5% and the above formula picks up this number in its calculation.)

The / (slash) sign here signifies divide. The sub-total shown in G16 (139.67) has been multiplied by the rate of discount shown in A17 (5) and then expressed as a percentage.

The net discount figure can be shown in cell G19. Move to that cell and subtract the discount from the previous sub-total.

+G16–G17   (ENTER)

The result is 132.6865.

Next VAT has to be calculated in a similar fashion to the discount. Move to cell G20 and type:

+G19*A20/100

VAT at 17½% on £132.6865 is £23.22014.

Finally the Sale Total is found by adding VAT to the Net amount. In cell G22 type:

+G19+G20

The result is 155.9066 (approximately) and the worksheet looks as follows.

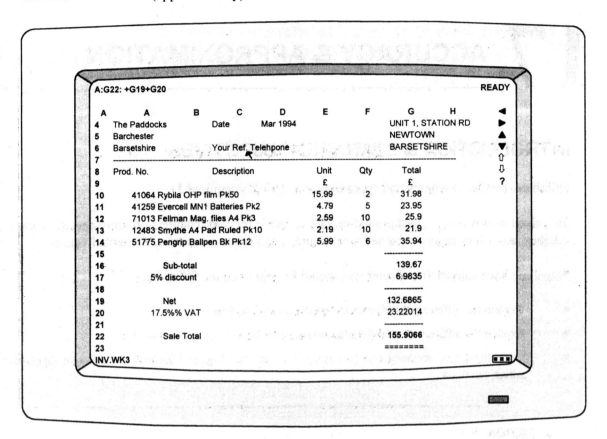

4   SPREADSHEETS AND THEIR USERS

4.1   Uses of a spreadsheet

Spreadsheets are used within many organisations, and some of their uses are outlined below.

> Cashflow forecasts
> Profit and loss accounts
> Calculation of VAT
> Financial reports

4.2   Users of spreadsheets

Spreadsheets are used by many areas of the organisations but they have tended to be used mostly by financial departments.

In reality, spreadsheets can be used by anybody, and many individuals now use spreadsheets packages to maintain their personal finances.

5   SELF TEST QUESTIONS

5.1   What is a spreadsheet? (1.1)

5.2   Which symbol is used to show multiplication on a spreadsheet? (2.1)

5.3   Which symbol is used to show division on a spreadsheet? (2.1)

5.4   What does @ AVERAGE(A1..A3) mean? (2.1)

5.5   What are spreadsheets used for? (4.1)

17 ACCURACY & APPROXIMATION

INTRODUCTION & LEARNING OBJECTIVES

Syllabus area 2e. Accuracy and approximation. (Ability required 3).

This chapter provides the background needed to tackle the later chapters on more specific areas of the syllabus, and is primarily concerned with accuracy and approximation of numerical values.

When you have studied this chapter you should be able to do the following:

- Explain the difference between continuous and discrete data.
- Explain the difference between independent and dependent data.
- Understand how accuracy can be distorted due to rounding, and identify the different types of errors which can occur.

---

1 NOTATION

1.1 Variables

These are the characteristics that are being measured. They can be classified in two different and distinct ways:

(a) Variables can be either **continuous** or **discrete**.

A continuous variable is one that can assume any value, including all fractional values (eg, height, weight, temperature), whereas a discrete variable is one that can only assume certain specific values, ususally integer (whole number) values (eg, the number of children in a family, shoe sizes).

(b) Variables can alternatively be classified as **independent** or **dependent**.

An **independent variable** is a variable which is not affected by changes in another variable, whereas a **dependent variable** is affected by changes in another, eg, changes in advertising expenditure in a year can be expected to affect sales, but a change in sales will not directly affect advertising expenditure. Hence, advertising is the independent variable and sales the dependent.

1.2 Accuracy and approximation

No measurement of a continuous variable is ever exact. If the length of a page of a book is measured, the result may be given as 21.6cm when, in fact, the length could lie between 21.55 and 21.65 because 21.6cm may have been rounded up or down to one decimal place. Measurements should not be quoted with greater accuracy than they merit; in this case the answer is said to be correct to three significant figures (3sf). Another method of indicating the accuracy of a number is to quote the limits of possible error, eg, to say that a boy's height is 163cm to the nearest cm means that his height lies between 162.5 and 163.5cm and may be written as 163 ± 0.5cm.

Even when a figure may be computed to, say, 4 significant figures it will sometimes be better to give the final answer to, say 3 significant figures. This will depend upon the accuracy of the original data on which the computations are based. It is important not to mislead the reader of the final results by making them spuriously accurate.

An example of a particular area where it would be incorrect to be too accurate is the computation of price indices as an estimate for the rate of inflation.

1.3   **Rounding errors**

The term error is used here not in the sense of mistakes, but in the same sense that we speak of experimental errors, that is, lack of precision.

Errors can be divided into two groups:

(a)   **Biased and unbiased errors**

Biased errors arise whenever individual items are rounded **in the same direction**. They are cumulative, which means that the total error will increase as more items are added together. For example, £10.30, £11.40, £14.60 and £15.90 rounded up to the nearest pound above become £11, £12, £15 and £16 respectively. When added together they give £54 compared with the true answer of £52.20.

Unbiased errors arise when individual items are rounded in **either direction**. They tend to cancel each other out so that the total error does not increase as more items are added together. For example, using the data of the previous example but rounding to the nearest pound, the figures become £10, £11, £15 and £16 respectively. When added together they give £52 compared with the true answer of £52.20.

(b)   **Absolute and relative errors**

An absolute error is the difference between the actual, or true, value and the approximate (rounded or estimated) value. For example, 3,752.9 kg becomes 3,800 kg when rounded to the nearest hundred kilograms.

$$\text{Absolute error} = (3,800 - 3,752.9)\text{kg}$$

$$= 47.1\text{kg}$$

A relative error is the absolute error expressed as a percentage of the actual, or true value. For example, using the data of the previous example:

$$\text{Relative error} = \frac{47.1}{3,752.9} \times 100$$

$$= 1.26\%$$

If the actual value is not known the error is expressed as a percentage of the approximated value. For example, if a length has been recorded as 125cm to the nearest whole number, before rounding it could have had any value form 124.5 to 125.5. Hence the maximum absolute error is $\pm$ 0.5cm and the maximum relative error $= \frac{0.5}{125} \times 100 = 0.4\%$.

1.4   Rounding errors in calculations

If calculations are made using values that have been rounded, the results of such calculations will themselves be only approximate. The effect of such errors is often overlooked, but is important, and it can be estimated as shown in the following examples. It will be assumed that all the values used have been rounded.

(a)   Addition

Eg, 4.782 + 3.42

Before rounding:

4.782   must have had a value in the range 4.782 ± 0.0005

3.42   must have had a value in the range 3.42 ± 0.005

The highest possible result is obtained by taking the two upper limits, viz:

4.7825 + 3.425 = 8.2075

The lowest possible result is obtained by taking the two lower limits, viz:

4.7815 + 3.415 = 8.1965

The result can therefore have any value in the range 8.1965 to 8.2075 which can be expressed as 8.202 ± 0.0055.

The upper and lower limits do not agree if expressed to 3 sf. (8.21 and 8.20 respectively). Strictly speaking, therefore, the result cannot be expressed meaningfully to more that 2 sf., although in practice, 3 sf. would probably be used. Expressing the result to a greater accuracy than 3 sf. would be quite unjustified.

Note that the absolute error in the result (0.0055) is equal to the sum of the absolute errors in the original values (0.0005 and 0.005). This is a general rule for addition and can be used as a quick method for estimating the error in the result.

(b)   Subtraction

Eg, 4.782 – 3.42

In this case, the highest result is obtained when the first value is as high as possible, and the second value as low as possible, and vice versa for the lowest result, hence:

Highest result: 4.7825 – 3.415 =   1.3675
Lowest result: 4.7815 – 3.425 =   1.3565

The result can therefore be expressed as 1.362 ± 0.0055.

The upper and lower limits agree only if expressed to 2 sf. or less, so that strictly speaking, the result cannot be expressed to more than 2 sf. (1.4), although in practice, 3 sf. (1.36) would be acceptable, but not more than 3 sf.

Note that, as with addition, the absolute error in the result is the **sum** of the absolute errors in the original values.

(c)   **Multiplication**

Eg, 3,260 (3 sf.) × 125

Highest result: 3,265 × 125.5 = 409,757.5

Lowest result: 3,255 × 124.5 = 405,247.5

The result can be expressed as 407,502.5 ± 2,255.

The upper and lower limits do not agree if the result is expressed to 3 or more sf., so that it cannot be expressed to a greater accuracy than 2 sf. (ie, 410,000).

Note that the error in the result is no longer equal to the sum of the errors in the original values. It can be shown, however, that the **relative** error in the result is approximately equal to the sum of the **relative** errors in the original values provided, as is usually the case, the errors are small compared with the values in which they occur.

Relative error in 3,260 $=$ $\dfrac{5}{3,260} \times 100\%$ $=$ 0.153% (3 sf.)

Relative error in 125 $=$ $\dfrac{0.5}{125} \times 100\%$ $=$ 0.4%

Relative error in result $=$ $\dfrac{2,255}{407,502.5} \times 100\%$ = 0.553%

0.553 = 0.153 + 0.4, demonstrating the truth of the above statement.

(d)   **Division**

Eg, 3,260 (3 sf.) ÷ 125

The highest result is obtained when the numerator has its maximum value and the denominator its minimum value, and vice-versa for the lowest result.

Highest result: 3,265 ÷ 124.5 = 26.22490

Lowest result: 3,255 ÷ 125.5 = 25.93626

The result can therefore be expressed approximately as 26.08 ± 0.15, but without error limits, only 2 sf. is justified (ie, 26).

As with multiplication, the relative error in the result is approximately equal to the sum of the relative errors in the two numbers. The demonstrating of this is left as an exercise.

These laws of errors provide the best method of calculating errors in practice, provided the errors are not unduly large, and are independent.

1.5   Activity

Calculate the result of each of the following and the error in the result, if the figures used have been rounded to three significant figures.

(a)   32.6 + 4.32

(b)   32.6 − 4.32

(c)   32.6 × 4.32

1.6   **Activity solution**

(a) $(32.6 \pm 0.05) + (4.32 \pm 0.005)$ $=$ 36.92 ± 0.055 (adding the absolute errors)

(b) $(32.6 \pm 0.05) - (4.32 \pm 0.005)$ $=$ 28.28 ± 0.055 (adding the absolute errors)

(c)   Highest result: $=$ 32.65×4.325 $=$ 141.211

Lowest result: $=$ 32.55×4.315 $=$ 140.453

The result can be expressed as 140.83 ± 0.38 (to 2 dp.)

Alternatively the problem can be solved by adding the relative errors:

Relative error in 32.6 $=$ $\dfrac{0.05}{32.6} \times 100$ $=$ 0.153%

Relative error in 4.32 $=$ $\dfrac{0.005}{4.32} \times 100$ $=$ 0.116%

Hence relative error in product $=$ $(0.153 + 0.116)\%$

$=$ 0.269%

Product $=$ 32.6×4.32

$=$ 140.83

Absolute error in product $=$ $\dfrac{0.269}{100} \times 140.83$

$=$ 0.38 (2 dp.)

Hence 32.6×4.32 $=$ 140.83 ± 0.38 (2 dp.)

1.7   Activity

Calculate the result of $32.6 \div 4.32$ and its error limits.

1.8   Activity solution

$32.6 \div 4.32$ $=$ 7.5463 (4 dp.)

Relative error $=$ 0.269% (as in (c) above).

Absolute error $=$ $\dfrac{0.269}{100} \times 7.5463$

$=$ 0.0203

Hence result is 7.5463 ± 0.0203

$=$ 7.55 ± 0.02 (2 dp.)

Conclusion The error in the result in any calculation due to the use of rounded values in that calculation can be estimated and it will always be greater than the rounding errors in the original values. The result of any calculation will, therefore, always be less precise than the **least** accurate value used in the calculation. This should be taken into account in deciding to how many significant figures the result should be expressed. Conversely, if a result is required to, say, three significant figures, all values used in calculating that result must have **at least** four significant figures. Indiscriminate rounding or chopping of intermediate values is a frequent mistake made in answering examination questions, and **must be avoided.**

2   SELF TEST QUESTIONS

2.1   What is the difference between a continuous and a discrete variable? (1.1)

2.2   What is the difference between an independent and a dependent variable? (1.1)

2.3   What are unbiased errors? (1.3)

18 SOURCES, COLLECTION & TABULATION

INTRODUCTION & LEARNING OBJECTIVES

Syllabus area 2e. Sources of data; collection and tabulation. (Ability required 3).

      2f. Random and non-random sampling methods. (Ability required 2).

This chapter is concerned with the collection of data, its conversion into meaningful statistics and the communication of those statistics into tabular form.

When you have studied this chapter you should be able to do the following:

- Identify the different ways of collecting primary data.

- Distinguish between descriptive and mathematical statistics.

- Classify data.

- Tabulate data.

---

1 POPULATION AND SAMPLE

1.1 Definitions

[Definition] The term **population** is used to mean all the items under consideration in a particular enquiry. A **sample** is a group of items drawn from that population. The population may consist of items such as metal bars, invoices, packets of tea, etc; it need not be people.

[Definition] A **sampling frame** is a list of all the members of the population. It can be used for selecting the sample. For example, if the population is electors, the sampling frame is the electoral register.

The purpose of sampling is to gain as much information as possible about the population by observing only a small proportion of that population, ie, by observing the sample.

For example, in order to ascertain which television programmes are most popular, a sample of the total viewing public is interviewed and, based on their replies, the programmes can be listed in order of popularity with all viewers.

There are three main reasons why sampling is necessary:

(a) The whole population may not be known.

(b) Even if the population is known the process of testing every item can be extremely costly in time and money.

For example, checking the weight of every packet of tea coming off a production line would be a lengthy process.

(c)   The items being tested may be completely destroyed in the process.

In order to check the lifetime of an electric light bulb it is necessary to leave the bulb burning until it breaks and is of no further use.

The characteristics of a population can be ascertained by investigating only a sample of that population provided that the following two rules are observed:

(a)   The sample must be of a certain size. In general terms the larger the sample the more reliable will be the results.

(b)   The sample must be chosen in such a way that each member of the population has an equal chance of being selected. This is known as random sampling and it avoids bias in the results.

There are several methods of obtaining a sample and these are considered in turn.

1.2   Random sampling

A simple random sample is defined as a sample taken in such a way that every member of the population has an equal chance of being selected. To achieve this, every item in the population must be numbered in order. If a sample of, say 20, items is required then 20 numbers from a table of random numbers are taken and the corresponding items are extracted from the population to form the sample, (a table of random numbers, Table 13, is supplied in the exam), eg, in selecting a sample of invoices for an audit. Since the invoices are already numbered this method can be applied with the minimum of difficulty.

This method has obvious limitations when either the population is extremely large or, in fact, not known. The following methods are more applicable in these cases.

1.3   Systematic sampling

If the population is known to contain 50,000 items and a sample of size 500 is required, then 1 in every 100 items is selected. The first item is determined by choosing randomly a number between 1 and 100, eg, 67, then the second item will be the 167th, the third will be the 267th . . . up to the 49,967th item.

Strictly speaking, systematic sampling (also called quasi-random) is not truly random as only the first item is so selected. However, it gives a very close approximation to random sampling and it is very widely used, eg, in selecting a sample of bags of sugar coming off a conveyor belt.

There is danger of bias if the population has a repetitive structure. For example, if a street has five types of house arranged in the order, A B C D E A B C D E . . . etc, an interviewer visiting every fifth home would only visit one type of house.

1.4   Stratified sampling

If the population under consideration contains several well defined groups (called strata), eg, men and women, smokers and non-smokers, different sizes of metal bars, etc, then a random sample is taken from each group. This is done in such a way that the number in each sample is proportional to the size of that group in the population and is known as sampling with **probability proportional to size** (pps).

For example, in selecting a sample of people in order to ascertain their leisure habits, age could be an important factor. So if 20% of the population are over 60 years of age, 65% between 18 and 60 and 15% are under 18, then a sample of 200 people should contain 40 who are over 60 years old, 130 people between 18 and 60 and 30 under 18 years of age, ie, the subsample should have sizes in the ratio 20 : 65 : 15.

This method ensures that a representative cross-section of the strata in the population is obtained, which may not be the case with a simple random sample of the whole population.

The method is often used by auditors to chose a sample to confirm debtors' balances. In this case a greater proportion of larger balances will be selected.

1.5   Multi-stage sampling

If a nationwide survey is to be carried out, then this method is often applied.

Step 1   The country is divided into areas (counties) and a random sample of areas is taken.

Step 2   Each area chosen in Step 1 is then subdivided into towns and cities or boroughs and a random sample of these is taken.

Step 3   Each town or city chosen in Step 2 is further divided into roads and a random sample of roads is then taken.

Step 4   From each road chosen in Step 3 a random sample of houses is taken and the occupiers interviewed.

This method is used for example, in selecting a sample for a national opinion poll of the type carried out prior to a general election.

1.6   Cluster sampling

This method is similar to the previous one in that the country is split into areas and a random sample taken. Further sub-divisions can be made until the required number of small areas have been determined. Then every house in each area will be visited instead of just a random sample of houses. In many ways this is a simpler and less costly procedure as no time is wasted finding particular houses and the amount of travelling by interviewers is much reduced.

1.7   Quota sampling

With quota sampling the interviewer will be given a list comprising the different types of people to be questioned and the number or quota of each type, eg, 20 males, aged 20 - 30 years, manual workers. 15 females, 25 - 35, housewives (not working). 10 males, 55 - 60, professional men . . . etc. The interviewer can use any method to obtain such people until the various quota are filled. This is very similar to stratified sampling, but no attempt is made to select respondents by a proper random method, consequently the sample may be very biased.

1.8   Sampling methods compared

The objective of a sample is to collect data upon which an opinion can be formed, and a conclusion drawn in respect of the population of which the sample is representative.

Ideally the sample would be chosen at random, and would be large enough so as to be representative of the population. Unfortunately both of these aspects introduce costs which are often unacceptably high.

Alternatives to the truly random sampling method have been outlined above. They are all concerned with minimising costs whilst maintaining the representative nature of the sample compared to the population.

In order to use these alternatives it is often necessary to have some knowledge of the population. Systematic sampling should not be used if the population follows a repetitive pattern. Quota sampling must be used with caution because the data collector may introduce bias because they choose how to fill the quota.

1.9   Statistical enquiries

Many of the problems met in a business situation are capable of being treated statistically. The steps in a statistical enquiry are as follows:

Step 1   Define the problem. The population to be investigated must be clearly defined at this stage as well as the problem itself.

Step 2   Select the sample to be examined. The size of the sample and the method used to select the sample will have to be determined, and will depend on the degree of accuracy and budgeted cost of the enquiry.

Step 3   Draft the questionnaire. A pilot survey is conducted to test the questionnaire before it is finalised, as it cannot be amended once distributed.

Step 4   Collect the data. Data is collected in various ways where it has not already been collected for some other statistical purpose.

Step 5   Check the returned questionnaires. Responses to questionnaires are checked an sometimes coded before data tabulation can take place.

Step 6   Organise the data. Some data will need to be reorganised before it can be tabulated, ie, items counted or values totalled.

Step 7   Analyse and interpret the data. Information collected has to be presented in a form that is easy to understand, ie, tables, charts and graphs from which conclusions can be reached about the sample collected.

Step 8   Write the report. The conclusions arrived at in (7) above will form the basis of a report which will recommend a certain course of action.

As will now be discussed there are many ways of collecting data - censuses, questionnaires, postal inquiries, personal interviews, random samples, public opinion polls etc, it is obviously very important to use a method that is suitable for the purposes of the inquiry, so that time and hence money is not wasted.

1.10   Survey methods

Primary data can be collected in the following ways:

(a)   **Postal questionnaire**

This allows respondents to remain anonymous if desired. The main disadvantage is that many people will not bother to return the questionnaire, resulting in a low response rate. Those who do respond may do so because they have a special interest in the subject, resulting in bias.

    (b)   **Personal interview**

Questions are asked by a team of interviewers. A set questionnaire is still used to ensure that all interviewers ask the same questions in the same way, to minimise interviewer bias. The response rate is usually higher than (a), but employment of trained interviewers is costly.

    (c)   **Telephone interview**

Similar to personal interview, but only suitable where all members of the population have a telephone (eg, business surveys). It is cheap and produces results quickly.

    (d)   **Observation**

Only suitable for obtaining data by counting (eg, number of cars passing a traffic census point) or measuring (eg, time taken to perform a task in work study).

Questionnaires consist of a series of questions which the recipient may answer without being under any pressure. As a consequence the answrs may be more informed than those obtained by interview but will be less spontaneous. Difficulties arise if the question is misread or misunderstood. This is because the answers do not match with any of those expected.

The response rate is generally much lower for a postal questionnaire than for an interview. This too is due to the absence of a physical presence. It is also true to say that the responses received may not be representative. Respondents may be particularly interested in the subject matter and take time to respond, others who are less interested may simply not bother to reply.

Cost is also an important factor. Once designed, the costs associated with postal questionnaires are small compared to interviewing costs. Interviewing is very time consuming both in organisation as well as carrying out the interviews. Such costs may be prohibitive.

2   INTRODUCTION TO STATISTICS

2.1   Statistics

        Definition   The word **statistics** refers to collections of numerical facts or estimates. It may be construed either as a singular or as a plural word. Statistics (plural) are the figures (more usually called data) together with any secondary statistics such as percentages or averages from them. Statistics (singular) is the study which deals with the collection, analysis and interpretation of these figures.

2.2   Descriptive statistics

This deals with the compilation and presentation of data as actually recorded during an investigation or from a questionnaire. The purpose of descriptive statistics is to provide concise, well presented information on which decisions can be taken: it is not intended to provide a refined and detailed analysis of the situation under consideration.

2.3   Mathematical statistics

This is based on the theory of probability and attempts to draw precise general conclusions from the data already collected. It may also help to decide how the data can be collected efficiently and economically.

2.4   Use and value of statistics

The main purpose of statistics is to provide estimates or comparisons on which decisions can be made. Also estimates based on present knowledge are essential for future planning in both the public and private sectors, eg, the number of school places needed in five years time (say), the demand for a particular product in three months time, the level of gas consumption at different times of day and at different times of year etc. These are known as 'inferential' statistics.

Such estimates may be based partly on statistics of population, incomes, employment etc and partly on a mathematical analysis of past records, which are then projected forward.

Since statistics deal only with measurable quantities they form a basis for judgement but not the whole judgement. Many other factors may need to be taken into account depending on the nature of the problem under consideration.

3   NATURE OF STATISTICAL DATA

3.1   Classification of data

There are two types of statistical data:

(a)   **Primary data**

[Definition]   This is data which has been expressly collected for a particular enquiry, for example, by observation or interviews.

(b)   **Secondary data**

[Definition]   This is data which has been collected for some other enquiry than the one of immediate interest. For example, data collected by a government department for national statistics would become secondary data when used by a company for an enquiry of its own.

Primary data is usually more difficult, more costly and more time consuming to collect; but secondary data should be used with caution as it may not really be appropriate to the enquiry, for example, it may not cover the exact time period required.

The terms primary and secondary data are also used to distinguish between raw data that has not been analysed and that data after it has been sorted, categorised, grouped, in the ways that will be described later in this chapter.

3.2   Sources of economic statistical data

There is a wealth of published statistical data covering many aspects of the nation's economy: population, manpower, trade, agriculture, price levels, capital issues, and similar matters.

The primary purpose of this data is to provide information for economic planning at the national level. The data serves the secondary purpose of providing industry with useful background information for deciding on future policies such as raising new finance or recruiting specialised labour. The data is only published in general terms, eg, for a particular industry or geographical area.

The following list shows some of the main sources. Copies are generally available in reference libraries and should be examined to appreciate the type of data published. The style and layout of the tables should also be noted.

Title	Frequency of publication	Main topics covered
Employment Gazette	Monthly	Earnings, basic wage rates, unemployment, indices of wholesale and retail prices.
British Business	Weekly	Wholesale and retail prices, production for specific sectors of industry, capital expenditure.
National Income and Expenditure Blue Book	Annually	Personal income and expenditure, gross national product.
Financial Statistics	Monthly	Money supply, interest rates, hire purchase liabilities, building societies.
Bank of England Quarterly Bulletin	Quarterly	} Both summarise many of the above statistics.
Monthly Digest of Statistics	Monthly	
Economic Trends	Monthly	} Similar coverage to Monthly Digest, but given information stretching back over a long period.
Annual Abstract of Statistics	Annually	
Price Indices for Current Cost Accounting	Annually, but updated by monthly supplement	Retail price index, also industry specific and asset specific price indices.

All the above publications relate to the UK. Publications concerned with statistics relating to the Common Market include *European Economy Annual Statistical Yearbook*, *Eurostat* (monthly) and *OECD Main Economic Indicators* (monthly). Information on the World Economy is available from the United Nations (*Demographic Yearbook* and *Statistical Yearbook*), the International Labour Organisation (*Yearbook of Labour Statistics*) and UNESCO (*Statistical Yearbook*).

3.3 Activity

Visit your local library and extract the values of the money supply from one of the sources listed above for the last six months.

3.4 Misleading statistics

Before leaving the topic of published statistics, it is necessary to mention a word of caution when dealing with statistical data.

All graphs, charts, tables, diagrams, etc must be carefully studied for units, scales, dates, etc.

All statements must be read and analysed for ambiguities and bias.

The following example may help to underline this last point.

3.5 Example

Badly worded statements can bring the subject of statistics into disrepute.

You are required to consider the following statements and:

(a)   explain briefly where they mislead or fail to make sense; and

(b)   re-word them in a more acceptable form.

    (i)   'Nine out of ten people in this country would oppose a policy of state intervention in the Z industry'.

    (ii)   'Unemployment up 10% . . .' as stated in newspaper A,

        'Unemployment down 10% . . .' as stated in newspaper B, both on the same day.

    (iii)   'There are 2.41 children per family in the country of Y'.

    (iv)   '80% of car accidents occurred within three miles of the driver's home, therefore, longer journeys must be safer'.

3.6   Solution

  (i)   (a)   The statement presumably gives the opinion of a **sample** of people, and the proportion of 'nine out of ten' must be an **average** figure. With the present wording, the statement implies, however, that **exactly** nine out of ten people in the population **as a whole** would oppose state intervention in the Z industry.

      (b)   A better wording would be:

          'In a sample of 2,500 people interviewed recently, about 90% said that they were opposed to state intervention in the Z industry'.

  (ii)   (a)   Although the statements seem at first sight to be incompatible, this is not necessarily the case since no base dates are given. Also, it may be that one newspaper was quoting actual unemployment and the other was quoting seasonally adjusted values.

      (b)   The alternative wordings:

          'Unemployment up 10% since July 1988'; 'Unemployment down 10% since March 1993' renders the statements compatible.

  (iii)   (a)   The figure of 2.41 is clearly an average: no family can have exactly 2.41 children: Further, the precise figure is not particularly helpful.

      (b)   An adequate wording would be:

          'On average, there are between two and three children per family in the country of Y'.

  (iv)   (a)   Longer journeys might perhaps be safer, but such an inference cannot be drawn from the first part of the statement. If the majority of journeys are made within three miles of people's homes, then one would expect the majority of accidents to occur there.

      (b)   The false conclusion should be omitted so that the statement reads: 'The majority of car accidents occurred within three miles of the driver's home'.

4   TABULATION OF DATA

4.1   Principles of data construction

When tabulating data to make it easier to comprehend, the following principles need to be borne in mind.

(a)   **Simplicity**: the material must be classified and detail kept to a minimum.

(b)   **Title:** the table must have a comprehensive and self explanatory title.

(c)   **Source:** the source of the material used in drawing up the table should always be stated (usually by way of a footnote).

(d)   **Units:** the units of measurement that have been used must be stated, eg, *000s* means that the units are in thousands. This can be done in the title, to keep the number of figures to a minimum.

(e)   **Headings:** all column and row headings should be concise and unambiguous.

(f)   **Totals:** these should be shown where appropriate, and also any subtotals that may be applicable to the calculations.

(g)   **Percentages and ratios:** these are sometimes called **derived statistics** and should be shown if meaningful, with an indication of how they were calculated.

4.2   Example

The following example illustrates the type of problem that may be set in the examination.

Alpha Products plc has two departments, A and B. The total wage bill in 19X7 was £513,000, of which £218,000 was for department A and the rest for department B. The corresponding figures for 19X8 were £537,000 and £224,000. The number employed in department A was 30 in 19X7 and decreased by 5 for the next year. The number employed in department B was 42 in 19X7 and increased by 1 for the year 19X8. Tabulate this data to bring out the changes over the two year period for each department and the company as a whole.

Solution

Alpha Products plc
Changes in Labour Force 19X7 to 19X8

	Dept A			Dept B			Total		
	19X7	19X8	Change %	19X7	19X8	Change %	19X7	19X8	Change %
Wage Bill (£'000s)	218	224	+2.8	295	313	+6.1	513	537	+4.7
Number employed	30	25	–16.7	42	43	+2.4	72	68	–5.6

Source *Company records*

4.3   Classification of data

Before data can be tabulated and interpreted it must be **classified**, since, in its raw form, data is impossible to handle quickly and easily. Classification is the **bringing together of items with a**

common characteristic.

4.4   Example

Fifty university students were selected at random and their heights were measured in inches. The following values were found and recorded:

67	71	61	70	66
68	72	71	76	72
77	71	66	70	72
71	64	70	72	66
70	67	71	66	69
73	74	68	70	73
67	69	69	70	71
69	74	68	72	70
70	65	69	75	67
72	70	68	73	67

By careful inspection of the above **raw** or **ungrouped data** it is possible to ascertain the height of the tallest student (77") and that of the shortest student (61"), but very little else. It is necessary, therefore, to arrange the data in a tabular form. This may involve a loss of detail, but will result in a gain in comprehensibility.

4.5   Grouped frequency distribution

In statistics, the term **total frequency** means the number of items being considered. A class frequency is the number of items in the class.

A grouped frequency distribution is constructed as follows:

Step 1   Pick out the highest and lowest figures from raw data.

Step 2   Determine the range of values, ie, the difference between the highest and lowest values.

Step 3   Decide upon the class intervals. There should normally be between 5 and 15 classes and, wherever possible, 'the intervals' should be equal and of a 'convenient' width.

Step 4   Take each figure in the raw data and insert a tally (or check) mark against the appropriate class, eg,

2 is represented by   11

5 is represented by   ‖‖

11 is represented by   ‖‖ ‖‖ 1

Step 5   By totalling the tally marks find the class frequencies. The totalling is made easier by grouping the tally marks in five's as shown above. This may seem unnecessary for fifty items, but becomes more important in practice where often tens of thousands of items have to be classified.

4.6   Example

Using the data given in the last example, a grouped distribution is constructed of the university student's heights.

Highest value is 77", lowest value is 61"; therefore, range of values = 16".

Taking 3" class intervals of 60" and less than 63", 63" and less than 66", etc the distribution becomes:

Class interval	Tally	Frequency
Height (inches)		Number of students
60" and less than 63"	1	1
63" and less than 66"	11	2
66" and less than 69"	++++ ++++ 111	13
69" and less than 72"	++++ ++++ ++++ ++++	20
72" and less than 75"	++++ ++++ 1	11
75" and less than 78"	111	3
Total		50

4.7 Class intervals and class limits

The following points should be **carefully** noted as regards the construction of such a frequency distribution:

(a) **Number of classes**

The number should be **relatively few** so that the information given is easily grasped and retained, but not so few that the inevitable loss of detail from grouping becomes too pronounced. Often it will be found that 6 or 7 classes are appropriate.

(b) **Class intervals (or width)**

These should all be **equal if possible**. The exception is generally for opening and closing classes where there may be one or two extreme values. Thus, in the above example, if there was a student of height 81" the final class would probably be 78" and above in order to include him and yet not have one class interval with zero frequency in between 78" and 80". It may also be more informative to divide one of the central classes into smaller intervals in order to retain some detail of the original data.

(c) **Open ended class intervals**

Classes such as '78 and over' or 'less than 60', which have only one boundary specified, are said to be open ended. For the purpose of statistical calculations, each such class is assumed to have the same interval as the class next to it. In this example, 'less than 60' would be taken as '57 and less than 60' to make it have the same interval as '60 and less than 63', and '78 and over' would be taken as '78 and less than 81' to have the same interval as '75 and less than 78'. Since open ended classes are only used when the number of items in the class is small, any error resulting from this assumption will usually be negligible.

(d) **Class limits (their mathematical meaning)**

The limits of a class indicate what values from the original data will be included in each class, and therefore it is important to clarify the various ways in which class limits can be stated.

The most commonly used method of defining classes is shown in the following example (the actual numbers used are an example only, and in practice would depend on the total range of values):

    0   and less than   10

10 and less than   20

20 and less than   30 etc.

This may also be shown as

≥ 0 but < 10

≥ 10 but < 20

≥ 20 but <30

The upper class boundary is thus inferred from the lower boundary of the next class.

The above method is unambiguous; a value of exactly 10 (say) would be put in the second class. For discrete whole number data, 'less than 10' would mean 'up to and including 9' so that in this case, the classes could be:

0 - 9

10 - 19

20 - 29 etc.

This must not be used for continuous data, as there would be nowhere to put values between 9 and 10, 19 and 20, etc.

The following is sometimes used, but should be avoided.

0   to   10

10   to   20

20   to   30 etc.

In this case, we cannot logically decide in which group a value of exactly 10 (say) should be put.

It is important not to round the data before classifying it. In the above example, if the data had been rounded before classifying, any value between 9.5 and 10 would have been rounded to 10 and then classified in the group 10 and less than 20 instead of the correct group of 0 and less than 10.

If the data has been rounded before classifying, it would be more correct to define the group intervals as 0 to 9.5, 9.5 to 19.5, 19.5 to 29.5 etc. Such boundaries are awkward and mean that the first group has a different class interval (9.5 units) to subsequent groups (10 units), which will present problems later on.

5   SELF TEST QUESTIONS

5.1   What is a population? (1.1)

5.2   Explain systematic sampling. (1.3)

5.3   When is multi-stage sampling most used? (1.5)

5.4   What are the steps to follow in statistical enquiry? (1.9)

5.5   List four ways of collecting primary data. (1.10)

19 PRESENTATION OF DATA

INTRODUCTION & LEARNING OBJECTIVES

Syllabus area 2e. Presentation: summarisation and interpretation of collected data. (Ability required 3).

Graphs and diagrams. (Ability required 2).

This chapter is concerned with communication of tabulated statistics into a diagrammatic representation, graphical representation, and incorporation into business reports.

When you have studied this chapter you should be able to do the following:

- Represent data using diagrams and charts.
- Represent data using graphs.
- Incorporate data in business reports.

---

1 DIAGRAMMATIC REPRESENTATION OF DATA

1.1 Introduction

There are several advantages of presenting a mass of data in tabular form. The figures can easily be located, comparisons between classes can be made at a glance, patterns of figures are highlighted and tables are easily understood by non-statisticians.

However, charts, diagrams and graphs are more popular ways of displaying data simply. Such visual representation of facts plays an important part in everyday life since diagrams can be seen daily in newspapers, advertisements and on television. These can be misleading and give entirely the wrong impression. It is, therefore, important to adhere to the same basic principles as were listed under table construction.

1.2 Construction of graphs and diagrams

Principles to be followed are:

(a)   All diagrams (and graphs) must have a title.
(b)   The source of data must be stated.
(c)   The units of measurement that have been used must be given.
(d)   The scale must be stated.
(e)   The axes must be clearly labelled.
(f)   Neatness is essential.

1.3   Advantages of diagrams and graphs

If these principles are followed than a diagram will have several advantages over a table:

(a)   It is easier to understand the mass of figures from a table.
(b)   Relationships between figures are shown more clearly.
(c)   A quick, lasting and accurate impression is given of the significant and pertinent facts.

1.4   Types of diagram

There are various methods of representing data diagrammatically. The first set of methods to be considered are:

(a)   Pictograms.
(b)   Bar charts - simple, component and multiple.
(c)   Pie charts.

Each of these is considered in turn with examples to illustrate the method of construction.

1.5   Pictograms

These are, as the name implies, pictures (or symbols) which can readily be associated with the data under consideration. One picture or symbol is used to represent a unit of the variable.

1.6   Example

The following pictogram represent the car sales for British Mayland for the three consecutive years 19X1 to 19X3:

Car sales British Mayland, 19X1 to 19X3

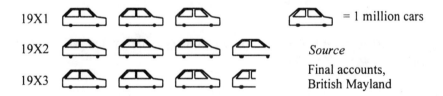

A higher value should be shown by a greater number of pictorial units, (as in this example) not by increasing the size of the pictorial units, as this can be deceptive.

If the latter approach, increasing the size, is used, bear in mind that if both the width and the height of a picture double, its area increases by a factor of 4. (In general the method should be avoided.)

1.7   Bar charts

When information is of a quantitative form, it is often represented by a bar chart. Bars of equal width, either vertical or horizontal, are constructed with their lengths proportional to the value of the variable.

1.8 Simple bar chart

Example

The following bar chart represents the production of wheat in the UK for the years 19X1 to 19X3:

Wheat production UK, 19X1 to 19X3

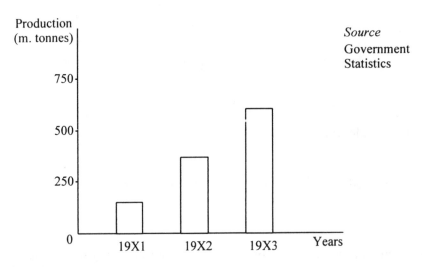

Note: it is bad practice to use a base line, horizontal axis, other than zero. If in the above chart the base line had started at (for example) 150 with the object of saving space, the relative heights of the bars would be visually incorrect and the chart misleading.

1.9 Component bar chart

A component bar chart is drawn when each total figure is built up from several component parts.

Example

The following bar chart represents the grain production (rye, barley and wheat) in the UK for the years 19X4 to 19X6:

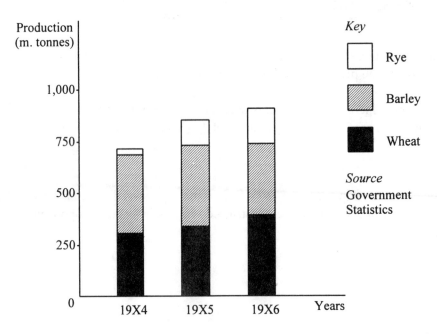

Notes:

(i)   The rectangle for barley must start at the top of the rectangle for wheat, and rye start at the top of barley, so that the total height represents the total production of all three cereals. A common mistake is to commence all rectangles from the same base line so that they overlap instead of appearing one above the other. (This would then form another type of bar chart shown later.)

(ii)   The components of a bar, when taken together, should form a logical whole, in this case, total grain production each year. This would not be the case if the data was plotted the other way round using each bar to represent a different type of grain instead of different years.

1.10   Percentage component bar chart

This is a component bar chart in which the component values are expressed and drawn as percentages of the bar total. Each bar will have the same total height, representing 100%. They can be misleading: an actual increase can appear as a decrease and vice-versa in relative terms.

1.11   Multiple bar chart

This is drawn where two or more related items are to be compared. The bars are placed next to each other and each represents a different item.

Example

The following bar chart represents the sales of root vegetables (turnips, carrots and parsnips) in Noddy Land for the years 19X4 to 19X6:

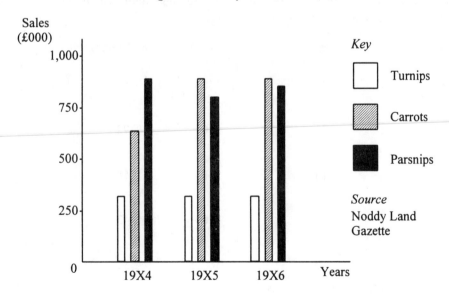

Root vegetables Noddy Land, 19X4 to 19X6

1.12   Pie charts

These are usually drawn when the proportion of each class to the whole is important rather than the absolute value of each class. A circle is drawn, and divided into sectors such that the area of each sector is proportionate to the size of the figure represented. They are analogous to the component bar chart.

1.13   Comparison with component bar charts

Advantage: with bar charts, all components have the same base line, making comparison within and across years easier.

Disadvantage: they do not show the total for each year. This is achieved in pie charts by ensuring that the area of each circle is proportional to this total.

1.14   Example

The following pie chart represents the proportion of each type of grain produced in Disney Land in the year 19X5:

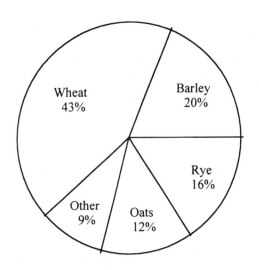

Source

Disney Land
Ministry of
Home Affairs

Construction of pie chart

The angles are calculated as proportional parts of 360° and then drawn on the diagram using a protractor. Eg, in the above example, given the %ages:

Grain	%	Angle of sector (degrees)
Wheat	43	$360 \times \dfrac{43}{100} = 155$
Barley	20	$360 \times \dfrac{20}{100} = 72$
Rye	16	$360 \times \dfrac{16}{100} = 58$
Oats	12	$360 \times \dfrac{12}{100} = 43$
Other	9	$360 \times \dfrac{9}{100} = 32$
	100	360

If two or more years are to be compared, a separate pie chart would be needed for each year. The area of each circle should be proportional to the total, which means that the radius must be proportional to the square root of the total. Thus if the total grain production for 19X5 was 5 million tonnes and for 19X6 was 6 million tonnes, the radii should be in the ratio $\sqrt{5} : \sqrt{6}$ or $1 : \sqrt{6/5}$ which equals 1 : 1.095. If the circle for 19X5 was constructed with a radius of 3cm, the circle for 19X6 should have a radius of 3.3cm.

1.15   Diagrams and charts compared

Pictograms are tedious to draw and lack accuracy. They are attractive to the eye but should really only be used to convey simple information.

Bar charts are the easiest type of diagram to understand and to draw. They are accurate, and actual values can be read off the vertical scale.

Pie charts are more difficult to draw than bar charts. They are less accurate, and actual values cannot usually be read off the chart. It is also very difficult to compare pie charts, especially if different sized circles have been drawn.

1.16   Diagrams and spreadsheet packages

Most spreadsheet packages developed for use in microcomputers have a facility to generate charts and diagrams directly from data in a spreadsheet.

The following example is a bar chart from closing cash balances using an 'Excel' spreadsheet.

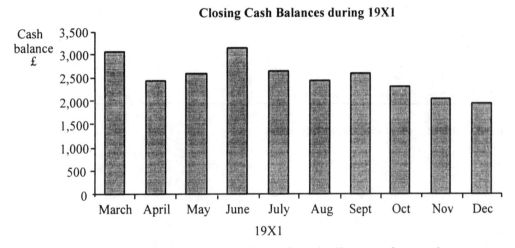

Closing Cash Balances during 19X1

The next example, using the same spreadsheet, is a pie diagram of area sales.

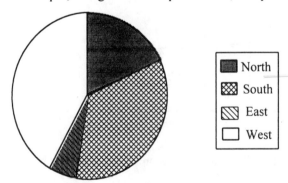

The main problem, given the wide availability of these packages, is to discourage users from filling reports with diagrams.

2   GRAPHICAL REPRESENTATION OF DATA

2.1   Types of graph

The graphical representation of data may take the following forms:

(a)   histograms;
(b)   frequency curves;
(c)   Z charts;
(d)   semi-logarithmic graphs.

3   HISTOGRAMS

3.1   Introduction

[Definition]   A **histogram** is a special form of column or bar chart that is used to represent data given in the form of a grouped frequency distribution. The important difference is that the area of each rectangle rather than the height represents the frequency of a particular class interval.

Types of histogram:

3.2   Equal class intervals

If all the class intervals are of the same size (as in the example below) then the rectangles have the same length of base (or width) and the heights will be proportional to the frequencies (just as in a bar chart).

3.3   Example

Class interval	Range of class	Frequency
Age (years)		No of people
11 and less than 16	5	9
16 and less than 21	5	17
21 and less than 26	5	22
26 and less than 31	5	18
31 and less than 36	5	10

The standard width of a class interval is five years.

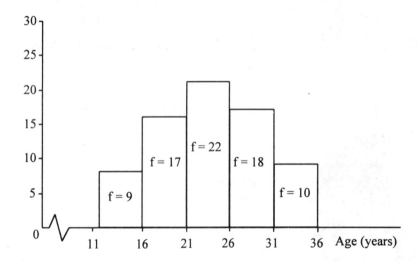

Part of the horizontal axis has been omitted for clarity. The omission is shown by a jagged line.

Note: that the vertical lines are always drawn at the mathematical class limits, so there are no gaps as in a bar chart. If class intervals are equal, as here, there is no need to put the frequency in each bar (except for additional accuracy reading the diagram). It is a useful technique if class intervals are unequal.

3.4   Unequal class intervals

If the distribution has unequal class intervals, eg, in the example below, the third and fourth class intervals have twice the range of the others, it is necessary to adjust the heights of the bars to compensate for the fact that the rectangles do not have all the same length of base. Only by doing this will the area of the rectangle represent the frequency.

3.5   Example

The following data refers to the weights (in kg) of 42 crates of frozen fish landed at Grimsby:

Class intervals	Range of class	Frequency	Height of bar
Weights (kgs)		No of crates	
10 and less than 15	5	2	2
15 and less than 20	5	5	5
20 and less than 30	10	12	12/2 = 6
30 and less than 40	10	16	16/2 = 8
40 and less than 45	5	7	7

The standard width of a class interval is 5kg. Therefore, since the third and fourth intervals are twice as wide, it is necessary to halve the frequencies of these two classes to find the actual heights of the rectangles.

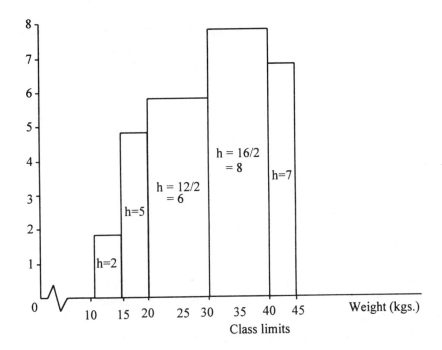

Similarly, if a distribution has a class interval that is three times the width of the standard class interval, the frequency of that class must be divided by three to find the height of the rectangle.

In the above example it was the central classes which were wider than standard. Usually it will be the tail-end classes which are wider, in order to avoid classes with no members if possible.

Interpretation must always be in terms of the standard width of class interval. For example, the height of the third rectangle is 6 units. This does not mean that there are 6 items in the class 20 to 30 kg, but that there is an average of 6 in **each** of the classes 20 to 25kg and 25 to 30kg. The vertical axis no longer represents frequency, but 'frequency density'.

3.6   Activity

A frequency distribution of a sample of incomes is as follows:

£	Frequency
40 and less than 80	7
80 and less than 100	16
100 and less than 120	28
120 and less than 130	21
130 and less than 140	8
	80

In the histogram of this data, the rectangle for the £80 - £100 class has a height of 8cm.

What should be the height of the rectangles for the following classes:

(a)   £100 to 120?
(b)   £130 to 140?

3.7   Activity solution

(a)   14cm
(b)   8cm

3.8   Frequency polygons

If the mid-points of the tops of the rectangles in the histogram are joined by straight lines, the figure is known as a **frequency polygon**. The lines at each end of the diagram must be taken to the base line at the centres of the adjoining corresponding class intervals. This is because these two class intervals have, in effect, a zero frequency since they contain no items.

Example

A frequency polygon is constructed using the data from 3.3 above.

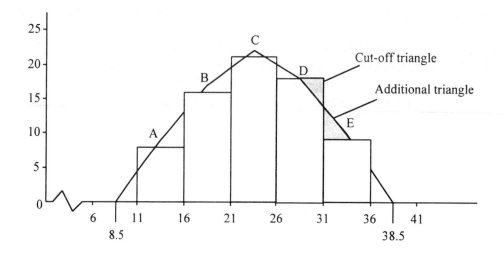

3.9   Area of a frequency polygon

Compared to the histogram, some areas are cut off when the polygon is drawn and some extra areas are enclosed. The area of the frequency polygon is equal to the area of the histogram because the areas of the cut-off triangle and of the additional triangle (shaded areas) are equal at each stage.

3.10   Frequency curves

If a smooth, freehand curve is drawn rather than joining up the mid-points with straight lines, this is known as a frequency curve and it is especially useful if two or more frequency distributions are to be compared and contrasted.

The area of a frequency curve should be the same as that of the original histogram.

A frequency polygon tends to a frequency curve as more data is collected to allow more class intervals to be shown of progressively smaller widths.

3.11   Cumulative frequency curves

These are often called **ogives**. The cumulative frequencies are plotted against the **upper class limits**.

3.12   Example

The following is the frequency distribution of the weights (to the nearest gram) of 100 articles. They have been grouped into intervals of 10 grams.

Class interval	Frequency	Cumulative frequency
Weight (grams)	No of articles	
100 and less than 110	1	1
110 and less than 120	2	1 + 2 = 3
120 and less than 130	5	3 + 5 = 8
130 and less than 140	11	8 + 11 = 19
140 and less than 150	21	19 + 21 = 40
150 and less than 160	20	40 + 20 = 60
160 and less than 170	17	60 + 17 = 77
170 and less than 180	11	77 + 11 = 88
180 and less than 190	6	88 + 6 = 94
190 and less than 200	6	94 + 6 = 100

The cumulative frequencies are plotted against the upper class limits because:

1 article weighs less than 110g

1 + 2 = 3 articles weigh less than 120g

1 + 2 + 5 = 8 articles weigh less than 130g

1 + 2 + 5 + 11 = 19 articles weigh less than 140g etc.

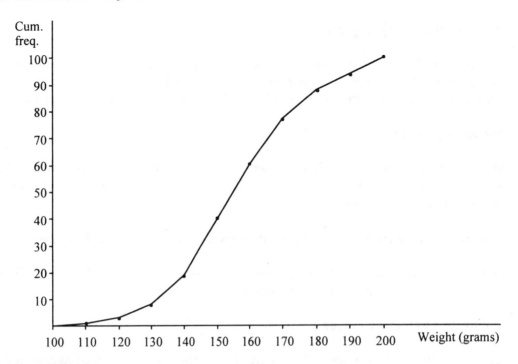

Note: that the cumulative frequency is always plotted at the upper mathematical class limit. It is only at this stage that the cumulative class frequency has been attained.

The above curve is called a 'less than' ogive because it shows the number of items less than a given value of the variable. Alternatively, the frequencies can be cumulated from the bottom upward and plotted against the **lower** class boundaries, ie,

$$\begin{array}{ll} 6 & \text{items weigh 190 grams or more} \\ 6 + 6 = 12 & \text{items weigh 180 grams or more} \\ 12 + 11 = 23 & \text{items weigh 170 grams or more, etc.} \end{array}$$

The curve obtained by plotting these values is called a 'more than' ogive.

Plot the complete graph for yourself and compare it with the 'less than' curve.

Notes:

A cumulative frequency curve has the points joined with one smooth continuous curve. A cumulative frequency polygon has the points joined by a series of straight lines.

Sometimes it is necessary to compare the ogives of two different distributions, but, unless the total frequencies of the two distributions are the same, the above method does not yield much useful information. For comparison purposes, it is better to plot cumulative percentage graphs, ie, the cumulative frequencies are expressed as percentages of the total frequencies.

Ogives can be used to estimate the value of any item in the distribution (say, the 20th item) by identifying the item on the vertical axis and reading off the value on the horizontal axis. The main use, however, will be met in the next chapter when medians and quartiles are being calculated. These are defined and explained elsewhere.

A common mistake is to use the class mid-points for the graph. This is always wrong for an ogive. For a 'less than' ogive the upper class boundaries, and for a 'more than' ogive the lower class boundaries must be used.

4   Z CHARTS

4.1   Introduction

Definition   A **Z chart** consists of three lines drawn on one set of axes and is often drawn to indicate sales performance. The graph extends over a single year and incorporates:

(a)   separate monthly figures;
(b)   cumulative monthly figures for the year; and
(c)   a moving annual total.

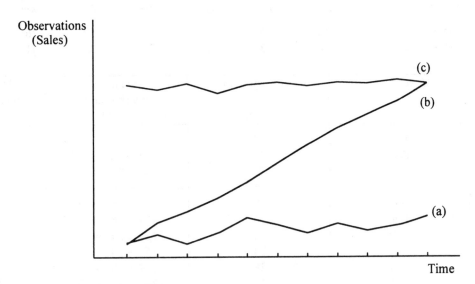

This chart takes its name from its appearance.

The aims of a Z-chart are:

(a)   To show monthly sales figure and any seasonal fluctuations.

(b)   To show cumulative monthly figures and indicate any substantial increases and trends in the current year.

(c)   To show the totals of figures for the preceding 12 months and trends over the past 12 months.

The graph of the separate monthly figures shows the fluctuations in sales from month to month, including seasonal effects. The graph of the cumulative monthly figures shows total sales for the year to date. This can usefully be compared with a sales target which can also be inserted on the chart. The graph of the moving annual total shows sales over the whole of the previous year, thus eliminating seasonal effects. Where the graph is rising, performance is better than in the previous year, and where it is falling, performance is not so good.

4.2   Drawing a Z-chart

In order to make the information clearer, a double scale can be used on the vertical axis. One scale is used for line (a) and a second scale for lines (b) and (c), since the figures used to draw these two lines are roughly 12 times larger than those used for drawing (a).

4.3   Example

The following table shows the monthly sales (in £'000) of Zabra Ltd for 19X4 and 19X5.

A Z chart will be drawn from this information of 19X5.

Month	Jan	Feb	Mar	Apr	May	Jun
19X4	20	20	25	18	16	25
19X5	18	21	26	16	20	26

Month	Jul	Aug	Sep	Oct	Nov	Dec
19X4	18	17	19	18	19	26
19X5	24	28	28	32	33	41

Month 19X5	Monthly sales £'000	Cumulative monthly sales £'000	Moving annual total* £'000
Jan	18	18	239
Feb	21	21 + 18 = 39	240
Mar	26	39 + 26 = 65	241
Apr	16	65 + 16 = 81	239
May	20	81 + 20 = 101	243
Jun	26	101 + 26 = 127	244
Jul	24	127 + 24 = 151	250
Aug	28	151 + 28 = 179	261
Sep	28	179 + 28 = 207	270
Oct	32	207 + 32 = 239	284
Nov	33	239 + 33 = 272	298
Dec	41	272 + 41 = 313	313

*Moving annual totals are easy to calculate, being simply the total of 12 months' figures.

239 is the total of the 12 months from Feb 19X4 to Jan 19X5 inclusive.

240 is the total of the 12 months from Mar 19X4 to Feb 19X5 inclusive.

It is found by omitting the February 19X4 value (20) and including the February 19X5 value (21) instead, giving an increase of 1 to 240.

241 is the total of the 12 months from Apr 19X4 to Mar 19X5 inclusive.
Omit 25 and include 26 instead, an increase of 1, giving 241.

They are called moving annual totals because the initial month moves on one each time.

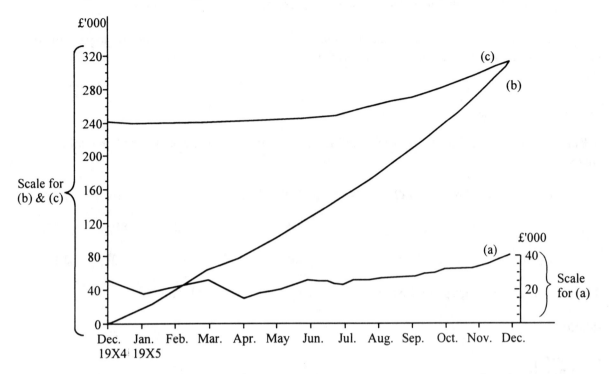

All points are plotted at the end of their time intervals since they are totals rather than averages.

Line (a) starts at the Dec 19X4 figure of 26.

Line (b) starts at zero.

Line (c) starts at 241 which is the total of sales up to the end of Dec 19X4.

Since the moving annual total is the total of the preceding 12 months' sales, the moving annual total for Dec 19X5 must be the same as the cumulative monthly total up to Dec 19X5 and the two lines will meet at this point.

The graph (a) shows that sales tended to be higher in autumn and early winter than for the rest of the year. This is also shown by the increasing slope of line (b).

Graph (c) shows that sales were approximately the same as in the previous year for the first half of the year, but steadily improved on the previous year's performance over the second half of the year. This suggests that the surge in performance in the second half of 19X5 had not also been achieved in 19X4.

5   SEMI-LOGARITHMIC (RATIO-SCALE) GRAPHS

5.1   Introduction

Normally the scales on graphs are drawn such that the distance between 50 and 60 is the same as that between 5 and 15, because each gap represents an increase of 10 units.

The effect of this is that if a graph is drawn where the y variable is increasing at a constant percentage rate vis-a-vis the independent x variable, then the curve becomes increasingly steep. Furthermore, as will be seen later, it is often easier to recognise straight-line relationships rather than more complicated functions. A ratio scale graph is a graph drawn in such a way that a constant rate of increase (or decrease) gives a straight line.

To show this straight-line relationship special log-linear graph paper (semi-log paper) may be used where one scale, normally the y axis, is drawn such that equal intervals on the scale represent equal percentage increases in the variable. For example the distance between y = 4 and y = 20 is the same as the distance between y = 100 and y = 500 both representing an increase of 500%.

If log-linear graph paper is not available, the same effect is obtained by plotting the logarithms of the y values against the x variables on ordinary graph paper, as illustrated in the following examples.

5.2   Example

In Ruritango (a country suffering accute inflation) the retail price index has had the following values:

Year;	19X0	19X1	19X2	19X3	19X4	19X5	19X6	19X7
RPI;	35	53	79	118	224	426	810	1,539
Log RPI;	1.54	1.72	1.90	2.07	2.35	2.63	2.91	3.19

Plot a semi-logarithmic graph of the retail price index for the period under review.

5.3   Solution

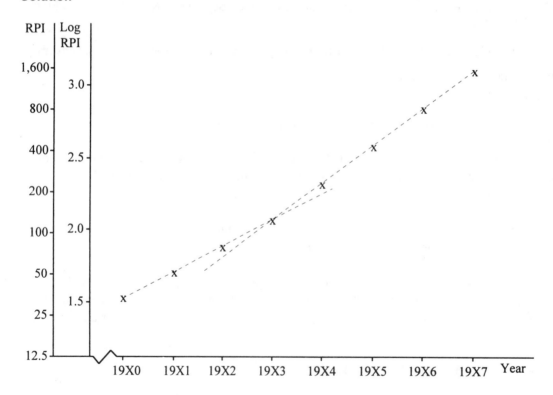

Note: from the graph that:

(a)   The RPI increased at one rate from 19X0 to 19X3, and thereafter the rate of increase was greater, but still constant, from 19X3 to 19X7.

(b)   The y scale will never have a zero value.

(c)   The intermediate values on the y scale have been approximated. The calculation of the actual position is based on logarithms.

(d)   The non-logarithmic scale has equal intervals as the RPI doubles, then doubles again.

5.4   Interpretation of ratio scale graphs

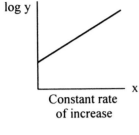

Constant rate
of increase

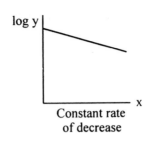

Constant rate
of decrease

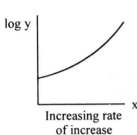

Increasing rate
of increase

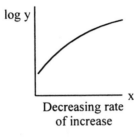

Decreasing rate
of increase

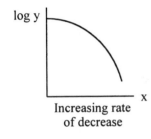

Increasing rate
of decrease

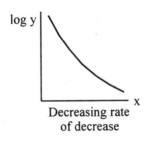

Decreasing rate
of decrease

5.5   Activity

The Central Statistical Office, Financial Statistics in August 19X9 contained the following information about exchange rates.

Average of daily telegraphic transfer per £1 sterling in London.

	Date	Swiss francs	Deutsch mark
19X7	January	4.2701	4.102
	July	4.1543	3.934
19X8	January	3.8398	4.094
	July	3.4143	3.892
19X9	January	3.3479	3.708
	July	3.7205	4.122

Plot the value of £1 in Swiss and German currencies on a semi-logarithmic scale.

5.6   Activity solution

To plot the data on semi-logarithmic scale, it is necessary first of all to determine the logs of the two sets of data.

Date		SF	Log	DM	Log
January	19X7	4.2701	0.6304	4.102	0.6130
July	19X7	4.1543	0.6185	3.934	0.5948
January	19X8	3.8398	0.5483	4.094	0.6121
July	19X8	3.4143	0.5333	3.892	0.5902
January	19X9	3.3479	0.5248	3.708	0.5691
July	19X9	3.7205	0.5706	4.122	0.6151

The values are plotted on the accompanying graph.

Semi-logarithmic graph of transfer rates per £1 sterling

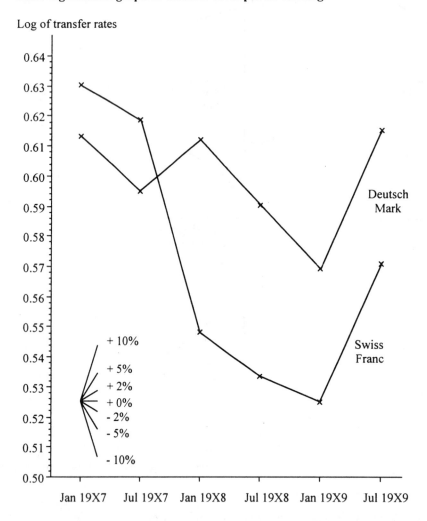

This semi-logarithmic graph represents the rate of change of data. In this example, sterling is normally moving at the same rate against both the Swiss Franc and the German Mark. The exception was the second half of 19X7, when the Swiss Franc graph fell and the German mark graph increased.

Thus a semi-log graph shows rates of changes; a natural graph shows absolute changes.

Two parallel lines on a semi-logarithmic graph imply equal percentage changes during a particular period whereas on a natural scale graph, two parallel lines would imply equal absolute increases. For the data given, the two graphs show almost parallel lines for 19X9 because the percentage increases are 11.13% and 11.17%. On the other hand, the absolute increases are quite different, being 0.3726 and 0.414.

5.7   Conclusion

Conclusion   A semi-logarithmic graph may be slightly misleading in that most people are used to interpreting natural scale graphs and as a consequence misread a semi-logarithmic graph. This makes it important to be perfectly clear whether or not a graph is drawn on a logarithmic basis. To achieve this correctness of interpretation, there may be a case for not labelling the scale of the vertical axis of a semi-logarithmic graph because one is not really interested in these values, merely in the slope of the lines. Furthermore, if a scale of slopes is provided, as on the above graph, it should serve to focus attention on this aspect of the graph rather than the vertical scale.

By their very nature, semi-logarithmic graphs can accommodate a large range of values much more readily than a natural scale graph. On the other hand, however, it is not possible to represent negative values on a logarithmic scale, although this is not a problem with the data of this question which has no negative figures.

6   DATA IN BUSINESS REPORTS

6.1   Introduction

Typically, numerical data is not well communicated. Neither statisticians nor accountants are particularly concerned with communications. Yet ultimately data is only effective when it is communicated. Targett (1984) suggests a series of rules for data presentation to improve their communication effectiveness particularly to the layman. These are reproduced below.

6.2   Rules for data presentation

In presenting statistical data, the usual form is a table. The object of a table is to enable the reader to see quickly and easily patterns and relationships between the data. In order to achieve this objective most effectively certain rules should be observed.

(a)   Round numbers to 2 significant figures.

(b)   Reorder the numbers - sort the data so as to highlight significant relationships.

(c)   Interchange rows and columns - significant relationships should be shown down columns, not across rows.

(d)   Use summary measures, eg, averages.

(e)   Minimise use of spaces and lines - grid lines, eg, from a spreadsheet, interfere with visualising patterns.

(f)   Labelling should be clear but not obtrusive - abbreviated labels may lead to lack of understanding.

(g)   Use a verbal summary - a brief summary of the main points emerging is often useful.

6.3   Using graphs and diagrams

In general, people find information in graphs and diagrams much easier to quickly grasp and interpret. However, such diagrams have their limitations, especially when handling more complex data, or being used to further analyse the data.

In summary:

(a)   **Advantages of graphs/diagrams**

   •   good at attracting attention and adding variety to reports

(b)   **Limitations of graphs/diagrams**

   •   can be confusing if used for too complex data

   •   not suitable for reference purposes

6.4   Data analysis

Accountants are expected to analyse data, to 'read figures'. This requires a systematic approach to handling any tabulated data. The following provides a general step by step approach to the problem.

Step 1   **Reduce the data**

Generally, tables contain too many numbers, usually because they are available and the producer is unclear what is important. Therefore, the data should be reduced to that which is essentially required for the analysis.

Step 2   **Represent the data**

The seven rules for representing data were set out above, as:

(a)   Round numbers to 2 significant figures
         (Take care when tabulating figures of different magnitudes)

(b)   Order rows and columns
         (Think about alternative arrangements for the table in 3.2)

(c)   Interchange rows and columns if appropriate

(d)   Use summary measures
         (Averages, index number, measures of spread)

(e)   Minimise spaces and grid lines
         (Some will be needed so that the eye does not slip a line in a table of figures)

(f)   Ensure labelling is clear

(g)   Provide verbal summary
         (Make it clear what conclusions you have drawn from the figures)

These same rules should be applied in representing the data for analysis.

Step 3   **Build a 'model'**

This means looking for relationships, eg, sales grew at 5% pa; production per employee in factories A and B both grew at 2% pa, but that in B remained 20% higher than that in A. Alternatively, the model may be a mathematical one eg, sales y, are related to time, t, by

$$y = 1,459 + 0.023t$$

A good model summarises a great deal of data. It can be used to identify exceptions. With caution, it can form the basis of a predictive model for saying what will happen in future.

Step 4   **Exceptions**

Having established a pattern, it becomes meaningful to look for exceptions. In management these can be most important.

When an exception is found, note that the first stage is to look for an error in recording data as the cause. If this is eliminated, management faces three choices in relation to an exception: correct it, leave it alone, or conduct a management investigation.

Step 5   **Comparisons**

The opportunity should always be sought to compare data. There is nearly always some possible source of comparison, eg, other companies, other countries, or simply the same company for earlier periods. If the results coincide, this further validates the model. If they differ, then the reasons may be investigated - is the model wrong, or are there some different factors? If the latter, are there some lessons that can be learnt?

7   CHAPTER SUMMARY

This chapter has considered the compilation of statistics from data and the various forms that the presentation of such data may take. Finally the use of such presentation techniques was considered in connection with the preparation of business reports.

8   SELF TEST QUESTIONS

8.1   What is a pictogram? (1.5)

8.2   How does a simple bar chart differ from a component bar chart? (1.9)

8.3   What is a pie chart? (1.12)

8.4   What is a histogram? (3.1)

8.5   What is a frequency polygon? (3.8)

8.6   What is an ogive? (3.11)

8.7   What is a Z chart? (4.1)

8.8   What is the benefit of using a semi-logarithmic graph to present data? (5.1)

9   EXAMINATION TYPE QUESTIONS

9.1   Pie charts and bar charts

The following data has been extracted from the annual report of a manufacturing company:

Annual Sales (£m)

	19X8	19X7
United Kingdom	35.0	31.5
EC (other than UK)	47.4	33.2
North America	78.9	40.3
Australia	18.2	26.1

Represent this data by:

(a)   pie charts;
(b)   component bar charts.

State the advantages and disadvantages of the two types of chart for representing this data.

(20 marks)

9.2   Students' statistics

From the following data prepare:

(a)   a histogram;
(b)   a frequency polygon; and
(c)   an ogive.

Height of students (ins)	*Number of students*
≥ 60 < 63	5
≥ 63 < 66	18
≥ 66 < 69	42
≥ 69 < 72	27
≥ 72 < 75	8
	100

(20 marks)

10   ANSWERS TO EXAMINATION TYPE QUESTIONS

10.1   Pie charts and bar charts

(a)   **Pie charts**

Calculation of angles of sections:

	19X8		19X7	
	Sales	Angles (degrees)	Sales	Angles (degrees)
UK	35.0	70.2	31.5	86.5
EC	47.4	95.1	33.2	91.2
NA	78.9	158.2	40.3	110.7
AUS	18.2	36.5	26.1	71.6
	179.5	360.0	131.1	360.0

Note:

The angles are calculated as $\dfrac{\text{Sales value}}{\text{Total sales}} \times 360$ degrees.

Thus the angles for UK in 19X8 is

$$\dfrac{35.0}{179.5} \times 360$$

$$= \quad 70.2°$$

Calculation of radii of circles

The radii 19X7 and 19X8 must be in the ratio

$$\sqrt{131.1} : \sqrt{179.5}$$

$$= \quad 11.4 : 13.4$$

Thus if the radius for 19X7 is 3cm, the radius for 19X8 must be

$$3 \times \dfrac{13.4}{11.4} = 3.5\text{cm}.$$

Annual Sales 19X7 - 19X8

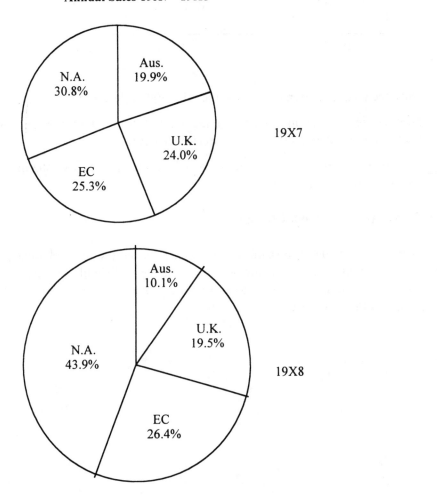

Note: time would have been saved by entering actual sales data rather than percentages.

(b)   **Component bar charts**

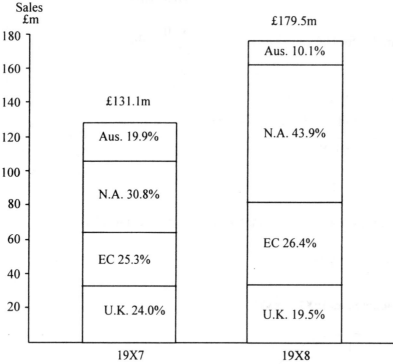

Annual Sales 19X7 to 19X8

Notes:

(i)   Once the chart has been completed the left hand scale could be erased.

(ii)   Neatness is essential in any chart, but do not go to great artistic lengths. There is not time in the examination and the examiner will not expect it.

(iii) If there is no room to write the details in each section, use shading and a key although this will take longer.

Comparison of pie charts and bar charts

The pie chart can be made to look more attractive, for example by exploding one or more sectors or by drawing it in 3 dimensions, but it is very difficult to make comparisons between areas of sectors. It is easier to compare the heights of rectangles in a bar chart, which also shows the total for each year.

10.2   Students' statistics

(a) & (b)   **Histogram and frequency polygon**

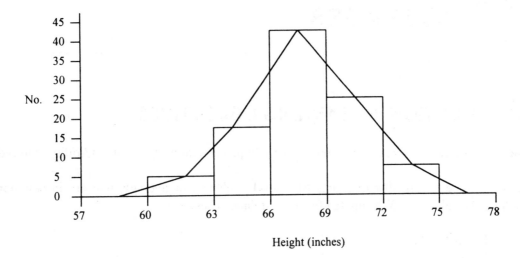

Height (inches)

Note: the frequency polygon is achieved by joining up the mid-points of the histogram. Note the correct treatment of the two ends of the polygon.

(c)   **Ogive**

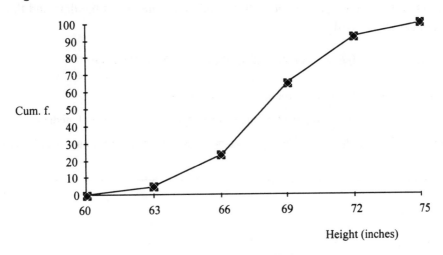

Height (inches)

Note: the cumulative frequency is plotted against the upper class limit.

20 AVERAGES

INTRODUCTION & LEARNING OBJECTIVES

Syllabus area 2e. Averages and variation for grouped and ungrouped data. (Ability required 3).

There are three examinable measures of central tendency, or average, that are in common use and which can be calculated or estimated for a set of data. These are:

(a)   The arithmetic mean.
(b)   The median.
(c)   The mode.

Each is a different method of choosing a single number to represent the items under consideration.

In any given situation the choice of average will depend on the nature of the data and the purposes for which the average is being calculated.

When you have studied this chapter you should be able to do the following:

●   Understand the four methods of central tendency discussed.

●   Define and explain the advantages and disadvantages of the mean, mode and median.

●   Calculate the values for the three measures of central tendency using information and data supplied.

---

1   AVERAGES

1.1   Choice of average

In the sections that follow the four measures stated in the introduction are examined in detail, and the calculations for both grouped and ungrouped data are explained. Students should bear in mind the following points:

(a)   The choice of average depends on the purpose for which the average is required.

(b)   All are correct measures; they are simply different ways of summarising the same data.

(c)   Measures for grouped data are always estimates, because of the loss of information when the raw data is grouped into classes.

Study the techniques, then consider carefully the last section comparing the different measures of average.

2   ARITHMETIC MEAN

2.1   Definition

[*Definition*]   The arithmetic mean is the best known type of average. It is defined as **the total value of the items divided by the total number of items**.

2.2   Calculation for ungrouped data

Assuming a set of data consists of n items, $x_1, x_2, \ldots x_n$, then the arithmetic mean (denoted by $\overline{x}$) is given by the formula:

$$\overline{x} = \frac{x_1 + x_2 + x_3 + \ldots + x_n}{n}$$

ie, $\overline{x} = \dfrac{\sum x}{n}$

where $\sum x$ (sigma x) denotes the sum of the individual values.

2.3   Example

The arithmetic mean of 3, 6, 10, 14, 17, 19 and 22 is calculated as follows:

$$\overline{x} = \frac{\sum x}{n}$$

where $x_1 = 3, x_2 = 6, \ldots$ etc and $n = 7$

$$\overline{x} = \frac{3 + 6 + 10 + 14 + 17 + 19 + 22}{7}$$

$$= \frac{91}{7}$$

$$\overline{x} = 13$$

2.4   Estimation of mean for grouped data

For a grouped frequency distribution, it is necessary to decide on one value that best represents each class interval. The mid-value of each class is conventionally taken, ie, it is assumed that the items in each class are spread evenly about the mid-value.

The formula is:

$$\overline{x} = \frac{f_1 x_1 + f_2 x_2 + \ldots + f_n x_n}{f_1 + f_2 + \ldots + f_n}$$

ie, $\overline{x} = \dfrac{\sum fx}{\sum f}$

where $x_1, x_2, \ldots x_n$ denote the mid-values of the class intervals and $f_1, f_2 \ldots f_n$ denote the corresponding frequencies and $\sum f$ is the total frequency.

This is an example of a weighted average; the x-values are weighted with the class frequencies. The general formula for a weighted average is:

$$\bar{x} = \frac{\sum wx}{\sum w}$$

where $w_1, w_2, w_3 \ldots$ are the weights of $x_1, x_2, x_3 \ldots$ respectively.

2.5   Example

The following table shows the frequency distribution of 100 articles.   The arithmetic mean is calculated as follows:

Class interval	Mid-value	Frequency	
Weight (grams)	x	f	fx
100 and less than 110	105	1	105
110 and less than 120	115	2	230
120 and less than 130	125	5	625
130 and less than 140	135	11	1,485
140 and less than 150	145	21	3,045
150 and less than 160	155	20	3,100
160 and less than 170	165	17	2,805
170 and less than 180	175	11	1,925
180 and less than 190	185	6	1,110
190 and less than 200	195	6	1,170
Totals		$\sum f = 100$	$\sum fx = 15,600$

$$\bar{x} = \frac{\sum fx}{\sum f}$$

$$= \frac{15,600}{100}$$

$$= 156 \text{ grams}$$

Notes:

(a)   Because 'less than 110' means 'up to 109.999. . .' the difference between the upper limit and 110 is infinite simal. The error is infinite simal in taking the class interval as 10 and the interval mid-point as 105. Similarly for the other classes.

(b)   If the data was discrete whole numbers, '100 and less than 110' would have meant '100 to 109'. In this case, the mid-value would have been:

$$\frac{100 + 109}{2} = 104.5$$

Similarly for the other classes. Take care in identifying the mid points and note this difference between discrete and continuous variables.

(c)   Open ended classes are closed by assuming that they have the same class interval as the adjacent closed classes.

2.6   Advantages and disadvantages of the mean

	Advantages		*Disadvantages*
(a)	It is easy to understand and calculate	(a)	It may give undue weight to or be influenced by extreme items, ie, high or low values. For example, the mean life of a sample of 100 electric light bulbs might be 2,000 hours, but it would only require one additional 'dud' bulb with a life of zero to reduce the mean to 1980 hours, a drop of 20 hours.
(b)	All the data in the distribution is used, and so it can be determined with arithmetical precision, and is representative of the whole set of data.	(b)	The value of the average may not correspond to any item in the distribution. For example, the average number of children per family is approximately 1.8, but there is no family with that number of children.
(c)	It can be calculated when nothing more than the total value or quantity of items and the number of items are known.		
(d)	It can be used in more advanced mathematical statistics.		

2.7   Activity

The following table shows the heights of a sample of 100 cabinets. Calculate the arithmetic mean.

Class interval Height (cms)	Frequency f
$\geq 150 < 160$	1
$\geq 160 < 170$	9
$\geq 170 < 180$	12
$\geq 180 < 190$	16
$\geq 190 < 200$	26
$\geq 200 < 210$	19
$\geq 210 < 220$	8
$\geq 220 < 230$	6
$\geq 230 < 240$	2
$\geq 240 < 250$	1
	$\Sigma f = 100$

2.8   Activity solution

Step 1   Find the mid point of each class interval, x, and produce a table showing x, f and fx.

Step 2   Multiply (x) by (f) and calculate Σfx.

Mid-value	Frequency	
x	f	fx
155	1	155
165	9	1,485
175	12	2,100
185	16	2,960
195	26	5,070
205	19	3,895
215	8	1,720
225	6	1,350
235	2	470
245	1	245
Totals	$\Sigma f = 100$	$\Sigma fx = 19,450$

Step 3   Calculate the arithmetic mean.

$$\text{The arithmetic mean} \quad = \quad \frac{\Sigma fx}{\Sigma f} \quad = \quad \frac{19,450}{100} = \quad 194.5\text{cms}$$

Notice that, if the original data had units so the mean should have units.

It might be worth practising calculating means on your scientific calculator.

2.9   When not to use the arithmetic mean

The arithmetic mean is the most generally used measure of central tendency. There are however situations where it is not appropriate. Three examples are as follows:

(a)   Distortion of the mean by extreme values, eg, a company where 10 employees earn £6,000 pa, and the managing director £40,000 pa.

(b)   The arithmetic mean is not always the correct average to use for rates of change and care has to be taken when finding averages of percentages (or averages of averages). For example, if one group of workers has a wage increase of 10% and another group 20%, the average increase is not 15% unless both groups are the same size.

(c)   If the data is split into 'clusters' the arithmetic mean is not suitable, eg, the number of people seeing a given number of episodes of a TV series tends to cluster at the very low and very high ends.

2.10   Arithmetic mean of combined data

If one group of 10 people has a mean height of 175cm, and another group of 15 people has a mean height of 172cm, the mean of the whole group is found as:

$$\text{Mean} \quad = \quad \frac{\text{Sum of heights of all people in combined groups}}{\text{Total number of people in combined groups}}$$

The sum of the heights of the 10 in the first group is 175×10 $=$ 1,750cm

The sum of the heights of the 15 in the second group is 172×15 $=$ 2,580cm

The sum of all 25 heights is therefore $1,750 + 2,580 =$ 4,330cm

The mean height is therefore $\dfrac{4,330}{25}$ $=$ 173.2cm

This should be recognised as another example of a weighted average. The average for the whole group is the weighted average of the individual groups, using the number of people in the group as the weight.

3   MEDIAN

3.1   Definition

[Definition]   The median is the value of the middle item in a distribution once all the items have
been arranged in order of magnitude.

3.2   Calculation for ungrouped data

Once the items have been arranged in order, starting with either the largest or smallest, then:

(a)   If the number of items is odd, the median is simply the value of the middle item.

(b)   However, if the number of items is even, the median is the arithmetic mean of the two
middle items.

3.3   Example

The median of 3, 6, 10, 14, 17, 19 and 22 is 14 since this is the value of the middle item.

Therefore, median   =   14.

3.4   Example

The median of 3, 6, 10, 14, 17, 19, 22 and 25 is found by taking the arithmetic mean of 14 and 17.

$$\text{Therefore, median} = \frac{14+17}{2}$$

$$= 15.5$$

If there are n items in the distribution:

the median is the value of the $\frac{n+1}{2}$th item.

3.5   Estimation of median for grouped data

When data has been categorised into classes, each containing a range of values, then:

the median is the value of the $\frac{n}{2}$th item.

n is taken rather than n + 1 because, for grouped data, n is always large, otherwise the data would
not have been grouped, and when n is large, the difference between n and n + 1 is negligible.

The median can be estimated from a cumulative frequency graph (ogive):

The value of the middle item is read off the horizontal axis:

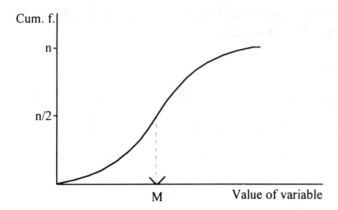

where n is the total frequency (Σf) and M is the median value.

Clearly, for reasonable estimates of the median to be made it is necessary to draw an accurate graph.

Note: the calculation of the median of grouped data by use of a formula is not examinable.

3.6   Example

Using the same data as in 2.5, the median is estimated as follows:

Weight (grams)	Frequency	Cumulative frequency
100 and less than 110	1	1
110 and less than 120	2	3
120 and less than 130	5	8
130 and less than 140	11	19
140 and less than 150	21	40
150 and less than 160	20	60
160 and less than 170	17	77
170 and less than 180	11	88
180 and less than 190	6	94
190 and less than 200	6	100

The cumulative frequency curve has already been drawn earlier, but is included again here.

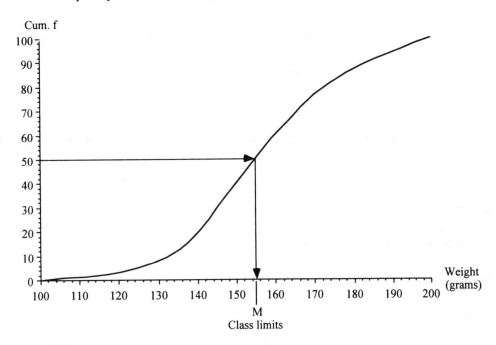

The median (M) is approximately 155 grams.

For accurate readings to be taken from the graph, it is essential that graph paper is used.

3.7   Advantages and disadvantages of the median

	Advantages		*Disadvantages*
(a)	It is simple to understand.	(a)	If there are only a few items, it may not be truly representative.
(b)	It is not affected by extreme values of the variable. For example in 3.3, Example 4, changing the last item from 22 to, say, 50 would have no effect on the median.	(b)	It is unsuitable for use in mathematical statistics.
(c)	It can be obtained even when the values of the extreme items are not known. It is unaffected by unequal class intervals or open-ended classes.	(c)	Data has to be arranged in order of size which is a tedious operation.
(d)	It can be the value of an actual item in the distribution.		

4   MODE

4.1   Definition

Definition   The mode is the value that occurs most frequently amongst all the items in the distribution.   When dealing with data grouped into class intervals, it is usual to refer to the modal class.

Note: it is possible to have two (or more) modal values or modal classes.

4.2   Calculation for ungrouped data

The mode can usually be determined by observation and no real calculation as such is necessary, although it is much easier if the data has been presented as a frequency distribution.

However, it is possible for a distribution to have more than one mode or, indeed, no mode at all.

4.3   Example

11 boys were asked what size shoes they were wearing. The following distribution resulted:

$$5, 7\frac{1}{2}, 6, 6, 7, 5\frac{1}{2}, 6, 5, 6, 5, 5.$$

$5\frac{1}{2}$, 7 and $7\frac{1}{2}$ occur once.

5 occurs four times and 6 occurs four times.

The modal values are therefore 5 and 6.

4.4   Example

An interviewer called at ten houses and enquired as to how many children there were in each family. The following data resulted:

$$0, 4, 1, 2, 2, 0, 1, 2, 3, 2.$$

3 and 4 occur once.

0 and 1 occur twice.

2 occurs four times.

The modal value is therefore 2.

The mode is the value with the highest frequency.

4.5   Estimation of mode for grouped data

In a grouped frequency distribution, the modal class is the class with the largest frequency. This can easily be found by observation. The value of the mode within the modal class can then be estimated from a histogram.

Having located the modal class it is necessary to draw in the dotted lines shown in the following diagram:

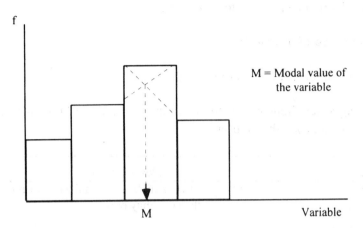

Students should appreciate that it is normally continuous variables which are summarised using class intervals. For continuous variables, no two items can ever be said to have exactly the same value and therefore when dealing with continuous variables the mode should be used with extreme caution, and preferably only discussed in terms of the modal class.

4.6   Example

Using the same data as 3.6 the mode is estimated from a histogram.

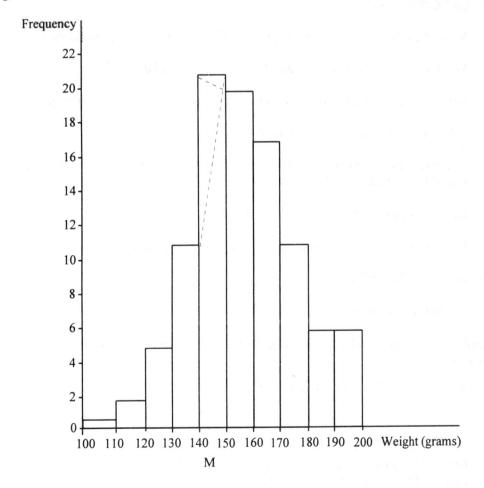

The mode (M) is 149 grams (approximately).

In order to estimate the mode graphically it is only really necessary to draw the modal class and the two adjoining classes. However, it is usual to be asked to draw the complete histogram. For an accurate reading, graph paper must be used, and the width of the rectangles be made as large as possible. It is worth noting before performing any calculation that the mode lies in the interval 140 grams to 150 grams, but is clearly much closer to 150 grams.

4.7   Advantages and disadvantages of the mode

The mode has many uses in both business and government.

For example, when planning a new housing estate, the architect needs to know the modal size of family in order to be able to design suitable houses.

	Advantages		*Disadvantages*
(a)	It is easy to understand.	(a)	There may be no modal value or more than one may exist.
(b)	It is not affected by extreme values.	(b)	Data has to be arranged to ascertain which value occurs most frequently and this can be tedious.
(c)	It can be calculated even if not all the values in the distribution are known.	(c)	It is not suitable for mathematical statistics.
(d)	It can be the value of an actual item in the distribution.		

5   SELF TEST QUESTIONS

5.1   What is the formula for calculating the arithmetic mean of ungrouped data? (2.2)

5.2   What does x denote when finding the mean of grouped data? (2.4)

5.3   Give two circumstances when use of the arithmetic mean is not appropriate. (2.9)

5.4   What is the definition of the median? (3.1)

5.5   The median can be estimated by use of a cumulative frequency graph or ogive. Explain how this is achieved. (3.5)

5.6   Give one disadvantage of using the median. (3.7)

5.7   Explain how the mode can be determined from a histogram.(4.5)

6   EXAMINATION TYPE QUESTIONS

6.1   Automatic filling machines

A sample of 12 packets taken from an automatic filling machine had the following weights in kilograms:

   504, 506, 501, 505, 507, 506, 504, 508, 503, 505, 502, 504

Find:

(a)   (i)   The median weight.
       (ii)   The modal weight.
       (iii) The arithmetic mean weight.

(b)   The effect on the median, mode and arithmetic mean if one extra value of 495 were included.

(15 marks)

6.2   Frequency distributions II

The production of each manufacturing department of your company is monitored weekly to establish productivity bonuses paid to members of that department.

250 items have to be produced each week before a bonus will be paid. The production of one department over a forty week period is shown below:

382	367	364	365	371	370	372	364	355	347
354	359	359	360	357	362	364	365	371	365
361	380	382	394	396	398	402	406	437	456
469	466	459	454	460	457	452	451	445	446

You are required

(a) to form a frequency distribution of five groups for the number of items produced per week.

(5 marks)

(b) to construct the ogive or cumulative frequency diagram for the frequency distribution established in (a).

(5 marks)

(c) to establish the value of the median from the ogive.

(2 marks)

(d) to contrast the use of the median and the mean as measures of location.

(2 marks)

(Total: 14 marks)

7   ANSWERS TO EXAMINATION TYPE QUESTIONS

7.1   Automatic filling machines

Arrange in numerical order:

501, 502, 503, 504, 504, 504, 505, 505, 506, 506, 507, 508

(a) (i) The median weight is $\dfrac{504 + 505}{2} = 504.5$kg.

(ii) The modal weight is 504 kg (it occurs three times).

(iii) To make calculating the arithmetic mean easier subtract 500.

$$\text{Mean} = 500 + \frac{1+2+3+4+4+4+5+5+6+6+7+8}{12}$$

$$= 500 + \frac{55}{12}$$

$$= 504.58 \text{ kg}$$

(b) Median becomes 504 kg. (The additional item appears at the beginning of the sequence.)

Mode remains as 504 kg.

Arithmetic mean:

The mean becomes $500 + \dfrac{55-5}{13} = 503.84$ kg.

7.2 Frequency distributions II

(a)   Highest value = 469, Lowest value = 347, Range = 122.

Hence for 5 groups (122 ÷ 5 = 24.4), a class interval of 25 will be satisfactory

Production (units)	Tally	Frequency	Cumulative Frequency
345 and less than 370	‖‖‖ ‖‖‖ ‖‖‖ I	16	16
370 and less than 395	‖‖‖ III	8	24
395 and less than 420	IIII	4	28
420 and less than 445	I	1	29
445 and less than 470	‖‖‖ ‖‖‖ I	11	40
	Total	40	

(b)   **'Less than' ogive of weekly production**

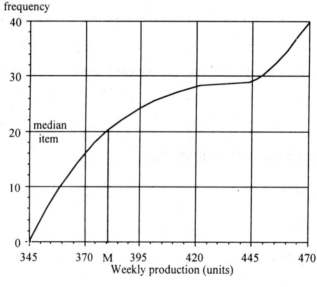

(c)   The median as read from the graph is 380 items.

(d)   The mean uses all the data and is therefore representative of all the data. It is easy to understand and calculate; it can be used in more advanced statistical theory.

It has the disadvantage that it can be unduly affected by a few extreme values, and it may not correspond to an actual value in the set if the set is discrete.

The median is also easy to understand. It is unaffected by extreme values, it can exist even if the items cannot be quantified, provided they can be ranked. It is a useful compromise between the mean and the mode.

As it does not use all the data, it may not be representative. Data has to be arranged in order of magnitude. It is not suitable for more advanced statistical theory.

21 VARIATION OF GROUPED & UNGROUPED DATA

INTRODUCTION & LEARNING OBJECTIVES

Syllabus area 2e. Averages and variation for grouped and ungrouped data. (Ability required 3).

When, for example, making cylinders for car engines, it is impossible, for a number of technical reasons, to produce all cylinders with exactly the same diameter. The designer must therefore specify not only the average diameter, but the limits to which variation about this average can be tolerated between cylinders. Such variation about the average is called **dispersion** and it is just as important to be able to measure this dispersion as to obtain the average.

Students should note that within the jargon of statistics, measures of averages, dispersion, and so on, are often referred to as the **parameters** of a distribution.

When you have studied this chapter you should be able to do the following:

- Calculate the range of a set of data items.
- Calculate the quartile deviation or semi-interquartile range of a set of data items.
- Calculate the standard deviation of a set of data items.
- Explain the use of each of these measures of dispersion.
- Distinguish between symmetrical and skewed distributions.

1   MEASURING DISPERSION

1.1   Types of measure of dispersion

There are four commonly used measures that can be calculated for a set of data. They are:

(a)   The range.   } used for presenting data
(b)   The semi-interquartile range.   } to non-statisticians
(c)   The standard deviation.

Each is a different method of choosing a single number to measure the spread of the items. Of these, (c) is by far the most important.

2   RANGE

2.1   Definition

Definition   This is by far the simplest measure of dispersion, being the difference between the extreme values of the distribution.

2.2   Calculation for ungrouped data

Range = Highest value – lowest value

2.3   Example

The range of values 3, 5, 8, 11 and 13 is simply 10, since the highest and lowest values are 13 and 3 respectively, and $13 - 3 = 10$.

2.4   Advantages and disadvantages of the range

Since this measure yields no information about the dispersion of items lying in the interval between the highest and lowest values, it is of very little practical use except in elementary quality control, where a measure is required that can be calculated very quickly. It is rarely calculated for a frequency distribution.

	Advantages		*Disadvantages*
(a)	It is very simple and quick to calculate.	(a)	It can be very misleading if the data contains one extremely high or low value.
(b)	It is very simple to understand.	(b)	Only two values are used from the distribution, it is not therefore representative of the whole data.
(c)	It is used as a measure of dispersion in quality control work, where rapid results are essential.	(c)	It cannot be used precisely in mathematical statistics.

2.5   Activity

Calculate the range of the following data:

9, 6, 8, 2, 4, 7, 3.

2.6   Activity solution

$9 - 2 = 7$

3   SEMI-INTERQUARTILE RANGE

3.1   Definition

Definition   The median divides a distribution into two equal parts since it is the value of the middle item; it divides the area of a histogram in half. Similarly, the **quartiles** divide the distribution into four equal parts. Once the data has been arranged in order of magnitude, the lower quartile (Q_1) is the value at one-quarter of the total frequency and the upper quartile (Q_3) is the value at the three-quarters of the total frequency.

The **semi-interquartile range (or quartile deviation)** is half the difference between the upper and lower quartiles.

Note: that there are only **three** quartiles, Q_1, Q_2 and Q_3, the middle one (Q_2) being the median.

3.2   Calculation for ungrouped data

Q_1 is the value of the $\frac{1}{4}(n + 1)$th item

Q_3 is the value of the $\frac{3}{4}(n + 1)$th item

$$\text{Semi-interquartile range} = \frac{(Q_3 - Q_1)}{2}$$

3.3 Example

Considering the set of data 3, 5, 8, 11 and 13, the semi-interquartile range is calculated as follows:

$n = 5$ ∴ Q_1 is the value of the $\frac{1}{4}(5+1) = 1\frac{1}{2}$ th item

ie, taking the arithmetic mean of the 1st and 2nd item

$$Q_1 = \frac{3+5}{2} = 4$$

Also Q_3 is the value of the $\frac{3}{4}(5+1) = 4\frac{1}{2}$ th item.

ie, taking the arithmetic mean of the 4th and 5th items.

$$Q_3 = \frac{11+13}{2} = 12$$

∴ Semi-interquartile range $= \dfrac{12-4}{2} = 4$

3.4 Activity

Calculate the semi-interquartile range from the following data:

1, 4, 9, 12, 15, 19, 21

3.5 Activity solution

$n = 7$ ∴ Q_1 is the value of the $\frac{1}{4}(7+1) = $ 2nd item

$$Q_1 = 4$$

Q_3 is the value of the $\frac{3}{4}(7+1) = $ 6th item

$$Q_3 = 19$$

Therefore the semi-interquartile range $= \dfrac{19-4}{2} = 7.5$

3.6 Calculation for a frequency distribution

When data has been classified into groups, the quartiles are calculated as follows:

Q_1 is the value of the $\frac{1}{4}n$ th item

Q_3 is the value of the $\frac{3}{4}n$ th item

$$\text{Semi-interquartile range} = \frac{(Q_3 - Q_1)}{2}$$

The quartile values can be estimated from a cumulative frequency graph.

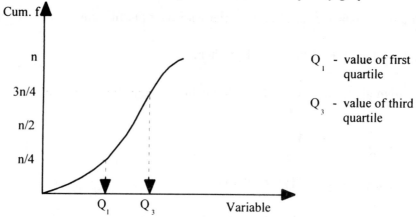

Q_1 - value of first quartile

Q_3 - value of third quartile

Having determined the quartile values then:

$$\text{Semi-interquartile range} = \frac{(Q_3 - Q_1)}{2}$$

3.7   Example

The following table shows the frequency distribution of the weights of 80 students.

Weight (stones)	Frequency (f)	Cumulative frequency
8 and less than 9	4	4
9 and less than 10	10	14
10 and less than 11	14	28
11 and less than 12	22	50
12 and less than 13	16	66
13 and less than 14	12	78
14 and less than 15	2	80

3.8   Solution

The quartiles are estimated from a cumulative frequency curve:

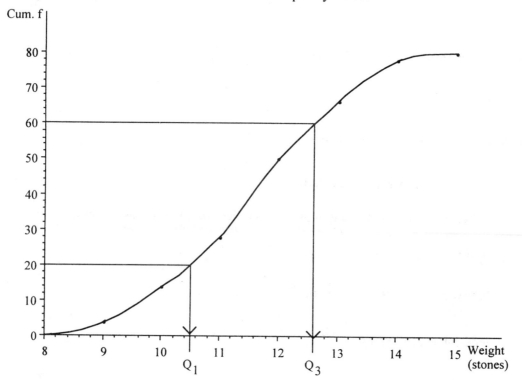

$Q_1 = 10.5$ stones (the 20th item)

$Q_3 = 12.6$ stones (the 60th item)

$$\therefore \text{Semi-interquartile range} = \frac{12.6 - 10.5}{2}$$

$$= \frac{2.10}{2}$$

$$= 1.05$$

$$= 1.1 \text{ stones (to same degree of accuracy)}$$

3.9   Advantages and disadvantages of the semi-interquartile range

	Advantages		*Disadvantages*
(a)	It is simple to understand.	(a)	It does not take all the values into account.
(b)	It is not affected by extreme values.	(b)	Data may have to be arranged in order of size.
(c)	It can be obtained even when the values of the extreme items are not known.	(c)	It cannot be used in mathematical statistics.

3.10   Deciles and percentiles

Just as the quartiles divide the distribution into four equal parts so that **deciles** divide it into ten equal parts and the **percentiles** into a hundred equal parts. These are usually estimated from a cumulative frequency graph. There are **nine** deciles and **ninety-nine** percentiles.

4   STANDARD DEVIATION

4.1 [Definition] This is the most valuable and widely used measure of dispersion. However, it is also the most complex to calculate and the most difficult to understand. It is defined as the **square root of the mean square deviations of the values from the mean.** The defining formula is therefore:

$$\text{Standard deviation} = \sqrt{\frac{\Sum(x - \bar{x})^2}{n}}$$

where n is the number of x values. The standard deviation is usually denoted by σ (the Greek lower case sigma).

While the above formula defines the standard deviation, it is rarely used for calculations, as there is an alternative formula which is algebraically equivalent, but is easier for computation. This formula is:

$$\sigma = \sqrt{\frac{\Sum x^2}{n} - \left(\frac{\Sum x}{n}\right)^2}$$

It will be noticed that the first of these formulae is preceded by a different version in the CIMA list of formulae, which uses $n - 1$ as the divisor instead of n. The reason for the difference is that in this section we are defining the standard deviation of any set of items. Sometimes the set of items is a sample from a larger population ; $n - 1$ is used as the divisor when it is the standard deviation of the **population** that is being **estimated from the sample**. This is covered later.

4.2   Example

Calculate the standard deviation of 3, 5, 8, 11, 13.

4.3   Solution

Statistical calculations of this nature are always best set out in columns thus:

x	x^2
3	9
5	25
8	64
11	121
13	169
$\Sigma x = 40$	$\Sigma x^2 = 388$

$$
\begin{aligned}
\text{Hence } \sigma &= \sqrt{\frac{388}{5} - \left(\frac{40}{5}\right)^2} \\
&= \sqrt{77.6 - 64} \\
&= \sqrt{13.6} \\
&= 3.69 \text{ to 2dp}
\end{aligned}
$$

4.4   Activity

Calculate the standard deviation for the data 3, 4, 6, 8, 9.

4.5   Activity solution

$$\Sigma x = 3 + 4 + 6 + 8 + 9 = 30, \qquad \Sigma x^2 = 9 + 16 + 36 + 64 + 81 = 206,$$

$$
\begin{aligned}
\sigma &= \sqrt{\frac{206}{5} - \left(\frac{30}{5}\right)^2} \\
&= 2.28
\end{aligned}
$$

4.6   Calculation for a frequency distribution

The defining formula now becomes:

$$\sigma = \sqrt{\frac{\Sigma fx^2}{\Sigma f} - \left(\frac{\Sigma fx}{\Sigma f}\right)^2} \quad \text{or} \quad \sqrt{\frac{\Sigma fx^2}{\Sigma f} - \bar{x}^2} \quad \text{(as given in CIMA tables)}$$

4.7   Example

Using the data of the earlier example (shown below)

Weight (stones)	Mid-value x	frequency f	fx	fx²
8 - 9	8.5	4	34	289.0
9 - 10	9.5	10	95	902.5
10 - 11	10.5	14	147	1,543.5
11 - 12	11.5	22	253	2,909.5
12 - 13	12.5	16	200	2,500.0
13 - 14	13.5	12	162	2,187.0
14 - 15	14.5	2	29	420.5
Totals		80	920	10,752.0

Note: that algebraically, $fx^2 = fx \times x$, therefore:

Column 5 = column 4 × column 2

(It is worth working across this table in rows to reduce the amount of button-clicking needed on the calculator.)

Substituting in the computational formula:

$$\sigma = \sqrt{\frac{10,752}{80} - \left(\frac{920}{80}\right)^2}$$

$$= \sqrt{134.4 - (11.5)^2}$$

$$= \sqrt{2.15}$$

$$= 1.47 \text{ stones.}$$

Note: that only one additional column (fx^2) is required to the calculation of the arithmetic mean. In practice, both parameters are usually calculated at the same time from the same table. It is again worth checking how the standard deviation function on your scientific calculator works.

4.8   Advantages and disadvantages of the standard deviation

	Advantages		*Disadvantages*
(a)	It is the most commonly used measure of dispersion in statistical work.	(a)	The calculation is complex.
(b)	The value of every item of data is used.	(b)	It is difficult for the layman to understand.
(c)	It is the only measure that can be used in mathematical statistics.	(c)	It can give more than a proportional weight to extreme values because of squaring the deviations.

4.9   Variance

[Definition]   The variance is the square of the standard deviation.

$\therefore$ Variance $= \dfrac{\Sigma(x - \bar{x})^2}{n}$ for ungrouped data.

Variance $= \dfrac{\Sigma fx^2}{\Sigma f} - \bar{x}^2$ for a frequency distribution.

This is of importance when combining frequency distributions.

Certain problems involve more than one distribution. As long as the distributions are independent, the following relationships can be used.

The mean of a sum   =   the sum of the means.

The variance of a sum   =   the sum of the variances.

4.10   Example

Bloggs Ltd, an engineering firm, produces an item which, in the course of assembly, has to pass through three workshops - A, B and C. A record of the times taken in each workshop was kept and the following summary shows the mean and standard deviations of these times (all in hours).

	Mean	*Standard deviation*
Workshop A	3.48	0.25
Workshop B	4.56	0.30
Workshop C	1.91	0.20

Assuming that these times are independent, the mean and the standard deviation of the time taken to completely assemble the items is:

Mean (A + B + C)   =   3.48 + 4.56 + 1.91

                       =   9.95 hours

Variance (workshop A)   = $(0.25)^2$ =   0.0625

Variance (workshop B)   = $(0.30)^2$ =   0.0900

Variance (workshop C)   = $(0.20)^2$ =   0.0400

$\therefore$ Variance (A + B + C)   =   0.0625 + 0.0900 + 0.0400

                       =   0.1925

Standard deviation   = $\sqrt{0.1925}$ =   0.44 hours
(A + B + C)

If the problem involves a **difference** rather than a **sum** then:

The mean of a difference   =   the **difference** of the means
The variance of a difference   =   the **sum** of the variances

4.11 Conclusion

Of all the measures of dispersion that have been calculated, the standard deviation is by far the most important, its main uses and applications being in the field of more advanced statistics.

In general, the mean and standard deviation are calculated for a distribution, however the median and semi-interquartile range are sometimes used. These are the most common 'pairings' of average and dispersion.

4.12 Coefficient of variation

When comparing the dispersion in two or more sets of data, the mean of each set of data must be taken into account. For example, a variation of 2 units in a set of data with a mean of 5 is of much greater significance than a variation of 2 units in a set of data with a mean of 50. To compare the amount of variation, or dispersion, between sets of data, the coefficient of variation is often used, which expressed the standard deviation as a percentage of the mean.

$$\text{Coefficient of variation} = \frac{\text{Standard deviation} \times 100}{\text{Arithmetic mean}}$$

4.13 Example

Two machines are used for filling bags of fertiliser. One machine is set to deliver a nominal weight of 1 kilo, and the other machine, 7 kilos. Tests on the actual amounts delivered gave the following results:

Machine	Mean weight (kilo)	Standard deviation (kilo)
1	1.05	0.062
2	7.13	0.384

Which machine varies most in weight delivered?

4.14 Solution

In absolute terms the answer is clearly machine 2, but:

Machine 1:   Coefficient of variation $= \dfrac{0.062 \times 100}{1.05} = 5.9\%$

Machine 2:   Coefficient of variation $= \dfrac{0.384 \times 100}{7.13} = 5.4\%$

Therefore machine 1 has a slightly greater variation in weight of output than machine 2, relatively speaking.

4.15 Activity

Given the following data concerning A and B, which has the higher coefficient of variation?

	Mean	Standard deviation
A	5.46	1.29
B	16.38	4.21

4.16   Activity solution

A	Coefficient of variation	=	$\dfrac{1.29 \times 100}{5.46}$	=	23.63%
B	Coefficient of variation	=	$\dfrac{4.21 \times 100}{16.38}$	=	25.70%

B has the higher coefficient of variation.

5   SYMMETRY AND SKEWNESS

5.1   Introduction

If a frequency curve is drawn for a distribution, then the position of the peak of the curve is very important. If the peak is in the centre of the distribution, then it is said to be **symmetrical**.

If the peak of the curve lies to one side of the centre, the distribution is said to be **skewed**.

The further the peak lies form the centre, the greater is the degree of skewness of the distribution.

5.2   Types of distribution

(a)   **Normal distribution**

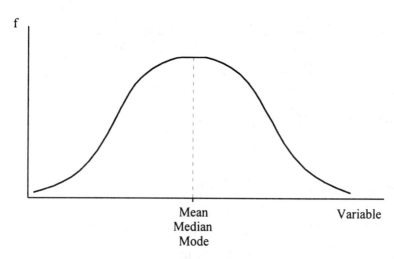

The peak of the frequency curve is at the centre of the distribution, the curve on either side of this being the same shape, ie, the curve is symmetrical about the dotted line.

The mean, median and mode all coincide at this point.

(b)   **A positively skewed distribution**

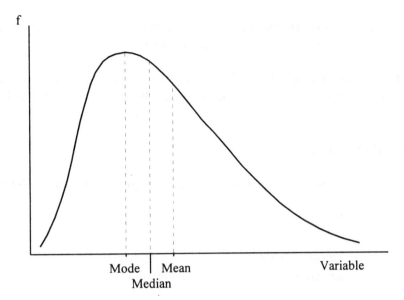

This occurs when the majority of the frequencies are located at the lower values of the variable. The peak of the curve therefore lies to the left of the centre of the distribution.

An example could be the distribution of salaries within a company.

(c)   **A negatively skewed distribution**

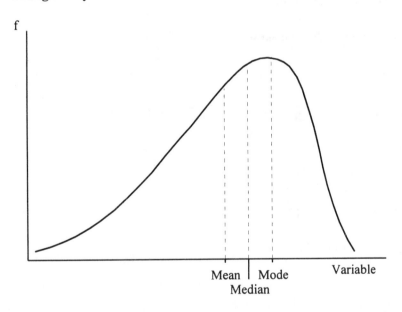

This is the exact opposite of (b); it occurs when the majority of the frequencies are located at the higher values of the variable. The peak of the frequency curve will be to the right of the centre of the distribution.

An example would be age at death.

These diagrams are not drawn to scale. In actual fact, the mean, median and mode would be much closer to each other than as shown, and the median will be nearer to the mean than to the mode.

5.3   Relationship between skewness and averages

(a)   In a **symmetrical distribution**, the mean, median and mode will all have the same value, and are located at the same point on the frequency curve.

(b)   In a **skewed distribution**, the mean will be drawn away form the mode, which is always found at the peak of the curve.   The median lies between the mean and the mode. (Remember the order mean, median, mode - alphabetical order.)

5.4   Pearsonian measure of skewness

One measure of the degree of skewness of a distribution is **Pearson's coefficient of skewness**.

The formula is:

$$\text{Skewness} \quad = \quad \frac{\text{mean - mode}}{\text{standard deviation}} \quad = \quad \frac{3(\text{mean - median})}{\text{standard deviation}}$$

The formula gives the direction of skew, (ie, positive or negative) as well as the magnitude.

The value will always lie between ± 3 since:

+3 indicates maximum positive skew

0 indicates symmetry, ie, no skew

−3 indicates maximum negative skew

5.5   Activity

The following figures have been calculated for a frequency distribution:

Mean   34

Median   32

Standard deviation   12

Calculate Pearson's coefficient of skewness.

5.6   Activity solution

$$\text{Skewness} \quad = \quad \frac{3 \times (34 - 32)}{12}$$

$$= \quad 0.5$$

6   CHAPTER SUMMARY

This chapter has considered the different measures of dispersion which may be used to analyse data and shown how each of them are calculated.

7   **SELF TEST QUESTIONS**

7.1   What are the advantages of the 'range' as a measure of dispersion? (2.4)

7.2   What is the quartile deviation? (3.1)

7.3   What is the formula for calculating the semi-interquartile range of ungrouped data? (3.2)

7.4   What are the disadvantages of the semi-interquartile range as a measure of dispersion? (3.9)

7.5   What is the standard deviation? (4.1)

7.6   What is the variance? (4.9)

7.7   What is the coefficient of variation? (4.12)

7.8   If a frequency distribution is said to be positively skewed, which value would be greater, the mode or the mean? (5.2)

8   **EXAMINATION TYPE QUESTIONS**

8.1   **Dispersion of sales values**

The following sales values were recorded per month over a period of 12 months in £'000s:

225, 227, 222, 227, 224, 225, 223, 220, 219, 221, 225, 228.

For this data calculate the standard deviation.

8.2   **Manco plc**

The price of the ordinary 25p shares of Manco plc quoted on the Stock Exchange at the close of business on successive Fridays is tabulated below:

126	120	122	105	129	119	131	138
125	127	113	112	130	122	134	136
128	126	117	114	120	123	127	140
124	127	114	111	116	131	128	137
127	122	106	121	116	135	142	130

Required

(a)   Group the above data into eight classes.   **(5 marks)**

(b)   By constructing the ogive calculate the median value, quartile values and the semi-interquartile range.   **(10 marks)**

(c)   Calculate the mean and standard deviation of your frequency distribution.   **(10 marks)**

(d)   Compare and contrast the values that you have obtained for:

   (i)   the median and mean; and
   (ii)   the semi-interquartile range and the standard deviation.

(5 marks)
(Total: 30 marks)

9   ANSWERS TO EXAMINATION TYPE QUESTIONS

9.1   Dispersion of sales values

Note: The standard deviation is unaffected by subtracting a constant. Hence the data can be simplified by subtracting 200. This will not affect the spread of the data.

Calculations:

x	x − 200 (=d)	d^2	$\lvert d - \bar{d} \rvert$
225	25	625	1.17
227	27	729	3.17
222	22	48	1.83
227	27	729	3.17
224	24	574	0.17
225	25	625	1.17
223	23	529	0.83
220	20	400	3.83
219	19	361	4.83
221	21	441	2.83
225	25	625	1.17
228	28	784	4.17
	286	6,908	28.34

$$\text{Standard deviation} = \sqrt{\frac{\Sigma d^2}{n} - \left(\frac{\Sigma d}{n}\right)^2}$$

$$= \sqrt{\frac{6,908}{12} - \left(\frac{286}{12}\right)^2}$$

$$= 2.76 \text{ (£'000)}$$

9.2   Manco plc

(a)   The smallest value in the distribution is 105, the largest value in the distribution is 142.

The range to be spanned is 142 − 105, ie, 37. Class intervals should be of the order of 37 ÷ 8 = 4.625; 5 is recommended. The following grouping is a suggestion.

The classes should be of equal width.

Share price	*Tally*	*Frequency*
105 but less than 110	I I	2
110 but less than 115	₩	5
115 but less than 120	I I I I	4
120 but less than 125	₩ I I I	8
125 but less than 130	₩ ₩	10
130 but less than 135	₩	5
135 but less than 140	I I I I	4
140 but less than 145	I I	2

(b)   To construct the ogive it is first necessary to calculate the cumulative frequency:

Share price	Frequency	Cumulative
105 but less than 110	2	2
110 but less than 115	5	7
115 but less than 120	4	11
120 but less than 125	8	19
125 but less than 130	10	29
130 but less than 135	5	34
135 but less than 140	4	38
140 but less than 145	2	40

Ogive - The price of ordinary 25p shares of Manco plc

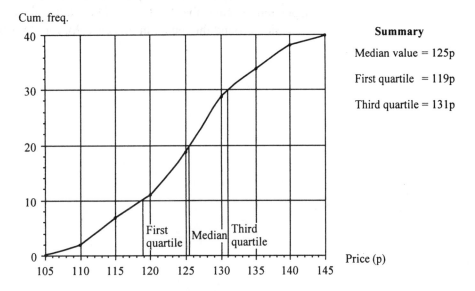

Summary

Median value = 125p

First quartile = 119p

Third quartile = 131p

The semi-interquartile range is given by the formula ½ (Third quartile value – First quartile value).

Thus, the semi-interquartile range $= \frac{1}{2}(131 - 119)$

$= \frac{1}{2} \times 12$

$= 6p$

(c)

Share price	Mid point x	f	fx	fx^2
105 - 110	107.5	2	215.0	23,112.50
110 - 115	112.5	5	562.5	63,281.25
115 - 120	117.5	4	470.0	55,225.00
120 - 125	122.5	8	980.0	120,050.00
125 - 130	127.5	10	1,275.0	162,562.50
130 - 135	132.5	5	662.5	87,781.25
135 - 140	137.5	4	550.0	75,625.00
140 - 145	142.5	2	285.0	40,612.50
		40 = Σf	5,000.0 = Σfx	628,250.00 = Σfx^2

Arithmetic mean $= \dfrac{\Sigma fx}{\Sigma f} = \dfrac{5,000}{40}$

$= 125p$

$$\text{Standard deviation} = \sqrt{\frac{\sum fx^2}{\sum f} - \left(\frac{\sum fx}{\sum f}\right)^2}$$

$$= \sqrt{\frac{628,250}{40} - \left(\frac{5,000}{40}\right)^2}$$

$$= \quad 9.01$$

(d)   (i)   This distribution is very nearly symmetrical and so consequently the mean, at 125, and the median, at just over 125, are close to one another.

(ii)   The semi-interquartile range and the standard deviation both measure dispersion.   The semi-interquartile range, in this case 6p, gives the dispersion around the median.   The standard deviation measures the dispersion around the mean, in this case 9p, for the whole distribution.

22 INDEX NUMBERS

INTRODUCTION & LEARNING OBJECTIVES

Syllabus area 2e.   Index numbers and their uses. (Ability required 3).

Indexing is a technique for comparing, over time, changes in some property of a group of items (price, quantity consumed etc) by expressing the property each year as a percentage of some earlier year, a base year.

Examples of index numbers are frequently seen in everyday life. The most well known is probably the Retail Price Index (RPI), which measures changes in the prices of goods and services supplied to retail customers. This index is often thought of as a 'cost of living' index. Index numbers may also measure quantity changes (eg, volumes of production or trade) or changes in values (eg, retail sales, value of exports).

Since much of the information needed to compile index numbers is the result of surveys of the population, sampling methods are used. These methods were included in detail in an earlier chapter.

When you have studied this chapter you should be able to do the following:

- Understand why indexing is used, and some of its uses.

- Calculate simple, weighted, Laspeyre, Paasche and chain base indices.

- Understand and be able to explain the effects of inflation, and its link to indexing.

- Have a general understanding of the Retail Price Index (RPI).

1   INDEX NUMBERS AND INFLATION ACCOUNTING

1.1   Inflation

Inflation has been a familiar feature of life for a number of years albeit currently running at a relatively low level. It explains the ever-increasing prices paid over time for the same commodity. The cause of and the cure of inflation have been much argued over by economists.

1.2   Index numbers

Most accountants acknowledge that the accounts of businesses are distorted when no allowance is made for the effects of inflation. The use of index numbers is often required for the preparation of inflation-adjusted accounts.

This is discussed later after consideration of the various types of index numbers and their calculation.

1.3   Types of index number

The following types of index number will be considered:

(a)   Simple indices.
(b)   Weighted indices.
(c)   Laspeyre indices.
(d)   Paasche indices.
(e)   Chain base indices.

2   SIMPLE INDICES

2.1   Price and quantity percentage relatives

These are also called percentage relatives and are based on a single item. There are two types:

(a)   Price relatives.
(b)   Quantity relatives.

The formulae for calculating them are:

$$\text{Simple price or price relative index} = \frac{P_1}{P_0} \times 100$$

$$\text{Simple quantity or quantity relative index} = \frac{Q_1}{Q_0} \times 100$$

Where P_0 is the price at time 0
P_1 is the price at time 1
Q_0 is the quantity at time 0
Q_1 is the quantity at time 1

Note: the concept of time 0, time 1 and so on is simply a scale counting from any given point in time. Thus, for example, if the scale started on 1 January 19X0 it would be as follows:

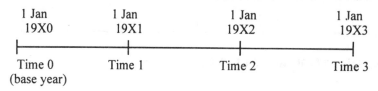

The starting point is chosen to be most convenient for the problem under consideration.

2.2   Example

If a commodity costs £2.60 in 19X4 and £3.68 in 19X5, calculate the simple price index for 19X5, using 19X4 as base year (ie, time 0).

2.3   Solution

$$\text{Simple price index} = \frac{P_1}{P_0} \times 100$$

$$= \frac{3.68}{2.60} \times 100$$

$$= 141.5$$

This means that the price has increased by 41.5% of its base year value, ie, its 19X4 value.

2.4   Example

6,500 items were sold in 19X8 compared with 6,000 in 19X7. Calculate the simple quantity index for 19X8 using 19X7 as base year.

2.5   Solution

Simple price index $\quad = \dfrac{Q_1}{Q_0} \times 100$

$$= \frac{6{,}500}{6{,}000} \times 100$$

$$= \quad 108.3$$

This means that the quantity sold has increased by 8.3% of its 19X7 figure.

2.6   Activity

A product which cost £12.50 in 19X0, cost £13.65 in 19X1. Calculate the simple price index for 19X1 based on 19X0.

2.7   Activity solution

Simple price index $\quad = \dfrac{P_1}{P_0} \times 100 \quad$ where P_1 is the price in 19X1 and P_0 is the price in 19X0

$$= \frac{13.65}{12.50} \times 100$$

$$= \quad 1.092 \times 100$$

$$= \quad 109.20$$

This means that the price has increased by 9.2% on its base year price of £12.50.

2.8   Multi-item indices

Usually, an index number is required to show the variation in a number of items at once rather than just one as in the examples above. The Retail Price Index (RPI) is such an index and consists of a list of items as diverse as the price of bread, the cost of watch repairs, car repairs and cinema tickets.

By using appropriate weights, price relatives can be combined to give a multi-item price index.

3   WEIGHTED INDICES

3.1   Weighted average of price relatives

An index number based on price relatives compares the price of each item in one year with the price of each item in the base year, expressing each as a percentage relative, and then finds the weighted average of the percentage relatives.

3.2   Example

From the following information, construct an index of the weighted average of price relatives, with 19X5 as the base year:

Item	Price (pence) 19X5	19X6	Weights
A	10	20	100
B	25	26	182
C	35	33	132
D	12	13	13
			427

3.3   Solution

Index of the weighted average of price relatives

$$= \frac{\sum W \frac{P_1}{P_0} \times 100}{\sum W} = \frac{52,783.5}{427} = 123.6$$

Where W = weight, p_1 = prices in 19X6, p_0 = prices in 19X5.

Workings

P_0	P_1	Price relative $\frac{P_1}{P_0} \times 100$	W	$W \times (\frac{P_1}{P_0} \times 100)$
10	20	200.0	100	20,000.0
25	26	104.0	182	18,928.0
35	33	94.3	132	12,447.6
12	13	108.3	13	1,407.9
			427	52,783.5
			$\sum W$	$\sum W \times \frac{P_1}{P_0} \times 100$

3.4   Selecting weights

The weights applied to price relatives should, in general, reflect the **amount spent** or total value of each item purchased, rather than simply the quantities purchased (however standardised). The reason is that this eliminates the effect of a relatively low-priced item having a very high price relative from only a small price rise.

3.5   Example

The price of peas and bread, and the amount consumed in both years is as follows:

Item	19X5 price	19X6 price	Units consumed (both years)
Peas	2p	3p	2
Bread	15p	16p	5

You are required

(a)   to construct a price-relative index using:

(i)   quantity weights;
(ii)   value weights.

(b)   to explain why the value weighted price relative is the more useful.

3.6   Solution

(a)   (i)

Item	19X5 P_0	19X6 P_1	q(same consumption pattern for both years)	Quantity weight only $W_A(= Q)$	Value weight $W_B(= P_0 \times Q)$
	pence	pence			
Peas	2	3	2	2	$2 \times 2 = 4$
Bread	15	16	5	5	$15 \times 5 = 75$
				7	79

$$\Sigma W_A \qquad\qquad \Sigma W_B$$

Item	$\dfrac{P_1}{P_0} \times 100$	$W_A \times \dfrac{P_1}{P_0} \times 100$	$W_B \times \dfrac{P_1}{P_0} \times 100$
Peas	150.0	300.0	600.0
Bread	106.7	533.5	8,002.5
		833.5	8,602.5

$$\Sigma W_A \times \frac{P_1}{P_0} \times 100 \qquad\qquad \Sigma W_B \times \frac{P_1}{P_0} \times 100$$

Therefore, using quantity weights only, the index is:

$$\frac{\Sigma W_A \dfrac{P_1}{P_0} \times 100}{\Sigma W_A} \quad = \quad \frac{833.5}{7} \quad = 119.1$$

(This would imply an average increase in prices of 19.1%.)

(ii)   using value weights, the index is

$$\frac{\Sigma W_B \dfrac{P_1}{P_0} \times 100}{\Sigma W_B} \quad = \quad \frac{8,602.5}{79} \quad = \quad 108.9$$

(This implies an average increase of 8.9%.)

(b)   The fact that the **value** weighted average of price relatives is the more realistic can be shown by considering total expenditure.

Item	Expenditure 19X5	Expenditure 19X6	% increase
Peas	$2 \times 2 = 4p$	$2 \times 3 \ = \ 6p \Rightarrow$	50%
Bread	$5 \times 15 = 75p$	$5 \times 16 \ = \ 80p \Rightarrow$	6.7%
Total Budget	79p	$86p \Rightarrow$	8.86%

Thus, an equal **money** price rise for two items will cause a higher percentage price rise for the lower priced item which is compensated for when the weights used are the value or expenditure on each item, since this reduces the importance of the lower priced item.

Algebraically, as $W = Q \times P_0$ then the weighted average of price relatives, which is:

$$\frac{\sum W \frac{P_1}{P_0} \times 100}{\sum W}, \text{ becomes } \frac{\sum QP_0 \times \frac{P_1}{P_0}}{\sum QP_0} \times 100 = \frac{\sum QP_1}{\sum QP_0} \times 100$$

3.7   Activity

A production process uses 10 sacks of product A and 30 of product B per year. The costs are as follows:

Item	19X1	19X2
Product A	£6.50	£6.90
Product B	£2.20	£2.50

Construct a price relative index using:

(a)   quantity weights
(b)   value weights

3.8   Activity solution

Lets start by preparing a table of all the information required to answer the question ie,

Item	P_0 19X1	P_1 19X2	Q	Quantity weight only $W_A (= Q)$	Value weight $W_B (= P_0 \times Q)$
Product A	6.5	6.9	10	10	65
Product B	2.2	2.5	30	30	66
$\sum$				40	131

Item	$\frac{P_1}{P_0} \times 100$	$W_A \frac{P_1}{P_0} \times 100$	$W_B \frac{P_1}{P_0} \times 100$
Product A	106.2	1,062	6,903.0
Product B	113.6	3,408	7,497.6
$\sum$		4,470	14,400.6

(i)   To calculate the index using quantity weights, we need to insert the data into the formula

$$\frac{\sum W_A \times \frac{P_1}{P_0} \times 100}{\sum W_A} = \frac{4,470}{40} = 111.75$$

(ii)   To calculate the index using value weights, we need to insert the data into the formula.

$$\frac{\sum W_B \times \frac{P_1}{P_0} \times 100}{\sum W_B} = \frac{14,400.6}{131} = 109.93$$

4   LASPEYRE AND PAASCHE INDICES

4.1   Introduction

These are sometimes referred to as aggregative indices.

An aggregative price index compares the total expenditure in one year (ie, at that year's prices) on a particular collection of goods with the total expenditure in the base year, at base year prices, on the same collection of goods.

By using the term **total expenditure**, this statement assumes that the weights used are the quantities purchased (students should note that this is not invariably the case, and quite often the weights used will bear no relationship to either numbers, weights or volumes purchased).

Given this assumption, a choice of weights arises between the quantity purchased in the **base year** and the quantity purchased in the **current year** for which the index is being prepared. Both choices are acceptable and both have their respective merits and demerits. The resultant indices are named after their 'inventors'.

The **Laspeyre** price index uses base year quantities, the Paasche uses current year quantities. The Paasche index, for instance, compares the cost of buying current year quantities at current year prices with buying them at base year prices.

4.2   Formulae

(a)   Laspeyre price index $= 100 \times \dfrac{\sum Q_0 P_1}{\sum Q_0 P_0}$

(using base year quantities as weights)

(b)   Paasche price index $= 100 \times \dfrac{\sum Q_1 P_1}{\sum Q_1 P_0}$

(using current year quantities as weights)

4.3   Example

The Laspeyre and Paasche Price Indices will be calculated for the following data, using 19X4 as base year:

Item	19X4		19X5	
	Price (P_0)	*Quantity (Q_0)*	*Price (P_1)*	*Quantity (Q_1)*
Milk	19p a pint	50,000 pints	26p a pint	70,000 pints
Bread	39p a loaf	30,000 loaves	40p a loaf	40,000 loaves
Soap	42p a pack	20,000 packs	64p a pack	25,000 kilos
Sugar	60p a kilo	10,000 kilos	68p a kilo	8,000 boxes
Eggs	84p a box	3,000 boxes	72p a box	2,500 boxes

4.4   Solution

(a)   **Laspeyre index**

Item	Weight (Q_0)	Price (P_0)	$Q_0 \times P_0$ £	Price (P_1)	$Q_0 \times P_1$ £
Milk	50,000	19p	9,500	26p	13,000
Bread	30,000	39p	11,700	40p	12,000
Soap	20,000	42p	8,400	64p	12,800
Sugar	10,000	60p	6,000	68p	6,800
Eggs	3,000	84p	2,520	72p	2,160
			38,120		46,760

$\sum Q_0 P_1 = 46,760 =$ last year's buying pattern at today's prices.

$$\Sigma Q_0 P_0 = 38,120 = \text{last year's buying pattern at last year's prices.}$$

$$\therefore \text{Index} = \frac{\Sigma Q_0 P_1}{\Sigma Q_0 P_0} \times 100$$

$$= \frac{46,760}{38,120} \times 100$$

$$= 122.7$$

The cost of buying 19X4 quantities at 19X5 prices shows an increase of 22.7% over 19X4 costs.

(b)   **Paasche index**

Item	Weight (Q_1)	Price (P_0)	$Q_1 \times P_0$ £	Price (P_1)	$Q_1 \times P_1$ £
Milk	70,000	19p	13,300	26p	18,200
Bread	40,000	39p	15,600	40p	16,000
Soap	25,000	42p	10,500	64p	16,000
Sugar	8,000	60p	4,800	68p	5,440
Eggs	2,500	84p	2,100	72p	1,800
			46,300		57,440

$$\Sigma Q_1 P_0 = 46,300 = \text{today's buying pattern at last year's prices.}$$
$$\Sigma Q_1 P_1 = 57,440 = \text{today's buying pattern at today's prices.}$$

$$\therefore \text{Index} = \frac{57,440}{46,300} \times 100$$

$$= 124.1$$

The 19X5 index shows an increase of 24.1% over 19X4 prices when buying 19X5 quantities.

Note: in calculating either type of index, a common mistake made by students is to add all the prices and all the quantities and multiply the two totals, ie, $\Sigma Q \times \Sigma P$ is calculated instead of $\Sigma (Q \times P)$. To do so is quite wrong and will be severely penalised in the marking of the examination.

4.5   Comparison of Laspeyre and Paasche indices

In a period of inflation, there is a general increase in prices. In addition, there will be relative price changes. Thus, for example, in the 1980s petrol became relatively more expensive and electric goods became relatively cheaper.

The effect of these changes is a changing pattern of consumption, with consumers switching to relatively less expensive goods, eg, from large to small cars, and buying more electric goods.

This switching minimises the effect of inflation on individual consumers. However, if a Laspeyre index is used it will fail to take account of the changing pattern of consumption. As a result, a Laspeyre index tends to overstate the real impact of inflation on individuals.

On the other hand, a Paasche index involves recalculating data for all preceding years each year. With a large number of indices to maintain, this is not practicable. Also, because a Paasche index is based on current consumption patterns it tends to understate the overall effect of inflation on consumers.

The relative merits and demerits of the indices are summarised below:

Relative merits of types of indices

Laspeyre index	**Paasche index**

Advantages

1 Cheaper, as the obtaining of new quantities each year may be costly.

2 Easier to calculate where a series of years are being compared, since the denominator remains the same for all years, eg 19X7 index would be calculated

$$\frac{\sum Q_0 P_7}{\sum Q_0 P_0} \times 100$$

where P_7 = prices in 19X7 and P_0 prices in 19X0.

3 Each year in a series of Laspeyre indices is directly comparable with all previous years.

Disadvantages

1 The major disadvantage of using Laspeyre indices is that an out-of-date consumption pattern may be used. In practice this is overcome by a periodic revision of the base year to keep it up to date, but this makes very long-term comparison almost impossible as the continuity of the series is destroyed.

2 As prices rise, quantities purchased tend to diminish if there are alternative goods available. This decrease is not reflected in the Laspeyre index which tends, therefore, to overestimate the effect of rising prices.

Advantage

1 Since current year weights are used, it results in an index being based on the current pattern of consumption so that a less frequent revision of base year is needed.

Disadvantages

1 Where a series of years is involved, the amount of calculation is greater as both numerator and denominator need calculating each year, eg, 19X7 index would be calculated

$$\frac{\sum Q_7 P_7}{\sum Q_7 P_0} \times 100$$

where P_7 = prices in 19X7

Q_7 = quantities in 19X7 and

P_0 = prices in 19X0

2 Each Paasche index in a series is only directly comparable with the base year (ie, 19X7 does not bear comparison with 19X6; only with base year 19X0).

3 The Paasche index can only be constructed if up-to-date information is available. The RPI is a Paasche index but, although it is produced monthly, quantities are only updated annually.

4 Rising prices have the opposite effect on the weights and the Paasche index therefore tends to underestimate the effect of inflation.

4.6 Quantity index

A quantity index measures changes in the volume of goods produced or sold. An example is the UK **Index of Industrial Production** which measures changes in the volume of goods produced in the United Kingdom and is therefore a measure of the industrial activity of the UK.

Just as a price index needs to be weighted with the quantities purchased, so a quantity index must be weighted with prices. A change in the volume of gold or other precious metal would have a greater effect on the economy that the same change in the volume of sand and gravel produced, because volume for volume it is much more valuable.

A quantity index is therefore calculated in the same way as a price index, with the role of price and quantity reversed. Hence:

$$\text{Laspeyre quantity index} = 100 \times \frac{\Sigma Q_1 P_0}{\Sigma Q_0 P_0}$$

$$\text{Paasche quantity index} = 100 \times \frac{\Sigma Q_1 P_1}{\Sigma Q_0 P_1}$$

4.7   Example

Laspeyre and Paasche quantity indices will be calculated for the data in example 4.3.

From paragraph 4.4.

$$\Sigma Q_1 P_0 = 46,300$$

$$\Sigma Q_0 P_0 = 38,120$$

$$\Sigma Q_1 P_1 = 57,440$$

$$\Sigma Q_0 P_1 = = 46,760$$

4.8   Solution

Hence   the Laspeyre index for 19X5 with 19X4 as base is $100 \times \dfrac{46,300}{38,120} = 121.5$

and   the Paasche index for 19X5 with 19X4 as base is $100 \times \dfrac{57,440}{46,760} = 122.8$

4.9   Value index

For a price index or a quantity index the weights are the same in both the numerator and the denominator of the formula. A value index uses current year weights for the numerator and base year weights for the denominator. Thus:

$$\text{Value index for year 1} = 100 \times \frac{\Sigma Q_1 P_1}{\Sigma Q_0 P_0}$$

$\Sigma Q_1 P_1$ = value of all goods in year 1

$\Sigma Q_0 P_0$ = value of all goods in the base year

Using the data of 4.3

$$\text{Value index for 19X5 with 19X4 as base} = \frac{57,440}{38,120} \times 100$$

$$= 150.7$$

Hence the value of all goods purchased increased by 50.7% from 19X4 to 19X5.

4.10   Activity

Taking 19X0 as the base year, calculate base year and current year weighted index numbers for prices and quantities for year 19X1 for the following data:

| | 19X0 | | 19X1 | |
Item	Price (£)	Quantity	Price (£)	Quantity
A	0.20	20	0.22	24
B	0.25	12	0.28	16
C	1.00	3	0.98	2

4.11   Activity solution

Item	P_0	Q_0	P_1	Q_1	Q_0P_0	Q_1P_0	Q_0P_1	Q_1P_1
A	0.20	20	0.22	24	4.0	4.8	4.40	5.28
B	0.25	12	0.28	16	3.0	4.0	3.36	4.48
C	1.00	3	0.98	2	3.0	2.0	2.94	1.96
					10.0	10.8	10.70	11.72

$$\text{Laspeyre price index for 19X1} = 100 \times \frac{\Sigma Q_0 P_1}{\Sigma Q_0 P_0}$$

$$= 100 \times \frac{10.7}{10.0}$$

$$= 107.0$$

$$\text{Paasche price index for 19X1} = 100 \times \frac{\Sigma Q_1 P_1}{\Sigma Q_1 P_0}$$

$$= 100 \times \frac{11.72}{10.8}$$

$$= 108.5$$

$$\text{Laspeyre quantity index for 19X1} = 100 \times \frac{\Sigma Q_1 P_0}{\Sigma Q_0 P_0}$$

$$= 100 \times \frac{10.8}{10.0}$$

$$= 108.0$$

$$\text{Paasche quantity index for 19X1} = 100 \times \frac{\Sigma Q_1 P_1}{\Sigma Q_0 P_1}$$

$$= 100 \times \frac{11.72}{10.70}$$

$$= 109.5$$

Thus prices increased by 7% or 8.5% and quantities by 8% or 9.5% depending on which method of weighting is used.

5   CHAIN BASE INDEX NUMBERS

5.1   Definition

> **Definition**   If a series of index numbers are required for different years, such that the rate of change of the variable from one year to the next can be studied, the chain base method is used. This means the each index number is calculated using the previous year as base. If the rate of change is **increasing** then the index numbers will be rising; if it is **constant**, the numbers will remain the same and if it is **decreasing** the numbers will be falling.

5.2   Example

A shopkeeper received the following amounts from the sale of radios:

19X1	£1,000
19X2	£1,100
19X3	£1,210
19X4	£1,331
19X5	£1,464

Is it correct to say that the annual rate of increase in revenue from sales of radios is getting larger?

5.3   Solution

Year	Sales	Chain base index
19X1	£1,000	$\dfrac{1,100}{1,000} \times 100 = 110$
19X2	£1,100	$\dfrac{1,210}{1,100} \times 100 = 110$
19X3	£1,210	$\dfrac{1,331}{1,210} \times 100 = 110$
19X4	£1,331	$\dfrac{1,464}{1,331} \times 100 = 110$
19X5	£1,464	

Although the sales revenue from radios has increased each year, the chain base index numbers have remained static at 110. Therefore, the annual rate of increase of sales revenue from radios is remaining constant rather than increasing.

The chain base is also a suitable index to calculate if the weights ascribed to the various items in the index are changing rapidly. Over a period of years, this index would have modified itself to take account of these changes whereas in a fixed-base method after a number of years the whole index would have to be revised to allow for the changed weighting.

5.4   Conclusion

In order to avoid the worst problems of Laspeyre indices, it is normal to periodically revise the commodities and weights used as a basis for index calculation. In order to maintain comparability, the new index is **linked** to the old series so as to establish one single index series with periodic revision of the weights.

In using any index, consideration should be given to the basis of revision, and whether the current weights are appropriate. Thus, for example, the Cost of Living Index (now the Retail Price Index) was not revised from 1914 to 1947. Towards the end of the period, the index was, arguably, meaningless, and indeed this was used deliberately by the government in the Second World War which, by controlling the price of a few commodities in the index was able to hold down the rate of increase of the index and claim a much lower rate of inflation than was actually taking place.

The weights used in the Retail Prices Index are now revised annually. However, other indices, both in the UK and overseas, may not be subject to regular revision.

6   OTHER PROBLEMS IN CONSTRUCTING INDICES

6.1   Obtaining prices

With many intermediate products used in industry, prices are the results of negotiation rather than a price list. Even for other products, there is the problem of discounts to be taken into account in establishing prices for index calculation.

6.2   Technical changes

Over time, most products are improved, and a direct price comparison ignores that improvement. For example, the hi-fi system at the end of the 1980s included a compact disc player and stereo video recorder; the 1960 model would have included little more than a gramophone and a wireless. The same problem exists with most products.

There are no simple answers to these problems. What they do mean in total is that index numbers, if carefully constructed, provide valuable information. They certainly do not, however, provide any absolute measure of price changes even in relation to a limited group of commodities.

7   INDEX NUMBERS AND INFLATION

7.1   Measuring changes in the value of money

The examination of indices above has concentrated on the measurement of price changes of specific groups of commodities. The more general problem is to measure the rate of inflation itself - the change in the value of money.

The *Sandilands Report*, published in 1975, which dealt with the weaknesses of historical cost accounts in times of inflation, went so far as to doubt whether such a measure was meaningful in a business context, in that it is merely an aggregation of individual price changes. The measurement of the general inflation rate (and hence the decline in the purchasing power of money) does present problems.

Theoretically, the purchasing power of money is its ability to purchase a fraction of all the goods and services within an economy. This could be found by revaluing the gross national product at constant price and calculating the implicit price deflator used. No such index is readily available in the UK, though it is published, for example, in the United States.

Instead, resort must be made to indices which are sufficiently widely based to provide a reasonable sample of all goods and services so as to provide a good estimate of the rate of inflation. In the UK, the Retail Price Index is generally regarded as the most appropriate such index.

7.2   The Retail Price Index (RPI)

The RPI measure the percentage changes month by month in the average level of prices of good and services purchased by most households in the UK. It is not, strictly speaking, a cost of living index, as it includes non-essential items such as leisure and entertainment and there are a number of payments not included, such as income tax, national insurance contributions, savings, charitable subscriptions, etc, but it is the best measure of the cost of living available.

For the prices, a representative list (basket) of items and services has been selected, and prices are collected (where appropriate) by a monthly sample survey among typical retail outlets in some 180 urban and rural centres. The prices noted are those actually charged, where these differ from published prices.

The index is calculated as a weighted average of price relatives, the weights being the proportional parts of each £1,000 spent by the average household on each item (ie, value weights). These weights are updated annually and are obtained from the *Family Expenditure Survey* which is a continuous survey among an annual sample of about 7,000 householders, who are asked to keep a diary of all their expenditure for a period of two weeks. For the purpose of the Retail Prices Index, very high and very low income families are excluded from the calculations.

For the structure of the index, the most recent issue of the *Monthly Digest of Statistics* should be examined.

The index is divided into fourteen main groups (food, catering, alcoholic drink, . . etc). These are subdivided into subgroups, (eg, food is divided into bread, cereals, biscuits and cakes, beef . . etc). Separate index numbers are given for each subgroup, each group and for all groups combined.

The current base is January 1987 = 100 and information is available for splicing the index right back to 1914 when it was originally published as a 'cost of living' index.

The pattern of expenditure by pensioners is different from that of other sections of the population, so the general index does not accurately reflect the effect of price changes on this group of consumers.

For this reason, a separate index is compiled for one and two pensioner households, and it is published quarterly.

Uses of the index:

(a)   Measurement of cost of living.
(b)   Measurement of inflation, used for wage negotiations, etc.
(c)   Index linked pensions, wages.
(d)   Current cost accounting.
(e)   Deflation of monetary series to obtain value in 'real terms', time series deflation.

7.3   Index splicing

As explained previously, it is sometimes necessary to revise the base year to take account of changing patterns in demand. This produces a discontinuity in the series, as the Index reverts to 100 for the new base. Splicing restores the continuity by either changing the new series to the old base or the old series to the new base.

7.4   Example

For a certain commodity the price index is as follows:

Year	Index (19X0 = 100)	
19X0	100	
19X1	105	
19X2	110	
19X3	115	
19X4	120	
19X5	125	
19X6	100	(New base, 19X6 = 100)
19X7	106	
19X8	112	

How can the discontinuity be removed in 19X6?

7.5   Solution

To remove the discontinuity in 19X6, the new series can be converted to the old base provided we know what the index for 19X6 was under the old base. We will assume that this was 140. Hence:

Year	Index (19X6 = 100)	Index (19X0 = 100)
19X6	100	140
19X7	106	$140 \times \dfrac{106}{100} = 148$
19X8	112	$140 \times \dfrac{112}{100} = 157$

We now have a complete unbroken series for 19X0 - 19X8. It should be noted that this method is only approximate, as the index with the new base will have used different weights to the old base, and this has not been taken into account in the calculation.

7.6   Deflating a monetary series

If wages, for example, increase at exactly the same rate as inflation, the earner's purchasing power is not changed. In real terms, the wage has remained constant. Deflating a monetary series shows the 'real term' effect. The following example illustrates the method, using the Retail Prices Index as the measure of inflation to deflate a set of sales values.

7.7   Example

Year	Actual sales (£'000)	RPI	Deflated sales (£'000)
1	275	100	$\dfrac{275}{100} \times 100 = 275$
2	305	112	$\dfrac{305}{112} \times 100 = 272$
3	336	122	$\dfrac{336}{122} \times 100 = 275$
4	344	127	$\dfrac{344}{127} \times 100 = 271$
5	363	133	$\dfrac{363}{133} \times 100 = 273$

It will be seen that although actual sales have increased in value by a fairly large amount, in real terms there has been a slight decrease.

Note: Deflated sales $= \dfrac{\text{Actual sales}}{\text{RPI}} \times 100$

7.8   Index numbers: Conclusion

Despite the problems involved in their calculation, index numbers have an important role nowadays both in everyday life and in the development of improved accounting information.

8   CHAPTER SUMMARY

Indexing is a technique for comparing changes over a period of time, by expressing current quantities as a percentage of a base year.

The most well known of indices is the Retail Prices Index (RPI), where the index is calculated as a weighted average of price relatives.

We have discussed and calculated the following types of indices, which you should now be able to calculate confidently:

Simple Indices
Weighted Indices
Laspeyre Indices
Paasche Indices
Chain Base Indices

You should also be able to answer questions on surveys and the various methods of sampling.

9   SELF TEST QUESTIONS

9.1   Distinguish between a Laspeyre and a Paasche Index. (4.1)

9.2   Give one advantage of the Laspeyre Index over the Paasche Index. (4.5)

9.3   What does a quantity index measure? (4.6)

9.4   What is the Retail Prices Index (RPI)? (7.2)

10   EXAMINATION TYPE QUESTIONS

10.1   Constructing an index number

(a)   What are the main considerations to be borne in mind when constructing an index number?

(5 marks)

(b)   The following table shows the total weekly expenditure on four commodities in June 19X1 and June 19X8, based on a representative sample of 1,000 households:

Commodities	Quantities purchased (lbs)	Total expenditure £
June 19X1:		
Butter	3,500	280
Potatoes	8,500	85
Apples	2,000	100
Meat	6,000	1,200
	20,000	£1,665
June 19X8:		
Butter	3,500	700
Potatoes	7,000	700
Apples	2,500	250
Meat	6,500	3,250
	19,500	£4,900

You are required to compute a Laspeyre index showing the extent of the rise in prices of all four commodities.

(5 marks)

(c)   Explain briefly the major weakness of the Laspeyre index in this case, and suggest an alternative.

(5 marks)

(Total: 15 marks)

10.2   Salaries of systems analysts

You have been requested by a UK based client to research into the area of salaries paid to their systems analysis team, to prepare a report in order that a pay review may be carried out.

The following table shows the salaries, together with the retail price index (or consumer price index) for the years 19X0 to 19X8.

Year	Average Salary £	Retail Price index* (1987 = 100)
19X0	9,500	89.2
19X1	10,850	94.6
19X2	13,140	97.8
19X3	14,300	101.9
19X4	14,930	106.9
19X5	15,580	115.2
19X6	16,200	126.1
19X7	16,800	133.5
19X8	17,500	138.5

Required

(i)   What is the purpose of an index number?

(2 marks)

(ii)   Tabulate the percentage increases on a year earlier for the average salary and the retail price index;

(7 marks)

(iii)   Revalue the average salary each year to its equivalent 19X8 value using the retail price index;

(7 marks)

(iv)   Using the results of (ii) and (iii) above, comment on the average salary of the systems analysts of your client.

(4 marks)

(Total: 20 marks)

11 ANSWERS TO EXAMINATION TYPE QUESTIONS

11.1 Constructing an index number

(a) There are four main considerations to be borne in mind when constructing an index number:

    (i) **The purpose of the index number**

        Unless the purpose is defined clearly, the eventual usefulness of the final index will be suspect. In other words it must be designed to show **something in particular**.

    (ii) **Selection of items for inclusion in an index**

        The main principles to be followed here are that the items selected must be unambiguous, relevant to the purpose, and of ascertainable value.

        Since index numbers are concerned largely with making comparisons over time periods, an item selected one year must be clearly identified (ie, in terms of size, weight, capacity, quantity, etc) so that the same items can be selected the following year for comparison.

    (iii) **Selection of appropriate weights**

        Deciding on the level of importance to attach to each change from one year to the next, or the relative importance of each item to the whole list.

    (iv) **Selection of a base year**

        Care must be exercised so that an 'abnormal' year is not chosen in relation to the characteristic being measured. If an abnormally 'high' year is chosen, all subsequent changes will be understated; whereas if an abnormally 'low' year is chosen, all subsequent changes will be overstated in percentage terms.

(b) **Laspeyre Price Index**

$$100 \times \frac{\sum Q_0 P_1}{\sum Q_0 P_0}$$

	Q_0 (19X1 quantities)	$Q_0 P_0$ (19X1 total expenditure)	$Q_1 P_1$ (19X8 total expenditure)	Q_1 (19X8 quantities)	$P_1 = \dfrac{Q_1 P_1}{Q_1}$	$Q_0 P_1$
	lbs	£	£	lbs	£	£
Butter	3,500	280	700	3,500	0.20	700
Potatoes	8,500	85	700	7,000	0.10	850
Apples	2,000	100	250	2,500	0.10	200
Meat	6,000	1,200	3,250	6,500	0.50	3,000
Total	20,000	£1,665	£4,900	19,500		£4,750

$$100 \times \frac{\sum Q_0 P_1}{\sum Q_0 P_0} = 100 \times \frac{£4,750}{£1,665}$$

$$= 285.3\%$$

Note: in column 6, the 19X8 prices are obtained by dividing the 19X8 total expenditure (column 4) by the 19X8 quantities (column 5).

(c) The major weakness of a Laspeyre Index is that it uses a consumption pattern that may well have changed considerably over the years. Since, when the price of a particular commodity rises considerably, there is usually some slackening in demand (providing it is not totally inelastic), a Laspeyre Index, still using the original quantities as weights, may place too much importance on this item and therefore will tend to overstate the general level of price increases.

An alternative index to be considered is the Paasche Index, which uses a current pattern of consumption to weight its prices. However, while it overcomes the weakness of a Laspeyre Index it does have its own weaknesses, which should be considered before changing over.

11.2 Salaries of systems analysts

(i) The purpose of an index number is to show the changes in prices, quantities, wages, etc, over a period of time. Many items can be included in the index, combining them as a weighted average. By expressing this as a percentage of the weighted average in the base year, the index becomes independent of units, so that different items with different units can be compared. For example, prices (£) can be compared with quantities which are not in monetary units.

(ii)

	Comparison with Previous Years			
	Average salary		*Index of Retail Prices*	
Year	*Increase*	*%*	*Increase*	*%*
19X0	–	–	–	–
19X1	1,350	14.2	5.4	6.1
19X2	2,290	21.1	3.2	3.4
19X3	1,160	8.8	4.1	4.2
19X4	630	4.4	5.0	4.9
19X5	650	4.4	8.3	7.8
19X6	620	4.0	10.9	9.5
19X7	600	3.7	7.4	5.9
19X8	700	4.2	5.0	3.7

(iii) To convert the salary for year n into the equivalent salary in year 19X8, multiply by I_{19X8}/I_n.

Year	Average salary At 19X8 values
19X0	14,751
19X1	15,885
19X2	18,608
19X3	19,436
19X4	19,343
19X5	18,731
19X6	17,793
19X7	17,429
19X8	17,500

Note:

The value for 19X0 is $\dfrac{9,500 \times 138.5}{89.2}$

The value for 19X1 is $\dfrac{10,850 \times 138.5}{94.6}$ and so on.

(iv) In real terms, based on 19X8 prices, the average salary has steadily decreased from a maximum of £19,436 in 19X3 to £17,500 in 19X8. Comparison of the % increase columns in section (ii) shows that this effective decrease is because in every year since 19X4, the index of retail prices has increased at a greater rate than the average wage. In the first three years, from 19X0 to 19X3, the reverse was the case, and salaries increased in real terms.

23 PROBABILITY

INTRODUCTION & LEARNING OBJECTIVES

Syllabus area 2f. Probability: simple addition and multiplication rules; expected values; payoff tables. (Ability required 3).

Probability is an important topic, especially in relation to sampling theory and decision-making. A business may be faced with choosing one of several alternative courses of action. If it could be certain which was the correct one to take, there would be no problem. However, managers will normally need to know (or estimate from past experience) the relative probabilities of success or failure resulting from each possible action so that they may choose the course which offers the best overall chance of success.

When you have studied this chapter you should be able to do the following:

- Understand why probability is used.

- Understand the laws of probability and be able to explain them.

- Calculate the probability of certain events when supplied with data, using the laws of probability.

- Identify when probability trees will be of help, and be able to construct them as necessary.

- Calculate expected values.

- Understand conditional probabilities and the methods for dealing with them.

---

1   DEFINITIONS OF PROBABILITY

While it is easy to understand that some events have a higher probability than others because they are more likely to occur, a mathematically rigorous definition of probability is surprisingly difficult. Two definitions are given here, neither of which is mathematically rigorous, but they both help in understanding and explaining probability.

1.1   Definition 1

  The probability of an event occurring in a single trial is the value to which the relative frequency tends in a large number of trials. (The relative frequency of an event is the ratio of the number of times the event occurs to the number of trials.)

For example, if an unbiased coin is spun in an unbiased way, it seems obvious that the outcome is equally likely to be heads or tails. However, if the coin is spun a small number of times (say 10) then it does not means that exactly 5 heads and 5 tails would be obtained, because random influences often result in repeated heads or repeated tails. However, as the number of tosses increases, these random effects are smoothed out so that the greater the number of tosses, the more equal will the number of heads and the number of tails become. Hence in the long run the relative frequency of heads and of tails will each become 0.5. Therefore the probability of heads in a single toss is 0.5.

This definition clearly cannot be applied in situations where repeated trials cannot be made, for example, the probability that the works allegedly written by Shakespeare were in fact written by Marlowe, or that a given horse will win the next race. However, it is useful in explaining to the layman the meaning of probability values. If the probability of a new product being successful when marketed is 0.6, this value can be explained as meaning that if it was possible to repeat the launching of the product a large number of times under identical conditions on average 6 launches out of every 10 would be successful.

1.2   Definition 2 (The 'classical' definition)

Definition   If there are m equally likely outcomes to a trial, n of which result in a given outcome, then the probability of that outcome is $\dfrac{n}{m}$.

For example, if an unbiased die is thrown in an unbiased way, each of the scores 1 to 6 is equally likely. Three of these scores would result in an even number (2, 4 or 6), hence the probability of scoring an even number is $\dfrac{3}{6}$ or $\dfrac{1}{2}$.

The problem with this definition is that it depends on the concept of 'equally likely events', or, in other words 'events of equal probability'; thus the concept of probability has to be assumed in order to define it, which is illogical. Also, it is not possible to know whether different outcomes are equally likely without carrying out repeated trials.

However, one of the main applications of probability theory is in the interpretation of results from random samples. As, by definition, all members of the population are equally likely to be included in a random sample, the above definition of probability is applicable to random sampling theory, and is the one that will be used in this course.

1.3   Measurement of probability

Probability is measured on a scale from 0 to 1, where 0 represents impossibility and 1 represents certainty.

<pre>
                        ⎧   1   –   Absolute certainty
                        ⎪   –
                        ⎪   –
            The   ⎪   –
            scale   ⎨ 0.5   ≡   50 : 50 chance (eg, an unbiased coin landing 'heads')
            of   ⎪   –
            probability ⎪   –
                        ⎪   –
                        ⎩   0   –   Impossibility
</pre>

1.4   Example

When an unbiased die is thrown, each of the numbers 1 to 6 has an equal chance of falling uppermost. Using this information, the following will be calculated; the probability that the outcome of a single throw is:

(a)   the number 4;
(b)   an even number;
(c)   a number less than 3;
(d)   a number greater than 6; and
(e)   a number less than 7.

When an unbiased die is thrown, there are six equally likely outcomes: 1, 2, 3, 4, 5, 6.

1.5   Solution

For each answer, (a) to (e) above, the number of 'favourable' outcomes must be determined, and this is expressed as a proportion of the total number of possible outcomes.

The probability of event 'A' occurring is represented by the symbol P(A) (some authors use Pr(A); it is often safer to write Prob (A) or Probability (A)).

(a)   P(number 4):

P(4) = 1/6, because one of the six possible outcomes is the number 4.

(b)   P(even) = 3/6 (or 1/2), because three of the six outcomes are even numbers: 2, 4 and 6.

(c)   P(a number less than 3):

P(<3) = 2/6 (or 1/3), because two of the six outcomes are less than 3, ie, 1 and 2.

(d)   P(a number greater than 6):

P(>6) = 0/6 (or 0), because none of the six outcomes is greater than 6.   This is an impossible situation.

(e)   P(a number less than 7):

P(<7) = 6/6 (or 1), because all six outcomes are less than 7.   It is therefore certain that the result will be a number less than 7.

1.6   Example

An ordinary pack of playing cards consists of fifty-two cards. If the pack is well shuffled and one card selected at random, the following probabilities can be calculated.

(a)   the card is the ace of clubs;
(b)   the card is a king;
(c)   the card is a heart; and
(d)   the card is red.

1.7   Solution

When a card is selected at random, there are fifty-two equally likely outcomes.

(a)   P(ace of clubs) = 1/52 because there is only one ace of clubs in the pack.
(b)   P(king) = 4/52 (or 1/13) because there are four kings in a pack.
(c)   P(heart) = 13/52 (or 1/4) because there are 13 hearts in a pack.
(d)   P(red) = 26/52 (or 1/2) because there are 26 red cards out of the total of 52.

1.8   A priori, empirical and subjective probability

The discussion of the scale of probability suggests that the concept of probability is always the same. This is not so; probabilities can be arrived at by different methods, and have quite different significance for their users. The simplest way of explaining this is in terms of the way in which probability estimates are obtained. These may be summarised as follows:

(a)   **A priori**

The probability of an event is calculated by a process of logical reasoning. In the scale of probability above, it was stated that there was a 0.5 probability of an unbiased coin landing 'heads'. This was deduced without any reference to any experiment, but is confirmed from personal experience of the way coins behave. This is a form of objective probability, but based on logic, ie, 'a priori' probability.

(b)   **Empirical probability**

Where a particular situation can be repeated a large number of times, an experimental approach may be used to derive probabilities. An example would be using meteorological records to estimate the probability of rain on the 30th June. Again this is a form of objective probability, but based on the relative frequency in a large number of experiments, ie, 'empirical probability'.

(c)   **Subjective probability**

These are estimates made by individuals of the relative likelihood of events occurring. Thus as an individual we may estimate that the likelihood of the Conservative Party winning the next British election is 0.4. This is a personal view, though it may be based on the individual's own predictive model of the political future. It cannot be confirmed by either a priori reasoning or experimentation, ie, it is 'subjective probability'.

It is the view of some statisticians that this type of probability is invalid. On the other hand, many business problems are of this nature, and it is difficult to find any other method of quantifying the relative likelihood of forecasts. Students will find that, irrespective of the theoretical arguments, accountants widely use subjective probability forecasts.

Subjective probabilities are assumed to follow the same laws as objective probabilities. This is why we study the behaviour of dice, coin tossing, etc; not because we are interested in such problems for themselves, but because the mathematical laws derived from them are applied to subjective probabilities which are of much greater importance in business.

(d)   **Conclusions**

The initial examination of statistical probability will be based on **objective** situations - either a priori or experimental - mainly because these are easier to visualise and describe.

However, many of the important business applications of probability are in its application to **subjective** probabilities.

When handling probabilities, the user should be aware of what type of probability is involved, so that the degree of reliance that can be placed on the results may be assessed. It is important to remember when using probabilities that, however sophisticated the analysis, the results will still be dependent on the reliability of the original assignment of probabilities.

Finally, it should be noted that the categories of probability are not absolute. Very often business forecasts will combine elements of all three types of probability.

1.9   Activity

A batch of electronic components had the following composition:

Type of component	Total quantity	Number defective
A	1,000	20
B	500	15
Total	1,500	35

If a component is selected at random, state the probability of each of the following ,using only basic definition of probability.

(a)   It is of type A.
(b)   It is defective.
(c)   It is of type A or defective.
(d)   It is of type A and defective.
(e)   It is of type A if defective.
(f)   It is defective if of type A.

1.10   Solution

$$\text{Probability} = \frac{\text{number of times a particular event occurs}}{\text{number of tests for that event}} = \frac{n}{m}$$

(a) $n = 1,000, m = 1,500,$ $P(A) = \dfrac{1,000}{1,500} = \dfrac{2}{3}$ or 0.667

(b) $n = 35, m = 1,500,$ $P(D) = \dfrac{35}{1,500} = 0.023$

(c) $n = 1,000 + 15 = 1,015$ (do not count defective A's twice)

m = 1,500

$$P(A \text{ or } D) = \frac{1,015}{1,500} = 0.677$$

(d) $n = 20, m = 1,500,$ $P(A \text{ and } D) = \dfrac{20}{1,500} = 0.013$

(e)   The effect of the condition 'defective' is to limit the population, and hence the value of *m*, to those fulfilling that condition.

$n = 20, m = 35,$ $P(A \text{ if } D) = \dfrac{20}{35} = 0.571$

(f) $n = 20, m = 1,000,$ $P(D \text{ if } A) = \dfrac{20}{1,000} = 0.020$

2   **LAWS OF PROBABILITY**

2.1   **Addition law**

(a)   **Mutually exclusive events:** two or more events are said to be mutually exclusive if the occurrence of any one of them precludes the occurrences of all the others, ie, only one can happen. For example, when a die is thrown once, it can only show one score. If that score is 6 (say), then all the other possible outcomes (1, 2, 3, 4 or 5) will not have occurred. Hence the six possible outcomes are all mutually exclusive. On the other hand, the outcomes 'score 6', and 'score an even number' are not mutually exclusive because both outcomes could result form one throw.

Mutually exclusive events may be written in symbols as:

$$P \text{ (A and B)} = 0$$

The probability of a 6 and a 1 in a single throw of one dice is clearly zero. In terms of set theory, this statement corresponds to ' the intersection of A and B is the empty set'.

If A and B are two mutually exclusive events, then the probability that either A or B occurs in a given experiment is equal to the sum of the separate probabilities of A and B occurring, ie,

$$P \text{ (A or B)} = P \text{ (A)} + P \text{ (B)}$$

This law can cover any number of events, as long as they are mutually exclusive:

$$P \text{ (A or B or C or D or ...)} = P \text{ (A)} + P \text{ (B)} + P \text{ (C)} + P \text{ (D)} + ...$$

2.2   **Example**

A bag contains 4 red, 6 blue and 10 black balls; the probability of selecting either a red or a black ball when one ball is drawn from the bag is calculated as follows:

Clearly, the events are mutually exclusive, since if the ball is red, it cannot be black, and vice versa.

$\therefore$ P(red) = 4/20   P(black) = 10/20

$\therefore$ P(red or black)   =   P(red) + P(black)

                        =   4/20 + 10/20

                        =   14/20 (or 0.7)

2.3   **Example**

The probability of drawing an ace or king, when one card is drawn from a pack of fifty-two playing cards is calculated as follows:

$\therefore$ P(ace) = 4/52   P(king) = 4/52

$\therefore$ P(ace or king)   =   P(ace) + P(king)

                        =   4/52 + 4/52

                        =   8/52 (or 0.15)

2.4   Addition law for non-mutually exclusive events

Non-mutually exclusive events: two events are not mutually exclusive if they can occur at the same time. This is sometimes regarded as an 'overlap situation'.

If A and B are two non-mutually exclusive events, then the probability that either A or B occurs in a given experiment is equal to the sum of the separate probabilities minus the probability that they both occur.

ie,   P (A or B) = P (A) + P (B) – P (A and B)

The term P(A and B) must be subtracted to avoid double counting. This is best illustrated by an example.

2.5   Example

The probability of selecting a heart or a queen, when one card is drawn at random from a pack of playing cards, is calculated as follows

The probability of selecting a heart or a queen is an overlap situation, as the Queen of Hearts would be included in both events. To avoid including this probability twice, it must be subtracted once.

P(any heart) = 13/52   P(any queen) = 4/52   P(queen of hearts) = 1/52

∴ P(heart or queen)   =   P(heart) + P(queen) – P(queen of hearts)

                        =   13/52 + 4/52 – 1/52

                        =   16/52 (or 0.31)

This situation may also be illustrated by reference to set theory

Drawing the Venn diagram of this situation, we have:

Universal set (= cards in the pack)

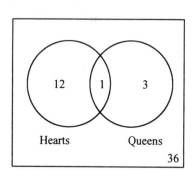

From this diagram it can be seen that, using the symbol n(A) to denote the number of occurrences of A:

n(hearts)	=	13
n(queens)	=	4
n(hearts and queens)	=	1
n(heart or queen)	=	16

2.6   Example

Twenty identical discs are marked one to twenty and placed in a large box. One is drawn at random from a box. The following probabilities will be calculated; that the number on the disk is:

(a)   a multiple of 2.
(b)   a multiple of 5.
(c)   a multiple of 2 or 5.

2.7   **Solution**

(a)   P(multiple of 2)   =   P(2 or 4 or 6 . . . 20) = 10/20 (or 0.5) ie, all even numbers

(b)   P(multiple of 5)   =   P(5, 10, 15, or 20) = 4/20 (or 0.2)

(c)   P(multiple of 2 and 5)   =   P(10 or 20) = 2/20 (or 0.1)

∴ P(multiple of 2 or 5) =   P(multiple of 2) + P(multiple of 5) – P(multiple of 2 and 5)
=   10/20 + 4/20 –2/20
=   12/20 (or 0.6)

This is easily verified from the fact that there will be 12 such discs (2, 4, 5, 6, 8, 10, 12, 14, 15, 16, 18, 20).

2.8   **Multiplication law**

(a)   **Independent events:** two or more events are said to be independent if the occurrence or non-occurrence of one event does not affect the occurrence or non-occurrence of the other.

For example, consider the events:

A   =   'I will be successful in the examination.'

B   =   'I will undergo a course of study for the examination.'

C   =   'I have blue eyes.'

Clearly A will have a higher probability if B occurs than if it does not occur. A is therefore dependent on B. But the colour of ones eyes has no known effect on the ability to pass examinations or vice versa, hence A and C are independent.

If any two events, A and B, are independent, then the probability of both A and B occurring is the product of the separate probabilities.

P (A and B) = P (A) × P (B)

(i)   **Example**

The probability of drawing an ace from a pack of cards and throwing a six with an unbiased dice is calculated as follows:

P(ace) = 4/52   P(6)   = 1/6

∴ P(ace and 6)   =   P(ace) × P(6)

=   1/13 × 1/6

=   1/78 (or 0.013)

The two events are independent because which card is drawn from the pack will have no influence on which score will be given by the die and vice versa.

(ii)   **Example**

A case contains twelve valves of which four are defective and the rest are non-defective. The probability of drawing two non-defective valves, the first valve being replaced before the second one is selected, is calculated as follows:

Since four are defective then the remaining eight are non-defective.

So P(defective) = 4/12, P(non-defective) = 8/12

∴ P(valve 1 non-defective) = 8/12 = 2/3, P(valve 2 non-defective) = 8/12 = 2/3

P(valves 1 and 2 non-defective)   =   P(valve 1 non-defective) × P(valve 2 non-defective)

                                  =   2/3 × 2/3

                                  =   4/9 (or 0.44)

(b)   **Dependent events:** two or more events are said to be dependent when the probability of the second event occurring is conditional on the first event having taken place.

If A and B are two events such that B is conditional on A, then the probability of A and B occurring is the product of the probability of A and the conditional probability of B occurring.

Thus, P(A and B) = P(A) × P(B given that A has occurred)

The probability that event B occurs given that A occurs is denoted by the symbol $P(B \mid A)$. The ' | ' is read as 'given' or 'if'.

(i)   **Example**

Two cards are drawn from a pack, the first card is not replaced before the second is drawn. The probability that they are both aces is calculated as follows:

P(first card is an ace) = 4/52

This is not replaced, therefore three aces remain, out of fifty-one cards.

P(second card is an ace, given that the first card is an ace) = 3/51.

∴ P(both aces)   =   P(first card is an ace) × P(second card is an ace, given that first card is an ace)

                 =   4/52 × 3/51

                 =   1/221 (or 0.0045)

(ii)   **Example**

A bag contains 3 black, 4 red and 13 blue marbles. The probability that if three are selected without replacement then they will be red, blue, black in that order is calculated as follows:

P(first red)   =   4/20

P(second blue given first red)   =   13/19

P(third black, given that the first two were red and blue) =   3/18

$$P(\text{red, blue, black}) = \frac{4}{20} \times \frac{13}{19} \times \frac{3}{18} \qquad = \qquad 13/570 \text{ (or 0.023)}$$

2.9 Complementary probabilities

When a single event has only two possible outcomes, usually denoted as success and failure, then, if p and q are the probabilities of success and failure respectively, it follows that:

$$p = 1 - q$$

This is because $p + q = 1$, since they are the only possible outcomes of the event.

2.10 Example

When an unbiased die is thrown, a six is regarded as success and any other number as failure.

$$\therefore \quad p \quad = \quad P(\text{success}) \quad = \quad 1/6$$

and q =   P(failure)   = $1 - 1/6$ =   5/6

2.11 Example

The probability that a job will be finished on time is 0.8, therefore the probability that it will not be finished on time is 0.2 because:

p   =   P(success)   =   0.8

q   =   P(failure)   = $1 - 0.8$ =   0.2

The event 'A does not occur' is called the **negation** of A and is denoted by $\overline{A}$ or A'. Hence:

$$P(\overline{A}) = 1 - P(A)$$

$P(\overline{A})$ is called the **complement** of P(A).

When several events are being considered then the probability that at least one of them occurs is given by:

P (at least one) = $1 - $ P (none of them)

This is because either none of the events occurs or at least one of them does therefore:

P(none of them) + P(at least one)   =   1

2.12 Example

If three dice are thrown together, then the probability of obtaining at least one six is calculated as follows:

P(at least one six) = $1 - $ P(no sixes)

Assuming independence then:

P(no sixes)   = P(not six on first die and not six on second die and not six on third die)

                    = $5/6 \times 5/6 \times 5/6$

                    = $\dfrac{125}{216}$

P(at least one six) = $1 - 125/216$

                    = $\dfrac{91}{216}$ (or 0.42)

2.13   Example

If a coin is tossed five times then the probability of obtaining at least one head is calculated as follows:

Assuming that the coin is fair (unbiased) then:

$P(\text{head}) = \dfrac{1}{2}$ and $P(\text{tail}) = \dfrac{1}{2}$

P(at least one head)   =   1 – P(no heads)

                        = $1 - (\dfrac{1}{2} \times \dfrac{1}{2} \times \dfrac{1}{2} \times \dfrac{1}{2} \times \dfrac{1}{2})$

                        = $1 - 1/32$

                        = $31/32$ (or 0.97)

2.14   Combination of addition and multiplication laws

The examples given so far in this section have been kept simple in order to illustrate the basic laws. When it comes to solving more complex problems it is important to work out and write down the outcomes that are favourable to a particular situation and then calculate the corresponding probabilities.

2.15   Example

A bag contains five white, four red and three blue balls.   Three balls are drawn without replacement.

Events A, B, C and D are defined as follows:

          A: at least one white ball is drawn
          B: exactly two white balls are drawn.
          C: one ball of each colour is drawn.
          D: the third ball is white.

(a)   Which two events are mutually exclusive?

(b)   Calculate the probabilities of A, B, C and D respectively.

2.16   Solution

(a)   B and C are mutually exclusive because the probability of drawing exactly two whites excludes the possibility of drawing each colour and vice versa.

A and B are not mutually exclusive.
A and C are not mutually exclusive.
A and D are not mutually exclusive.
B and D are not mutually exclusive.
C and D are not mutually exclusive.

(b)   (i)   P(A)   =   P(at least one white)

=   1 – P(no whites)

The bag contains five white and seven non-white balls ie, the red and blue can be grouped together as non-white.

∴ P(non-white on first ball)   =   7/12

∴ P(A)   =   1 – (7/12 × 6/11 × 5/10)

= $1 - \dfrac{210}{1,320}$

= $\dfrac{1,110}{1,320}$

= $\dfrac{37}{44}$ (or 0.84)

(ii)   P(B) = P(exactly two whites)

Exactly two whites can be drawn in any one of three possible ways:

Possibility	First ball	Second ball	Third ball
1	White	White	Non-white
2	White	Non-white	White
3	Non-white	White	White

P(1)   =   5/12 × 4/11 × 7/10   = $\dfrac{140}{1,320}$

P(2)   =   5/12 × 7/11 × 4/10   = $\dfrac{140}{1,320}$

P(3)   =   7/12 × 5/11 × 4/10   = $\dfrac{140}{1,320}$

∴ P(exactly two whites)   =   P(1 or 2 or 3)

= $\dfrac{140}{1,320} + \dfrac{140}{1,320} + \dfrac{140}{1,320}$

= $\dfrac{420}{1,320}$

= $\dfrac{7}{22}$ (or 0.32)

Note: the table showing the various ways of achieving the desired result, exactly two white balls, is an essential working for this type of probability problem.

(iii)   P(C) = P(one ball of each colour)

One of each colour can be drawn in any one of six possible ways.

Possibility	First ball	Second ball	Third ball
1	Red	Blue	White
2	Red	White	Blue
3	Blue	Red	White
4	Blue	White	Red
5	White	Red	Blue
6	White	Blue	Red

$$P(1) = 4/12 \times 3/11 \times 5/10 = \frac{60}{1,320}$$

$$P(2) = 4/12 \times 5/11 \times 3/10 = \frac{60}{1,320}$$

$$P(3) = 3/12 \times 4/11 \times 5/10 = \frac{60}{1,320}$$

$$P(4) = 3/12 \times 5/11 \times 4/10 = \frac{60}{1,320}$$

$$P(5) = 5/12 \times 4/11 \times 3/10 = \frac{60}{1,320}$$

$$P(6) = 5/12 \times 3/11 \times 4/10 = \frac{60}{1,320}$$

P(one of each colour) = P(1 or 2 or 3 or 4 or 5 or 6)

= 60/1,320 + 60/1,320 + 60/1,320 + 60/1,320 + 60/1,320 + 60/1,320
= 6 × 60/1,320 = 360/1,320
= 3/11 (or 0.27)

Note: work out the probability of achieving the required result in **one particular order** (60/1,320); then find the **number of orders;** then multiply the two.

(iv)   P(D)   =   P(third ball is white)

There are now four possibilities to consider:

Possibility	First	Second	Third
1	Not white	Not white	White
2	Not white	White	White
3	White	Not white	White
4	White	White	White

$$P(1) = 7/12 \times 6/11 \times 5/10 = \frac{210}{1,320}$$

$$P(2) = 7/12 \times 5/11 \times 4/10 = \frac{140}{1,320}$$

$$P(3) = 5/12 \times 7/11 \times 4/10 = \frac{140}{1,320}$$

$$P(4) = 5/12 \times 4/11 \times 3/10 = \frac{60}{1,320}$$

$$P(\text{third ball is white}) = P(1 \text{ or } 2 \text{ or } 3 \text{ or } 4)$$
$$= 210/1{,}320 + 140/1{,}320 + 140/1{,}320 + 60/1{,}320$$
$$= 550/1{,}320$$
$$= 5/12 \text{ (or } 0.42)$$

Note: a fatal mistake to make here is to say, 'it doesn't matter what the first ball is, therefore the probability is 1'. This makes it impossible to think clearly about the various ways of achieving the desired result (third ball white).

This example can also be represented diagrammatically by a probability tree. All possible outcomes of the experiment are shown, together with their related probabilities.

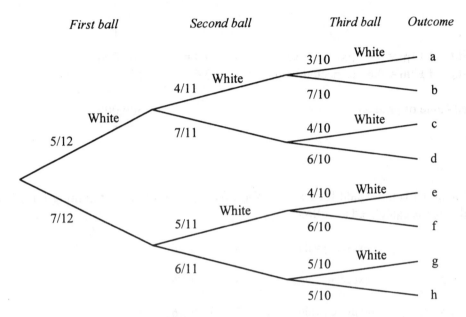

For example, event B, where exactly two white balls are drawn is represented by outcomes b, or c, or e. Because these are mutually exclusive events, we can compute the probabilities of each and add them together.

To compute the probability of going along a particular path through the tree, multiply the probabilities of all the branches along that path.

$$P(b) = 5/12 \times 4/11 \times 7/10 = \frac{140}{1{,}320}$$

$$P(c) = 5/12 \times 7/11 \times 4/10 = \frac{140}{1{,}320}$$

$$P(e) = 7/12 \times 5/11 \times 4/10 = \frac{140}{1{,}320}$$

$$\text{Hence } P(\text{exactly 2 whites}) = \frac{420}{1{,}320} \text{ (as before)}$$

3   EXPECTED VALUE

3.1   Introduction

If the probability of winning £x is p then the expected value is £px.

This is rather a mathematical (or theoretical) concept as will be seen from the following example.

3.2   The general formula

Where there is more than one possible outcome each with a probability attached, the expected value of the outcome (E(x)) will be the sum of the expected values of the individual possible outcomes.

Thus $E(x) = \Sigma px$.

3.3   Example

A company plans to introduce a new product to the market. There is a 0.4 probability that the profit from the product will be £1m and a 0.6 probability that the profit will be £2m. What is the expected value of the product?

3.4   Solution

	£
Probability of £1m = 0.4. Expected value = £1m × 0.4 =	400,000
Probability of £2m = 0.6. Expected value = £2m × 0.6 =	1,200,000
Expected value of product	£1,600,000

3.5   Example

On the throw of a die £5 is to be paid for a six, £4 for a five, £3 for a four and nothing for a 1, 2 or 3. The expected value is calculated as follows:

P(6)	=	1/6	∴	expected value = £1/6 × 5	=	£5/6
P(5)	=	1/6	∴	expected value = £1/6 × 4	=	£4/6
P(4)	=	1/6	∴	expected value = £1/6 × 3	=	£3/6
P(1, 2 or 3)	=	3/6	∴	expectation = £3/6 × 0	=	£0
				Total		£2

The expected value is £2.

In fact a person playing a game of this type will either win £5 or £4 or £3 or nothing. He cannot actually win £2. The expected value is the amount he can expect to win per game, on average, over a long series of games. It is also a fair price to pay for playing the game. Expected values are equivalent to conventional ideas of averages, arithmetic means.

This same approach can be applied to decision-making. Two or more possible courses of action may be open to a firm and the only basis on which they can make a decision is that of expected profits.

3.6   Example

A supermarket is opening a new store and two sites are available to them: A or B. From past experience, they calculate that the probability of success on Site A is 0.8 with an annual profit of £500,000. If not successful, the annual loss is estimated at £80,000.

For Site B the corresponding figures are 0.6 for the probability of success with an annual profit of £600,000, or an annual loss of £120,000.

Where should the branch be located in order to maximise expected profits?

To answer this it is necessary to calculate the expected profit on each site, and then choose the site giving the higher figure.

Site A

P(success) = 0.8 ∴ expectation	=	£0.8 × 500,000
P(failure) = 0.2 ∴ expectation	=	£0.2 × (−80,000)
∴ The expectation is £400,000 − £16,000	=	£384,000 per annum

Site B

P(success) = 0.6 ∴ expectation	=	£0.6 × 600,000
P(failure) = 0.4 ∴ expectation	=	£0.4 × (−120,000)
∴ The expectation is £360,000 − £48,000	=	£312,000 per annum

Note: it has been assumed that the only outcomes are profit or loss. Break-even (resulting in zero profit) has been ignored. It has also been assumed that the probability of profit or loss remains constant each year.

On the basis of these calculations, the new store should be located on Site A, because of the higher expected profit, ie, on average, the profits are expected to be £384,000 per annum over a number of years.

3.7   Activity

(a)   If three cards are drawn from a pack of fifty-two, without replacement, what is the probability that at least one is an ace?

(b)   If three cards are drawn from a pack of fifty-two, what is the probability that exactly two are aces, if the cards are drawn?

    (i)   with replacement; and
    (ii)   without replacement?

(c)   There are 10 horses in a race, each of which is equally likely to finish in any position. A punter places a stake of £20 on a horse that will earn £100 if first, £50 if second and £10 if third. What is his expected gain or loss?

3.8   Activity solution

(a)   P(no aces)   =   48/52 × 47/51 × 46/50

                  =   0.783

    P(at least one ace)   =   1 − P(no aces)

                  =   0.217

(b)   (i)   Probability (ace, then ace, then no ace) = $4/52 \times 4/52 \times 48/52$
              Number of arrangements of these cards =   3
              P (two aces) = $3 \times 4/52 \times 4/52 \times 48/52$ =   0.016

       (ii)   P(two aces, without replacement)

              = $(4/52 \times 3/51 \times 48/50) + (4/52 \times 48/51 \times 3/50) +$
                   $(48/52 \times 4/51 \times 3/50)$

              = $3 \times (4/52 \times 3/51 \times 48/50)$

              =   0.013

(c)

Position	Probability	Gain (£)	Probability × Gain (£)
1	0.1	100	10
2	0.1	50	5
3	0.1	10	1
Other	0.7	0	0

                                                    16 = Expected winnings
                                      Less stake   (20)

                                                    –4

Hence there is an expected loss of £4.

4   CONDITIONAL PROBABILITY

4.1   Introduction

This is a topic which has been implicitly considered earlier in the chapter when discussing dependent events, and the calculation of the probability of them both occurring. However, the methods will now be formalised further.

The symbol P(A|B) is read as 'the probability of A occurring given that B has already occurred' and we can say that:

P (A and B) = P (A|B) × P (B)

ie, the probability of both A and B occurring is equal to the probability of A occurring, given that B has occurred multiplied by the probability of B occurring in the first place.

Using Venn diagrams where the universal set is a pack of playing cards:

      A   =   queens   ⇒   n(A)   =   4   (Number of queens in a pack)

      B   =   hearts   ⇒   n(B)   =   13   (Number of hearts in a pack)

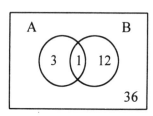

$$P(A|B) \quad = \quad \frac{1}{1+12} \quad = \quad \frac{1}{13} \qquad \text{(Probability of picking a queen, given that the card selected was a heart.)}$$

$$P(B) \quad = \quad \frac{1+12}{1+12+36+3} \quad = \quad \frac{13}{52} \qquad \text{(Probability of picking a heart)}$$

$$P(A|B) \times P(B) \quad = \quad \frac{1}{13} \times \frac{13}{52} \quad = \quad \frac{1}{52} \qquad \text{(Probability of picking the queen of hearts)}$$

and from the diagram:

$$P(A \text{ and } B) \quad = \quad \frac{1}{52}$$

Thus, the result is confirmed.

The formula is often turned around in order to enable the conditional probability to be computed, and becomes:

$$P(A|B) = \frac{P(A \text{ and } B)}{P(B)}$$

The use of this formula is demonstrated below.

4.2   Example

When a die is thrown, what is the probability that the number is greater than 1, given that it is odd?

4.3   Solution

$$P(>1|\text{odd}) \quad = \quad \frac{P(>1 \text{ and odd})}{P(\text{odd})}$$

$$= \quad \frac{2/6}{3/6} \quad \text{(The odd numbers} > 1 \text{ are 3 and 5)}$$

$$= \quad \frac{2}{3}$$

We know that $P(A \text{ and } B) \quad = \quad P(A|B) \times P(B)$

and by symmetry $P(A \text{ and } B) \quad = \quad P(B|A) \times P(A)$

This is so because if, after the event, we consider a situation and find that both A and B have occurred, it is irrelevant to ask 'which occurred first, A or B?'.

Hence:

$$P(A|B) \times P(B) = P(B|A) \times P(A)$$

4.4   Example

Two dice are thrown and the scores noted. What is the probability that:

(a)   at least one die shows a score greater than four given that the total score is eight or more; and

(b)   the total score is eight or more given that at least one die shows greater than a four.

4.5   Solution

Let event A = at least one die shows greater than 4.
Let event B = the total score is eight or more.

The problem may be described in terms of a 'sample space' made up of 36 'sample points', 36 possible outcomes each of which have an equal chance of occurring.

The sample space may be represented as:

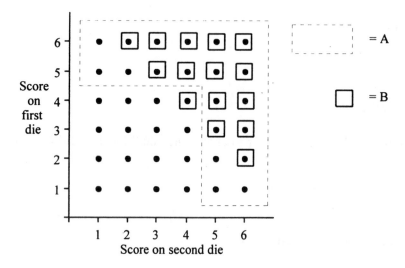

This type of diagram is very useful in problems such as this and saves becoming embroiled in rearranging formulae. Probabilities can be found by counting dots.

$$P(A) \quad = \quad \frac{20}{36}$$

$$P(B) \quad = \quad \frac{15}{36}$$

$$P(A \text{ and } B) \quad = \quad \frac{14}{36}$$

(a)   Hence $P(A \mid B) = \dfrac{P(A \text{ and } B)}{P(B)}$

$$= \quad \frac{14/36}{15/36}$$

$$= \quad 14/15$$

(Probability that you are in the dotted area given that you are marked by a solid box.)

(b) $P(B \mid A) \quad = \quad \dfrac{P(B \text{ and } A)}{P(A)}$

$$= \quad \frac{14/36}{20/36}$$

$$= \quad 14/20$$

(Probability that you are marked by a solid box given that you are in the dotted area.)

4.6   Contingency tables

Another method for dealing with conditional probabilities is by use of contingency tables. These are created by taking the given probabilities and then by multiplying by some convenient number, typically 100 or 1,000, drawing a table to show the various combinations of factors which may exist. This technique will be demonstrated by means of the following example.

4.7   Example

40% of the output of a factory is produced in workshop A and 60% in workshop B. Fourteen out of every 1,000 components from B are defective and six out of every 1,000 components from B are defective. After the outputs from A and B have been thoroughly mixed, a component drawn at random is found to be defective.

Calculate the probability that it came from workshop B.

4.8   Solution

The problem will be solved by drawing a contingency table, showing defective and non-defective components and output from workshops A and B.

A suitable multiple will be 10,000 (because the probabilities of components being faulty are quite small and yet we wish to end up working with whole numbers, the multiple must be high).

Consider 10,000 components, we know that of these 4,000 are from workshop A and 6,000 from workshop B. Of the 4,000 from workshop A, 1.4%, that is 56 will be defective, and from workshop B 0.6%, that is 36 will be defective. Hence the table can be completed so far:

	Workshop		
	A	B	Total
Defective	56	36	
Non-defective	3,944	5,964	
Total	4,000	6,000	10,000

Finally, the total number of defective items can be inserted into the table, and the final contingency table becomes:

	Workshop		
	A	B	Total
Defective	56	36	92
Non-defective	3,944	5,964	9,908
Total	4,000	6,000	10,000

Hence, the problem may now be solved, which, to remind you, was what is the probability that a component came from workshop B, given that it is defective?

Given that it is defective, we know that we are dealing with one of the ninety two components in the top row of the table. We can see that of these ninety-two components, thirty-six come from workshop B.

Hence P(came from workshop B given that it is defective) $= \dfrac{36}{92}$

$$= 0.39$$

The above problem could have been dealt with using conditional probabilities.

Thus, let

A   =   item came from workshop A
B   =   item came from workshop B
D   =   item is defective
N   =   item is non-defective

We require $P(B \mid D)$

$$P(B \mid D) = \frac{P(B \text{ and } D)}{P(D)}$$

We are told that $P(B) = 0.6$

$P(D)$ must be computed as:

$$P(D) = (P(D \mid A) \times P(A)) + (P(D \mid B) \times P(B))$$

$$= (0.014 \times 0.4) + (0.006 \times 0.6)$$

$$= 0.0056 + 0.0036$$

$$= 0.0092 \qquad \text{(This is out of 92 out of 10,000 defectives)}$$

$$P(B \text{ and } D) = P(D \mid B) \times P(B) = 0.006 \times 0.6 = 0.0036.$$

Hence $P(B|D) = \dfrac{0.0036}{0.0092}$

$$= 0.39$$

It is expected that most students will find the method using the contingency table easier to follow and therefore, this is the recommended method.

4.9   Activity

30% of the new cars of a particular model are supplied from a factory X, the other 70% from factory Y. 10% of factory X's production has a major fault, 12% of factory Y's production has such a fault.

A purchaser's new car has a major fault: what is the probability that it was made at factory Y?

4.10   Solution

Using 1,000 as a suitable multiple, ie, considering 1,000 cars are manufactured, the contingency table is:

	Made at factory		
	X	Y	Total
Has major fault	30	84	114
No major fault	270	616	886
Total	300	700	1,000

Hence P(made at factory Y/major fault exists) $= \dfrac{84}{114}$

$$= 0.737$$

4.11   Example

A product is manufactured in a two-stage process, the stages being designated A and B. Each process has two machines, named A_1 and A_2 for process A, and B_1 and B_2 for process B.

Each unit of finished product must pass through either one of the two machines in process A, and then through either one of the two machines in process B. (50% go through A_1 and 50% through A_2. Similarly for B_1 and B_2).

(a)   How many different ways may a product be manufactured?

(b)   If the probabilities of a defective product from each machine are as follows:

2% for A_1, 6% for A_2, 4% for B_1, 2% for B_2.

and the defectives are thrown out as they occur, what is the probability of a perfect item being produced?

(c)   The total production is 10,000 items started pa, the loss on each defective item is £10, and the profit on each item is £80. Calculate the expected net profit.

4.12   Solution

(a)

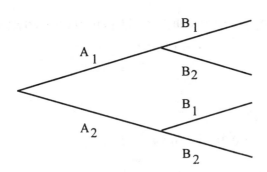

The product can be manufactured in four different ways, as shown on the above tree diagram:

$$A_1B_1, \quad A_1B_2, \quad A_2B_1, \quad \text{or} \quad A_2B_2$$

(b)   A perfect item can similarly be manufactured in any of the four different ways. Along each route the probability of it being perfect can be shown on the following tree:

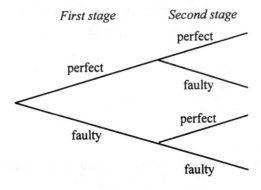

However, the probabilities depend on which route in the earlier diagram is being followed.

It is known that:

$P(\text{Defective}|A_1)$	$=$	$2/100$	$=$	0.02
$\therefore P(\text{Perfect}|A_1)$	$=$	$1 - 0.02$	$=$	0.98

$P(\text{Defective}|A_2)$	$=$	$6/100$	$=$	0.06
$\therefore P(\text{Perfect}|A_2)$	$=$	$1 - 0.06$	$=$	0.94

$P(\text{Defective}|B_1)$	$=$	$4/100$	$=$	0.04
$\therefore P(\text{Perfect}|B_1)$	$=$	$1 - 0.04$	$=$	0.96

$P(\text{Defective}|B_2)$	$=$	$2/100$	$=$	0.02
$\therefore P(\text{Perfect}|B_2)$	$=$	$1 - 0.02$	$=$	0.98

Thus, considering route A_1B_1

The probability that an item goes through A_1 and is perfect, is:
$$P(A_1) \times P(P|A_1) = 0.5 \times 0.98 \qquad = \quad 0.49$$

The probability that an item goes through B_1 and is perfect, is:
$$P(B_1) \times P(P|B_1) = 0.5 \times 0.96 \qquad = \quad 0.48$$

$\therefore$ the probability of an item having gone through A_1 and B_1 and being perfect is:
$$0.49 \times 0.48 \qquad\qquad = \quad 0.2352$$

Similarly for A_1B_2:

$$P(A_1) \times P(P|A_1) \quad = \quad 0.49$$
$$P(B_2) \times P(P|B_2) \quad = \quad 0.5 \times 0.98 \quad = \quad 0.49$$

$\therefore$ the probability of an item having gone through A_1 and B_2 and being perfect is:
$$0.49 \times 0.49 \qquad\qquad = \quad 0.2401$$

And for A_2B_1:

$$P(A_2) \times P(P|A_2) \quad = \quad 0.5 \times 0.94 \quad = \quad 0.47$$
$$P(B_1) \times P(P|B_1) \quad = \quad 0.48$$

$\therefore$ the probability of an item having gone through A_2 and B_1 and being perfect is:
$$0.47 \times 0.48 \qquad\qquad = \quad 0.2256$$

And finally A_2B_2:

$$P(A_2) \times P(P\,|\,A_2) \qquad\qquad = \quad 0.47$$
$$P(B_2) \times P(P\,|\,B_2) \qquad\qquad = \quad 0.49$$

$\therefore$ the probability of an item having gone through A_2 and B_2 and being perfect is:
$$0.47 \times 0.49 \qquad\qquad = \quad 0.2303$$

$$\therefore \text{P (Perfect item)} = P(A_1B_1 \text{ or } A_1B_2 \text{ or } A_2B_1 \text{ or } A_2B_2)$$

$$= P(A_1B_1) + P(A_1B_2) + P(A_2B_1) + P(A_2B_2)$$

$$= 0.2352 + 0.2401 + 0.2256 + 0.2303$$

$$= 0.9312$$

(The problem could be solved by saying that 4% fail at the first stage, 400 leaving 9,600; 3% of these fail, 288 leaving 9,312).

(c) Since the total production is 10,000 items pa, the expected number of perfect items is $0.9312 \times 10,000 = 9,312$.

The profit on each of these is £80, therefore the expected profit on the perfect items is $9,312 \times £80 = £744,960$.

$$\text{P(perfect item)} = 0.9312$$

$$\therefore \text{P(defective item)} = 1 - 0.9312 = 0.0688$$

$\therefore$ expected number of defects is $0.0688 \times 10,000 = 688$. The loss on each of these is £10, therefore the expected loss on the defective items is $688 \times £10 = £6,880$.

$$\text{The expected net profit} = £744,960 - £6,880$$

$$= £738,080.$$

This is the average profit that the company might expect to make per annum.

4.13 Example

A mad professor has invented and produced a revolutionary new two-stage rocket to take his wife to Mars. Problems have, however, developed in its ignition system. The ultimate failure of either stage to ignite means that the rocket blows up.

Three attempts at ignition of the first stage are possible. The first attempt has a probability of successful ignition of 60%, the second attempt 40% and the third attempt 20%. If all three attempts fail, the rocket blows up.

To ignite the second stage three attempts are also possible. The probability of success of the first attempt at igniting the second stage depends on whether the first stage ignited at the first attempt or not. If the first stage ignited at the first attempt then the probability of the second stage igniting at the first attempt is 65%. If not the probability is only 50%.

The probability of successful ignition at the second attempt is 30% and at the third attempt 25% irrespective of whether the first stage ignited at the first attempt or not.

What is the probability of the professor's wife surviving ignition?

4.14   Solution

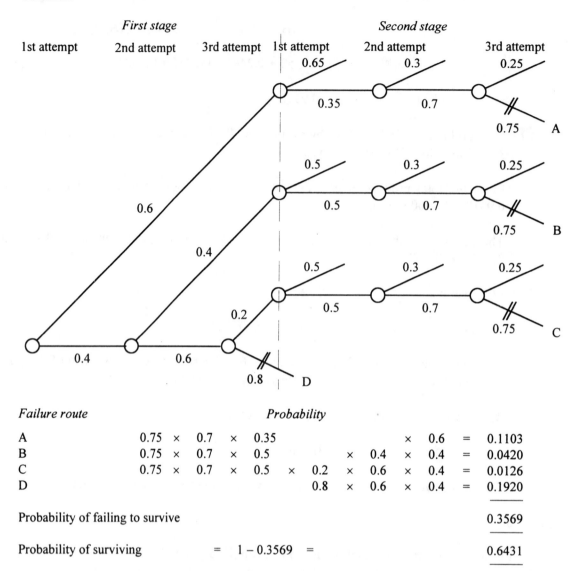

Failure route   *Probability*

A	0.75 × 0.7 × 0.35			× 0.6	= 0.1103
B	0.75 × 0.7 × 0.5	× 0.4	× 0.4		= 0.0420
C	0.75 × 0.7 × 0.5 × 0.2	× 0.6	× 0.4		= 0.0126
D	0.8 × 0.6 × 0.4				= 0.1920

Probability of failing to survive   0.3569

Probability of surviving   =   1 – 0.3569   =   0.6431

You should check this final probability by tracing the 9 survival routes.

5   PAY-OFF TABLES

5.1   Introduction

A pay-off table is a tabular layout showing the result (pay-off) in monetary value of a combination of different decisions against the 'state of the world'.

The monetary value can be either a cost or profit depending on the information used to construct the table.

5.2   Expected values

When pay-off tables are used to calculate expected values it is often easier to prepare the pay-off table first, which will then show the net costs or profits associated with the alternative combinations of information, and then to calculate the expected monetary value afterwards.

5.3   Example

A grocer buys fresh tomatoes, which have to be sold on the date purchased or thrown away. Each tomato costs 10p to buy and sells for 15p. The levels of demand per day and their associated probabilities are as follows:

Demand per day	Probability
200	0.2
220	0.2
240	0.3
260	0.2
280	0.1
	___
	1.0
	___

How many tomatoes should the grocer buy?

5.4   Solution

Pay-off table

Demand	Purchased per day				
	200	220	240	260	280
200	(W1) £10	(W4) £8	£6	£4	£2
220	(W2) £10	£11	£9	£7	£5
240	(W3) £10	£11	£12	£10	£8
260	£10	£11	£12	£13	£11
280	£10	£11	£12	£13	£14

W1   =   The grocer purchased 200 tomatoes and sold 200 tomatoes, and on each tomato he made 5p profit (ie, 15p − 10p).

Therefore his total profit is 5p × 200 = £10.

W2   =   The grocer purchases 200 tomatoes, and although demand is 220, he still has only 200 tomatoes.

Therefore his total profit is 5p × 200 = £10.

W3   =   The grocer purchases 200 tomatoes and although demand is 240, he still has only 200 tomatoes.

Therefore his total profit is 5p × 200 = £10.

W4   =   If the grocer buys 220 tomatoes the cost =   220 × 10p = £22.

If he only sells 200 tomatoes the revenue   =   200 × 15p = £30

Hence profit = 30 − 22 = £8.

The table can be filled in using the same process.

To calculate the Expected Value (EV):

Demand per day	Probability	Production per day				
		200	220	240	260	280
200	0.2	(W1) 2.0	1.6	1.2	0.8	0.4
220	0.2	2.0	2.2	1.8	1.4	1.0
240	0.3	(W2) 3.0	3.3	3.6	3.0	2.4
260	0.2	2.0	2.2	2.4	2.6	2.2
280	0.1	1.0	1.1	1.2	1.3	1.4
EV		10	10.4	10.2	9.1	7.4

(W1) =   Using the pay-off table value of £10, this is multiplied by the probability of 0.2 ie, £10 × 0.2 = 2.

(W2) =   Using the pay-off table value of £10, this is multiplied by the probability of 0.3 ie, £10 × 0.3 = 3.

All the values are calculated by multiplying the pay-off table value by its respective probability.

Conclusion   The grocer should buy 220 tomatoes per day, giving him an expected profit of £10.40.

6   CONCLUSIONS

The basic laws of probability have been outlined with many detailed examples to show the methods of calculation.

When solving complex problems, it is very important to decide on the possible outcomes and then calculate the corresponding probabilities.

Answers may be left in fractional or decimal form: in the latter case give two or three decimal places.

7   SELF TEST QUESTIONS

7.1   Probability is measured on a scale from 0 to 1. What do these figures represent? (1.3)

7.2   What are mutually exclusive events? (2.1)

7.3   Explain the Addition Law. (2.1)

7.4   Define a dependent event. (2.8)

7.5   What is a contingency table used for? (4.6)

8   EXAMINATION TYPE QUESTION

8.1   Red, blue and yellow beads

A box contains 4 red beads, 1 blue bead and 2 yellow beads. Three beads are selected at random.

If there is no replacement between each selection find the probability of selecting:

(a)   one of each colour;   **(5 marks)**

(b)   three of the same colour   **(5 marks)**

                                                                                                      (Total: 10 marks)

9   ANSWER TO EXAMINATION TYPE QUESTION

9.1   Red, blue and yellow beads

Notes:

(1)   At the start, there are 4 reds and 7 beads, hence P(red) = $\dfrac{4}{7}$. If the first is red, there will

only be 3 reds left out of 6 beads. Hence in this case P(red) = $\dfrac{3}{6}$. As there is only 1 blue

bead, it cannot be selected more than once; similarly yellow cannot be selected more than twice.

(2)   The probability of traversing a path is the product of all the probabilities along it, the 'joint probability'.

(a)   There are six outcomes that give one of each colour (all those except that marked * below),

each having the probability $\dfrac{(4 \times 2 \times 1)}{(7 \times 6 \times 5)}$.

Hence probability of one of each colour = $6 \times \dfrac{4 \times 2 \times 1}{7 \times 6 \times 5}$

$$= \frac{8}{35} = 0.23$$

(b)   There is only one colour that can be selected three times, red, see (a) above.

P(3 reds) $= \dfrac{4}{7} \times \dfrac{3}{6} \times \dfrac{2}{5}$

$$= \frac{4}{35} = 0.11$$

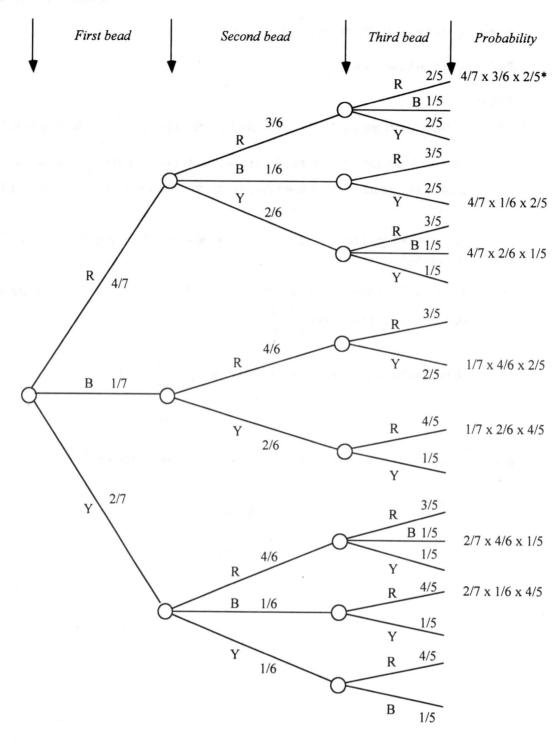

24 THE NORMAL DISTRIBUTION

INTRODUCTION & LEARNING OBJECTIVES

Syllabus area 2f. Properties and characteristics of the normal distribution. (Ability required 3).

When you have studied this chapter you should be able to do the following:

- Recognise when to use the normal distribution.

- Apply the distribution to solve particular problems.

- Understand and be able to calculate confidently required outcomes by using the appropriate formulae.

---

1 PROPERTIES OF THE NORMAL DISTRIBUTION

1.1 Introduction

The normal distribution is a continuous probability distribution meaning that it can take non-integer values. We wish to consider how to solve problems such as:

If the length of metals bars is normally distributed, calculate the probability that a metal bar is between 2.63 and 2.74 cm long.

The normal distribution can be used to answer such questions as this.

When continuous data has been collected and a frequency distribution formed, it is often shown diagrammatically in a histogram, where the total frequency of the distribution is represented by the total area of the rectangles. When **comparing** histograms based on different sample sizes it is necessary to make the total area of each diagram the same or comparison is impossible. This is quite simply achieved by letting the area of each rectangle be equal to the **relative frequency** rather than the **absolute frequency** of the class.

If f_1 = frequency of the first class, then the relative frequency for the first class is $\dfrac{f_1}{n}$ or $\dfrac{f_1}{\sum f}$

where $n = \sum f$ is the total frequency. For the second class the relative frequency is $\dfrac{f_2}{n}$ etc.

A particular type of histogram that is commonly met is the bell-shaped diagram, ie,, the highest column is in the centre of the histogram with decreasing columns spread symmetrically on either side of this peak. If the class intervals are **very** small, the histogram (figure 1) becomes a frequency curve (figure 2).

Figure 1

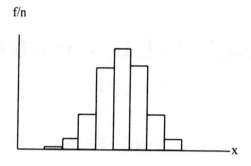

Figure 2

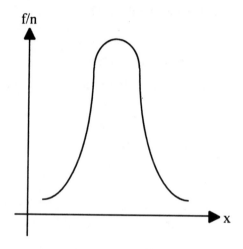

It is mathematically convenient to fix the total area under a histogram as one unit of area.

Since the area of the original histogram was one unit, the area under the curve will also be equal to unity. The **normal distribution curve** is a theoretical relative frequency curve which has a shape as in figure 2. Its actual shape can be defined mathematically, and therefore the area under any particular part of the curve can be computed, albeit with some difficulty.

1.2   Features of the normal curve

(a)   It is a mathematical curve, calculated from a complex equation, but which closely fits many naturally occurring distributions, such as heights of men.

(b)   It is symmetrical and bell-shaped.

(c)   Both tails of the distribution approach, but never meet, the x-axis. This is its chief difference from naturally occurring distributions. No man, for example, has an infinite height, (or a negative height).

(d)   The mean, median and mode lie together on the axis of symmetry of the curve.

(e)   The area under the curve is one unit of area and, by symmetry, the area to the left of the mean equals the area to the right of the mean which equals 0.5 units of the area.

1.3   Mathematical formula

Since the total area under the curve is one unit, the probability that a value of the variable lies between certain limits will be the corresponding proportion of the total area.

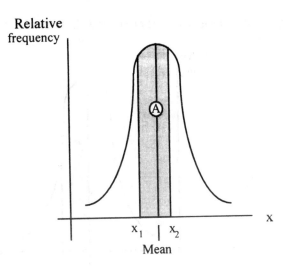

So the probability that x lies between x_1 and x_2 is the area A (shaded)

or $P(x_1 < x < x_2) = A$

This area can be found by using the normal distribution tables given at the front of the text and issued in the exam.

In order to use these tables it is necessary to know the mean (μ) and the standard deviation (σ) of the distribution being studied. Knowing these, the values (x_1 and x_2) of the variable can be standardised, ie, they can be expressed in terms of the number of standard deviations by which they differ from the mean. When the variable is transformed in this way, all normal distributions become identical, so that only the one set of tables is required.

The formula for calculating the standardised variables (usually given the letter z to distinguish them from the original data) is:

$$z = \frac{x - \mu}{\sigma}$$

1.4   Applications of the normal distribution

This distribution has many applications in life; eg, height, weight, intelligence of the population and other related matters have this type of distribution. However, one of its main uses is in sampling theory which will be studied in the next chapter.

In solving problems it is **always** advisable to **draw a sketch** of the distribution to ensure that the correct area is being calculated.

1.5   Example

A normal distribution has a mean of 68 and a standard deviation of 3. The area under the curve between the mean and 74 is calculated as follows:

First the curve is sketched and the required area shaded. It need not be to scale.

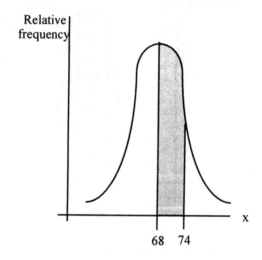

In order to find the area between $x_1 = 68$ and $x_2 = 74$ it is necessary to standardise the values of the variables using the formula.

For $x_1 = 68$ and with $\mu = 68$ and $\sigma = 3$

$$z_1 = \frac{68 - 68}{3} = 0$$

For $x_2 = 74$ and $\mu = 68$ and $\sigma = 3$

$$z_2 = \frac{74 - 68}{3} = 2$$

z_1 and z_2 simply measure the number of standard deviations between each value of the variable (ie, 68 and 74) and the mean, so 68 is zero standard deviations from the mean, since it is the mean, and 74 is two standard deviations above the mean (ie, $2 \times 3 = 6$ and $68 + 6 = 74$).

Standardising is a logical process that enables one set of standard normal distribution tables to be used. These tables give the area under the curve between the mean ($z = 0$) and the value calculated using the formula. (See Table 4 in the front of the text.)

From the table:

z_1 =   0   gives an area of 0, and
z_2 =   2   gives an area of 0.4772   (*Note* that the total area to the right of the mean is only 0.500)

$\therefore$ the probability that x lies between 68 and 74 is 0.4772 since that proportion of the area is enclosed between these limits. This is the shaded area in the sketch above.

$$\therefore P(68 < x < 74) = 0.4772$$

It is not usual to standardise the mean as it will always result in a zero value and this is understood in the working.

1.6   Example

A normal distribution has a mean of 12, and a standard deviation of 3. The probability that a randomly chosen value of x lies between the values of 6 and 15 is calculated as follows:

Again, the curve is drawn and the appropriate area shaded.

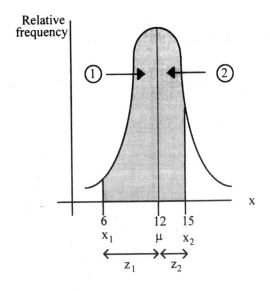

Since the area lies on both sides of the mean it is calculated in two steps.

Step 1   The area from 6 to the mean of 12 will be found; and

Step 2   the area from the mean of 12 to 15 will be found.

(a) $z_1 = \dfrac{6-12}{3} = \dfrac{-6}{3} = -2$ The minus sign merely indicates that 6 is 2 standard deviations below the mean. It can be ignored for the purposes of the calculation, since the distribution is symmetrical, and the area for $z = -2$ is therefore the same as for $z = +2$.

(b) $z_2 = \dfrac{15-12}{3} = \dfrac{3}{3} = 1$

From tables:

$z_2 = 1$ gives an area of   0.3413

$z_1 = 2$ gives an area of   0.4772

∴ total area   0.8185

∴   Probability that a randomly chosen value of x lies between the values of 6 and 15 is 0.8185

or $P(6 < x < 15) = 0.8185$

1.7   Example

Jam is packed in tins of nominal weight 1 kg (1,000 g). The actual weight of jam delivered to a tin by the filling machine is normally distributed about the set weight with a standard deviation of 12 g.

If the set, or average, filling of jam is 1 kg, calculate the proportion of tins containing:

(a)   less than 985 g;
(b)   more than 1,030 g;
(c)   between 985 g and 1,030 g.

1.8   Solution

(a)   Less than 985 g,   ie,   P (x < 985)

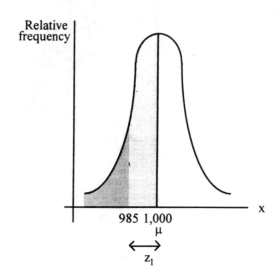

In order to calculate the proportion of tins containing less than 985 g it is necessary to find the area between 985 and 1,000 (lightly shaded) and subtract this from the area under half the curve, ie, 0.5.

$$\therefore z_1 = \frac{985 - 1,000}{12} = -1.25 \quad \text{(again the minus sign can be ignored)}$$

From the table $z_1 = 1.25$ gives an area of 0.3944, found in the row labelled 1.2 and the column headed 0.05.

∴ Area of darker shaded part of diagram = 0.5 – 0.3944 = 0.1056

So P (x < 985) = 0.1056

∴ Proportion of tins is 0.1056 (or 10.56%).

(b)   More than 1,030 g,   ie,   P (x > 1,030)

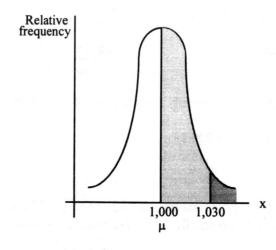

This is calculated in a similar way to part (i) ie, area under half the curve less area with light shading is the required area (shaded darkly).

$$z_2 = \frac{1,030 - 1,000}{12} = 2.5$$

From the table $z_2 = 2.5$ gives an area of 0.4938

∴ Area of dark shaded part of diagram = 0.5 – 0.4938

so P (x > 1,030) = 0.0062

∴ Proportion of tins is 0.0062 (or 0.62%).

(c)   Between 985 g and 1,030 g, ie, P (985 < x < 1,030)

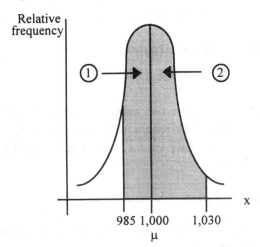

The area will again be calculated in two steps:

(i)   the area between the mean and 985;
(ii)   the area between the mean and 1,030.

These areas have already been calculated in (a) and (b).

Area 1 is 0.3944
Area 2 is 0.4938

So P (985 < x < 1,030) = 0.3944 + 0.4938 = 0.8882

∴ Proportion of tins is 0.8882 (or 88.82%).

1.9   Expected frequencies

These are derived in exactly the same way as for the other two distributions. The probabilities must be calculated first, and then the corresponding frequencies can be found.

1.10   Example

Considering the data of the previous example with jam tins, if 50,000 tins a week pass through the filling machine the number of tins expected to contain:

(a)   less than 985 g;
(b)   more than 1,030 g; and
(c)   between 985 g and 1,030 g,

is calculated as follows:

(a)   P (x < 985)   =   0.1056

∴   expected number of tins   =   50,000 × 0.1056

=   5,280

(b)   P (x > 1,030)   =   0.0062

∴   expected number of tins   =   50,000 x 0.0062

=   310

(c)   P (985 < x < 1,030)   =   0.8882

∴   expected number of tins   =   50,000 x 0.8882

=   44,410

(Check: 5,280 + 310 + 44,410 = 50,000)

2   COMBINED NORMAL DISTRIBUTIONS

2.1   Introduction

Many circumstances exist where two or more normal distributions are combined together. When this happens the resulting distribution will again be normal and therefore probabilities may be determined in the usual way once values have been obtained for the mean and standard deviation of the combined distribution.

2.2   Mean and standard deviation

The mean of the combined distribution is arrived at by simply adding together the means of the distributions that are combining.

In general terms:

Mean $(A + B)$ = Mean A + Mean B

The same is not true of the standard deviation, although it is true for the variance of a distribution. Remember the variance of a distribution is the square of its standard deviation.

Variance = σ^2

Variance $(A + B)$ = Variance A + Variance B

∴ $\sigma (A + B) = \sqrt{\sigma_A{}^2 + \sigma_B{}^2}$

2.3   Example

Over a period of time, a certain branch of Richquick Bank has analysed its daily note issue and found that demands for five pound, ten pound and twenty pound notes on any day of the week have approximately normal distributions with the following parameters:

Denominations	Number of notes	
	Mean	Standard deviation
£ 5	1,200	250
£10	600	100
£20	50	5

The demand for the three denominations are independent of one another.

What is the probability that the demand for cash exceeds £15,000 on any one day?

Mean daily demand (£) = $1,200 \times £5 + 600 \times £10 + 50 \times £20$

$$= 6,000 + 6,000 + 1,000$$

$$\doteq £13,000$$

Standard deviation of demand = $\sqrt{(250 \times £5)^2 + (100 \times £10)^2 + (5 + £20)^2}$ (£)

$$= \sqrt{1,250^2 + 1,000^2 + 100^2}$$ (£)

$$= \sqrt{2,572,500}$$ (£)

$$= £1,603.90$$

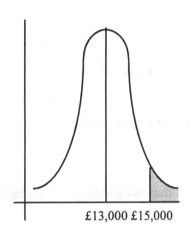

£13,000 £15,000

$$z = \frac{15,000 - 13,000}{1,603.90} = 1.2470 = 1.25$$

Since normal distribution tables are only produced for values of z to 2 decimal places, there is no point in calculating z more accurately (although σ should be found to several decimal places to avoid rounding). Since the normal distributions is not a triangle but a bell-shaped curve, there is little point in interpolating.

Area of tail (from tables) = 0.3944

∴ Probability that demand is greater than £15,000 is $0.5 - 0.3944 = 0.1056$.

3 **SELF TEST QUESTIONS**

3.1 What are the features of the normal curve? (1.2)

3.2 What is the formula for the value of z? (1.3)

3.3 What are the formulae for the mean and standard deviation of combined normal distributions? (2.2)

4   EXAMINATION TYPE QUESTION

4.1   Workers' weekly wages

A group of workers has a weekly wage which is normally distributed with mean £120 and standard deviation £15.

Find the probability of a worker earning:

(a)   more than £110;
(b)   less than £85;
(c)   more than £150;
(d)   between £110 and £135;
(e)   between £125 and £135.

Find the limits which enclose the middle:

(f)   95%;
(g)   98%.

What is the value of the interquartile range?

(20 marks)

5   ANSWER TO EXAMINATION TYPE QUESTION

5.1   Workers' weekly wages

Note: it is always advisable to draw sketch diagrams for this type of problem. They need not be to scale.

(a)

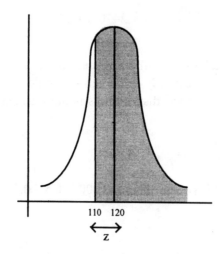

Standardise 110 to give $z = \left(\dfrac{110 - 120}{15} \right)$ =   −0.67

From tables, area from 110 to 120   =   0.2486

(The negative value of z means that the area is to the left of the mean.)

$\quad\quad\quad\quad$ P(> 110)   =   0.2486 + 0.5

$\quad\quad\quad\quad\quad\quad\quad\quad\quad$ =   0.7486

(b)

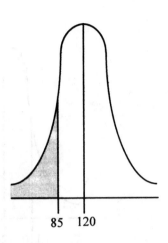

$$z = \frac{85 - 120}{15}$$

$$= -2.33$$

From tables, the area from 85 to 120 is 0.4901

$$P(< 85) \quad\quad = \quad 0.5 - 0.4901$$

$$= \quad 0.0099$$

(c)

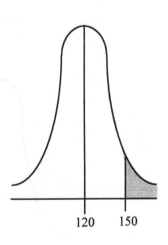

$$z = \frac{150 - 120}{15}$$

$$= \quad 2.0$$

From tables, the area from 120 to 150 is 0.4772

$$P(> 150) \quad\quad = \quad 0.5 - 0.4772$$

$$= \quad 0.0228$$

(d)

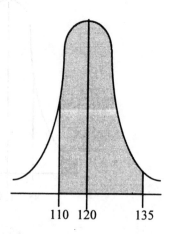

The area from 110 to 120 has already been found (0.2486)

For 135, $z = \dfrac{135-120}{15}$

                                         $= 1.0$

Area from 120 to 135 is 0.3413

Hence   P(> 110 and < 135) $= 0.2486 + 0.3413$

                                      $= 0.5899$

(e)

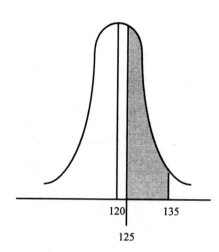

The required area = area from 120 to 135 (= 0.3413) minus the area from 120 to 125.

For 125, $z = \dfrac{125-120}{15}$

                                      $= 0.33$

Area from 120 to 125 is 0.1293

Hence   P(125 to 135) $= 0.3413 - 0.1293$

                                      $= 0.212$

(f)

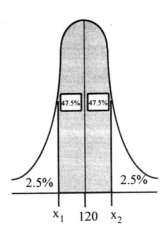

$$x_1 \quad 120 \quad x_2$$

To find this, the tables must be used in the opposite way, ie, work outwards from the area found in the body of the table to find the value of z.

For an area of 0.475, z = 1.96

$$\frac{x_2 - 120}{15} \qquad = \quad 1.96$$

$$\therefore \qquad x_2 = 120 + 1.96 \times 15 \qquad = \quad 149.4$$

By symmetry, the lower limit is given by $\dfrac{x_1 - 120}{15} = -1.96$

$$\therefore \qquad x_1 = 120 - 1.96 \times 15 \qquad = \quad 90.6$$

Hence the middle 95% lies between £90.6 and £149.4

(g)   For an area of 0.49, z = 2.33 (actual area = 0.4901)

$$\therefore \qquad \frac{x - 120}{15} \qquad = \quad \pm 2.33$$

$$x \qquad = \quad £120 \pm £15 \times 2.33$$

$$= \quad £(120 \pm 34.95)$$

Hence the middle 98% lies between £85.05 and £154.95

The interquartile range is the range of the middle 50% of items.

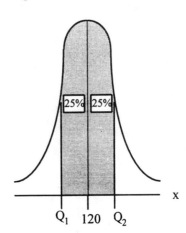

$$Q_1 \quad 120 \quad Q_2$$

From tables, the value of z cutting off 25% of the area under the normal curve is 0.675 (0.25 is sufficiently close to the mid point between 0.2486 and 0.2518 to justify this rough interpolation).

The interquartile range is therefore the range from (£120 – £15 × 0.674) to (£120 + £15 × 0.675). The interval = 2 × £15 × 0.675   =   £20.25

25 STATISTICAL INFERENCE

INTRODUCTION & LEARNING OBJECTIVES

Syllabus area 2f.   Standard errors and confidence intervals for means and percentages. (Ability required 3).

Problems of sample size. (Ability required 2).

It is often necessary to draw conclusions about a whole population by examining only a small sample taken from that population. In order to be able to do this successfully, it is very important that the sample is truly representative of the population.

The mean, median, standard deviation etc. of the sample are known as **statistics**; the corresponding population values are called **parameters**.

From now on, it becomes important to distinguish carefully between sample data and population data. The usual method is to use Greek letters for the population parameters (μ = mean, σ = standard deviation) and English letters for the sample statistics ($\overline{x}$ for mean, s for standard deviation).

When you have studied this chapter you should be able to do the following:

- Estimate the mean and standard deviation of a population from sample data.

- Calculate a confidence interval for the estimate of a population mean.

- Determine the confidence interval for the estimate of a population percentage.

- Calculate the most appropriate sample size for producing these estimates

---

1   THE THEORY OF SAMPLING (MEANS)

1.1   Unbiased estimates

Any sample statistic can be used to estimate the corresponding population parameter and this is then known as a **point estimate of the parameter**. The most commonly used statistics are the mean and standard deviation.

If one sample is randomly selected from a given population the mean ($\overline{x}$) of the sample will give the best (ie, unbiased) estimate of the population mean (μ).

When the standard deviation of a population is estimated from a sample rather than from measuring every member of the population, this is denoted by placing the symbol $^\wedge$ over the symbol for standard deviation. Thus:

σ =   Exact population standard deviation, obtained by measuring every item in the population.

$\hat{\sigma}$ =   Population standard deviation estimated from a sample (called 'sigma hat').

s =   Sample standard deviation (ie, the standard deviation of the items in the sample).

It is a proven fact that the sample standard deviation tends to underestimate the population standard deviation. It is said to be a **biased estimator**. A better, unbiased, estimate is obtained by multiplying the sample standard deviation by:

$$\sqrt{\frac{n}{n-1}}$$

This is known as **Bessel's correction**. However, when $n \geq 30$, this correction factor makes little difference and its use is then optional:

$$\hat{\mu} \;=\; \bar{x} \text{ for all values of } n$$

$$\hat{\sigma} \;=\; s \times \sqrt{\frac{n}{n-1}} \text{ for all values of } n$$

$$\simeq\; s \text{ for } n \geq 30$$

Note on formulae for calculating standard deviations

By definition, $s \;=\; \sqrt{\dfrac{\Sigma(x-\bar{x})^2}{n}}$ or $\sqrt{\dfrac{\Sigma x^2}{n} - \left(\dfrac{\Sigma x}{n}\right)^2}$

Applying Bessel's correction:

$$\hat{\sigma} \;=\; \sqrt{\frac{\Sigma(x-\bar{x})^2}{\not{n}}} \times \sqrt{\frac{\not{n}}{n-1}} \quad\text{or}\quad \sqrt{\frac{\Sigma x^2 - \frac{(\Sigma x)^2}{n}}{\not{n}}} \times \sqrt{\frac{\not{n}}{n-1}}$$

$$=\; \sqrt{\frac{\Sigma(x-\bar{x})^2}{n-1}} \;\begin{matrix}\text{(as in CIMA} \\ \text{formulae)}\end{matrix} \quad\text{or}\quad \sqrt{\frac{\Sigma x^2 - \frac{(\Sigma x)^2}{n}}{n-1}}$$

Thus, when $n-1$ is used as the divisor for calculating the standard deviation, it is $\hat{\sigma}$ that is being calculated, not s.

1.2 Example

A random sample of 15 metal bars is taken from a day's production. The weights of the bars in kg are:

1,205, 1,205, 1,208, 1,215, 1,260, 1,270, 1,271, 1,272, 1,283, 1,286, 1,289, 1,290, 1,291, 1,292, 1,293.

Using this data, the best possible point estimates of the mean and standard deviation of the weights of *all* such bars are calculated as follows:

$$\bar{x} \;=\; \frac{\Sigma x}{n}$$

$$=\; \frac{1{,}205 + 1{,}205 + 1{,}208 + \ldots + 1{,}293}{15} \text{ kg}$$

$$= \frac{18,930}{15} \text{ kg}$$

$$= 1,262 \text{ kg}$$

$\therefore \quad \bar{x} \quad = \quad 1,262$ kg can be used as an estimate of the population mean.

ie, $\quad \mu \quad = \quad 1,262$ kg $\quad$ (based on sample data)

$x^2 \quad = \quad$ 1,452,025, $\quad$ 1,452,025, $\quad$ 1,459,264, $\quad$ 1,476,225, $\quad$ 1,587,600,
$\quad$ 1,612,900, $\quad$ 1,615,441, $\quad$ 1,617,984, $\quad$ 1,646,089, $\quad$ 1,653,796,
$\quad$ 1,661,521, $\quad$ 1,664,100, $\quad$ 1,666,681, $\quad$ 1,669,264, $\quad$ 1,671,849

$\sum x^2 \quad = \quad$ 23,906,764

$$s \quad = \quad \sqrt{\frac{\sum x^2 - \frac{(\sum x)^2}{n}}{n}} \quad = \quad \sqrt{\frac{\sum x^2}{n} - \left(\frac{\sum x}{n}\right)^2}$$

$$= \quad \sqrt{\frac{23,906,764}{15} - \left(\frac{18,930}{15}\right)^2}$$

$$= \quad 33.77 \text{ kg}$$

$$\hat{\sigma} \quad = \quad 33.77 \times \sqrt{\frac{15}{14}}$$

$$= \quad 34.96 \text{ kg}$$

or $\quad \hat{\sigma} \quad = \quad \sqrt{\frac{\sum x^2 - \frac{(\sum x)^2}{n}}{n-1}}$

$$= \quad \sqrt{\frac{23,906,764 - \frac{(18,930)^2}{15}}{14}}$$

$$= \quad 34.96 \text{ kg as before}$$

$\therefore$ the unbiased estimate of the population standard deviation = 35 kg (2 sf.).

A further example illustrating when to use n and when to use $n - 1$ in the calculation of standard deviations:

1.3   Example

A random sample of 5 wooden tables was selected from a large production run (the 'population'). The lengths of the 5 tables, in metres, were found to be:

$\qquad$ 1.25, 1.30, 1.32, 1.26, 1.21.

It is required to obtain

(a) $\qquad$ The mean length of the 5 tables selected (ie, the sample mean).

(b)   The standard deviation of length of the 5 tables selected (ie, the standard deviation of the sample).

(c)   The mean length of all tables in the production run (ie, the population mean).

(d)   The standard deviation of length of all tables in the production run (ie, the population standard deviation).

1.4   Solution

Note that as every table made in the large production run was not measured, it is not possible to calculate the exact mean and standard deviation of the population; they must be estimated from the sample of 5 selected, which is why the sample was taken.

Initial calculations:

$$\Sigma x \quad = \quad 1.25 + 1.30 + 1.32 + 1.26 + 1.21 = 6.34 \text{ metres}$$

$$\Sigma x^2 \quad = \quad (1.25)^2 + (1.30)^2 + (1.32)^2 + (1.26)^2 + (1.21)^2 = 8.0466 \text{ sq. metres}$$

(a)   The mean length of the five tables is $\bar{x}$, where

$$\bar{x} = \frac{\Sigma x}{n} = \frac{6.34}{5} = 1.27 \text{ metres (to 3 sig. figs.)}$$

This is the sample mean.

(b)   The standard deviation of length of the five tables is s. This is where n is used as the divisor, hence

$$s \quad = \quad \sqrt{\frac{\Sigma x^2}{n} - \left(\frac{\Sigma x}{n}\right)^2}$$

$$= \quad \sqrt{\frac{8.0466}{5} - \left(\frac{6.34}{5}\right)^2}$$

$$= \quad 0.0387 \text{ metres (3 s.f.)}$$

This is the sample standard deviation.

(c)   The estimated mean length of the whole production run is the same as the mean of the sample, hence

Estimated population mean = 1.27 metres.

(d)   The estimated standard deviation of length of table for the whole production run is $\hat{\sigma}$. This is where $n - 1$ is used as the divisor, hence

$$\hat{\sigma} \quad = \quad s\sqrt{\frac{n}{n-1}} = 0.0387 \times \sqrt{\frac{5}{4}}$$

$$= \quad 0.0433 \text{ metres (3 s.f.)}$$

This is the estimated population standard deviation.

In sampling theory, it is usually the estimated population standard deviation rather than the sample standard deviation that is required so if you are still in doubt as to which formula to use, use the one with $n - 1$ as the divisor, as this will more likely be the correct one.

1.5   Distribution of sample means

If two samples of the same size are drawn from a given population they will not be identical, even though each has been randomly selected. So if the mean of each sample is calculated, two different values will result, each of which could be used to estimate the population mean.

If a large number of samples of the same size (n) are drawn from a given population and the mean of each calculated, a distribution of values will be obtained. This is known as the **sampling distribution of the mean** or the **distribution of sample means.**

When large samples are taken (ie, $n \geq 30$) this distribution is found to be normally distributed irrespective of the form of the distribution of the parent population.

Furthermore, the mean of all the sample means is the population mean. So the distribution of sample means will be of the type:

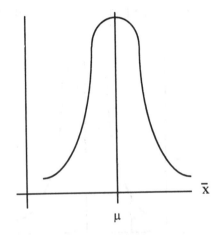

Any normal distribution is completely defined by its mean and standard deviation. To avoid confusion, the standard deviation of **this** sampling distribution is called the **standard error** and its value is $\dfrac{\sigma}{\sqrt{n}}$ (ie, the population standard deviation divided by the square root of the sample size).

The larger the sample size (n) the smaller will be the value of the standard error $\dfrac{\sigma}{\sqrt{n}}$ and the less dispersed will be the sample means about the population mean.

So the distribution of sample means is normal with mean μ and the standard deviation (or standard error) related to the population standard deviation as shown above and therefore the standardised variable becomes:

$$z \quad = \quad \frac{\overline{x} - \mu}{\frac{\sigma}{\sqrt{n}}}$$

The following points should be noted:

(a)   The population from which the samples are drawn need not itself be normally distributed. It is the sample means that are normally distributed about the population mean.

(b)   The standard error, $\dfrac{\sigma}{\sqrt{n}}$ of the means is **not** the sample standard deviation **nor** the population standard deviation; it is an entirely separate value that measures the spread (or dispersion) of the sample means. It happens to depend on σ and n which is not surprising, though it need not be proved at this level.

(c)   *n* is the size of each sample and **not** the number of samples that are taken. In general, only one sample is available and all conclusions are based on the one set of data as will be seen shortly.

(d)   The main reason for taking samples is so that inferences can be made about the population under consideration. It is, therefore, very likely that σ will not be known and therefore *s*, the sample standard deviation, must be used to estimate σ.

(e)   It is assumed that the population is very large, so that any sample forms only a very small proportion of that population (less than 5%).

(f)   A further necessary assumption is that the sample size is ≥ 30.

1.6   Example

The mean length of a component is specified as 20cm with a standard deviation of 0.51cm. The probability that a sample of 100 rods will have a mean less than 19.85cm is calculated as follows:

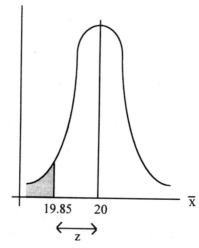

$\mu = 20$, $\sigma = 0.51$, $n = 100$, $\bar{x} = 19.85$

standard error $= \dfrac{\sigma}{\sqrt{n}} = \dfrac{0.51}{\sqrt{100}} = 0.051$ cm

Standardising: z $= \dfrac{19.85 - 20}{0.051}$

                        $= \dfrac{-0.15}{0.051}$

                        $= -2.94$ Area $= 0.5 - 0.4984$

                                                $= 0.0016$

(ie, 19.85 is 2.94 standard errors below the population mean of 20.)

$\therefore P(\bar{x} < 19.85)$ $= P(z < -2.94)$ $= 0.0016$

                                $= 0.16\%$

1.7   Confidence intervals (means)

Instead of giving just a point estimate of the population mean, it is possible to give a probable range of values in which the population mean lies and the probability that it does in fact lie within this range. This range of values is known as a **confidence interval**. The lower and upper limits of this interval are called **confidence limits, or precision limits**. The probability that the population value lies within this range is known as the **confidence level**.

In order to calculate the limits of a confidence interval, the following critical values must first be understood.

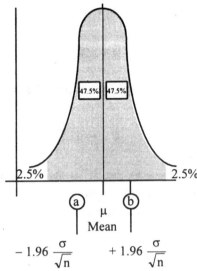

95% of the area under any normal curve is contained within ± 1.96 standard deviations of the mean. This can be checked from normal curve tables. 1.96 standard deviations corresponds to 0.475 or 47.5 % of the area; twice this (remembering that the tables are one-sided) gives 95%.

So, for a sampling distribution, the range from $\mu - 1.96 \dfrac{\sigma}{\sqrt{n}}$ to $\mu + 1.96 \dfrac{\sigma}{\sqrt{n}}$

((a) to (b) above) contains 95% of all the sample means. Therefore, the probability that a sample mean lies within this range is 0.95 and the probability that a sample mean lies outside this range is 0.05. So ninety-five samples out of every 100 would yield a mean value in this range and only five samples in every 100 would yield a value outside this range.

Also:

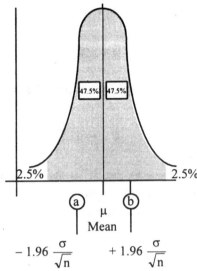

99% of the area under any normal curve is contained within ± 2.58 standard deviations of the mean. So for a sampling distribution the range from

$$\mu - 2.58 \dfrac{\sigma}{\sqrt{n}} \qquad \text{to} \qquad \mu + 2.58 \dfrac{\sigma}{\sqrt{n}} \qquad \text{((c) to (d) above)}$$

contains 99% of all sample means. Therefore, the probability that a sample mean lies within this range is 0.99 and the probability that it falls outside the range is 0.01. So out of every 100 samples ninety-nine would yield a value within the range and only one would give a value outside it.

It therefore follows that there is a 95% probability that the population mean lies within ± 1.96 standard errors of a sample mean, ie, in the range:

$$\bar{x} - 1.96 \, \frac{\sigma}{\sqrt{n}} \qquad \text{to} \qquad \bar{x} + 1.96 \, \frac{\sigma}{\sqrt{n}}$$

There is a 99% probability that the population mean lies within ± 2.58 standard errors of a sample mean, ie, in the range

$$\bar{x} - 2.58 \, \frac{\sigma}{\sqrt{n}} \qquad \text{to} \qquad \bar{x} + 2.58 \, \frac{\sigma}{\sqrt{n}}$$

These ranges of values are known as the 95% and 99% confidence intervals for the population mean. Any size of confidence interval can be set up, by using the appropriate number of standard errors, but these are two very commonly used values.

1.8   Summary

95% confidence limits $= \quad \bar{x} \pm 1.96$ standard errors

99% confidence limits $= \quad \bar{x} \pm 2.58$ standard errors

where the standard error $= \quad \dfrac{\sigma}{\sqrt{n}}$

If σ is not known, use $\hat{\sigma}$ $= \quad s\sqrt{\dfrac{n}{n-1}}$

1.9   Example

The mean and standard deviation of the height of a random sample of 100 students are 168.75 cm and 7.5 cm, respectively. The 95% and 99% confidence intervals for the mean height of all students are calculated as follows

1.10   Solution

As the standard deviation of the population is not known, and $n > 30$, the standard deviation of the sample can be used to calculate the standard error. Hence:

$$\text{Standard error} \quad = \quad \frac{7.5}{\sqrt{100}} \text{cm}$$

$$= \quad 0.75 \text{ cm}$$

The 95% confidence limits are 168.75 ± 1.96 Standard errors

$$= \quad 168.75 \pm 1.96 \times 0.75$$

$$= \quad 168.75\text{cm} \pm 1.47 \text{ cm}$$

This means that there is a 95% probability that the mean height of all students is between 167.28 and 170.22 cm.

The 99% confidence limits are 168.75 ± 2.58 Standard errors

$$= \quad 168.75 \pm 2.58 \times 0.75$$

$$= \quad 168.75\text{cm} \pm 1.94 \text{ cm}$$

This means that there is a 99% probability that the mean height of all students is between 166.81 and 170.69 cm.

It is important to note that it is impossible to infer an exact value of the population mean from a sample. We can only state that there is a specified probability that the population mean is within specified limits. This uncertainty is known as sampling error. The only way to eliminate sampling error and obtain an exact value for the population mean is to measure every item in the population.

The result of **increasing** the degree of confidence (from 95% to 99%) is that the precision of the estimate is reduced, ie, a wider interval is calculated for μ.

1.11   Sample size for a given error

$1.96 \dfrac{\sigma}{\sqrt{n}}$ and $2.58 \dfrac{\sigma}{\sqrt{n}}$ are known as **errors** in the estimates of μ. It is possible to reduce the size of this error by increasing the value of n, the sample size.

1.12   Example

In measuring the reaction time of individuals, a psychologist estimates that the standard deviation of all such times is 0.05 seconds.

Calculate the smallest sample size necessary in order to be (a) 95% and (b) 99% confident that the error in the estimate will not exceed 0.01 seconds.

(a)   95% confidence limits are $\bar{x} \pm 1.96 \dfrac{\sigma}{\sqrt{n}}$

$\therefore$ error in estimate $= 1.96 \dfrac{\sigma}{\sqrt{n}} = 1.96 \times \dfrac{0.05}{\sqrt{n}}$

and this must be less than or equal to 0.01 seconds.

$\therefore \qquad 1.96 \times \dfrac{0.05}{\sqrt{n}} \ \leq \ 0.01$

$\therefore \qquad \dfrac{1.96 \times 0.05}{0.01} \ \leq \ \sqrt{n}$

$\qquad\qquad 9.80 \qquad \leq \ \sqrt{n}$

$\qquad\qquad 96.04 \qquad \leq \ n \qquad$ (squaring both sides to remove square root)

The sample size should be 97 since n must be greater than or equal to 96.04.

(b)   99% confidence limits are $\bar{x} \pm 2.58 \dfrac{\sigma}{\sqrt{n}}$

$\therefore \qquad$ error in estimate $= 2.58 \dfrac{\sigma}{\sqrt{n}} = 2.58 \times \dfrac{0.05}{\sqrt{n}}$

and this must be at most 0.01 seconds.

$\therefore \qquad \dfrac{2.58 \times 0.05}{\sqrt{n}} \ \leq \ 0.01$

$\qquad\qquad \dfrac{2.58 \times 0.05}{0.01} \ \leq \ \sqrt{n}$

$$12.90 \quad \leq \quad \sqrt{n}$$

$$166.41 \quad \leq \quad n \qquad \text{(squaring both sides)}$$

The sample size should be 167.

By increasing the sample size from 97 to 167, we can be more confident that the mean reaction time is within the required limits.

1.13   Activity

A sample of 100 items from a production line has a mean length of 8.4 cm with standard deviation 0.5 cm.

What is the 95% confidence interval for the mean length of all items from that production line?

1.14   Activity solution

$$\text{95\% confidence interval} \quad = \quad \bar{x} \pm 1.96 \, \frac{\sigma}{\sqrt{n}}$$

Using s to estimate σ,

$$\text{95\% confidence interval} \quad = \quad 8.4 \pm 1.96 \times \frac{0.5}{\sqrt{100}} \text{cm}$$

$$= \quad 8.4 \pm 1.96 \times 0.05 \text{ cm}$$

$$\therefore \qquad 8.302 < \mu < 8.498 \text{ cm}$$

2   THEORY OF SAMPLING (PROPORTIONS)

2.1   Introduction

It is often necessary to estimate a population proportion from a sample, rather than estimating a mean. For example, in public polls, sample enquiries are made to estimate the proportion of people in favour of Government policies. In consumer research, it may be required to estimate the proportion of consumers who would use a new product in order to estimate the demand. This type of enquiry is known as **sampling for attributes**, as the object is to estimate the proportion of the population who possess the attribute under investigation.

If $n \geq 30$, the normal distribution can be used. The theory is the same as that for means, except that a different formula is used for the standard error.

$$\text{Standard error of a proportion} = \sqrt{\frac{pq}{n}}$$

where p = proportion of the population possessing the attribute

q = $1 - p$ = proportion not possessing the attribute

n = size of sample

If the proportion of the population is not known, the proportion of the sample can be used as an estimate.

2.2 Example

Past experience with an examination in Law has shown that only 50% of the students pass. The probability that 55% or more of a group of 200 students will pass is calculated as follows:

The population proportion is 50%, ie, $\dfrac{50}{100} = 0.5$. Hence:

$p = 0.5, \quad \therefore q = 1 - 0.5 = 0.5 \quad$ and $\quad n = 200$

$$\text{Standard error} \;=\; \sqrt{\dfrac{pq}{n}} \;=\; \sqrt{\dfrac{0.5 \times 0.5}{200}}$$

$$= \sqrt{0.00125}$$

$$= 0.03536$$

Given sample proportion $\quad = \quad 0.55$

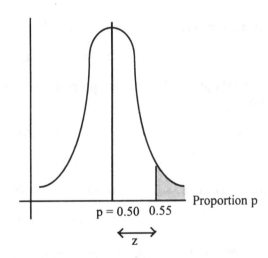

Standardising the value 0.55:

$$z \quad = \quad \dfrac{0.55 - 0.5}{0.03536}$$

$$= \quad 1.41 \qquad \text{Area} = 0.4207 \quad \text{(from table at front of text)}$$

$\therefore$ the required probability $\quad = \quad 0.5 - 0.4207 = 0.0793$

The chances of 55% (or more) passing are 0.0793 or approximately 8 in 100.

2.3 Confidence intervals (proportions)

The 95% and 99% confidence limits for the population proportion are obtained in the same way as those for the sample mean, using the formula for the standard error of a proportion, ie,:

$$95\% \text{ confidence limits} \quad = \quad \text{sample proportion} \pm 1.96 \text{ SE}$$

$$99\% \text{ confidence limits} \quad = \quad \text{sample proportion} \pm 2.58 \text{ SE}$$

$$\text{where } \text{SE} \quad = \quad \sqrt{\dfrac{pq}{n}}$$

If the population proportion is not known, use the sample proportion to calculate the standard error.

2.4   Example

Calculate the 95% and 99% confidence limits for the proportion of all voters in favour of candidate A if a random sample of 100 voters had 55% in favour of A.

2.5   Solution

As the population proportion is not known the sample proportion must be used to calculate the standard error; Hence:

$p = 0.55,$ $q = 1 - 0.55 = 0.45$ and $n = 100$

Standard error $= \sqrt{\dfrac{pq}{n}} = \sqrt{\dfrac{0.55 \times 0.45}{100}}$

                                                        $= 0.04975$

95% confidence limits $= 0.55 \pm 1.96 \times 0.04975$

                                                        $= 0.55 \pm 0.0975$

The 95% confidence interval is therefore $(0.55 - 0.0975)$ to $(0.55 + 0.0975)$

                                                        $= 0.45$ to 0.65 (2 d.p.)

This means that there is a 95% probability that the proportion of all voters in favour of candidate A is between 45% and 65%.

The 99% confidence limits $= 0.55 \pm 2.58 \times 0.04975$

                                                        $= 0.55 \pm 0.128$

The 99% confidence interval is therefore $(0.55 - 0.128)$ to $(0.55 + 0.128)$

                                                        $= 0.42$ to 0.68 (2 d.p.)

This means that there is a 99% probability that the proportion of all voters in favour of candidate A is between 42% and 68%.

There is obviously a very large sampling error, indicating that a larger sample should have been used.

Note again the nature of the inference that can be drawn from the sample. It does not follow that because 55% of the sample were in favour, 55% of the population will be in favour. We can only infer that there is a specified probability that the proportion will be within specified limits. If the candidate assumed from the sample result that he would win the election, he might well be disappointed.

2.6 **Sample size and proportions**

The standard error and hence the error in the estimate can again be reduced by increasing the sample size n.

2.7 **Example**

An advertising firm claims that its recent promotion reached 30% of the families living in the city. The company who hired the firm doubts this assertion and wishes to take a sample survey of its own. Calculate the sample size necessary to be at least 95% confident that the estimate will be within 3% of the true value.

Here, the only estimate available of the population proportion is 30% or 0.3. This value must therefore be used to calculate the standard error.

Hence: $\quad\quad p \;=\; 0.3$

$$q \;=\; 1 - 0.3 = 0.7$$

Standard error $\quad=\quad \sqrt{\dfrac{pq}{n}}$

$$=\quad \sqrt{\dfrac{0.3 \times 0.7}{n}}$$

but we require the value of n to be such that 1.96 standard errors = 0.03 (ie, 3%)

$$\therefore \quad 0.03 \;=\; 1.96 \times \sqrt{\dfrac{0.3 \times 0.7}{n}}$$

$$\therefore \quad \sqrt{n} \;=\; \dfrac{1.96 \times \sqrt{0.3 \times 0.7}}{0.03}$$

$$\therefore \quad n \;=\; \dfrac{1.96^2 \times 0.3 \times 0.7}{0.03^2} \qquad \text{(squaring both sides)}$$

$$=\quad 896.4$$

A sample size of 897 should be taken.

Note that in order to calculate the standard error, it is necessary to have an assumed value of the population proportion p. If the survey is completely new, there will be no means of knowing what value of p would be reasonable to assume. In this case, the method used is to take the worst possible case giving the highest standard error. This is when $p \;=\; q \;=\; 0.5$.

Thus in the previous example, if it was not valid to assume $p \;=\; 30\%$, the calculation would be as follows:

Take $\quad p = q = 0.5$

Standard error $\quad\quad=\quad \sqrt{\dfrac{0.5 \times 0.5}{n}} \quad=\quad \sqrt{\dfrac{0.25}{n}}$

We require $0.3 = 1.96 \sqrt{\dfrac{0.25}{n}}$

$$n = \left(\dfrac{1.96}{0.03}\right)^2 \times 0.25$$

$$= 1{,}067.1$$

A sample of size 1,068 would be required.

2.8   Activity

In a random sample of 144 people, 63% preferred the flavour of a new brand of instant coffee to that of the other brands tested.

What are the 99% confidence limits for the proportion of the total population preferring the new brand?

2.9   Activity solution

Estimated $p = 0.63$, $q = 1 - 0.63 = 0.37$, $n = 144$

99% confidence limits = sample proportion ± 2.58 standard errors

$$= 0.63 \pm 2.58 \sqrt{\dfrac{0.63 \times 0.37}{144}}$$

$$= 0.63 \pm 0.10$$

$$\therefore \quad 0.53 < p < 0.73$$

$$\text{or} \quad 53\% < p < 73\%$$

2.10   Illustration

A manufacturer of electric light bulbs needs to estimate the average 'burning life' of the bulbs he makes. A random sample of 100 bulbs was found to have a mean life of 340 hours with a standard deviation of 30 hours.

Calculate

(a)   the standard error of the mean;
(b)   the 95% and 99% confidence intervals for the population mean;
(c)   the sample size necessary to provide a degree of accuracy within 3 hours at the 95% level.

2.11   Solution

$\bar{x} = 340$ hours, $s = 30$ hours $= \hat{\sigma}\ (n > 30)$ $n = 100$

(a)   Standard error $= \dfrac{\hat{\sigma}}{\sqrt{n}}$

$$= \dfrac{30}{\sqrt{100}}$$

$$= 3 \text{ hours}$$

(b)   95% confidence interval for μ:

$$\bar{x} \pm 1.96 \times \frac{\hat{\sigma}}{\sqrt{n}}$$

$= \quad 340 \pm 1.96 \times 3$

$= \quad 340 \pm 5.88$

$= \quad 334.12$ to 345.88 hours

$= \quad 334$ hours to 346 hours

99% confidence interval for μ:

$$\bar{x} \pm 2.58 \times \frac{\hat{\sigma}}{\sqrt{n}}$$

$= \quad 340 \pm 2.58 \times 3$

$= \quad 340 \pm 7.74$

$= \quad 332.26$ to 347.74 hours

$= \quad 332$ hours to 348 hours

(c)   The error in the estimate $= 3$ hours

$\therefore \quad 1.96 \times \dfrac{\hat{\sigma}}{\sqrt{n}} \quad = \quad 3$

$\therefore \quad 1.96 \times \dfrac{30}{\sqrt{n}} \quad = \quad 3$

$\therefore \quad \dfrac{1.96 \times 30}{3} \quad = \quad \sqrt{n}$

$\qquad 19.6 \quad = \quad \sqrt{n}$

$\qquad 384.16 \quad = \quad n$

$\therefore$ it is necessary to use a sample of at least 385.

2.12   Conclusions

As can be seen, the normal distribution has many applications. It can be used as an approximation to the binomial probability distribution under certain given conditions. It is also fundamental to much of the work on sampling.

So far, two sampling distributions have been covered – for the mean and for proportions. Whilst sample statistics can be used to give point estimates of the corresponding parameters, it is more realistic to give a range of values within which the parameter probably lies. This is known as a confidence interval and the degree of confidence is the probability that the range contains the population parameter.

3   SELF TEST QUESTIONS

3.1   What is Bessel's correction? (1.1)

3.2   What is a distribution of sample means? (1.5)

3.3   What are confidence intervals? (1.7)

3.4   What confidence level is given by the interval $\bar{x} \pm 1.96$ standard errors? (1.8)

4   EXAMINATION TYPE QUESTIONS

4.1   Sampling computer records

A mail-order company is analysing a random sample of its computer records of customers. Among the results are the following distributions:

Size of order £	Number of customers
Less than 1	8
1 and less than 5	19
5 and less than 10	38
10 and less than 15	40
15 and less than 20	22
20 and less than 30	13
30 and over	4
Total	144

You are required

(a)   to calculate the arithmetic mean and standard deviation order size for the sample;

(10 marks)

(b)   to find 95% confidence limits for the overall mean order size for the customers and explain their meaning;

(6 marks)

(Total: 16 marks)

4.2   Mail-order customers

(a)   A simple random sample of 400 of a large mail-order company's customers showed that the mean value of orders in the first quarter of 19X7 was £31 with a standard deviation of £10.

Find 95% confidence limits for the population mean and interpret your answer.

(6 marks)

(b)   (i)   The sample of 400 comprises 80 pensioners. Find a 99% confidence interval for the population percentage of pensioner customers and interpret your answer.

(6 marks)

(ii)   What size of sample would have to be taken to be at least 95% confident that the population percentage of pensioner customers would be estimated to within $\pm 2\%$?

(8 marks)

(Total: 20 marks)

5 ANSWERS TO EXAMINATION TYPE QUESTIONS

5.1 Sampling computer records

Notes:

(i) Take the upper group boundaries as 1, 5, 10 . . . etc.

(ii) Close the final group by assuming the same interval as the previous group, ie, '30 and less than 40'.

Size of order (£)		Mid-point x	f	fx	fx²
0 and less than	1	0.5	8	4	2.0
1 and less than	5	3.0	19	57	171.0
5 and less than	10	7.5	38	285	2,137.5
10 and less than	15	12.5	40	500	6,250.0
15 and less than	20	17.5	22	385	6,737.5
20 and less than	30	25.0	13	325	8,125.0
30 and less than	40	35.0	4	140	4,900.0
			144	1,696	28,323.0

$$\text{Mean} = \frac{\Sigma fx}{\Sigma f}$$

$$= \frac{1,696}{144}$$

$$= £11.78$$

$$\text{Standard deviation} = \sqrt{\frac{\Sigma fx^2}{\Sigma f} - \left(\frac{\Sigma fx}{\Sigma f}\right)^2}$$

$$= \sqrt{\frac{28,323}{144} - \left(\frac{1,696}{144}\right)^2}$$

$$= £7.61$$

Note: you are reminded that column 5 = column 2 × column 4.

(b) Standard error $= \dfrac{\sigma}{\sqrt{n}}$

$$= £\frac{7.61}{\sqrt{144}}$$

$$= £0.6342$$

95% confidence limits = mean ± 1.96 standard errors

$$= £(11.78 \pm 1.96 \times 0.6342)$$

$$= £11.78 \pm £1.24$$

$$= £10.54 \text{ to } £13.02$$

This means that there is a 95% probability that the mean size of all orders in April was between £10.54 and £13.02.

5.2   Mail-order customers

(a)   Standard error

$$= \frac{\sigma}{\sqrt{n}}$$

$$= \frac{£10}{\sqrt{400}}$$

$$= £0.5$$

95% confidence limits   = sample mean ± 1.96 standard errors

$$= £(31 \pm 1.96 \times 0.50)$$

$$= £31 \pm 0.98$$

$$= £30.02 \text{ and } £31.98$$

This means that there is a 95% probability that the mean value of all orders lies between £30.02 and £31.98.

Note: a common mistake, particularly under the stress of examination conditions, is to omit to divide the standard deviation by $\sqrt{n}$ to obtain the standard error.

(b)   (i)   Standard error of a proportion $= \sqrt{\dfrac{p(1-p)}{n}}$

where p = population proportion. As the population proportion is not known and the sample is a large one, the sample proportion is used as an estimate. Hence;

$$p \quad = \quad 80/400 \quad = \quad 0.2$$

$$\text{Standard error} \quad = \quad \sqrt{\frac{0.2 \times 0.8}{400}}$$

$$= \quad 0.02$$

99% confidence limits   = sample proportion ± 2.58 standard errors

$$= \quad 0.2 \pm 2.58 \times 0.02$$

$$= \quad 0.2 \pm 0.0516$$

Hence 99% confidence limits for the percentage

$$= \quad (20 \pm 5.16)\%$$

This means that there is a 99% probability that the percentage of all customers who are pensioners is between 14.84% and 25.16%.

Note: to convert a proportion to a percentage, it is multiplied by 100. This applies equally to confidence limits for proportions.

(ii)   To be 95% confident that the proportion would be estimated to within ± 2%, we require

1.96 Standard errors of the proportion = 0.02 (ie, 2%)

If it is assumed that the population proportion is 0.2, as obtained from the sample,

$$1.96 \sqrt{\frac{0.2 \times 0.8}{n}} = 0.02$$

where n is the size of the sample.

This gives n $\quad = \quad \left(\dfrac{1.96}{0.02}\right)^2 \times 0.2 \times 0.8$

$\qquad\qquad\quad = \quad 1{,}537$

However, if it cannot be assumed that the population is 0.2, then the value of p that gives the highest standard error (p = 0.5) should be taken.

In this case

$$1.96 \times \sqrt{\frac{0.5 \times 0.5}{n}} \quad = \quad 0.02$$

giving n $\qquad = \quad \left(\dfrac{1.96}{0.02}\right)^2 \times 0.5 \times 0.5$

$\qquad\qquad\quad = \quad 2{,}401$

Notes:

(i)   The sample size must always be rounded to the nearest whole number above; rounding down will not achieve the required accuracy of sample prediction.

(ii)   In b (ii), strictly speaking, 2,401 is the correct answer, but it is doubtful whether a candidate would be penalised for the answer 1,537. You should make sure you understand the reason for the different answers.

26 INTRODUCTION TO FINANCIAL MATHEMATICS

INTRODUCTION & LEARNING OBJECTIVES

Syllabus area 2g.   Simple interest; compound interest; Annual Percentage Rate (APR).   (Ability required 3).

Discounting. (Ability required 3).

Simple applications (eg, annuities and perpetuities, investments and depreciation). (Ability required 3).

A knowledge of financial mathematics is vital not just for the conventional and the multiple choice questions that appear in this exam but in the financial management topics that appear in later papers.

This chapter is concerned with the relationships between numbers in a series where the differences between the values in the series can be identified, and how this relates to the principles of simple and compound interest.

The principle of compound interest is then applied to the discounting of future money values to find a present value used in the evaluation of projects.

When you have studied this chapter you should be able to do the following:

- Distinguish between arithmetic and geometric progressions.
- Calculate the sum of a series and identify the value of a specific term within the series.
- Distinguish between simple and compound methods of calculating interest.
- Use the theory of compound interest and apply it to the discounting of future cash flows.
- Evaluate projects using the net present value discounting technique.

1   SEQUENCES AND SERIES

1.1   **Definition**   A **sequence** is a succession of numbers, of which each number is formed according to a definite law which is the same throughout the sequence. When each term in the sequence is summed the result is called a **series**.

The series of most relevance are known as **arithmetical** and **geometrical** progressions.

2   ARITHMETICAL PROGRESSIONS

2.1   **Definition**   An **arithmetical progression** is one in which each term is formed from the preceding one by adding or subtracting a constant number, eg,

(a)   2, 3, 4, 5, . . .
(b)   −7, 3, 13, 23, . . .

The constant number which is added or subtracted is known as the **common difference**.

For (a) the common difference is +1.
For (b) the common difference is +10.

An arithmetical progression can be written in general terms as:

$$a, a + d, a + 2d, \ldots a + (n - 1)d,$$

where a is the first term and d is the common difference.

The nth term is:

$$a + (n - 1)d$$

The sum of the first n terms of an arithmetical progression (S_n) is given by the following formulae:

$$S_n = \frac{n}{2} [\text{First term} + \text{nth term}]$$

$$= \frac{n}{2} [2a + (n - 1)d]$$

2.2   Example

(a)   Find the tenth term and the sum of the first ten terms of the series 22, 20.5, 19 . . .

(b)   The first term of an arithmetic progression is 7 and the fourth term is 16. Find:

   (i)   The sum of the first four terms.
   (ii)   The sum of the first ten terms.

2.3   Solution

(a) $a = 22, d = -1.5$

   10th term $= a + 9d$

   $= 22 + (9 \times -1.5)$

   $= 8.5$

   $S_{10} = \frac{10}{2} [2 \times 22 + (9 \times -1.5)]$

   $= 152.5$

(b)   (i) $S_4 = \frac{4}{2} [\text{1st term} + \text{4th term}] = \frac{4}{2} [7 + 16]$

   $= 46$

   (ii)   4th term $= a + 3d$ where $a = 7$

   $\therefore 7 + 3d = 16$

   $d = 3$

   $S_{10} = \frac{n}{2} [2a + (n - 1)d] = \frac{10}{2} [2 \times 7 + 9 \times 3]$

   $= 205$

2.4   Activity

(a)   Find the twenty-first term of the following series: 3, 5, 7, . . .

(b)   A new company makes 250 products in the first week. If the rate at which these are produced increases by 6 each week, find:

(i)   How many will be produced in their 40th week of manufacture.
(ii)   The expected total produced after 12 weeks.

2.5   Activity solution

(a) $a = 3$ The first term

$d = 2$ The common difference

$n = 21$ The number of terms

The nth term in the series will be $T_n = 2 + (n-1)d$

So $T_{21} = 3 + (21-1)2$

$= 3 + 40$

$= 43$

(b)   (i) $a = 250$

$d = 6$

$n = 40$

$T_{40} = 250 + (40-1)6$

$= 250 + 234$

$= 484$

(ii) $a = 250$

$d = 6$

$n = 12$

The sum for the first n terms is

$S_n = \dfrac{n}{2}(a + \text{nth term})$

where the nth term is $(a + (n-1)d)$

Step 1   Calculate the 12th term in the series:

$250 + (12-1)6 = 316.$

Step 2   Calculate Sn.

$$Sn = \frac{12}{2}(250 + 316)$$

$$= 6(566)$$

$$= 3,396 \text{ units}$$

3   GEOMETRICAL PROGRESSIONS

3.1   **Definition**   A geometrical progression is a series in which each term is found by multiplying the previous term by a constant number. The constant is known as the **common ratio**, eg:

(a)   1, 2, 4, 8, 16, ... common ratio =   2

(b) $\frac{1}{3}, \frac{1}{9}, \frac{1}{27}, \frac{1}{81}, \ldots$ common ratio = $\frac{1}{3}$

A geometrical progression may be written in general terms as:

A, AR, AR^2, AR^3, ... common ratio = R

the nth term is AR^{n-1}

The formula for calculating the sum of the first n terms of a geometrical progression is:

$$S_n = \frac{A(1 - R^n)}{1 - R} \quad \text{for R} < 1$$

$$S_n = \frac{A(R^n - 1)}{R - 1} \quad \text{for R} > 1$$

(The formulae are essentially the same, although they have been presented in ways that are convenient to use depending on the size of R).

3.2   **Example**

Calculate the sixth term and sum of the first six terms of the series:

5, 2.5, 1.25 . . .

3.3   **Solution**

Here   A   =   5

R   =   0.5

Hence 6th term   = $5 \times (0.5)^5$

= 5×0.03125 = 0.15625

$$S_6 = \frac{5 \times (1 - 0.5^6)}{(1 - 0.5)}$$

$$= \frac{5 \times (1 - 0.015625)}{0.5}$$

=   9.84375

3.4   Activity

Calculate the 10th term and the sum of the first 10 numbers of the following series.

5, 7.5, 11.25, . . .

3.5   Activity solution

A	=	5
R	=	1.5

The 10th term $= AR^{10-1}$

$\qquad\qquad = 5 \times 1.5^9$

$\qquad\qquad = 192.22$

The sum of the first ten terms $= \dfrac{A(R^n - 1)}{R - 1}$

$$= \frac{5 \times (1.5^{10} - 1)}{1.5 - 1}$$

$$= \frac{5 \times (56.665)}{0.5} = \frac{283.325}{0.5}$$

$$= 566.65$$

3.6   Summing an infinite geometrical progression

Where the series is infinite it may still have a finite sum. This will only occur if $-1 < R < +1$. (NB if this is the case then each term in the series is smaller than the last, although of itself this latter condition is not a sufficient condition to give a finite result.)

Substituting back into the formula given above gives:

$$S_\infty = \frac{A(1 - R^\infty)}{(1 - R)} \quad \text{where } \infty \text{ means infinity.}$$

but if $-1 < R < +1$, as n gets larger, R^n gets smaller, hence R^∞ becomes zero,

$$\therefore \quad S_\infty = \frac{A}{1 - R}$$

This formula will be important in your later studies and should be learnt.

3.7   Example

Calculate the sum to infinity of the following series:

(a) $\dfrac{8}{3} + \dfrac{4}{9} + \dfrac{2}{27} \ldots$

(b) $5 - 1 + \dfrac{1}{5} \ldots$

3.8   Solution

(a) $A = \dfrac{8}{3}$, $R = \dfrac{4/9}{8/3} = \dfrac{4}{9} \times \dfrac{3}{8} = \dfrac{1}{6}$

$S = \dfrac{8/3}{(1 - \frac{1}{6})}$

$= \dfrac{8/3}{5/6}$

$= \dfrac{16}{5} = 3.2$

(b) $A = 5$, $R = \dfrac{-1}{5}$

$S = \dfrac{5}{(1 - (-\frac{1}{5}))}$

$= \dfrac{5}{(\frac{6}{5})}$

$= \dfrac{25}{6} = 4.167$

3.9   Activity

Calculate the sum to infinity of the following series

8, –1, 1/8,...

3.10   Activity solution

$A = 8$

$R = \dfrac{-1}{8}$

$S_{\infty} = \dfrac{A}{1-R} = \dfrac{8}{1 - (\frac{-1}{8})} = \dfrac{8}{\frac{9}{8}} = \dfrac{64}{9} = 7\frac{1}{9}$ or 7.11

4   SUMMARY

Arithmetic progressions:

The 'nth' term is $a + (n-1)d$

The sum of the first 'n' terms is $\dfrac{n}{a}[2a + (n-1)d]$

Geometric progressions:

The 'nth' term is AR^{n-1}

The sum of the first 'n' terms   is $\dfrac{A(1-R^n)}{1-R}$ for $R < 1$

or $\dfrac{A(R^n-1)}{R-1}$ for $R > 1$

The sum to infinity is $\dfrac{A}{1-R}$ for $-1 < R < 1$

5   INTRODUCTION TO SIMPLE AND COMPOUND INTEREST

5.1   Simple interest

When money is invested it earns interest; similarly when money is borrowed interest is payable. The sum of money invested or borrowed is known as the **principal**.

With simple interest, the interest is payable or recoverable each year but it is not added to the principal. For example, the interest payable (or receivable) on £100 at 15% pa for 1, 2 and 3 years will be £15, £30 and £45.

The usual notation is:

$I = Xrt$

where   X   =   initial sum invested/borrowed (principal)

r   =   interest rate % pa (expressed as a decimal; 15% = 0.15)

t   =   time in years

I   =   interest in £

5.2   Example

A man invests £160 on 1 January each year. On 31 December simple interest is credited at 12% but this interest is put in a separate account and does not itself earn any interest. Find the total amount standing to his credit on 31 December following his fifth payment of £160.

Year (1 January)	Investment (£)	Interest (31 December)
1	160	$\dfrac{12}{100} \times 160 = £19.20$
2	160 + 160 = 320	$\dfrac{12}{100} \times 320 = £38.40$
3	160 + 320 = 480	$\dfrac{12}{100} \times 480 = £57.60$
4	160 + 480 = 640	$\dfrac{12}{100} \times 640 = £76.80$
5	160 + 640 = 800	$\dfrac{12}{100} \times 800 = £96.00$
Total		£288.00

Total amount at 31 December, Year 5   =   £(800 + 288)   (Principal and simple interest)

=   £1,088

5.3   Activity

Calculate:

(a)   the total amount of interest if a lump sum of £5,000 is invested for 5 years at 12% per annum simple interest;

(b)   the rate pa of simple interest if the amount of interest over 10 years on £800 is £400.

5.4   Activity solution

(a) $X = £5,000, \; r = 0.12, \; t = 5$

$I = Xrt = 5,000 \times 0.12 \times 5 = £3,000$

(b) $X = £800, \; t = 10, \; I = £400$

$r = \dfrac{I}{Xt} = \dfrac{400}{800 \times 10} = 0.05$ or 5% pa

5.5   Compound interest

With compound interest, the interest is added each year to the principal and for the following year the interest is calculated on their sum. For example, the compound interest on £1,000 at 10% pa for four years is calculated as follows:

Year	Principal (£)	Interest (£)	Total amount (£)
1	1,000	$\dfrac{10}{100} \times 1,000 = 100$	$1,000 + 100 = 1,100$
2	1,100	$\dfrac{10}{100} \times 1,100 = 110$	$1,100 + 110 = 1,210$
3	1,210	$\dfrac{10}{100} \times 1,210 = 121$	$1,210 + 121 = 1,331$
4	1,331	$\dfrac{10}{100} \times 1,331 = 133.1$	$1,331 + 133.1 = 1,464.1$

An alternative way of writing this is now shown:

Year	Principal (£)	Total amount (£)			
1	1,000	$1,000(1 + 0.1)$			$= 1,100$
2	$1,000(1 + 0.1)$	$1,000(1 + 0.1)(1 + 0.1)$	$=$	$1,000(1 + 0.1)^2$	$= 1,210$
3	$1,000(1 + 0.1)^2$	$1,000(1 + 0.1)^2(1 + 0.1)$	$=$	$1,000(1 + 0.1)^3$	$= 1,331$
4	$1,000(1 + 0.1)^3$	$1,000(1 + 0.1)^3(1 + 0.1)$	$=$	$1,000(1 + 0.1)^4$	$= 1,464.1$

So the value (V) at the end of the nth year is given by:

$$V = X(1 + r)^n$$

So the amounts at the end of successive years form a geometrical progression with common ratio $(1 + r)$ ie,$(1 + r),(1 + r)^2,(1 + r)^3 \ldots$

5.6   Example

(a)   Calculate the compound interest on £624 at 4% pa for 10 years.

(b)   Find the sum of money which, if invested now at 5% pa compound interest, will be worth

£10,000 in 10 years' time.

5.7   Solution

(a)   Using $V = X(1 + r)^n$ with $X = £624$

$r = 0.04$

$n = 10$

then $V = £624 (1 + 0.04)^{10}$

$= £624 (1.04)^{10}$

$= £923.67$

So the compound interest $= £(923.67 - 624)$

$= £299.67$

(b)   Using $V = (1 + r)^n$ with $V = £10,000$

$r = 0.05$

$n = 10$

then $£10,000 = X(1 + 0.05)^{10}$

$X = \dfrac{£10,000}{(1.05)^{10}}$

$X = £6,139.13$

So £6,139.13 is the necessary sum of money.

5.8   Example

A country's population at the end of each year is greater by 2% than at the beginning of the year. Calculate the number of years required for the population to double.

Although this question is concerned with population rather than money it is still a *compounding* problem and the same basic formula can be adapted.

Using $V = X(1 + r)^n$ with $X =$ present population, p say
$V =$ double population, 2p

$r = 0.02$

$2p = p(1 + 0.02)^n$

$\therefore \quad 2p = p(1.02)^n$

$2 = (1.02)^n$ (Dividing both sides by p)

This type of equation can be solved in two ways:

(a)   With a calculator powers of 1.02 can be multiplied out until the appropriate power corresponding to an answer of 2 is found.

This is rather a tedious and inaccurate method.

(b)   It is necessary to take logs of both sides of the equation. This has the effect of bringing the index, n, down on to the line.

$$2 \ = \ 1.02^n$$

$$\therefore \quad \log 2 = \ \log(1.02^n)$$

$$\log 2 = \ n \log 1.02$$

From log tables $0.3010 \ = \ n \times 0.0086$

$$\therefore \quad n \ = \ \frac{0.3010}{0.0086}$$

$$n \ = \ 35$$

Do not take the antilog as the log tables have not been used for any multiplication or division - merely as a device to obtain n.

This method is always used when the unknown is an index (a power).

5.9   Activity

In how many years will £1,000 amount to £3,207 at 6% pa compound interest?

5.10   Activity solution

Using $V \quad = \quad X(1+r)^n$ with $V \ = \ £3,207$

$$X \ = \ £1,000$$

$$r \ = \ 0.06$$

$$3,207 \ = \ 1,000 \times (1+0.06)^n$$

$$\frac{3,207}{1,000} \ = \ (1.06)^n$$

$$3.207 \ = \ 1.06^n$$

Taking logs of both sides gives: $\log 3.207 \ = \ \log(1.06^n)$

$$= \ n \log 1.06$$

From tables $\quad\quad\quad\quad 0.5060 \ = \ n \times 0.0253$

$$n \quad = \ \frac{0.5060}{0.0253}$$

$$n \quad = \ 20$$

5.11   Activity

Find the rate percent at which £552 amounts to £896 in 11 years at compound interest.

5.12   Activity solution

Using V = $X(1 + r)^n$ with V =   £896

X =   £552

n =   11

∴ 896 = $552 \times (1 + r)^{11}$

∴ $\dfrac{896}{552}$ = $(1 + r)^{11}$

1.623 = $(1 + r)^{11}$

∴ $\sqrt[11]{1.623}^{\,*}$ = $1 + r$

1.045 = $1 + r$

so r = $1.045 - 1$

r = 0.045

*Using logs

No	Log
1.623	0.2103
$\sqrt[11]{1.623}$	0.2103 ÷ 11
1.045	= 0.0191

So the rate of interest is $100 \times 0.045 = 4.5\%$

Note

The eleventh root can easily be obtained from an electronic calculator if it has an x^y or $x^{\frac{1}{y}}$ key making use of the fact that $\sqrt[11]{x} = x^{\frac{1}{11}}$.

If your calculator has an $x^{\frac{1}{y}}$ key put $y = 11$.

If it only has an x^y key, put $y = \dfrac{1}{11}$ $(= 0.090909)$

5.13   Annual percentage rate (APR)

For simplicity purposes previous compound interest examples have assumed that interest is calculated only once per year. However, this is not always the case, interest may be calculated on a monthly or even daily basis. The same formula can still be used, but there is a need to distinguish between the nominal and annual percentage rates.

There are usually two rates quoted by financial institutions, the first is the nominal rate, and the other, the rate actually earned, is known as the annual percentage rate (APR).

5.14   Example

A credit card company charges 3.5% interest per month. Assume a customer has purchased £100 worth of goods on his card and does not pay anything against this sum for a full year, calculate the amount he will owe after one year, and also the annual percentage rate (APR).

5.15   Solution

At the end of a 12 month period the amount which will be owed is:

$$V = X(1 + r)^n$$

where:
$$X = \text{original sum}$$
$$r = \text{interest rate}$$
$$n = \text{time period}$$
$$V = \text{amount at end of period}$$

So
$$100 \times (1 + 0.035)^{12} = £151.11$$

(Note that in the formula r is always expressed as a decimal, hence 3.5% is expressed as 0.035.)

The APR (which we shall call r_1 to avoid confusion with the r above) is therefore:

$$100 \times (1 + r_1) = 151.11$$

Hence:
$$100\, r_1 = 51.11$$

$$r_1 = 0.5111 = 51.11\%.$$

The APR is 51.11%.

5.16   Compound depreciation

If a machine costs £1,000 and depreciates in value by 10% per annum on written down value, its value in successive years is shown in the following table (all values in £).

Year	Amount of depreciation			Depreciated value		
0				1,000		
1	10% of 1,000	=	100	1,000 – 100	=	900
2	10% of 900	=	90	900 – 90	=	810
3	10% of 810	=	81	810 – 81	=	729
4	10% of 729	=	72.90	729 – 72.90	=	656.10

etc.

This is known as the **reducing balance** method of depreciation, as distinct from 'straight line' depreciation, which is depreciation by the same amount each year on cost (rather than on written down value.)

Compound depreciation is similar to compound interest except that instead of adding interest, we subtract depreciation. The law is therefore:

$$D = X(1 - r)^n \qquad \text{where} \qquad$$
$$D = \text{the depreciated value}$$
$$X = \text{the initial value}$$
$$r = \text{rate of depreciation}$$
$$n = \text{number of periods}$$

5.17   Activity

A new machine costs £5,000 and is depreciated by 8% per annum. What is the book value of the new machine when it is five years old?

5.18   Activity solution

$X = £5,000$

$r = 8\% = \dfrac{8}{100} = 0.08$

$n = 5$

$$
\begin{aligned}
D &= X(1-r)^n \\
&= £5,000 \times (1-0.08)^5 \\
&= £5,000 \times 0.6591 \\
&= £3,295
\end{aligned}
$$

5.19   Activity

A new machine costs £8,000 and has a useful life of ten years, after which it can be sold as scrap for £100. Calculate the annual rate of compound depreciation.

5.20   Activity solution

$D = £100$

$X = £8,000$

$n = 10$

So

$$100 = 8,000 (1-r)^{10}$$

$$(1-r)^{10} = \frac{100}{8,000} = 0.0125$$

$$(1-r) = \sqrt[10]{0.0125}$$

$$= 0.6452$$

$$r = 1 - 0.6452$$

$$= 0.3548 \text{ or } 35.48\%$$

Note: to find the 10th root, use the $x^{\frac{1}{y}}$ function on a calculator, putting y = 10. Alternatively, divide the logarithm of 0.0125 by 10 and take the anti-log.

5.21   Conclusion   Interest is not always calculated on an annual basis: it may be calculated daily, weekly, monthly, quarterly, half-yearly or at any other interval of time.

It is important that the rate of interest and the time are in compatible units.

For example, if the time is in months, then the rate of interest needs to be r% per month. If the time is in half-years, then the rate of interest must be r% per half-year.

As has already been shown, the general compounding formula can be applied to situations other than money problems.

For example, it can be applied to population statistics, index numbers or rates of increase and decrease generally.

5.22   Graphical representation

Consider £500 invested at 10% pa for 6 years at (a) simple interest and (b) compound interest.

(a) $I = 0.1 \times 500 = £50$ pa.

So the total amount at the end of the years 1 - 6 is:

Year	Principal and interest	Amount
1	500 + 50	£550
2	500 + 2 × 50	£600
3	500 + 3 × 50	£650
4	500 + 4 × 50	£700
5	500 + 5 × 50	£750
6	500 + 6 × 50	£800

(b)   Using $V = X(1 + r)^n$ to calculate the amount at the end of the nth year where n = 1, 2, 3, 4, 5, 6.

Year	Principal and interest	Amount
1	$500 (1 + 0.1)$	550
2	$500 (1 + 0.1)^2$	605
3	$500 (1 + 0.1)^3$	665.5
4	$500 (1 + 0.1)^4$	732.05
5	$500 (1 + 0.1)^5$	805.26
6	$500 (1 + 0.1)^6$	885.78

Showing these graphically gives the following:

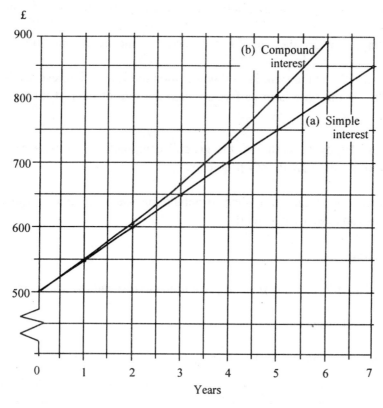

Notes on the graph

(a)   The simple interest graph is a straight line.

(b)   The compound interest graph is a curve.

(c)   At any point in time, after the end of the first year, the amount at compound interest is greater than that at simple interest.

(d)   The difference between these amounts becomes greater at later points in time.

5.23   Sinking fund

[Definition]   A sinking fund is money put aside periodically to settle a liability or replace an asset. The money is invested to produce a required sum at an appropriate time. **(CIMA Official Terminology).**

5.24   Example

£2,000 is invested at the end of each year for five years at 8% compound interest. What is the accumulated amount at the end of five years?

The first contribution to the fund will earn interest for four years, the second contribution for three years and so on. Summarising in a table:

Instalment	Amount (£)	Duration (yrs)	Accumulated amount (£)
1	2,000	4	$2,000 (1 + 0.08)^4$
2	2,000	3	$2,000 (1 + 0.08)^3$
3	2,000	2	$2,000 (1 + 0.08)^2$
4	2,000	1	$2,000 (1 + 0.08)^1$
5	2,000	0	2,000

The total amount in the fund at the end of the period is the sum of the values in the final column.

Thus, taking these from the bottom upwards:

Total $= 2,000 + 2,000(1 + 0.08) + 2,000(1 + 0.08)^2 + 2,000(1 + 0.08)^3 + 2,000(1 + 0.08)^4$

This is a geometrical progression with $A = 2,000$, $R = 1.08$, $n = 5$.

Hence the total is $\dfrac{A(R^n - 1)}{R - 1}$ (R is the common ratio of the GP)

$$= \frac{2,000 \times (1.08^5 - 1)}{1.08 - 1}$$

$$= \text{£}11,733$$

If the instalments are paid into the fund at the start of each year instead of the end, the first term will become $2,000 (1.08)^5$ and the last, $2,000(1.08)$. Each term is therefore increased by a factor 1.08, so that the total would then be £11,733 × 1.08 = £12,672.

5.25   Activity

Joe, saving to pay for his daughter's wedding in five years' time intends to save £400 each year in a building society account which will earn interest at 9% (effective rate).

How much will he have by then?

5.26   Activity solution

The question is ambiguous as to whether the final instalment will be saved immediately prior to the wedding or twelve months in advance.

Therefore, we may assume that the former is the case. If faced with such uncertainty in the exam, read the question again to check that the information is missing then STATE your assumption clearly. In total there will be six instalments and the amount saved will be:

$$S_n = \frac{A(R^n - 1)}{R - 1} \qquad \text{where} \quad A = \text{£}400,$$

$$R = 1.09,$$

$$n = 6$$

$$= \frac{\text{£}400 \times (1.09^6 - 1)}{1.09 - 1}$$

$$= \text{£}3,009$$

5.27   Activity

Charlotte, an ambitious young student accountant, has put her name down on the waiting list for a Morgan Plus 8 sports car. The delivery time is seven years and she expects the price to be £35,000 at that time.

How much does she need to invest annually in a savings account earning 11% pa in order to be able to buy the car outright at that time?

5.28   Activity solution

Rearranging the previous formula we have:

$$A = \frac{S_n(R-1)}{(R^n-1)} \quad \text{where} \quad S_n = \text{£35,000}$$

$$n = 8$$

$$R = 1.11$$

$$A = \frac{\text{£35,000} \times 0.11}{(1.11^8 - 1)} \quad \text{≤ 3108}$$

$$= \text{£2,951}$$

6   PRESENT VALUES AND DISCOUNTING

6.1   Discounting

Discounting is the reverse of compounding. It answers such questions as:

'I need £500 in two years time. How much will I need to invest now at 10% compound to achieve this'?

and

'I have been offered an investment opportunity requiring an immediate single outlay of £850. It will generate cash inflows of £388 per annum for the next three years. I will need to borrow the initial sum from the bank at 8%. Is it worthwhile?

The second of these will be considered later in the text.

Consider the first - we want to know the value of x where

$x(1.1)(1.1) = 500$, or $x(1.1)^2 = 500$

(this just uses the compound interest formula where V = 500, r = 0.1 and n = 2)

ie, $x = \dfrac{500}{(1.1)^2} = \text{£413}$ (to the nearest £)

Thus £413 will need to be invested for 2 years at 10% in order to yield £500.

£500 has been **discounted** to £413, which is known as its **present value**.

6.2   Present values

Definition   The present value is the cash equivalent now of a sum receivable or payable at a future date. **(CIMA Official Terminology).**

The general formula for the present value (PV) of an amount A receivable/payable in n years' time at a discount rate of r% (as a decimal) is:

$$PV = \frac{A}{(1+r)^n}$$

The present value (PV) of an amount A receivable in n years' time is thus defined as that amount that must be invested now at r% pa to accumulate to A at the expiry of n years.

6.3   Example

Calculate the present value of £2,000 at 10% pa for 1 year, 2 years, or 3 years.

1 year: $PV = \dfrac{2,000}{(1+0.1)} = \dfrac{2,000}{1.1} = £1,818.18$

2 years: $PV = \dfrac{2,000}{(1+0.1)^2} = \dfrac{2,000}{1.1^2} = £1,652.89$

3 years: $PV = \dfrac{2,000}{(1+0.1)^3} = \dfrac{2,000}{1.1^3} = £1,502.63$

This means that £1,818.18 must be invested now to yield £2,000 in one year's time, £1,652.89 must be invested now to yield £2,000 in two years' time, etc.

6.4   The use of PV tables

Because discounting is so widely used in business problems, present value (PV) tables are available to shortcut the computations. A PV table is included at the start of this text (Table 11).

This table provides a value (the 'discount factor') for a range of years and discount rates. Thus, the discount factor is the factor by which the future sum (A) is multiplied to get its present value:

$$\frac{1}{(1+r)^n}$$

where r is the discount rate
        n is the number of years

In this table, the values are to three decimal places. This involves some rounding and loss of accuracy, but is adequate for most purposes.

Students should note the time scale:

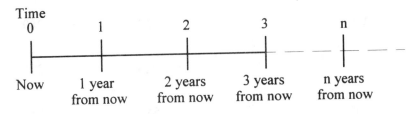

(the discount factor for time 0 is always 1, so this is not included in the table)

Calculations involving discounting using PV tables are best laid out in tabular form.

6.5   Example

Calculate the present value of the given cash flows using a 15% discount rate.

Time	Cash flow £	Discount factor	PV £
0	(60,000)	1.000	(60,000)
1	(10,000)	0.870	(8,700)
2	15,000	0.756	11,340
3	20,000	0.658	13,160
4	20,000	0.572	11,440
5	20,000	0.497	9,940
6	20,000	0.432	8,640

The above cash flows may represent the outflows and inflows of a particular investment project - this will be taken up later.

Finally, it should be noted that some electronic calculators now directly calculate present values. Any reasonable scientific calculator, an essential tool in the exam, can calculate $(1+r)^{-n}$ quickly. If these are used in the examination, students should show all their workings, as in the above table, except that there will be no PV factors; it is important to state that a calculator has been used to obtain the present values.

6.6   Annuities

> **Definition**   An annuity is a fixed periodic payment which continues either for a specified time, or until the occurrence of a specified event. **(CIMA Official Terminology).**

A ground rent is an example of an annuity, the holder of the freehold receiving an annual payment for the number of years specified in the lease.

Annuities and ground rent are constantly being bought and sold and the method of present values can be used to calculate a fair price for the transaction.

6.7   Example

Find the present value of an annuity of £300 for 5 years, using compound interest at 4% pa, the first receipt being in one year's time.

This can be tackled using the simple discount factor identified in the previous section using the tabular approach; the factors can either be calculated directly or taken from the tables:

Time	Cash flow £	Discount factor	PV £
1	300	$\dfrac{1}{(1.04)^1} = 0.962$	289
2	300	$\dfrac{1}{(1.04)^2} = 0.925$	277
3	300	$\dfrac{1}{(1.04)^3} = 0.889$	267
4	300	$\dfrac{1}{(1.04)^4} = 0.855$	256
5	300	$\dfrac{1}{(1.04)^5} = 0.822$	247
Total present value			1,336

This means that if £1,336 were invested now at a compound rate of 4%, the investor would be able to withdraw £300 a year for 5 years (at the end of which the investment would be down to nil). You can check this for yourself.

This type of calculation can get quite time-consuming, especially if the annuity continues for a lifetime! A quicker way is by the use of *annuity factors* or *cumulative discount factors*, which can again be obtained from a formula or from tables.

6.8   Annuity factor formula

The calculation in the table above could be written as:

$$\text{Total PV} = \frac{300}{1.04} + \frac{300}{(1.04)^2} + \frac{300}{(1.04)^3} + \frac{300}{(1.04)^4} + \frac{300}{(1.04)^5}$$

These terms form a GP with $A = \frac{300}{1.04}$, $R = \frac{1}{1.04}$ and $n = 5$

$$\text{Using } S_n = \frac{A(1-R^n)}{1-R}$$

$$= \frac{\frac{300}{1.04}\left(1-\left(\frac{1}{1.04}\right)^5\right)}{\left(1-\frac{1}{1.04}\right)}$$

This can be shown to rearrange to:

$$300\left[\frac{1}{0.04} - \frac{1}{0.04(1.04)^5}\right]$$

The expression in the square brackets represents the sum of the first five years' simple discount factors at 4%, with a value of 4.452.

Thus the Total PV may be calculated as:

$300 \times 4.452 = £1,336$, as above.

The general formula for the annuity discount factor, which is given in the Mathematical Tables, can be seen from the above to be:

$$\frac{1}{r} - \frac{1}{r(1+r)^t}$$

where r = discount rate (as a decimal)
       t = number of years for which the annuity continues

6.9   Annuity (cumulative) factor tables

The annuity or cumulative discount factors for a range of values of r and t are given in Table 12, which can be found at the front of this text (t is denoted as n).

For $n = 5$, $r = 4\%$ cumulative factor from table = 4.452 as before. Cumulative factors are sometimes denoted as a $n\overline{}r$ where a = annuity (n, r as before). Thus:

$$a\,5\overline{}\,0.04 = 4.452$$

6.10   Activity

Calculate the amount to be invested now at 6% pa to provide an annuity of £5,000 pa for ten years commencing in five years time.

6.11   Activity solution

The first income payment will be received at the end of five years from now and has a present value of $\frac{£5,000}{(1.06)^5}$.

The second payment has a present value of $\frac{£5,000}{(1.06)^6}$, etc.

The total PV of the ten payments will therefore be:

$$PV = 5,000\left[\frac{1}{(1.06)^5}+\frac{1}{(1.06)^6}+\frac{1}{(1.06)^7}+.....+\frac{1}{(1.06)^{14}}\right]$$

The terms inside the square brackets can be regarded as the cumulative PV of £1 for the first fourteen years minus the cumulative PV of £1 for the **first four** years. It is worthwhile checking that years 5 to 14 inclusive correspond to years 1 to 14 less years 1 to 4. Thus:

$$PV = £5,000 \times [9.295 - 3.465] \text{ (from the tables)}$$
$$= £29,150$$

6.12   Amortisation

Definition   The term amortisation can be used to mean the repaying of a debt by regular instalments as with a mortgage. Such repayments consist partly of interest and partly repayment of some of the loan. The amount of each instalment remains constant, but as the amount of the outstanding debt decreases, the proportion of the instalment which goes to paying the interest decreases, and the proportion which goes to paying off the outstanding debt increases.

From the point of view of the lender (mortgagee) it is equivalent to an annuity. He invests a lump sum in the borrower (mortgager) and receives a regular income in return.

6.13   Example

To find the annual repayment on a building society loan of £40,000 over five years at 12% pa.

This is equivalent to an annual income derived from an investment of £40,000.

Let the amount of each repayment = £A.

The first repayment is made at the end of the first year, the second at the end of the second year, and so on, so that:

$$£40,000 = \text{Present value of all repayments}$$
$$= A\left[\frac{1}{1.12^1}+\frac{1}{1.12^2}+\frac{1}{1.12^3}+\frac{1}{1.12^4}+\frac{1}{1.12^5}\right]$$
$$= A \times 3.605 \text{ (from cumulative PV table)}$$
$$\therefore A = \frac{40,000}{3.605}$$
$$= £11,096$$

The correctness of the result can be demonstrated by following through each transaction:

Year	Debt b/f	Interest	Debt & interest	Repaid	Debt c/f
	£	£	£	£	£
1	40,000	4,800	44,800	11,096	33,704
2	33,704	4,044	37,748	11,096	26,652
3	26,652	3,198	29,850	11,096	18,754
4	18,754	2,250	21,004	11,096	9,908
5	9,908	1,189	11,097	11,096	1

Thus the debt has been cleared by the end of the fifth year. The small residue of £1 is due to the use of tables which only run to 3 decimal places and rounding errors in the calculations. You could rework the calculations using the formula for the sum of a GP to find the cumulative discount factor as 3.6048 to get more accuracy.

6.14   Activity

What is the annual repayment on a bank loan of £50,000 over eight years at 9% pa.?

6.15   Activity solution

Let annual repayment be A.

Present value of 8 repayments of A at 9% = £50,000.

A × 5.535   =   £50,000

∴ A   =   £9,033

Note: as the calculations in 6.12 show, there is no point in stating results to the nearest penny since the tables do not allow for that accuracy.

6.16   Perpetuities

Definition   A perpetuity is a periodic payment continuing for a limitless period. **(CIMA Official Terminology).**

Referring back to the formula for the annuity discount factor:

$$\frac{1}{r} - \frac{1}{r(1+r)^t}$$

if t gets very large (tends to infinity) the second term gets very small, and will be zero at t = infinity.

Thus the perpetuity discount factor is $\dfrac{1}{r}$

6.17   Activity

How much need to be invested now at 5% to yield an annual income of £4,000 in perpetuity?

6.18   Activity solution

The PV of the perpetuity is £4,000 × $\dfrac{1}{0.05}$ = £80,000

If £80,000 is invested now at 5%, £4,000 could be withdrawn each year indefinitely (this represents the withdrawal of the annual interest, ie 5% of £80,000 = £4,000).

6.19   The relevance of discounting to business problems

One of the difficulties in many business problems is to evaluate, on a common scale, cash flows occurring at different points in time. Since businesses normally are either borrowing or lending money, interest is the cost/benefit to the business of cash at different points in time. Therefore, discounting provides a method of adjusting cash flows to a common base through the device of the notional interest charges.

For this reason discounting is widely used for financial evaluations, especially of new capital investment projects.

6.20   Example

We return to the problem posed at the beginning of this section.

An investment opportunity is available which requires a single cash outlay of £850. Cash inflows of £388 will then arise at twelve month intervals for three years commencing in one year's time.

Bank overdraft finance is available at 8% pa.

You are required

(a)   to show the movement on the firm's bank account assuming that all cash flows associated with the project are paid into or out of the overdraft account;

(b)   to compute the net terminal value of the project;

(c)   to compute the net present value of the project;

(d)   to comment upon your results and show the relationship between the numerical solutions derived in (a), (b) and (c).

Solution

(a)

Beginning of year	Opening balance £	Interest @ 8% £	Less repayments £	Closing balance £	End of year
1	(850)	(68)	388	(530)	1
2	(530)	(42)	388	(184)	2
3	(184)	(15)	388	189	3

Closing balance is £189 in hand.

(b)   **Net terminal value**

The net terminal value of a project is equal to the net amount of all the cash flows associated with the project compounded forward to the end of the project's life.

Time	Cash flow	Compounding factor	Terminal value £
*0	(850)	$1.08^3 = 1.26$*	(1,071)
1	388	$1.08^2 = 1.17$	453
2	388	$1.08^1 = 1.08$	419
3	388	$1.08^0 = 1.00$	388
			189

* For convenience, in almost all investment appraisal methods cash flows are assumed to arise at twelve monthly intervals, at the end of an integral number of years. By convention, 'now' is denoted as time 0 (the end of year 0, the beginning of year 1); twelve months' time is the end of year 1, the beginning of year 2 or, more particularly, time 1, and so on.

Although only 2 decimal places are shown it is worth using the figure that your calculator produces for 1.08^3 (1.259712) but then round the result for the terminal value (1,070.7552) to the nearest whole number.

(c)   **Net present value**

The net present value of a project is the net amount of all cash flows associated with the project discounted back to the beginning of the project.

The neatest way to lay out the problem is to use the table seen in 6.5.

Year	Cash flow £	PV factor @ 8%	Present value £
0	(850)	1.000	(850)
1	388	0.926	359
2	388	0.857	333
3	388	0.794	308

Net present value £150

(d)   As can be seen from (a) and (b), the net terminal value of the project is also equivalent to the net amount which would be in the bank if all cash flows associated with the project were paid into/out of a single bank account. Both of these are positive - ie, there will be money left over after meeting all interest charges. Thus the project is worth considering.

The net present value (NPV) of £150 is related to the net terminal value (NTV) of £189 by:

$$£150 = \frac{£189}{(1.08)^3}$$

ie, $$NPV = \frac{NTV}{(1+r)^3}$$

= the present value of the net terminal value.

It follows that if the NTV is positive, then the NPV will be also. Thus a positive NPV indicates a worthwhile investment.

6.21   Internal rate of return

For so-called conventional projects, that is those where a single cash outflow is followed by subsequent cash inflows, it is often useful to compute the internal rate of return (IRR) of the project. This indicates the maximum discount rate at which the project is still worthwhile (positive NPV).

> **Definition**   The internal rate of return is the annual percentage return achieved by a project, at which the sum of the discounted cash inflows over the life of the project is equal to the sum of the discounted cash outflows. **(CIMA Official Terminology).**

In general, it is necessary to compute the IRR by trial and error, that is to compute NPVs at various discount rates until the discount rate is found which gives an NPV of zero.

6.22   Example

Find the IRR of the project in the example above.

Solution

The NPV was computed at 8% and found to be £150. Our next estimate of the discount rate must be greater than 8% since the larger the discount rate, the lower the present value of future cash receipts. Initially, try 15%; and since the 3 amounts of £388 represent an annuity, we can reduce the size of our calculation.

Year	Cash flow £	Discount factor @ 15%	Present value £
0	(850)	1.000	(850)
1 – 3	388	2.283	886
Net present value			36

The NPV of £36 is lower than previously computed but still positive.

Therefore, increase the discount rate again a little more to say 20%:

Time	Cash flow £	PV factor @ 20%	Present value £
0	(850)	1.000	(850)
1 – 3	388	2.106	817
Net present value			£(33)

The IRR lies between 15% and 20%. A closer estimate can be found by linear interpolation.

If   A is the lower discount rate (15%)
B is the higher discount rate (20%)
N_A is the NPV at rate A (£36)
N_B is the NPV at rate B (– £33)

The IRR is given by:

$$\text{IRR} \approx A + \left(\frac{N_A}{N_A - N_B}\right) \times (B - A)$$

Note that this is only an approximate relationship (as will be shown later). Also note that N_B is negative, which means that care must be taken with the signs.

$$\text{IRR} \approx 15 + \left(\frac{36}{36-(-33)} \right) \times 5$$

$$\approx 17.6\%.$$

Since this is only an approximate relationship there is no point in quoting several decimal places. Even the first decimal place is suspect, 17½% might be more appropriate. The result could be found more accurately if two discount rates closer to 17½% were used.

6.23   Investment decisions

It is now possible to develop criteria for accepting or rejecting investment opportunities. Consider the situation where management can acquire funds at a known rate of interest and are considering whether to accept or reject an investment project. There are two possible approaches:

(a)   **Internal rate of return approach** – is the IRR on the project greater than the borrowing rate? - if so, accept.

(b)   **Net present value (NPV) approach** – at the borrowing rate, is present value of cash inflows, less initial cash outflows (ie, the net present value) positive? - if so, accept.

6.24   Activity

An initial investment of £2,000 in a project yields cash inflows of £500, £500, £600, £600 and £440 at 12 monthly intervals. There is no scrap value. Funds are available to finance the project at 12%.

You are required to decide whether the project is worthwhile, using:

(a)   Net present value approach.

(b)   Internal rate of return approach.

6.25   Activity solution

(a)   **Net present value approach**

Year	Cash flow	Discount factor @ 12%	Present value
	£		£
0	(2,000)	1.000	(2,000)
1	500	0.893	447
2	500	0.797	399
3	600	0.712	427
4	600	0.636	382
5	440	0.567	249
Net present value			£(96)

Since the present value is negative, the project should be rejected.

(b)   **Internal rate of return approach**

Calculating IRR requires a trial and error approach. Since it has already been calculated in (a) that NPV at 12% is negative, it is necessary to decrease the discount rate to bring the NPV towards zero - try 8%.

Year	Cash flow	Discount factor @ 8%	Present value @ 8%
	£		£
0	(2,000)	1.000	(2,000)
1	500	0.926	463
2	500	0.857	429
3	600	0.794	476
4	600	0.735	441
5	440	0.681	300
Net present value			+109

Thus, the IRR lies between 8% and 12%. We may estimate it by interpolation:

$$\text{IRR} \approx A + \frac{N_A}{N_A - N_B} \times (B - A)$$

$$\approx 8\% + \left(\frac{109}{109 - (-96)}\right) \times (12\% - 8\%)$$

$$\approx 8\% + \left(\frac{109}{109 + 96}\right) \times 4\%$$

$$\approx 10.13\%$$

The formula produces an IRR of 10%. *Note:* however, that a linear relationship is assumed between discount rates and NPV. This is not accurate and, in fact, the actual rate of return is somewhat lower at almost exactly 10%. We can conclude that the project should be rejected, ie, the same conclusion as in (a) above, because the IRR (10.13%) is less than the cost of capital to finance the project (12%).

6.26   Relationship between IRR, NPV and discount rate

Example

Using the data in the previous activity, calculate additionally the NPV at 0%, 5% and 20%. Plot these, plus those already calculated, on a graph of net present value (y axis) against discount rate (x axis).

Solution

Year	Cash flow (= PV @ 0%)	Discount factor @ 5%	PV @ 5%	Discount factor @ 20%	PV @ 20%
	£		£		£
0	(2,000)	1.000	(2,000)	1.000	(2,000)
1	500	0.952	476	0.833	417
2	500	0.907	454	0.694	347
3	600	0.864	518	0.579	347
4	600	0.823	494	0.482	289
5	440	0.784	345	0.402	177
NPV	640		287		(423)

Graph of NPV against discount rate

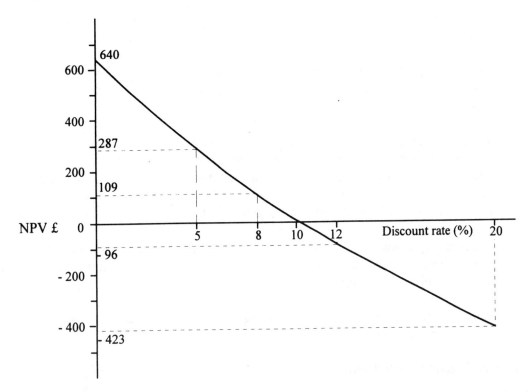

The graph shows that the higher the discount rate, the lower the NPV. Where the NPV is zero (ie, cuts the x-axis), then we may read off the IRR.

Note that the 'curve' is nearly, but not quite, a straight line.

Thus, if a 'cut-off discount rate' is selected (eg, the borrower's rate) of 12%, using the NPV criterion, we see that the NPV is negative; using the IRR criterion the x axis is cut at a lower discount rate than 12%. Either way the project is rejected.

7   FURTHER POINTS IN PROJECT APPRAISAL

7.1   Why cash flows rather than profits

(a)   **Cash is what ultimately counts** - profits are only a guide to cash availability, they cannot actually be spent.

(b)   **Profit measurement is subjective** - which time period income or expenses are recorded in, and so on.

(c)   **Cash is used to pay dividends** - the ultimate method of transferring wealth to equity investors.

Students should note that in practice the cash flows of a project are likely to be similar to the project's effects on profits. Major differences will be:

(a)   Changes in working capital; and

(b)   Asset purchase and depreciation.

7.2   Problems in establishing which cash flows are relevant

(a)   **Considering all alternatives** - any project becomes attractive if it is compared with a sufficiently bad alternative.

(b)   **Opportunity costs** - if a project occupies premises which could otherwise be let at £1,000 pa, then that £1,000 pa could be regarded as a cash outflow (in fact it is a cash inflow forgone).

(c)   **Interest payments** - since the analysis is based on discounting, it would be double counting to include the interest payments of the finance used to fund the project in the cash flows. Interest payments arise because money has a time value and it is precisely this time value which discounting/compounding is designed to account for. The only exception is when debt finance is raised specifically in connection with the acquisition of a particular asset.

(d)   **Taxation payments** - are a cash outflow when they are paid; savings in tax payments through capital allowances or tax losses may be treated as cash receipts at the point in time when they reduce a tax payment.

(e)   **Scrap or terminal proceeds** - where any equipment used in a project is scrapped, then the proceeds are a cash inflow.

7.3   Absolute and relative cash flows

When deciding between two projects (known as **mutually exclusive projects**) two approaches are possible.

(a)   Discount the cash flows of each project separately and compare NPVs; or

(b)   Find the **differential** cash flow year by year, ie, the **difference** between the cash flows of the two projects. Then discount those differential cash flows.

Either approach will give us the same conclusion, although the second is only valid if you know that you **must** adopt one of the **two** projects.

7.4   Example

Two projects A and B, are under consideration. Either A or B, but not both, may be accepted. The relevant discount rate is 10%. You are required to recommend A or B by:

(a)   discounting each cash flow separately, and
(b)   discounting relative (or differential) cash flows.

The cash flows are as follows:

Year	A	B
	£	£
0	(1,500)	(2,500)
1	500	500
2	600	800
3	700	1,100
4	500	1,000
5	NIL	500

Solution

(a) **Discounting each cash flow separately**

Year	Discount factor at 10%	Project A Cash flow	Project A PV of cash flow	Project B Cash flow	Project B PV of cash flow
		£	£	£	£
0	1.000	(1,500)	(1,500)	(2,500)	(2,500)
1	0.909	500	455	500	455
2	0.826	600	496	800	661
3	0.751	700	526	1,100	826
4	0.683	500	341	1,000	683
5	0.621	NIL	NIL	500	311
NPV's			£318		£436

Project B is preferred because its NPV exceeds that of A by £(436 – 318) = £118.

(b) **Discounting relative cash flows**

Year	Project A	Project B	Relative cash flow B – A	Discount factor at 10%	PV of relative cash flow
0	(1,500)	(2,500)	(1,000)	1.000	(1,000)
1	500	500	NIL	0.909	NIL
2	600	800	200	0.826	165
3	700	1,100	400	0.751	300
4	500	1,000	500	0.683	342
5	NIL	500	500	0.621	311
NPV of relative cash flow					£118

In other words, the net present value of the cash flows of project B are £118 more than those of project A. B is preferred. *Note* the result is exactly the same in (a) and (b). This gives a useful shortcut to computation when comparing two projects.

(However, method (b), whilst indicating that B is better than A, does not indicate that either are worthwhile. B may simply be less bad than A.)

8 CHAPTER SUMMARY

This chapter has considered both arithmetic and geometric progressions and their relationships with simple and compound interest.

The principles of compound interest have then been used to discount future cash flows and thereby evaluate investment projects.

9 SELF TEST QUESTIONS

9.1 What is the formula for the nth term of an arithmetic progression? (2.1)

9.2 What is meant by simple interest? (5.1)

9.3 What is compound interest? (5.5)

9.4 What is a sinking fund? (5.23)

9.5 Explain the meaning of 'present value'. (6.2)

9.6   What is an annuity? (6.6)

9.7   What is the meaning of 'net present value'? (6.20)

9.8   Explain the meaning of 'internal rate of return'. (6.21)

9.9   Explain the relationship between IRR, NPV and the discount rate. (6.26)

10   EXAMINATION TYPE QUESTIONS

10.1   Sum of a series

(a)   Find the 20th term and the sum of 20 terms of the series

20, 17.5, 15 . . .

(b)   Find the number of terms in an arithmetic progression whose first term is 2, common difference is 6 and sum is 420.

(c)   Find the 10th term, sum of ten terms and the sum to infinity of the series

3, 1.2, 0.48 . . .

(15 marks)

10.2   Cash flows for projects A and B

The cash flows for two projects are expected to be as follows:

Project A		Project B	
Time	*Cash flow* £'000	*Time*	*Cash flow* £'000
0	−25	0	−25
1	10	1	0
2	10	2	5
3	10	3	10
4	10	4	30

(a)   Use present value tables or first principles to compute the present values for each project at discount rates of 10%, 20%, 30% and 40%.

(b)   Plot the two sets of points on a single sheet of graph paper, and join the two sets of points to produce two smooth curves.

(c)   Use the graphs to read off the internal rate of return for the two projects.

(20 marks)

11   ANSWERS TO EXAMINATION TYPE QUESTIONS

11.1   Sum of series

(a)   20th term   = $a + 19d$ where $a = 20$; $d = -2.5$

= $20 + 19 \times (-2.5)$

= -27.5

$$S_{20} = \frac{n}{2}[2a + (n-1)d] \quad \text{where } n = 20$$

$$= \frac{20}{2}[2 \times 20 + 19 \times (-2.5)]$$

$$= -75$$

(b)   Using the S_n formula,

$$420 = \frac{n}{2}[2 \times 2 + (n-1) \times 6]$$

multiplying by 2 and multiplying out the inner bracket:

$$840 = n[4 + 6n - 6]$$

$$= 4n + 6n^2 - 6n$$

$$= 6n^2 - 2n$$

$$\therefore 6n^2 - 2n - 840 = 0$$

Solving by the quadratic formula:

$$n = \frac{+2 \pm \sqrt{2^2 - 4 \times 6 \times -(840)}}{2 \times 6}$$

$$= \frac{2 \pm \sqrt{4 + 20,160}}{12} = \frac{2 \pm 142}{12}$$

$$= 12 \text{ or } -11.67$$

As a fractional or negative number of terms is not admissible, the number of terms is 12.

(c)   10th term $= AR^9$ where $A = 3$; $R = 0.4$

$$= 3 \times (0.4)^9$$

$$= 0.0007864$$

$$S_{10} = \frac{A(1 - R^{10})}{1 - R}$$

$$= \frac{3 \times (1 - 0.4^{10})}{1 - 0.4}$$

$$= 4.999$$

$$S_\infty = \frac{A}{1-R}$$

$$= \frac{3}{1-0.4}$$

$$= 5$$

Note: to evaluate $(0.4)^9$ and $(0.4)^{10}$, use the x^y function on your calculator.

11.2   Cash flows for projects A and B

(a)

Project A

Cash flow £'000	Time	Present values			
		10%	20%	30%	40%
(25)	0	(25.0)	(25.0)	(25.0)	(25.0)
10	1 – 4	31.7	25.9	21.7	18.5
Net present value		6.7	0.9	(3.3)	(6.5)

Project B

Cash flow £'000	Time	Present values (£'000)			
		10%	20%	30%	40%
(25)	0	(25.00)	(25.00)	(25.00)	(25.00)
0	1	0.00	0.00	0.00	0.00
5	2	4.15	3.45	2.95	2.55
10	3	7.50	5.80	4.60	3.60
30	4	20.40	14.40	10.50	7.80
Net present value		7.05	(1.35)	(6.95)	(11.05)

(Tutorial note: The discount factors for 10% and 20% can be read directly from the PV tables, eg Project A at a discount rate of 10% has a PV of -25 + (3.170 × 10) = 6.7. For 30% and 40% the factors must be read from your calculator or calculated from first principles, eg Project B at a discount rate of 30% has a PV of $-25 + \frac{5}{(1.3)^2} + \frac{10}{(1.3)^3} + \frac{30}{(1.3)^4} = -6.95$.)

(b)

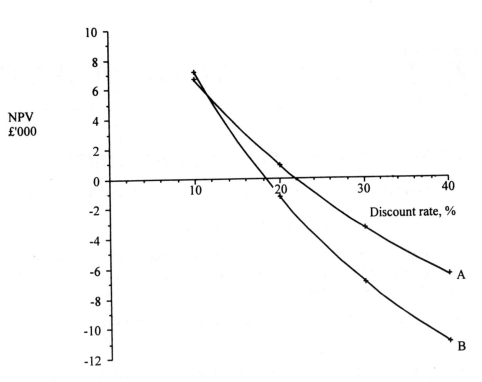

NPV
£'000

Discount rate, %

A

B

(c)   The internal rate of return is the point on the graph where the curve cuts the horizontal axis.   For Project A this is approximately 22%, and for Project B approximately 18%.

To obtain these values, graph paper must be used.

Note: for practice students may wish to calculate the approximate IRR by interpolation:

$$\text{IRR} \approx A + \left(\frac{N_A}{N_A - N_B}\right)(B - A)$$

Project A (using 20% & 30%)   Project B (using 10% & 20%)

$$20\% + (30\% - 20\%) \times \frac{0.9}{(0.9 - (3.3))} \qquad 10\% + (20\% - 10\%) \times \frac{7.05}{(7.05 - (1.35))}$$

$20\% + 0.214 \times 10\%$ $10\% + 0.839 \times 10\%$

$= \quad 22.1\%$ $= \quad 18.4\%$

The differences are due to the fact that the interpolation method assumes a straight line relationship between NPV and discount rate and also because it is difficult to plot and read the graph accurately.

27 CORRELATION AND REGRESSION

INTRODUCTION & LEARNING OBJECTIVES

Syllabus area 2h. Establishing a line of best fit, either by eye or regression. (Ability required 3).

Correlation. (Ability required 3).

This chapter is concerned with analysing the relationships between one data variable and another, and between data and the passage of time. This chapter will consider the techniques known as scatter diagrams, regression and correlation.

When you have studied this chapter you should be able to do the following:

- Prepare a scatter diagram and interpret it.
- Use regression to find the line of best fit between data variables.
- Distinguish between the regression lines of x on y and y on x.
- Calculate and explain the coefficient of correlation.
- Calculate and explain the coefficient of determination.
- Calculate and explain rank correlation.

---

1 SCATTER DIAGRAMS

1.1 Introduction

Information about two variables that are considered to be related in some way can be plotted on a scatter diagram, each axis representing one variable. For example, the amount of rainfall and the crop yield per acre could be plotted against each other, or the level of advertising expenditure against sales revenue of a product.

It is important, however, to decide which variable can be used to predict the other – ie, which is the **independent** and which the **dependent variable**. In many cases it is quite clear, eg, the amount of rainfall obviously causes a particular crop yield, and not vice-versa. Here, rainfall is the independent variable and crop yield the dependent variable, (ie, yield depends on the amount of rainfall). Some relationships have classic 'chicken and egg' characteristics; for example, advertising and sales revenue. Whether a given level of advertising causes a particular level of sales or whether a particular level of sales provokes a certain level of advertising is not quite so clear. In fact, advertising tends to **directly** affect sales levels whereas sales only have an indirect influence on decisions about advertising expenditure and therefore sales tends to be regarded as the dependent variable and advertising expenditure the independent variable.

The independent variable is usually marked along the horizontal (x) axis and the dependent variable up the vertical (y) axis.

Students are advised to think in terms of the x-axis being the cause, and the y-axis the effect.

The values of the two variables are plotted together so that the diagram consists of a number of points. The way in which these are scattered or dispersed indicates if any link is likely to exist between the variables.

For example:

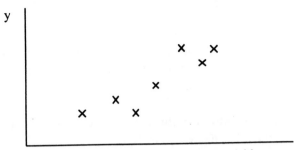

1.2   Correlation

One advantage of a scatter diagram is that it is possible to see quite easily if the points indicate that a relationship exists between the variables, ie, to see if any correlation exists between them.

It is not possible to establish how strong the relationship is (to measure the degree of correlation) from a scatter diagram. However, as will be seen later, there are methods of calculating a numerical value for this.

1.3   Types of correlation

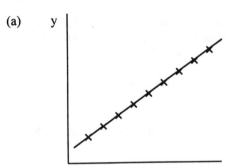

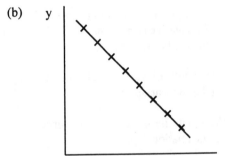

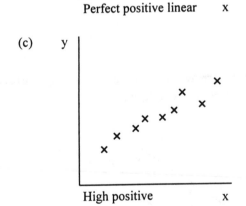

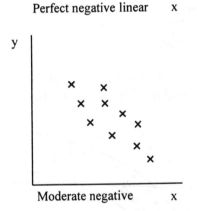

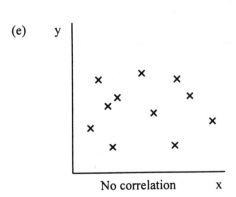

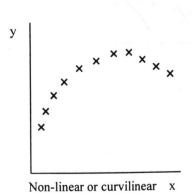

These six scatter diagrams illustrate some of the different types of correlation. Scatter graphs of non-linear correlation can assume many different types of curve.

If the points lie exactly on a straight line, then the correlation is said to be perfect linear correlation. In practice this rarely occurs and it is more usual for the points to be scattered in a band, the narrower the band the higher the degree of correlation.

Positive correlation exists where the values of the variables increase together. Negative correlation exists where one variable increases as the other decreases in value.

Thus, considering the six diagrams:

(a)   This is an example of perfect positive linear correlation since the points lie exactly on a straight line and as 'x' increases so 'y' increases.

(b)   This is an example of perfect negative linear correlation since the points again lie on a straight line, but as the x values increase so the y values decrease.

(c)   In this diagram, the points lie in a narrow band rather than on a straight line, but x and y still tend to increase together, therefore a high degree of positive correlation is evident.

(d)   This time the points lie in a much wider band and, as x increases, y tends to decrease, so this is an example of negative correlation where, because of the wider spread of the points than those in (c), the correlation is only moderate.

(e)   When the points are scattered all over the diagram, as in this case, then little or no correlation exists between the two variables.

(f)   Here the points lie on an obvious curve. There is a relationship between x and y, but it is not a straight line relationship.

2   REGRESSION

2.1   Linear correlation

When the points on a scatter diagram tend to lie in a narrow band, there is a strong correlation between the variables. This band may be curved or straight. For example:

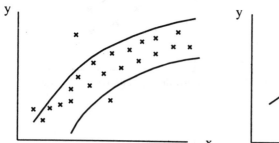 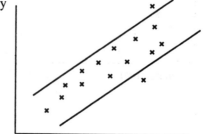

When the band is straight the correlation is linear and the relationship between the variables can be expressed in terms of the equation of a straight line. It is this type of correlation that will be studied throughout this chapter.

2.2   Line of best fit

To obtain a description of the relationship between two variables in the form of an equation in order to forecast values, it is necessary to fit a straight line through the points on the scatter diagram which best represents all of the plotted points. There are several ways of accomplishing this.

2.3   Establishing trend lines by eye

One method which can be used to fit a straight line through the points, is to fit it 'by eye'. To do this a line must be drawn, going directly through the centre of all the points. Obviously, the more correlated the points, the easier the line will be to draw. However this method does have the disadvantage that if there is a large amount of scatter, no two people's lines will coincide and it is, therefore, only suitable where the amount of scatter is only small.

2.4   Equation of a straight line

The equation for any straight line is of the form:

$$y = a + bx$$

where x and y are the variables and a and b are constants for the particular line in question.

a is called the **intercept** on the y-axis and measures the point at which the line will cut the y-axis.

b is called the **gradient** of the line and measures its degree of slope.

a and b can take any value, including zero, and may be positive or negative.

In order to locate any particular line, it is therefore necessary to determine the values of a and b for that line.

2.5   Parameters of a regression line by inspection

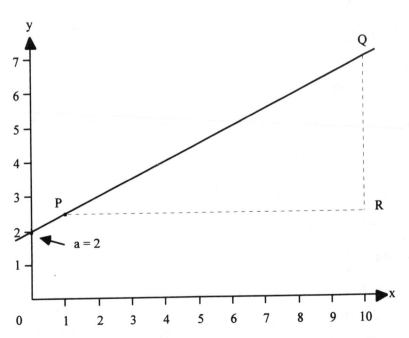

The diagram shows a line which has been fitted to a scatter graph by eye. The points of the scatter graph have been omitted for clarity. It is required to find the values of a and b for this line in the general equation y = a + bx.

Method

a is the intercept on the y-axis, ie, the value of y at which the line cuts the y-axis. Hence a = 2.

To find the slope, b, take any two points (P and Q) on the line.

The further apart P and Q are, the more accurate will be the result.

Draw horizontal and vertical lines through P and Q to meet at R.

The length of PR **as measured on the x-scale**   =   9 units

The length of RQ **as measured on the y-axis**   =   4.5 units

The slope $= \dfrac{RQ}{PR} = \dfrac{4.5}{9} = 0.5$, hence b = 0.5

The equation is therefore:

$$y = 2 + 0.5x$$

Note: that for this method, no part of the x-scale can be omitted, otherwise the vertical axis is not the true y-axis and the intercept will not be correct.

An alternative method which can be used if part of the x-scale needs to be omitted is to read off from the graph the values of x and y at P and Q, substitute these values into the general equation and solve the resulting simultaneous equations for a and b.

$$y = a + bx$$

at P,   x = 1,   y = 2.5, hence:

$$2.5 = a + b \times 1$$

ie,   a + b   =   2.5   .... (1)

at Q,   x = 10,   y = 7,   hence:

$$7 = a + b \times 10$$

ie,   a + 10b   =   7   .... (2)

Subtract (1) from (2) to eliminate *a*:

$$a + 10b = 7$$

$$a + b = 2.5$$

$$\overline{}$$

$$9b = 4.5$$

$$b = \frac{4.5}{9} = 0.5$$

Substitute in (1) to find a:

$$a + 0.5 = 2.5$$

$$a = 2.5 - 0.5$$

∴   a   =   2.0

Hence   a = 2.0 and   b = 0.5 as before.

2.6   **Least squares linear regression**

The method of least squares regression is the most mathematically acceptable method of fitting a line to a set of data.

It is possible to calculate two different regression lines for a set of data, depending on whether the horizontal deviations or the vertical deviations of the points from the line are considered. It is the sum of the **squares** of these deviations which is minimised; this overcomes problems that might arise because some deviations would be positive and some negative, depending on whether the point was above or below the line. It is not necessary to go into the theory of this method any more deeply at this level.

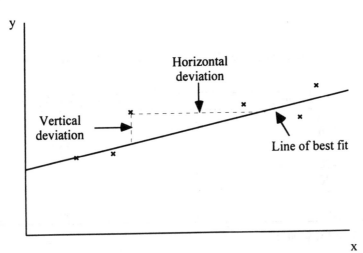

The regression line of y on x must be used when an estimate of y is required for a given value of x. This line minimises the sum of the squares of the vertical distances of the points from the line. The regression line of x on y must be used when an estimate of x is required for a known value of y. This line minimises the sum of the squares of the horizontal distances of the points from the line.

The scatter diagram has the following appearance when the regression lines are graphed:

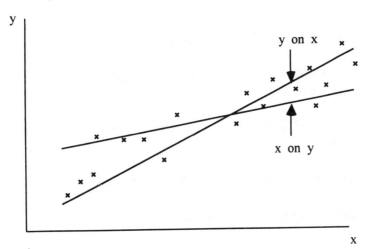

The two lines will intersect at the point $(\bar{x}, \bar{y})$, ie, the mean of the x-values and the mean of the y-values.

2.7   **The regression line of y on x**

Assuming that the equation of the regression line of y on x is:

$$y \quad = \quad a + bx$$

it is necessary to calculate the values of a and b so that the equation can be completely determined.

The following formulae may be used; a knowledge of their derivation is not necessary. They do not need to be memorised since they are supplied in the exams (using upper case X and Y).

$$a = \bar{y} - b\bar{x} = \frac{\sum y}{n} - \frac{b\sum x}{n}$$

$$b = \frac{n\sum xy - \sum x \sum y}{n\sum x^2 - (\sum x)^2}$$

n is the number of pairs of x, y values, ie, the number of points on the scatter graph.

The value of b must be calculated first as it is needed to calculate a.

2.8   Example

The following table shows the amount of fertiliser applied to identical fields, and their resulting yields:

Fertiliser (kg/hectare)	Yield (tonnes/hectare)
100	40
200	45
300	50
400	65
500	70
600	70
700	80

Calculate the regression line for y on x.

2.9   Solution

Notes on the calculation

(a)   A scatter diagram is always a useful aid in answering questions on correlation and regression. Even if it is not specifically requested, a sketch diagram can be included as part of a solution.

(b)   The calculation can be reduced to a series of steps:

Step 1   Tabulate the data and determine which is the dependent variable, y, and which the independent, x.

Step 2   Calculate $\sum x$, $\sum y$, $\sum x^2$, $\sum xy$; (leave room for a column for $\sum y^2$ which may well be needed subsequently.

Step 3   Substitute in the formulae in order to find *b* and *a* in that order.

Step 4   Substitute a and b in the regression equation.

The calculation is set out as follows, where x is the amount of fertiliser in units of **hundreds** of kg/hectare and y is the yield in tonnes/hectare.

x	y	xy	x^2	
1	40	40	1	
2	45	90	4	
3	50	150	9	
4	65	260	16	
5	70	350	25	
6	70	420	36	
7	80	560	49	
28	420	1,870	140	n = 7

$$b = \frac{n\sum xy - \sum x \sum y}{n\sum x^2 - (\sum x)^2}$$

(Try to avoid rounding at this stage since, although n Σxy and Σx Σy are large, their difference is much smaller.)

$$= \frac{(7 \times 1,870) - (28 \times 420)}{(7 \times 140) - (28 \times 28)}$$

$$= \frac{13,090 - 11,760}{980 - 784}$$

$$= \frac{1,330}{196}$$

$$= 6.79$$

(Ensure you make a note of this fraction in your workings. It may help later.)

$$a = \frac{\sum y}{n} - \frac{b\sum x}{n}$$

$$= \frac{420}{7} - 6.79 \times \frac{28}{7}$$

$$= 60 - 27.16$$

$$= 32.84$$

∴   the regression line for y on x is:

y   =   32.84 + 6.79x   (x in hundreds of kg per hectare
                                           y in tonnes per hectare)

(Always specify what x and y are very carefully.)

This line would be used to estimate the yield corresponding to a given amount of fertiliser. If, say, 250 kg/hectare of fertiliser is available, it is possible to predict the expected yield by using the regression line and replacing x with 2.5:

$$y \quad = \quad 32.84 + 6.79 \times 2.5$$

$$= \quad 32.84 + 16.975$$

$$= \quad 49.815$$

$$\therefore y = 50 \text{ tonnes/hectare (rounding to whole numbers in line with original data)}$$

2.10   Activity

If $\Sigma x = 560$, $\Sigma y = 85$, $\Sigma x^2 = 62,500$, $\Sigma xy = 14,200$ and $n = 12$, find the regression line of y on x (the line of best fit).

2.11   Activity solution

Equation of line is: $\quad y \quad = \quad a + bx$

$$b \quad = \quad \frac{12 \times 14,200 - 560 \times 85}{12 \times 62,500 - 560 \times 560} = \frac{122,800}{436,400} \quad = \quad 0.281$$

$$a \quad = \quad \frac{85}{12} - 0.281 \times \frac{560}{12} \qquad\qquad = \quad -6.03$$

Regression line is: $\quad y \quad = \quad -6.03 + 0.281x$

2.12   The regression line of x on y

If asked to find a line of best fit the calculations just shown are what is required. This second regression line is less likely to be needed in the exam, but it may be requested, and it gives some insight into correlation.

The method of finding the regresson line is the same as for the regression line of y on x, but with x and y interchanged. Thus the equation is:

$$x \quad = \quad a' + b'y$$

$$\text{where} \quad a' \quad = \quad \bar{x} - b'\bar{y} \qquad = \quad \frac{\Sigma x}{n} - \frac{b'\Sigma y}{n}$$

$$b' \quad = \quad \frac{n\Sigma xy - \Sigma x \Sigma y}{n\Sigma y^2 - (\Sigma y)^2}$$

To calculate the equation for the data in 2.8, Σy^2 is required.

y^2
1,600
2,025
2,500
4,225
4,900
4,900
6,400
26,550

$$b' = \frac{n\sum xy - \sum x \sum y}{n\sum y^2 - (\sum y)^2}$$

$$= \frac{1,330}{7 \times 26,550 - (420)^2} \quad \text{(1,330 and 420 come from the previous calculation)}$$

$$= \frac{1,330}{9,450}$$

$$= 0.141$$

$$a' = \frac{\sum x}{n} - \frac{b'\sum y}{n}$$

$$= \frac{28}{7} - \frac{0.141 \times 420}{7}$$

$$= -4.46$$

$\therefore$ The regression line of x on y is:

$$x = -4.46 + 0.141y$$

This equation would be used to estimate the amount of fertiliser that had resulted in a given yield. Eg, if the yield was 60 tonnes/hectare, the estimated amount of fertiliser would be given by:

$$x = -4.46 + 0.141 \times 60$$

$$= 4.0 \quad \text{(hundreds of kg/hectare)}$$

$\therefore$ 400 kg/hectare of fertiliser would have been used to give a yield of 60 tonnes/hectare.

2.13   Regression and correlation

The angle between the two regression lines y on x and x on y decreases as the correlation between the variables increases.

In the case of perfect correlation the angle between the lines is zero, ie, the two lines coincide and become one.

At the other extreme, the angle between the lines becomes 90^0 when there is no correlation between the variables. In this case one line is parallel to the x-axis and the other parallel to the y-axis.

Measures of correlation are discussed later in this text.

2.14   Interpolation and extrapolation

As has been shown, regression lines can be used to calculate intermediate values of variables, ie, values within the known range. This is known as **interpolation** and it is one of the main uses of regression lines.

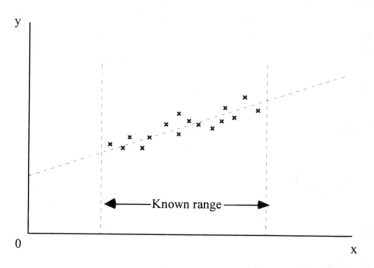

It is also possible to extend regression lines beyond the range of values used in their calculation. It is then possible to calculate values of the variables that are outside the limits of the original data, this is known as **extrapolation**.

The problem with extrapolation is that it assumes that the relationship already calculated is still valid. This may or may not be so.

For example, if the fertiliser was increased outside the given range there would come a point where it had an adverse effect on the yield. The seed might actually be damaged by too much fertiliser.

The resultant diagram could be of this form:

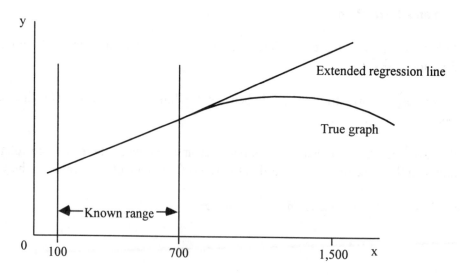

Therefore the yield from using 1,500 kg/hectare of fertiliser as estimated from the regression line may be very different from that actually achieved in practice.

Generally speaking, extrapolation must be treated with caution, since once outside the range of known values other factors may influence the situation, and the relationship which has been approximated as linear over a limited range may not be linear outside that range. Nevertheless, extrapolation of a time series is a valuable and widely used technique for forecasting.

3   CORRELATION

3.1   Introduction

Through regression analysis it is possible to derive a linear relationship between two variables and hence estimate unknown values.   However, this does not measure the **degree of correlation** between the variables, ie, how strong the connection is between the two variables. It is possible to find a line of best fit through any assortment of data points; this doesn't mean that we are justified in using the equation of that line.

3.2   Correlation coefficient

Pearson's correlation coefficient, r, is defined as:

$$r = \frac{n\sum xy - \sum x \sum y}{\sqrt{(n\sum x^2 - (\sum x)^2)(n\sum y^2 - (\sum y)^2)}}$$

This formula does not have to be memorised, since it is also supplied in the exam, but practice is needed at applying it to data and interpreting the result.

3.3   Example

Using the data of the example in 2.8 relating to fertiliser and crop yield calculate the correlation coefficient.

The totals required are:

$\sum x = 28$, $\sum y = 420$, $\sum xy = 1{,}870$, $\sum x^2 = 140$, $\sum y^2 = 26{,}550$, $n = 7$

3.4   Solution

$$\text{Thus} \quad r = \frac{(7 \times 1{,}870) - (28 \times 420)}{\sqrt{((7 \times 140) - (28 \times 28))((7 \times 26{,}550) - (420 \times 420))}}$$

$$= \frac{13{,}090 - 11{,}760}{\sqrt{(980 - 784)(185{,}850 - 176{,}400)}}$$

$$= \frac{1{,}330}{\sqrt{(196 \times 9{,}450)}}$$

$$= 0.98$$

(If you look at your calculations for b and b' you will notice that you've already found the terms in this section.)

3.5   Interpretation of coefficient of correlation

Having calculated the value of r, it is necessary to interpret this result. Does   r = 0.98   mean that there is high correlation, low correlation or no correlation?

r varies between +1 and −1 where:

       $r = +1$ means perfect positive linear correlation;

       $r = 0$ means no correlation; and

       $r = -1$ means perfect negative linear correlation

So in this case the value of 0.98 indicates a high degree of positive correlation between the variables.

In general, the closer that r is to +1 (or − 1) the higher the degree of correlation. This will usually be confirmed by the scatter diagram where the points will lie in a narrow band for such values.

It must be realised that r only measures the amount of linear correlation, ie, the tendency to a straight line relationship. It is quite possible to have strong non-linear correlation and yet have a value of r close to zero. This is one reason why it is important in practice to draw the scatter graph first.

The more data points the farther r may be from 1 and still indicate good correlation. If there are few data points, as here, we would wish to see r very close to 1 (clearly if there were only 2 points they will lie exactly on the line of best fit. In the exam you are supplied with tables (Table 7) which will enable you to get a feel for how close r has to be to 1, but at this stage no detailed knowledge of this analysis is required.

3.6   Coefficient of determination

The coefficient of determination is the square of the coefficient of correlation, and so is denoted by r^2. The advantage of knowing the coefficient of determination is that it is a measure of how much of the variation in the dependent variable is 'explained' by the variation of the independent variable. The variation not accounted for by variations in the independent variable will be due to random fluctuations, or to other specific factors which have not been identified in considering the two-variable problem.

In the example on fertiliser and yield, r had a value of 0.98 and so $r^2 = 0.96$.

Thus, variations in the amount of fertiliser applied account for 96% of the variation in the yield obtained.

3.7   Spurious correlation

Students should be aware of the big danger involved in correlation analysis. Two variables, when compared, may show a high degree of correlation but they may still have no direct connection. Such correlation is termed **spurious** or **nonsense** correlation and unless two variables can reasonably be assumed to have some direct connection the correlation coefficient found will be meaningless, however high it may be.

The following are examples of variables between which there is high but spurious correlation:

(a)   Salaries of school teachers and consumption of alcohol.
(b)   Number of television licences and the number of admissions to mental hospitals.

Such examples clearly have no direct **causal** relationship. However, there may be some other variable which is a causal factor common to both of the original variables. For example, the general rise in living standards and real incomes is responsible both for the increase in teachers' salaries and for the increase in the consumption of alcohol.

3.8   Activity

If r = 0.42, how much of the variation in the dependent variable is explained by the variation of the independent variable?

3.9   Activity solution

If r = 0.42, then $r^2 = 0.1764$, so about 17.6% of the variation is explained by variations in the independent variable (poor correlaton).

4   RANK CORRELATION

4.1   Introduction

For Pearson's correlation coefficient, (sometimes called a product moment correlation coefficient), x and y must both be quantifiable as numerical values. It is possible, however, to consider correlation between attributes which cannot be quantified numerically, such as artistic ability, skill, intelligence, beauty, etc.

Provided the items or people can be ranked, that is, placed in order of merit, ability, magnitude or any other relevant order, a correlation coefficient can still be obtained.

One method is to use Spearman's rank correlation coefficient (R).

$$R \quad = \quad 1 - \frac{6 \sum d^2}{n(n^2 - 1)}$$

where d   =   difference between ranks in each attribute
       n   =   number of items or people ranked

4.2   Example

To investigate whether correlation exists between ability in writing plays and ability in English, a group of 10 playwrights were set a test in English and also had the quality of their plays assessed by a panel of experts, who ranked them in order of merit.

The following results were obtained:

Candidate	A	B	C	D	E	F	G	H	I	J
Mark in English (%)	60	75	40	62	64	71	58	50	83	45
Rank in play writing	5	3	8	6	4	2	9	7	1	10

(Rank 1 is the best play and 10 the worst)

Is there any evidence of correlation?

4.3   Discussion

The quality of a play is not something that can be quantified, but plays can be placed in order of merit. As far as English is concerned, it is true that the examination mark could be used to quantify ability, but an examination does not really measure ability, it merely enables candidates to be compared and ranked. In any case, for Pearson's correlation coefficient to be used, both attributes would need to be quantified. This is clearly a case where ranking methods must be used.

4.4   Solution

First, the candidates must be ranked in English on the same basis as the rank for play writing, that is, the best (83%) is given a rank of 1, down to the worst (40%) with a rank of 10.

Candidate	A	B	C	D	E	F	G	H	I	J
Rank in English	6	2	10	5	4	3	7	8	1	9

The calculation can now be set out as follows:

Candidate	Rank in English	Rank in Play	Difference d	d^2
A	6	5	1	1
B	2	3	−1	1
C	10	8	2	4
D	5	6	−1	1
E	4	4	0	0
F	3	2	1	1
G	7	9	−2	4
H	8	7	1	1
I	1	1	0	0
J	9	10	−1	1
			$\Sigma d = 0$	$\Sigma d^2 = 14$

(Σd is not used, but serves as a check on your arithmetic.)

n = number of candidates = 10

$$\therefore \ R \ = \ 1 - \frac{6 \times 14}{10 \times (10^2 - 1)}$$

$$= \ 1 - \frac{84}{990}$$

$$= \ 0.92$$

4.5   Interpretation of R

Perfect positive correlation occurs when the ranks in both attributes are identical; the best in one is best in the other, etc.

Perfect negative correlation occurs when the ranks are in reverse order, ie, the best in one attribute is worst in the other, and so on.

If there is no tendency to either of these extremes, there is no correlation.

R behaves in the same way as r, ie,

For perfect positive correlation,   R = +1
For perfect negative correlation,   R = −1
For no correlation,   R ≃ 0

A value of R = 0.92 would therefore appear to indicate a high degree of positive correlation, showing that ability in English does tend to go with ability in play writing.

4.6   The problem of tied ranks

If two or more candidates have equal ranks (ie, they tie), errors will be introduced. A few ties can be tolerated provided they are treated correctly. Candidates who tie should be given the arithmetic mean of the ranks they would have had if they had not been quite equal. For example, if the marks in English had been:

Candidate	A	B	C	D	E	F	G	H	I	J
Mark in English (%)	83	70	70	65	60	52	52	52	50	45

Candidates B and C would have had ranks 2 and 3 if they had not been equal. They are both given a rank of (2 + 3)/2 = 2.5. Candidate D must follow on from 3 with a rank of 4. Candidates F, G and H would have had ranks of 6, 7 and 8 if they had not been equal. They are therefore given a rank of (6 + 7 + 8)/3 = 7. Candidate I must follow on from 8 with a rank of 9. Hence the ranks would be:

1, 2.5, 2.5, 4, 5, 7, 7, 7, 9, 10

4.7 Ranking of numerical data

Numerical data suitable for calculation of Pearson's correlation coefficient (r), can always be ranked in order of magnitude. Some of the information will be lost, and therefore Spearman's correlation coefficient will not give such an accurate result. However, it is much easier to calculate, and can be used as a quick method if only an approximate indication of the degree of correlation is required. If Spearman's coefficient indicates no correlation then Pearson's coefficient will give the same result, but if Spearman's coefficient indicates correlation, Pearson's coefficient may not confirm this if the correlation is weak.

4.8 Activity

Calculate a rank correlation coefficient for the fertiliser data in paragraph 2.8 seen earlier.

4.9 Activity solution

(Ranking 1, 2, 3 ... etc. is in order of increasing magnitude.)

Fertiliser x	Rank of x	Yield y	Rank of y	Difference in ranks d	d^2
100	1	40	1	0	0
200	2	45	2	0	0
300	3	50	3	0	0
400	4	65	4	0	0
500	5	70	5½	− ½	¼
600	6	70	5½	½	¼
700	7	80	7	0	0
				0	½

$$\therefore R = 1 - \frac{6 \times \frac{1}{2}}{7(7^2 - 1)}$$

$$= 1 - 0.0089$$

$$= 0.9911$$

The rank correlation coefficient shows almost perfect positive correlation, whereas Pearson's coefficient (0.98) indicates high but not so nearly perfect correlation. The latter is the more accurate conclusion.

5 CONCLUSIONS AND ILLUSTRATION

5.1 Conclusions

This chapter has been concerned so far with 'bivariate distributions', ie, the distributions of two variables. The three methods used to investigate the interrelationship of two distributions are:

(a) Scatter diagrams.
(b) Regression analysis.
(c) Correlation coefficients.

A number of formulae have been used; these must be well practised so that calculations can be made quickly and accurately.

5.2   Illustration

The following figures show the power to the nearest kilowatt and the top speeds to the nearest mile per hour, of twelve racing cars:

Power (kw)	70	63	72	60	66	70	74	65	62	67	.65	68
Top speed (mph)	155	150	180	135	156	168	178	160	132	145	139	152

(a)   Plot the information on a scatter diagram, showing top speed as the dependent variable.

(b)   Calculate the line of regression of y on x.

(c)   Estimate the top speed of a car with a power rating of 71 kw.

(d)   From the calculations carried out so far, is it possible to estimate the power rating of a car which has a top speed of 175 mph? Give reasons.

(e)   What would be the problems involved in estimating a top speed for a car with a power rating of 95 kw?

5.3   Solution

(a)   Since top speed is the dependent variable it is plotted on the vertical y-axis. Power is therefore plotted on the x-axis.

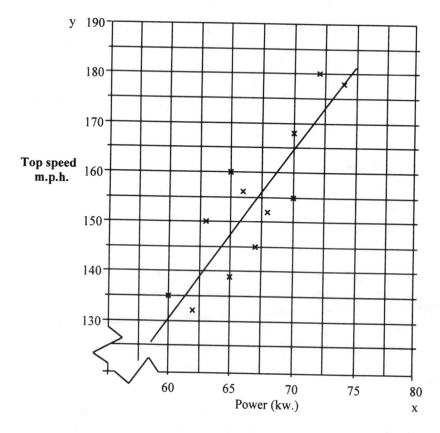

(b)

Power (kw)	Top speed (mph)		
x	y	xy	x^2
70	155	10,850	4,900
63	150	9,450	3,969
72	180	12,960	5,184
60	135	8,100	3,600
66	156	10,296	4,356
70	168	11,760	4,900
74	178	13,172	5,476
65	160	10,400	4,225
62	132	8,184	3,844
67	145	9,715	4,489
65	139	9,035	4,225
68	152	10,336	4,624
$\Sigma x = 802$	$\Sigma y = 1,850$	$\Sigma xy = 124,258$	$\Sigma x^2 = 53,792$

$$y = a + bx$$

Using $b = \dfrac{n\Sigma xy - \Sigma x \Sigma y}{n\Sigma x^2 - (\Sigma x)^2}$, and $a = \dfrac{\Sigma y}{n} - \dfrac{b\Sigma x}{n}$

$$b = \frac{(12 \times 124,258) - (802 \times 1,850)}{(12 \times 53,792) - (802 \times 802)}$$

$$= \frac{1,491,096 - 1,483,700}{645,504 - 643,204}$$

$$= \frac{7,396}{2,300}$$

$$\therefore \; b = 3.22 \text{ (3 s.f.)}$$

$$a = \frac{1,850}{12} - 3.22 \times \frac{802}{12}$$

$$= 154.2 - 215.2$$

$$\therefore \; a = -61.0$$

So the regression line is: $y = -61.0 + 3.22x$

(c)   If power rating is 71 kw then replacing x = 71 in equation gives:

$$y = -61.0 + 3.22 \times 71$$

$$= -61.0 + 228.62$$

$$\therefore \; y = 168 \text{ mph (to nearest whole number)}$$

(d)   Strictly speaking, it is not possible to estimate power rating for a given top speed without working out the line of regression of x on y, which has not yet been done.

(e)   As soon as a regression line is used to predict values of y for given values of x outside the observed range, there is an immediate risk of error which continues to increase the further away one goes from the observed values.

There is no reason why a particular relationship should remain linear for higher (or lower) values of the variables (in fact the reverse is often more likely as saturation point is reached).

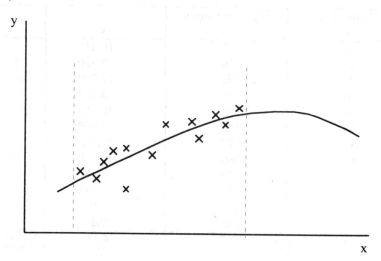

Thus, since 95 kw is a power rating well outside the present observed range, it would be unreliable to extrapolate in order to obtain an estimate of top speed for that rating.

6   FORECASTING USING CORRELATION AND REGRESSION

6.1   Causal forecasting

This is used where there is a causal relationship between the variable whose value is to be forecast and another variable whose value can be ascertained for the period for which the forecast is to be made. If, for example, there is correlation between the demand for sun roofs in a given year and the sales of new cars in the previous year, then this year's car sales could be used to predict sun roof demand for next year.

6.2   Example

Hi-Fi Videos plc has obtained the relationship between net profit (y) and number of sales outlets (x) as:

$$y \quad = \quad 0.25x - 1.9$$

where $y \quad = \quad$ net profit in £m.

It plans to increase sales outlets next year to 18. The forecast of net profit for next year will therefore be:

$$\text{Net profit} \quad = \quad 0.25 \times 18 - 1.9$$

$$= \quad £2.6m$$

This is subject to the limitations of extrapolation already discussed.

6.3   Trend extrapolation

The trend is the smoothed-out line through the data when plotted against a time scale. The time scale is taken as the x-variable, and the trend is the line of best fit.

6.4 **Example**

Year	Sales (£'000)
19X3	12.0
19X4	11.5
19X5	15.8
19X6	15.0
19X7	18.5

To forecast sales for 19X8:

The sales in £000 units are taken as the y-values. Year 19X3 is taken as $x = 1$, 19X4 as $x = 2$, 19X5 as $x = 3$, etc., in which case the forecast for year 19X8 will be the value of y when $x = 6$.

The least squares regression line of y on x (the line of best fit) for this data is:

$$y = 9.61 + 1.65x$$

(Students should check this for themselves.)

Hence, the forecast of sales for year 19X8 is obtained by putting $x = 6$ in this equation, giving:

$$y = 9.61 + 1.65 \times 6$$

$$= 19.51 \text{ (£000)}$$

$$= £19,510$$

Notes:

(i) Any consecutive numbers could be used for the year values; there are computational advantages in taking 19X3 as –2, 19X4 as –1, 19X5 as 0, etc as this makes $\Sigma x = 0$. In this case the forecast for 19X8 would be obtained when $x = 3$; and the regression line would be $y = 14.56 + 1.65x$.

(ii) To forecast future demands, previous demands should be used, not previous sales. These are not the same as there may have been unfulfilled demand due to stock-outs.

7 **SELF TEST QUESTIONS**

7.1 What is a scatter diagram? (1.1)

7.2 What is the difference between perfect positive linear correlation and perfect negative linear correlation? (1.3)

7.3 What is a 'line of best fit'? (2.2)

7.4 What is the equation of a straight line? (2.4)

7.5 What is the difference between interpolation and extrapolation? (2.14)

7.6 What is Pearson's correlation coefficient? (3.2)

8   EXAMINATION TYPE QUESTION

8.1   D & E Ltd

D & E Ltd produces brakes for the motor industry. Its management accountant is investigating the relationship between electricity costs and volume of production. The following data for the last ten quarters has been derived, the cost figures having been adjusted (ie, deflated) to take into account price changes.

Quarter	1	2	3	4	5	6	7	8	9	10
Production, X, ('000 units)	30	20	10	60	40	25	13	50	44	28
Electricity costs, Y, (£'000)	10	11	6	18	13	10	10	20	17	15

(Source: Internal company records of D & E Ltd.)

$$\Sigma X^2 = 12{,}614, \qquad \Sigma Y^2 = 1{,}864, \qquad \Sigma XY = 4{,}728$$

You are required

(a)   to draw a scatter diagram of the data on squared paper;   **(4 marks)**

(b)   to find the least squares regression line for electricity costs on production and explain this result;

(8 marks)

(c)   to predict the electricity costs of D & E Ltd for the next two quarters (time periods 11 and 12) in which production is planned to be 15,000 and 55,000 standard units respectively;

(4 marks)

(d)   to assess the likely reliability of these forecasts.

(4 marks)
(Total: 20 marks)

9   **ANSWER TO EXAMINATION TYPE QUESTION**

9.1   **D & E Ltd**

(a)   **Scatter graph of electricity cost against production**

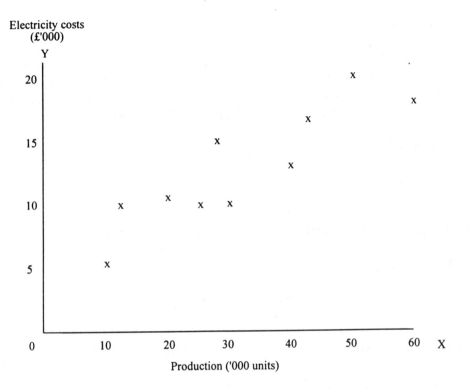

Production ('000 units)

Notes:

(i)   Do not confuse this with a time series graph.

(ii)   Choose the scales so that the graph fits the graph paper.

(iii)   Do not attempt to draw a line through the scatter graph unless the question requires it.

(iv)   Label the axes and state the units.

(b)   The regression line of Y on X is $Y = a + bX$ where

$$b = \frac{n\sum XY - \sum X \sum Y}{n\sum X^2 - (\sum X)^2} \quad \text{and} \quad \frac{\sum Y - b\sum X}{n}$$

$$\sum X = 320$$

$$\sum Y = 130$$

$$n = 10$$

$$b = \frac{10 \times 4,728 - 320 \times 130}{10 \times 12,614 - (320)^2} = \frac{5,680}{23,740}$$

$$= 0.239$$

$$a = \frac{130 - 0.239 \times 320}{10}$$

$$= 5.34$$

The least squares regression line of electricity costs (Y) on production (X) is therefore

$$Y = 5.34 + 0.239X$$

where y is in £'000 and x in '000 units.

Explanation

Assuming there is an approximately linear relationship between production and electricity costs, which is shown to be reasonable by the scatter graph, the electricity costs are made up of two parts, a fixed cost (independent of the volume of production) of £5,340 and a variable cost per unit of production of £239 per 1,000 units or 23.9p per unit).

(c)   For quarter 11, X = 15, hence

$$Y = 5.34 + 0.239 \times 15$$
$$= 8.93$$

The predicted electricity cost for quarter 11 is therefore £8,930.

For quarter 12, X = 55, hence

$$Y = 5.34 + 0.239 \times 55$$
$$= 18.5$$

The predicted electricity cost for quarter 12 is therefore £18,500.

(d)   There are two main sources of error in the forecasts:

(i)   The assumed relationship between Y and X.

The scatter graph shows that there can be fairly wide variations in Y for a given X. Also the forecast assumes that the same conditions will prevail over the next two quarters as in the last ten quarters.

(ii)   The predicted production for quarters 11 and 12.

No indication is given as to how these planned production values were arrived at, so that it is not possible to assess how reliable they are. If they are based on extrapolation of a time series for production over the past ten quarters, they will be subject to the errors inherent in such extrapolations.

Provided conditions remain similar to the past ten quarters, it can be concluded that the forecasts would be fairly reliable but subject to some variation.

Note: methods for calculation of confidence limits for forecasts are available, but are outside the scope of this syllabus. At this level it is impossible to quantify the reliability, so that comments can only be in general terms, although a correlation coefficient would be worth calculating **if time allowed**.

28 TIME SERIES

INTRODUCTION & LEARNING OBJECTIVES

Syllabus area 2h. Elementary time series analysis: trend, seasonality, random fluctuations. (Ability required 3).

This chapter is concerned with analysing the relationships between data and the passage of time.

When you have studied this chapter you should be able to do the following:

- Explain the use of time series analysis.

- Distinguish between additive and multiplicative time series models.

- Identify and quantify cyclical variations in time series data.

- Explain how the techniques of regression, correlation and time series analysis may be used in forecasting.

---

1 TIME SERIES

1.1 Introduction

A time series is the name given to a set of observations taken at equal intervals of time, eg, daily, weekly, monthly, etc. The observations can be plotted against time to give an overall picture of what is happening. **The horizontal axis is always the time axis.**

Examples of time series are total annual exports, monthly unemployment figures, daily average temperatures, etc.

1.2 Example

The following data relates to the production (in tonnes) of floggels by the North West Engineering Co. These are the quarterly totals taken over four years from 19X2 to 19X5.

	1st Qtr	2nd Qtr	3rd Qtr	4th Qtr
19X2	91	90	94	93
19X3	98	99	97	95
19X4	107	102	106	110
19X5	123	131	128	130

This time series will now be graphed so that an overall picture can be gained of what is happening to the company's production figures.

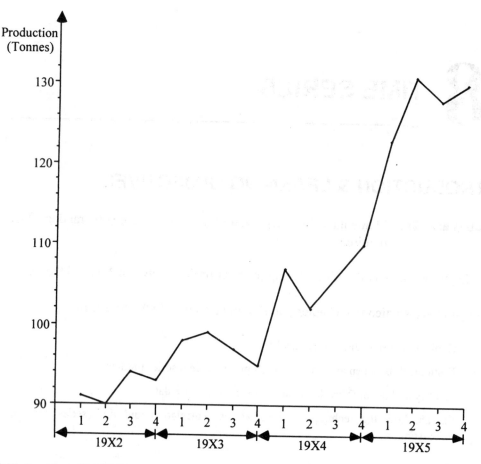

Note: that each point must be plotted at the **end** of the relevant quarter.

The graph shows clearly how the production of floggels has increased over the four-year time period. This is particularly true during the last year considered.

1.3   Variations in observations

A time series is influenced by a number of factors, the most important of these being:

(a)   **Long-term trends**

This is the way in which the graph of a time series appears to be moving over a long interval of time when the short-term fluctuations have been smoothed out. The rise or fall is due to factors which only change slowly, eg,

(i)   increase or decrease in population;
(ii)   technological improvements;
(iii)   competition from abroad.

(b)   **Cyclical variations**

This is the wave-like appearance of a time series graph when taken over a number of years. Generally, it is due to the influence of booms and slumps in industry. The distance in time from one peak to the next is often approximately 5 to 7 years.

(c)   **Seasonal variation**

This is a regular rise and fall over specified intervals of time. The interval of time can be any length – hours, days, weeks, etc, and the variations are of a periodic type with a fairly definite period, eg:

(i)   rises in the number of goods sold before Christmas and at sale times;

(ii)   rises in the demand for gas and electricity at certain times during the day;

(iii)   rises in the number of customers using a restaurant at lunch-time and dinner time.

These are referred to under the general heading of 'seasonal' variations as a common example is the steady rise and fall of, for example, sales over the four seasons of the year.

However, as can be seen from the examples, the term is also used to cover regular variations over other short periods of time.

They should not be confused with cyclical variations (paragraph b) which are long-term fluctuations with an interval between successive peaks greater than one year.

(d)   **Residual or random variations**

This covers any other variation which cannot be ascribed to (a), (b) or (c) above. This is taken as happening entirely at random due to unpredictable causes, eg:

(i)   strikes;

(ii)   fires;

(iii)   sudden changes in taxes.

Not all time series will contain all four elements. For example, not all sales figures show seasonal variations.

1.4   A time series graph

The graph in the example covered the quarterly production of floggels over a four-year time period.

The long-term trend (a) and seasonal (quarterly) (c) were obvious from the graph. However, in order to be able to observe any cyclical variations it is usually necessary to have data covering a much wider time-span, say 10 – 15 years minimum.

The following graph shows the production (in tonnes) of widgets for each quarter of the 18 years from 19X1 to 19Y8.

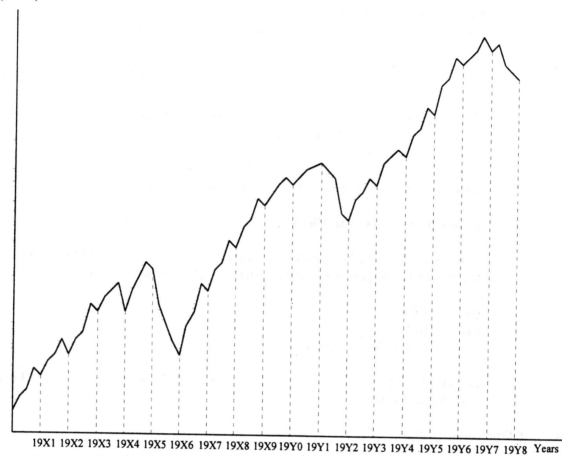

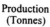

This time it is possible to detect:

(a)   The long-term trend – upwards in this case.

(b)   Cyclical variations – the wave like appearance of the graph shows that the cycle of production spans 6 years, ie, the distance in time between successive peaks (and successive troughs) is 6 years.

(c)   Seasonal variation – since these are quarterly production figures this is sometimes called **quarterly variation**. These are the small steps in each year which are evident on the first graph. They occur because some parts of the year are busier than others and the actual pattern will depend very much on the type of industry, eg, the building industry tends to be slack during the winter months because of the weather, whereas an engineering company may be quietest during the summer months due to holidays.

(d)   Residual variation – this is simply the difference between the actual figure and that predicted – taking into account trends, cyclical variations and seasonal variations. By its nature it cannot be fully explained.

1.5   Analysis of a time series

It is essential to be able to disentangle these various influences and measure each one separately. The main reasons for analysing a time series in this way are:

(a)   To be able to predict future values of the variable, ie, to make forecasts.

(b)   To attempt to control future events.

(c)   To 'seasonally adjust' or 'deseasonalise' a set of data, that is to remove the seasonal effect. For example, seasonally adjusted unemployment values are more useful than actual unemployment values in studying the effects of the national economy and Government policies on unemployment.

2   ANALYSIS OF A TIME SERIES

2.1   Additive and multiplicative models

To analyse a time series, it is necessary to make an assumption about how the four components described combine to give the total effect. The simplest method is to assume that the components are added together, ie, if:

$$A \quad = \quad \text{Actual value for the period}$$
$$T \quad = \quad \text{Trend component}$$
$$C \quad = \quad \text{Cyclical component}$$
$$S \quad = \quad \text{Seasonal component}$$
$$R \quad = \quad \text{Residual component}$$

Then $A = T + C + S + R.$ This is called an **additive model**.

Another method is to assume the components are multiplied together, ie:

$$A = T \times C \times S \times R$$

This is called a **multiplicative model**.

The additive model is the simplest, and is satisfactory when the fluctuations about the trend are within a constant band width. If, as is more usual, the fluctuations about the trend increase as the trend increases, the multiplicative model is used. Illustrated diagrammatically:

(a)   y

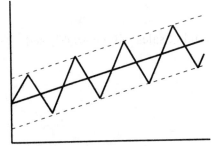

Time

Constant band width.
Use additive model.

(b)   y

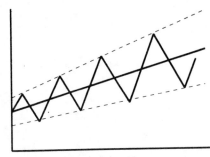

Time

Band width proportional to trend.
Use multiplicative model.

2.2   Trend

The trend can be obtained by using regression to obtain the line of best fit through the points on the graph, taking x as the year numbers (1, 2, 3.... etc.) and y as the vertical variable. It is not necessary for the trend to be a straight line, as non-linear regression can be used, but for this method it is necessary to assume an appropriate mathematical form for the trend, such as parabola, hyperbola, exponential, etc. If the trend does not conform to any of these, the method cannot be used.

An alternative, which requires no assumption to be made about the nature of the curve, is to smooth out the fluctuations by **moving averages**.

The simplest way to explain the method is by means of an example.

2.3   Example

The following are the sales figures for Bloggs Brothers Engineering Ltd for the fourteen years from 19X1 to 19Y4.

Year	*Sales* (£'000)
19X1	491
19X2	519
19X3	407
19X4	452
19X5	607
19X6	681
19X7	764
19X8	696
19X9	751
19Y0	802
19Y1	970
19Y2	1,026
19Y3	903
19Y4	998

Using the method of moving averages the general trend of sales will be established.

2.4   Solution

Step 1   First, it is advisable to draw a graph of the time series so that an overall picture can be gained and the cyclical movements seen.

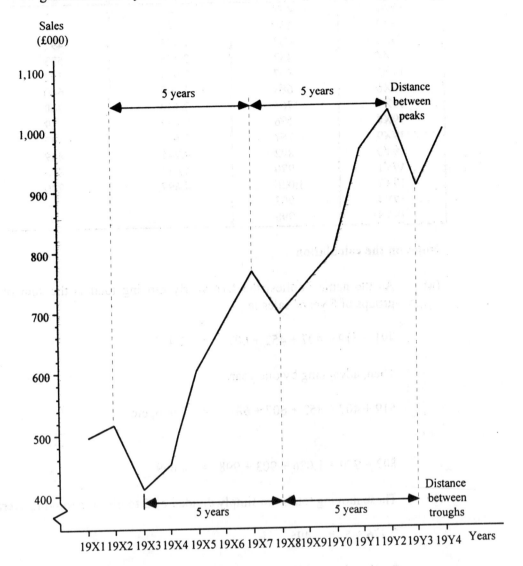

In order to calculate the trend figures it is necessary to establish the span of the cycle. From the graph it can easily be seen that the distance in time between successive peaks (and successive troughs) is 5 years; therefore a 5 point moving average must be calculated.

Step 2 A table of the following form is now drawn up:

Year	Sales (£'000)	5 yearly moving total	5 yearly moving average
19X1	491	-	-
19X2	519	-	-
19X3	407	2,476	495
19X4	452	2,666	533
19X5	607	2,911	582
19X6	681	3,200	640
19X7	764	3,499	700
19X8	696	3,694	739
19X9	751	3,983	797
19Y0	802	4,245	849
19Y1	970	4,452	890
19Y2	1,026	4,699	940
19Y3	903	-	-
19Y4	998	-	-

Notes on the calculation

(a)   As the name implies, the five yearly moving total is the sum of successive groups of 5 years' sales ie,

$$491 + 519 + 407 + 452 + 607 \ = \ 2,476$$

Then, advancing by one year:

$$519 + 407 + 452 + 607 + 681 \ = \ 2,666, \text{ etc.}$$

$$802 + 970 + 1,026 + 903 + 998 \ = \ 4,699$$

(b)   These moving totals are simply divided by 5 to give the moving averages, ie,

$$2,476 \div 5 \ = \ 495$$

$$2,666 \div 5 \ = \ 533$$

$$4,699 \div 5 \ = \ 940$$

(c)   Averages are always plotted in the middle of the time period, ie, 495 is the average of the figures for 19X1, 19X2, 19X3, 19X4 and 19X5 and so it is plotted at the end of 19X3, this being the mid-point of the time interval from the end of 19X1 to the end of 19X5. Similarly, 533 is plotted at the end of 19X4, and 940 is plotted at the end of 19Y2.

Step 3 A second graph is now drawn showing the original figures again and the trend figures, ie, the five yearly moving averages.

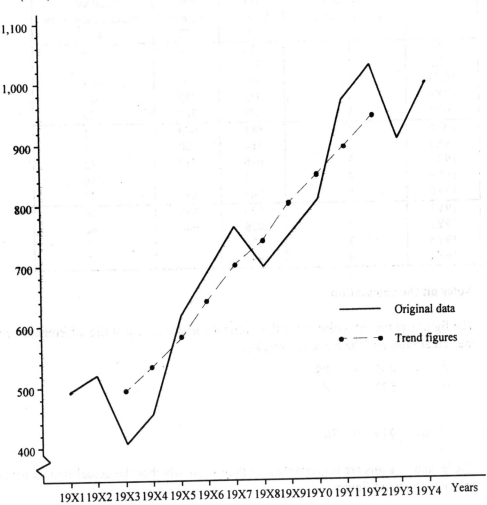

2.5   Cyclical variation

Having calculated the trend figures it is a simple matter to work out the cyclical variations.

For annual data, there cannot be a seasonal component. Hence, using the additive model,

$$A = T + C + R$$

Subtracting T from both sides,

$$A - T = C + R$$

So, by subtracting the trend values from the actual values, the combined cyclical and residual variation will be obtained.

If the multiplicative model is used, A must be divided by T,

$$A = T \times C \times R$$

$$\frac{A}{T} = C \times R$$

As before, this will be explained by way of an example.

2.6   Example

Using the same data, establish the cyclical variation, using the additive model.

2.7   Solution

Step 1   A table of the following type is drawn up:

Year	Period of moving averages	Sales (£'000) (A)	Trend figures (T)	Cyclical + Residual variation (A - T)
19X1	1	491	–	–
19X2	2	519	–	–
19X3	3	407	495	–88
19X4	4	452	533	–81
19X5	5	607	582	25
19X6	1	681	640	41
19X7	2	764	700	64
19X8	3	696	739	–43
19X9	4	751	797	–46
19Y0	5	802	849	–47
19Y1	1	970	890	80
19Y2	2	1,026	940	86
19Y3	3	903	–	–
19Y4	4	998	–	–

Notes on the calculation

The figures in the last column for the cyclical variation are just the differences between the actual sales and the trend figures, ie,:

$$407 - 495 = -88$$
$$452 - 533 = -81$$
$$\vdots$$
$$1,026 - 940 = 86$$

The '+' and '–' signs are important since they show whether the actual figures are above or below the trend figures.

Step 2   To remove the residual component from C + R, another table must now be drawn up in order to establish the average cyclical variations.

	Period 1	Period 2	Period 3	Period 4	Period 5
Cyclical variation calculated above	– 41 80	– 64 86	–88 –43 –	–81 –46 –	25 –47 –
(i) Totals	121	150	–131	–127	–22
(ii) Average cyclical variation (= (i)/2)	60.5 61	75	–65.5 –66	–63.5 –64	–11

The individual variations have been averaged out for each year of the cycle, ie,

$$\text{Year 1 of each cycle} = \frac{41+80}{2} = \frac{121}{2} = 60.5, \text{ rounded to } 61;$$

$$\text{Year 2 of each cycle} = \frac{64+86}{2} = \frac{150}{2} = 75$$

etc.

Step 3 One more step is necessary because the cyclical variation should total to zero, and $61 + 75 + (-66) + (-64) + (-11) = -5$.

The adjustment is made by dividing the excess ($- 5$ in this case) by the number of years in the cycle (5 in this case) and subtracting the result from each of the cyclical variations.

Adjustment is $-5 \div 5 = -1$

Cyclical variations within each cycle are:

Year 1	$61 - (-1)$	$=$	$61 + 1$	$=$	62
Year 2	$75 - (-1)$	$=$	$75 + 1$	$=$	76
Year 3	$-66 - (-1)$	$=$	$-66 + 1$	$=$	-65
Year 4	$-64 - (-1)$	$=$	$-64 + 1$	$=$	-63
Year 5	$-11 - (-1)$	$=$	$-11 + 1$	$=$	-10

(and just as a check, the revised cyclical variations do total zero: $62 + 76 - 65 - 63 - 10 = 0$)

2.8   Seasonal variations

When figures are available for a considerable number of years as in the examples above, it is possible to establish the trend and the cyclical variations.

Usually, however, monthly or quarterly figures are only available for a few years, 3 or 4, say. In this case, it is possible to establish the trend by means of a moving average over an annual cycle by a method very similar to that used above. The span of the data is insufficient to find cyclical variations, but average seasonal variations can be found.

2.9   Example

The following table gives the takings (£000) of a shopkeeper in each quarter of 4 successive years.

Qtrs	1	2	3	4
19X1	13	22	58	23
19X2	16	28	61	25
19X3	17	29	61	26
19X4	18	30	65	29

Calculate the trend figures and quarterly variations, and draw a graph to show the overall trend and the original data.

2.10   Solution

Again the additive model will be used, but as the data is now over too short a time for any cyclical component to be apparent, the model becomes:

$$A = T + S + R$$

Step 1 It is necessary to draw up a table as follows:

1 Year & quarter	2 Takings (£'000) A	3 4 quarterly moving average	4 Centred value T	5 Quarterly + Residual variation S + R
1	13	-	-	-
2	22		-	-
19X1		29		
3	58		30	28
		30		
4	23		31	-8
		31		
1	16		32	-16
		32		
2	28		33	-5
19X2		33		
3	61		33	28
		33		
4	25		33	-8
		33		
1	17		33	-16
		33		
2	29		33	-4
19X3		33		
3	61		34	27
		34		
4	26		34	-8
		34		
1	18		35	-17
		35		
2	30		36	-6
19X4		36		
3	65		-	-
4	29	-	-	-

Notes on the calculation

Column 3

To smooth out quarterly fluctuations, it is necessary to calculate a 4-point moving average, since there are 4 quarters (or seasons) in a year.

ie, $\dfrac{13 + 22 + 58 + 23}{4} = \dfrac{116}{4} = 29$

then, advancing by one quarter:

$\dfrac{22 + 58 + 23 + 16}{4} = \dfrac{119}{4} = 30$ (rounding to nearest whole number)

$\dfrac{18 + 30 + 65 + 29}{4} = \dfrac{142}{4} = 36$ (rounding to nearest whole number)

Step 2 29 is the average of the figures for the four quarters of 19X1 and so if plotted, would be at the mid-point of the interval from the end of the first quarter to the end of the fourth quarter, ie, half-way through the third quarter of 19X1.

Column 4

To find A – T, it is essential that A and T both relate to the same point in time. The four-quarterly moving averages do not correspond with any of the A values, the first coming between the second and third A values and so on down. To overcome this, the moving averages are 'centred', ie, averaged in twos. The first centred average will coincide with the third A value and so on.

Note: that this is necessary because the cycle has an even number of values (4) per cycle. Where there is an odd number of values per cycle, as in the previous example, the moving averages themselves correspond in time with A values, and centreing should not be done.

The centreing is as follows:

$$\text{ie} \quad \frac{29+30}{2} \quad = \quad 30 \qquad \text{(rounding up)}$$

$$\frac{30+31}{2} \quad = \quad 31 \qquad \text{(rounding up)}$$

$$\vdots$$

$$\frac{35+36}{2} \quad = \quad 36 \qquad \text{(rounding up)}$$

The first average now corresponds in time with the original value for the 3rd quarter, and so on.

These are the trend values.

Step 3 Column 5

A – T = S + R, hence the figures for the quarterly + residual variations are the differences between the actual figures and the centred values.

$$\text{ie,} \quad 58 - 30 \quad = \quad 28$$
$$23 - 31 \quad = \quad -8$$
$$\vdots$$
$$30 - 36 \quad = \quad -6$$

Step 4 In order to establish the quarterly variation another table must be drawn up (as in example 6 on cyclical variation), to remove the residual variation R.

	Quarter 1	Quarter 2	Quarter 3	Quarter 4
	–	–	28	–8
	–16	–5	28	–8
	–16	–4	27	–8
	–17	–6	–	–
Totals	–49	–15	83	–24
Seasonal variation	–16	–5	28	–8

The individual variations have been averaged out for each quarter of the cycle:

ie, Quarter 1 $\dfrac{-16+(-16)+(-17)}{3}$ = $\dfrac{-49}{3}$ = -16

Quarter 2 $\dfrac{-5+(-4)+(-6)}{3}$ = $\dfrac{-15}{3}$ = -5

Step 5 The quarterly variations should total to zero again, but $-16 + (-5) + 28 + (-8) = -1$. However, the adjustment would only be $-1 \div 4$, ie, -0.25 which means using a spurious accuracy of two decimal places. To avoid this one value only need be adjusted, choosing the greatest value as this will give the lowest relative adjustment error.

1st	Quarter	=		−16
2nd	Quarter	=		−5
3rd	Quarter	=	28 + 1	=	29
4th	Quarter	=		−8
				0

Step 6

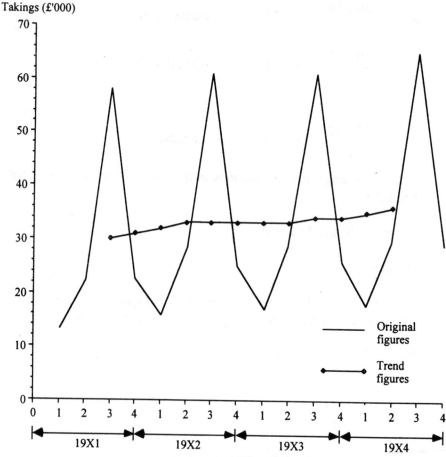

Step 7 **Comment**

As can be seen from the calculations and the graph, the takings show a slight upward trend and the seasonal (quarterly) variations are considerable.

2.11   Seasonally adjusted figures

A popular way of presenting a time series is to give the seasonally adjusted or deseasonalised figures.

This is a very simple process once the seasonal variations are known.

For the additive model:

Seasonally adjusted data	=	Original data	–	Seasonal variation	=	A – S

For the multiplicative model:

Seasonally adjusted data	=	Original data	÷	Seasonal indices	=	A ÷ S

The main purpose in calculating seasonally adjusted figures is to remove the seasonal influence from the original data so that non-seasonal influences can be seen more clearly.

2.12   Example

The same shopkeeper found his takings for the four quarters of 19X5 were £19,000, £32,000, £65,000 and £30,000 respectively. Has the upward trend continued?

2.13   Solution

De-seasonalising the figures gives:

Seasonally adjusted figures (£'000)

Quarter 1	19 – (–16)	=	35
Quarter 2	32 – (–5)	=	37
Quarter 3	65 – 29	=	36
Quarter 4	30 – (–8)	=	38

So, as can be seen from comparing the seasonally adjusted figures with the trend figures calculated earlier, the takings are indeed still increasing, ie, there is an upward trend.

2.14   Example

Having mentioned a multiplication model (or proportional model) this now needs illustrating.

The following data will be seasonally adjusted using 'seasonal indices.'

	Quarter			
	1	2	3	4
Sales (£'000)	59	50	61	92
Seasonal variation	–2%	–21%	–9%	+30%

If $A = T \times S \times R$, the deseasonalised data is A/S.

A decrease of -2% means a factor of 0.98. Similarly, an increase of 30% means a factor of 1.3. Hence the seasonal factors are 0.98, 0.79, 0.91, 1.30 respectively. The actual data, A, must be **divided** by these values to remove the seasonal effect. Hence:

A	Seasonal factor (S)	Seasonally adjusted figure (= A/S)
59	0.98	60
50	0.79	63
61	0.91	67
92	1.30	71

While actual sales are lowest in spring and highest in winter, the seasonally adjusted values show a fairly steady increase throughout the year.

2.15   Forecasting using time series

It has been shown in the above sections how data can be de-seasonalised in order to identify the underlying trend. However, it is often the case that predictions are required to be made about the future, but taking into account seasonal factors.

This can be done in two ways:

(a)   by fitting a line of best fit (straight or curved) by eye (preferably through the trend found by moving averages); and

(b)   by using linear regression. This will be considered below.

The line is then extended to the right in order to estimate future trend values. This 'trend' value is then adjusted in order to take account of the seasonal factors.

Hence, the forecast $= T_e + S$,   where $T_e =$ extrapolated trend.

Residual variations are by nature random and therefore unforecastable.

2.16   Example

Using the data from the shopkeeper predict the takings of the shop for the first and second quarters of 19X5.

2.17   Solution

Takings (£000)

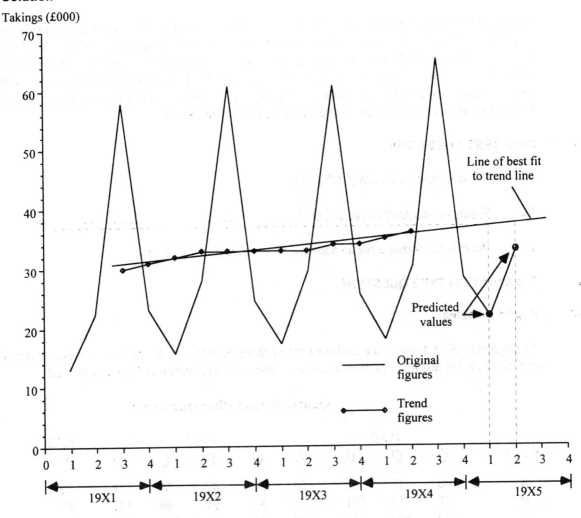

From the graph it can be seen that the trend line predicts values as follows:

Quarter in 19X5	(i) Trend value	(ii) Seasonal variation	(i) + (ii) Final prediction
1	37,000	−16,000	21,000
2	38,000	−5,000	33,000

The predicted values of £21,000 and £33,000 have been plotted on the graph.

For the multiplicative model, the extrapolated trend must be **multiplied** by the appropriate seasonal factor. Thus in the example in paragraph 2.14, if the predicted trend value for the first quarter of the following year was £65,000, the appropriate seasonal factor for this quarter being 0.98, the forecast of actual sales would be £65,000 × 0.98 = £64,000 (to the nearest £000).

2.18   Time series applied to forecasting models – alternative method

An alternative method for making predictions is to use linear regression in order to establish the trend line in the first place (rather than using the method of moving averages), and then on the basis of this regression line it is possible to predict the figures for the underlying trend. These are then used to estimate seasonal variations and the extrapolated trend values are calculated from the regression equation.

2.19 Conclusion

It is important to appreciate that although the various methods which have been used to identify seasonal (and cyclical) factors and hence predict future values of a particular variable will give different results, it is often not possible to say that any one answer is more valid than another. All methods essentially assume that whatever has caused fluctuations and trends to occur in the past will continue similarly into the future. Clearly this is often not the case and therefore any value forecast by any of the methods should be treated with due caution.

3 SELF TEST QUESTIONS

3.1   What is time series analysis? (1.1)

3.2   What is a seasonal variation? (1.3)

3.3   What is the formula for an additive time series model? (2.1)

4 EXAMINATION TYPE QUESTION

4.1 Report on sales

As the result of a takeover, the performance of three brands – A, B and C – is being reviewed. The unit sales for the last nine quarters are shown below. Contribution is 10 pence per unit.

Quarterly sales (thousand units)

Brand	19X0				19X1				19X2
	Q_1	Q_2	Q_3	Q_4	Q_1	Q_2	Q_3	Q_4	Q_1
A	40	33	60	104	56	45	80	136	72
B	78	63	101	158	81	59	98	162	80
C	400	290	460	700	335	240	380	575	270

You are required to analyse these data and to write a management report of your main findings, including at least five clear points.

Note: no technical statistical analysis is required but graphs, diagrams or simple tables may be included as necessary.

(20 marks)

5   ANSWER TO EXAMINATION TYPE QUESTION

5.1   Report on sales

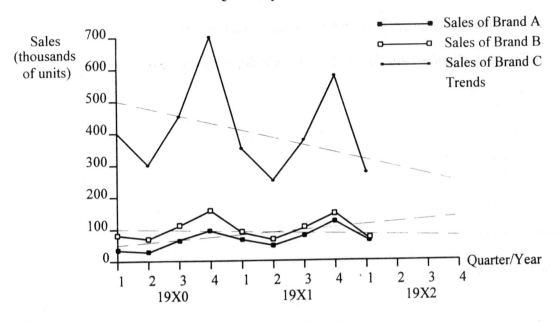

Quarterly sales of brands A, B & C

Summary table

	A			B			C			Total		
	19X0	*19X1*	*19X2**	*19X0*	*19X1*	*19X2**	*19X0*	*19X1*	*19X2**	*19X0*	*19X1*	*19X2**
Annual sales ('000 units)	237	317	397	400	400	400	1,850	1,530	1,210			
Annual contribution (£'000)	23.7	31.7	39.7	40	40	40	185	153	121	248.7	224.7	200.7
% of total for group	9.5	14.1	19.8	16.1	17.8`	19.9	74.4	68.1	60.3			

* Estimated.

*(**Tutorial note:** there is no time in the examination for a detailed time series analysis and the question specifically stated that this was not required.*

The values for 19X2 were therefore predicted by the crude method of assuming the same difference in the annual values from 19X1 to 19X2 as there was from 19X0 to 19X1.

The fact that the first quarter sales for 19X2 show the same trend as the previous first quarters for each brand (this can be seen from the graph) indicate that this is a reasonable assumption.)

Points to note (at least five are required)

(i)   Each brand has a strong seasonal variation.

(ii)   The seasonal variation occurs at the same time for each brand, being lowest in Q_2 and highest in Q_4.

(iii)   Brand A has an increasing trend of approximately 80,000 units per year.

(iv)   Brand B has a constant trend (ie, no increase or decrease).

(v)   Brand C has a decreasing trend of approximately 320,000 units per year.

(vi)   The total market is decreasing by approximately £24,000 per year.

(vii)   Brand C at present has the largest share of the market, but this is decreasing.

(viii) Brands A and B have an increasing share of a decreasing market.

(ix)   Sales of Brand A will probably overtake those of Brand B in 19X2.

(x)   The forecasts of performance for 19X2, as given in the summary table.

Student Questionnaire

Because we believe in listening to our customers, this questionnaire has been designed to discover exactly what you think about us and our materials. We want to know how we can continue improving our customer support and how to make our top class books even better - how do you use our books, what do you like about them and what else would you like to see us do to make them better?

1 Where did you hear about AT Foulks Lynch CIMA Textbooks?

☐ Colleague or friend   ☐ Employer recommendation   ☐ Lecturer recommendation

☐ AT Foulks Lynch mailshot   ☐ Conference   ☐ CIMA literature

☐ CIMA Student   ☐ Management Accountant   ☐ Pass Magazine

☐ Internet   ☐ Other ....

2 Overall, do you think the AT Foulks Lynch CIMA Textbooks are:

☐ Excellent   ☐ Good   ☐ Average   ☐ Poor   ☐ No opinion

3 Please evaluate AT Foulks Lynch service using the following criteria:

	Excellent	Good	Average	Poor	No opinion
Professional	☐	☐	☐	☐	☐
Polite	☐	☐	☐	☐	☐
Informed	☐	☐	☐	☐	☐
Helpful	☐	☐	☐	☐	☐

4 How did you obtain this book?

☐ From a bookshop   ☐ From your college   ☐ From us by mail order

☐ From us by telephone   ☐ Internet   ☐ Other ....

5 How long did it take to receive your materials? .... days.

☐ Very fast   ☐ Fast   ☐ Satisfactory   ☐ Slow   ☐ No opinion

6 How do you rate the value of these features of the CAQM Textbook?

		Excellent	Good	Average	Poor	No opinion
1	Syllabus referenced to chapters	☐	☐	☐	☐	☐
2	Syllabus guidance notes	☐	☐	☐	☐	☐
3	Hotline to the examiner	☐	☐	☐	☐	☐
4	Introductions and learning objectives	☐	☐	☐	☐	☐
5	Chapter summaries	☐	☐	☐	☐	☐
6	Self test questions	☐	☐	☐	☐	☐
7	Examination type questions	☐	☐	☐	☐	☐
8	Index	☐	☐	☐	☐	☐

Continued/...

7 Have you purchased any other AT Foulks Lynch CIMA titles?
If so, please specify title(s) and your rating of each below:

Title	Excellent	Good	Average	Poor	No opinion
....	☐	☐	☐	☐	☐
....	☐	☐	☐	☐	☐
....	☐	☐	☐	☐	☐
....	☐	☐	☐	☐	☐

8 Have you used publications other than AT Foulks Lynch CIMA titles?
If so, please specify title(s) and your rating of each below:

Title and Publisher	Excellent	Good	Average	Poor	No opinion
....	☐	☐	☐	☐	☐
....	☐	☐	☐	☐	☐
....	☐	☐	☐	☐	☐
....	☐	☐	☐	☐	☐

9 Will you buy the AT Foulks Lynch CIMA Textbooks again?

☐ Yes   ☐ No   ☐ Not sure

Why? ....

10 Please write here any additional comments you might have on any of the above areas or tell us what you would like us to do to make the books even better:

....

....

....

....

11 Your details: these are for the internal use of AT Foulks Lynch Ltd only and will not be supplied to any outside organisations.

Name
....

Address
....

....

Telephone
....

Do you have your own e-mail address?   ☐ Yes   ☐ No

Do you have access to the World Wide Web?   ☐ Yes   ☐ No

Do you have access to a CD Rom Drive?   ☐ Yes   ☐ No

Please send to:

Quality Feedback Department
FREEPOST 2254
AT Foulks Lynch Ltd, 4 The Griffin Centre, Staines Road, Feltham, Middlesex, TW14 0BR.

Thank you for your time.

CIMA

HOTLINES

AT FOULKS LYNCH LTD

Telephone: 0181 844 0667
Enquiries: 0181 831 9990
Fax: 0181 831 9991

Number 4, The Griffin Centre
Staines Road, Feltham
Middlesex TW14 0HS

Intended Examination Date: November 97 ☐ May 98 ☐	Textbooks	Exam Kits	Lynchpins	Distance Learning Includes all materials
Stage One				
1 Financial Accounting Fundamentals	£17.00 ☐	£8.95 ☐	£5.00 ☐	£85.00 ☐
2 Cost Accounting & Quantitative Methods	£17.00 ☐	£8.95 ☐	£5.00 ☐	£85.00 ☐
3 Economic Environment	£17.00 ☐	£8.95 ☐	£5.00 ☐	£85.00 ☐
4 Business Environment & Info Technology	£17.00 ☐	£8.95 ☐	£5.00 ☐	£85.00 ☐
Stage Two				
5 Financial Accounting	£17.00 ☐	£8.95 ☐	£5.00 ☐	£85.00 ☐
6 Operational Cost Accounting	£17.00 ☐	£8.95 ☐	£5.00 ☐	£85.00 ☐
7 Management Science Applications	£17.00 ☐	£8.95 ☐	£5.00 ☐	£85.00 ☐
8 Business & Company Law	£17.00 ☐	£8.95 ☐	£5.00 ☐	£85.00 ☐
Stage Three				
9 Financial Reporting	£18.00 ☐	£9.95 ☐	£5.00 ☐	£85.00 ☐
10 Management Accounting Applications	£18.00 ☐	£9.95 ☐	£5.00 ☐	£85.00 ☐
11 Organisational Mgt & Development	£18.00 ☐	£9.95 ☐	£5.00 ☐	£85.00 ☐
12 Business Taxation (Finance Act 1997)	£18.00 ☐	£9.95 ☐	£5.00 ☐	£85.00 ☐
Stage Four				
13 Strategic Financial Management	£18.95 ☐	£9.95 ☐	£5.00 ☐	£85.00 ☐
14 Strategic Mgt Accountancy & Marketing	£18.95 ☐	£9.95 ☐	£5.00 ☐	£85.00 ☐
15 Information Management	£18.95 ☐	£9.95 ☐	£5.00 ☐	£85.00 ☐
16 Management Accounting Control Systems	£18.95 ☐	£9.95 ☐	£5.00 ☐	£85.00 ☐
P & P + DELIVERY UK Mainland	£2.00/book	£1.00/book	£1.00/book	£5.00/pack
NI, ROI & EU Countries	£5.00/book	£3.00/book	£3.00/book	£15.00/pack
Rest of world standard air service	£10.00/book	£8.00/book	£8.00/book	£25.00/pack
Rest of world courier service*	£22.00/book	£20.00/book	£14.00/book	£47.00/pack

SINGLE ITEM SUPPLEMENT: If you only order 1 item, INCREASE postage costs by £2.50 for UK, NI & EU Countries or by £10.00 for Rest of World Service

TOTAL				
Sub Total £				
Post & Packing £				
Total £				

Telephone number essential for this service.

Order Total £ _____

DELIVERY DETAILS

☐ Mr ☐ Miss ☐ Mrs ☐ Ms Other

Initials _____ Surname _____

Address _____

Postcode _____

Telephone _____ Deliver to home ☐

Company name _____

Address _____

Postcode _____

Telephone _____ Fax _____

Monthly report to go to employer ☐ Deliver to work ☐

PAYMENT

1. I enclose Cheque/PO/Bankers Draft for £_____
   Please make cheques payable to AT Foulks Lynch Ltd.

2. Charge Access/Visa A/c No: Expiry Date ☐ ☐ ☐ ☐

☐ ☐ ☐ ☐ ☐ ☐ ☐ ☐ ☐ ☐ ☐ ☐ ☐ ☐ ☐ ☐

Signature _____ Date _____

DECLARATION

I agree to pay as indicated on this form and understand that AT Foulks Lynch Terms and Conditions apply (available on request). I understand that AT Foulks Lynch Ltd are not liable for non-delivery if the rest of world standard air service is used.

Signature _____ Date _____

Please Allow:	UK mainland	- 5-10 w/days
	NI, ROI & EU Countries	- 1-3 weeks
	Rest of world standard air service	- 6 weeks
	Rest of world courier service	- 10 w/days

Notes: All delivery times subject to stock availability. Signature required on receipt (except rest of world standard air service). Please give both addresses for Distance Learning students where possible.

All details correct at time of printing.

Source: CMTXJ7